Thomas Edward Satterthwaite

A Manual of Histology

.

Thomas Edward Satterthwaite

A Manual of Histology

ISBN/EAN: 9783742806109

Manufactured in Europe, USA, Canada, Australia, Japa

Cover: Foto ©Thomas Meinert / pixelio.de

Manufactured and distributed by brebook publishing software
(www.brebook.com)

Thomas Edward Satterthwaite

A Manual of Histology

HISTOLOGY

EDITED AND PREPARED BY

THOMAS E. SATTERTHWAITE, M.D.,

OF NEW YORK

Professor of Histological and Pathological Anatomy in the New York Post-Graduate Medical College, Pathologist to the St. Luke's and Presbyterian Hospitals, etc.

IN ASSOCIATION WITH

DRS. THOMAS DWIGHT, J. COLLINS WARREN, WILLIAM F. WHITNEY, CLARENCE J. BLAKE, and C. H. WILLIAMS, of Boston; DR. J. HENRY C. SIMES, of Philadelphia; DR. BENJAMIN F. WESTBROOK, of Brooklyn; and DRS. EDMUND C. WENDT, ABRAHAM MAYER, R. W. AMIDON, A. R. ROBINSON, W. R. BIRDSALL, D. BRYSON DELAVAN, C. L. DANA, and W. H. PORTER, of New York City

SECOND EDITION, ENLARGED AND REVISED, CONTAINING TWO HUNDRED AND TWO ILLUSTRATIONS, WITH AN APPENDIX

NEW YORK

WILLIAM WOOD & COMPANY

56 AND 58 LAFAYETTE PLACE

1882

PREFACE TO THE SECOND EDITION.

THE editor, in preparing the second edition, acknowledges that the favor with which the first edition was received, both at home and in Great Britain, has been a matter of pleasure and of surprise to him, and probably no less so to those who aided him in the work. But he was totally unprepared for the announcement, a few months after the publication of the volume, that a second edition would soon be needed. This task has now been accomplished, though not in a manner to satisfy the rigid requirements of such a book, which should be in all respects abreast of the time at which it is issued. Practically speaking, however, it has been the opinion of the collaborators that the positive advances that have been made in the field of Histology during the brief interval alluded to have not been sufficient to justify any extensive alterations in the text-matter, especially in view of the great expense attending such changes. The editor, in taking this occasion to thank his able reviewers for the many valuable suggestions they have offered, states at the same time that only such textual changes have now been made that were necessary to remedy those manifest errors that will unavoidably creep in. An appendix, however, is now added, and it is hoped that this new text-matter, illustrations, and recent bibliographical references will add to the usefulness of the book and make it continue to merit the favor of practitioners and students of medicine.

T. E. S.

PREFACE TO THE FIRST EDITION.

For some years past there has been a general demand among the members of our profession for a manual of Histology, summarizing, in concise and plain language, our present knowledge in this fundamental branch of medicine. It is true many books have been written on the subject, but their great brevity, on the one hand, or an unnecessary diffuseness on the other, have prevented them from meeting with acceptance at the hands of physicians and students. In the one class belong the little handbooks of Rutherford and Schaefer, which have done much to simplify and therefore popularize histology, but they were intended for beginners, and especially students doing class-work under the laboratory system now so much in vogue. But both physician and student need something of wider scope, and they have been compelled to turn to Klein & Smith, Stricker, or Frey, though no one of these excellent works is thoroughly adapted to their wants.

Apart from the expense of the two former, they all are deficient in matters relating to human histology.

The practical experience of a teacher made it evident also that the volume to fill such an obvious gap should take the form of a text-book. And the present time seemed opportune for its appearance, since we have latterly made much positive

advance in histological studies, while histologists themselves
are now more of one mind in microscopical matters. That such
a book should appear under American auspices seemed further
to be eminently proper, as we have in various parts of the country a goodly number of medical men who are either engaged
in teaching histology or in studying some special branch of it.

The advantages of utilizing their accumulated experiences
was therefore apparent to the editor, and he gladly applied
to them for assistance when it was found that one individual
could not prepare the volume within a reasonable time or
in a manner that would be satisfactory. It is hoped that
the names of the collaborators furnish a sufficient guarantee
that proper representatives of American histology have been
selected. In some respects the object sought for has not been
wholly attained, as, for example, in the effort to separate
purely human histology from the comparative. But this is
impossible at the present time, mainly because our knowledge is still too limited. It is a matter of regret, also, that the
original illustrations have been so few in comparison with the
total number, but the great expense attending their production
would not warrant any one in attempting much in this direction. Through the kind co-operation, however, of Messrs. William Wood & Co., the editor has been able to utilize many
excellent cuts that were in their possession.

As a further means of relieving the tedium associated with
a work that is so largely descriptive, the various authors have
aimed to intersperse here and there throughout the text matters of physiological or pathological import. Still, intelligent
practitioners do not have to be reminded that rational therapeutics has found a substantial support in the revelations of
pathological anatomy, which, in turn, rests upon histology,

so that the relation between microscopic anatomy and the scientific practice of medicine is readily appreciated.

Emanating as the volume does from American sources, the editor finds it a fitting place to give proper space to American contributions, and the reader may therefore find due notice of the physiological desquamation of blood-vessels, considerations on the nature of nerve-termini, matters relating to the intimate structure of the striped muscular fibre and nerves, with the results of studies on the structure and development of certain connective substances, and novelties in microscopic apparatus and methods. A special chapter is also given to the thick cutis vera, now for the first time described as a distinctive portion of the skin. In it will be found detailed the discovery of the *fat-columns*, which are calculated to explain certain pathological changes that have been imperfectly understood.

The first chapters of the book are devoted to the mechanism of the microscope, and to certain formal methods of work with which the beginner should be familiar. Of the illustrations, sixty-five were prepared for the volume, while forty have never, it is believed, appeared in book-form. The remainder are mostly from the manuals of Stricker and Frey.

A limited number of bibliographical references have been inserted where it was thought they were desirable in guiding the reader to the literature of the subject. For the preparation of these tables and much valuable assistance, the editor here desires to express his thanks to Dr. E. C. Wendt, of this city.

It was thought best to omit the subject of optical principles which figure so conspicuously in some of our histological manuals. Those who wish information on these matters are referred to any of the standard text-books on physics, where the subject is treated at greater length than was permissible in the present instance.

For a similar reason, and also because it would prove a needless expense, the price-lists of instrument-makers have been omitted. Full particulars relating to the various sorts of microscopes and their accessories can be obtained from any of the leading opticians, who from time to time issue lists containing ample illustrations of the most recent improvements in all that pertains to practical working of the instrument.

In conclusion, the editor finds himself compelled to reiterate the well-worn statement, that circumstances over which he has had no control have united to delay the press-work of the volume, and at the end have made its final revision rather hasty. A kind indulgence is therefore asked for any error that may, through oversight, have escaped his notice.

T. E. S.

TABLE OF CONTENTS.

PART I.

CHAPTER I.

By THOMAS E. SATTERTHWAITE, M.D.

CHAPTER II.

By THOMAS E. SATTERTHWAITE, M.D.

CHAPTER III.

By THOMAS E. SATTERTHWAITE, M.D.

CHAPTER IV.

By THOMAS E. SATTERTHWAITE, M.D.

CHAPTER V.

By THOMAS E. SATTERTHWAITE, M.D.

PART II.

CHAPTER X.

By THOMAS DWIGHT, M.D.

CHAPTER XI.

By EDMUND C. WENDT, M.D.

CHAPTER XII.

By W. R. BIRDSALL, M.D.

CHAPTER XIII.

By A. MAYER, M.D.

CHAPTER XIV.

By A. MAYER, M.D.

CHAPTER XV.

By J. HENRY C. SIMES, M.D.

CHAPTER XVI.

By J. HENRY C. SIMES, M.D.

PART III.

CHAPTER XXII.

By D. BRYSON DELAVAN, M.D.

CHAPTER XXIII.

By D. BRYSON DELAVAN, M.D.

CHAPTER XXIV.

By EDMUND C. WENDT, M.D.

CHAPTER XXV.

By C. L. DANA, M.D.

A

MANUAL OF HISTOLOGY

AND

HISTOLOGICAL METHODS.

CHAPTER I.

MATERIALS REQUISITE FOR HISTOLOGICAL WORK—HOW TO USE
THE MICROSCOPE—TESTING THE MICROSCOPE—ITS USES.

VERY little apparatus and few reagents are essential for general histological work. Such as are really needed may be so arranged as to fit in a box or bag, that can be carried in the hand. First of all, the student should be provided with a

FIG. 2.

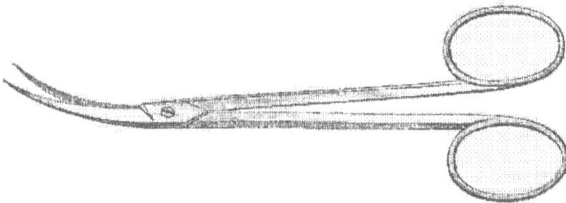

FIG. 1.

FIG. 3.—Curved Iris Scissors.

pair of small forceps, with either curved or straight points (Figs. 1, 2), according to individual fancy ; a pair of delicate *curved iris scissors* (Fig. 3) ; a few *pipettes;* a *glass rod* or

two ; a *spoon* (Fig. 4) for lifting sections of tissues from the
fluids in which they have been immersed ; a *pair of needles*
(Fig. 5) in handles for teasing or tearing tissues ; (the handles
used for crochet needles, or the pin-slides sold by jewelers,
may be fitted with ordinary milliner's needles, which are long,
delicate, and flexible, and therefore well adapted for this

FIG. 4.

FIG. 5.—Microscopic Needle-holder.

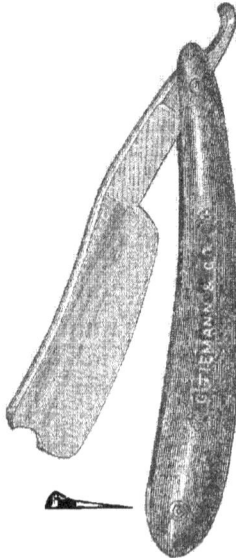

FIG. 6.—Microscopic Section Razor.

FIG. 7.—Capped Bottle.

work) a *sable* or *camel's hair brush* for removing cellular
elements, so as to bring particular parts into prominence ; *bibulous paper ;* a *sharp knife* (Fig. 6) for cutting thin sections ;[1]

[1] For this purpose the razors made by Le Coultre, in Geneva, have been highly
recommended, but good knives may be obtained of almost any cutler ; indeed, most
of the makers of surgical instruments furnish them ; they are usually flat on one
side and slightly concave on the other.

five or six *shallow porcelain dishes*, ounce gallipots, with flat bottoms, in which to soak the tissues when they have been cut ; *glass slides* for mounting specimens (the ordinary size is 3 × 1 inch) ; thin *glass* or *mica covers* (squares or circles) for covering the specimens (three-quarters of an inch is a good diameter).

Mica covers are much cheaper than glass, and are suitable for rapid work and when it is not desirable to make permanent preparations.

FIG. 8.—Beer's Cataract Knife.

In addition, a small *Beer's cataract knife* (Fig. 8) will be found useful for puncturing vessels and hollow organs to obtain samples of their fluid contents.   All of these articles may easily be contained in the drawer of a box 10 × 12 inches in size ; [1] the upper portion will hold the necessary reagents.   These latter should comprise a small amount of a three-fourths per cent. aqueous solution of *sodium chloride*, about an equal amount of *distilled water, dilute acetic acid, glycerine, and iodized serum;* [2] a fluid ounce of each will be all that is necessary, and for convenience of use they may be put in corked bottles provided with capped pipettes passing through the corks.   The vials and perforated corks may be obtained of almost any apothecary.   The cap being of rubber, very small quantities of the fluid can be withdrawn from the bottle and pressed out as desired, either upon the slide or otherwise.

Other reagents required are oil of cloves in a two-ounce stoppered bottle ; dammar varnish or Canada balsam, each in a capped bottle (Fig. 7), containing a glass rod ; a solution of logwood, and another of borax carmine,[3] in ordinary glass stoppered two-ounce bottles, and a small vial of asphalt or some similar cement.   It will be useful, in addition, to have a small bottle (4 oz.) of absolute alcohol, another (8 oz.) of commercial alcohol, some Müller's fluid [3] (8 oz.), and a solution of the bichromate of potassium (gr. xv.— ℥ j.).

---

[1] T. H. McAllister, optician, No. 49 Nassau Street, New York City, has made one for me which answers the purpose satisfactorily.   Miller Bros., No. 69 Nassau Street and 1213 Broadway, New York City, also make and furnish cases for the same purpose.

[2] See page 38.

[3] See page 14.

No good histological work can be done without a *note-book*
to record the results of observation. All such memoranda will
be very useful for subsequent reference. A *heating slide*, a
gas chamber and a *slide* arranged for conducting electric cur-
rents may also be desirable. They will be described in the
chapter on the Blood.

The following substances that cannot be contained in a box,
and are necessary in some forms of microscopic work, may be
mentioned: osmic acid (1 per cent.), nitric acid (C. P.), distilled
water, olive oil, caustic soda or potash, chloride of gold ($\frac{1}{2}$ per
cent. sol.).[1]

It is also very convenient to have at hand a *short wooden
rule* which is divided into inches and tenths of an inch. The
stage micrometer is also equally necessary. Other accessory
materials will be described in their proper places.

HOW TO USE THE MICROSCOPE.[2]

Illumination.—When the instrument is ready for use it
should be placed upon a firm and rather low table, near a
window, which does not receive the direct rays of the sun.   If
daylight is not to be obtained, a small kerosene hand-lamp will
answer sufficiently well for illuminating purposes. The flame
should be on a level with the reflecting mirror of the microscope, and quite near it. Sometimes a condenser is interposed,
but this is rarely necessary, and, indeed, it may be said that it
seldom comes into use in histological work.

A thin sheet of blue glass may sometimes be found to assist
the eye when artificial illumination is used, as the light is made
white. Some microscope makers furnish with their instruments a set of blue glasses varying in color from very light to
dark blue. They are rarely needed, as the eye soon becomes
accustomed to continuous work for long sittings, even when
strong light is employed. Those who work much with the
microscope keep both eyes open, and use first one and then

[1] See pages 28, 29.

[2] It is presumed that students engaging in histological work are more or less
familiar with the mechanism of the microscope. For this reason the subject of
optical principles and the description of the different parts of a microscope are
omitted here. Those who may wish special information on these points are referred to the standard text books on Physics.

the other. Some find it a great assistance to direct the unengaged eye upon a dark object, such as a blackened card, which they fasten to the tube of the instrument near its top.

As it is desirable that the lamp should only illuminate the reflector, a great many ingenious contrivances have been made to cut off the superfluous light. For this purpose some microscopists interpose a piece of thin board, or a thick card, having a circular opening between the lamp and the reflector.

Stage diaphragms.—When the pencil of light has been reflected from the mirror upon the opening in the stage, it is plain that a larger or smaller amount of light will pass, according to the size of the opening. The appliances that regulate this matter are called stage diaphragms—sometimes they are simply cylindrical tubes with capped upper extremities, each tube being provided with caps of varying aperture. The tubes are pushed into the stage from beneath. When polished they undoubtedly aid in converging the light upon the aperture. Other diaphragms are simply round holes in a circular revolving plate which is set into the stage.

The diameters of the apertures vary from that of a pin's point to about three-fourths of an inch or even more.

The revolving diaphragms have now come into general use, because they work simply and efficiently. Mr. Wale has devised one that is extremely ingenious. It has the advantage of a cylindrical diaphragm, in so far as it converges the pencil of light upon the diaphragmatic opening, while the size of the opening is regulated by the action of a single thumb-screw.[1] It acts as the iris does in enlarging or diminishing the pupil, and therefore its name, the *iris diaphragm.*

The mirrors.—Of these there should be two, one *plane,* when a diffuse light is needed ; the other *concave* for a concentrated beam. The latter is frequently used, the former seldom.

Direct and oblique light.—Thus far the descriptions have applied to direct light, and it is the only kind much used in histological work. In testing a lens, however, as with a diatom, it is often necessary to use oblique light in order to resolve a line or series of lines. In such cases the aperture in the stage should be made as large as possible, and the mirror, concave or plane, is to be carried well up under the stage, to the left or

---

[1] See illustrated catalogues of leading microscope makers.

right, so that the pencil of light may be thrown across the object. By this means, little inequalities of the surface which would be invisible under direct light are clearly demonstrated. The poorer lenses, however, are those which necessitate oblique light. When reference is made to the definition of the lens, direct light is intended.

Arrangement of the object.—When the object is to be examined, it should be placed upon the glass slide, which is usually one by three inches in superficial measurement, and as thin as is compatible with the usages to which it is put in ordinary microscopic work. The glass should be white in color, and free from any imperfections that can be detected by the eye. Usually a drop or two of water, a drop of glycerine, or a drop of water and glycerine in equal parts, is placed upon the slide.

The object is then immersed in the liquid. It takes some little time for the fluid to permeate the specimen, so that it is ready for study. When pure glycerine is used fully ten minutes will generally elapse before the specimen is transparent. A covering glass is then cautiously let fall upon the liquid, care being taken that no bubble of air enters. The cover is then pressed down. In such cases, when the object is studied with high powers, the cover will often slowly rise and separate itself from the slide, so that the forceps or the finger may be necessary to press it back. This inconvenience is obviated by painting a little Canada balsam or cement around the edge of the cover so as to hold it down.

The kind of a lens to be used.—For the first examination a low objective should be used, with a medium, not short, eyepiece. The tube should then be carried down until the object comes within the focus. Low powers should always be used at first, because they give a good idea of the object in its general features.

Then the tube may be withdrawn, and a higher power substituted, and so on, until the specimen has been studied in all its details. A convenient accessory is now made by most of the instrument makers; it is a "nose-piece"—a brass attachment which is screwed into the end of the tube, and carries two or more lenses.[1]

---

[1] The double angular nose-piece made by Schrauer, 46 Nassau Street, costs $6, the triple, $20; all of the microscope makers are now prepared to furnish them.

The first named is usually fitted with a $\frac{4}{5}$ and a $\frac{1}{5}$ inch lens; in addition to these a $\frac{1}{10}$ immersion may be used for the triple nose-piece.

How to keep the instrument clean.—After using the instrument it should always be wiped dry, as it is damp from the moisture of the breath and hands. The lenses should be returned to their cases, and, if necessary, the surfaces are to be rubbed off with a bit of soft chamois skin or fine linen. Water will remove almost all the dirt from the anterior lens, but occasionally it may be necessary to use alcohol. In such cases but very little is requisite, as it may penetrate behind the anterior lens and dissolve the Canada balsam that cements the different portions together.

It is well for the student to familiarize himself at first with certain common objects that are apt to be met with in all forms of microscopic work, such as the little foreign substances that go to make up the dust of rooms; these include minute bits of wood, cotton and linen fibres, particles of wool, hairs of various animals, feathers, etc.

The imperfections in the glass should also be noted, and especially the curious red figures sometimes resembling butterfly wings, caused by an accumulation in the flaws of the glass of a red substance—the red oxide of iron—used by manufacturers in polishing glass. These red figures are often wonderfully alike, and have given rise to singular errors among microscopical workers.

TESTING THE MICROSCOPE—ITS USES.

Magnifying power of a lens.—To determine the actual magnifying power of a lens in combination with the particular eye-piece that happens to be in use, the ordinary method is as follows:

The glass stage micrometer, which is ruled off into tenths, hundredths, and thousandths of an inch, is placed upon the stage and focussed. This having been done, the wooden rule, which we have already alluded to and which is divided into inches and tenths of an inch, is laid alongside of the micrometer-slide.

One eye, looking outside of the tube, reads off the number

of divisions of the wooden rule corresponding to a single division of the micrometer slide as seen with the other eye directed through the tube of the microscope.

By this method of double vision, as it were, a comparison is instituted between the two rules, and the ratio that one bears to the other may be estimated.

Suppose, for example, that $\frac{1}{1000}$ of an inch on the scale of the stage micrometer is equal to $\frac{2}{10}$ of an inch on the wooden rule. The ratio of $\frac{1}{1000}$ to $\frac{2}{10}$ will represent the magnifying power of that particular combination. Reducing these fractions to a common denominator they stand to one another as 1 to 200. The object has therefore been magnified two hundred times.

With a short eye-piece the power is greater and it increases in proportion as the tube is drawn out. It is customary however to assume a certain length of the draw-tube as the standard : this is twenty-five centimetres or about ten inches.

How to estimate the size of an object.—To estimate the size of an object is a much easier task. Place the stage micrometer upon the stage of the microscope and then slip the micrometer eye-piece into the draw-tube. The micrometer eye-piece is simply an ordinary ocular with a glass cover fitted into the diaphragm. The micrometer consists of a series of parallel lines ruled across it at regular distances apart. By focussing the lines on the stage micrometer one may readily count the actual fractions of an inch corresponding to a single division in the micrometer eye-piece.

Thus, for example, if we find that a single division of the micrometer eye-piece corresponds to $\frac{1}{1000}$ of an inch, and that a lymphoid corpuscle covers half a division, its diameter is necessarily $\frac{1}{2000}$ of an inch.

Testing a lens.—A lens should be free from certain defects, as we have already stated. First of all it should have no spherical aberration ; the objects seen upon the edge of the field should be sharply defined, and all objects having parallel sides should appear as such. In other words, they should not be distorted.

Secondly, they should have no color or, at least, as little as possible. This defect, however, has never been entirely overcome ; some glasses are over-corrected and then the prevailing color is blue ; others are under-corrected and then the prevailing color is red. ·

It is a matter of some indifference which color prevails. These defects are best seen by observing a bubble of air in a fluid specimen. The prevailing color is seen at the periphery of the bubble.

Thirdly, all objects in the field should appear with equal distinctness, whether at the periphery or in the centre. If a fine powder, such as lycopodium be strewn over the field, the granules should be seen as distinctly at the edges as at the centre ; an ordinary thin section of any microscopic object will also exhibit this defect, if it exist.

Fourthly, the glasses should have good resolution. This enables the observer to see the general aspect of bodies better, though it may not make him see objects quite as sharply ; the former depending upon a large angle of aperture, and the latter (definition) upon a small one.

To be able to have at the same time both great resolving and great defining power is the highest desideratum, and it has been the merit of our American makers to increase the angle of aperture and still maintain a high defining power.

For ordinary histological purposes, a lens that will show the oscillatory movement in the mucous or salivary corpuscles is sufficiently high for practical purposes. This is accomplished by the ordinary student's one-fifth of Grunow, for example. If, however, we are studying the delicate intercellular sub-stance of the brain and connective-tissue corpuscles, bacteria, etc., a somewhat higher power is needed.

For such studies it is desirable to have an immersion lens, such as the No. 10 or 12 Hartnack or Prazmowski, or a $\frac{1}{17}$ or $\frac{1}{18}$ of other good makers, such as Wale, Tolles, etc.

In using these high powers it is necessary to place a single drop of water on the anterior lens and depress the tube until the drop touches the circle or cover. The drop of water utilizes light that would otherwise be lost, mag-nifies slightly, and corrects, so that the image is made brighter and more distinct.

The new oil immersion of Zeiss is highly recommended by Woodward of Washington. In using such a lens, a drop of oil is substituted for water. We are hardly yet prepared to decide whether oil is preferable on the whole to water.

How to illuminate the microscope. —In doing ordinary microscopic work it is best to use day-light, such as is reflected from a clear sky. It is not well to use direct sun-light, but to receive illumination from a point opposite to the sun. North light is very excellent.

If artificial light is to be used, an ordinary kerosene burner will answer sufficiently well, even better than gas. Some of the highest lenses require artificial light.

Testing the eye-piece.—Eye-pieces are usually free from serious defects, but if we are desirous of testing one, the following method may be followed :

Select a combination of lens and eye-piece that gives a perfectly flat field. Then remove the eye-piece and substitute the one that is to be tested. If now the image is no longer flat, the eye-piece has *aberration of form* and should be rejected.

Testing high lenses.—In combinations that magnify about five hundred times, a good test is the *pleurosigma angulatum*, one of the diatoms. A lens that will demonstrate three sets of lines by direct light has a proper amount of defining power, and with the other qualifications already mentioned, is suitable for the finer sorts of microscopical work. This task is easily accomplished by either the No. 10 immersion of Hartnack or Prazmowski, the $\frac{1}{12}$ of Wale, and also by lenses of other good makers.

To test the resolving power of lenses even more accurately, Nobert's test plates may be used. They consist of bands of fine lines from nineteen to thirty in number.

It has usually been thought that the eighth or ninth of their series is a good test ; the nineteenth band,[1] however, has been defined by a ten immersion Hartnack, and probably by a goodly number of American lenses. (See Appendix.)

Measuring the angle of a lens.—Take an instrument of which the pillar is hinged, and which also revolves on its vertical axis.

Measure off on the table, in front of the instrument, a semicircle with the pillar as a fixed point. Divide the semicircle into the proper number of degrees, viz., 180.

Place opposite the instrument, and without the circle, a candle or lamp. Then interpose between the two a screen having an aperture to admit a small beam of light. Revolve the tube on its axis until the light can no longer be seen ; then

---

[1] According to Carpenter, the nineteenth band contains 113,595.13580 spaces to the inch.

count off the number of degrees which the instrument has passed over. Suppose, that, in a given case, the number be seventy ; then revolve the instrument in the opposite direction and count as before. The number of degrees will of course be the same.

Add the two figures together, and the total number of degrees (viz., 140) will represent the angle of aperture.

CHAPTER II.

General directions.—Microscopic work should be done at a rather low table, not more than thirty inches high, and resting squarely upon the floor, so that it cannot be jarred by movements in the room. In most laboratories small and short microscopes are preferred; they are now made by nearly every optician. The total height, when the stand is vertical, need not be more than eleven or twelve inches. For various reasons, which soon become apparent to those who do much histological work, it is seldom necessary to provide the stand with a hinge-joint, which allows the tube to be inclined toward the observer. A vertical and rigid stand is steadier, less expensive, and, except in very rare instances, all that is required in medical work.

When the microscopist is about to commence his examination, he should select the various materials that are likely to be needed, and place them near him on the table, so as to be within easy reach of his hand. Special tables for microscopic work may be provided with rows of drawers upon either side of the worker. In them should be kept all the microscopic accessories that he expects to use, such as glass slides and covers, wooden boxes for specimens, labels, a note-book for rough sketches and annotations, a bit of chamois skin for cleaning the lenses and other adjuvants which are found useful. By so doing, these materials are kept free from dust, and stand ready for use at any time. A small vessel holding clean water to wash the covers and slides, a receptacle of some kind for the waste, and a clean, fine, and soft towel should not be forgotten, as they are always useful for every kind of microscopic work.

The instrument is best kept under a bell-glass on the table. If, however, it has to be taken about from place to place, it should be packed in its box, and the accessories may also be kept in a suitable chest, such as has been described, and which is made by a number of opticians.

After the directions that have been given, it seems hardly necessary to add that everything pertaining to the work should be carefully cleansed after using, and put away in its proper place, so as to be immediately available at any future time. The expenditure of a little time in these details is more than counterbalanced by the greater rapidity and effectiveness of subsequent work.

How to prepare a fresh microscopic object for **rapid examination.**—When practicable, every specimen should be studied as early as possible after removal from the body, and this is important even if it is to be hardened and prepared for permanent preservation.

Take a clean slide, which, of course, should be reasonably thin ; place it before you upon a white ground (some microscopists have a square plate of marble set into the table); moisten the slide with a drop of some indifferent fluid, such as iodized serum or, perhaps, a three-fourths per cent. aqueous solution of common salt ; then place in the drop the fragment to be examined. Small particles are more easily studied than large ones. Usually the substance should be spread out a little with needles.

In one or two minutes it is ready for examination. By this method striped muscular tissue may easily be detected ; and it also happens to be a good example because it is very frequently brought to microscopists for examination. In certain forms of dyspepsia, especially in women, it is common for ingested meat to pass through the alimentary tract with very little change. Prepared for the microscope in this simple way the peculiar markings of striped muscle may be observed at once, and even if the meat has been boiled.

If, however, the material to be examined is opaque, we add to the drop of serum another of glycerine ; the latter alone refracts the light too much, and is therefore undesirable. When, however, it is combined with an equal amount of serum or the salt solution, the fluid has a proper refractive power for most histological purposes. The microscopist should now let fall upon the drop a cover glass, and place the slide upon the stage of the microscope. Nothing is required to keep the cover in place. Examine at first with a low power, and then with a higher one, until the specimen has been studied in all its details.

THE ORDINARY METHODS OF PREPARING TISSUES.

Müller's fluid.—It is customary to use Müller's fluid to render tissues firm, so that they may be easily cut with the knife, and made thin enough for microscopic studies. The formula is (by weight) bichromate of potassium, 2 parts, sulphate of soda, 1 part, distilled water, 100 parts. This fluid, which is of a brown color and transparent, is admirably adapted for hardening and preserving permanently nearly all the tissues of the body; though for the brain and cord it is unsatisfactory without the subsequent use of other reagents. It is, however, very cheap, and specimens may be preserved in it for years, and still retain the characteristics which make them suitable for microscopic study.

Potassium bichromate solution.—Some microscopists prefer simply a solution of the bichromate of potassium (gr. xv.— ʒ j.). It is well, in this case, to put the specimens into a fresh solution every day for several days. Subsequently they are to be hardened in alcohol. The strength of the latter should at first be eighty per cent., then ninety per cent., and finally may be ninety-five per cent. The alcoholic process requires a few additional days. Solutions containing chromic acid or the bichromates are objectionable if the specimen is to be used for coarse demonstration, because the yellow or brown color of the acids is difficult to remove. Prolonged soaking in distilled water will accomplish a great deal, but the final color is generally a clay brown. Of course this objection does not apply to microscopic sections, and indeed it appears as if the chromic acid and chromate solutions prepare them particularly well for the process of staining in various colors.

Ammonia bichromate solution.—Gerlach has recommended this reagent in one or two per cent. solutions for hardening the brain and cord. It is to be used as the preceding (Frey).

Alcohol and acetic acid mixture (Lockhart Clarke).—Two objects were sought by their combination: one to coagulate albuminous matters by the alcohol, the other to render them transparent. The proportion was alcohol three parts and acetic acid one part. It is said that by this method sections of the cord may be made transparent in a few hours (Frey).

Alcohol and acetic acid mixture (Moleschott).—This "strong acetic acid mixture," of which the formula is strong acetic acid (1.070 sp. gr.), 1 vol.; alcohol (.815 sp. gr.), 1 vol.; distilled water, 2 vols., causes the connective-tissue substances to become very transparent. Delicate textures do not tolerate it well (Frey).

Molybdate of ammonia has been recommended by Krause for hardening specimens. It has met with some favor.

Solution of osmic and chromic acids.—Flesch recommends a union of these acids for hardening and decalcifying bone. It is also useful for hardening other tissues. His formula is as follows: osmic acid, 10 parts; chromic acid, 25 ; distilled water, 100.

Alcohol and acetic acid and muriatic acid solution.— Beale gives the following formula: water, 1 oz.; glycerine, 1 oz.; spirit, 2 oz.; acetic acid, 2 drachms; hydrochloric acid, ½ drachm. This is said to harden well and be suited for epithelial structures (Frey).

Method of hardening the brain.—Hamilton recommends the following method: pieces of brain and cord cut into sections not more than an inch in length, or length and breadth, are immersed in a fluid containing three parts of Müller's fluid and one of methyl alcohol, and put away for some three weeks in a refrigerator. Then they are to be soaked in a solution of the bichromate of ammonia (1–400) for a week ; another week in a solution of 1–100; a third week in a solution of 1 to 50 ; and finally kept in chloral hydrate (12 gr. to the ounce). Before cutting, they are to be washed twelve hours or more in water ; they then are to stand forty-eight hours in a syrup containing two parts of refined sugar to one of water. He then cuts with Rutherford's microtome. Staining is done with osmic acid and carmine.

For clarification he uses oil of cloves or turpentine.

How to embed specimens.—When a piece of tissue is so small that it cannot be held in the hand, it is customary to embed it in some substance of about the same consistence. A combination of wax and oil answers the purpose very well ; they should be mixed in about equal proportions in a porcelain dish, and then heated together until the wax is thoroughly melted. This having been done, a mould should be at hand to receive both the embedding mixture and the piece of tissue. Various moulds are in use. Some are made of tin-foil, and are shaped like a common earthenware garden-pot.

A fine, long cambric needle should be passed through the tissue, and then (the mould being placed in position) the point of the needle is to be pushed through the bottom into the table beneath.

Then the mixture of the liquid wax and oil, which has been heated to the point of melting and no more, should be poured slowly into the mould, so as to slightly cover the specimen. During the process of hardening, minute bubbles of air will be liberated from the tissue ; they will escape more rapidly, and the embedding material will harden more quickly and thoroughly, if the microscopist blows gently and continuously on the surface of the liquid. Just at the moment when the mass is no longer liquid, the needle should be suddenly withdrawn.

As soon as it is hard throughout, the tin-foil mould may be torn off by breaking the edge at any point with the finger. The foil tears like paper.

When moulds are not at hand, an excellent substitute may be made with ordinary writing paper. Some confectioners make them of pressed paper.

Embedding in glycerine and tragacanth.—Mr. John Stevenson's plan is as follows : He takes two drachms of glycerine and mixes them with one drachm and a half of powdered gum tragacanth. The tissue to be cut is then placed in a small pill-box, and the mixture poured in. The box is then laid away in a cool place from eight to twelve hours, when sections may be made with the knife. In case the specimen is to be preserved for a longer time, the bottom of the box may be taken off, and the side slit up. The specimen will now be found embedded in a solid elastic cake, and may be slipped into alcohol until required. When it is to be kept in spirits less than twenty-eight hours, the mixture should be glycerine, 2 drachms ; powdered tragacanth, 1 drachm ; gum arabic, 15 grains. Tissues that have lain in spirit should be steeped in cold water a few hours before embedding.

The hand section-cutter is used by some microscopists. It is simply a cylinder which is designed to receive the object and the material in which it is embedded. A plunger, which is driven up from beneath by the revolution of a screw, pushes up the specimen so that it may be sliced off by an ordinary knife. For some purposes it is very useful.

Freezing section-cutters.—Of these there are many in use, and they have certain advantages. In conjunction with Dr. J. H. Hunt, of Brooklyn, I have devised a modification of the ordinary instrument.[1] (Fig. 9.)

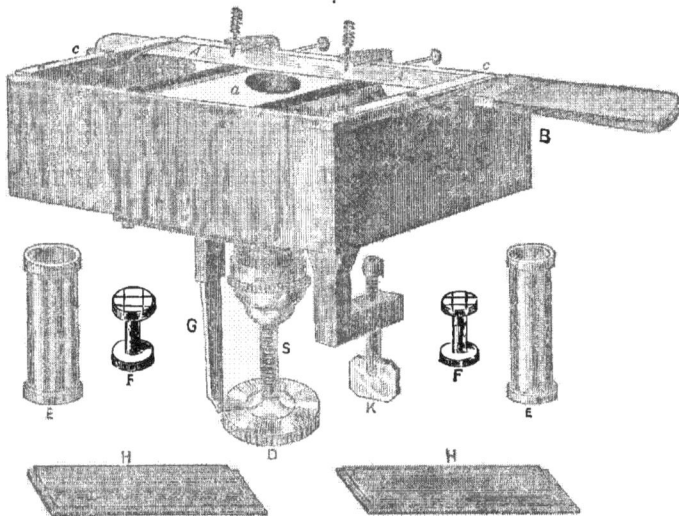

FIG. 9.—Freezing section-cutter: B, metallic box; S, cylinder; *a*, well; *c*, *c*, frame for holding knife A. A; G, indicator; D, milled head; F, F, plugs; E, E, tubes to fit in well; H, H, covers to metallic box; K, binding screw attaching box to table.

It consists of the brass cylinder, S, made of rather large size, and placed in the centre of a metallic box, B. The length of the cylinder, with driver, D, is about five inches. The diameter of the well, *a*, measures $1\frac{3}{8}$ inch. Fitted round and about the cylinder is a plate of glass which from its smoothness permits the knife to sweep it easily.

The knife, A, A, is large, measuring 13 inches in length, including handle; in breadth, $1\frac{3}{8}$ inch. It is fitted into a brass frame, *c*, *c*, $7\frac{1}{4}$ inches in length and $3\frac{1}{8}$ in breadth. Two strong brass springs, and two sliding clamps, hold it in place. The knife is slightly concave on both sides.

The well is so large that it will hold an ordinary kidney after hardening, or at least so much of it that a transverse sec-

---

[1] Made by Miller Bros., 1213 Broadway, New York city.

2

tion may be made of the whole organ at one sweep of the knife. The knife and frame are modifications of those devised by Dr. E. Curtis of this city, and the section-cutter and box are not different in any essential particulars from those in common use.

They are larger, however, and the indicator, G, enables the observer to determine with accuracy the thickness of his sections. Thus, in my own instrument thirty-one turns of the milled head drives the plug forward one inch.

Each revolution consequently drives the specimen forward $\frac{1}{31}$ inch. Now, the circumference of the milled head is marked off into thirty divisions.

When the indicator marks that the plug has been driven forward one division, the distance traversed will be $\frac{1}{930}$ inch.

It is easy, therefore, to determine the thickness of any section with considerable accuracy.

When it is desirable to put the instrument in use, the plug that is to be used is well oiled, as also the thread of the driver, and the metallic box is filled with a mixture of ice and snow.

It is necessary to be particular and oil the bearings thoroughly, else they will bind and the instrument will be clogged while the freezing process is going on. The usual plan is to soak the tissue (as Dr. Pritchard suggests) in a thick solution of gum, which cuts like cheese when frozen. The soaking should continue for a number of hours, say until the next day.

When the tissue is ready, a thick solution of the gum should be poured into the well and the tissue held until it is fixed by the ice. Some non-conductor is to be placed over the well as soon as fixation has commenced, in order that access of heat may be prevented.

If ice is used it should be ground up finely and then packed tightly about the well; snow is better. The whole process takes only ten or fifteen minutes. The freezing section-cutter is of use when we are desirous of making a rapid examination of fresh tissues.

It is obvious that they are seen under more natural circumstances than when they have passed through the bichromate or chromic acid solutions, or alcohol, all of which cause more or less change in such delicate substances.

It has been hoped that by the freezing method we should

learn much that is new about the finer structures of the brain and the character of the corpuscular elements of the body, but as yet it has not reached our expectations.

Hailes's microtome.—A very ingenious and excellent instrument (Fig. 10) has been devised by Dr. William Hailes, Professor of Histology and Pathological Anatomy at the Albany Medical College. Objections to it will be mainly on the ground of price.

Dr. Hailes uses it as a simple instrument or as a freezing microtome, arranged either for ice and salt, ether-spray, rhigoline, etc.

The employment of ice and salt (coarse) is preferred, because it costs but little and freezes the mass solidly and quickly, and, if desired, 500 or 1,000 sections can be obtained in a few moments, depending, of course, upon the rapidity and skill of the operator.

The time of freezing is about seven minutes, except in very warm weather, when it requires a few moments longer.

The instrument does not work quite so satisfactorily in very warm weather, owing to the rapid melting at the surface of the preparation.

It is absolutely necessary that the mass should be frozen solid, or the sections cannot be cut smoothly.

An extra freezer may be employed, and while one specimen is being cut the other is being frozen; by exchanging cylinders (they being interchangeable) no delay is necessary.

The art of cutting is readily acquired. Two hundred or two hundred and fifty sections have been made in a minute, and of a uniform thickness of $\frac{1}{7300}$ of an inch. It is not necessary to remove the sections from the knife each time, but twenty or thirty may be permitted to collect upon the blade. They lie curled or folded up upon the knife, and when placed in water, straighten themselves out perfectly in the course of a few hours. The knife employed is an ordinary long knife from an amputating case.

Perfectly fresh tissues may be cut without any previous preparation, using ordinary mucilage (acacia) to freeze in, but most specimens require special preparation.

If preserved in Müller's fluid, alcohol, etc., they require to be washed thoroughly for several hours, and then, according to the suggestion of Dr. David J. Hamilton, F.R.C.S., etc., of

the University of Edinburgh, Scotland, the specimen is placed in
a strong syrup (sugar, two ounces; water, one ounce) for twenty-
four hours; it is then removed to ordinary mucilage for forty-
eight hours, and finally is cut in the freezing microtome.

These sections may be kept indefinitely in a preservative

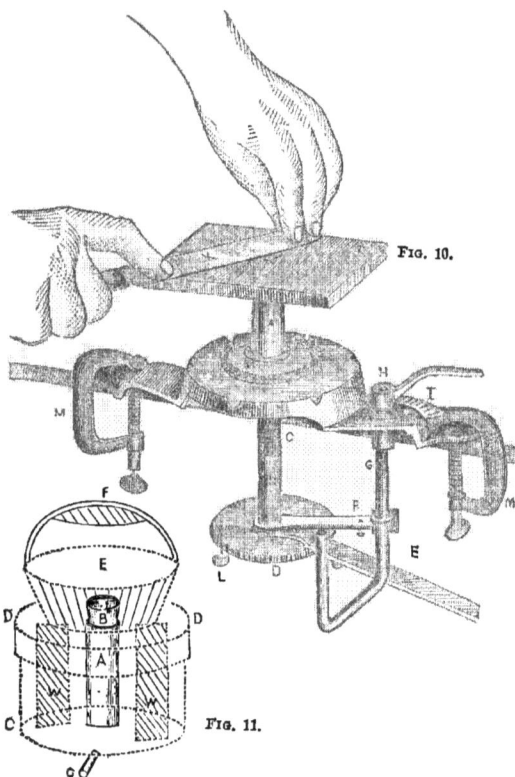

FIG. 10.

FIG. 11.

FIG. 10.—Poly-microtome (without freezing apparatus): A, small well fitting on pyramidal bed-plate;
B, pyramidal bed-plate containing different sizes; C, micrometer screw; D, ratchet-wheel attached to
screw: E, lever actuating the micrometer screw by means of a pawl engaging in teeth of ratchet-wheel;
F, arm carrying a dog, which prevents back motion of screw; G, regulator for limiting the throw of
lever, and consequently governing the micrometer screw; H, lever-nut for fixing regulator; I, index with
pointer and graduated scale, from 1/2400 inch to 1/200 inch; K, knife for cutting sections; L, knob to
turn micrometer screw direct when pawls are detached; M, table clamp; T, table of microtome, with
glass top to facilitate cutting.

FIG. 11.—(Very much reduced in size). A, B, tube containing specimen which is surrounded by freezing mixture in tin receiver C, D; E, F, revolving hopper with wings, W, W, for stirring the ice; G, outlet for melted ice.

fluid recommended by Dr. Hamilton: ℞. Glycerin., aquæ
destil., āā. ℥ iv.; acid. carbolic., gtt. iij. Boil and filter. The
addition of alcohol, ℥ ij., is advisable.

The Vincent microtome.—This instrument, which was devised by Dr. Vincent, of New York city, is a flat piece of steel (Fig. 12) 12 inches long by 2—2½ inches wide, with a bevelled cutting edge, 6 inches long. The handle is simply the rounded and smoothed extremity of the knife.

It has been in use at the School of Histology connected with the Columbia Veterinary College, and has proved to be a very efficient knife.

The mode of action is very simple. The object having been previously placed in any ordinary hand-cylinder and mounted

Fig. 12.

in wax, paraffine, or pith, the sections are made by a stroke of the knife, which is pushed straight forward. As will be readily seen, the larger the section the wider the knife must be.

The blade is made of the best plate steel, and is easily kept in order.

STAINING FLUIDS.

Ammonia carmine.—This is one of the oldest and best known solutions. Take one part, by weight, of the best carmine, which is known as "No. 40," dissolve it in 100 parts of distilled water, and add one part of aqua ammoniæ. The previous dull color now gives place to a most brilliant and deep red. It is necessary, however, that the carmine be either neutral or very faintly alkaline, else the color will diffuse and the tissues will not be differentiated. Expose the fluid, therefore, for some weeks to the air, or evaporate over the water-bath until the odor of ammonia is no longer perceptible.

The nuclei should be deeply and brightly stained, while the intercellular substance is in no way affected. If, however, diffusion has taken place, a great deal of it may be removed by soaking the section in a saturated alcoholic solution of oxalic acid. When a brick-red color has in this way been obtained, the object has been accomplished. Crystals of oxalic acid are apt to be found in specimens that have been prepared in this way. It is therefore desirable, after using the acid, to wash thoroughly in alcohol or water.

Borax carmine (Arnold's formula).—The following method is given by Dr. M. N. Miller as the one in use by students in the histological laboratory of the New York University. It originated with Prof. J. W. S. Arnold. A saturated solution of borax is prepared in a wide-mouthed pint bottle. The borax should be in some excess. "No. 40" carmine is now added to the solution under constant agitation, until after a while it no longer dissolves, and an excess remains at the bottom of the vial, mingled with the crystals of borax. After twenty-four hours the supernatant fluid is decanted. To this clear portion f. ℥ ij. of alcohol are added, and f. ℨ j. of caustic soda solution (U. S. P.). The staining solution is now ready. Or, the alcohol may be omitted (Arnold), and the liquid evaporated to dryness; the red amorphous mass is then powdered. Of this, 15 grains are placed in an ounce of water, to which f. ℨ j. of alcohol is added.[1]

Sections, after staining, should be washed in alcohol to remove the superfluous coloring fluid, and then transferred to a saturated solution of oxalic acid in alcohol to fix the color. The oxalic acid is then washed out in alcohol; finally the sections are cleared up in oil of cloves, and mounted in balsam or dammar.

Double staining by borax carmine and indigo carmine.—Drs. W. T. Norris and E. O. Shakespeare, of Philadelphia, have recommended a method which is a modification of Merkel's. Two staining fluids are made, one red and the other blue. The red one contains carmine, gr. 7½; borax, ℨ ss.; distilled water, ℥ j. The blue contains indigo carmine, ℨ ss.; borax, ℨ ss.; and distilled water, ℥ vij.

After thorough trituration the ingredients are mixed and left in a vessel; the supernatant fluid is then poured off. The sections, if previously hardened in bichromate, picric acid, or chromic acid, should be well washed; they then are to be placed for a few minutes in a mixture (equal parts) of the red and blue fluids, then transferred, without washing, to a saturated solution of oxalic acid and allowed to remain in it rather less time than in the staining fluid. When sufficiently bleached

---

[1] [This preparation of borax carmine is the best that I have ever used.—T. E. S.]

the sections should be washed in water until every trace of oxalic acid is removed. Sections thus prepared may be mounted in balsam or dammar. Connective-tissue substances are blue, while the nuclei are red. The osseous lamellæ of bone are blue, the cells in the lacunæ red, while the marrow is applegreen.

Picro-carmine (Miller's).—Add one part of a saturated solution of picric acid to two parts of the 15-grain borax carmine solution (Arnold's). The epithelium of the glands and the muscles are stained yellow, while the nuclei of the cells and the connective tissues acquire the carmine color. Sections should remain in the picro-carmine solution for about twenty-four hours. Next they are washed quickly in water, then in alcohol, after which they are transferred to the oil of cloves. (For Ranvier's method of making picro-carmine, see the chapter upon the Histology of the Nervous System.)

Hæmatoxylon solution (Boehmer's).—Dissolve 20 grains of hæmatoxylon in one-half an ounce of absolute alcohol; then dissolve 2 grains of alum in an ounce of water. Some drops of the first solution are added to the second, which, after a short time, becomes a beautiful violet. It improves after keeping for a few days, and should always be filtered before using (Thin).

Hæmatoxylon solution (Kleinenburg's).—First make a saturated solution of the chloride of lime in seventy per cent. alcohol, and add alum to saturation.

Then make a saturated solution of alum in seventy per cent. alcohol. Add the first to the second in the proportion of one to eight. To the mixture add a few drops of a saturated solution of hæmatoxylon in absolute alcohol (Thin).

Hæmatoxylon solution (Miller's method).—Take a pint bottle, as in the former process, fill with water, and add about an ounce of common extract of logwood in coarse powder. Allow this to remain in a warm place for twenty-four hours, with occasional stirring. After the expiration of this time add powdered commercial alum until the liquid changes from the muddy brown color given by the logwood to a brilliant purple.

The alum is to be added until no change is produced. An excess of the salt will do no harm. Add about f. ℥ j. of alcohol, and after decanting or filtering it is ready for use. One may omit the alcohol at this stage, and evaporate to dryness as in the borax-carmine process. The powder thus obtained is added to water when required. Three grains to the ounce of water will give a fluid that will stain alcohol-hardened tissue in from ten to fifteen minutes. A solution containing ten grains to the ounce will stain very quickly. If it is desired to keep the solution, add f. ℥ j. of alcohol for each ounce. Hæmatoxylon stainings are soaked in water for a few minutes to wash out the alum, then transferred to alcohol, clarified in the clove oil, and finally mounted in balsam or dammar.

Klein's formula for hæmatoxylon.—Mix in a mortar 5 grammes of the officinal extract of hæmatoxylon, with 15 grammes of alum, and pulverize carefully. To this add gradually 25 c.c. of distilled water, and filter. To the residue add 15 c.c. of distilled water and again mix in a mortar, and filter; to this filtrate add 2 grammes of alcohol. Now mix the two filtrates and keep in a glass-stoppered bottle. If the liquid should at any time become muddy, filter again. Care must be taken to prevent any acid from intermingling with the fluid. Acids cause the hæmatoxylon to turn red ; for this reason, sections which have been hardened in chromic acid should be placed in a watch-glass and covered with distilled water, to which add a drop or two of a 30 per cent. solution of caustic potassa ; allow it to remain therein 10 to 15 minutes. To use the hæmatoxylon fluid, add a few drops to an ounce of distilled water, so as to make a pale violet solution ; allow sections to remain in this solution for 12 to 24 hours. Or, a stronger solution may be employed which will stain specimens in 10 to 30 minutes, and still give good results. Mount in glycerine, acetate of potassa, balsam, or better, resinous turpentine.

Eosine solution.—Eosine, first introduced by Fischer in 1875, is much used in staining fresh preparations. It is customary to have a strong solution of one to ten or twenty on hand. A few drops are then added to a watch-glassful of water or alcohol. Fresh tissues are both stained and hardened. It affects the body of the cells, together with the nuclei. It is apt to diffuse, unless special care is taken, and long soaking, say for twenty-four hours, is practised.

Double-staining with eosine and other aniline colors.— Schiefferdecker first stains in an alcoholic solution of eosine and then in a one per cent. watery solution of an aniline color (dahlia, methyl violet, or aniline green). Care must be taken not to extract the color when dehydrating the specimen in alcohol according to the usual method; very deep staining is therefore desirable.

Green coloration of the nuclei.—To effect this, Tafani employs a fluid containing three or four parts of a saturated watery solution of aniline blue to some six or seven parts of a saturated watery solution of picric acid.

Eosine and hæmatoxylon for staining bone.—Busch recommends eosine and hæmatoxylon for double-staining the zone of ossification in growing bone. The sections of decalcified bone are first immersed a few days in a one-half per cent. chromic acid solution, or in a one per cent. solution of the bichromate of potassium, and then, after washing with water, in a watery solution of eosine. In young bone, where ossification is progressing, the cartilage matrix is blue, while the nuclei of the cartilage-cells adjoining the line of bone are red; the contents of the medullary spaces are also bright red, while in the bone trabecles there is a combination of blue and red.

Eosine for permanent specimens.—Renaut has employed eosine to differentiate all forms of protoplasm, whether bodies or their processes. He either employs a watery solution alone, or with the admixture of one-third its volume of alcohol. The coloration is obtained after immersion of the sections from one-half minute to one minute. They are then washed in distilled water, and may be preserved in a neutral solution of glycerine to which one per cent. of chloride of sodium has been added to prevent the glycerine dissolving the eosine. These preparations will then remain unchanged for months.

In examining the fixed corpuscles of the subcutaneous tissue, the same author injects beneath the skin a solution of eosine and water (1–500), and then removes a portion of the infiltrated tissue with the scissors. The fibrous fascicles are unaffected, while the elastic fibres take the color deeply.

The fixed corpuscles appear as red granular plates, while their nuclei take a very intense color. This reagent, therefore, is well suited for the study of connective tissues. In special instances the silver method may be used first, and then the eosine.

Preparation of the cornea.—Klein has adopted the following plan for exhibiting this most delicate tissue. He first burns the centre of the cornea of a kitten with caustic potash, and then, twenty-four hours later, brushes the surface with nitrate

of silver, and, half an hour afterward, immerses it in water
acidulated with acetic acid ; after a day or two it is found to
have a glutinous appearance. The lamellæ are then easily
stripped off, and in the middle portions, the corneal corpuscles
assume a purplish-brown color while their nuclei are uncolored. The outlines of the lymphatic channels are also sharply
defined.

Picro-hæmatoxylon and eosine (triple-staining).—Wendt
has described a method of double-staining by picric acid and
hæmatoxylon. Only the very thinnest sections, however, give
satisfactory results. A strong solution of hæmatoxylon is first
employed. In this the sections are allowed to remain about
twelve hours. After washing them in water, they are placed
in a saturated solution of picric acid and carefully watched.
They may be removed from time to time, examined with a low
power, and, when properly stained, put in alcohol and mounted in Canada balsam with as little delay as possible. To obtain triple-staining, eosine may be conveniently combined with
this picro-hæmatoxylon method. To insure good results some
amount of practice is necessary.

Double, triple, and quadruple staining.—Dr. Gibbes recommends for double-staining, immersion first in picro-carmine
and then in logwood, or which is better, immersion first in a
spirituous solution of rosine or aniline violet, and then in an
aqueous solution of aniline blue or iodine green. In obtaining
more than two colors there is considerable difficulty. To accomplish it he uses first the chloride of gold or picro-carmine
and then the spirituous and aqueous solutions of the ani-
lines.

Staining with Bismark brown.—Make a watery solution of
gr. ij.— ℨ j., heat and filter ; soak in the solution about three
minutes ; set the color with glacial acetic acid (4 per cent).
for half a minute. After dehydrating with alcohol mount in
dammar varnish. Weigert prepares the Bismark brown as
follows : he makes a concentrated aqueous solution by boiling in water, filtering from time to time. He also uses a weak
alcoholic solution, and combines with other colors.

[To combine with eosine—put the sections in a strong aqueous solution of
Bismark brown ; remove after about two minutes, set in weak acetic acid (four
per cent.), then place in a weak alcoholic or aqueous solution of eosine, and
then again in the acetic acid solution.—T. E. S.]

Solution of alum-carmine.—Grenacher recommends this fluid: Take a one to five per cent. solution of ordinary alum, or ammonia alum ; boil with one-half to one per cent. powdered carmine for twenty minutes. Filter, and add a little carbolic acid to preserve.

Naphthaline yellow for bone.—In sections of the femur from a fœtal pig, three and a half inches in length, the following method was found to yield very excellent results :

After immersion for three days in Müller's fluid, sections were made, and, after washing in water, immediately dipped in an alcoholic solution of naphthaline yellow (gr. iv.— ℥ j.) ; after eight to ten minutes the sections were removed, and dipped in a watery solution of acetic acid of three per cent.; then they were immersed for about ten minutes in the ordinary solution of ammonia-carmine, rendered neutral by exposure to the air.

The sections were again dipped in the acetic acid solution in order to set the color, and then placed in alcohol of eighty per cent., and subsequently in absolute alcohol.

The specimens thus stained showed a matrix of deep transparent chrome yellow. The young bone-corpuscles and osteoblasts, on the other hand, together with the fibrous tissue, assumed a brilliant rose color, thus affording an excellent contrast between forming and formed bone.

Staining with methyl-green and induline.—Calberla has introduced two new substances into use, viz., methyl-green and induline. The one stains the nuclei of the cells of the subcutaneous tissue, the nuclei of vessels and nerve-sheaths rose color, while the cells of the corium and their nuclei are a violet red ; the other colors the cells of the Malpighian layer a greenish blue. Combinations of methyl green and eosine are also recommended. Eosine (one part) and methyl green (sixty parts) are to be dissolved in a thirty per cent. solution of warm alcohol. The epithelial nuclei take a violet blue, the nuclei of connective tissue a greenish blue, and the cell-body a red color. Singular differentiations are made ; thus, while the striated muscle is red, the nuclei are green. On the other hand, smooth muscular tissue is green, and the intercellular substance red. In the salivary glands the cells of the excretory ducts are blue, while the so-called secretory cells are red. Induline dissolves in warm water and in dilute alcohol. Take a

concentrated watery solution, dilute it with six times its
volume of water, then immerse the preparations from 5 to 20
minutes, wash them out and clarify in oil of cloves or glycerine.
The peculiarity of this material is that it never affects the
nucleus, but only the cell-body. More frequently, however, it
is the intercellular substance that is colored blue.

Purpurine.—Ranvier has recommended this dye, which is
extracted from madder. Alum (one part) is dissolved in distilled water (two hundred parts); the fluid is then heated to
the boiling point in a porcelain dish. Then a small quantity
of purpurine is dissolved in distilled water and added to it.
Sufficient purpurine should be added to leave a residue, by
which it is certain that the solution is saturated. While still
hot it is to be filtered into alcohol of one-fourth the total
volume. The fluid has an orange red color, and is more efficient when fresh. Sections should be immersed from 24 to 48
hours.

French archil—Staining with extract.—Wedl uses this
substance, which, after the loss of the ammonia, is dissolved
in 20 c.c. absolute alcohol, 5 c.c. acetic acid of 1.070 sp. gr.,
and 40 c.c. of distilled water so as to make a saturated solution. Protoplasm and matrix, but not nuclei, are colored a
beautiful red.

Alizarine.—This aniline color is recommended by Thanhoffer, but experience is limited with reference to it. It has a
golden yellow color, and is easily fixed by the tissues.

METALLIC SOLUTIONS.

Staining with osmic and oxalic acids.—Broesicke adopts
the following method :

Little pieces of fresh or freshly dried preparations are left
for an hour in a one per cent. solution of osmic acid ; then
they are carefully washed and soaked in a cold saturated solution of oxalic acid, and finally examined in water or glycerine. Elastic fibres are yellow, fat is black, while the walls
of capillaries and many connective-tissue substances are
red.

Chloride of gold and lemon juice. — Ranvier is in the
habit of demonstrating the corneal nerves by using lemon-

juice in which the tissue is left five minutes. Then it is soaked for 15 to 20 minutes in 3 c.c. of a one per cent. solution of the gold chloride, and finally 25 to 30 minutes in distilled water to which one or two drops of acetic acid has been added. After two or three days' exposure to the sun, the fibres become distinct.

Nitrate of silver in solution (gr. j.—iv.— ℥ j.) is much used. The details of the method will be found in the Chapter on the Lymphatics.

Chloride of gold has also been much used in studying the so-called lymph-canalicular system of the cornea. The method of employing it will be found in the section relating to the cornea.

Osmic acid in solution is also very useful. Its effects are given in the chapter on the General Histology of the Nervous System.

Methyl-green for showing waxy change.—Curschmann, of Hamburg, has recommended this reagent to effect the same object as the *violet de Paris* of Cornil. A solution of about five grains to the ounce is used. The specimens are bathed in the fluid a few minutes or hours. They take the color quickly. After staining they may be mounted in glycerine. The amyloid material assumes a brilliant rose color. The surrounding tissue takes a dull green.

Wickersheimer's preserving liquid.—This material has been extensively used of late, and there are several formulæ for it. Among the most recent modifications is that made by the firm of Poetz & Flohr, of Berlin. For immersing specimens the ingredients are : arsenious acid, 12 grains ; sodium chloride, 60 grains ; potassium sulphate, 150 grains ; potassium nitrate, 18 grains ; potassium carbonate, 15 grains ; water, 10 litres ; glycerine, 4 litres ; wood naphtha, ¾ litre. A modified fluid is used for injecting the blood-vessels. This is suitable for all fresh tissues, preserving them in their natural color and consistence.

If the tissues are to be used subsequently for the microscope, it is said that they should be washed thoroughly in water, but it seems from recent experiments that the fluid unfits them for minute examination. It is also rather expensive, and has an extremely pungent and unpleasant odor.

METHODS OF INJECTING THE BLOOD-VESSELS.[1]

Good injections are hard to make, requiring skill, patience, and practice. First of all, it is essential to have a perfectly transparent injecting material. This is usually made up with gelatine and colored by carmine or Prussian blue. When carmine is used it is customary to dissolve it in ammonia, filter, and then add it to the solution of gelatine. In order to obtain a neutral or faintly acid liquid, acetic acid is added, drop by drop, until the alkalinity is overcome, but there must, at the same time, be no precipitation of carmine, which is best detected by the granules of carmine seen in the field of the microscope. If alkaline, the color diffuses and the result is a failure.

It is difficult to lay down any rule in reference to the amount of acetic acid necessary ; the color of the liquid is the best and only satisfactory test. The ammoniacal odor, if very slight, cannot be detected, and therefore is useless as a test. A slight excess of acid, however, will do no harm.

The preparation of the blue injecting fluid is less difficult.

Usually Brücke's soluble Berlin blue is used ; it can be procured at most of the large drug stores, but if not obtainable, may be made as follows (Klein) :

"Take of potassic ferrocyanide 217 grammes, and dissolve in one litre of water (solution A). Take one litre of a ten per cent. solution of ferric chloride (solution B). Take four litres of a saturated solution of sulphate of soda (solution C). Add to A and B two litres of C. Then, with constant stirring, pour the ferric chloride mixture into a vessel, collect the precipitate upon a flannel strainer, returning any blue fluid which at first escapes through the pores of the flannel ; allow the solutions to drain off. Pour a little distilled water over the blue mass, returning the first washing if colored, and renew the water from day to day until it drips through permanently of a deep blue color. This is a sign that the salts are washed away, and all that is further necessary is to collect the pasty mass from the strainer and allow it to dry."

Having obtained the soluble Berlin blue, it will be much

---

[1] Prepared for the editor by Dr. W. H. Porter, Curator of the Presbyterian Hospital, New York city.

simpler to inject both arteries and veins with the same solution. If a small animal is to be employed (as the rabbit, for instance) it will be found most convenient to inject through the aorta. If, however, an organ from the human body is to be injected, through the main vessels of that part. To commence with, the kidney is probably the best, as it is small and of firm consistence.

For injecting with the red gelatine liquid the following rules will be found of service, and yield good results:

Take 40 grammes of Cox's best English gelatine, place it in a jar, and add just water enough to cover it; let it stand for several hours, when it will imbibe the water, being hygroscopic; it may then be dissolved over a water-bath.

Take of the carmine 22 grammes and dissolve in 40 c.c. of aqua ammoniæ, then add 240 c.c. distilled water, and filter. The preparation of the carmine solution had better be commenced the day before, as it takes about twenty-four hours to filter. The gelatine and carmine solutions are raised, separately, to the same temperature, when the gelatine solution is gradually added to the carmine solution, under constant stirring. The injection fluid, which is now of a deep cherry-red color and alkaline reaction, is precipitated with acetic acid until the deep cherry color gives place to a bright red, and the ammoniacal odor is exchanged for that of acetic acid. At this point a little more acid may be added without doing harm. In case the liquid should be found too concentrated, a little more water may be added. For the blue mass the following method may be adopted:

Take 66 grammes of gelatine, and prepare as in the former case. Add 4 grammes of soluble Berlin blue in substance and 360 c.c. of water.

The blue will also be found slow in filtering. When both are heated to the same temperature add the gelatine to the blue solution, with constant stirring. When this has been done, a solution of the iron salts may be added to intensify the blue color, care being exercised not to add enough of the iron to coagulate the gelatine. This liquid also may be diluted if found so concentrated that it will not flow easily. The liquids having been prepared, the organ carefully removed from the body, thoroughly washed out and heated to a temperature of 98° F., everything is ready for injection. The filling of the vessels may be accomplished in one of two ways: either by forcing in the fluid with a syringe or by the pressure of a column of water. The syringe is the simplest, but requires practice and skill in manipulation.

Having inserted the canula into the artery, the kidney may be entirely filled with either the red or blue injecting liquid. When the organ is seen to be swollen, tense, and well colored the vessels must be tied off, and the kidney placed in a freezing mixture until the gelatine has set. When this is accomplished, the organ should be cut into small pieces, and placed first in a weak solution of alcohol (seventy per cent. or less), and the strength of the alcohol gradually increased until the specimen is sufficiently hard for cutting. The object of using weak alcohol is to prevent too great shrinkage of the gelatine. If two colors are used, it is impossible to tell beforehand how much fluid will be necessary to fill the arterial and venous systems, and not have the one encroach on the other. For an ordinary kidney, about 250 c.c. of the injecting liquid should be prepared to fill the arterial vessels, and nearly double to fill the veins. The following rules must be observed in injecting: keep the gelatine solutions and the organ as nearly as possible at the same temperature. Immerse the organ in warm water during the process. Avoid the entrance of air into the canula when connecting the syringe. Inject slowly, and give the fluid time to work its way into the minute capillary ramifications.

The above rules can be applied to any organ, with such modifications as will suggest themselves to the operator.

BIBLIOGRAPHY.

KLEIN. Handbook of the Physiological Laboratory. Edited by Sanderson. Vol. I. 1873.

BUSCH. Arch. f. Mikroskop. Anat. XIV. 1877.

NORRIS and SHAKESPEARE. American Journal of the Medical Sciences, Oct., 1877.

RENAUT. Archives de physiol. 2me Série, T. IV. 1877.

SCHAEFER. Histology and the Microscope. Philadelphia, 1877.

THIN. Practical Histology. London, 1877.

WENDT. Ueber die Hardersche Drüse, etc. Strassburg, 1877.

RANVIER. Traité technique d'histologie. Paris, 1877-8.

BROESICKE, J. Med. Centralblatt. 46. 1878.

CALBERLA. Morpholog. Jahrb. III. H. & S.'s Jahrb. I. 1878.
HAMILTON. Journal of Anatomy and Physiology. Vol. XII. 1878.
MILLER. New York Medical Record, Feb. 2, 1878, p. 97.
RANVIER. Journ. de micrographie. H. & S.'s Jahrb. 1878.
SCHIEFFERDECKER. Arch. f. mikrosk. Anat. XIV. 1878.
TAFANI. Journal de micrographie. 1878.
WEDL. Virchow's Archiv, 74. 1878.
WEIGERT. Arch. f. mikrosk. Anat. XV., p. 259. 1878.
FLESCH. Archiv f. mikrosk. Anat. XVI., p. 300. 1879.
GRENACHER. Arch. f. mikrosk. Anat. XVI., p. 463. 1879.
KLEIN and E. NOBLE SMITH. Atlas of Histology. 1879–80.
CURSCHMANN. Archiv f. Path. Anat. LXXIX., III. 1880.
FREY. The Microscope and Microscopical Technology. New York, 1880.
GIBBES. Lancet, March 20, 1880.
HAILES. An Improved Microtome. New York Medical Record, July 24, 1880.
THANHOFFER, L. v. Das Mikroskop u. seine Anwendung. Stuttgart, 1880.
VINCENT. New York Medical Record, June 12, 1880.
WICKERSHEIMER. Arch. f. Pharm. New Remedies, May, 1880.
GIBBES. Practical Histology and Pathology. Philadelphia, 1881.
SEILER. Compendium of Microscopical Technology. Philadelphia, 1881.
STOWELL. The Student's Manual of Histology. Detroit, 1881.
HARRIS and POWER. Manual for the Physiological Laboratory. New York, 1881.

CHAPTER III.

THE BLOOD.

In man and most vertebrates the blood consists of a clear fluid, the *liquor sanguinis* or *plasma*, in which a large number of corpuscles are very evenly distributed. Of these there are two prominent varieties, differing much in character—the *red* and the *colorless* or *white*. The former are greatly in excess, and give to the liquid its characteristic red appearance.

In relative proportion the two vary greatly within certain limits. Usually there is but one of the white to 600 or 1,200 of the red ; but these numerical relations are disturbed by various diseases, and the white may equal the red, or even, in rare cases, exceed them.

In fresh liquid blood the corpuscles are the only solid matters visible under the microscope ; nor is there any difference in this respect with coagulated blood, when the quantity is large. If, however, a little should be allowed to dry, fibrin may be deposited under the form of delicate filaments, which are superimposed on one another without definite order.

In one hundred volumes of blood there are said to be thirty-six volumes of corpuscles and sixty-four of plasma. This ratio, however, is altered somewhat by different conditions, such as the age and health of the individual.

The *red corpuscles* in man and other mammals, with very few exceptions, are bi-concave bodies, circular in outline. In birds, amphibia, and almost all fishes they are also bi-concave or hollowed out at the centre, but have an elliptical contour. In the human species nuclei or central bodies appear at a very early period of life, but subsequently are invisible, unless artificial means are used to display them. In birds, amphibia, and fishes a rounded prominence is also seen at the centre, which is particularly well marked when the corpuscle happens to be turned so that its edge meets the eye. This prominence corresponds to the ordinary nucleus of other elementary bodies or cells. In this position the peculiar shape of the corpuscles, with their constricted centres and rounded extremities, has suggested a comparison between them and the little cakes known as lady's-fingers. (See Fig. 13.)

It is obvious also that this varying thickness of the disk will have some effect upon the microscopic image, for the whole superficies cannot be in focus at one time, even when the cor-

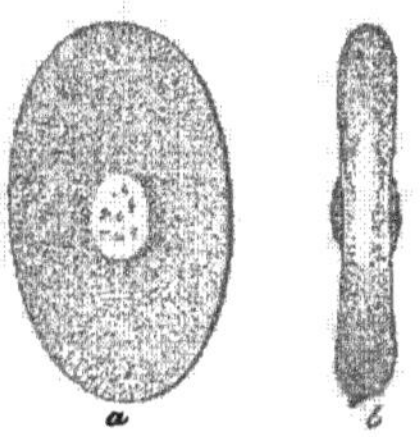

FIG. 13.—Red corpuscles of the frog. Rollett.

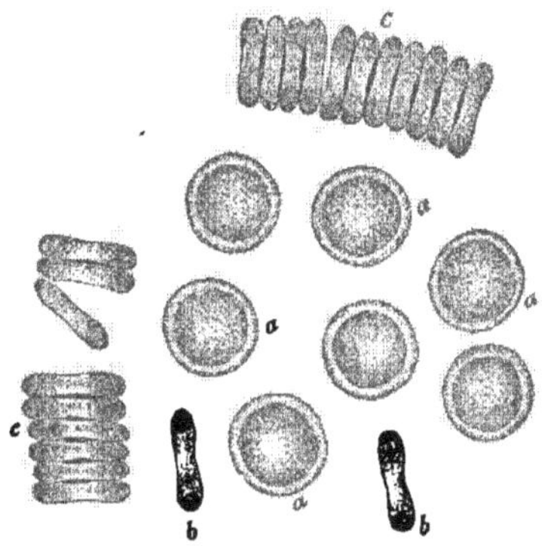

FIG. 14.—Human red blood-corpuscles: *a*, globules showing the double contour; *b*, globules turned on edge; *c*, the same in rouleaux like coin. Rollett.

puscle is turned flatwise to the eye. There will be some difference between the level of the thickest and thinnest portions. As a result, when one is dark the other is bright, when one is well defined the other is blurred. This statement serves for an explanation of the double contour that is sometimes observed in human blood (see Fig. 14), though it has also been offered in support of the theory that the semi-solid and elastic matter of which the disk is mainly composed has an external envelope or limiting membrane of different density. It is to be remembered, however, that the property of double refraction which explains the double contour, belongs to all transparent bodies that have rounded edges, such as drops of water or oil, in which cases there is plainly no enveloping or peripheral wall. When the lens and eye-piece are suitably combined, as in the best microscopes, the double marking is often difficult or impossible to discover. On the other hand a poor optical combination will generally exhibit it to an unpleasant degree, and

especially if great amplification is aimed at. Lenses of very
high power are also apt in any case to exhibit the same appearances.

*Measurements of the red corpuscles in man and ani-
mals.*—The average diameter of the human red globule is still
a matter of discussion. The faulty measurements of the older
writers have led to some misconception on these points, and the
matter has required new study. Welcker, who has long been
an authority on the Continent, gave .00774 mm. as the average
breadth in the human male, with a minimum of .0045 mm., the
latter from personal observation. A maximum of .010 mm.
has been given by Max Schultze, while Frey places the average
thickness at .0018 mm. Later investigations by Hayem show
that a diameter of .012 mm. or even .014 mm. may be reached,
while he has known it to fall as low as .0022 mm. Elsberg
gives the mean diameter of the red blood-corpuscle at .0075
mm., agreeing very nearly with Welcker. He has observed a
maximum of .01016 mm., and a minimum of .00422 mm.

Measurements of single corpuscles have no value in determining the particular animal from which the blood has been
obtained, and this is an object of prime importance in medico-
legal cases. It is common, therefore, to make a hundred or
more single measurements, and then take the average of them.
And yet this figure may vary considerably in different individuals, or even in the same one. In the blood of the puppy, for
instance (the size of the dog's corpuscle being very nearly
that of man's), a recent observer found that the average diameter of fifty corpuscles varied only two-millionth of an inch
from a like average of fifty taken from his own blood. In
another instance, taking forty from a puppy, he found that
the average differed only seven-millionth of an inch from a
similar average of his own (Woodward).

Opposite is given a table of blood-corpuscle measurements
by Welcker and others.

By referring to it, the cat's and rabbit's corpuscles will be
found to have an average diameter which is not far distant
from man's and dog's, while the minimum and maximum
diameters of each show conclusively that a large number of
their corpuscles would be likely to equal man's, and therefore make it impossible to distinguish one from the other. To
obviate this source of error a very large number of corpuscles

would have to be measured separately, as we have already seen, and then an average taken of them all, before even a guarded opinion could be given as to the source of the blood. Still other difficulties, however, are apt to beset the microscopist. The blood is usually dried and in small quantity. The disks are then shrunken. If we endeavor to restore them to their original shape, as by soaking in blood-serum, we are never sure of having accomplished the object, or that we have not overdone it. This statement will be better understood by experiments that will be detailed at another point in this chapter. Where blood-corpuscles are elliptical, as in birds, there is much less opportunity for error.

Measurements of red Blood-corpuscles.

	Maximum diameter.	Minimum diameter.	Average diameter.
	mm.	mm.	mm.
Dog	.0082	.0065	.0073
Cat	.0074	.0058	.0065
Rabbit	.0080	.0062	.0069
Sheep	.0056	.0038	.0050
Goat (old)	.0046	.0036	.0041
" (eight days old)	.0066	.0039	.0054
Moschus javanicus	.0030	.0022	.0025
Elephant	.0106	.0084	.0094
Pigeon (old)	.0160	.0132	.0147
" (fledgling)	.0140	.0116	.0126
Chicken	.0132	.0104	.0121
Duck	.0140	.0118	.0129
Vespertilion	.0066	.0054	.0061
Triton cristatus	.0327	.0259	.0293
Salamandra cryptobranchus	.0415	.0302	.0378
Japonicus	.0579	.0460	.0512
Lepidosiren annectens	.0440	.0360	.0410

	Average length.	Average breadth.
	mm.	mm.
Protens anguineus	.058	.034
Amphiuna tridactylum (Schmidt)	.075	.047

The number of the red globules.—It has commonly been held that the blood of an adult man contains 5,000,000 red corpuscles in each cubic millimetre. In anæmic conditions this number may be reduced below 3,000,000, while in fair physical health it has reached 6,000,000 and over. Under ordinary circumstances 4,500,000 is thought to argue a fair bodily condition (Keyes).

Quite recently Hayem has given an instance where the number was reduced to 800,000. This extraordinary state he has called *aglobulie intense;* the name *aglobulie extrême* was given to a condition observed on another occasion where he counted only 450,000 corpuscles.

The blood-globules in an indifferent fluid.—In order to get a proper conception of the various influences that act upon the red corpuscles, so as to alter their form, size, and internal appearance, it is essential to subject them to some of the more common, such as water, acids, alkalies, electricity, etc. In no other way can the student appreciate the extraordinary changes which these bodies suffer, and indeed a knowledge of such matters is quite necessary in studying the histology of either normal or diseased tissues.

Unfortunately we are not always able to use human blood for these demonstrations because the corpuscles are too small, and consequently the alterations do not admit of easy observation. We naturally turn to an object that has larger corpuscles and may be procured with little trouble or expense.

The frog is therefore selected, or, even better still, the newt, which is especially well suited for this purpose. At first the blood may be examined in a menstruum similar to the liquor sanguinis or plasma, and the frog's aqueous humor is usually found satisfactory.

To a drop of this latter add an equal quantity of the blood, mix them well with a glass rod, and adjust an ordinary ¼ inch circle. The aqueous humor exerts no special influence over the corpuscles, and is therefore called an *indifferent* fluid. If it be impossible to obtain aqueous humor, an excellent substitute may be found in the fresh fluid from a hydrocele or ovarian cyst, or we may use serum to which iodine has been added, which is then called *iodized serum.* To six ounces of the fluid twenty grains of finely powdered iodine are added. After prolonged agitation the iodine will be dissolved, and the mixture thus prepared may be kept for a number of months. Suspended in this liquid the blood is studied to advantage with a lens of moderate power, such as an ordinary

$\frac{1}{3}$ inch. The contents of the disk will appear *homogeneous*, which is a term that merely indicates an *apparent* absence of structure. The nucleus and nucleolus should also be invisible. The shape of the corpuscles is oval, and they are flattened and have rounded edges, with hollowed centres, in which a prominence is usually seen (Fig. 13). The *protoplasm* is the substance of which the disk is made ; it has a light yellow color, and is dull or pellucid in appearance, much like semi-solid jelly.

Brownian and amœboid movements. — Using the same method of preparation the *white corpuscles or leucocytes* are seen to good advantage. They are much smaller than the red disks (in the frog—the reverse of human blood), and there is wide range in size, one histologist (Klein) having described as many as thirty varieties. In the interior, little dark spots are sometimes seen in constant vibration. By a skilled observer they are readily detected, even with a good $\frac{1}{4}$ inch glass. When such specks are numerous the bodies are said to be granular. In the newt's blood this phenomenon is usually best seen. The word *granule* has been applied in these cases from the notion once prevalent that the little dots were molecules suspended in a menstruum of some sort that filled the corpuscle. This subject is now eliciting much study, but the movement, whatever its significance may be, is called the *Brownian movement*.

Klein, who states that the newt's leucocyte is traversed by an intracellular network, believes that the movement just described is due to the motion of the "disintegrated network" under the stimulus of imbibed water. Under this explanation the oscillatory movement in the corpuscles of the human saliva would indicate death rather than life. When fluid has been withdrawn by evaporation the phenomenon ceases. According to other histologists this vibratile motion is an indication of vital action.

The remarkable change in form which these corpuscles undergo is a more positive indication of vital power in the leucocyte. When the little body is placed under conditions which imitate those of its natural state it commences to put forth processes and then withdraw them, carrying on these movements slowly, but with a certain degree of regularity. While this is being accomplished the corpuscle is observed to move about from place to place.

In Fig. 15 the leucocytes are seen. Those marked with the letter *a* are engaged in amœboid motion. The one marked *b* is in a state of contraction. This phenomenon is called *amœboid movement*, because it resembles that of the amœba—the little microscopic organism found in stagnant water. In order to permit these changes to continue for some length of time, it is well to paint a little oil or glycerine around the edge of the circle. Evaporation is thus prevented.

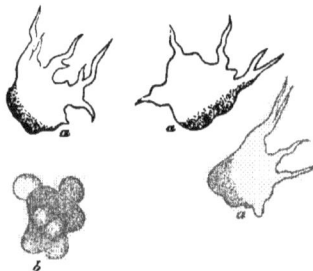

Fig. 15.—Leucocytes: *a*, putting out processes; *b*, having withdrawn them.　Rollett.

If the *warm slide* be used the changes will follow with greater rapidity. Both Brownian and amœboid movements are usually confined to a limited number of the corpuscles, and the former often to only a small portion of the interior.

The *slide*[1] *for heating* consists of an ordinary glass slide (Fig. 16) upon which is riveted a thin copper plate (*b*) perforated in the centre, so as to allow space for the drop of blood which is to be examined. From the copper plate extends an arm (*c*) over which is slipped a spiral copper wire (*e*), that is heated by the flame of an alcohol lamp. By this means the glass plate is kept warm and with it the drop of blood. In order to secure a proper amount of heat and no more, it is customary to put a little bit of cocoa butter upon the corner of the slide. The butter melts at the temperature of the body, and after this point has been reached the lamp should be carried along

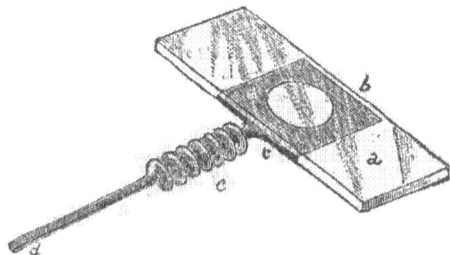

Fig. 16.—Slide for heating : *a*, slide; *b*, copper plate; *c*, arm over which the spiral wire (*d*) is slipped

the wire away from the slide until the precise distance is found at which this particular degree of heat will be maintained.

Action of a dilute salt solution.—It is often difficult, and,

---

[1] Made by T. H. McAllister, 49 Nassau Street, New York City.

indeed, impossible, to obtain aqueous humor or even an animal
fluid such as has been described, and microscopists have accordingly made use of a substitute that can be prepared at any time
and kept indefinitely. This is a solution of common salt in
distilled water (1—400). Add a drop of fresh frog's blood to a
drop of the salt solution, mix them well, and it will be seen
that the delicate protoplasm of the red blood-corpuscle, most
susceptible of change, is not altered in appearance, though the
body itself will change in form from the elliptical to the spherical. This salt solution has been found, in practice, an excellent
substitute for blood-serum, and is very generally used in examining fresh specimens, where it is important to avoid any
material change in the corpuscle.

Action of distilled water—Irrigation.—The effect of water
is also noteworthy, as it is a very important consideration in
both histological and pathological work, especially the latter.
Take a drop of frog's blood, add to it an equal quantity of
distilled water and apply a cover. The nucleus or central body
will now be readily seen, surrounded by a yellow border ; the
body of the corpuscle or peripheral part will at the same time
gradually become paler and larger. Now add distilled water
slowly, drop by drop, in the following way : Take a long strip
of tissue or filter paper about half the length of the slide and in
breadth equal to one-half the diameter of the cover. Apply
the water with an ordinary minim dropper, close to the edge of
the cover, on the side opposite to the paper strip. This latter
will now take up the excess of water and cause a stream to
pass through the specimen. This process is called *irrigation*.
Push the paper a short distance under the edge of the cover,
and the solid particles in the fluid will be carried to the edge
of the paper, where they will remain at rest and may be observed at one's leisure.

This plan is often useful in other sorts of microscopic work, as in looking
for renal casts, urinary crystals, etc. It may save much valuable time. I first
learned it from my friend, Dr. Edward Curtis, of this city.

Continued addition of water will cause the corpuscles to
swell and after a time burst, or, at any rate, become so expanded that they can scarcely be seen. When water is applied
slowly to human blood, the corpuscles soon begin to lose their

disk-like form and assume a spheroidal, perhaps spherical contour. The coloring matter then escapes, in most instances, and
they become quite transparent (see Fig. 17). Such corpuscles are
often seen in human urine where they appear as colorless rings.
In frog's or newt's blood the body of the disk first imbibes the

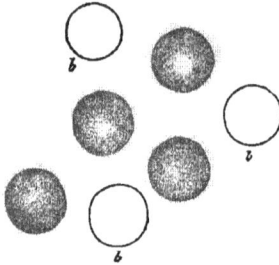

FIG. 17.—Human red blood-globules:
a, with hæmoglobin; b, without it.   Rollett.

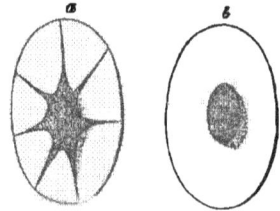

FIG. 18.—Red corpuscles of the frog
that have imbibed water.   Rollett.

water ; later, the nucleus, which then has a sharply defined
outline. Sometimes the material of which the body is largely
composed (hæmoglobin) is gathered about the nucleus, sending
off radiating prolongations to the periphery, while the imbibed
fluid is stored in the intervening spaces (see Fig. 18).

Action of carbonic acid gas.—This experiment requires a
special apparatus. First of all it is essential to have a *moist
chamber* (Fig. 19).

Take a small, flat bit of wood about 1½ inch wide, 3 inches
long, and ⅔ inch thick ; make a square opening in the centre,
sufficiently large to admit an ordinary ¾ inch cover-glass ; this
is to be pressed to the bottom and firmly fixed, thus making a

FIG. 19.—Moist chamber.

shallow well with a glass
bottom. Into this cham-
ber are admitted, through
side holes, glass tubes (one
on each side), so that air
or gases can be carried into the chamber. When in use, the
chamber is kept moist by a drop of water, which is put in
one corner of the well, while the specimen of blood to be examined is dropped upon a large glass cover, and the latter in-
verted over the mouth of the well. In determining the effect
of carbonic acid gas upon animal life, we have merely to connect the gas-chamber just described with a jar in which carbonic

acid gas is generated. Fig. 19 illustrates a *gas* or *moist chamber* of the same general character, and devised by Dr. J. H. Hunt, of Brooklyn. Take a large gallon flask, fill it partly full of pulverized marble-dust, attach it by means of a rubber tube through a perforated stopper to a Wolff's bottle, which latter must be connected with the moist chamber. Now generate the carbonic acid gas in the flask by pouring muriatic acid upon the marble-dust. When the gas is being evolved it will be known by the ebullition of the water in the Wolff's bottle. Now place the moist chamber upon the stage of the microscope. Take a drop of newt's blood, dilute it with serum or an indifferent fluid, and mount it upon a glass cover, which invert over the well, first seeing that the edge of the cover is oiled, so that it will remain in place. Now connect the tube of the moist chamber with the tube of the gas-generator, and the carbonic acid gas will enter and pass through the chamber. The rapidity with which the current moves may be regulated by a spring clip. As soon as the gas enters, the central body or nucleus becomes distinctly visible, and is surrounded by a yellow halo; when, however, the gas is withdrawn and atmospheric air is admitted, the nucleus and colored zone disappear. This double experiment may be repeated a number of times. Finally a point will be reached where all action will cease. This central body, under such circumstances, has been called the *zooid*, and the corpuscle proper the *oikoid* (Bruecke).

Action of acids upon the blood.—Acetic acid is commonly used in observing the changes that are produced by an acid solution.

Take the ordinary dilute watery solution of acetic acid (1 per cent.) so much used in laboratories, add a drop of it to an equal amount of frog's blood. The red globules instantly exhibit nuclei. The colorless globules also cease their motion, if any has existed, and they become granular and shrivelled. The term granular is used merely in a relative sense and has no special reference to granules whether present or not, but merely to an appearance that has already been explained.

These phenomena are more marked if the solution is concentrated. The red bodies, also, in such case, are apt to crack and split up. A good way of determining the proper strength for the ordinary acetic acid solution is to pour a little into an ordinary watch-glass, and then add chemically pure acetic acid drop by drop until the solution is faintly acid to the taste.

Action of alkalies upon the blood.—Take a drop of the newt's blood and mount it in a drop of serum or of salt solution. Then, affixing a strip of bibulous paper in the way that has been described, add drop by drop a weak solution of aqua ammoniæ. A similar strip of paper, somewhat larger in size, upon the other side, will cause a current and carry the corpuscles to the side of the field where the paper strip is largest, and there the corpuscles may be observed at rest, and the alterations effected by the alkali duly noted. It will be seen that after a little time the corpuscles, both red and colorless, will swell up and finally, after a time, provided the alkali be in sufficient amount, disappear or become so expanded as to be invisible. Sometimes they will burst, leaving the field evenly stained with a homogeneous glutinous-looking substance.

Action of electricity.—It seems to make little difference, so far as the microscope is concerned, whether the continuous or interrupted current is employed, as in either case the phenomena observed are the same in quality. Take bits of tinfoil and attach them to an ordinary glass slide, in such a way that they are just ¼ inch distant from one another. The pieces of foil should be triangular in shape and have their pointed extremities turned to one another. The specimen should be a drop of newt's blood diluted with an equal amount of serum, both perfectly fresh. They should be intimately mixed with a glass rod.

Depositing a drop of this solution upon a cover-glass, it should be inverted and placed upon the slide in such a way that it occupies an intermediate position between the bits of tin-foil. The ordinary stage clips of the microscope are then to be used in holding the slide firmly in position and to press upon the tin-foil. The only remaining task is the attaching of conducting wires from the electrical instrument, one to each clip. The bits of tin-foil are easily fastened to the slide ; they have merely to be hammered out flat, when they will adhere by simple pressure. Sometimes it may be desirable to approximate the poles. In such cases it is necessary to use two fine bits of platinum wire. They should be flattened, and shaped like the letter S. Rest them upon the bits of tin-foil, opposite to one another and at the required distance apart. The cover-glass should press on them. Some little mechanical dexterity is required to get them in position, and they are apt, after using, to become so charged that their action upon the corpuscles commences before they are connected with the battery. The phenomena at the negative pole are those of an acid ; at the positive, those of an alkali. At a distance from the line of the current, secondary changes occur of a less regular character.

Harting has devised an apparatus which is somewhat more elaborate, but in principle the same.

Other changes in the red corpuscles.—If a drop of blood be taken from the finger, by pricking with a needle (the triangular or glover's is the best), it will be seen after a time that the exterior of the corpuscle is indented or *crenated*, as this change is called. It is well shown in Fig. 20.

Examination of the circulation in the web of a frog's foot.—Take a medium-sized frog and curarize him by injecting beneath the skin, with an ordinary hypodermic syringe, two drops of a weak solution of curara (1—2,000 in water) or a few minims of a 50 per cent. solution of chloral hydrate (Schaefer). After a variable time the animal will be completely paralyzed, but the circulation will go on as before.

FIG. 20.—Human blood : red corpuscles crenated. Rollett.

There are many difficulties in the use of curara, depending on the variable strength of the drug, the idiosyncrasies of the animal, and other causes that we do not appear to understand. A solution which will produce a proper amount of paralysis in a frog on one day will rapidly kill another frog the next day. To ensure any reliability of action, it is well to have a specimen of which the strength has been properly tested. Then, if time enough is at one's disposal, a weak solution, such as the above, may be injected every hour until the symptoms of the drug are apparent. If the subsequent recovery of the animal is not of vital importance, the amount may be increased, for the circulation will often be well shown, even if the animal does not eventually survive.

My friend, Dr. W. H. Welch, who is in charge of the Histological Laboratory at the Bellevue Medical College, employs a watery solution of curara. He keeps on hand a ¼ per cent. solution of the drug (1 gramme to 200 c.c. of distilled water), and then dilutes it as occasion may warrant to ⅛ per cent., or even $\frac{1}{5}$ per cent. (1—500 or 1—1,000). Of this diluted solution he injects four or five drops into the dorsal lymph-sac of the frog. A still more dilute solution he is often in the habit of using, so that the frog does not come under the influence of the drug for an hour or an hour and a half. After twenty-four to forty-eight hours the animals entirely recover, but if a stronger solution is used, he finds the results are frequently fatal, though the animals may survive long enough to permit a ready demonstration of the circulation, emigration of leucocytes, etc.

Now envelop his body in a damp cloth and extend him upon a cork plate about a quarter inch thick and large enough to support the entire body. Make a small opening in the cork, and over it place the web of the frog's foot, fastening the latter by ordinary pins.

The circulation may in this way be studied at one's leisure. The red and white blood-corpuscles are seen in the arteries, veins, and capillaries. While the red bodies pass rapidly through the central portions of the vessels, the white creep slowly along the walls, altering their shape as they meet with any obstruction. Where, however, a small artery divides, it will sometimes be seen that the corpuscles, especially the red, are caught at the bifurcation; part bending to go down one branch, and part down the other; taking, in fact, the shape of a saddle-bag. Such a phenomenon exhibits the elastic and distensile properties of the corpuscle. Apply an irritant, such as a weak solution of nitrate of silver, and after prolonged and careful watching, the gradual exit of both white and red corpuscles may be seen. This procedure requires extreme patience and a co-operation of peculiarly fortunate conditions, which are not likely to favor the beginner in microscopy.

Internal structure of the red corpuscles.—As yet the intimate structure of blood-corpuscles is a matter little understood, though an abundance of theories are rife about it. Klein maintains that these corpuscles, in common with others in the body, are traversed by an intracellular network. In the red corpuscles of the newt, especially, he says there is a network of fibrils, with an interfibrillar hyaline ground substance, both together forming the so-called *stroma.* The nucleus contains a network of fibrils in connection with the network of the corpuscle proper; the hæmoglobin, a colored fluid, is contained in the substance of the meshes of the network of the corpuscle proper. Drs. Cutter, of Boston, and Heitzmann, of this city, also state that there is an intracellular network. The former regards it as due to the mycelium of a parasitic growth.

Dr. Elsberg, of this city, also states that he finds a reticular appearance after using a solution of the bichromate of potash (30 per cent. to 50 per cent. of a saturated solution in water).

Real granules are often present in the corpuscles, as may be proved by adding water in large quantity. They will then become greatly distended, and bursting, the granules will be scattered throughout the field.

If finely ground vermilion is sprinkled in the liquid, some of the white corpuscles will take up the granules, perhaps without losing their amœboid character ; finally, they may eject them after a longer or shorter sojourn.

According to Boettcher, the human red blood-corpuscle has a nucleus. He exhibits it in the following way : Taking a saturated solution of corrosive sublimate in alcohol (96°), he diffuses about fifty volumes with one of blood. The corpuscles are deprived of their hæmatin, but at the same time are preserved. The mixture is frequently agitated, but in about twenty-four hours it is allowed to subside, when the superincumbent fluid is poured off and alcohol added. By further agitation for another twenty-four hours the corpuscles are thoroughly washed, and then settle at the bottom of the vessel. Prof. Boettcher claims in this way to have found three classes of red globules. The first are homogeneous and shiny throughout ; the second are clear externally, but granular within ; the third variety exhibit a nucleus and nucleolus.

Development of the blood-corpuscles.—In early fœtal life all the corpuscles are colorless (Klein). According to Balfour and Foster, both colored and colorless corpuscles, at least in the chick, are developed from solid sprouts of protoplasm, derived from the middle germinal layer. There seems good reason, however, to believe that the leucocytes are formed in part, at least, from the lymphatic glands, and Klein thinks that they are thrown off from the "germinating buds" of serous membranes. Later, the red ones make their appearance, and for a time are nucleated. The investigations of Neumann and Bizzozero, showing that the red corpuscles in the medulla of bones are also nucleated, favor the theory that bone-marrow is one of the theatres for such corpuscular metamorphosis.

According to Hayem the production of red corpuscles in the blood is accomplished through the agency of *hæmatoblasts*, *i.e.*, minute red corpuscles. In convalescence from acute fevers, or after a considerable loss of blood, these smaller bodies may be observed in the blood for a variable time, even some weeks.

According to Recklinghausen, the colorless corpuscles may be generated from the red corpuscles, but it is probable that they may be formed in the tissues at many points, and the connective substances through their intimate association with the lymphatics are capable of manufacturing them in almost any quantity. Neither of the two varieties of corpuscles, the red or the white, have a cell-wall or outer investing membrane that can be demonstrated, though it is not unlikely that the outer layer of protoplasm has greater density than the more internal portions.

White or colorless blood-corpuscles.—The white blood-corpuscle is much larger, on an average, in the human species, than the red. It is rounded in form, and is estimated as varying between .0077 and .0120 mm. The average is .0091 mm. (Frey). In contour they are apt to be more or less rough, and exhibit processes. In some of these corpuscles the nucleus is distinct, though when quite fresh a nucleus is rarely seen. If the eye of the observer can watch the corpuscle when it is upon a heated stage and under suitable conditions, its division may be seen. The number contained in the system is variable, as we shall see, depending upon a great number of conditions.

The personal observations of the author do not incline him to regard the network which has attracted so much attention of late years as satisfactorily shown to exist in living corpuscles, although there is no question but that it has been seen in corpuscles after exposure to chemical reagents.

According to Dr. Richard Norris, there is, in mammals, a third corpuscular element which is usually invisible and of the same size as the red ones. Some doubt is thrown upon his alleged discovery, by the fact that the method he employs is likely to produce artificial appearances, and therefore leads to the supposition that the alleged bodies were merely red corpuscles decolorized.

Mode of counting the blood-corpuscles.—Thanks to the instruments of Malassez, Hayem and Nachet, and Gowers, we are in a position to count the red blood-corpuscles with a fair degree of accuracy.

The methods are somewhat different, but are not difficult to understand.

Schaefer describes his plans as follows : In order to separate the corpuscles and prevent coagulation, the blood used is first diluted to a definite extent—say a hundred times—with a 10 per cent. solution of sulphate of soda. The mixing can be performed in a measuring-glass if the blood is in sufficient quantity, but if only a small drop is obtainable, such, for example, as is got by pricking the finger, a mixer is better. This consists of a capillary tube terminating in a bulb, the capacity of the bulb between the marks 1 and 101 being exactly 100 times that of the tube from its point to the mark 1. A small glass ball is inclosed in the bulb, and serves, by its movements, to facilitate the mixing. The capillary tube is allowed to fill with blood as far as the mark 1 ; sulphate of soda solution is then sucked up as far as the mark 101. As it passes in, it of course pushes the blood before it into the bulb, and the two are there thoroughly mixed by gentle agitation.

The next thing is to count the corpuscles in a known quantity of the mixture. The most convenient plan is that of Hayem and Nachet. A slide is used, having a glass ring $\frac{1}{5}$ mm. in depth, cemented on to its upper surface. A drop of the mixture, but not enough to fill the cell so formed, is placed in the middle of the ring, and a perfectly flat cover-glass is so laid on that the drop touches and adheres to it without reaching the sides of the cell. The slide is placed on the microscope, and as soon as the corpuscles have settled down to the bottom of the drop, the number in a definite area is counted. If the area chosen is $\frac{1}{5}$ mm. square, this will give the number which were contained in $\frac{1}{5}$ mm. cube of the mixture, and multiplying this by the number of times the blood was diluted, the result will be the number of corpuscles in $\frac{1}{5}$ mm. cube of blood. Schaefer thinks that it is more convenient to have the quadratic markings upon the micrometer glass of the eye-piece than upon the slide, which is a practical point. The quadratic markings are shown in Fig. 22. To measure any square, it is only necessary to take the stage micrometer, ruled in millimetres and decimals, and adjusting the draw tube, make the side of one square correspond exactly to an interval of $\frac{1}{5}$ mm. on the stage micrometer. It will then be convenient to mark the tube at this point, and then, in all subsequent work, if the tube be kept at this line and a slide is used of the thickness of the micrometer and the same lens and eye-piece, the side of a square will always be $\frac{1}{5}$ mm. This method is the one in general use.

Another less frequently employed is that of Malassez, which is also described by Schaefer as follows : A little of the mixture of blood and sulphate of soda is transferred to a very fine flat-

4

tened capillary tube, the capacity of a given length of which has
been ascertained previously and marked on the slide to which
the tube is fixed. Thus, in his capillary tube a length of 400 mi-
cromillimetres represents the $\frac{1}{189.8}$ part of a cubic millimetre
of the mixture. The counting is performed with the aid of a
squared ocular micrometer, the microscope tube having been
previously so adjusted by the aid of a stage micrometer that
the side of the square shall have the value of one of the lengths
(400 μ[1] for example) marked on the slide. The result of the

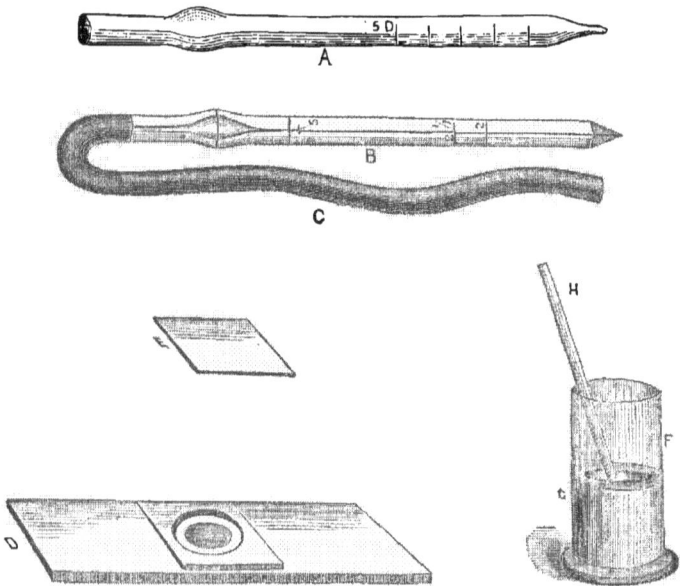

FIG. 21.—Hayem and Nachet's apparatus for blood-counting.

counting gives the number of corpuscles in a known quantity
($\frac{1}{189.8}$ c.mm.) of the mixture, and the number in a whole cubic
millimetre can therefore be readily determined.

Dr. Keyes uses a modification of the method of Hayem and
Nachet, making a dilution of 1 to 250, in order to render the
counting more easy. In Fig. 21 the pipette, A, is filled up to
the mark, 5 D ; it is then emptied into the glass vessel, F. The
pulp of the finger of the patient whose blood is to be tested
should be pierced with a triangular needle (glover's). Quick

---

[1] A micromillimetre (μ) = $\frac{1}{1000}$ mm.

but firm pressure down the finger will at once force out a drop
from the punctured spot. The blood must be drawn immediately into the capillary pipette lest it coagulate. When the
pipette is full to the mark 2, its point should be rapidly wiped
clean of any blood adhering to the outside, and the contents at
once blown into the artificial serum in the cup, F. A little
suction back and forth clears the tube of any blood-corpuscles
which may have adhered to the glass within. Both tubes
should be carefully washed before being put away.

The mixture is now to be thoroughly agitated with the glass
rod, and before it has time to settle, a drop is placed in the
middle of the cell on the slide, D, care being taken that the
drop is not large enough to touch any part of the circumference
of the cell. The covering glass, E, should at once be placed
upon the cell. Should the drop be too large, so that when the
thin cover is adjusted it spreads out too much, the glass should
be cleansed and the attempt made anew. Finally, a small drop
of water or saliva is applied to the edge of the covering glass,
under which it circulates around the top of the cell, serving to
hold the cover in place and pre-
vent evaporation. The slide is
then put in position and when
the corpuscles have all settled
to the bottom of the fluid, the
counting should begin. The
following detailed plan is then
given by Dr. Keyes:

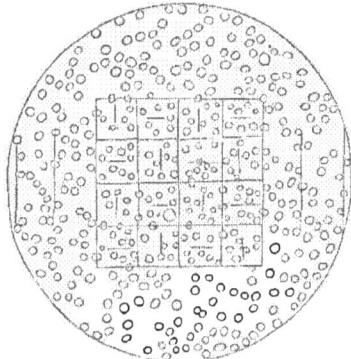

"It is better to count each
of the sixteen squares and write
down its number separately,
so that in counting the square
beneath it, should there be any
doubt about counting a given

Fig. 22.—Blood corpuscles as seen with the squared ocular micrometer. Keyes.

corpuscle lying upon the line, a glance at the number recorded
for the square above may remove all doubt. Many corpuscles
will be found lying upon the outside lines bounding the large
square. I have adopted the rule of rejecting all those lying
upon the upper and right-hand outside lines (of the large
square) and counting all those lying on the lower and left-
hand outside lines.

After having thus obtained the number of red corpuscles

situated within the large square, it becomes easy, by a simple equation, to find the number in a cubic millimetre. A single count, however, exposes to sources of error, and in order to approach more nearly to exactness, I have uniformly counted the number contained in the large square in five different portions of the field (sometimes ten), and have taken a mean of the whole number of counts as the standard.

The computation is as follows : The glass cell on the slide is $\frac{1}{5}$ mm. deep. The eye-piece micrometer marks off $\frac{1}{5}$ mm. square, therefore the count of red corpuscles (or white, as the case may be) must indicate the number contained (in the dilution used) in $\frac{1}{5}$ mm. cube. But $\frac{1}{5}$ mm. cube is $\frac{1}{125}$ of a c.mm., therefore the number counted must be multiplied by 125 ; and the blood was diluted by adding 250 parts of fluid to 1 of blood (2 c.mm. to 500 c.mm.), therefore the product above obtained must be again multiplied by 251 to get the number of corpuscles in a c.mm. of pure blood. Instead of multiplying twice, a single multiplication by the product of 125 × 251, 31,375, will give the same result.''

This method should, theoretically, be absolutely accurate, but there are various errors which will unavoidably creep in. First of all, the tubes should be verified as to accuracy. This has been done for me at the Winchester Observatory, of Yale College, by Leonard Waldo, Esq., the astronomer in charge. My *larger glass tube* is slightly different in shape from the one here represented, and is marked so that the line at $\frac{1}{2}$ indicates a capacity of 500 cubic millimetres (0.5005 grammes of distilled water at 26.4° C.). The cubical contents of the reservoir from the point to the line $\frac{1}{4} = 0.2425 + 0.008 = 2505$ grammes = 250 c.mm., approximately. Accordingly, the marks $\frac{1}{4}$ and $\frac{1}{2}$ indicate $\frac{1}{4}$ and $\frac{1}{2}$ a cubic centimetre, within a limit of error so small as to be practically insensible. The smaller glass tube, which is capillary, is marked 2, 2$\frac{1}{4}$, 4, and 5. The level 5 indicates a capacity of 5 c.mm. The capacity between the pointed extremity and 2 is 2 c.mm., less $\frac{3}{100}$ c.mm.; the space between 2 and 2$\frac{1}{4}$ contains .55 c.mm.; the space between 2$\frac{1}{4}$ and 4 contains 1.45 c.mm.; the space between 4 and 5 contains exactly 1 c.mm. (Waldo). The determination of these capacities was made by using distilled water, and comparing the weight, when filled to the various levels, with the same tube after careful drying.

These estimates are given to show one of the errors which may be met with, and that an instrument, before using, should be verified by some one who has special means for determining capacities of this kind. My eye-piece micrometer was made for me by Rogers, of Cambridge, and the entire field was subdivided into squares, so that every portion of it may be counted without moving the slide. My method has been practically the same as that of Dr. Keyes, except that I prefer diluting with one thousand parts of the diluent, and use iodized serum in place of urine. The ordinary ¼ per cent. solution of common salt in water will also answer sufficiently well.

Recent investigations, such as those conducted by Drs. Cutter and Bradford, of Boston, have established that there is great variation in the number of globules of an individual, depending on various causes, such as the locality from which the blood is drawn, the loss of fluids, as by diarrhœa, sweating, increased urinary secretion, etc., and even the period of the day, week, or year. These general conclusions have also been sustained by Hayem, of Paris, in researches which are still being prosecuted.

When one further considers that we have no definite standard of comparison; that the instrument is apt to be imperfect; that there is a liability of errors to the amount of 10 per cent.; that skill and practice are required in manipulation, it is by no means difficult to see that the hæmatometer is not calculated at present to introduce much scientific precision into medicine, unless the most extraordinary precautions are taken in every case, and these all duly noted.

Blood crystals.—The pigment of the blood occurs usually in an amorphous form, and is called hæmatine. The brownish red needles found in extravasated blood are known as hæmatoidine.

Hæmoglobin also occurs in most mammalian blood, and is deposited under the form of rhombic plates. It is estimated that about 125 grammes are present in the blood of a healthy adult.

THE HÆMOCHROMOMETER.

According to Mantegazza and others, richness in hæmoglobin indicates a corresponding richness in red corpuscles, and any special depth of color in the blood may be regarded as implying a certain given number of red corpuscles to the cubic millimetre. While this ratio appears to hold true in health, it fails in disease. Thus, a condition which we recognize as anæmia may be almost wholly due to a loss of hæmoglobin in the corpuscle, or an actual loss of red corpuscles, together with a diminished amount of hæmoglobin in those that remain. In the cachexia of cancer the number of the corpuscles may be sustained, but their hæmoglobin diminished. In diabetes mel-

litus, on the other hand, there may be an excess of red corpuscles, while there is a diminution of their hæmoglobin. In
anæmia, from hemorrhage, there is an actual loss both of corpuscles and of hæmoglobin in those that remain.

To facilitate the estimation of hæmoglobin, an instrument
has been devised by Malassez and Verick (Paris), called the
hæmochromometer,[1] which is easily manipulated, and bids fair
to establish some facts of practical utility (see *Archives de
Phys.*, 1877, p. 1).

It consists of a hand-screen, to which a movable prismatic
trough, containing a colored fluid, is attached, and a modified
Potain pipette. By means of this apparatus the richness of
the blood in hæmoglobin, and the maximum quantity of oxygen which it can absorb, may be determined. To use the apparatus the pipette is first filled up to a certain point with the
blood to be examined, and then diluted with 100 parts of water.
The reservoir of the pipette is then filled with the diluted
blood. The screen has two holes; behind one of these the
prismatic trough is made to slide up and down, the color of the
fluid contained in it of course varying in intensity, according
to the extent of the upward and downward motion. Behind
the other opening the reservoir of the pipette is secured by
means of a little elastic ring. The screen is now held against
the light (preferably white light; sunlight is to be especially
avoided), and the trough moved until the color of the blood
mixture is matched by its own color. Then the figure on the
scale attached to one side of the trough is read off, and this
indicates, by reference to the table annexed to the apparatus,
the points to be determined. If the blood to be examined be
deeply colored, the aqueous blood-mixture is made in the proportion of ½ to 100; if it be but slightly colored, in the proportion of 2 to 100.

BIBLIOGRAPHY.

WELCKER. Pragervierteljahreschr. XLIV., p. 60. 1854. Zeitschr. f. rat. Med.
    3, XX., p. 280.
SCHULTZE, MAX. Archiv f. mikrosk. Anat. I., p. 35. 1865.
ROLLETT. Stricker's Manual of Histology. New York, 1872.
WOODWARD. Am. Jour. of the Med. Sci., Jan., 1875. N. Y. Med. Rec., Jan. 31, 1880.

---

[1] To be obtained of J. F. Reynders & Co., New York city.

KELSCH.   Arch. de Phys.   Vol. II.   1875.

KEYES.   Am. Jour. of the Med. Sci., Jan., 1876.

HEITZMANN.   New York Med. Jour., April, 1877.

MANTEGAZZA.   Berl. Klin. Woch., April 1, 1878.

RANVIER.   Traité technique d'histologie.   Paris, 1877 et seq.

HAYEM.   Archives de Puys.   2 Ser., T. VI., p. 201 et seq.   1879.

BIZZOZERO, G., and SALVIOLI, G.   Centralb. f. d. Med. Wiss.   16, p. 273.   1879.

POUCHET.   Gaz. Med. de Paris.   14, 16.   1879.

CUTLER, E. G., and BRADFORD, E. H.   Journal of Phys.   Vol. I.   1878—1879.

BOETTCHER.   Archiv f. mikrosk. Anat.   Bd. XIV.   p. 73.   1877.

KLEIN and E. NOBLE SMITH.   Atlas of Histology.   1879.

ELSBERG.   Annals of the N. Y. Academy of Sciences.   Vol. I., Nos. 9 and 10.   1879.
(A very extensive bibliography.)

SATTERTHWAITE, T. E.   Arch. of Comp. Med.   N. Y.   II.   1880.

BAXTER and WILLCOCK.   Lancet, March 6, 13, 20, 1880.

BIZZOZERO.   L'examen microscopique du Sang.   Ann. Soc. méd.-chir. de Liège.
XX. 201-216.   1881.

HAYEM.   Contribution à l'étude de la structure des hématoblastes et des hématies.
G. Ac. Med. de Paris.   6. S., III. 479-481.   1881.

THOMA, R.   Die Zählung der weissen Zellen des Blutes.   Arch. f. Path. Anat., etc.
LXXXVII. 201-209.   1882.

VIBERT.   Possibilité de distinguer le sang de l'homme de celui des mammifères.
Arch. de phys. norm. et path.   2. S.   IX. 48-58.   1882.

CHAPTER IV.

EPITHELIUM.

THE skin, mucous surfaces of the body and various passages in connection with them, are evenly coated with bodies of peculiar shape, which are united together to form a covering of one or more layers.

In some places, as upon the external portions of the epidermis, the corpuscles are more or less flattened. Elsewhere, as in the ducts of secreting glands and in the trachea and fallopian tubes, they are cylindrical, and the free extremities are often surmounted by cilia—fine, hair-like processes, which have a vibratile movement that propels solid matters, such as sputa and ova, in some special direction. In other parts, again, as in the collecting tubes of the kidney, near the apices of the pyramids, a cuboidal variety is found. Intermediate or transitional forms are also frequently met with in all parts of the body.

A characteristic of epithelium which is especially noteworthy is that the same species is not found uniformly in the same position. Sometimes this mutation of type is governed by the physical laws that regulate the growth and development of the subject, or it may be a consequence of disease. An example of the former peculiarity is to be noted in the larynx, where the ciliated corpuscles of infancy part with their cilia from advancing age, or indeed may become flattened.

As an example of pathological change it is not uncommon to find villosities covered with the most beautifully marked cylindrical epithelium, springing from the ordinary mucous membrane, just where the superficial corpuscles happen to be somewhat flattened in their normal state.

The use to which the part is put has also an important influence in governing the shape and other attributes of the corpuscles. Where they are exposed to the drying action of the air, to harsh usage, and continued friction, as upon the hands and feet, they become flattened, dry, and horny ; in the interior of the body, on the other hand, where such conditions do not exist, they are succulent and pliable.

Ordinary flattened or squamous epithelium.—This is best obtained by scraping the back of one's tongue with a blunt instrument. The scrapings should then be mounted in equal parts of the common salt solution ($\frac{1}{4}$ per cent.) and glycerine. The epithelial bodies may in this way be readily studied. They are separate or grouped together in collections of two or more. In diameter they vary between $\frac{1}{1500}$ and $\frac{1}{600}$ inch. The surfaces are all bevelled, and at the same time are uneven or ridged ; consequently they overlap one another to a certain degree, and the inequalities of one corpuscle fit into those of another. The most superficial epithelium is the thinnest, and, conversely, the deepest is apt to be the most nearly spheroidal.

Intermixed in the mucus will be seen the so-called mucous or salivary corpuscles. They are not very numerous, but are detected by the "molecular" or Brownian movement of their interior. In size they closely resemble the white corpuscles of the blood, but, as a rule, exhibit no amœboid motion ; the white globules, on the other hand, rarely have any Brownian movement.

The surfaces of the epithelia are often so covered with bacteria that they are only recognized with some difficulty. These little bodies are wonderfully uniform in size, and are disposed in the most regular manner. Looking straight down upon them they appear to be minute spheres with a diameter averaging between $\frac{1}{25000}$ and $\frac{1}{27000}$ inch. Closer inspection and examination of the corpuscles at their free edges shows that the bacteria are in reality rod-shaped, and that they adhere to the corpuscles by their extremities, standing in such cases vertical to the surface. A high power, such as the immersion $\frac{1}{12}$, develops this point quite clearly.

Incidentally the mucin of the mucus may be seen to advantage in the scrapings of the mouth or tongue. To a drop or two add another drop of commercial alcohol and a drop of the ordinary hæmatoxylon solution. The alcohol will coagulate the mucin, which then takes the form of filaments and branching networks ; the logwood will make them distinctly visible.

Epithelium from the skin may be studied in one of two methods. Take a fresh specimen from the palmar surface of the hand or plantar of the foot, freeze it in a section cutter,

take off a thin slice with a knife, immerse for a few seconds in
a dilute solution of acetic acid (¼ per cent.), and then mount in
glycerine and water ; or a similar portion of the skin may be
steeped in a weak, sherry-colored, watery solution of the bichromate of potassium (gr. ij.—iij.—f. ℥ j.) for several days and then
hardened in alcohol, first of 80 per cent., then of 90 per cent.,
finally of 95 per cent. strength ; this latter process taking several
days, and ending when the specimen is thoroughly hard. Sections may then be made in the usual way. By the use of acetic
acid the nuclei will readily be seen in the lower strata of the epidermis, while the outermost layers have none, or, at least, none
that can be demonstrated by the usual histological methods.

Three different strata can now be recognized : 1, the *stratum corneum*, or corneous layer, in which the corpuscles are
flattened, and appear to have no nuclei ; 2, the *rete mucosum*,
or malpighian layer, immediately underlying the former, and
composed of cuboidal elements, armed with *spines* or *prickles*,
as they are often called ; lastly, 3, there is the *pigmented layer*,
which overlies the papillæ. The bodies of the latter corpuscles
are infiltrated with particles of *melanine*, which is the cause of
the dark color in the skin of the negro and swarthy races.

Maceration of the epidermis in liquor potassæ is an excellent
method for exhibiting the individual elements ; after a few minutes they will swell up and detach themselves from one another.

It was thought, until quite recently, that these prickle cells interdigitate
with one another, but Ranvier has claimed that they are continuous with those
of adjacent corpuscles (see chapter on the Skin). This point is difficult to settle, as it requires a special method and lenses of high power. Ranvier injected
a one-fourth per cent. solution of osmic acid into the lower layers of the epidermis, using a hypodermic syringe, and driving the fluid right and left.

There is a form of flattened and pigmented epithelium that
may be seen by examining the external surface of the choroid,
the ciliary processes, and the posterior surface of the iris. In
the choroid these bodies look like a mosaic of polyhedral cells.
Such specimens may be permanently preserved by simply drying them, and then mounting in dammar or Canada balsam.

Ciliated epithelium.—The movement of living cilia is readily
seen. All that is necessary is to take the common frog (Rana
temporaria), draw out his tongue, and then observing the teat-
like projections at the posterior part, snip one off.

This little piece is then to be mounted in a one-fourth per cent. salt solution, or serum, and examined. Along the free edge of the mucous membrane the cilia will be seen engaged in active vibratile motion. The appearance presented by a broad expanse of moving cilia has been aptly described as resembling a field of grain which is being swept by the wind, though the motion is often much more rapid than this comparison would imply. It will be seen that various substances, such as blood globules, are propelled in a definite direction. When the frog's mouth is open, all solid particles that are lodged upon the mucous membrane are carried quietly but inevitably toward the gullet, and down toward the stomach. The power of the ciliary movement may be estimated, in a measure, by placing some light but adhering body upon the anterior portion of the roof of the mouth, and then inverting the animal. The substance immediately begins to ascend against gravity, and soon is wedged in the gullet. The same force, though acting in an opposite direction, expels mucus, pus, and indeed all solid matters, from the cavities of the human lungs; it also propels the ova through the Fallopian tubes into the uterus. In excessive catarrh from mucous membranes the epithelial bodies may themselves be expelled, so that they are not infrequently found with their cilia attached, as in the nasal discharges. After death cilia are hard to recognize; they contract down to little knobs on the surface of the cells, and can only be demonstrated when the eye looks directly down upon them. Osmic acid is useful to preserve them in their natural condition. Take a fresh specimen and immerse it for twenty-four hours in a one-fourth per cent. osmic acid solution, and for another twenty-four hours in dilute alcohol; then tease and mount in glycerine and water. It will be observed that each cilium is a slim, straight rod, which is apparently structureless; they rest upon a band, which, with a high power, may be seen to have vertical striations.

Effect of reagents.—By making use of the moist chamber (Fig. 19, p. 42), and placing a drop of chloroform in the corner of the cell, it will be seen that the action of the cilia rapidly stops, while, if the chloroform be removed, it will again resume its activity.

If carbonic acid gas is admitted, the action of the cilia will at first be accelerated, but subsequently retarded, and eventually stopped (Kuehne).

After shutting off the carbonic acid gas and admitting oxygen, the action will again commence. When the ordinary motion has ceased, the gradual application of heat will cause it to return ; but if the temperature be raised continuously, a point will soon be reached where the excessive heat will cause the motion again to stop.

Columnar or cylindrical epithelium.—This is the epithelium *par excellence* of the digestive tract, clothing the mucous membrane from the cardiac orifice of the stomach to the anus. It is also found at the orifices of the ducts of the large excretory glands, such as the liver and pancreas, in the milk-passages of the nipple, and in some parts of the generative system. These cells are tall and narrow, standing vertical to the surface of the mucous membrane. Sometimes they are broadest at their free extremity, at other times about the middle, so that when viewed from above they appear to be separated from one another. The nuclei are rounded, and are either placed about the middle of the cell or near the attached border. They admit of considerable variation, however, as to size and shape, some of those in immediate contact being broad at one extremity, and some broad at the others ; the free edge also may be uneven.

Scrape the surface of a frog's tongue or a rabbit's intestine after washing ; the cells will be seen to advantage. Place some of the scrapings in a drop of glycerine and water to which another drop of dilute acetic acid ($\frac{1}{4}$ per cent.) has been added, and mount. In this way the nuclei will be brought clearly into view. The cells closely resemble in their shape the columnar variety, except that they have no cilia. Among them will almost always be found *chalice* or *goblet* cells. They lie among the columnar corpuscles, and are usually shorter, but broader, expanding in the centre, and terminating at their attached extremities in a single or double process. The surface is cupped. They contain one or more nuclei ; whether they are a distinctive cell or not is as yet uncertain. Some suppose them to be the ordinary columnar cell undergoing mucoid degeneration ; others that they are not epithelial at all. Frey regards them as artificial productions.[1]

---

[1] The most rational explanation is that furnished by F. E. Schultze. The intrafibrillar substance is, according to this observer, converted into hygroscopic mucin, which swells up. This constitutes a change in the cell which, from being columnar, becomes goblet-shaped. The wall finally ruptures, and the mucin is poured out.

Other varieties of epithelium will be taken up in connection with the different organs. As already stated, many transitional varieties occur, even in direct association with the typical forms we have described.

Structure of epithelial corpuscles.—According to the views of Heitzmann, Klein, and others, the substance of the corpuscle is pervaded by a network, the minute fibres of which may be seen under a lens of high power. The nucleus or central body is also similarly provided. Within the meshes of this network there is a hyaline substance, the abundance or paucity of which determines the size of the meshes.

The "granules," which have often been described, are, according to this view, the nodal points of the meshwork. It is also stated that the epithelial cells sometimes have a fine limiting membrane (Klein); but even in such instances it is merely a condensation of the outer part of the corpuscle. Within the nucleus there are also, according to the same observers, fibres, within the meshes of which are not infrequently real granules (nucleoli). The epithelial corpuscles are attached together, either by an interlacement of their processes, as in the liver, or by a peculiar cement substance, as in pavement epithelium, or by a continuity of their processes, as in the rete mucosum.

Recent histological studies have narrowed the field formerly occupied by the epithelial bodies, and, in accordance with these views, the flattened corpuscles which cover serous membranes, such as the pleura and peritoneum, will be arranged under the connective-tissue series, rather than under the epithelial. The reasons for this change will be given in a subsequent chapter. On the other hand, the enamel of teeth finds a more fitting position among epithelial structures, as it is largely if not wholly developed from them.

BIBLIOGRAPHY.

RANVIER. Traité technique d'histologie. Paris, 1875.

DELAFIELD. Studies in Pathological Anat. New York, 1878 et seq.

KLEIN and E. NOBLE SMITH. Atlas of Histology. 1879-80.

HEITZMANN. New York Medical Record. July 31, 1880. p. 133.

FREY. The Microscope and Microscopical Technology. New York, 1880.

CHAPTER V.

THE CONNECTIVE SUBSTANCE GROUP.

MUCOUS OR GELATINOUS TISSUE; ADENOID TISSUE; NEUROG-
LIA; FAT TISSUE; FIBROUS TISSUE PROPER; CORNEAL TIS-
SUE; INTERMUSCULAR TISSUE; TENDON TISSUE; ELASTIC
TISSUE.

THE term *connective substance* was first proposed by Reichert in 1845, and is now applied to a class of animal tissues whose
offices are very important in the economy. Prominent among
them is bone, which forms the solid framework of the body,
gives it strength, and supplies points of attachment for muscles
and tendons; another group comprises the ligaments, which
assist in holding the bony parts, and also some organs, in their
proper relations; others again, of a more delicate nature, furnish support or protection for epithelial bodies, blood-vessels,
and nerves. Just at the present time the histology of connective substances has an important bearing on many points that
relate to inflammation, degeneration, and the development of
certain new growths, and it is therefore desirable to have a clear
conception of them. This object is best effected by studying
each variety separately, not only in its normal condition, but
under the changes it exhibits when acted on by the factors that
are concerned in the processes of disease.

It is a property of these substances that they supplant one
another at different times or under peculiar circumstances. As
an example, the hyaline cartilage of young life may change
into true bone in old age, while, on the other hand, there is
always a tendency for fully formed tissue, if inflamed, to re-
vert toward the embryonic type.

The connective substances may be subdivided as follows:
1, mucous or gelatinous tissue; 2, adenoid tissue; 3, neurog-

lia ; 4, fat tissue ; 5, fibrous tissue proper ; 6, corneal tissue ; 7, intermuscular tissue ; 8, tendon tissue ; 9, elastic tissue ; 10, bone ; 11, cartilage ; 12, cement ; and 13, dentine. The word *connective tissue* was first proposed by Johannes Mueller, and is sometimes used as synonymous with *connective sub-stance*, but erroneously. The former is merely a variety of the' latter, and is usually intended to indicate one or other of the flexible connective substances that form the interstitial material of the body, and in that sense we shall use it for convenience sake, but without implying any special histological character.

In precise histological descriptions it is always best to use the special name of the variety intended, such as *mucous tis-sue*, *adenoid tissue*, and the like, where the structure happens to be known.

It is also well to state here that the term "cellular" tissue, found in many of our anatomies, is apt to mislead the student. The word "cellular" has no reference to cells, *i.e.*, corpuscles, but to the large cavities or spaces that exist in all loose connec-

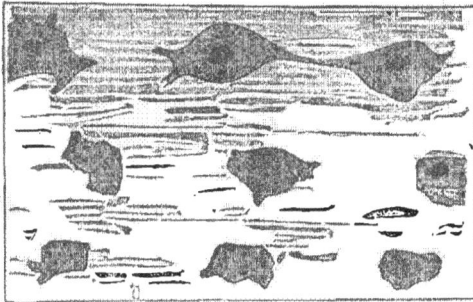

Fig 23.—Gelatinous or mucous tissue. Human umbilical cord.

tive tissues, of which the subcutaneous is an example. These spaces are easily seen by the naked eye, when inflated with air.

Mucous or gelatinous tissue.—This is the most simple form that is met with. It is seen to great advantage in the embryonic umbilical cord, which also contains several other varieties of connective tissue.

The following method has been found best suited to demonstrate it. Take a small piece of cord at about the third month and immerse it a few weeks in Mueller's fluid ; make a thin section through the very soft gelatinous part, then soak it a few minutes in distilled water, to which subsequently a few drops of acetic acid are to be added so that the solution shall not contain more than 1 per cent. of acid, and then mount in glycerine. It will then be seen that the softest portion contains numbers of irregularly-shaped, thin plates, some provided with an oval, flattened nucleus, others having none that are apparent (Fig. 23). Some of these flattened bodies anastomose by these processes with those of other plates, others are quite free. The substance lying between the cells, the intercellular substance, is quite homogeneous, or slightly granular, in the softest portions, and has at first no defined fibrillation. In the neighborhood of the former tissue, lines of fibrillation occur, while at the same time these flattened bodies become smaller, although they are still flattened (Fig. 24, b). Mucous or gelatinous tissue,

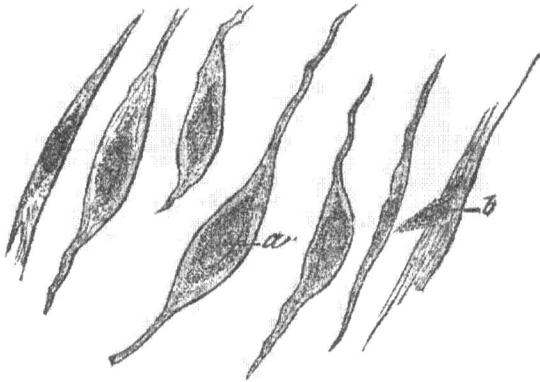

FIG. 24.—Connective tissue in an advancing stage of development. From the umbilical cord.

as it is seen in the umbilical cord of an embryo, is properly an embryonic or developmental form of connective tissue which is never found in normal adult life. All the phases of development may here be seen, from the most primitive, comprised in Wharton's jelly, to the firm, fibrous fascicles that encircle the vessels.

Properly speaking, the true mucous tissue is, as its name implies, a viscid material, and, indeed, is much like half-set glue, in which the corpuscles are scattered with little or even no cohesion.

The intercellular substance differs from albumen in not containing sulphur; from chondrin and gelatin, in not being precipitated by boiling, tannin, or the bichloride of mercury.

At an early stage there are no marks of fibrillations in the intercellular substance, but later fibrils are seen in the vicinity of the corpuscles, and are some of the early signs that organization of the tissue is commencing.

The corpuscles at the same time become smaller, and about the central body or nucleus we see a delicate expansion (Fig. 24 *a*), which is the envelope of the connective-tissue corpuscle—a film of great tenuity. Klein believes that in these corpuscles there are two portions, a granular or firmer part continuous with the processes, and a delicate expansion that is hardly visible. It is certain that the connective-tissue corpuscle is frequently in connection with one or more of its fellows by a mutual anastomosis of processes. The fibrillation appears to be at first limited to certain areas about the cellular elements, so that the long, flattened and pointed lamellæ of fibrous tissues on which the corpuscles are attached look like large corpuscles with correspondingly large nuclei. Using a camel's-hair brush and pencilling off the specimen under examination, after soaking in a 10 per cent. watery solution of common salt, the apparent nuclei with their delicate envelopes are partially (Fig. 24 *b*) or wholly removed. We then see small strips of more or less fibrillated tissue, having no central body that can be recognized, even with the use of strong staining solutions. These and similar observations tend to establish a conviction that the fibrillated portion arises from the soft, gelatinous material by a process of fibrillation inaugurated by the presence and under the formative action of the connective-tissue corpuscle. It is not impossible that the fibrin of the blood, which, though fluid in the blood-current, is often known to be deposited in delicate filaments, may contribute largely, if not wholly, to the formation of the fibrillæ. As the tissue becomes firmer, the little plates with their anastomosing branches form a loose network which separates the fibrils into distinctive bundles or fascicles, and encircles them more or less completely.

There is another view which is offered as an explanation of the process by which connective tissue becomes organized. It is this. The change is derived wholly from the corpuscles. Some of them split up into fibrils, constituting the fibrous part of the tissue; the others remain, and are developed into connective-tissue corpuscles. This view has the support of excellent histologists.

5

The white corpuscles of the blood are pre-eminently suited for building tissue. When blood is organized, which occurs not infrequently, the white corpuscles at once assume an important rôle, while the red are soon melted down into a homogeneous mass, that is usually absorbed. This change is observed under various pathological conditions.

Fibrous tissue.—This substance, which is also known as fibrillated connective tissue, is the fully developed material that has just been described. It occurs either in parallel

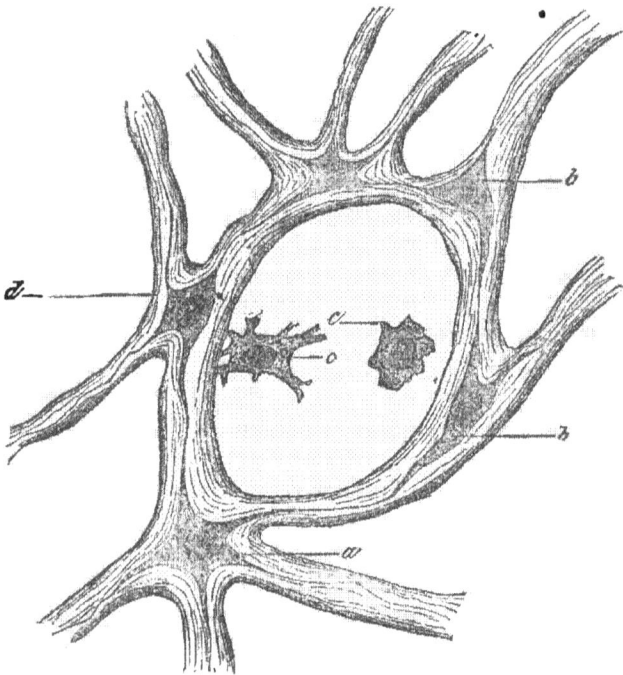

Fig. 25.—Reticular form of connective tissue. From the human umbilical cord.

bundles or fascicles, in interlacing lamellæ, or as a fenestrated material containing larger or smaller openings. A special variety, the *reticular*, is seen to great advantage in the umbilical cord of an infant at birth (Fig. 25).

If a cut be carried through the spongy portions of the cord, it will be seen that the tissue is composed of bright, shining, branching bundles, *d*, superimposed upon which are a number of oval, flattened plates, *a*, at intervals; about them is a delicate envelope, *b*, which appears to be highly elastic, so that it will stretch or relax, according as the networks are compressed or dilated. By teasing with needles or immersion for a few days in a 10 per cent. watery solution of common salt, these corpuscles can often be separated from the bundles, and then they will be seen to form a connected system. When entirely isolated from one another, they often appear spindle-shaped. That this is not their character may be shown by passing a current of fluid through the specimen—a method already described under the name of *irrigation*. It is accomplished in this way: having affixed small strips of filter-paper to the edges of the cover on either side, and moistened one side with fluid, the excess will be absorbed by the other slip, causing a current by which the corpuscles may be made to roll over. We then learn that they are disks of an irregularly flattened form, having longer or shorter processes (*c*, *c*, Fig. 25)—variations in form which seem to depend, in a great measure, upon the tension to which they are exposed, and the position they occupy in the tissue. This explanation will serve to show why all measurements of such corpuscles are merely approximative, and have but little value.

They are shrunken by immersion in alcohol, swollen by the imbibition of water, are drawn out into long, flattened spindles when the tissue is put on the stretch, or become rounded, perhaps nearly spherical, during relaxation. They may assume almost any form as the result of pressure.

The nucleus may be regarded as more of an exception to this rule; at any rate it seems that in fresh specimens, when the substance has been swollen by immersion in water, it is always oval and flattened.

The bundles upon which these bodies lie are somewhat cylindrical in form, branched, and composed of separate filaments, that can be separated by Mueller's fluid, or a 10 per cent. watery solution of common salt.

Two other forms of corpuscles may also be noticed: (1) the kind observed by Waldeyer, and called *plasma cells*, and thought by him to be corpuscles peculiarly prone to take up fat to make fat tissue, bodies four or five times the size of a lymphoid corpuscle, and rounded in form, containing a central body; and (2) the ordinary lymphoid corpuscles, seen at times in all tissues.

The form of fibrous tissue that occurs in parallel lamellæ is well shown in the mesentery of the frog, and in serous mem-branes generally. No great difficulty will be met with in pre-paring this tissue, for it is only necessary to remove it from the frog in the fresh state, acidulate it in a weak (1 per cent.) watery solution of acetic acid, and mount it in glycerine.

It will be seen that these so-called spindle-cells are really flattened plates, when viewed flat-wise, and generally irregu-larly quadrilateral, though the form varies somewhat in each instance.

It is not improbable that some which appear spindle-shaped, and lie in the interfascicular spaces, have a double office, one of which is to guard the nutrition of the tissue, and the other to form a partial lining of a lymphatic channel. The researches

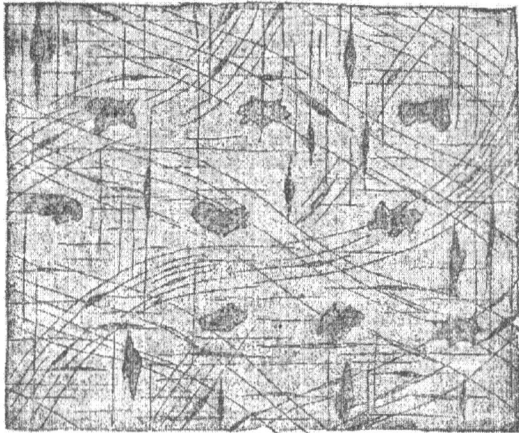

FIG. 26.—Connective tissue in the mesentery of the frog.

of Klein tend to establish this double relation, for they show that these corpuscles lie in the walls of the lymphatic radicles, which are themselves in direct communication with the perito-neal cavity by breaks in the endothelial connective-tissue cor-puscle coating and in actual apposition with the endothelial elements of the serous membranes.

During the last few years there has been a tendency to regard the serous membranes, especially such as have large openings and slight reticula, as having no connective-tissue corpuscles, other than the endothelial, which form a covering over them. In the larger trabecles, however, there are connective-tissue corpuscles, in addition to those just mentioned; they are well seen in profile, interposed between the bundles (Fig. 26).

Adenoid tissue (Fig. 27).—Adenoid tissue is the name given to the delicate substance that forms the framework of the lymphatic glands. It consists of fibres in networks which form an

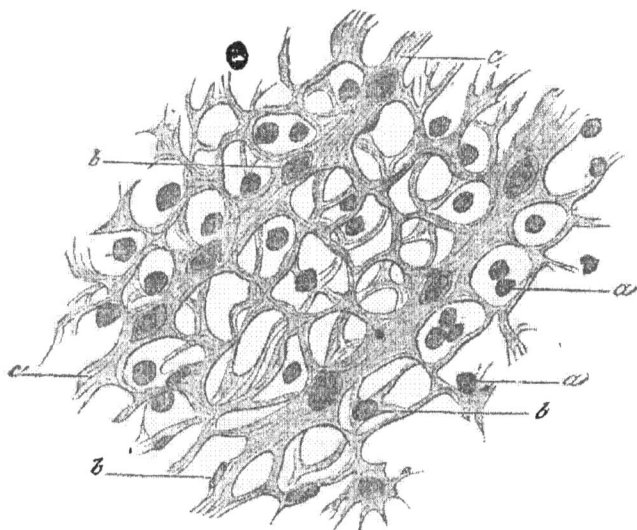

FIG. 27.—Adenoid tissue from a human lymphatic gland.

intricate texture, that is filled with the rounded bodies commonly known as lymphoid cells. It is exceedingly difficult to analyze these tissues, because it is not easy to demonstrate anything that conveys to the eye our idea of a cell, *i. e.*, excepting, of course, the lymphoid corpuscle. The best mode of procedure is the following: Take a lymphatic gland—such as the inguinal in the early stage of inflammation: harden at first, in Mueller's fluid, and then in alcohol, and make sections through it.

On viewing such a specimen under the microscope it will exhibit a delicate meshwork, packed with lymphoid corpuscles (Fig. 27, *a*). Now, if we take such a section and agitate it in a test-tube with water for a considerable length of time, and then place it upon a glass slide, pencilling it with a camel's-hair brush, most of the lymphoid cells will be removed, and the delicate network, c, will be very thoroughly exposed.

It will be seen that, at certain parts of this meshwork, there are flattened bodies, b, of small size, lying upon the larger cords of the meshes. It has been held by Klein and other histologists that the reticulum is made of branching corpuscles; but this statement must be modified. In some instances the appearance of netted corpuscles is well seen in those portions of the glands that are regarded as the lymph passages, where the adenoid tissue forms the framework of the part. The network seems to be comprised of delicate, silk-like cords, enclosing vast numbers of lymphoid corpuscles, and exhibiting, at the nodal points of the meshes, flattened corpuscles. These delicate fibres, however, are often replaced by heavy trabecles, c, such as are seen in the figure, and after continual inflammations the diameter of these latter may be found greater than that of the spaces.

In these latter instances it is often difficult to find any corpuscular elements that may not be separated from the fibres; and, indeed, large areas of these fibrous networks may, by diligent pencilling with a camel's-hair brush, be swept clean of corpuscles. But neither this rough method, nor agitation in a test-tube, will always succeed in separating all the corpuscles from the fibres, even after an immersion in common salt solution for many weeks. The sum of the whole matter is, that adenoid tissue does not generally consist of a network of branching corpuscles, as has been claimed, but rather of a network of fibrous cords, on which the corpuscles are superimposed; they may anastomose, but this point seems difficult to demonstrate in most cases.

Possibly higher powers than those now in use, or some new method may solve the question. Where the fibrous networks have attained some thickness, there is no doubt that we find the ordinary flattened connective-tissue plates lying on the bundles and surrounded by a delicate envelope.

Neuroglia (Fig. 28).—But a short time since it was not known positively whether the delicate, supporting substance of the nervous system, especially of the brain, was granular or fibrous. Even after Virchow insisted that this substance was like the other tissues, known as connective, doubt was thrown upon the matter, for the defining power of most objectives then

used was insufficient to make out such delicate objects. At
the present time the actual existence of a network is hardly
called in question, for it may be demonstrated with really good
glasses, such as some of the immersion lenses (No. 10) of Hartnack's system, and, indeed, by other lenses made both at home
and abroad. As to the question of the corpuscular elements
there is more doubt, and it can hardly be said that their exact
form and shape have been definitely agreed upon by histologists. We find, it is true, that where there is a considerable
deposit of connective mate-
rial along the central canal of
the spinal cord, we have the
ordinary fibres and corpuscles
already described, and so, too,
near the surface of the convolutions. When, however,
we examine the supporting
substances of the white and
gray masses there is less certainty. The actual condition
may be tolerably well seen
by adopting the following
plan. Place any portion of
the brain or cord a few days
in a weak solution of bichromate of potash (5 per cent.)

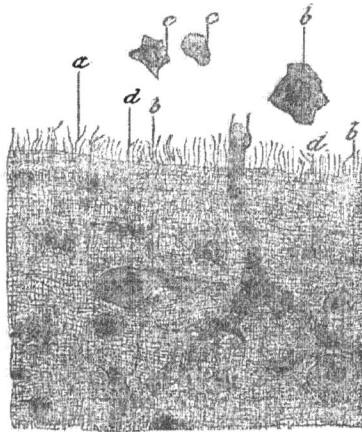

FIG. 28.—Human brain showing neuroglia.

or Mueller's fluid, then immerse it in alcohol until hard ; make
thin sections and stain for twenty-four hours with the following solution of hæmatoxylon: hæmatoxylini, gr. lij. ; aluminis,
℥j. ; aquæ, ℥ viij. ; mix and strain.

Wash in distilled water and mount in glycerine, tease with
needles and examine with a high power; there will then be
little difficulty in seeing that the delicate supporting substance
of both gray and white matter consists of fibres. They may
even be distinctly isolated, for the coloring matter darkens them
somewhat and they become hardened at the same time so as to
be somewhat stiff and unyielding. It will be seen that many
fibrils are disposed in parallel rows which perhaps can hardly
be called bundles, but rather thin laminæ; other similar fibrils
cross them at various angles, giving to the whole, with a
moderately high power, the appearance of a very delicate

meshwork, *a*. It does not appear as if the fibrillæ anastomose with one another, though this point cannot now be definitely settled. It must be stated that some of these fibrils are possibly nerve-elements, and yet this is doubtful, because they do not even seem to be connected with the nerve-fibres [1] that are distinctly shown by this method of preparation.

Granular appearances are always noted in the brain, which is to be expected when cross-sections are made of the delicate fibrillæ. Three kinds of corpuscles are met with in the brain and medulla. The first are the variously shaped *ganglionic corpuscles* or *cells*, Fig. 28, *b*, *b*, *b* ; secondly, the *ordinary lymphoid cells*, *c*, *c*, which are generally seen to have a pale envelope about them ; lastly, smaller *corpuscles, d, d, of irregular shapes*, and many of them undoubtedly flattened and appearing to have branching processes. They may be found in considerable numbers, and can be isolated so that there is no doubt that they exist.

The fibrillæ of the neuroglia do not differ substantially in size from the fibrillæ of fibrous tissues elsewhere.

Tendon-tissue (Fig. 29).—Tendon-tissue may be well studied

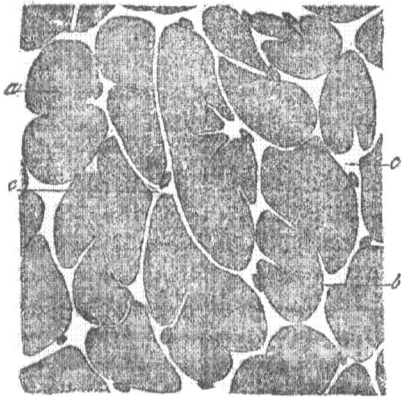

FIG. 29.—Tendon-tissue from the frog.

in the gastrocnemius of the frog. It is prepared like the preceding. If, however, it is desirable to show the nuclei in adult tissue, it is well to use nitrate of silver. Cut a thin section of a fresh tendon and expose it for a few minutes in a $\frac{1}{2}$ per cent. solution of nitrate of silver, until the section is turbid or milky, then place in the sunlight, and in a few minutes the turbid color will give place to dark brown or black, owing to the deposit of silver, and the tissue may then be mounted in glycerine and examined.

This method will show the corpuscular bodies to advantage.

---

[1] To avoid confusion they are not represented in the drawing.

In some cases better results are obtained by the use of chloride of gold. The method is as follows: Freeze a small portion of a tendon, then make the thinnest possible section, acidulate it slightly and immerse in a ½ per cent. solution of chloride of gold until a strong yellow color has been obtained, then soak in a ¼ per cent. solution of dilute acetic acid and expose to the sunlight until a purple or reddish color has been obtained. This will take a variable time, and is not always successful, for reasons which are not easy to understand.

At considerable distances from one another there will be seen small dark bodies, which are the corpuscles already described. It is difficult to determine whether or not these corpuscles are connected together. To isolate them, take a small piece of young tendon-tissue, immerse three or four days in a 10 per cent. solution of common salt, and then tease. In this way the cells may be liberated, and they will prove to be irregularly flattened plates.

Sometimes they lie at the intersection of several bundles and then have separate expansions for each bundle; the plates then lie at various angles with one another, and if one be seen edgewise it looks as if the corpuscle proper were traversed by a line.

Silver or gold, the latter especially, is generally necessary to show the corpuscles in old tendons. The same method shows the fibrillated tissue to advantage. The large tendon bundles are often covered with endothelium (connective-tissue corpuscles), which are continuous and form a complete investment.

For the smaller bundles the tendon-corpuscles do not by any means form a connected sheath. In very young tendons they are quite near to one another, though even at this time they only form a partial investment for the bundles; but as the tendon grows older the corpuscles become smaller, withdraw from one another, and sometimes almost disappear.

Tendon bundles, like other forms of connective tissue, are often encased in a transparent, delicate membrane, not unlike the sarcolemma of striped muscular tissue. It is well shown by immersing the tendon in a dilute solution of acetic acid.

Fat tissue.—The ordinary fibrillated connective tissue often becomes the deposit for oil, which fills the corpuscles, making them swell out enormously. This is fat tissue. An excellent way of showing it consists in making a section through fat tissue that has been hardened in alcohol or Mueller's fluid, or both. The phenomena will, in this way, be well shown. After immersion in an acid solution, it will be seen that the **fatty acids crystallize in the centre** of the sac.

The nature of the evidence that fat corpuscles are really the altered corpuscles of the fibrous tissues is as follows: They occupy the same position, being in rows, between the bundles, just as the other corpuscles that we have mentioned ; a few oil drops at first appear, then others, until finally they coalesce into a single large drop, which fills the corpuscle ; if fat tissue be pressed, and the oil escapes, the walls of the fat-corpuscles collapse, and then the flattened **nuclei may be observed on** the side of the cell-body.

Waldeyer believes that there is a peculiar corpuscle, three to five times the size of the lymphoid, and roundish, which is especially prone to take up fat, and be converted into a fat-corpuscle.

This body, known as the *plasma cell*, is the second element that forms the fat-cell. The change is said to occur only occasionally, and under favorable conditions of alimentation (Klein).

The same author states that there is also a third way in which fat is formed : In many parts of serous membranes, especially in connection with the large vessels, there appear "nodules or cords, which are made up of multiplying connective-tissue cells." The cells increase, the matrix is converted into a network, lymph-corpuscles appear, the tissue is supplied with arteries, veins, and capillaries, and resembles lymphatic tissue. Sometimes these structures persist as they are ; in other cases they are converted into fat-tissue.

Ranvier recommends the following plan of demonstrating fat-tissue: He injects beneath the skin a weak solution of osmic acid (1–1000). The connective-tissue corpuscles may be seen to be more or less filled with oil-globules.

The property of taking up oil is not peculiar to these corpuscles already described, but belongs, physiologically, to the liver, to adult cartilage, the glandular elements of the female breast during lactation, and the glandular epithelium of the sebaceous glands.

Intermuscular tissue.—It has been claimed by some that

there is a form of spindle-cell in the intermuscular tissue of the frog's thigh. This, however, is apparent rather than real. We find broad plates, in which are oval, flattened bodies, placed at certain distances apart (Fig. 31). These, seen in profile, appear spindle-shaped. There is something peculiar about such bodies, for they seem to bear a close relationship to the elastic networks, *a*, so that, in some cases, it appears as if the flattened central bodies were directly connected with the elastic fibres, as stated by Boll.

In many instances these elastic fibres lie upon the plates, *b*, which themselves rest in a homogeneous, intermediate, and apparently structureless substance.

This tissue is therefore similar, in some respects, to mucous tissue.

Corneal tissue.—The cornea consists of thin, fibrous bands, each one partly anastomosing with its adjacent neighbor. Between them are well-marked corpuscles lying in clefts—the corneal spaces.

The term corneal corpuscles, however, is even now applied to the spaces by some of the best-known writers, and it seems evident that there is doubt as to whether real corpuscles exist or not. Recently the subject has been restudied by Waldeyer, and the author has been able to verify his conclusions in a great measure, both as to the character of the corpuscles and the spaces in which they lie.

In general, these bodies appear, as stated by Waldeyer, to be flat, having a considerable amount of protoplasmic material about their nuclei (Fig. 30), though in the direction of the periphery they gradually taper off into thin expansions, which are nearly homogeneous, and extending from them are distinct processes which in part unite with those of other corpuscles, not materially differing in this respect from tendon-tissue and the other varieties. In them is the same flattened, oval body, which, when seen on the side, is rod-shaped, *b*, and is surrounded by an irregular envelope that assumes almost any shape. Thus the corpuscles are not always flat, though they are usually so. Their shape depends upon many different causes, such as the method of preparing the tissue, the amount of laceration to which it is subjected, etc. The best method of examining the cornea consists in preparing it by the gold method, already described.

After the tissue has been properly stained, which is known when it has taken a mauve or violet tint, as already stated, the specimen should be allowed to stand in the sun.　Thin lamellæ are then torn off with the forceps and mounted in dammar varnish or Canada balsam.

After the specimen has been made thoroughly transparent by soaking in oil of cloves, it will then be seen that there are bodies within certain well-defined areas—the corneal spaces,

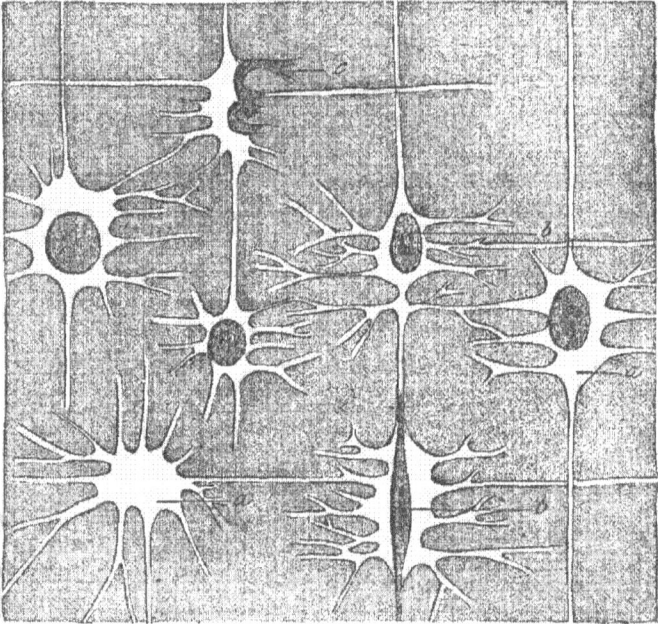

FIG. 30.—Corneal tissue.　From the rabbit.

as they have been called by Recklinghausen and others.　These bodies are disposed at quite regular intervals throughout the cornea, and are generally flat with rounded contours, though often they have processes extending from them in various directions.　In the accompanying drawing the spaces may be distinctly seen, as well as the variously shaped corneal corpuscles. One, c, is crowded into the prolongation of a corneal space, while another, b, is connected by its processes with a neighboring corpuscle.　One corneal space, a, is entirely empty.　These differing conditions are in a measure due, probably, to the laceration of the tissue in preparing it, some of the bodies having been torn out and others forced to the side of the corneal space. There seems to be a very general agreement that the intercellular substance may be separated into independent fibrils; but I have seen no decisive proof bearing on this point.

Elastic tissue.—This differs from the other forms microscopically and chemically, though it is often combined with them in the body. It is also convenient to class it by itself for other reasons, chief of which are, that its corpuscular elements have not yet been definitely shown in adult tissue. Virchow, some years ago, stated that this tissue, as well as other connective substances, was composed of networks, the substance of the fibres containing certain markings, and he inferred that these latter might be the corpuscles of the tissue. Elastic fibres were, however, according to him and others, nothing but the ordinary fibrous tissue condensed. Each fibre was hollow and capable of conveying the nutritive juices.

Henle, in his earlier writings, regarded the elastic fibres as emanating from the nuclei, of which, in fact, he stated they were prolongations. Subsequently, he seems to have believed that the fibres originated in the basis substance.

Reichert could not trace the connection between the nuclei and the elastic fibres, and, when the latter had formed, the former had disappeared.

Boll, however, distinctly stated that the elastic fibres, each one constituting an "elastic cord," arise from the plate-like cells.

Ranvier examined tendon-tissue, as mentioned before, but he was only able to find the elastic fibres after boiling the tissue from eight to ten hours. It is proper, however, to add here, that elastic fibres are very uncommon in tendon-tissue, at least they have not often been observed.

The fibres of the elastic substance are pretty readily recognized by the fact that they are not colored by carmine or hæmatoxylon, and do not swell with acetic acid; they branch dichotomously, these branches forming, with similar branches of other elastic fibres, networks.

Elastic tissue prevails in the ligamentum nuchæ of the ox, in the serous membranes generally, and in the subcutaneous connective tissue of the skin, as well as in the delicate inter-

muscular substance already described. It will generally be
found that where this material occurs in bundles it is not because there are no meshes, but rather because they are compressed laterally, so as not to be apparent unless most carefully
teased apart. When such fibres are broken off, their extremities curl up ; further, the fibres are unaffected by being boiled
in solutions of strong acids and alkalies, such as 35 per cent.

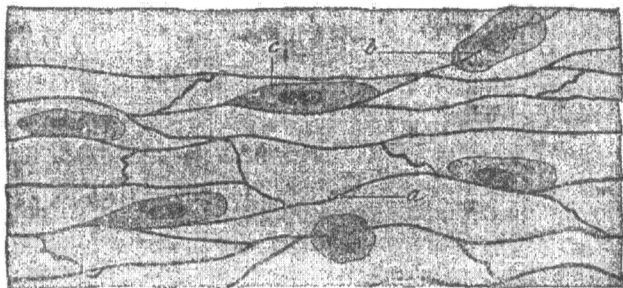

FIG. 31.—Elastic tissue networks. From the frog.

solutions of caustic potash, or nitric acid (standard preparations commonly used in laboratories), unless the action is prolonged for a considerable time. These networks are beautifully
shown by taking the mesentery of the frog when slightly contracted after immersion in acetic acid. The fibrillated connective tissue will then swell up and become invisible, while the
elastic fibres are unaffected.

The ligamentum nuchæ also affords an excellent opportunity for studying this tissue by itself. To render the work
more easy, the specimen may be allowed to soak a few days in
a 10 per cent. watery solution of common salt, so that it may
be the more easily teased. In the subcutaneous connective
tissue of the skin the elastic fibres are well shown by hæmatoxylon preparations. Being unaffected by this staining solution they appear as bright, silk-like cords, which lie in close
apposition with the wavy bundles, and the branches arch over
the bundles, to anastomose with corresponding branches of
other bundles, so that in this way meshes are formed. Some
writers have spoken of little knobs at the nodal points of the
meshes, but these appearances have been illusory.

Recklinghausen seems to have believed with Virchow, that
the elastic fibres contain peculiar nuclei of their own, which in

adult tissue become extremely small, and are represented by the dark markings seen in them. Thin, of London, has claimed that they originate in branching corpuscles, which by their coalescence form the network, and the remains of the nucleus may be shown by hæmatoxylon. These markings may, it is true, be seen in the ligamentum nuchæ of the ox, but it is doubtful whether they are nuclei or mere clefts in the tissue. Examination by the author, with such high powers as Gundlach's No. 15 immersion, and Wale's $\frac{1}{10}$, have failed to clear up the matter.

Good examples of human elastic tissue are found in the sloughs of ulcers and in the sputa of phthisical patients.

In some portions of the body these networks are stouter, as in the bronchi and trachea ; here they almost form a layer by themselves ; some of the fibres are even said to have a sheath.

There is a variety that has been called, by Henle, *perforated membrane*. It is found in arteries and veins. The fibres are broad and the meshes very small. There are also "continuous elastic membranes." They are made up of fibrils, react chemically like elastic tissue, and have no meshes. Such is Bowman's elastic membrane in the human cornea, which is very distinct in man, also Descemet's membrane—the posterior elastic membrane of the cornea.

In various parts of the body, beneath the epithelium, there are other elastic membranes which will be noticed in their proper places. The elastic membrane, made of endothelium, and forming the basement membrane of gland-ducts, must not be confounded with those first described.

The growth and development of connective tissue varies according to the particular type. It is probable, however, that all the corpuscles are first round, but soon become flattened and have a delicate envelope (Fig. 32, *b*).

About this is a further lightly attached investment, which, uniting with those of other similar bodies, is the commencement of the intercellular substance. At first the plate-like bodies lie in niches, as it were, in the intercellular substances, and if one is brushed out it leaves a socket behind it (Fig. 32, *c*). They are often arranged in rows, as in the drawing, which was taken from a fibroma of the scalp. As the intercellular substance increases the corpuscles become smaller, while immediately under them thin laminæ are formed, probably from the effused fibrine—the commencement of fibrillation.

As the corpuscles become smaller their envelope shrinks, and they recede from one another. Yet, in many cases, they may retain connection with one another by means of their processes. In advanced life these corpuscles are generally more or less flattened, but their form is also considerably modified by the age of the tissues and various mechanical alterations to which they are subjected, according to the particular locality in which they occur or the province they have to fill.

By referring to Fig. 32 it will be seen that the delicate protoplasm, *b*, has processes which come clearly into view where the corpuscles are isolated.

Pavement endothelium (epithelium).—From the views that have been advanced it is plain that we are prepared to abandon the old idea that the mesentery, peritoneum, the pleura, endocardium, serous cavities, and tendinous sheaths are lined with epithelium. It is becoming more and more evident from studies in the lymphatics that they are lined with connective-tissue corpuscles, which, on the one hand, are in actual continuity with the interfascicular connective-tissue corpuscles, and, on the other, with the pavement corpuscles of the serous cavities. It is but a step farther and in the same direction to trace the endothelium of the endocardium out through the arteries and veins into the capillaries and recognize the connective-tissue corpuscle as the one cellular element of all these tissues. The special methods by which these parts are studied may be found described in the chapters more especially devoted to these topics. Nitrate of silver and chloride of gold are still prominent among the reagents that demonstrate them most distinctly.

Ehrlich has recently described peculiar connective-tissue

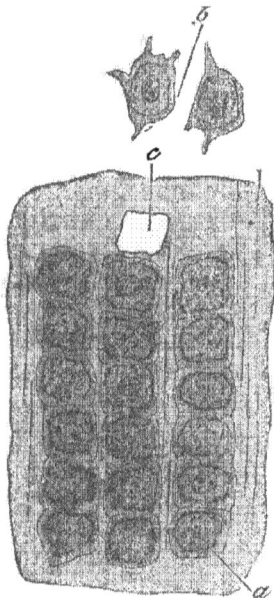

FIG. 32.—Development of fibrous tissue. Fibroma of the scalp.

corpuscles, which he previously supposed to be identical with Waldeyer's plasma cells, but which he is now inclined to regard as a distinctive group of bodies. They are characterized by a special power of intense coloration in specimens treated with certain of the aniline dyes. Red and violet colors appear to be best suited to reveal the presence of these bodies, called by Ehrlich *granular cells.* Acetic acid produces a diffuse staining of the nucleus in these aniline stained cells. At the same time the conspicuous granules lose their color. The same author also states that the granular cells commonly found in such great abundance in inflammatory processes are not modified leucocytes, but are derived from the fixed connective-tissue corpuscles.

According to Ravogli, the connective-tissue corpuscles of the corium and subcutaneous tissue are branching cells, whose processes unite to form anastomoses. With advancing age these cells undergo structural alterations, and their processes begin to form reticula of elastic tissue. Simultaneously with this metamorphosis the cell-bodies are said to become flattened, elongated, and united in longitudinal rows. At length the cells as well as their processes are transformed into ordinary elastic tissue.

BIBLIOGRAPHY.

SATTERTHWAITE, T. E. On the Structure and Development of Connective Substances (Prize Essay). New York Med. Jour., July, 1876, and Monthly Microscop. Jour., October and November, 1876.

FLEMMING. Arch. f. Anat., etc. 1879. 401—454.

STRICKER. Allg. Wien. med. Ztg. 1879. XXIV., 547.

KOLLMANN. Centralbl. f. d. med. Wiss. 1878. XVI., 881.

EHRLICH. Verhandl. d. Berliner phys Gesell. Jan. 17, 1879; Arch. f. Anat. u Phys Phys. Abtheil. pp. 166—169. 1879.

RAVOGLI. Wien. med. Jahrb. Heft 1, p. 49. 1879.

Also the more recent text-books of Klein and Ranvier.

6

CHAPTER VI.

CARTILAGE.

CARTILAGE is divided into three prominent varieties: 1, *hyaline;* 2, *fibrous;* and 3, *elastic* or *yellow.* There is, in addition, a form called *ossifying,* which will be described in connection with the development of bone.

Hyaline cartilage is the tissue from which the bones of the skeleton are first made; it is also found in the articular and costal cartilages, and in the cartilages of the larynx, trachea, and bronchi; possibly also in some of the nasal cartilages, and in portions of the sternum. All of these tissues consist of a solid material or matrix, in which are capsules which contain the true cartilage corpuscles.

The character of the intercellular substance determines the particular variety. Thus, hyaline cartilage appears, under the microscope, to be structureless and homogeneous. Fibrous cartilage, on the other hand, has distinct lines of fibrillation extending through it. Elastic cartilage is permeated by networks of elastic fibrils.

Hyaline cartilage, though so-called because of its apparent absence of structure, is now known to be less often structureless than has been supposed, for the researches of Tillmanns have revealed distinct marks of fibrillation in some adult articular and costal cartilages. Soaking the tissue in a 10 per cent. solution of common salt will dissolve out the cement substance and isolate fibrils, though the tissue has previously appeared homogeneous. Staining with the picro-carminate of. ammonia (Ranvier's formula) will also demonstrate the fibrils.

Each capsule is probably invested by a delicate membrane, which is thicker in some instances than in others. Extending from this cavity are minute canals, which communicate with those of other capsules in many instances, and thus, in all probability, establish a system of serous channels which convey the plasmatic fluid, *i.e.*, the lymph.

Many years ago H. Mueller gave a description of minute passages radiating out from the cartilage capsules. Since this time the matter has been studied by numbers of observers, but opinions have been divided as to their existence. More recently A. Budge has detailed a method by which he claims that a complete lymphatic system can be demonstrated in hyaline cartilage. Employing a solution of Berlin blue, he injected the cartilage of an epiphysis from which the articular lamella had been cut off. Having thus opened and exposed the substance of the cartilage, he found it permeated with minute blue networks that were in communication with the cartilage capsules. A connection with the lymphatics of the bone was also shown.

Nykamp, who prosecuted his investigations about the same time (1876-77), verified the work of Budge, though his methods were different. He experimented on rabbits, injecting one gramme of indigo carmine (in substance) into the abdominal cavity. Blue granules appeared in certain spaces, which had shown themselves to be hollow passages by a previous soaking in the neutral chromate of ammonia. The cartilage commonly known as hyaline was also, by this means, shown to be fibrillated.

Round about every cartilage capsule there is usually an area of hyaline material. When very thin sections of cartilage are made, these areas sometimes become visible ; soaking in acids is said also to bring them into prominence (Klein).

The amount of intercellular substance in comparison with the capsules varies ; as a rule, there is less of this substance near the periphery of the cartilage. When the amount is so very small that the tissue is almost cellular, it is called *parenchymatous cartilage;* this condition is observed in all cartilages, at an early stage of development, and in some portions of the adult forms. The cartilage corpuscles are rounded bodies, sometimes oval and sometimes pyriform. In the normal condition they fill up the capsule, but after the application of reagents that shrivel, such as alcohol, they are withdrawn from the walls of the capsules, being only attached at a few points (perhaps where their processes extend out through the canaliculi).

The cell-corpuscles and nuclei are said, by some recent observers, to exhibit networks in their interior (Schleicher and Flemming). They frequently contain, in addition, moving bodies, which are often oil-globules of minute size.

The cartilage capsules do not usually appear to have any connection with one another when examined in an indifferent fluid, though in the episternal cartilage of the frog, immediately beneath the perichondrium, a connection may occasionally be seen.

Division of the cartilage corpuscle.—One of the prominent features seen in cartilage is the division of the cartilage corpuscle. First we notice the splitting of the nucleus; then of the corpuscle itself. When such a division has taken place the corpuscles are called *daughter-cells* (Fig. 33). As a next step each daughter-cell may divide and again subdivide, and

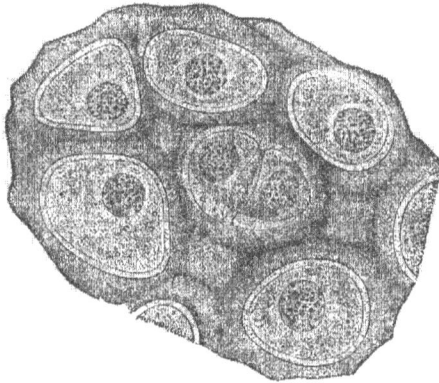

FIG. 33.—Fresh cartilage from the triton.   Rollett.

thus we have developed in one capsule four or eight corpuscles. Sometimes it will be observed in the same specimen that with each division of a corpuscle, hyaline matter from without the capsule pushes in, and so from the original capsule two are now formed.

Calcification of hyaline cartilage.—Hyaline cartilage in old age is infiltrated by a deposit of the salts of lime, which, when seen under the microscope, have a granular appearance. The deposit occurs first round about the cartilage capsule (Ranvier).

Nerves and blood-vessels are not supplied to hyaline cartilage proper, though blood-vessels which belong to adjacent tissues sometimes dip into it or pass through it.

Methods of studying hyaline cartilage.—An excellent and simple plan is to snip off the tip of the episternal cartilage from the frog ; strip it of perichondrium and mount in serum. The shoulder-girdle of the triton (newt) may also be employed.

It will then be seen that there are numbers of granular corpuscles, with nuclei scattered irregularly throughout an apparently homogeneous, *i.e.*, structureless matrix. If now a little water be added to the preparation, it will be seen that the corpuscles are made to shrivel, and in so doing they expose the wall of the cavity or capsule in which they lie. The corpuscles do not appear to have any uniform size or shape : sometimes they are single ; again they are double (daughter-cells) ; occasionally they are united with the corpuscles in adjacent capsules. The nucleus is apt to be round and full ; the corpuscles are apt to be filled with dark spherical bodies which are usually fatty molecules, as may be shown by employing a dilute solution of osmic acid (1 per cent.).

Using the silver method it will be seen that there exist, in the apparently homogeneous matrix, numbers of corpuscles whose nature is not fully understood. Incidentally it may be mentioned that the silver method often exhibits curious markings in all tissues.

Sometimes these appearances are due to the silver itself, and some caution is therefore necessary in deducing conclusions from the method.

The *gold method*[1] shows that there are concentric rings about the capsules, but it is highly probable that this phenomenon is artificial.

Ranvier recommends, as a staining fluid, *purpurine*, the formula of which is as follows : Take one gramme of powdered alum and add to it two hundred grammes of distilled water, which boil, in a porcelain dish. To this solution add some powdered purpurine diluted with water. If the boiling be now continued, a portion of the purpurine will dissolve. Filter while warm, and receive the colored fluid in a flask which contains 60 c.c. of alcohol. This liquid has a rose-orange color. The nuclei of the corpuscles will be colored red and have a double contour ; the cell-body will be bright red.

Hyaline cartilage may be well exhibited in the respiratory tract of young children, as in the cricoid cartilage of an infant two or three years old.

Yellow elastic or *reticular* cartilage is a very distinctive form. It consists of the hyaline variety permeated with elastic networks. Examples of it may be obtained from the human

---

[1] See pages 28–29.

epiglottis, laryngeal cartilages, and the pinna of the ear (Fig. 34). The presence of elastic fibres is proved by their resistance to boiling in acids and alkalies, and their failure to color with carmine. Sections may be made with the knife and prepared in almost any of the ways already mentioned.

The appearances already described are not seen in the early development of elastic tissue, but are easily identified in adult

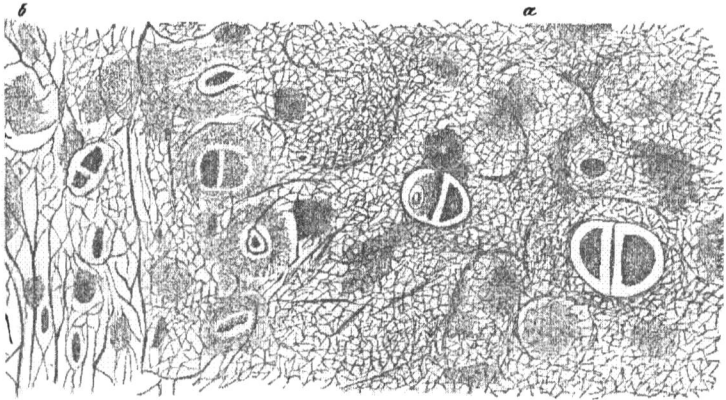

Fig. 34.—Section of the boiled and dried auricle of the human ear : a, retiform cartilage; b, connective tissue. Rollett.

life. Even then the elastic fibrils may only be found in the interior of the cartilage, while at the periphery the matrix is hyaline. Elastic cartilage is coated over with a delicate membrane—the *perichondrium*.

Fibrous cartilage.—This variety is also known as fibrillated or fibro-cartilage. The matrix has probably no elastic fibrils, but is interspersed with connective-tissue bundles. It is found in the cartilages which make the lips of the joints, the inter-articular cartilages, the cartilaginous deposits in tendons, the cartilage of the symphysis pubis and of glenoid fossæ, and possibly in the intervertebral ligaments and sesamoid cartilages. There is often more or less hyaline material about them. In many instances the line of distinction between cartilage and fibrous tissue is difficult to make out. Where, however, distinct corpuscles can be demonstrated, the tissue may properly be regarded as cartilage. These bodies are similar to those seen in hyaline and reticular cartilage.

Division of the cartilage-corpuscle.—A problem that has

attracted the study of various histologists for a number of years, since Leidy, in 1849, first directed attention to it, is the mode in which cartilage-corpuscles divide. Various theories have been afloat, each with its special supporters.

Dr. W. S. Bigelow, of this country, in 1878 reviewed the subject carefully, pursuing his investigations on the hyaline cartilage of the triton, tree-toad, frog, various fishes, the guinea-pig, fœtal pig, and the human embryo in health and disease. His inquiries were especially concerned with reference to the statement of Buetschli, that in the divisions of the corpuscles, the splitting of the nucleus and cell-body are simultaneous. As the result of Dr. Bigelow's work, he concludes that the old theory is still tenable, viz., that at first there is a division of the nucleus, and that subsequently a septum is found in the cell-body. After division takes place the matrix of the cartilage penetrates between the corpuscles, and thus two cavities are formed. This view has received confirmation from very extended and elaborate researches by Schleicher, to which Flemming has also expressed a provisional assent.

Structure of the cartilage-corpuscle.—According to Schleicher the nuclei are provided with peculiar filaments and granules which undergo amœboid movements when they are in the act of dividing. In the cell-body of young cartilage-corpuscles he has seen no network, such as has been described by some later writers (Heitzmann, Klein, etc.), though in the adult tissue peculiar linear markings are evident. He thinks that the nucleus is not permeated by a network, but is homogeneous. Reticulated appearances are apt, he thinks, to be the result of using reagents that alter the natural quality of the tissues. According to Flemming, the nucleus of the cartilage-corpuscles contains a network which gives the appearances described as "coarsely granular."

In the drawings of this author the cell-bodies nowhere exhibit a network, but, on the contrary, linear markings, which have often a concentric direction. In many, the internal structure is represented as homogeneous. The conflict of opinion now apparent in this matter, and the marked differences in the microscopic drawings of the same object, make it apparent that these topics are still to be regarded as *sub judice*.

Structure of the intercellular substance.—According to Spina there is an *intracellular* substance in cartilage which is directly continuous with the *intercellular* substance, which itself exhibits an extremely delicate network. This condition, which he regards as an early form of cartilage, undergoes changes, in so far that the intercellular network is enlarged and narrowed so as to give the appearance of fascicles or bundles of parallel fibres. The meshes are filled with a finely granular substance which is thought to be partly formed at the expense of the network. The method employed in demonstrating these appearances consisted in taking the articular extremities of frog's bones, immersing them three to four days in alcohol, then cutting thin sections, and finally, examining them in alcohol.

BIBLIOGRAPHY.

TILLMANNS. Archiv f. mikrosk. Anat. X. Bd. X. p. 401. 1874.

BUDGE, A. Archiv f. mikrosk. Anat. Bd. XIV., S. 65. 1877.

NYKAMP. Archiv f. mikrosk. Anat. Bd. XIV., S. 492. 1877.

HEITZMANN. Studien am Knochen u. Knorpel. Wien. med. Jahrb. 1872. V. and H.'s Bericht.

BIGELOW, W. S. Arch. f. mikrosk. Anat. XVI., 2. 1878.

SCHLEICHER. Ibid.

FLEMMING. Ibid.

KLEIN and E. NOBLE SMITH'S Atlas of Histology. 1879—1880.

RANVIER. Traité technique d'histologie. 1877.

BUETSCHLI. Zeitschr. f. wiss. Zool. 29, p. 206.

SPINA, A. Sitzb. de k. Akad. der Wiss. Bd. LXXX., LXXXI. 1879, 1880.

CHAPTER VII.

BONE.

THERE are two principal varieties of bone known to anatomists, the compact and the cancellous or spongy. The former is found in the shafts of all the long bones of the body and along the outer surface of all the short and flat bones. The latter occurs in the articular extremities of all long bones and in the interior of all short and flat bones.

Compact tissue consists of an unyielding, almost inelastic, massive framework, which is traversed by networks of blood-vessels and lymphatics, and perhaps by nerves. The dense organic substance forming the groundwork of all bone—*ossein* —is in reality nothing but a form of connective substance almost precisely resembling ordinary fibrous tissue, but which is evenly infiltrated with minute molecules of the carbonates and phosphates of lime and some other inorganic salts. These insoluble matters are so thoroughly intermixed with the fibrous tissue that they give it great solidity, though at the same time they restrict its flexibility, and therefore increase its susceptibility to fracture.

Like other forms of the connective-tissue series, it contains corpuscles that are disposed in a regular way between lamellæ, which here correspond to the fascicles of fibrous tissue. The province of these corpuscles is doubtless the same as that of other connective-tissue corpuscles, viz., to preside over the nutrition of the tissue in which they are found.

After decalcification by strong acids, such as the nitric or muriatic, if the residue be boiled it will yield gelatin or chondrin.

These corpuscles that have just been described are not al-

ways easily recognized, and, in fact, have often been ignored
by writers of anatomical text-books. They were not detected
for a long time, because the capsules in which they are embedded received all the attention, and were even called *bone-
corpuscles*. But when it was discovered by Virchow that
these bodies had nuclei, and that they could be separated, together with their processes, from the bone, it was supposed
that the nutrition of the tissue was maintained through them,
acting in the capacity of hollow tubes. This view Virchow at
one time supported. Subsequently it was discovered that injection fluids could be forced into the canaliculi and round
about the corpuscles, so that three facts became assured : (1)
the existence of capsules in the bony substance with radiating
and anastomosing passages, the lacunæ and canaliculi ; (2) the
presence of nucleated and branched corpuscles in the lacunæ;
and of spaces (3) about the nucleated corpuscles and their
processes, suitable for the movement of fluids designed for the
nutrition of the part.

The structure of bone then became clear, and its similarity
with other connective substances well established. These bony
canaliculi extend to the wall of the Haversian canal, the great
channel conveying the blood-vessels and larger lymphatics.
Thus a lymph-canalicular system permeates the bone in close
connection with the blood-vessels, bathing every bone-corpuscle.

When a cross-section is made of any long bone, it will be
observed that most of the lamellæ have a concentric arrangement about each Haversian canal (Fig. 35, *b*). But it will also
be seen that there are other groups of lamellæ whose arrangement is slightly different. For example, at the periphery of
the bone their direction is parallel with the surface.

Such lamellæ may be represented at *a*. They are known as
the *intermediate* or *circumferential* (Tomes and De Morgan).
Another group, only partly encircling each canal, is known as
the *peripheric* or *interstitial*, *c*. The first mentioned, immediately about the canal, are the *concentric*, *b*.

Schaefer believes with Sharpey that each lamella consists of fibres crossing
each other diagonally, and separated on either side by a homogeneous layer.
According to Von Ebner, the peculiar cross striations belong only to Canada
balsam preparations that are old. These markings are due to the peculiar
refractive power of the balsam which fills the canaliculi.

The arrangement just described is found in all compact bone where there is any considerable thickness, but when, as in flat bones, the cortex is very thin, the lamellæ often pursue a straight and parallel course. Some of these lamellæ or plates exhibit transverse striations ; others are homogeneous.

In Fig. 35 may be seen the lacunæ lying between the lamellæ. They appear as dark spaces disposed at quite regular intervals and, having their long axes parallel with the course of the lamellæ. Laterally each corpuscle gives off numbers of processes, many of which branch, while all, or nearly all, anastomose with corresponding branchlets of other corpuscles. A branchlet is also given off from the end of each corpuscle, and forms a connection with the adjacent bodies lying in the same interlamellar space and in the same plane.

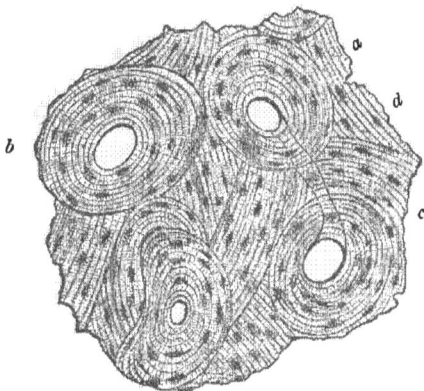

FIG. 35.—Transverse section of human femur, deprived of inorganic material by hydrochloric acid. Rollett.

The Haversian canals form a broad-meshed network throughout the bone, establishing a communication between the central marrow cavity and the external surface of the bone (Fig. 36).

The arrangement of parts comprised by each Haversian canal, with its investing lamellæ, and interposed lacunæ and their anastomosing canaliculi constitutes an *Haversian system.* Though found mainly in the compact tissue, they may also be seen in the large trabeculæ of the spongy substance. As seen in Fig. 36, the Haversian canals form a network of which the longitudinal tubes are the larger and longer. Besides conveying blood-vessels and lymphatics they have a certain amount of connective tissue which varies according to the locality, and establishes a more or less complete connection between the connective tissue of the marrow cavity and of the periosteum.

In young bone this is well seen ; in adult bone the direct continuity can with difficulty be traced, as the vessels are apt to fill the tubes pretty completely.

Preparation of dry bone.—In order to study the characteristics which have just been described, any human long bone may be taken. It should be stripped of its soft parts, bleached, and well dried. Thin sections are then to be made both in a longitudinal and transverse direction, with a watch-spring saw.

Next, cleanse them well in water to which a little bicarbonate of soda has been added; then place on a whetstone and grind down by rubbing backward and forward with the finger until they are sufficiently thin; or the sections may be placed between two plates of ground glass and rubbed down.

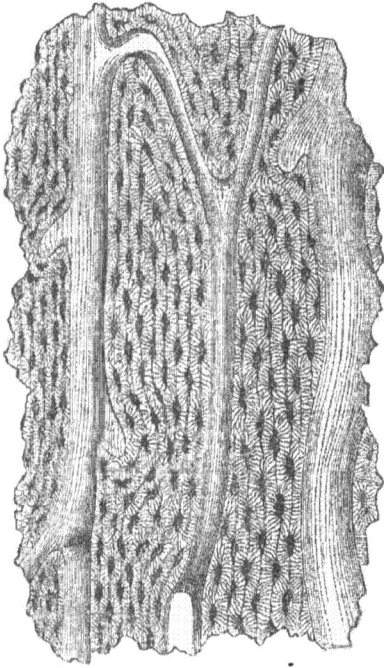

Finally, when so thin that type may be read through them, mount either dry or in Canada balsam or dammar varnish. All the characteristics already described may then be seen.

Preparation of decalcified bone.—Another method consists in first removing the earthy salts. If it is desirable to accomplish the work rapidly, cut the bone to be prepared into the smallest available pieces and immerse from four to five days in a 10 per cent. watery solution of hydrochloric acid.

FIG. 36.—Longitudinal section of human ulna, showing the Haversian canals forming meshes.   Rollett.

The completion of this process may be determined by testing the bone with a fine cambric needle. So long as it meets with resistance, the presence of the bone-earths is certain; on the other hand, if it enter easily, the process of decalcification is over, and the piece ready for cutting.

Now wash thoroughly in water, so as to remove the acid, place in 80 per cent. alcohol, gradually increasing the strength to 95 per cent. The specimen is then ready for use and may be treated precisely as any other tissue of the body. If more time is at the disposal of the student, chromic acid may be used in a ¼ per cent. solution. This process is rather slow, requiring several months. It may be materially hastened by the use of nitric acid (2 per cent.). It has been found that after immersion in chromic acid for a few days, the soft parts are rendered insensible to the action of other strong acids, such as nitric and hydrochloric, when used in the dilute form. These chromic acid preparations are exceedingly beautiful objects

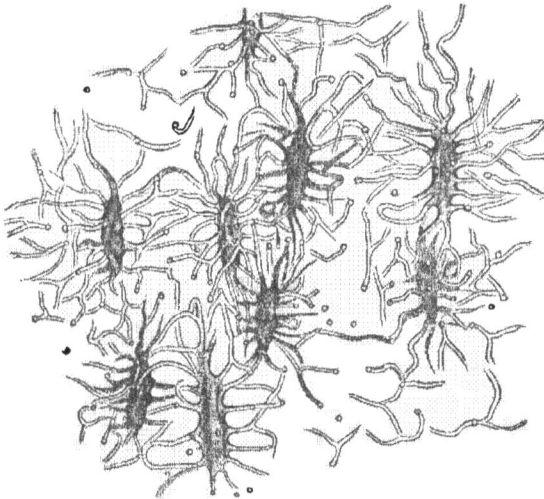

FIG. 37.—Bone lacunæ with their processes.   Rollett.

when seen with low powers. The matrix is of a deep grass green. If a thin section is stained with borax-carmine (Arnold's formula) the bone-corpuscles and connective tissue are stained red, and the contrast of color brings out the finer elements very distinctly.

Picro-carmine may also be used, and then the muscular tissue, if any chance to adhere to the bone, is stained yellow ; or eosine and hæmatoxylon may be used instead of borax carmine, and thus very excellent examples of triple staining procured. Sometimes a saturated solution of picric acid is employed to decalcify, but the excess of acid, after taking out the bone-earths should be thoroughly removed by soaking in water before immersion in any staining fluid. In preparing a specimen for cutting with the knife it may conveniently be held in the hand, or, if the microtome is used, the bone may be embedded in the ordinary mixture of wax and oil, pith, or liver, according to methods already described. Rutherford recommends glycerine jelly for this purpose.

Any of these plans of preparing decalcified bone will reveal the presence of the bone-corpuscles within the lacunæ. These will be found to correspond quite closely in size and shape with the cavities. They may also be shown to have a direct continuity with the connective-tissue corpuscles of the periosteum. In growing bone this is more evident. A nucleus can also sometimes be seen in the bone-corpuscle. In Fig. 36 the lacunæ, with their canaliculi, are well shown.

Sharpey's perforating fibres.—Attached to the outer surface of compact tissue, and penetrating the bone at right angles, are certain fibres which have been named after Sharpey, their discoverer.

Take a flat bone of the skull that has been decalcified, seize pieces with the forceps, tear them out from the surface, and examine in water. In some of the fragments the bundles of fibres will be seen; in others the lamellæ, perforated for the fibres. If a portion of tendon adhere to the bone, and a section be made through the two at their line of apparent junction, it will be seen that the tendon-fibres are continuous in the bone with Sharpey's fibres.

A very prevalent view is that they constitute the remains of the *periosteal processes*, which we shall see are largely concerned with the ultimate development of bone.

Cancellous tissue.—All of the elements of bone, that go to make up a Haversian system, are found in the cancellous tissue, so that, in this respect, it does not differ from the compact. The chief peculiarity lies in the *marrow cavities*, or *channels*, as they might appropriately be called, and they indicate either, on the one hand, that the bone is passing through a developmental stage; or that it is being rarefied by a process of retrograde metamorphosis; or, finally, that it has reached a stadium of repose in either of the first-named changes. These points will be further particularized when the growth and development of bone is explained, but the reader is now prepared for the rather remarkable proposition that compact bone is formed out of spongy, and spongy out of compact.

These marrow channels are a series of branching and anastomosing tubes, rich in corpuscular elements and vessels. In young bone the latter are known as *red marrow*. When a longitudinal section has been made through a tubular bone, it will be seen that the channels are enclosed in an osseous network, whose meshes differ much in shape. In the articular extremities they are long and narrow; at other points, more nearly quadrilateral.

There is a second variety of marrow, known as *yellow*, which is found in the central cavity of the long bones. The yellow color is due to the presence of fat, though it also contains peculiar, small, colorless corpuscles, not unlike the leucocytes of the blood, and known as *marrow-cells*, together with the ordinary branched and nucleated connective-tissue corpuscles, also large multi-nucleated bodies that are usually granular and sometimes striated, and blood-vessels. The large corpuscles are the *myeloplaxes* of Robin (giant-cells).

The red marrow also contains marrow-cells, though but few fat-cells. It is remarkable for being the seat of the peculiar nucleated blood-corpuscles that have been described by Neumann and Bizzozero. They are transitional between the white and the red in size, and have a uniform yellowish green color (Klein).

The authors above referred to found the nucleated corpuscles in the red marrow of the ribs and bodies of the vertebræ; they resembled blood-corpuscles that are found in the human embryo, and were regarded as evidence that the bones have bloodmaking properties. Later researches (Orth and Litten) have seemed to corroborate these views, and to have shown that in certain morbid states of the blood, as in carcinoma, phthisis, and syphilis, an effort of this kind is made for the relief of the constitutional infection. Experiments upon dogs have also added further testimony and have shown that after extreme artificial anæmia there is a new formation of blood-globules, in which the nucleated bodies play an active part, together with other elements, such as the *giant-corpuscles* of Hayem, etc. These views, however, have met with opposition, and Rutherford ("Pract. Histology," p. 88) maintains that the nucleated corpuscle is an indication of corpuscular disintegration rather than of new-formation.

The periosteum is a layer of dense fibrous tissue closely covering the bone, and connected with it by a thinner layer of looser texture. The external portion may be composed of single, double, or treble laminæ of varying thickness. The inner or *osteogenetic* portion is of great interest and importance, as it contains the *osteoblasts*, which are active agents in the formation of a great part of all bones, as we shall presently see.

Development of bone.—Views as to the method by which bone is formed have undergone great changes within the past few years, and it may be stated that most modern observers have given in their adhesion to the theory that bone is not developed by a calcification of cartilage, but by a long and complicated series of changes inaugurated by the corpuscles of the marrow cavities, on the one hand, and those of the periosteum, on the other. These conclusions have been the result of very extended researches conducted by a variety of methods and upon many kinds of animals.

As the mode of growth in man and horned cattle is identical, a good method of procedure is as follows. Take the hoof of a yearling bullock, and, removing the bones, macerate them a few days in a 10 per cent. watery solution of hydrochloric acid and then in chromic acid (gr. ij.— ℥ j.). In a few days they will be decalcified sufficiently to allow of a thin section being shaved off from the surface so as to include parts where ossification has already commenced. The sections may then be stained in a neutral solution of carmine and mounted. The gradual stages between the advancing bone and the liquefying cartilage can now be studied. Following the changes from the surface of the articulation toward the centre of the bone, there is seen at first, beneath the fibrous layer, a stratum of hyaline cartilage. The corpuscles are long, flattened, and lie parallel with the surface. Passing to a greater depth they become larger, and increase in number by gradual progression. As these capsules enlarge and their contents multiply, they begin to be arranged about the wall of the cavity, while the matrix gradually wastes away. A little farther and there is a deposit of calcific material in the intercapsular substance. Another step internally and the cartilage capsules have in part coalesced, and now they are beginning to be filled by the marrow tissue pushing up from the central parts of the bone. When the connective tissues and vessels that constitute this arborescent growth have entered the capsules, the corpuscles that line them are called osteoblasts. Whether or not they are identical with the cartilage-corpuscles, or belong to the budding marrow-processes, seems to be a matter of doubt. Klein intimates that the cartilage-corpuscles disintegrate. Ranvier has seen no proof of it. It is probable that some of the cartilage-corpuscles persist, certainly to a limited extent, and preside over the remains of the calcified cartilage. The bulk of the new bone is made up, however, of new material which is deposited under the form of concentric lamellæ about the marrow cavities, most likely by a proliferation of the osteoblasts.

These changes may all be observed to advantage in the specimen just mentioned, and the successive gradations of the process can be conveniently magnified, so as to be easily seen, by making sections obliquely to the surface of the bone. With a low power the specimens will have uncommon beauty, as the corpuscles take the carmine well, while the interstitial tissue is of a bright, transparent grass-green.

In a vertical section of a long bone, while the process is essentially the same, there are some modifications in the successive steps. Thus the spongy bone of the epiphysis encroaches on the cartilage, causing it to be absorbed in the manner already described, but the *intermediary cartilage*, lying between the epiphysis and diaphysis, is seen to have its corpuscles arranged in long lines parallel with the axis of the bone ("*step-ladders*"). The bone meshes of the encroaching bone are also shaped in correspondence with the cartilage capsules, that is, they are long and narrow.

Formation of bone through the medium of cartilage.—The successive changes in this species of bone development have been best described by Klein. According to him the hyaline cartilage that is destined to prepare the way for bone is covered with perichondrium, consisting like the periosteum of two layers. This membrane does not at first contain mature fibrous tissue, but merely the rudiments of it, under the form of spindle-shaped corpuscles; its internal layer, however, is early provided with spherical corpuscles, the future osteoblasts, and is rich in vessels.

Subsequently this osteogenetic envelope puts out processes (*periosteal processes*, Virchow) that penetrate into the cartilage-capsules, which, melting as the external growth makes its

7

way inward, develop communications between the capsules, so
that in this way a cartilaginous network is formed that is filled
with the arborescent tissue. This change in the cartilage,
which is characterized by absorption and rarefaction, is called
chondro-porosis.

At a more advanced stage the cartilage around the oldest
channels has become transparent in places, while the walls are
irregular, because portions of calcified trabeculæ project into
them. These irregular spaces are called *primary marrow
cavities*. Now upon the walls may be seen, not the cartilage-
corpuscles, but the *osteoblasts*, which are proceeding to develop
concentric layers of osseous tissue.

When this process has been completed, the osseous tissue
will be found to have replaced the calcified cartilage, and true
bone has been formed. But this action may be no sooner
completed than absorption will again commence, and at first in
the last or most internal layer of the Haversian system. This
process is essential for the development of the central marrow
cavity. After an Haversian system has been removed, the
matrix will also disappear.

Now, while this cavity is filling up with marrow a gradual
development of bone is taking place from the periosteum,
which slowly encroaches upon the bone whose formation we
have just described.

This last stage results in the formation of adult bone.
When it has been completed all the first formed bone has
been absorbed before it. This periosteal or *metaplastic* bone
is at first spongy, as is all new bone; in the fulfilment of its
task it next appears to form compact bone, and then part of
this latter is rarefied, as, for example, along the wall of the
central cavity. Thus, as we have already seen, compact bone
is formed from spongy, and spongy from compact. The peripheric or interstitial lamellæ are either the remains of calcified
and unabsorbed trabeculæ, or perhaps the walls of other Haversian systems forming sides of the bony network.

Formation of bone from membrane.—This second method
of bone-formation is seen in the bones of the skull and face.
The steps are precisely similar to those already described. The
inner layer of the periosteum, which is lined with osteoblasts,
produces both matrix and bone corpuscles by a process of budding. The change first begins at the *points of ossification*.

At first the bone is spongy, but later absorption takes place—*osteoporosis*. Around some of the marrow-tubes concentric lamellæ are formed, and in this way a Haversian system develops. The unabsorbed portions of the trabeculæ are thought to constitute the lamellæ known as the intermediary. Compact tissue is thus formed from spongy. This theory, which has been placed in its present acceptable light by Klein, is very simple and appears to accord with observation, and explains all the phenomena. Yet those who have believed in the direct transmutation of cartilage into bone are still in the field. Kölliker maintains that both views are correct.

According to this last named author the differences between primary or primordial and the tegumentary or secondary bones are, from a morphological point of view, sharp and complete. The former are ossifications of the cartilaginous skeleton.

The tegumentary are never cartilaginous at first; the primordial bones, on the other hand are, without exception, formed from cartilage. The method and manner in which bony tissue is formed is the same in both bones. The primordial skeleton in the lower vertebrates ossifies only in part from the perichondrium, in part perichondrally, and, in part, endochondrally.

According to Kassowitz, in the tuberosities and spines of the bones the periosteal processes of the periosteum, which develop the bone, are primarily cartilaginous, the fibrillated tissue being converted into hyaline cartilage, which is at first calcified and then undergoes direct conversion into bone.

According to the experiments of Strawinsky a transplanted periosteum will develop either bone or cartilage, when the conditions are favorable. The conditions of nutrition determine which it shall be. When the supply is best, cartilage is formed ; when poorest, bone.

The earliest evidences of ossification were seen by this observer between the fourth and fifth days. The formation of vessels preceded that of bone. Absorption commenced between the second week and the second month. The new formation of periosteum is partly derived from the border of the wound and partly from the Haversian canals, which contain a small amount of connective tissue.

Development of bone and absorption.—It has been seen that these two processes go on hand in hand. As soon as the periosteum has commenced to deposit new layers of bone on the surface of the primary spongy bone, absorption takes place along the marrow canal. First of all, as we have already said, the innermost of the concentric lamellæ yield. In this way the Haversian canals are widened and become Haversian spaces, as they were at first ; then the interstitial lamellæ, and finally the spaces disappear, and in place of them there is a single dilated central cavity.

Howship's lacunæ are the pits or lacunæ seen in bone beneath the periosteum. They usually contain a multinuclear corpuscle (giant-cell), which is in some way related to absorption, and, therefore, has received the name *osteoclast* (Kölliker). It has been surmised (Klein) that they are the agents by which an acid is formed that dissolves the lime-salts. Whether they are developed out of the osteoblasts or not is a matter of uncertainty.

All the steps, both in development and absorption of bone, have been carefully studied and placed upon a most satisfactory foundation (Lieberkühn and Bermann). The absorption of bone has also been actually proved by measurements of the bones in children (Schwalbe). By comparing the bones of the third and fourth years of life, it was found that the marrow cavity had enlarged in the latter, while the compact bone had diminished in thickness. The change commenced at the sixth month. This physiological process is closely allied to the pathological one exhibited in rachitis; in the latter the development of bone from the periosteum has the character of fœtal bone, but the formation of the lamellæ is slow and incomplete.

It has been claimed that the growth of bone takes place by an expansion of the intercellular substance (Strelzoff), but this is denied (Kölliker, Wegener, Schwalbe, and others). The ossein appears to increase somewhat, but it is at the expense of the bone-corpuscles, which are thereby diminished in size.

Formation of callus.—The method is the same as in the development from periosteum. A corpuscular blastema is developed from the periosteum and intermuscular tissue. This presses in between the fibres and bundles of the loose connective tissue, pressing them asunder, assuming considerable volume. This new tissue is hyaline cartilage. In from three to six weeks it ossifies, being in part directly transformed into bone, in part mediately, *i.e.*, through the agency of medullary spaces and osteoblasts. Where the extremities of the bone are widely separated there is a formation of bone in the medullary spaces of the broken ends of the bones. The pre-existing bone-corpuscles have no part in the new-formation. This compact bone thus formed will be absorbed in a few months, in its internal portions, by rarefying ostitis, so that the marrow cavities of the broken diaphysis will be in communication.

BIBLIOGRAPHY.

The student is referred, for further particulars, to Klein's Atlas of Histology, Ranvier's Traité technique d'histologie, Stricker's Manual of Histology, and also to the following recent writers:

SCHAEFER. Pract. Histology. 1872.

LIEBERKÜHN and BERMANN. Ueber Resorption der Knochensubstanz. 1877.

AUFRECHT. Ueber Riesenzellen in Elfenbeinstiften. Med. Centralblatt, No. 26. Jahresb. d. Fortschritte der Anat. und Phys. 1878.

ARNOLD, J. Virchow's Archiv. Bd. 71, p. 17. 1877.

VON EBNER. Sitzungsbericht der Wiener Akad. III. Abtheil. Bd. 75. Hofmann und Schwalbe's Jahresb. 1878.

KASSOWITZ. Med. Centralblatt, No. 5. Hofmann und Schwalbe's Jahresb. 1878.

SCHWALBE. Sitzungsb. der med. naturwiss. Gesellschaft zu Jena. 1877. H. und S.'s Jahresb. 1878.

STRAWINSKY. Ueber Knochenresorption. H. und S.'s Jahresbericht, p. 109, 1878.

LITTEN, M., and ORTH, J. Berliner klin. Woch. No. 51, p. 743. 1877.

KÖLLIKER. Entwickelungsgeschichte. V. und S.'s Jahresb. 1878.

TOURNEUX, F. Application de l'acide osmique à l'étude du tissu osseux. Gaz. méd. de Paris. G. S. III. 318. 1881.

CHAPTER VIII.

THE TEETH.

From the standpoint of descriptive anatomy, every tooth is composed of three parts : (1) the crown, that portion which stands above the level of the mucous membrane of the gum ; (2) the neck, a constricted part at the level of the gum ; and (3) the root, which terminates in one or more fangs, and is firmly embedded in the alveolar process of the jaw. Each fang also is pierced from below by a canal, which extends up into the crown, and is filled by a soft material rich in nerves and vessels, called the *pulp*, which has the special province of supplying nutriment to the dense tissue about it.

From a histological point of view, every tooth may be divided into : 1, enamel ; 2, dentine, or ivory ; 3, cement, or true bone. The enamel forms the covering for the crown, the cement for the root ; but they meet at the neck, and there the cement slightly overlaps. The ivory or dentine lies intermediate between the outer coatings and the pulp.

The enamel.—This substance, which is the hardest met with in the body, consists of a series of long polyhedral columns grouped in bundles and disposed mostly at right angles to the surface of the dentine which lies beneath it. Each column or pillar is a hexagonal prism, having a diameter varying between $\frac{1}{10000}$ and $\frac{1}{8250}$ inch. When viewed in cross-section these columns look like a tesselated pavement. They are not, however, closely applied to one another, but have interspaces which are said to be filled with a homogeneous substance or fluid.

All of the groups of columns do not stand vertical to the dentine ; some are parallel to it, and thus are interwoven with the vertical ones. This crossing of the fibres produces an alternation of light and dark bands (Fig. 38, 1). But there are other systems of markings. In the same figure are wavy lines running parallel to the surface. These are the "brown, *parallel stripes of Retzius*." They pursue a somewhat curved course. No unity of opinion exists about their significance, one (Hertz) attributing them to deposits of pigment, another (Von Bibra) to the presence of the oxide of iron. Still other striæ are observed, and are thought to represent the zigzag or spiral course of the enamel prisms. It is observed that when the prisms are isolated, which can be accomplished by immersion in a dilute hydrochloric acid solution, they have a somewhat spiral form, and have bulging sides and cross markings, the significance of which will be alluded to at another place.

Near the line of the dentine there are spaces between the prisms which are continuous with the cavities in the dentine. These are called the *interglobular spaces of Czermak*. They also occur at irregular intervals in the dentine.

In young subjects there is a delicate membrane covering the sur-

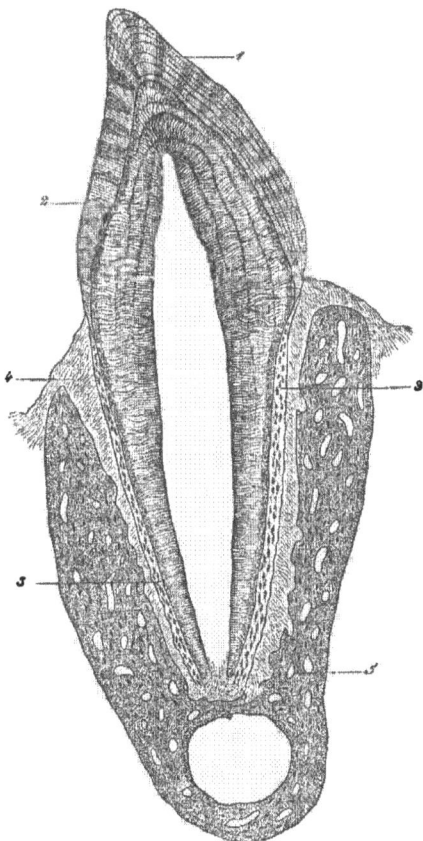

Fig. 38.—Premolar tooth of the cat, *in situ*. Vertical section, magnified 15 diameters. 1, enamel with decussating and parallel striæ; 2, dentine with Schreger's lines; 3, cement; 4, periosteum of the alveolus; 5, inferior maxillary bone. Waldeyer.

face of the enamel. It is composed of laminated epithelial scales, and corresponds to the corneous layer of the skin, of which, indeed, it represents the vestiges.

The *dentine* or *ivory* (Fig. 38, 2) consists of a dense and hard matrix impregnated with the salts of lime. It contains numerous passages having, like the enamel prisms, a direction at right angles to the surface of the bone. These passages, the *dentinal canals*, are united with one another laterally by minute oblique branches, and form undoubtedly open channels of communication between the pulp cavity and the spaces between the enamel prisms in the crown and the bone lacunæ of the cement in the fang. Each canal is lined with a particularly delicate and resistant membrane, the *dentinal sheath of Neumann*.

Upon the internal surface of the dentine, or the external surface of the pulp-tissue, is the layer of *odontoblasts* (Schwann). These corpuscles, according to Waldeyer, have long branching processes extending in three directions, inward into the pulp-cavity, outward through the dentinal channels, forming the *dentinal fibres of Tomes*, and laterally so as to form connections with adjacent corpuscles. On the outer surface of the dentine the canals connect with the interglobular spaces of Czermak, and they in turn are continuous with interstices between the enamel prisms. The dentinal tubules never appear to be in direct communication with the enamel spaces, but only mediately, as has been described. These cavities are filled with protoplasmic material. Those immediately adjoining the cement are small in size, and form what is known as the *granular layer of Tomes or Purkinje.*

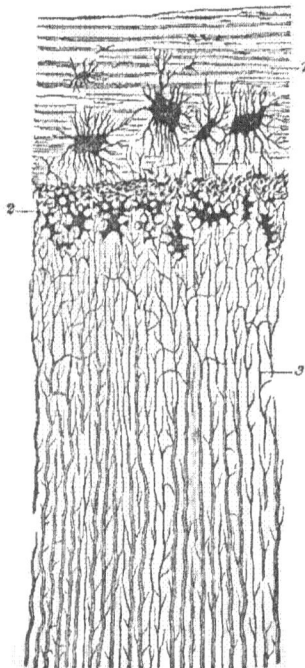

FIG. 39.—Canine tooth of man, presenting a portion of the transverse section of the root: 1, cement with large lacunæ and parallel striæ; 2, interglobular substance; 3, dentinal tubules. Magnified 300 diameters. Waldeyer.

Dentinal globules (Fig. 39, 2) is the name given to certain spheroidal masses that are regarded (Waldeyer) as calcified remains of the corpuscles in the spaces. The contours of these masses correspond in outline with those of the interglobular spaces.

Beneath the cement the intercommunication of interglobular spaces and bone-lacunæ is well shown. The *interglobular substance* is apt to be present in layers ; the lines which are then called the *incremental lines* of Salter, are supposed to show that there has been growth by successive stages. The *lines of Schreger* (Fig. 38, 2) are also waving parallel lines ; they are thought to be due to the curvature of a series of adjacent fibres. In some instances vascular channels have been found in the dentine, which has acquired the name *osteo* or *vasodentine*. In pathological conditions masses have also been found containing bone-lacunæ. They have been called *odontomata* by Virchow.

The *cement* is true bone-tissue, containing lacunæ and canaliculi, and in them the bone-corpuscles with their processes. The matrix is also subdivided into lamellæ. The periosteum of the gum dipping down into the bony socket from the surface of the gum forms a coating over the cement. Occasionally Haversian canals and blood-vessels are seen where the cement is thick (Salter). Sharpey's fibres may also be seen, according to Waldeyer.

The *pulp* is a substance that belongs to the connective-tissue series. Adjoining the dentine are two layers of corpuscles. The nearest are long cylindrical bodies whose oval nuclei are distant from the dentine. Wedged in between them, and forming a layer intermediate between them and the pulp, are peculiar branched corpuscles of a spindle or pyramidal shape. According to Klein, these latter send processes into the dentinal tubules, while, according to Waldeyer and Boll the odontoblasts send the fibres, and are also connected to one another by lateral processes. The pulp tissue is very rich in non-medullated nerves ; their prolongations penetrate between the odontoblasts, but it is a matter of question whether they enter the dentinal canals.

Capillaries are abundant and form close networks in the pulp. The lymphatics are said to accompany the blood-vessels and to be surrounded by endothelial sheaths.

Development of the teeth.—Waldeyer, whose views on the teeth are the most complete and satisfactory extant, makes the following succinct statement:

"The anatomical model of a tooth of a vertebrate animal is a large papilla of the mouth or of the pharyngeal mucous membrane, which in consequence of chemical and histological conversion of its constituents has acquired a remarkable degree of hardness, and according to whether the connective-tissue substance of the papilla participates in the hardening or not, two large groups of teeth are distinguished—*dentinal teeth* and *horny teeth*. The horny teeth are by far the most simple in

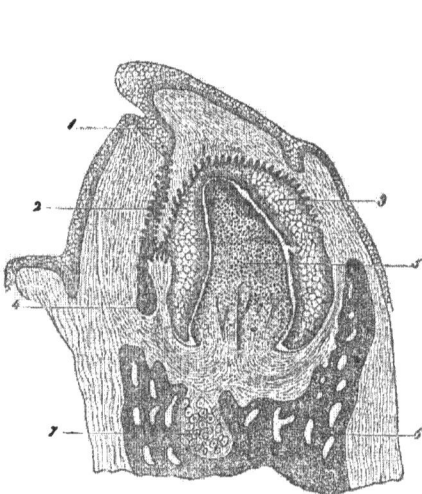

FIG. 40.—Vertical section of the inferior maxilla of a human fœtus, measuring 11 ctms. from the vertex to the coccyx. Magnified 25 diameters. 1, dental groove; 2, remains of the enamel germ; 3, enamel organ presenting externally epithelium, as also where it forms the enamel germ of the papillæ of the dental sacculus; 4, secondary enamel germ: rudiment of the permanent tooth; 5, dental germ; 6, lower jaw; 7, Meckel's cartilage. Waldeyer.

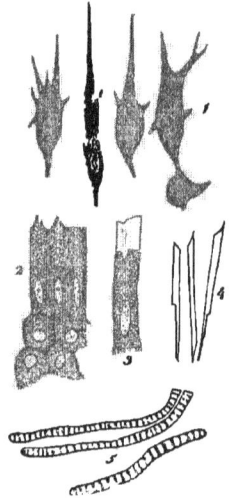

FIG. 41.—1, various forms of odontoblasts, with the three kinds of processes; 2, three enamel cells, with a few cells of the stratum intermedium attached; 3, an enamel cell, with a small portion of enamel; 4, fragments of enamel fibres from young and soft enamel; 5, old enamel fibres with transverse striæ and rounded extremities. Waldeyer.

their structure. They appear as more or less developed papillæ covered with a thick horny investment. They are never continuous with portions of the skeleton, but constitute the transition to other horny formations, as hairs, stings, etc."

"In the dentinal teeth the connective-tissue matrix of the papillæ plays a most important part in the hardening process, which here proceeds in a manner precisely similar to the ossifying process, except that no true bone is formed, but only an allied substance, of much harder consistence, and differing more or less in histological structure, termed *dentine*. The epithelium of the tooth papillæ either atrophies to a rudimentary horny investment—the *cuticula* (membrane of the enamel)—or it becomes elongated in a remarkable manner into long, petrified prisms, which collectively invest the dentine and are known as the enamel."

Preparations for the development of the teeth take place at a time when the epithelium of the mucous membrane of the mouth is found growing downward, like a solid peg, with a rounded extremity.

This has been called the *primary enamel organ.* As a next step, the material which is to give form to the tooth pushes upward as a papillary growth, and meeting the epithelial peg, pushes in or invaginates its rounded extremity. This is the *tooth papilla*, and as it pushes upward the *primary enamel organ* becomes the *secondary* enamel organ, or the *enamel cap.* We have now two tissues which are embedded in the soft embryonic substance, that happens at this early period to be gelatinous. That portion of it immediately surrounding the papilla and cap is called the *tooth-sac.*

The papilla, which becomes highly vascular, is covered, on its outer surface, by the odontoblasts, a layer of columnar epithelial corpuscles, which elongating, are transformed directly into the dentinal substance at their outer extremity.

According to Kölliker and others, they excrete the dentine. The former view seems to have the most weight of argument in its favor, but it seems less likely that the odontoblasts both make the matrix and send fibres into the tubulæ. The view of Klein already given seems to be preferable, and in conformity with what we know of other connective substances.

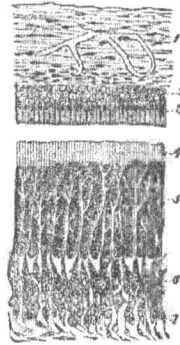

FIG. 42.—Longitudinal section of a milk tooth from the fœtal sheep, carried through the margin of the dentine pulp and adjoining portion of the enamel organ. Magnified 200 diameters. 1, dental sacculus; 2, external epithelium and stratum intermedium here united to the internal epithelium or enamel cells; 3, after the disappearance of the enamel pulp; 4, young layer of enamel detached from the enamel cells; 5, dentine; 6, odontoblasts; 7, part of the dentine pulp. Waldeyer.

The separation of the tooth-sac from the mucous membrane is effected by the gelatinous tissue, which, gradually closing in the neck of the sac, finally cuts it off. The epithelium of the enamel cap is abundant and of various kinds; into it push a number of papillary processes downward from the gelatinous tissue. Later the enamel cap is changed into three membranes.

The middle membrane is a peculiar cellular network, formed by the transformation of the middle epithelium layer into a network of cells, below which there is a deposit of a hyaline material. The inner membrane is formed of cylindrical epithelial bodies, which are called enamel-cells; outside of them are one or more layers of polygonal cells; they form the *stratum intermedium* of Hannover. The *outer membrane* is composed of several layers. Finally, the middle membrane disappearing, the outer and inner membranes are brought into close apposition.

Development of the enamel.—This is formed by the enamel-cells (*inner epithelium*, Kölliker), presumably in the same way as the dentine by the odontoblasts. There is a direct conversion of the outer extremities of the enamel-bodies into enamel. Kölliker, Hertz, and Kollmann, however, regard the enamel as an excretion from the enamel-cells. The former view appears the more natural, especially as the enamel-prisms are continuous with the enamel-cells, having the same form and shape. The successive stages of growth, it is believed, give rise to the transverse markings.

Whether or not, in the interstitial substance of the enamel, there are corpuscular elements (Boedecker), is a matter that will require further investigation. The outer membrane eventually gives rise to the cuticle covering the enamel.

The development of the cement takes place precisely as bone is produced, viz., from the periosteum, or, which is the same in this instance, from the fibrous tissue of the tooth-sac, the *periodontium*.

BIBLIOGRAPHY.

The following systematic works and journal articles may be consulted :
RETZIUS. Müller's Archives. 1837.
NASMYTH. Med.-Chir. Trans. Vol. 22. 1839.
KÖLLIKER. Man. of Human Histology. 1853.
WENZEL. Arch. d. Heilkunde. 1868.
HENLE. Anatomie. 1871.
STRICKER. Manual of Histology. Am. Ed. 1872.
TOMES. Manual of Dental Anatomy, Human and Comparative. Lond., 1876.
OWEN. Comparative Anat. and Phys. of Vertebrates. 1866.
BOEDECKER. Dental Cosmos. XXI., 409—416. Phil., 1879.
HEITZMANN. Microscopic Anat. of Human Teeth. Med. Rec., N. Y., 1879. XV., 187.
KLEIN. Atlas of Histology. 1879—80.

CHAPTER IX.

WE may gain a clear conception of the nervous system in its general outlines by remembering that it consists essentially of a series of delicate cords which, on the one hand, proceed from the nucleated bodies of the gray matter, conveying volitional impulses to the periphery of the organism ; or, on the other hand, of sensitive peripheral extremities that take up the impression of external objects and carry them back to the central gray substance.

In either case both the conducting cords and the central corpuscles of the gray matter possess no distinctive differences, such as may be appreciated by the microscope, while, on the other hand, the peripheral termini appear under many different forms, the peculiarity of ending being dependent in part upon the type of tissue in which they are found, partly upon the office they have to perform, and partly upon other causes that are unknown to us. The nerve-centres are located in the brain, spinal cord, and in the ganglia of the cerebro-spinal and sympathetic system.

The methods of nerve-terminations that have been described may be briefly enumerated here. They are by (1) *peculiar terminal bodies*, (2) *loops*, (3) *networks*, (4) *end bulbs*, (5) *protoplasmic bodies* (cells), (6) *free or pointed extremities*.

Nerve-fibres.—Of these there are three kinds that have distinctive differences : 1. *The myelinic* or *medullated* fibres. 2. *Fibres of Remak*. 3. *Ultimate fibrils*. Intermediate forms, such as have been described by various writers, under the names of protoplasmic processes, primitive fasciculi or naked axis-cylinders, varicose cylinders, etc., will be noticed in other connections.

Myelinic fibres.—These are also known as the medullated.

To the naked eye they appear white and glistening, and are the main constituents of the peripheric nerves, though they occur in less number in the sympathetic and also in the brain and cord. Each fibre is made up of three distinct parts : (a) a central cylindrical cord, the *axis-cylinder*, about which is a (b) coating of soft homogeneous fatty material, called *myeline* (medulla, white substance of Schwann), forming for the axis-cylinder a sort of tubular sheath, while exterior to both is a delicate membrane or envelope (c), the *sheath of Schwann* or primitive sheath.[1] These fibres run a parallel unbranching course, except near their termini or origin, and are surrounded by a connective-tissue coating of varying thickness. Their diameter varies also according to their situation and the degree of their tension or relaxation. In the nerve-trunks the average diameter lies between $\frac{1}{90}$ and $\frac{1}{130}$ millimetre. In the brain they are described as having sometimes a diameter of $\frac{1}{500}$ millimetre, but it is difficult to determine the presence of a medulla in such small fibres.

To study the properties of a myelinic nerve, we may take a portion of the sciatic from a frog that has just been killed. Having removed it with care and placed it in a drop of water on a slide, we should separate the fibres carefully with needles, taking care not to tear them. Then adjusting a covering glass, it will be seen that from the broken end of the nerve a soft substance is exuding (Fig. 43, b) ; in a few minutes it is pushed off in the form of drops of irregular shapes (Fig. 43, c). This material is the myeline or medulla. It will be seen to re-fract the light strongly, and show concentric markings. It will also be seen that each fibre has a double contour and is divided at tolerably regular intervals by transverse divisions, which are now known as *Ranvier's nodes.* (See Fig. 47.) Midway be-tween each node we may perhaps see an oval body surrounded by a broad expansion of protoplasm. In a few fibres we may even see that a fine thread-like process is projecting from the broken ends of the nerve-fibre—the axis-cylinder (Fig. 43, d)—while the whole fibre is enclosed by a delicate tightly investing membrane, the sheath of Schwann. Possibly we may also see the

---

[1] A most unfortunate source of confusion among histologists has arisen from the use of the word neurilemma, which by some is spoken of as synonymous with Schwann's sheath (Frey), and by others as the connective tissue which binds the nerve-fibres together (Klein, Rutherford). We shall avoid the term altogether.

oblique or *arrow markings* (incisures of Schmidt) (Fig. 43, *f*), which seem first to have been accurately described by Schmidt, of New Orleans, later by Lantermann of Cleveland, Shaw, and others.   The same appearances can be also obtained by the use of iodized serum.

The double contour is not visible in all the myelinic nerves, but is most marked where they show varicose swellings, a condition that is due to a preponderance of myeline at the enlarged point.   From this fact and another, that the drops of myeline when separated from the fibre show the same double contour, it is argued that the double marking in the fibre is due to a refracting (double) of the myeline, and has nothing to do with the membranous sheath. These varicosities just mentioned are not to be confounded with the bulgings of the ultimate fibrils, or with the "necklace" appearances seen in the course of the fibres of Remak, both of which latter may probably be regarded as artificial productions, either from stretching in the act of teasing or from the imbibition of water.   In the brain of the calf they are frequently seen, and they are said to be found in the intracranial part of the olfactory, optic, and acoustic nerves.   The fibres in which this change occurs are usually quite small.

Staining in picro-carmine.—

This reagent has been recommended by Ranvier.   It is satisfactorily prepared by Rutherford's process.[1]   Taking precautions not to injure the nerve in removing it, mount in the solu-

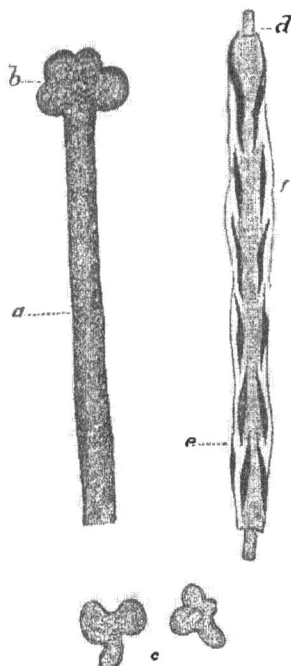

Fig. 43.—*a*, Myelinic fibre in a state of "coagulation;" *b*, myeline exuding from the broken end of the fibre; *c*, drops of myeline separated from the nerve-fibre; *d*, axis cylinder; *e*, nucleus of Henle's sheath; *f*, arrow markings.

[1] He takes 100 c.c. of a saturated solution of picric acid.   Next he prepares an ammoniacal solution of carmine by dissolving one gramme in a few c. c. of water, with the aid of an excess of ammonia and heat.   He then boils the picric acid solution on a sand-bath, and when boiling adds the carmine solution.   The mixture is

tion.   The nuclei will then be stained a brick-red, while the sheath of Schwann, and, in fact, the whole nerve, will be stained yellow.   It is said that, if the axis-cylinder projects, it will be stained a bright red, though twenty-four hours may be required to effect the staining.   In my hands picro-carmine has not proved so successful a coloring agent as some others.

Staining with the nitrate of silver.—The sciatic or any peripheral nerve may be employed.   Expose it without removal in a frog that has just been killed.   Then dry up all fluid from about it, and pour on a solution of the nitrate (1 to 1,000).   In this way the nerve-fibres will be made rigid.   They are then to be removed with a pair of delicate scissors, and placed in a flat vessel containing a little more of the solution. After a few minutes the nerve will look turbid, and then it should be cut out and washed in distilled water, and exposed to the sunlight.   In a variable time (ten to fifteen minutes) the turbid appearance will give way to a brown coloration.   Examining a single funiculus or bundle in glycerine, it will be seen that it has an endothelial coating of one or more layers (Fig. 44).

If another funiculus be separated with fine needles,[1] the same care being taken to spread the fibres apart and not tease, and so lacerate them, it will be seen that each fibre contains a series of *Latin crosses* at certain pretty regular intervals.   The transverse bar of the cross corresponds to the "annular constriction" seen in Ranvier's node, while the axis-cylinder forms the longitudinal bar.   Close observation with high powers will show that this latter is marked by transverse lines of a dark brown or

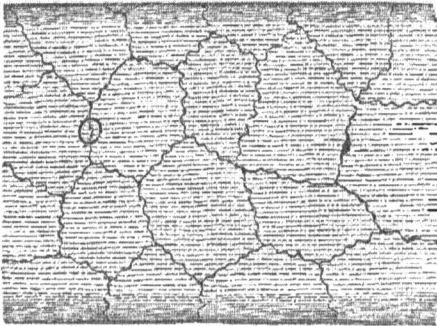

FIG. 44.—Funiculus or Nerve Bundle covered with Endothelium (Epithelium).   From the sciatic of the frog.—Hartnack, object. 4, oc. 2.

then evaporated to dryness, the residue dissolved in 100 c.c. of water, and filtered. If the solution is not clear, he adds more ammonia, evaporates, and then dissolves as before.

[1] Milliners' are the best.

black (*Frommann's lines*).   It appears probable, as Ranvier explains, that, owing to the break in the myeline, at the "annular constriction," the particles of silver gain an entrance to the axis-cylinder at this the only unprotected spot.   If the action of the salt is long continued, the axis-cylinder is col-
ored for a somewhat longer
distance.   The transverse bar
seems to be formed of two
conical segments set base to
base.   The position of this biconical segment usually corresponds in position with the
"annular constriction," but
it would appear that they may
be separated, for, when the

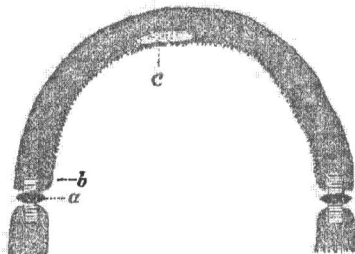

FIG. 45.—*a*, Ranvier's disk; *b*, Frommann's lines; *c*, nucleus of interannular segment.

tissue of the nerve has been put upon the stretch, the biconical segment, may be drawn away from the annular constriction. (See Fig. 45.)

Now, as Schwann's sheath is understood to end at the annular constriction, where it is cemented to the next adjoining segment just as epithelial cells are joined together, the biconical disk may belong to the axis-cylinder exclusively, and merely constitute a dividing line between its segments.   According to Engelmann, the axis-cylinder is divided up into portions corresponding with the interannular segments.

According to Rawitz, Schwann's sheath does not end at the nodes, but is continuous with the sheath of the adjacent interannular segment.

Staining of the nerve in osmic acid—semi-desiccation.— Osmic acid is one of the most valuable reagents for histological work, and the method now to be described (a modification of Ranvier's[1]) succeeds well.   Take the frog's sciatic, or any other peripheral nerve, carefully remove a portion with the surrounding tissue, keep the whole extended with pins, upon a flat bit of cork, and then dip it into a vessel containing a 1 per cent. watery solution of osmic acid.[2]   The vessel is then to be exposed to the light.   The whole nerve will be more or less thoroughly

[1] Leçons sur l'Histologie du Système Nerveux, Paris, 1878.
[2] The solution should, of course, have been kept in a dark bottle away from the light.

stained in a few hours. The external portions, however, will be stained in a few minutes, and they may be removed by careful separation with fine needles. To mount, take a glass slide and slip it under the nerve-fibres, while the needle is employed to carry them up on to a dry part of the slide where they can be placed side by side. Then remove the excess of water with bibulous paper, and let the fibres get so dry that they adhere to the slide. Place about them a ring of tissue-paper, so that when the cover is adjusted it will not press upon the fibres. Fix the cover at different points with paraffine, then put a drop of glycerine upon one side, and a drop of water upon the other. The union of water and glycerine should be allowed to go on for twenty-four hours in a damp place. The constrictions and arrow-markings are usually well seen. The nuclei also are occasionally to be found in a niche of the myeline. These bodies, however, are better seen in specimens that have been a short time (fifteen or twenty minutes) in osmic acid, and then in picro-carmine a few hours. It still is a question among histologists whether the arrow-markings are artificial or not; each of the sections lying between the markings is called the cylindro-conical segment (*Hohlcylinder*, Kuhnt). (See Fig. 43.)

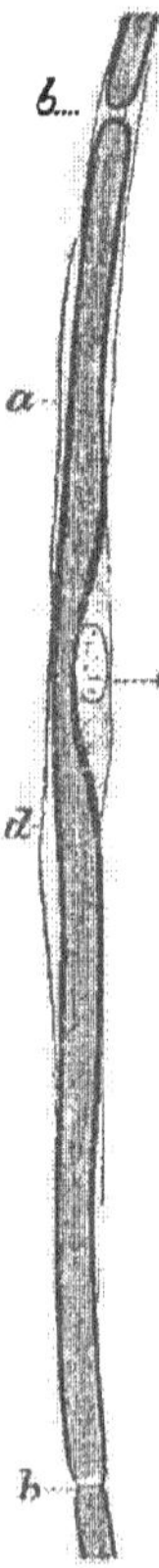

Transverse sections of myelinic nerves.— Certain points are best seen by making transverse sections. Prepare the sciatic of a frog or any of the human peripheral nerves by immersing a few days in a sherry-colored solution of bichromate of potash, or in Mueller's fluid,[1] and then in 90 per cent. of alcohol, until the tissue is hard enough to cut. Then it is to be mounted in the microtome with wax and oil of about its own consistence. Sections are to be made with the razor; or it may be mounted in elder-pith in the following way: bore out from the centre of the pith-cylinder a cylindri-

FIG. 46.— Human myelinic nervo: *a*, Interannular segment; *b*, Ranvier's node; *c*, nucleus of the interannular segment surrounded by granular protoplasm; *d*, Henle's sheath with nucleus.

[1] The well-known eye-fluid, of which the composition is: Bichromate of potash, 2 to 2½ grammes; sulphate of soda, 1 gramme; distilled water, 100 grammes.

cal hole a little larger than the trunk of the nerve, then immerse the whole in water, and the pith will begin to swell. As soon as it has firmly embraced the nerve, sections may be made with the knife. Ammonia-carmine will stain the axis-cylinder well, but the outline of the cut will appear irregular rather than round. This appearance is doubtless artificial. In my hands, borax-carmine [1] has proved much better than the ammonia-carmine, as it diffuses very little, and much of the excess may be removed by dilute acetic acid (about ¼ per cent.), in which the specimen should remain, from a few seconds to a minute or two, until it has become bright to the eye. The further steps in the process of making a permanent preparation are the same as those for other specimens; *i.e.*, it may be mounted in glycerine and water, or clarified by clove-oil and mounted in dammar varnish or Canada balsam.

Preparation by the bichromate of ammonia.—Ranvier employs of this a 2 per cent. solution, allowing the specimen to remain, with frequent changes of the fluid, from two or three months to a year. The sections are to be stained in ammonia-carmine or picro-carmine, and mounted in glycerine. It will then be seen that immediately about the axis-cylinder is a sheath. This is called by Ranvier the *sheath of Mauthner*, from the author who described it. (See Fig. 46, *b*.) Specimens prepared in the ordinary way, by long immersion in Mueller's fluid alone, or sub-

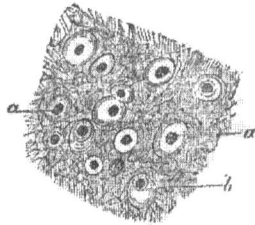

FIG. 47.—Cross-section of the human cord just below the decussation: *a*, axis-cylinder; *b*, sheath of Mauthner.

sequently in the chromic acid solution (gr. ij.— ℥ j.) and stained with ammonia-carmine, occasionally show the same thing.

Sometimes histologists find that embedding in gum succeeds best in securing these transverse sections of nerves. The difficulty of the task is one of considerable moment. The method is as follows: Take a fresh nerve, harden it in osmic acid (1 per cent., if it is desirable to expedite the process, or $\frac{1}{10}$ per cent. if it is not necessary to conclude the examination the same day). Then, when the nerve is thoroughly blackened all through, [1]

---

[1] The powder is prepared by Eimer & Amend, of this city (205 to 211 Third Avenue), according to Arnold's formula. The strength required is gr. xv.— ℥ j. distilled water.

it is to be immersed in water for a few hours ; then in 90 per cent. alcohol, and then in a weak solution of gum-arabic, which fills the interstices between the bundles, and finally in strong alcohol (95 per cent.), which hardens the gum sufficiently. The sections, cut as thin as possible, should be placed on a slide to remove the excess of alcohol, which may be done with filter-paper. A drop of water is then to be added ; about the cover put a few drops of carbolized water ; remove to a damp place. At the end of twenty-four hours the gum will have dissolved, and then the glycerine may be allowed to enter slowly without displacing the elements (Ranvier).

In examining such cross-sections, the medullated nerves will present various diameters, and the contour of the myelinic sheath will vary in width and outline according as the cut comes through the broadest part of the arrow-marking, or through the thin overlapping parts. (See Fig. 43.) If the cut chances to pass close to the annular constriction, no myeline will of course be seen. For these reasons, the cross-sections of such nerves, when stained with osmic acid, are very different.

Modern conceptions of myelinic nerves.—The specimens that have been studied according to the methods given will not have shown any termination of the nerves, or any division, either into trunks of any considerable size or into the fibrils of which they are said to be composed. They do, however, as we have already said, divide both near their origin and near their termination. It is presumed that each fibril of which the axis-cylinder is composed passes directly through from its point of origin of the nerve-centres, to its final point of distribution, without branching. It is difficult, however, with the instruments in ordinary use, to see any distinct marks of fibrillation in cross-sections of the axis-cylinder, and it is in them that we should expect to see them best. The ideas of Ranvier are well worthy of consideration, as he has given more form and solidity to our conception of the intimate structure of a myelinic nerve-fibre than any previous writer. According to him, each section of nerve between the annular constrictions represents an ultimate morphological element. It is, in fact, a tubular cell, whose proper external portion (the membrane of the cell, according to common phraseology) is the sheath of Schwann, while the myeline or medulla fills the interior, just as in adipose tissue a globule of oil fills out and distends an ordinary connective-tissue corpuscle. Each of these bodies, which he calls an interannular segment, begins and ends at the constriction. It contains a single ovoid flattened nucleus, which fills a niche in the myeline, and is surrounded by a broad, thin expansion of protoplasm (the body of the corpuscle). The axis-cylinder has nothing to do with this body that we have described, except that it pierces it. Instead of stopping short at each constriction, it goes on indefinitely. As we have already seen, the annular constriction and the biconical disk are not always at the same point, which argues strongly for Ranvier's views. The myelinic sheath probably protects the delicate fibre from external injury, but whether it also insulates it, is problematical. In the fœtus all nerves are devoid of myeline.

Fibres of Remak.—These are called by some the amyelinic or non-medullated fibres, by others the pale, gray, or gelatinous fibres. The term Remak's fibres has come into use recently as the distinctive name for certain nerve-fibres abounding in the sympathetic, as distinguished from others which also contain no myeline, and are found in the cranial portions of the optic, auditory, and olfactory nerves. Each fibre is marked with oval nuclei at pretty short intervals, and has an indistinct longitudinal striation, probably the evidence of fibrils such as are believed to exist in the axis-cylinder. The nuclei are imbedded in a homogeneous sheath. There being no breaks in the continuity of the fibre, there can be no sheath of Schwann in the sense that has been described. In diameter each fibre varies between $\frac{1}{250}$ and $\frac{1}{120}$ millimetre. In 1838 Remak first called attention to them, but his views were received with disfavor. More recently, Max Schultze, Frey, Leydig, and Henle have joined in representing them as long, cylindrical, continuous, slightly striated, and dotted with nuclei.

The fibres of Remak are found in great abundance in all the nerves of the organic system, but they also exist in all the mixed nerves, varying with the kind of nerve and the animal. They are not found in special nerves. The pneumogastric of the cat is well adapted for the study of them, as the myelinic fibres are present in considerable quantity, and make the mechanical separation of the bundle easy. Associated with them, fibres are often seen, that are shown in Fig. 48, *c.* They are delicate, run a wavy course, and sometimes exhibit curious varicosities (*a*), (necklace appearance). The nuclei are placed at about the same distances apart as in the other form of fibre already mentioned.

Preparation in osmic acid and picro-carmine.—Remove the pneumogastric in the following way, from a cat that has just been killed : Having exposed the nerve, slip under it *in situ* a long narrow strip of cork, to which, pin down the nerve with some adjacent tissue, all of which may be removed at once and placed in a solution of osmic acid (1—1,000) for twenty-four hours ; the nerve may then be separated from its attachments and placed in the picro-carmine solution for still another twenty-four hours. The excess of the coloring agent may be removed by dipping for a few seconds in acetic-acid solution ($\frac{1}{4}$ per cent.), and then the nerve may be placed in alcohol, afterwards in water, and finally mounted in glycerine. It will be seen that the nerve-fibres are stained a reddish yellow, while the nuclei are brick-red. The picric-acid yellow is apt, however, to diffuse. Careful separation of the fibres may show that they branch, as shown in Fig. 48, *A, B ;* and yet this characteristic, which Ranvier insists upon, is by no means easy to see in most of the fibres, in fact it requires much careful work before it is apparent. The myelinic nerves will be distinguished by their greater average size, their dusky, granular medulla, broken at points, and by the axis-cylinder, which, if it does not project, may be seen winding spirally along beneath its medullary coat. In them, too, as a rule, each interannular segment contains but one nucleus.

Preparation of Remak's fibres in hæmatoxylon.—One of

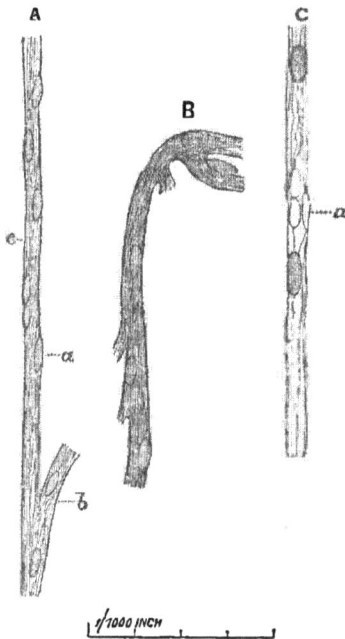

FIG. 48.—Fibres of Remak. *A,* Pneumogastric of the cat—hæmatoxylon specimen : *a,* nerve nuclei ; *b,* appearances of branching ; *c,* connective-tissue sheath. *B,* Same. Picro-carmine specimen. The branching in this case is more evident. *C,* Same—hæmatoxylon specimen. The necklace appearance is shown at *a.*

the most rapid and successful methods is by the use of hæma-toxylon. The pneumogastric nerve of a cat is removed and immediately placed in the hæmatoxylon solution; then, after thorough staining, which may only take a few minutes, in dilute acetic acid ($\frac{1}{2}$ per cent.), and finally mounted in gly-cerine. In this way the nuclei will be stained a beautiful pur-ple, while the fibres will be unaffected. The number of nuclei and absence of medulla will serve to distinguish the fibres of Remak from the medullated. It is difficult by any method of preparation to see that there are any precise limits to the lon-gitudinal lines in the fibres, i.e., that the striation is due to little, short, narrow rods, lying side by side (Ranvier). The nitrate of silver demonstrates no transverse markings and no constrictions or crosses. There is but little likelihood in these specimens to mistake the fibres for connective-tissue bundles. In the first place, the nuclei, and what cell-bodies happen to be about them, of the one, are small, flattened, ovoid bodies occurring at pretty regular intervals, while the connective-tis-sue corpuscles are usually larger, longer, and, though they may appear oat-shaped, when the side is turned to the observer, are broad plates with irregular edges when seen flatwise. In the second place, the fibres run their course in long, narrow bundles, as no connective tissue does.

Ganglionic bodies.—Of these there are three kinds: 1. Those that are connected with the spinal and some cerebral nerves. 2. Those found in the gray substance of the brain and spinal cord. 3. Those in the ganglia of the sympathetic sys-tem. These bodies are of such large size that they may often be seen with the naked eye. In the human species they are usually in close connection with the origin of the nerves, though they also may be interspersed at points through the course of the fibres or may be present near their points of distribution (*ganglia of Auerbach*). Their immediate connection with the nerve-fibre is made in the following ways: 1. A large process, which does not at first appear to branch, passes off, and is continuous with the axis-cylinder. 2. Fine branches are given off from one or more corpuscles, and, uniting, contrive to form a nerve-fibre (either a fibre of Remak or a myelinic fibre). 3. These branches after combination may pass through a gangli-onic corpuscle, which then is called bipolar (Gerlach, Wal-deyer). In the sympathetic system we have the unbranched process and the superficial or spiral fibre, which corresponds to the branched fibre of the ganglionic bodies of the brain and spinal nerves.

Ganglia of the cranial and spinal nerves.—These organs, which appear to the naked eye as nodular enlargements of the nerves with which they are connected, consist of groups of peculiar large corpuscles which are interspersed among the nerve-fibres. In shape they are usually large and ovoid, or pear-shaped. About and between them are bands of connective tissue studded with nuclei, forming for each separate body a kind of capsule ; the vascular supply to them is liberal. The contents of these bodies are soft, elastic, and beset with granules. They have a large, globular, or ovoid nucleus or nucleolus, and may appear to have no process, or to be unipolar or bipolar, as in the lower animals.[1]

Examination of the Gasserian ganglion in the frog.—Take a frog that has just been killed, or, better still, one that has been some time in Mueller's fluid ; trace the fifth nerve into the skull. On it will be seen, just within the bone, a yellow enlargement. This is to be removed with forceps and teased with needles. The ganglionic bodies usually appear to have no processes (apolar), but they probably have one or more, and the apparent absence of them is because they have been torn off in teasing.

Examination of the ganglia of the spinal cord.—Take the cord of a bullock, and prepare it while fresh, or after it has been a greater or less time in Mueller's fluid, or a weak solution of the bichromate of potash (gr. xv.— ℥ j.). Having cut it into transverse segments, the gray substance may be easily seen. Snip out with fine curved scissors small pieces from the anterior horns in the lumbar regions where the corpuscles are very numerous ; if the specimen be fresh, immerse in osmic acid (1—1,000) for twenty-four hours. Then, by careful brushing in water with the camel's-hair brush, or by teasing, or agitation in a test-tube with a little distilled water, some of the ganglionic corpuscles will be successfully removed. They will be seen to vary much in size, and be multipolar, i.e., they will exhibit a very large number of branches (*Deiter's protoplasmic*

---

[1] According to Key and Retzius, they are probably all unipolar. Stud. in der Anat. d. Nerven-Syst., 2 Hälfte, V. and H.'s Jahresb., 1878.

processes) which divide and subdivide, and, it is said, form a network which unites with a similar one proceeding from the ganglionic bodies of the posterior roots.

There is, in addition, a single straight process (naked axis-cylinder), which, proceeding outward, soon receives a medullary sheath. The nucleus is very large and circular, and usually displays a nucleolus. The contents of the body of the corpuscles are more or less granular, and a mass of pigment in granules is usually seen piled up in some one portion. The corpuscles thus separated may be preserved in glycerine and water, or, after staining in borax-carmine, in dammar varnish or Canada balsam. In the posterior horns the corpuscles are similar in character, but smaller. Gerlach claims that the ganglionic bodies of the anterior horns are connected together through networks formed of the branching processes given off from each. Carrière, working under Prof. Kollman, of Munich, has examined the spinal cord of the calf in the fresh condition, and has satisfied himself that the ganglionic corpuscles are connected together by their fine processes, being thus in agreement with Stilling, Wagner, Remak, and many others.— *Arch. f. mikroskop. Anat.*, xiv., 2, 1877.

Ganglionic bodies in the human brain.—Thin sections made through the cortex of the human brain show that there are conical ganglionic corpuscles of medium size, whose base is directed toward the white substance, and apex toward the superficies. From either end processes are given off, from the broad end several, and from the apex a single one ; both subsequently branch. In the upper strata the corpuscles are smallest. Disseminated throughout this substance are two other forms of corpuscles, one star-shaped (spider-cells),[1] and the other the lymphoid corpuscles that belong to all tissues of the body. Possibly the *spider-cells*, which have a variable number of processes, are the cells of the neuroglia. *Brush-cells*[2] have also been described. Perhaps they should also be regarded as a variety of the spider-cells.

Ganglionic bodies of the sympathetic system.—They occur either singly or in groups, interspersed among the nerve-fibres, or in lines, or form enlargements in the nerve-plexuses, as

---

[1] Described by Jastrowitz.
[2] Arch. f. mikrosk. Anat., 1874, LXI., p. 93.

in the digestive tract. Preparations of the cœliac ganglion of the frog may be made according to the methods that have already been described. The aorta and bulbus arteriosus of the frog are recommended by Klein, and the gold method is the best to show them. It was in these corpuscles of the green tree-frog that Beale noticed a *spiral fibre*. It was a delicate one, winding round the axis-cylinder, finally going off in an opposite direction. He also thought, from an examination of the ganglia in the mammalia, that the same fibre existed in them. Subsequently Julius Arnold corroborated his views, and even described a network of fibres which was connected with the nucleolus, and extended through the corpuscle, at its final exit forming the spinal fibre. Recent observers, however, have failed to confirm Arnold's opinion, and even the existence of a spiral fibre is held to be in doubt.[1] These corpuscles, which are either globular or oblong, may appear to be apolar, unipolar, bipolar (when two processes are given off in the opposite directions), or multipolar (when two are given off in the same direction, or several are given off in various directions).

Meissner's plexus.—This network, named after its discoverer, is situated in the submucous tissue, and consists of nerve-bundles of medium size, which have nodular enlargements studded with nuclei at certain points. An excellent way of securing them is the following : Take a piece of cat's intestine, three or four inches in length ; cleanse thoroughly by passing through it a stream of water ; then ligate one extremity. Fill an ordinary two-ounce syringe with a solution of the chloride of gold ($\frac{1}{2}°$). Slip the nozzle into the other end of the intestine, and, tying it in, inject with such force as to distend the gut to its utmost extent without bursting. Then pass another ligature round the gut beyond the nozzle, and draw it tight. Remove the syringe, and place the specimen in an open vessel containing the same solution, but allowing fully one-half of it to be uncovered by the liquid. After twenty-four hours the part thus exposed will have taken a mauve or violet color. Then remove from the liquid, and open with scissors, let it partly dry, and, seizing the mucous membrane with the forceps, tear it off in pieces. The submucous tissue will then

---

[1] Key and Retzius did not find the spiral fibre in the human species, but in the frog occasionally. Op. cit. Many other excellent observers agree with them.

be exposed, and small bits are to be torn out in a similar way They may be mounted in glycerine or dammar varnish. The nerve-trunks can be readily seen; they will contain, on an average, from two to three fibres perhaps, and form a large-meshed plexus. The ganglionic enlargement may be found where three or four bundles meet, or in the course of a single bundle. The diameter of the enlargement is three to five times the size of the bundle.

Auerbach's plexus, called after its discoverer, is seen by taking the same specimen, and tearing out thin laminæ from the muscle, at the junction of their longitudinal and transverse coats. The ganglionic bodies are nodular, and contain numerous nuclei. It is said that they may be isolated by immersion of the muscular tissue eight to ten days in a 10 per cent. solution of common salt. Guinea-pigs furnish the best specimens.[1] There are both coarse and fine networks.

Termination of nerves.—There are various methods which have been described, and these are: 1, by undivided or free endings (tendons, conjunctiva); 2, by end bulbs (cornea); 3, by terminal loops; 4, in corpuscles (seminal canals—Letzerich); 5, by networks (peritoneum); or, finally, 6, in a special apparatus (Pacinian or Meissner's corpuscles). When nerves terminate by networks, the meshes may be formed from the medullated fibres, or those of Remak, and may consist of one or more fine fibrils. They have been found in the skin, and are to be seen in the submucous tissue of the intestines, in the cornea, and elsewhere. Termination by bulbs has been closely investigated by Krause. The bulbs are described as having a diameter of $\frac{1}{20}$ millimetre, and ovoid-shaped in man, with a thin capsule of connective tissue. One or more fibres appear to enter the bulb, and, penetrating some distance, end in a knob. They have been found in the conjunctiva, in the mucous membrane of the floor of the mouth, lips, soft palate, and tongue, and in the glans penis and clitoris. In the cavity of the mouth they are placed in the papillæ. The bodies Krause has observed in the clitoris are somewhat peculiar; they are variously shaped, and have a mulberry-like surface.

These corpuscles, about which there has been so much discussion, and which some excellent observers (Waldeyer, Arnold)

---

[1] Frey: Das Mikroskop., Leipzig, 1877.

had failed to see, were investigated a few years ago by Longworth, of Cincinnati, and their existence established as a matter
of no doubt. He took the human eye, freshly removed with
the conjunctiva, and made the examination immediately. Attaching the conjunctiva with threads, so that it preserved its
natural tension, he immersed it in a ½ per cent. solution of osmic acid, or exposed it to the vapor of the same solution.
After twelve to twenty-four hours the membrane was deeply
stained, and the epithelium could usually be removed with
a brush or the finger-nail. Next, a thin piece of cornea was
removed and examined in water, or in 1 to 2 per cent. acetic-
acid solution. It was then mounted in glycerine. This method
was preferred to the gold chloride. In some conjunctivæ they
were found almost entirely absent ; in others, or in certain portions, quite numerous. The entire interior was seen to be filled
with nucleated corpuscles. Waldeyer, in commenting on the
work of Dr. Longworth, agreed to it fully, and retracted his
former opinions. He places these bodies intermediate between
the tactile and Pacinian bodies.

The *tactile corpuscles* of the skin (called also Meissner's
or Wagner's corpuscles) are to be seen in the papillæ, and
especially well in the tips of the fingers, and in the internal
genitals. They have a length of about $\frac{1}{16}$ millimetre. Specimens hardened and preserved in the ordinary way show them
well. They are oblong, rounded, and marked by transverse
wavy lines. A nerve-fibre may be seen running into their
centre.

The *Pacinian bodies*, discovered by Vater, in 1741, but first
carefully described by Pacini, of Pisa, are oval or pear-shaped
bodies, attached to the nerves like berries to a stem. They are
found in the subcutaneous tissues of the finger (Kölliker), in
the labia majora, prostate, corpora cavernosa, and in many
other places. They are seen to the best advantage, however,
in the mesentery of the cat, where they are so large as to be
easily visible to the naked eye.

Cut out a small piece of the mesentery, place it in a weak
solution of osmic acid (1—100), and after a few minutes, when
it has become brown, detach the capsule carefully with needles.
Mounting at once in glycerine, the whole interior of the Pacinian will be superbly shown, constituting one of the most beautiful specimens in histology. The medullated nerve may be

seen winding in at one end (Fig. 49), covered with a dense coating of connective tissue, and accompanied by a small artery. After penetrating a variable distance, it leaves its medulla and is continuous with a straight fibrillated band that is called the core. It terminates in one or more granular expansions, apparently. In two cases, however, I saw the nerve passing through the body, giving off its medulla on entering it, and assuming it again on leaving. This has been observed by Klein, Pappenheim, and others. Round about the core, forming a series of pretty regularly oval markings, are concentric tunics. Toward the periphery they are at a pretty even distance apart. Between them, applied closely to the tunics,[1] are small ovoid nuclei. The spaces between the lamellæ are probably filled with a clear fluid. In my experience these bodies are not successfully preserved in glycerine, even after hardening in osmic acid. The chloride of gold may answer better.

Nerve - terminations in muscle are quite easily seen. It is only necessary to take a bit of muscle from the thigh

Fig. 49.—Pacinian body from the cat's mesentery.

of a frog just dead, and immerse it in dilute acetic acid, and then in glycerine. When the tissue is thoroughly transparent, as it will be in a few minutes (ten or fifteen), there will be little difficulty in finding a medullated nerve, and then in tracing it into a muscle-fibre. Reaching the sarcolemma, it

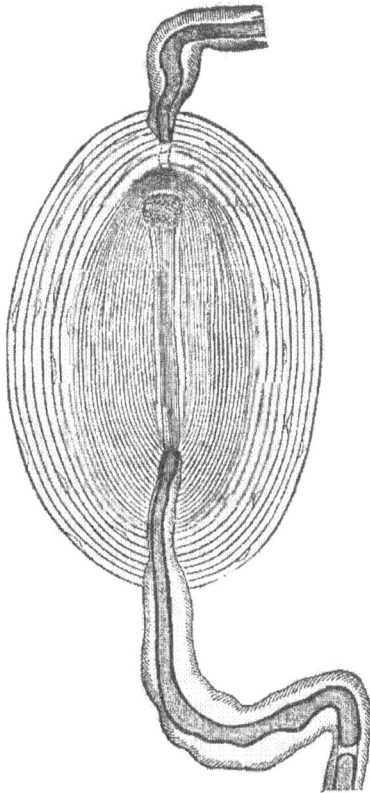

[1] According to Schaefer, the nuclei belong to epithelioid corpuscles which cover the tunic on both sides. Practical Histology, p. 134; Quarterly Microscop. Journ., 1875.

penetrates it at a prominence (*Doyère's eminence*). From this point it divides into fibrils, which form delicate networks, and one, or possibly two filaments will be seen to enter an irregular body placed in the centre of the fibre. This body is highly nucleated, and may without much difficulty be distinguished from the muscle nucleus, which lies either on the bundle or in it. This body is called the *motorial plate*. It is not certain, however, that the ultimate fibrils actually end there, for in some instances one is in connection with one side, and one with the other. Varicosities are described in the primitive fibrils when osmic acid or chloride of gold is used.

Gschleiden, of Breslau, one of the most recent writers on this subject, has traced (in the leech) the ultimate fibrils to the cement substance between the contractile muscle-corpuscles (unstriped muscular tissue). He never saw them end in plates or in networks. Ganglion-cells are closely attached to the fibres near their termination, and they may be unipolar, bipolar, or even multipolar, the former being the most numerous.

Termination of nerves in epithelial bodies has been described by a good many observers. The demonstration of such endings, however, is extremely difficult. The ultimate fibrils are liable to be confounded with elastic tissue, possibly with connective-tissue fibres. To be quite sure of their character they should be traced into connection with nerve-trunks, on the one hand, or ganglionic bodies on the other.

Connective tissue of nerves.—In our description we have adhered to the idea that the sheath of Schwann is the one that immediately incloses the medulla, without any intervening substance. Ranvier has called the first sheath, exterior to Schwann's, "the *sheath of Henle*." (Fig. 43, *e.*)

The term *perineurium* is often applied to the sheaths of the funiculus or bundle. The connective tissue separating the funiculi in a large trunk has been called the *endoneurium*, while *epineurium* is the great sheath of the whole trunk. Each bundle or funiculus, the smallest element that we see in making a gross dissection of a nerve, is covered with one or more layers of endothelium, forming a special sheath. These funiculi do not run parallel without anastomosing, but two, joining, form a third, which again divides.

There is much practical difficulty in the way of giving precise limits to these sheaths, from the fact that they are apt to be continuous with one another, while one or more may be absent, according to the size or quality of the nerve.

BIBLIOGRAPHY.

COHNHEIM. Virchow's Archiv. Vol. XXXVIII., p. 343. 1867.

CLEVELAND. Ueber d. feineren Bau d. Markhült. Nervenfasern. Arch. f. mikrosk. Anat., 1870. Vol. XIII., p. 1.

SCHULTZE, MAX. Stricker's Histology, p. 117. 1872.

SCHMIDT. On the Construction of the Dark or Double-bordered Nerve-fibre. Month. Micros. Journ., May 1, 1874.

LONGWORTH. Arch. f. mikrosk. Anat. Vol. II. 1875.

SCHAEFER. Practical Histology. Quart. Micr. Journ., p. 134. 1875.

KRAUSE. Arch. f. mikrosk. Anat. Vol. XII. 1876.

SHAW. Some Peculiarities in the Myelinic Peripheral Nerves, etc. Jour. of Nerv. and Ment. Dis., Jan., 1876.

GSCHLEIDEN. Arch. f. mikrosk. Anat. Vol. XIV. 1877.

RANVIER. Leçons sur l'histoire du système nerveux. 1878.

KEY and RETZIUS. Stud. in d. Anat. d. Nerv.-Syst. V. & H.'s Jahresb. 1878.

HIS, W. Arch. f. Anat. u. Phys., p. 455. 1879.

RAWITZ, B. Arch. f. Anat. u. Phys. 1879.

RUMPF. Zur Histol. d. Nervenfaser, etc. Unt. d. Phys. Inst. d. Univ. Heidelberg. Vol. II.

SCHULTZE, H. Axencylinder u. Ganglienzelle. Arch. f. Anat. u. Phys. 1879.

KÜHNE, W. Zur Histol. d. motor. Nervenendig. Unt. d. phys. Inst. d. Univ. Heidelberg. Vol. II.

HESSE, FR. Zur Kennt. d. peripher. Markhält. Nervenfaser. Arch. f. Anat. u. Phys. 1879.

KÜHNE, W., and STEINER, J. Beobacht. ueber Markhältige u. Marklose Nervenfasern. Unt. d. Phys. Inst. d. Univ. Heidelberg. Vol. III.

HIS, W. Ueber d. Anfänge d. peripher. Nerven-System. Arch. f. Anat. u. Phys., p. 455. 1879.

WALDEYER. Ueber die Endig. d. sensiblen Nerven. Arch. f. mikros. Anat. Vol. XVII., pp. 367–382. 1880.

RANVIER. Leçons d'anat. gén. App. nerveux term., etc. Paris, 1880.

KRAUSE, W. Die Nervenendigung in den Tastkörperchen. Arch. f. mik. Anat. XX. 212–221. 1881–82.

LUSTIG, A. Ueber die Nervenendigung in den glatten Muskelfasern. Sitzungst. d. k. Akad. d. Wiss., math. naturw. cl. 3. Abtheil. Wien. LXXXIII. 186–194. 1881.

WOLFF, W. Ueber freie sensible Nervenendigungen. Arch. f. mikr. Anat. XX. 382–412. 1881–82.

PFITZNER, W. Nervenendigungen im Epithel. Morphol. Jahrb., Leipzig. VII. 726–745. 1882.

PART II.

CHAPTER X.

MUSCULAR FIBRE.

By THOMAS DWIGHT, M.D.,

Instructor in Topographical Anatomy and in Histology at Harvard University.

THE physiological attribute of muscular tissue is contractility. This may or may not be under the control of the will. The structure of voluntary muscular fibre is very different from that of the involuntary.

This distinction, however, is not absolute. The muscular fibre of the heart presents a structure intermediate between the two typical forms. Striped fibres are found in some places, as, for instance, in the upper part of the œsophagus, over which most people have little or no control. There is also an undoubted difference in the manner of contraction among voluntary muscles. Whether this is associated with a difference of structure is an interesting but very uncertain question that will be alluded to later.

INVOLUNTARY MUSCULAR FIBRE.

Unstriped muscular fibre is shown with great advantage in the bladder of the frog. It should be stained with gold chloride, logwood, or carmine.[1] After the specimen has lain two

---

[1] If one's object is to study the muscular tissue only, gold has no advantages over the other agents, and should not be used, because it is less certain. The writer has obtained remarkably beautiful stainings of the bladder by using carmine, following Beale's method.

or three days in glycerine, the lining epithelium is easily brushed off. The bladder of the frog is peculiarly favorable, because it affords an opportunity of studying the fibres, both

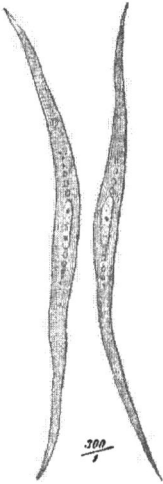

FIG. 50.

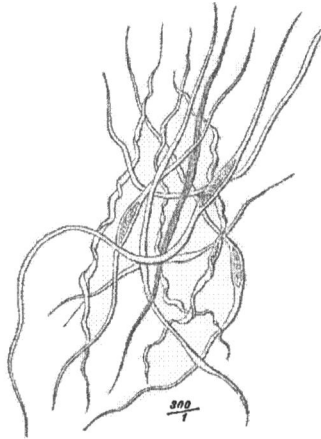

FIG. 51.

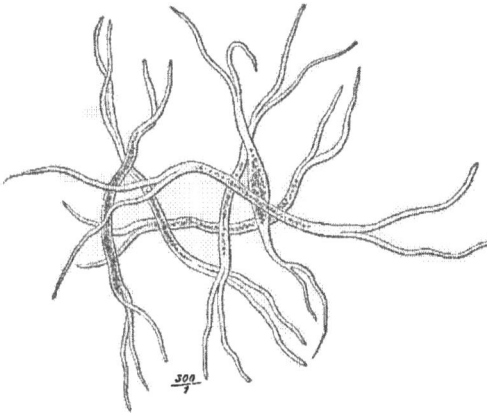

FIG. 52.

FIG. 50.—Muscular fibres treated with serum. FIG. 51.—Muscular fibres from the muscular tissue of the intestine, isolated by means of nitric acid. FIG. 52.—Muscular fibres from a pleuritic membrane. J. Arnold.

separately and in bundles, in its walls and in the coats of the minute arterioles which nourish it.

The plain fibre is composed simply of one or more elongated

9

cells. (Fig. 50.) The nucleus is at about the middle. The cell swells out around the nucleus, and quickly contracts again beyond it. A small cell, such as is found in the wall of a small blood-vessel, is consequently spindle-shaped, but we find many in the frog's bladder that run out into fine threads of indefinite length. Sometimes one end of a cell divides into two fibres. (See Figs. 51 and 52.)

The nucleus sometimes appears to be homogeneous, though it usually contains one or more granules, sometimes considered to be nucleoli. When using a high power the writer has sometimes found that the nucleus contained many granules, so arranged as to suggest very strongly a transverse striation. A row of granules at each end of the nucleus is sometimes found. Muscular fibres in the walls of small, transparent blood-vessels are very instructive objects, because by changing the focus we can observe them as they curve round the vessel, both in longitudinal and in transverse section. At those places where a transverse section of one end of the cell is in focus we see what appears to be a granule merely. If another part near the nucleus is brought into focus, it shows as a small circle, while if the nucleus happens to be cut transversely, it gives the effect of a dark spot inside a circle.

VOLUNTARY MUSCULAR FIBRE.

No tissue is more easily recognized than striped muscular fibre, yet none is more difficult to understand.[1]

The fibres are cylinders or irregular prisms of varying length. Their diameter in the human body varies, according to Frey, from .0113 to .0563 mm. Each fibre is tightly inclosed in a structureless elastic membrane, called the *sarcolemma*. This sheath is not very easily demonstrated ; but if fresh muscle be roughly picked to pieces in water, shreds of it may be seen at the torn ends of fibres, and sometimes it can be made out where the muscular substance has been injured in the course of a fibre.

---

[1] Any attempt at an account of the many views that have been and are held, would make this article far too long. A few only will be mentioned, and these incidentally. It is hoped that this defect, if it be one, will be compensated for by the fulness of the bibliography.

The existence of a sarcolemma being admitted, it is clear
that it must be highly elastic so as to accommodate itself
to the changes both of length and breadth which the fibre
undergoes. The phenomena of contraction show, moreover,
that it must be attached at definite points to the muscular
substance.

Fresh muscular fibre of a vertebrate animal, when teased
out and examined under a moderately high power, presents a
series of alternate black and white cross stripes, which are
held to be characteristic of voluntary muscle. (Fig. 53.) This
appearance is beautifully distinct in some
fibres, and very vague in others. It may
vary greatly in different parts of the same
fibre ; the stripes may run perfectly straight
across the fibre ; they may present a uniform curve, or they may be interrupted at
intervals, some parts of the line being in
advance of others. (See Fig. 53.)

As a fibre taken from an animal immediately after death naturally draws itself together (without, however, necessarily
presenting the phenomena of physiological contraction), it is desirable to ascertain
whether this modifies the appearances. To

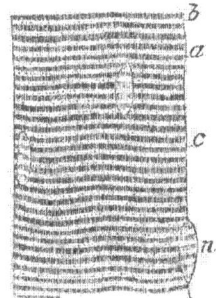

FIG. 53.—Striped muscular
fibre: *a*, black stripe: *b*, intermediate stripe: *c*, white
stripe; *n*, nucleus. After
Ranvier.

do this, fibres from a recently killed animal should be examined in a state of extension. A cut should be made in the
body of a muscle, a few fibres teased out and stretched on the
slide under the covering glass before their attached ends are
divided.

It will be seen that the light stripe is more affected by the
stretching than the dark one, though both are broader than in
the non-extended fibre ; but the most important effect is the
appearance, often seen with high powers, of a very narrow, interrupted black line in the middle of the light band.

Beside this cross striation, the fibres of vertebrates show
more or less plainly minute longitudinal lines. It is to be noticed that when the cross stripes are very distinct the longitudinal ones are very faint, or even invisible, and that when the
latter are well marked the former are the reverse of it. Some
reagents tend to divide a fibre into disks, others into fibrillæ.
Among the former are solutions of acetic acid in water (1 in

100—200), hydrochloric acid (1 in 50—200), and among the latter
a solution of chromic acid (1 in 200). It is very probable that
the amount of longitudinal striation varies in different muscles,
being related, perhaps, to physiological properties, or possibly
the result of mechanical causes. It is certain that both kinds
of striation may be found in great perfection in fibres treated
with almost any reagent that does not destroy them. Sometimes muscle is seen to be split into fibrillæ, each of which
shows the transverse stripe, though the shreds are so fine that
each disk is represented by a dot merely.[1] This may be detected very well in the muscle of the lobster after it has been
picked to pieces in glycerine.

Returning to the transverse stripes in vertebrates, the striæ
are very near together in the frog, and thus this useful animal
is not specially desirable. The muscle of the rabbit is much
better, and human muscle is, perhaps, better still. The muscle
of the human embryo in the last months of pregnancy is particularly good. A very high power will often show the narrow
black line in the midst of the white band. Sometimes one edge
of each black stripe will be very sharply marked against the
glaring white, while the other side will present a less marked
contrast. If the stage of the microscope admits of rotation,[2] instructive effects can also be obtained. As the field turns round,
the brightness at the sharp border of the black stripe gradually
decreases, to return on the other side. Again, this change may
not occur. Sometimes, when the upper edge of the fibre is precisely in focus, the black and white stripes may be made to apparently exchange places, if the lens is slightly depressed. This
is probably to be accounted for as follows: First, we may for
the present assume that the black and white bands are caused
by disks of different nature. Take a series of such disks and
imagine them somewhat inclined to one side, like a roll of
coins on their edges leaning against a support. A vertical line,
representing the line of vision, that passes through a black disk
at the upper border of the roll will strike a light one at a
deeper level. A peculiar effect may be obtained by removing
the diaphragm and employing very oblique light. The black

---

[1] The fact that muscle removed from the body can be reduced to fibrillæ does not
prove that these are pre-existing elements.
[2] It is to be regretted that this movement is not more common.

band then is often replaced by two narrow black lines with a light space between them. This is more frequently observed when the rays strike the fibre longitudinally.

The fibres of invertebrates, though on the same plan as those of higher animals, are better fitted for study, because the elements are farther apart, and because the phenomena of contraction may, in some cases, at least, be observed under the microscope,

The muscles from the thorax and legs of large flies are very good. Merkel recommends that they be examined in fresh albumen from the egg, in which they will continue to contract. The fibre is crossed by narrow black stripes which, be it remembered once for all, correspond to the black stripes of vertebrate muscle. On each side of these stripes there is a bright, glittering border, which gradually shades off into a dull band, midway between the two stripes. The substance between the black stripes is all of one nature, the difference between its middle and end portions being an optical effect. The dull band corresponds to the fine line which high powers reveal in vertebrate muscle. Its greater breadth is due to the greater distance of the black stripes.

Fibres from the legs and wings of the large water-beetles (Hydrophilus and Dytiscus) are admirable objects. Schäfer's valuable observations were made on those of the legs. He found the black stripe to consist of a double row of highly refracting granules, which were the ends of dumb-bells embedded in the contractile substance. These structures are arranged side by side, the

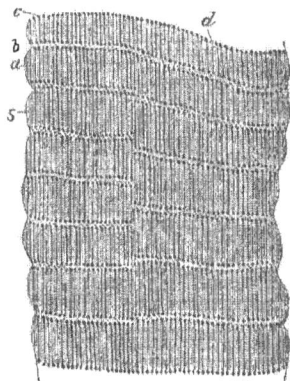

Fig. 54.—Muscle of large water-beetle (Dytiscus): *a*, dull band; *b*, bright space around; *c*, the highly refractive ends of the dumb-bells; *d*, the handles of the dumb-bells; δ, sarcolemma. After Schäfer.

adjacent ends of the dumb-bells forming the stripe, while the handles constitute the slight longitudinal striations. (See Fig. 54.) The bright borders are due to the refraction of light from the spherical heads of the dumb-bells. It is clear that they must cause a greater amount of rays to pass through the substance directly beside them than go through the substance midway between them, which latter appears dark in consequence. Some years before Schäfer's theory was advanced Heppner had shown that the bright borders of the black stripe must be due to the reflection of rays through them from the surface of the stripe. The phenomena observed on rotating the stage of the microscope are in accordance with this theory. There are, no doubt, some apparent exceptions, but these lose their weight when we consider how many elements there are that complicate the problem. If, for instance, as is often the case, the disks do not present their edges quite evenly to the eye of the observer, but are somewhat inclined, like the roll of coins above mentioned, the conditions are at once changed. Again, light thrown up vertically through a small diaphragm must produce different effects on the object from light striking it very obliquely.

Some years ago the writer was fortunate enough to discover an excellent object for the study of living muscular fibre in the detached legs of the Gyrinus. This is a small beetle, known in the country as the "lucky bug," which describes most eccentric figures on the surface of ponds. A leg should be cut off close to the body, and examined in a drop of water under a very thin covering glass. The shell is transparent, and as the muscles are undisturbed, except in the segment cut in removing the leg, they are in a perfectly normal condition, lacking only their vascular and nervous supply. They will frequently contract for more than an hour, if the covering glass be lightly tapped occasionally. The part of the leg known as the tibia, which is easily recognized by a large Y-shaped air-tube, has the thinnest shell, and is usually the best place for study, though occasionally better views are obtained in the two parts next above it, in which it is easier to find a single layer of fibres. The leg is very apt to flex itself between the femur and tibia, thus obscuring one of the best places. If necessary, this can be prevented by putting a thin piece of paper against the inner side of the leg. The anterior pair of legs, which project forward, are made on another plan, and are less desirable. A very high power is necessary, as, for instance, Hartnack's 10 immersion lens. Much practice also is needed to follow the steps of contraction, and indeed this can be done only when it has become very slow.

The fibre, when at rest and moderately stretched, appears to be a cylinder with straight edges, and composed of a semi-

fluid, transparent ground-substance. This is crossed by the
black stripes with shining borders, such as have been described.
The black stripe usually appears
granular, and may be divided into
two parallel rows of granules. Sometimes the two borders are equally
bright; sometimes one much out-
shines the other. Some fibres are
found which, not being subjected
to any tension, are much more
drawn together. The black bands
are, perhaps, only half so far apart
as in the case just described. They
are never divided into two, and
though some appear granular,
others are homogeneous. The edges
of the fibre are no longer straight,
but slightly scalloped, the centre
of each projection being midway
between the black stripes. (See
Fig. 55.)

When active contraction takes
place, the whole fibre is involved,
and presents nothing but a series
of transverse black and white bands
with scalloped edges. To study the
successive stages of contraction we
must wait until it is feeble and in-
volves but a small part of the fibre.
It runs like a wave from one end of
the fibre to the other, pauses a moment, and then runs back again,
and sometimes starts anew, but with
diminished force. It is hard to follow the steps, for the elements are
changing their shape and position
at the same time; the black stripes
become broader, less granular, and
each runs toward its neighbor in
the direction of the wave; the gray band disappears, and the
edge of the fibre bulges. As the elements in front of the

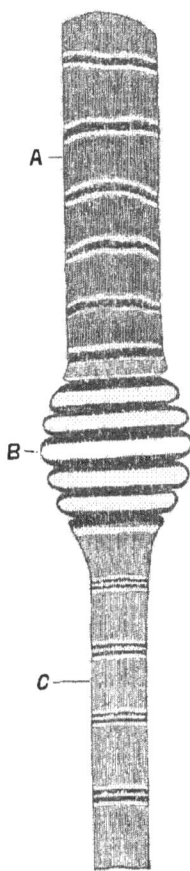

FIG. 55. — Semi-diagrammatic repre-
sentations of muscular fibres of Gyrinus.
Fibre supposed to be *in situ* and showing
the different appearances which the black
stripe may present. The wave of contraction is travelling toward A. At C we
notice that a part of the fibre, after contraction, has been subjected to stretching
after the passage of the wave; at B the
elements are in a state of active contraction. The longitudinal striation made
unavoidable in the woodcut, does not, as a
rule, exist in the living fibre.

wave enter into the contracted condition, those behind assume their normal state at first, but do not retain it, for they are immediately subject to a severe stretching by the course of the wave, and present new and very instructive appearances. The fibre becomes much narrower, the black stripes are resolved into two rows of granules some distance apart. The whole substance of the fibre is lighter than in the other conditions, and though the bright borders of the stripes are still there, they are much less glaring, and present less contrast with the intermediate portion.

In some of these fibres an indistinct longitudinal striation is seen, but the writer is not satisfied that it is in the substance of the fibre.

FIG. 56. — Transverse section of frozen frog's muscle showing Cohnheim's areas. Frey

Transverse sections of muscle have been appealed to for elucidation of the structure of the fibre. Cohnheim showed a network of whitish lines surrounding small, dull-colored polygons on cross-cuts of frozen muscle (Fig. 56). The muscles of the crab are said to show this particularly well. Schäfer found in the muscles of the water-beetle the appearance of granules on a clear ground. A similar appearance is seen in the fibres of vertebrates. The writer has observed in the cross-section of fibres from the tongue of the mocassin snake, granules which presented, at least, the suggestion of bright points in their centre. In some fibres these were collected into groups, separated by clear spaces.

Cohnheim's areas cannot be considered equivalent to fibrillæ, but rather, as Kölliker claims, to bundles of them, supposing always, we would add, that fibrillæ exist at all. It is pointed out in the account of the transverse striæ that these are often interrupted, and there is no doubt that this may be due to the limits of the muscle-columns. Of course, we must assume that there are many more columns than would be inferred from these interruptions ; for if the transverse stripes of two neighboring columns exactly correspond, no break will appear.

Nuclei and muscle-corpuscles.—In mammalian muscle acetic acid demonstrates a number of oval nuclei which may contain one or more nucleoli. Their long axis runs in the same direc-

tion as that of the fibre. A small amount of granular matter
may be seen at their extremities. Cross cuts of fibres show
that, with possibly some exceptions, they lie directly beneath
the sarcolemma. In the frog, and in many invertebrates, as the
beetles, they lie in the substance of the fibre, and, especially
in the latter class of animals, are surrounded by a mass of
granular protoplasm. Weber denies that in the adult frog
they are surrounded by this mass.

Conclusions.—From what precedes, it seems demonstrated
that striped muscular fibre consists of a transparent, semifluid
ground-substance, which is the contractile element. At certain
intervals a double layer of minute granules or spherules is
placed, which practically forms a transverse disk. The refraction of the light causes the substance bordering this disk to
appear brighter than the intermediate portion, which is only
occasionally seen in mammalian muscle as an indistinct and
usually a broken line, because the black stripes are so near together that the bright borders of two neighboring ones coalesce.
In invertebrates, as beetles, for instance, they are so far apart
that the dim stripe is proportionally broad, but it necessarily
disappears when by contraction the black stripes are brought
nearer together. Variations in the direction of the light, or
any obliquity of the disks, will cause peculiar effects, well-
nigh defying analysis. The writer's views coincide, in the main,
with Schäfer's, except that he cannot accept the "handles" of
the latter's dumb-bell-shaped structures. As the writer has
stated in another paper, muscles in the leg of the Gyrinus
which have been exhausted by electricity show the stripes very
indistinctly, and contain a number of stray granules. Klein
has pointed out that if fresh muscular fibre of the frog is
teased out in salt solution, when a break of the substance occurs inside the sarcolemma, "inside this tube a greater or less
number of granules are observed in active molecular movement." These observations appear to confirm the views given
above.

A good deal has been written about the effect of polarized
light on muscular fibre, and very different results have been
reached. Ranvier thinks it of no value in the discussion, because the same substance may be either doubly or singly refracting, according to the pressure to which it is subjected.
This is certainly a strong argument against its value, espe-

cially in view of the discrepancy of the observations made
with it.

Each fibre is, moreover, divided longitudinally into a varying number of what are called muscle-columns, held together
probably by a delicate cement. Between these are lodged the
muscle-corpuscles in the lower forms of animals. In opposition
to most authorities, the writer is inclined to question the existence of fibrillæ in the living muscle, at all events, as essential
parts of its structure. The granular appearance of cross sections is in accord with the views given above, and does not
necessarily imply the presence of fibrillæ.

Peculiarities of voluntary muscles of different functions.
—Ranvier was the first to discover a physiological and structural difference in the red and white muscles of the rabbit's
leg and in some other animals where both kinds exist. He
found that the semitendinosus of the rabbit, a red muscle, if
acted on by an induction current, gradually contracted till it
became tetanized, and remained so until the current was
stopped, when it gradually relaxed. White muscles, on the
other hand, when treated in the same way, contracted suddenly, and continued to give jerks corresponding to the interruptions of the current as long as it was continued. With its
cessation the muscle instantly returned to its original length.
From this he concludes that the white muscles are those of
sudden action, while the red ones serve to regulate power and
to maintain equilibrium. As to structure, he found out that
the white muscles had a very distinct transverse striation, and
a very faint longitudinal one, while in the red the longitudinal
lines were very marked, interrupting the cross ones at many
points, and giving the fibre a granular appearance. The nuclei were much more numerous in the red fibres, and, instead
of being flattened and situated just beneath the sarcolemma, as
in the white, were oval and projected into the fibre, some even
lying in its interior.

Ranvier showed later that the vascular supply of the red
muscles differed from the usual arrangement, which consists
simply in elongated meshes of capillaries in the main parallel
with the fibres. In red muscle, not only were the minute vessels more numerous, but the longitudinal capillaries were more
varicose, the meshes nearly as broad as long, and the transverse
vessels, both of the capillaries and small veins, presented fusi-

form dilatations, the object being, as he points out, to keep the muscle supplied with oxygen during its long-continued contraction, which must interrupt the circulation.

E. Meyer has since shown that Ranvier was over-hasty in his generalization. What is true of the semitendinosus of the rabbit is not necessarily true of other red muscles.

The writer is able to confirm this statement. As to the difference between the semitendinosus and white muscle, he is inclined to admit the greater number of nuclei of the former, but the difference in the stripes did not seem to him conclusive. The peculiarity, however, of the minute blood-vessels of the semitendinosus is very striking ; but in another red muscle of the rabbit's thigh he did not find the same arrangement. The richness of the capillary network varies greatly in different muscles of the same animal. Future investigations will, perhaps, show that modifications in the arrangement of the minute blood-vessels correspond with the function of the muscle.

The termination of muscle in tendon.—This occurs in several ways. Sometimes the fibre divides again and again, ending in small bundles of fibrillæ which have lost all muscular characteristics. Again, instead of spreading out, a fibre may become pointed, and the enveloping sarcolemma, reinforced with more or less fibrous tissue, runs on as a delicate tendon. Both these modes of ending can be seen in the tongue.[1] The cases in which a fibre loses its striation, and is apparently continued as a tendon of about the same size, present greater difficulties. By separating the fibres of a frog killed

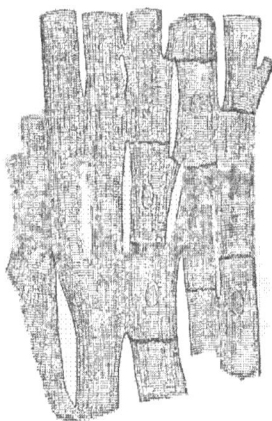

FIG. 57. — Anastomosing muscular fibre of the heart, seen in a longitudinal section. On the right, the limits of the separate cells with their nuclei are exhibited somewhat diagrammatically. After Schweigger-Seidel. J. Arnold.

by immersion in hot water, Ranvier has succeeded in demonstrating that the sarcolemma incloses the tendinous end of the fibre. The whole subject, however, of the ending of the fibres is not exhausted.

---

[1] Thin sections of the hardened tongue of a small animal are to be recommended, not only for the study of this point, but for that of striped muscle in general.

The muscular fibre of the heart.—This is transitional in structure between the voluntary and the involuntary. The fibres of the heart of the frog resemble chiefly the latter, being made of elongated, narrow, nucleated cells, which differ from it only in being transversely striped. In the mammalia the fibres are broader and composed of nucleated cells placed end to end. These cells frequently give off lateral processes which support others, thus forming a network of fibres. The cells have both a longitudinal and a transverse series of stripes, but the latter are not so clear as in well-marked voluntary muscle.

BIBLIOGRAPHY.

BOWMAN. On the Structure and Movements of Voluntary Muscle. Philosoph. Transactions. 1840–41.

AMICI. Ueber die Muskelfaser. Virchow's Archiv. Bd. XVI. 1859.

WEISMANN. Ueber die Muskulatur des Herzens beim Menschen und in der Thierreihe. Reichert & Du Bois-Reymond's Archiv. 1861.

IBID. Ueber die Verbindung der Muskelfasern mit ihren Ansatzpunkten. Zeitschrift für ration. Medicin. 3te Reihe. Bd. XII. 1861.

COHNHEIM. Ueber den feineren Bau der quergestreiften Muskelfaser. Virchow's Archiv. Bd. XXXIV. 1865.

DWIGHT. The Structure and Action of Striated Muscular Fibre. Proceedings Boston Soc. Nat. Hist. Vol. XVI. 1873.

SCHAEFER. On the Minute Structure of the Leg Muscles of the Water-Beetle. Philos. Transact. 1873.

ENGELMANN. Mikroskopische Untersuchungen über die quergestreifte Muskelsubstanz. Pflüger's Archiv. Bd. VII. 1873.

KÖLLIKER. Handbuch der Gewebelehre. Leipzig. 1867.

HENSEN. Arbeiten aus dem Kieler physiologischen Institut. 1868.

HEPPNER. Ueber ein Eigenthumliches Verhalten der quergestreiften Muskelfaser. Archiv für mikroscop. Anat. Bd. V. 1869.

DOENITZ. Beiträge zür Kenntniss der quergestreiften Muskelfaser. Reichert & Du Bois-Reymond's Archiv. 1871.

SCHWEIGER-SEIDEL. The Heart. Stricker's Histology. 1872.

MERKEL. Der quergestreifte Muskel. Archiv für mikro. Anatomie. Bd. VIII. 1872.

BRUECKE, E. The Behavior of Muscular Fibres when examined by Polarized Light. Stricker's Histology. 1872.

SACHS. Die quergestreifte Muskelfaser. Reichert & Du Bois-Reymond's Archiv. 1872.

WAGENER. Ueber die quergestreifte Muskelfibrille. Archiv für mikro. Anat. Bd. IX. 1873.

IBID. Ueber einige Erscheinungen an den Muskeln lebendiger Corethra plumicornis-larven. Archiv. für mikro. Anat. Bd. X. 1874.

KAUFMANN. Ueber Contraction der Muskelfaser. Reichert & Du Bois-Reymond's Archiv. 1874.

THIN. On the Minute Anatomy of Muscle and Tendon. Edinburgh Medical Journal. Sept., 1874.

WEBER. Note sur les noyaux des muscles striés chez la grenouille adulte. Archives de physiologie. 1874.

RANVIER. De quelques fait relatifs à l'histologie et à la physiologie des muscles striés. Archives de phys. 1874.

IBID. Note sur les vaisseaux sanguins et la circulation dans les muscles rouges. Archives de phys. 1874.

IBID. Traité technique d'histologie. Paris, 1875.

FRÉDÉRICQ. Génération et structure du tissu musculaire. Bruxelles, 1875.

MEYER. Ueber rothe und blase quergestreifte Muskeln. Reichert & Du Bois-Reymond's Archiv. 1875.

FRÉDÉRICQ. Note sur la contraction des muscles striés chez l'hydrophile. Bulletin Acad. Roy. de Belgique. Tome XL. 1877.

RENAUT. Note sur les disques accessoires des disques minces dans les muscles striés. Compt. rend. Tome LXXXV. No. 21. 1877.

BIEDERMANN. Zur Lehre vom Bau der quergestreiften Muskelfaser. Wiener Acad. Sitzungsbericht. Bd. LXXXV. No. 21. 1877.

SCHAEFER. Quain's Anatomy. Eighth edition. New York : Wm. Wood & Co. 1878.

NASSE. Zur microscopischen Untersuchung. des quergestreiften Muskels. Pflüger's Archiv. Bd. XVII. 1878.

FRORIEP. Ueber das Sarcolemm und die Muskelkerne. Archiv für Anatomie und Entwickelungsgeschichte. 1878.

ENGELMANN. Nouvelles recherches sur les phénomènes microscopique de la contraction musculaire. Archives Néanderlaises des Sciences exactes et naturelles. 1878.

FLEMMING. Ueber Formen und Bedeutung der organischen Muskelzellen. Zeitschrift für wissenschaftliche Zoologie. XXX. Supplement. 1878.

UNGER. Untersuchungen über die quergestreiften Muskelfasern des lebenden Thiers. Wiener medinische Jahrbücher. 1879. (Largely pathological.)

NEWMAN. New Theory of Contraction of Striated Muscle, and Demonstration of the Composition of the Broad Dark Bands. Journal of Anatomy and Physiology. Vol. XIII. 1879.

CHITTENDEN. Histochemische Untersuchungen über das Sarcolemm und einige verwandten Membranen. Untersuchungen aus der Physiol. Institut der Universität Heidelberg. Bd. III. 1879.

KLEIN and SMITH. Atlas of Histology. Part V. 1879-80.

RANVIER. Leçons d'anatomie générale sur le système musculaire. Paris, 1880.

VON THANHOFFER. Beitr. z. Hist. d. quergestreift. Muskels u. d. Nervenendigungen in demselben. Biol. Centralbl. I. 349-351. 1881.

CHAPTER XI.

THE BLOOD-VESSELS.

By EDMUND C. WENDT, M.D.,

Curator of the St. Luke's and St. Francis' Hospitals, etc., New York City.

IN man, a closed circuit of branching tubes, which proceed from a central organ, the heart, and, ramifying throughout the body, return the blood to this central organ, constitutes the blood-vascular system, as it has been named.

Of these vessels we recognize three different kinds: arteries, capillaries, and veins. The arteries convey the blood to the various capillary districts, whence it is again collected and carried back to the heart by the veins.

The arteries, highly elastic throughout, are composed of three superimposed layers or tunics. The veins, less elastic, and consequently more flaccid and compressible, likewise consist of three coats or tunics. In both sets of vessels these coats have received the names of *intima* for the inner, *media* for the middle, and *adventitia* for the external layer. The capillaries, intervening between the two, form minute branching tubules, which generally have but a single exceedingly thin and permeable membrane as the sole constituent of their walls.

Of course, all these vessels merge into one another, so that a sharp line of demarcation can nowhere be drawn; but in their typical forms they present clearly defined structural differences, necessitating a separate description of them. We begin with the simplest and yet most important class:

The capillary blood-vessels.—They are composed, as we have already said, of a single layer of cells, arranged in tubular form, and containing nuclei. These corpuscles are directly continuous, on the one hand, with the inner coat of the terminal arteries, and, on the other, with the intima of the veins, hence also with the lining membrane of the heart. They are called *endothelia*, and since they constitute the only structural elements which enter into the composition of all blood-vessels, we will first consider them and their relations to these vessels.

The vascular endothelium.—Histologists understand by the term *endothelium* a thin layer of flattened cells lining the free surface of various membranes, canals, sheaths, and cavities, all belonging to the serous type. *Epithelium*, on the other hand, is found covering the skin and mucous surfaces. All endothelia, in common with the blood, the blood-vessels, and connective tissues, are derived from the *mesoblast*, or middle of the three fundamental layers of the embryo. The epithelia, it will be remembered, originate in the two other layers, called *epiblast* and *hypoblast*, respectively—the former being the superior and the latter the inferior layer of the embryo.

In adult human subjects the vascular endothelia are made up of thin, polygonal, sometimes irregularly pentagonal, flattened cell-plates. Most of the elements are furnished with a rounded or ovoid nucleus, of central or more or less peripheral location (Fig. 58). Some have two nuclei. In general, the cells are somewhat elongated in the longitudinal direction of the vessel to which they belong. They also grow slightly narrower as the calibre of the vessel decreases. Their borders are serrated or scalloped, and dove-tailed into one another. An albuminoid substance, ordinarily invisible, cements their adjoining edges. This substance has the peculiar property of effecting an energetic reduction of silver nitrate. Hence, by proper management, the outlines of each individual cell may be made visible as a black zigzag surrounding a nucleus. Every cell represents a plate-like expanse of modified protoplasm. Remnants of this original substance may be seen to surround the nuclei of young vessels, where they appear in the shape of varying quantities of distinctly granular matter. Klein has described an *intracellular network*, formed by plexuses of minute fibrils, and associated with a second denser reticulum within the nucleus, called the *intranuclear network*. Whatever interpretation we choose to give these minute structures, the fact of their existence is indisputable. In man, however, their presence is not as readily demonstrable as in animals.

An isolated endothelial cell, when tilted up on its edge, presents the appearance of a straight or curved double contour, with a central thickening corresponding to its nucleus. Viewed *en face*, we observe the sinuous outline and the central or eccentric nucleus, with its surrounding granules of protoplasm. The shape and contour of endothelial cells are subject to con-

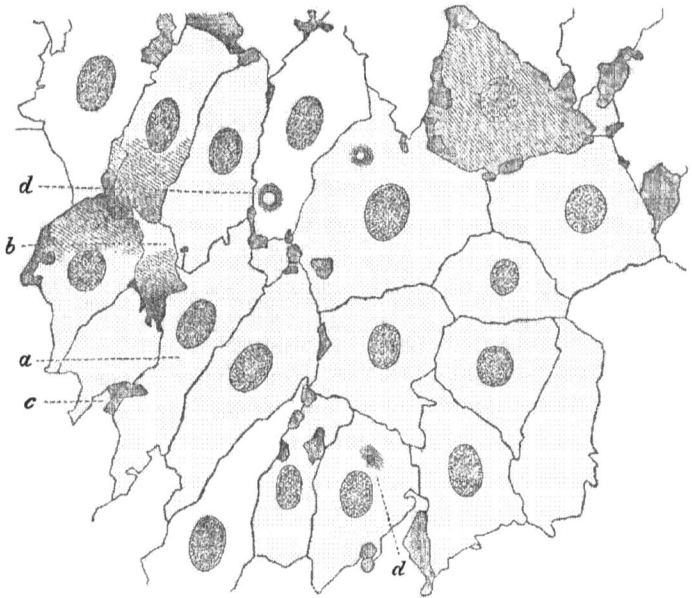

FIG. 58.—Endothelium of the carotid artery of man, after treatment with nitrate of silver: *a*, cells; *b*, clearer, *c*, darker intermediate spaces; *d*, intra-cellular circular and spotted markings. Eberth.

siderable variations in the different vascular districts. Such differences also occur in the same district, with the varying degree of expansion or contraction of the particular vessel under observation.

The capillaries proper.—In point of wideness of distribution, this variety of blood-vessels greatly exceeds all others. Indeed, the capillaries occupy a rank, in this respect, second only to the connective-tissue group of histological structures. As regards importance to the economy, it will only be necessary to advert to the vital processes of nutrition, secretion, respiration, and excretion, to recall the quality and extent of their physiological usefulness. Throughout the body [1] capillary plexuses are interposed between arteries and veins, which constitute a series of conveying and returning tubes. Thereby the direct continuity of these blood-channels is established.

It is in these intermediate territories, and in them only, that the blood serves its true function of giving and taking. True markets of exchange, then, these capillary districts, where the system is supplied with new material, and in return gets rid of useless or even deleterious by-products of tissue-life. Hence, the paramount importance of these vessels in the maintenance of life and health. Hence, also, the direct practical utility of knowing their minute anatomy and physiological dignity. Every practitioner of medicine will see the important relation this branch of histology holds to pathology, and therefore to therapeutics. At the same time we should not forget that the *rôle* played by the capillaries in the system is normally due to the inherent mechanical and physical properties of a finely elastic animal membrane, rather than to any specific action of their cellular constituents.

Robin, following Henle's example, distinguishes several varieties of these vessels. It seems to me proper to limit the term capillaries to those minute tubules which are entirely devoid of muscular elements. This corresponds to the classification adopted by Virchow, Kölliker, Eberth, Ranvier, Frey, and others. It is the one therefore that has generally been accepted, and is both simple and logical.

FIG. 59.—A rather large capillary from the hyaloid of the frog, presenting a membranous and nucleated tunica adventitia. Eberth.

The diameter of these tubules varies from 0.0045 to 0.0115 mm. Their structure is readily understood. Examined in the living animal with a high power, we see merely a delicate, hyaline, double-contoured membrane, having an

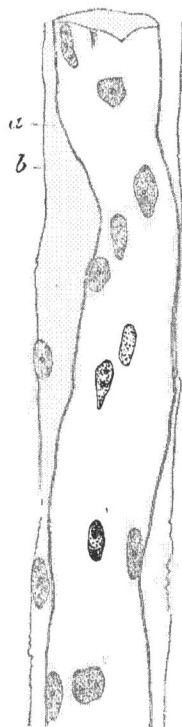

---

[1] Hoyer has shown that a direct communication of arterioles with venules occurs normally in the tips of the fingers, the matrix of the nails, the tip of the nose, and various other parts.

average thickness of 1 to 2 micro-millimetres (0.001—0.002 mm.). This membrane forms a tubule, the parietes of which are studded at intervals with rounded or oval nuclei, often containing one or more bright nucleoli. When oval, these nuclei have their long axis parallel with the direction of the vessel. Their average size is 0.0056 to 0.0074 mm. They possess the property of eagerly imbibing most of the staining fluids employed in histology, and of resisting the action of dilute acids, alkalies, and other reagents. (See Fig. 59.)

Besides nuclei, the capillary wall contains at various points peculiar granules, which indicate its protoplasmic nature. In addition, Stricker and Eberth have described lateral processes and pointed prolongations jutting out from the parietes of the

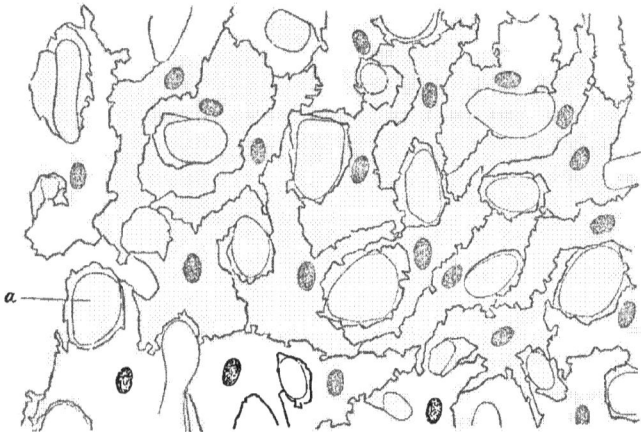

FIG. 60.—Capillaries of the lungs of the frog, with irregularly dentated cells: a, vascular meshes. Eberth.

capillary tubes. In growing tissue these are readily demonstrable, often forming thread-like connecting bridges between neighboring vessels; at a later period they are hollowed out into true capillaries. The shorter sprouts are also protoplasmic buds, capable of further development into similar vessels. (See Fig. 61.) By employing weak solutions of silver nitrate, the capillary-wall may be shown to consist of variously shaped areas, each one corresponding to a nucleated cell. They are the endothelia, and represent, as already stated, the sole essential constituents of all capillaries. Their form varies with the calibre of the vessel, the smaller capillaries being composed of corpuscles which are comparatively narrow, the larger vessels having broader cells. In man they have an average length of 0.0756—0.0977 mm., and an average breadth of 0.01—0.05 mm. The intercellular boundaries, brought out as dark lines by means of the silver salt, frequently exhibit little nodular swellings. (See Fig. 58.)

In addition to the ordinary endothelia, we find smaller areas, generally without nuclei ; they have rounded or somewhat dentate contours, and are interposed between the other cells. Eberth believes t h a t some of these *intercalated areas*, as Auerbach has called them, probably correspond to portions of strangulated vascular cells. It is more logical to regard them as the remnants of an incomplete endothelial desquamation, a process which is of physiological occurrence throughout the blood-vessels. These remaining bits are finally destined to become quite detached

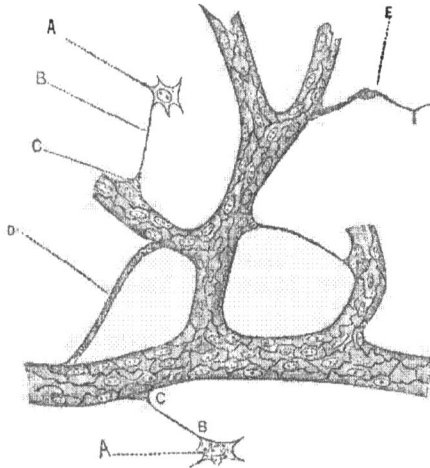

FIG. 61.—A,A, stellate connective-tissue cells connected by B,B, delicate protoplasmic threads to C,C, sprouts of endothelial tubes ; D. protoplasm connecting two capillaries : E, nucleus imbedded in a primitive sprout of protoplasm, budding from wall of capillary. Specimen prepared by silver nitrate.

from the vascular wall, and are then swept away by the rush and flow of the blood-current. The detached portions of such endothelia and their nuclei appear as free granules in the blood, where they have puzzled many observers, and have been variously called *microcytes*, *hæmatoblasts*, etc. From this description it is plain that Cohnheim's view, that these spaces are openings or stomata, is not sustained. True, we find in serous membranes of certain animals real openings, but these always appear of rounded shape, and are, to say the least, not commonly observed in human blood-vessels. This statement of the case does not militate against Cohnheim's well-known views that the corpuscles emigrate through the vessels, for, remembering the protoplasmic nature of the endothelial tubes, we can readily account for the phenomena in question. The capillary-wall is elastic, extremely thin, and permeable. By virtue of these qualities, it may allow the passage of a leucocyte or colored globule through its substance without suffering a permanent breach of continuity.

The writer's views on endothelial desquamation as a normal process of physiological import may strike the reader as insufficiently substantiated by known facts. But when we remember that similar processes have been actually observed taking place under the microscope, all doubts as to the probability of this endothelial desquamation should vanish. The author refers to the recent observations of Altmann (*Arch. f. mikros. Anat.*, Vol. XVI., p. 111). This histologist investigated the changes which take place in the serous epithelium (*i.e.*, endothelium) of the exposed frog's mesentery. Multiple swellings of the endothelia were seen to occur; then portions of these cells would become detached. Such detached bits were found to resemble in their appearance ordinary leucocytes. But, in spite of this apparent breaking up of the endothelia into these nucleated corpuscles, they often retained their individuality unaltered. The production of bodies resembling leucocytes from endothelia has, therefore, been actually observed in connection with serous membranes, and vascular desquamation is essentially the same process.

The capillary blood-vessels occupy the interstitial connective tissue of organs, without entering their parenchyma proper. Cartilage, the teeth, the hairs and nails, the cornea, and certain structures of the nervous system and organs of special sense are devoid of capillary supply.

Most of the larger tubes are invested by a delicate, external, sheath-like structure, called the *capillary adventitia* or *vascular perithelium*. It is composed of a rather close network of delicate connective-tissue fibrils. Prolongations of peculiar stellate cells, which clasp the capillary-tube, may sometimes be seen to join these fibrils. (Fig. 62.) Such branching cells are also encountered at some distance from the capillaries. They show delicate processes, which may anastomose with the offshoots of the adventitial corpuscles. In other places we only find external plates of connective-tissue cells (Krause's *inoblasts*), which have become more or less fused with the capillary-wall. In many instances the perithelium is inseparable from the connective-tissue stroma surrounding the vessel.

In reference to the manner of anastomosis, the forms and modes of ramification of different networks vary with the different tissues and organs of the body. Hence, a simple in-

spection of capillary reticula will generally enable us to decide
the nature of the tissue or organ in question. From a physiological point of view, we recognize a causal relation between
high capillary development and .great functional activity.
Therefore, the abundance of capillaries will determine the
physiological importance of an organ.

The chief forms of ramification may be grouped as follows :
1. Loops (*a*), simple or compound ; *e.g.*, the skin and the hard

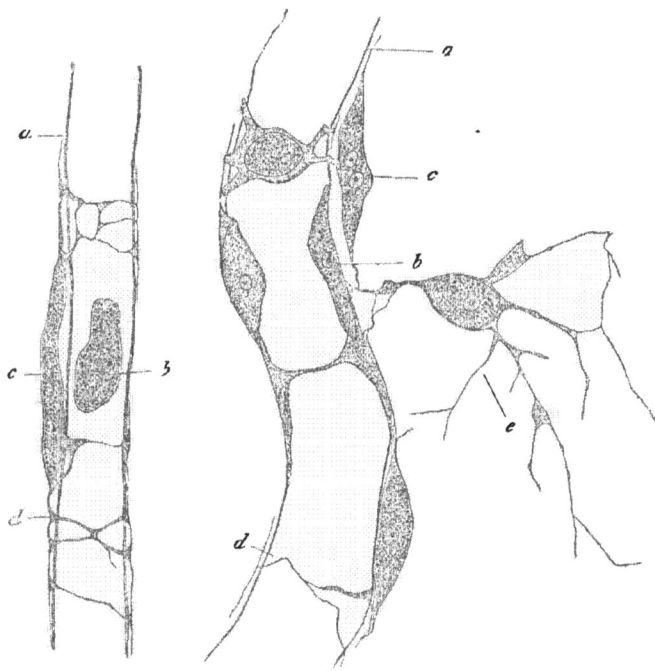

Fig. 62.—Capillaries from the hyaloid membrane of the frog : *a,a,* capillary-wall ; *b,b,* nuclei of the same ; *c,c,* cells of the tunica adventitia ; *d,d,* processes of these cells clasping the capillary-wall ; *e,* stel-late cell anastomosing with the cells of the tunica adventitia. Eberth.

palate ; (*b*) reticulated (the intestinal villi). 2. Tufts (the kidney). 3. Irregularly polygonal networks (the glands and the
mucous membranes). 4. Rounded reticula, with round or
polygonal meshes (adipose tissue). 5. Reticula with elongated
meshes (the muscles, bones, and tendons). There would be a
certain satisfaction in knowing that this or that vessel had a
precise breadth, and its coat a certain thickness. The precision
would be apparent, however, rather than real, because such

measurements vary greatly at different times in the same animal, and even more so in different animals. It may be stated, in general, that the calibre corresponds to the size of the largest blood-globules. In man, therefore, we have an average diameter of about 0.007 mm. The largest capillaries exist in the mucous membrane of the stomach and colon, the periosteum and bones, and the pituitary body. The smallest are found in the skin, the small intestine, the lungs, the muscles, the gray substance of the brain, and the retina (Valentin, Weber, and Henle).

The genesis, reproduction, and regeneration of capillaries. —There is still much uncertainty about the mode in which blood-vessels are first formed in the embryo. My personal

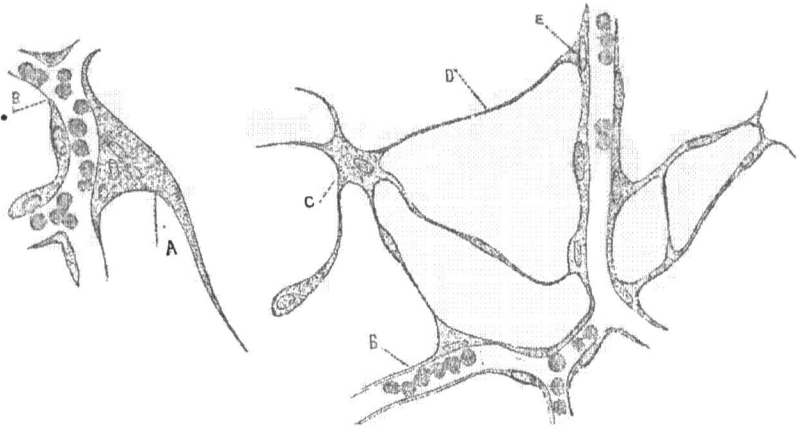

FIG. 68.—Growth and development of capillaries by nucleated sprouts of protoplasm: A, poly-nucleated large sprout with filiform process; B,B, blood-globules; C, branched cell; D, delicate protoplasmic tendril linking C with E, a smaller mono-nucleated sprout of endothelial wall.

observations on this subject, while working recently under the supervision of Kölliker, appear to confirm the view held by Foster and Balfour. These authors' account of the interesting process may be summed up as follows: About the second day of incubation in the chick, certain mesoblastic cells send out solid processes, which, uniting, form a protoplasmic network containing nuclei. A majority of the latter acquire a reddish tint, and are ultimately transformed into colored blood-globules. Other nuclei, however, remain unaltered, and, receiving an investment of protoplasm, form walls inclosing the reddened nuclei. The protoplasm of these central nuclei rapidly becomes liquefied, thus forming the blood-plasma. And now we have a system of communicating tubules, containing corpuscles floating in a plasma, their walls consisting of nucleated cells. Hence, the blood-vessels do not arise as intercellular spaces, but are hollowed out to form channels in an originally solid reticulum of protoplasm derived from mesoblastic cells.

This explanation of the way in which vessels are formed aids us in understanding both how capillaries are reproduced in the adult, and their regeneration under pathological conditions. The capillary-wall itself, under the influence of favoring circumstances, begins to bud, as it were ; the delicate protoplasmic sprouts send out more delicate filaments, which, uniting with similar offshoots from neighboring vessels, establish a connection between two capillaries. In due time these solid structures undergo the familiar process of hollowing out, and the newly formed vessel is complete. Frequently the proto plasmic threads communicate, forming a reticulum which Ran vier has called *vasoformative network*. This author also ob served that capillaries develop from special cells, termed *vasoformative cells*. They resemble leucocytes, and form by their prolongations a network of solid protoplasm. This is originally quite independent of already existing capillaries. Subsequently, however, a consolidation is effected, and the blood then flows through these new channels in the usual manner.

The author has been able to trace collections of emigrated leucocytes through various stages of progressive development, culminating in the formation of true capillaries. The experimental investigations on this subject were carried out in Professor v. Rindfleisch's laboratory, and have been fully described by his former assistant, Prof. Ziegler, of Berne.

The arteries.—If we follow the capillaries in a direction toward the heart, we soon find the endothelial tube receiving an investment of unstriped muscle-cells. These are wound transversely or obliquely around the capillary, thus forming a second tube, as it were, surrounding the first. External to the muscular layer there appears some connective tissue, mingling with which elastic elements may be observed. The direction of these additional fibres is mainly longitudinal. They form the third or external coat, called the *adventitia*, the second or middle being represented by the muscle-cells, and the first or internal by the endothelial tube. The latter now receives the name of *intima*. When the layers of its walls are arranged in this simple manner the vessel is called an *arteriole*, and this constitutes the type of all arteries.

Arterioles, however, commonly contain a few additional fibres between the intima and the media, as the first indication of what afterward becomes a special layer. This structure, known as the *internal elastic coat*, attains considerable development in the larger vessels. With the growth of an artery in calibre its individual coats are reinforced by additional layers. Hence the thickness of the entire wall increases at the same

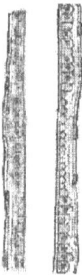 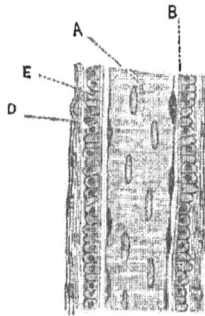 

FIG. 64.   FIG. 65.   FIG. 66.

FIG. 64.—Minute artery showing optical section of alternate groups of muscle-cells, and an external nucleated membrane, representing the tunica adventitia.
FIG. 65.—A, intima ; B, delicate internal elastic coat ; E, media (as in Fig. 64) ; D, adventitia. Arteriole, from a child's mesentery.
FIG. 66.—Elastic internal tunic of the basilar arteries. Eberth.

time that its structure is rendered more complex. But new tissues never appear. Moreover, the increased thickness is not uniformly proportionate to the enlarged calibre ; neither does it take place by equal participation of the different tissues mentioned. In vessels of small and medium size there is a preponderance of muscular over elastic elements. In the larger trunks the reverse condition obtains. It is, therefore, proper to distinguish arteries of the muscular from those of an elastic type. The latter class is represented by the principal distributing trunks, all the remaining arteries belonging to the muscular type. There exist, however, no abrupt lines of demarcation between these main forms—the one merging gradually into the other.

The interposition of the *internal elastic coat* between the intima and the media marks the transition of a minute into a small artery. This new layer consists at first of delicate fibrils of elastic tissue, or an apparently homogeneous membrane. Vascular contraction throws it into folds, which appear as longitudinal striæ or a transverse series of continuous festoons. As the vessel grows larger this coat gets thicker, becomes distinctly fenestrated, and presents a reticulated appearance. It is now made up of interlacing bundles of connective tissue and elastic fibres, with spaces left between them. The latter constitute the fenestræ of this layer, which in the large vessels becomes a double or triple lamellated membrane. Between it and the lining endothelium there appears still another structure, which has received various names from different authors. Thus, Kölliker has called it the *striated internal coat;* Remak, the *innermost longitudinal fibrous coat;* and Eberth, the *internal fibrous coat.* We shall employ the last term. The *internal fibrous coat* consists at birth of a granular substance, which becomes distinctly fibrillated in the adult. Embedded in this membrane lie numerous branching corpuscles, containing large, conspicuous nuclei. Besides these cells, smaller, so-called granulation-bodies are frequently seen. So far from regarding them as of pathological origin (Eberth, in "Stricker's Histology"), I prefer to consider them as matrix-cells for the regeneration of desquamated endothelia. My reasons for so doing are as follows: In the blood-vessels of young animals and newly born infants I have frequently noticed thick, dark, and granular bodies immediately below the endothelial lining. These subendothelial cell-plates were smaller and more polyhedral than ordinary endothelia, and invariably contained one or even two nuclei. They appeared to resemble germinating endothelial cells, such as Klein has described as occurring in serous membranes. They did not, however, occur in single layers, as Klein has seen them,

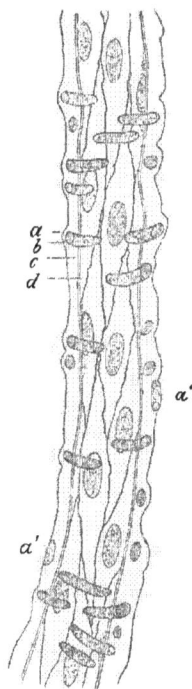

FIG. 67.—Small artery from the brain of man: *a*, tunica adventitia; *a'*, *a'*, nuclei of the tunica adventitia; *b*, muscle nucleus; *c*, elastic internal tunic; *d*, membrane formed of fusiform cells. Eberth.

but in strata. They were observed in particular vessels of young animals. It seems likely that these cells disappear or shrivel with the growth of the individual, but their sudden reappearance in pathological processes leads the author to believe that at least some of them persist through life. Talma (*Virchow's Arch.*, Vol. LXXVII., pp. 242–269) observed similar elements, but thinks they are derived from the ordinary endothelia, instead of *vice versâ*. He is also convinced that the latter are merely modified leucocytes; but this view has been shown to be erroneous by Virchow (*Archiv f. path. Anat.*, Vol. LXXVII., pp. 380–383). Endothelial desquamation is probably, as already stated, a physiological process of constant

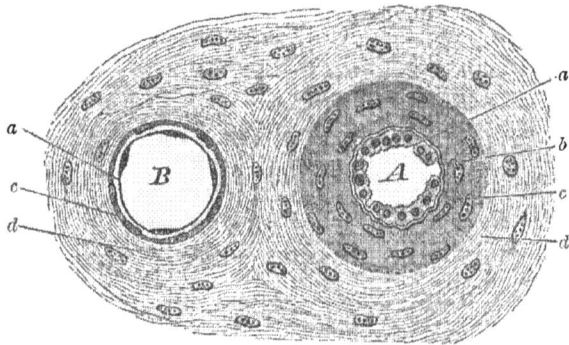

Fig. 68.—Transverse section through small artery and vein: *A*, artery; *a*, intima with bulging endothelial cells, the vessel being drawn in a state of contraction; *b*, internal elastic coat, wavy for same reason; *c*, media; *d*, adventitia. *B*, vein, same denominations.

occurrence, and in some respects analogous to the epithelial shedding from the surface of the skin and mucous membranes.

The *media, musculosa*, or middle coat, consists of superimposed layers of smooth muscle-elements disposed in groups. Most of them lie transversely to the course of the vessel. The intervals between neighboring groups are occupied by connective tissue and elastic fibres, arranged in networks. This interstitial substance becomes augmented with the increasing calibre of the artery. In the largest trunks it all but replaces the muscle-cells. Here, however, the elastic fibres also reach their maximum development, encroaching upon the connective-tissue elements until the latter become quite inconspicuous. Besides its principal transverse layer, the media also contains fusiform muscle-cells, placed in an oblique or longitudinal direction.

They are scattered irregularly throughout the middle coat. Sometimes the intima and the adventitia also contain sparsely distributed muscle-cells. The arterial muscular coat is distinctly separated from the intima by the interposition of the internal elastic coat. Externally a sharp boundary is formed either by the adventitia or by the *external elastic coat.* The latter appears as a separate membrane in arteries of small and medium size. There are, however, exceptions to this rule. The external elastic coat consists of a close network of delicate

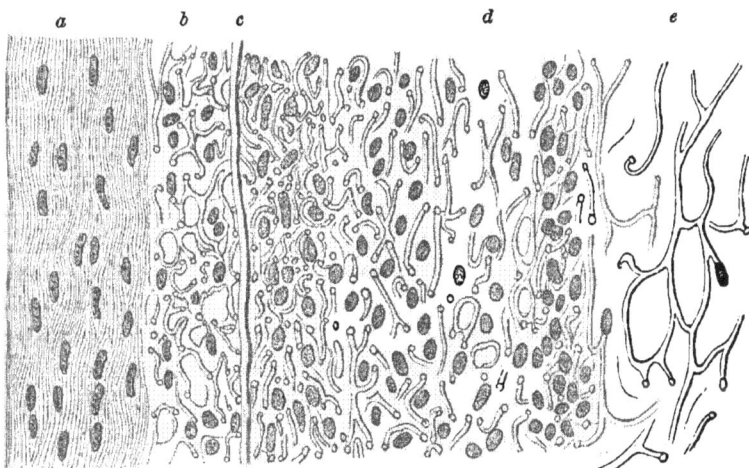

FIG. 69.—Longitudinal section of pulmonary artery. Mounted in glycerine and acetic acid after desiccation of the artery. *a,* Internal portion of intima; *b,* external portion of intima; *c,* internal elastic coat; *d,* media, showing cross sections of muscle fibres and elastic tissue; *e,* adventitia.

elastic fibrils, anastomosing with similar adventitial reticula. The *adventitia* is composed of interlacing bundles of connective tissue, commingled with elastic lamellæ of varying thickness.

The veins.—From their origin in the capillaries to the point where they enter the trunk proper, the veins preserve throughout a uniform type of structure. But no sooner have they penetrated into the visceral cavities of the body than we find them undergoing considerable alterations, which may either increase or diminish the complexity of their structure (Ranvier). The veins are far more numerous than the arteries. They are also, as a rule, wider and more dilatable, and have thinner coats. It is owing to the latter peculiarity that the color of the blood is seen through their semitranslucent walls. Finally, they branch more frequently than the arteries. Three main coats or tunics enter into the composition of most veins.

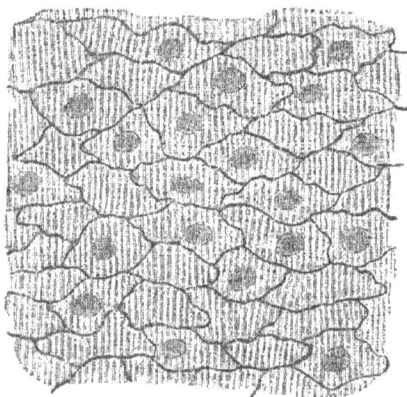

These resemble the corresponding arterial structures, and have likewise received the names of *intima*, for the internal endothelial lining ; *media*, for the middle muscular ; and *adventitia*, for the external connective-tissue coat.

Veins, however, differ from arteries in the feebler development of their muscular coat, in the comparative paucity of elastic elements, a greater laxity of their intima, and the presence in some of valves.

FIG. 70.—Portion of innominate vein of dog, after injection of a solution of silver nitrate. The endothelial cells and their nuclei are visible. The media shines through this layer.

We may distinguish veins of smaller calibre, or *venules*, from the vessels of medium and large size. The venules, like the arterioles, in certain respects resemble the capillaries. As

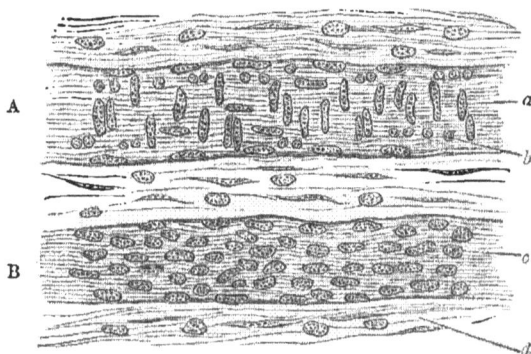

FIG. 71.—Arteriole and venule from child's mesentery, treatment by acetic acid and glycerine: A, artery ; *a*, nucleus of muscle-cell of media ; *b*, same in transverse section (optical). B, vein ; *c*, nucleus of connective tissue constituting media, which in these minute veins contains no muscle-cells ; *d*, nucleated connective tissue.

it may become important to differentiate the minuter forms of vessels, we will here briefly indicate the main points of distinction between full-sized capillaries, small veins, and arterioles. In the latter, the endothelial cells are more nearly fusiform, longer, and somewhat narrower than in the venules. In the capillaries, their form and dimensions hold an intermediate position between the arterial and venous types. The middle coat is entirely wanting in capillaries, and is much less conspicuous in the small veins than in the arterioles. In fact, under ordinary circumstances, the muscle-coat forms by far the most characteristic distinguishing feature between these vessels. Venules quite frequently have only a few sparsely scattered muscle-cells, in place of the continuous muscular layer which exists in minute arteries. The former also are either altogether deficient in the internal elastic coat, or the presence of this structure is barely indicated by delicate elastic fibres; these latter usually have a longitudinal direction. On the other hand, arteries of corresponding calibre are mostly furnished with a distinct elastic inner coat. Finally, with regard to the adventitia, we find it more highly developed proportionally in venous than in arterial vessels, whereas capillaries commonly have only a few faint fibres to denote the presence, in them also, of this coat.

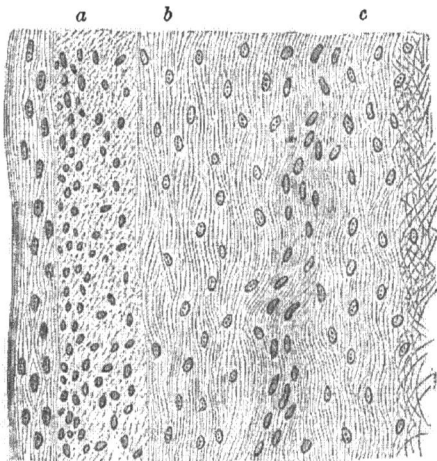

Fig. 72.—Longitudinal section of popliteal vein: a, intima; b, media; c, adventitia.

The *internal elastic coat* of the larger and largest veins is very feebly developed in comparison with that of the arteries. Distinct fenestrated membranes are scarcely ever encountered. Veins are likewise possessed of an *internal fibrous layer*, but here again we observe that comparatively feeble development of a coat which in the arteries is quite conspicuous.

Among the many special characteristics of the various veins in different regions, we will only mention the following: the jugular veins show well-marked elastic reticula, the meshes of which contain sparse muscular elements. In the femoral,

brachial, and subcutaneous branches there is a media of considerable dimensions. The inferior vena cava has, in addition
to a transverse layer of muscle-cells, a longitudinal one of
greater thickness, and, besides these, contains muscle-cells,
which are scattered through its elastic coat. The veins of the
meninges of the encephalon and cord, the retina, the bones,
and the muscles, and the jugular, the subclavian, the innominate, and the thoracic portion of the vena cava are all entirely
devoid of a true muscular coat. The veins of the gravid uterus have only longitudinal muscle-elements. In addition to an
outer longitudinal layer, the vena cava, the azygos, the renal,
the hepatic, the internal spermatic, and the axillary veins possess an inner circular layer. The iliac, the femoral, the popliteal, and several other veins contain a middle coat of transverse
muscle-cells, between internal and external longitudinal layers.

The *valves* of the veins consist of longitudinal bundles of
connective tissue commingled with scanty elastic fibrils, and
containing nucleated cells. The inner endothelial layer appears
to be a direct continuation of the intima of the vein. That
portion of the subendothelial tissue which does not face the
blood-current is less developed than the part turned toward it ;
the elastic fibres of the latter are also barely visible. The attached valvular border frequently presents transversely disposed muscle-elements. Eberth has denied their occurrence,
but they have been repeatedly observed by Ranvier and other
competent histologists.

Peculiar vascular structures.—The following structures are
remarkable for the conspicuous and characteristic development
of their blood-vessels, the *vascular membranes, tunicæ vascu-
losæ,* such as the pia mater of the brain and spinal cord, and
the choroid coat of the eye. In these we find that the excessive
vascularity is intended to nourish, not the membranes themselves, but the organs which they invest.

Blood-vascular glands, vascular plexuses.—In man, two
bodies of peculiar structure represent this group. They are
the *coccygeal gland* of Luschka, and a rudimentary organ
called the *intercarotid gland.* Both consist essentially of convoluted blood-vessels and nerves, imbedded in a nucleated connective-tissue stroma. The *coccygeal gland* is a small, rounded,
pinkish body, of rather firm consistence, and is connected by a
pedicle with the middle sacral artery. This pedicle contains

blood-vessels and nerves. The arteries entering the gland-like body become convoluted, and show numerous tubular, fusiform, or ampullar dilatations. Sometimes they have terminal sacculi, closely resembling minute aneurisms, and giving the organ its glandular appearance. Indeed, Luschka has called them gland-tubules and vesicles. After death they are com-

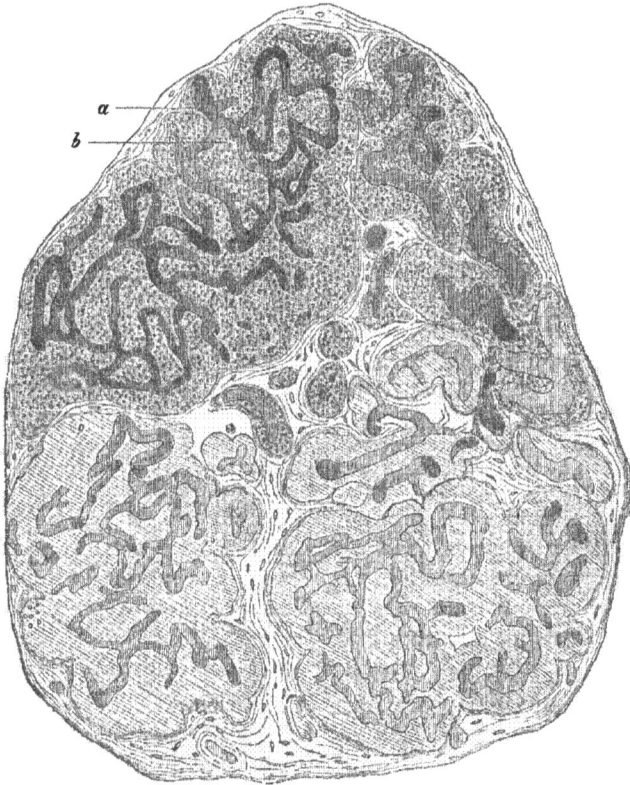

Fig. 78.—Section of a naturally injected coccygeal gland : *a*, vessels ; *b*, collection of cells. Eberth.

monly found to be empty, but by proper management a good natural injection with blood may be readily obtained. Both capillaries and veins also present lateral varicosities, studding them in great number. All these vessels have the usual endothelial lining. External to this there appear aggregations of rounded or polygonal cells. They are furnished with nuclei, and receive an investment corresponding to the vascular adventitia, but containing comparatively more nuclei than that structure.

The *intercarotid gland* differs from the coccygeal in its larger size, and because it contains accumulations of ganglionic nerve-cells. These are derived from the carotid plexus. Here the vascular sacculi also more nearly resemble dilated capillaries, whereas in the other body they approach the arterial type. In all other respects the structure of these vascular plexuses is identical. Some authors regard the spleen and the suprarenal capsule as belonging to this group of blood-vascular glands. The author sees no necessity for so considering them, and the subject may therefore be dismissed without further comment.

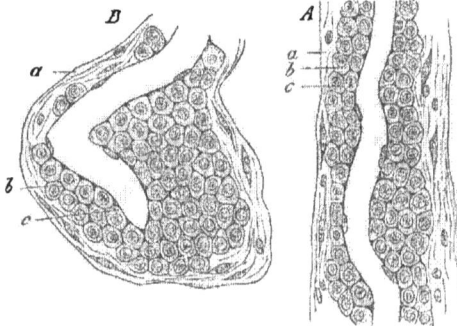

Corpora cavernosa.—They consist in great part of dilated blood-vessels, chiefly of the venous type. These intercommunicate very freely, and when filled with blood cause the organ to assume the peculiar condition known as *erection.* The penis and the clitoris are supplied with cavernous bodies. The urethra of the female and the vestibule also contain them. Interlacing bundles of muscle-fibres, together with similar bands of connective tissue, form a framework for the support of the vascular structures mentioned. The latter present the ordinary endothelial lining.

FIG. 74.—A, cellular vascular sheath, from the coccygeal plexus: *a*, connective tissue with scattered cells and nuclei; *b*, round and polygonal cells lying immediately upon the capillary wall, *c*; B, a capillary from the coccygeal plexus, with a vascular sheath very rich in cells. References as in A. Eberth.

Several years ago Dr. H. J. Bigelow succeeded in demonstrating the existence of cavernous tissue in the nasal fossæ. In a letter to the author, Dr. Bigelow states that his point was "the demonstration of an abundant and true cavernous structure and erectile tissue on and about the turbinated bones, occupying the place of what had been previously supposed to be only venous sinuses, the *loops* of Kohlrausch. The new result obtained was due to a different mode of preparation. Kohlrausch injected from the jugular vein ; I [Dr. Bigelow] inflated the tissue locally, as if it were in the penis."

Vasa vasorum, lymphatics, and nerves.—Nutrient vessels are found in the walls of all the larger arteries and veins, where they occupy the adventitia. Sometimes they are seen to dip down into the outermost portions of the media. *Lymphatics* occur as clefts or spaces between the various tissues of all arterial and venous trunks. Some vessels are ensheathed by a lymphatic membrane, which is sometimes furnished with a lining endothelium. Such structures are called *perivascular*, or, better, *circumvascular spaces*. They may be found in connection with the omental and the mesenteric vessels, also the splenic and the hepatic arteries, as well as certain meningeal vessels of the brain and cord.

Nerve-fibres are seen to pass to many of the blood-vessels. They enter the adventitia, and at its internal boundary suddenly appear to divide into numerous filaments, the ultimate distribution of which has not hitherto been satisfactorily ascertained. They seem to terminate in the muscle-cells of the media. Beale considers the presence of ganglion-cells in the vascular nerves as of constant occurrence. The author cannot admit the truth of this general statement, having discovered such cells in only exceptional instances. There is no discernible difference of structure between the vaso-constrictor and the vaso-dilator nerve-fibres.

BIBLIOGRAPHY.

In addition to the well-known standard treatises by Bichat, Kölliker, Henle, Sappey, Krause, Frey, Leydig, Teichmann, Stricker, Klein, Ranvier, Donders, Vierordt, Luschka, Pouchet et Tourneux, the following may be consulted :

LUDWIG. De arteriarum tunicis. Lipsine, 1739.
RÄUSCHEL. De arteriarum et venarum structura. Vratisl., 1836.
ROBIN. Sur la structure des artères. Compt. rend. 1847.
SCHULTZE. De art. struct. Gryph., 1850.
REMAK. Hist. Bemerk. ueber d. Blutgefässwände. Müller's Arch., p. 96. 1850.
SEGOND. Syst. capillaire sanguin. Thèse. Paris, 1853.
REMAK. Entwickelung d. Wirbelthiere. Berlin, 1855.
REMAK. Klappen d. Venen. Deut. Klinik. 1856.
HÄCKEL. Müller's Arch. 1857.
LUSCHKA. Virch. Arch. XVIII., p. 106. 1860.

162   MANUAL OF HISTOLOGY.

HOYER. Arch. f. Anat., p. 244. 1865.
KLEBS. Virch. Arch. Vol. XXXII., p. 172. 1865.
AEBY. Med. Cent. Zeit. No. XIV. 1865.
CHRZONSZCZEWSKY. Virch. Arch. Vol. XXXV. 1865.
EBERTH. Virch. Arch. Vol. XLIII., p. 136, and Centralblatt, p. 196. 1865.
AUERBACH. Virch. Arch. Vol. XXXIII. 1865. Med. Cent. Zeit. No. X.
GIMBERT. Structure et texture des artères. Thèse. Paris, 1865. Journ. de
    l'anat. et de la phys. Robin, p. 536. 1865.
FASCE, LUIGI. Istologia della arterie. Palermo, 1865.
LANGHANS. Virchow's Arch. Vol. XXXVI., p. 197. 1866.
HIS. Die Häute und Höhlen d. Körper's. Basel, 1866.
LEGROS. Journal de l'anat. et de la phys. No. III., p. 275. 1868.
TOLUBEW. Beitr. z. Kennt. d. Baues u. d. Ent. d. Capill. Arch. mikr. Anat., p.
    49. 1869.
ZIEGLER. Exp. Unt. ueber d. Herk. d. Tuberkelelemente. Würzburg, 1875.
ZIEGLER. Unt. ueber pathol. Bind. u. Gefässneubildg. Würzburg, 1876.
KÖLLIKER. Entwickelungsgeschichte. Leipzig, 1876.
DISSE. Arch. f. mikros. Anat. Vol. XVI., p. 1. 1879.
ILLTMANN. Arch. f. mikros. Anat. Vol. XVI., p. 111. 1879.

CHAPTER XII.

THE LYMPHATIC SYSTEM.

By Dr. W. R. BIRDSALL, New York City.

HISTOLOGICAL research has brought to light within recent years no more important or interesting facts than those connected with the lymphatic system ; interesting, in exhibiting entirely new features in tissues which had previously been carefully studied ; and important in their physiological, and, particularly, in their pathological relations.

Assisted by experimental pathology, it is still in this direction that we are to look for advancement in pathological histology, for there can be no doubt that heretofore too little attention has been paid to the lymphatic system, both in its histological details and in its topographical anatomy.

Present condition of the views on the structure of the lymphatic system—Relations to the connective tissues.—Unfortunately we have still a great variety of contradictory observations, and various interpretations of the same observations. Through this maze of uncertainties it is not easy to lead the student to a settled opinion, nor can all the phases of this many-sided subject be presented. It shall be our aim, however, to draw the outlines. If the student wishes to follow out the controversies, he will be aided by the references which are appended to this chapter.

It may be said that we have, to a great extent, returned to the views of the older anatomists and physiologists, and believe that the whole connective-tissue formation is a network of channels ; that its interstices are, directly or indirectly, connected with the lymphatic capillaries and larger vessels ; that, in short, the lymphatic system is pre-eminently a connective-tissue circulatory system, irregularly distributed, it is true, but found in one form or another wherever this tissue exists, and constituting in the serous membranes a great absorbent system, with its special connections, the lacteals, the lymphatic nodes or glands, and the fat-tracts. The important pathological processes, both acute and chronic, connected with these membranes are due principally to the fact that they are parts of this great lymphatic system.

Of course we must not lose sight of the connections of the latter with the complimentary blood-vascular system; the tendency has been too much in the opposite direction, however, and this more extensive, though less visible, system has been too often neglected in favor of its more prominent companion, in the consideration of processes of nutrition and of pathological changes.

General histology of the lymphatic system — Previous ideas.—In describing the lymphatic system, only its general histology will be considered, the details of its special distribution and arrangement being classed with the description of the different organs with which it is associated. Since the serous membranes have come to be regarded as important parts of the lymphatic system, being, in fact, great membranous expansions of that system, they are naturally and easily considered in connection with each other. It is not intended to treat of them here in their special details, but merely to make a general histological study of them as a class. It is convenient to begin with them in taking up the study of the origin of the lymphatic system.

With Virchow originated the theory that the starting-point of the lymphatics is from hollow anastomosing cells, the connective-tissue cells, whose prolongations communicate to form continuous tubes. He termed them *plasma cells.* Kölliker supported this doctrine, and a similar view was held by Leydig. Henle held a different opinion, whilst Brücke and Ludwig reverted to the ancient theory of Bichat, that the interstitial spaces of the connective tissue are the true sources of the lymphatics. Recklinghausen, introducing nitrate of silver as a reagent, showed that the lymphatic vessels are lined, and the serous membranes covered, with flat cells, forming an endothelial layer. He observed the passage of milk and fine granules, through openings in the central tendon of the diaphragm, from the peritoneal to the pleural surface. He believed also that he had discovered a system of canaliculi in connective tissue, which he termed *sap* or *juice canaliculi* (saftkanälchen). His views, as modified somewhat later, are, that the connective tissue is traversed by *serous canaliculi* or *plasmatic channels* which are directly continuous with the lymphatic vessels. "Not mere fissures in the connective tissue, but interstices of the fibrous fasciculi and lamellæ of connective tissue, cemented to one another by a tenacious, homogeneous, firm material, in which the serous canaliculi are buried."

The lymphatics of the mesentery.—A portion of the mesentery between the trabeculæ, taken fresh from a cat and stained with nitrate of silver, exhibits on both surfaces an endothelial layer, the cells of which possess an irregular outline, marked by the deposit of silver, either in a supposed intercellular substance or in crevices between the cells. Sometimes this outline is polygonal, sometimes sinuous, crenated, or even sharply dentated. It may be an even, fine line, or it may possess irregularities as if beaded. At the union of these lines, that is, where two or more cells terminate, a round, irregularly triangular, or spindle-shaped spot may be often observed, which is stained like the intercellular line, or in a lighter or darker shade. There are other spots of larger size, presenting the appearance of openings; we shall refer to them again. The surface of the cells may be clear, or granular, sometimes it is quite dark, varying with the degree of staining and the condition of the tissue; a nucleus can usually be seen at a slightly deeper level. This is plainly visible in unstained or slightly stained specimens, or where special reagents have been used to make the nuclei prominent, as hæmatoxylin or picro-carminate of ammonia. The granular appearance spoken of is sometimes confined to a series of cells which surround a *stoma*, or the black spots mentioned, while the neighboring cells may be clear; in other cases, several corpuscles in the form of an irregular tract may present this appearance.

Klein has observed cells which are club-shaped, undergoing a budding process, *i.e.*, giving off little bodies resembling lymphoid corpuscles. He has given the term *germinating endothelium* to these cells. Other histologists have made similar observations.

Underneath and around the nuclei a delicate, intricate, reticulum of elastic fibres may be seen plainly in unstained specimens, and by careful focussing in silver preparations. According to Ranvier, they are connected near their point of union by a very thin, elastic, fenestrated membrane. Below the layer of elastic fibres is the connective tissue which forms the basis of the membrane. It consists of fasciculi, which are straight, or wavy, according to the degree of tension of the membrane, or its fasciculi are held together by the elastic fibres, which penetrate from the reticulum on each side. They usually present a decidedly convoluted appearance in ordinary specimens, and in consequence of the contiguous fasciculi not possessing corresponding convolutions, clear interspaces are seen. Sometimes the fibres are very irregular in their arrangement. Ranvier claims that an interfascicular membrane can be demonstrated here also. Ordinary flat, branching connective-tissue cells are distributed through this tissue; they lie upon and between the fasciculi; they are particularly numerous under the endothelial layer. Lymphatic and blood-capillaries traverse the interspaces and run upon the fasciculi. In the mesentery and pleura they form a wide-meshed plexus; in the pericardium a close plexus.

To see the features of the deeper portions to advantage, we must remove the superficial endothelial layer before staining with silver.

Klein's method of studying the omentum.—Klein has described a very careful process for doing this, and as he claims it must be followed in detail to obtain the results at which he has arrived, we reproduce it : "To prepare the omentum, a rabbit is killed by bleeding; the stomach is exposed; after having pushed the intestine to the right side, the free surface of the omentum is pencilled several times from the large curvature toward the diaphragm, with a fine camel's-hair pencil moistened with fluid of the abdominal cavity. After that, a $\frac{1}{4}$ or $\frac{1}{2}$ per cent. solution of nitrate of silver is allowed to flow over the omentum from a large capillary-tube until the membrane has become slightly milky (one or two minutes are generally sufficient); after that, the stomach, together with the omentum, spleen, pancreas, and a portion of the duodenum is cut out and transferred to a large capsule with distilled water ; after some time the water is renewed and the omentum is separated under water, together with the spleen and pancreas, from the stomach, with scissors, and is transferred to common water. Those parts of the omentum which are seen to contain small patches are cut out and mounted. . . . . A failure is more frequent than a success. Either the surface has not been pencilled enough, and then the endothelium of both surfaces is colored, and consequently, hardly anything is to be seen of the cellular elements of the ground-substance; or the surface has been pencilled too hard, and then the arrangement of the ground-substance is altered, its bundles appear considerably stretched and distinctly fibrillar."

When these patches referred to, found in the mesentery, and particularly in the omentum, are examined, they are observed, according to Klein, to consist of systems of somewhat flattened, finely granular, nucleated, branched corpuscles connected together; the spaces which appear clear between them forming the lacunæ and canaliculi, corresponding to Recklinghausen's lymph canalicular system. The nuclei of these cells are sharply defined, oval, and possess one or two nucleoli. Lymphoid corpuscles are found in these spaces, and also slightly larger corpuscles, which are supposed to be derived, in part, at least, from the branched cells by a process of budding. Klein calls these patches *lymphangeal patches* or *nodules*, and *lymphangeal tracts*. He divides them into two classes.

The *perilymphangeal nodules* or *tracts* which lie closely connected with, but principally outside of, the lymphatic vessels, are accumulations of more or less flat, branched cells, which, by their growth and proximity to one another, make the canaliculi shorter or close them entirely. The second class develop within the lymphatic vessels, and are termed *endolymphangeal nodules* or *tracts*. They consist of those which perfectly resemble adenoid or reticular tissue, and those which are formed of a reticulum of branched cells, their spaces being filled with liquid or a few lymphoid corpuscles. The last form may have a rich blood-capillary plexus, and the branched cells may possess buds, pedunculated and non-pedunculated, supposed to represent different stages in the formation of a lymphoid corpuscle. These tracts and nodules are found most frequently in the neighborhood of the blood-vessels and trabeculæ. In young animals they are much less numerous and more isolated than in adults, where they have become fused into extensive tracts in consequence of the growth and division

of the branched cells. Ranvier has described similar structures under the name "*taches laiteuses.*"

Development of fat-tissue.—Their relation to the development of fat-cells is of extreme interest. If we accept the views
of Klein and Flemming, the branched cells are converted into
fat-cells, and the former observer has pointed out that, by following up a perilymphangeal tract into a vascularized fat-tract,
we may find all stages of conversion into fat-tissue. The fat-
tracts are found in the same location as the perilymphangeal
tracts, that is, along the larger blood-vessels, and the greater
the number of the former the less there are of the latter. The
conversion of branched cells into fat-cells varies in different
animals, and in different membranes of the same animal, and
under different conditions of nutrition. The formation of lymphoid corpuscles, supposed to go on from the branched cells,
must cease, necessarily, when they become converted into fat-
cells, and it is found that they are, in fact, present in less numbers when the latter process is going on. Let us consider the
relations of these branched cells to the lymphatics. The larger
blood-vessels are usually accompanied by a lymphatic on each
side, which gives off branches at irregular intervals, finally
breaking up into a capillary plexus, which may ensheath the
accompanying blood-vessels, or even enclose a blood-capillary
plexus. When the latter exists in a perilymphangeal nodule,
the lymphatic capillary may apparently communicate directly
with the lacunæ and canaliculi, the endothelial cells composing the capillary being continuous with those which invest the
spaces, and covering externally, it may be, the blood-capillary
as well (Klein, Delafield).

Course and termination of the lymphatic radicles.—In
tracing the lymphatic capillaries we find that they run in every
direction, branching irregularly, and vary in calibre and number in different parts. It is very difficult to trace one of them
to a positive termination. The interstices of the connective-
tissue fasciculi in brushed silver preparations sometimes present an irregular shape, as if they were enclosed by irregular
cells. This appears to me to be often due to the convolutions
of the fasciculi, made more irregular, perhaps, by a cement
substance, or an interfascicular substance, either fluid or semifluid, which has been coagulated by the processes following
death, and by the action of our reagents. The irregular action

of silver, which produces so many doubtful pictures, may aid in producing this appearance. The extreme mobility necessary in some forms of connective tissue demands extreme flexibility as a quality of its elements, thus facilitating great variation in structural arrangement under different conditions.

Artificial injection of the lymphatics.—If we inject this tissue, by puncture with a hypodermic syringe, we can fill the lymphatic vessels and also the interstices, so that they are continuous; but the question whether this is a natural or an artificial transition is one about which histologists still differ. Theoretically, we may consider that such communications exist to some extent, at least when greatly increased vascular tension takes place. But, at the same time, many, or even most of the interstices may be closed spaces.

FIG. 75.—From mesentery of cat; silver-stained right portion denuded of endothelium, showing, A. branched cells, with B, intervening spaces; left portion, endothelial layer preserved; C, pseudo-stomata; D, nuclei; E, elastic fibres.

It is not a matter of great consequence, physiologically speaking, since not only fluids but lymphoid corpuscles can penetrate partitions which fail to resist so slight an injecting force as is sufficient to unite these spaces and the lymphatic capillaries.[1] The fact that injections can be made without forming a communication (Frey) does not prove that the latter does not exist; it may be due to an imperfect injection. As we shall see later, the wandering propensities of the lymphoid corpuscles would almost exclude the possibility of the connective-tissue interstices remaining closed spaces everywhere.

Endothelium and stomata.—We have already referred to

[1] Thoma and Arnold have shown that injections into the veins, in a living animal, of insoluble coloring matters (not distending the vessels, however), pass between the endothelial cells and find their way into the clefts and channels of the deeper tissues. The possibility of absorption taking place through the intercellular substance which, after all, may only be a semifluid material filling a space which varies in size under different conditions, throws light on many of the difficult problems of absorption, secretion, and excretion, and numerous pathological processes.

Recklinghausen's observation, that communication exists between the abdominal and pleural cavities by means of small openings in the central tendon of the diaphragm. By injecting some insoluble coloring matter, held by fluid in suspension, into the abdominal cavity, he obtained a fine injection of the lymphatics of the central tendon, and was able to detect the substance on its pleural surface. The experiment may be reversed by injecting the pleural cavity. He was able to see the actual passage of milk-globules into these openings by removing a portion of the fresh tendon upon a cork ring, its pleural surface upward, placing a drop of milk upon it, and observing with the microscope the nearly round openings, large enough to admit at once two or three of the milk-globules which ran toward these openings in little eddies, and disappeared below. He stained this membrane with nitrate of silver, and found that the openings corresponded to perforations between the endothelial cells leading perpendicularly or obliquely to the lymphatics. Schweigger-Seidel and Doigiel observed similar openings leading from the abdominal cavity, through the retroperitoneal membrane, into the *cysternæ lymphaticæ magnæ* of the frog. Dybkowsky showed that colored fluids placed in the pleural cavity were absorbed by the lymphatics of the intercostal pleura. Schweigger-Seidel, Doigiel, and Ludwig confirmed the observations of Recklinghausen in connection with the central tendon of the diaphragm, and it is now generally admitted that such openings exist, not always freely open, however, but sometimes with a valve-like cleft. It must not be understood that the small bead-like spots and the dark spots between the cells are true stomata. It is not definitely known, in fact, what they really represent. Oedmannson first described them, not only on the serous membranes, but also on the endothelial layer of the chyle-vessels. They are very numerous directly over the lymph-vessels of the central tendon on its peritoneal surface (Dybkowsky).

Ranvier's views on false stomata.—Ranvier has an ingeneous theory explaining the formation of these objects, which have been termed *false stomata*, also of the true stomata and the fenestra of the omentum. He considers that the lymphoid corpuscles, which are always to be found in serous cavities, penetrate the membrane, making a depression or perforation, sometimes remaining, sometimes escaping again. In the majority of cases the black spots are formed by the albuminous serum which these openings retain by capillary attraction, having been coagulated and stained by the nitrate of silver, producing a plug. In other cases, a globular cell resembling a lymphoid corpuscle occupies the stoma, surrounded by a black margin due to the action of the silver. Other cells have a greater resemblance to small endothelial cells than to lymphoid corpuscles. The irregularity of their distribution in different membranes, in different animals, and at different ages, seems to favor the idea of such an accidental manner of formation.

Klein on true and false stomata.—Klein divides the *stomata vera*, or true stomata, into two classes: *a*, those which form the mouth of a vertical lymphatic channel leading to a superficial vessel (they have a special endothelial lining); and *b*, those formed by discontinuity between the endothelium of the surface leading into a simple lymphatic sinus near the surface, and lined only on the lower surface with endothelium. *Pseudo-stomata*, or false stomata, may be produced, according to this observer, by the prolongations of the sub-endothelial branched cells becoming free by projection outward between the endothelial cells.

Fig. 76.—Frond of fern (Osmunda Claytoniana), under-surface showing stomata.

In pathological conditions he has seen an extensive cell-proliferation going on from one of these projecting pseudo-stomata. Ranvier accounts for the origin of the fenestra of the omentum in a similar manner, as for the stomata. It is of interest to know that the openings do not exist before birth, but increase in size and number as age advances. Klein, on the other hand, considers that the openings in the omentum are produced by a process of vacuolation. The arrangement of the connective-tissue fasciculi around these openings is not that of complete rings, but is such that each opening is bordered by several fibres which take part in the formation of other openings in consequence of the irregularity in their arrangement. The endothelial cells may form a complete tube in some of the narrow trabeculæ, in which a single cell may complete the circumference. Klein states that when these openings take place, the connective-tissue cells previously situated between the connective-tissue bundles, come to lie on the lateral surface which is now free. This, he thinks, establishes the fact that the latter may be converted into true endothelial cells. Delafield, in considering the question of the re-formation of the endothelium on serous membranes, after hydrothorax, remarks that it would seem to be reproduced from the old endothelium, or from migrating white

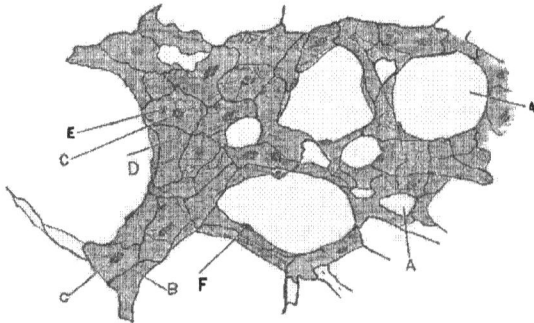

FIG. 77.—From silver-stained omentum of cat: A, fenestra; B, intercellular lines of upper surface; C, nuclei of same; D, intercellular lines of lower surface; E, nuclei of same; F, nuclei in wall of opening: corresponding cell-forms, part of upper and part of lower surface.

blood-cells, or from sub-endothelial connective-tissue cells, although he has not seen sufficient proof to establish any of these theories.

The nerves of the peritoneum have been studied by Cyon. They enter the mesentery with the blood-vessels as fasciculi of medullated nerve-fibres, and, dividing laterally, lose their medullary sheath and form a plexus, the fibres of which show projecting nuclei at various points. The walls of the arteries receive a rich supply of these fibres. A lymph-space, surrounding the fibres, can sometimes be demonstrated.

Intimate structure of lymphatic vessels.—A lymphatic vessel may be considered as a serous membrane with only one free surface, rolled in the form of a tube, its endothelial layer forming the intima, resting upon an elastic reticulum, and an adventitia or external envelope of connective-tissue fasciculi, as in the serous membranes. In the finest capillaries only the endothelial layer is independent, although they lie surrounded by elastic fibres and connective-tissue fasciculi. In the larger trunks, smooth muscular elements form a middle layer. The endothelial cells of the lymphatics have a more sinuous outline than the spindle-shaped cells of the blood-capillaries ; they are often irregularly dentated like the cranial sutures. The calibre of the lymphatics is also much more irregular than that of blood-vessels. As they increase in size, the tissues external to the endothelium assume more and more the character of ves-

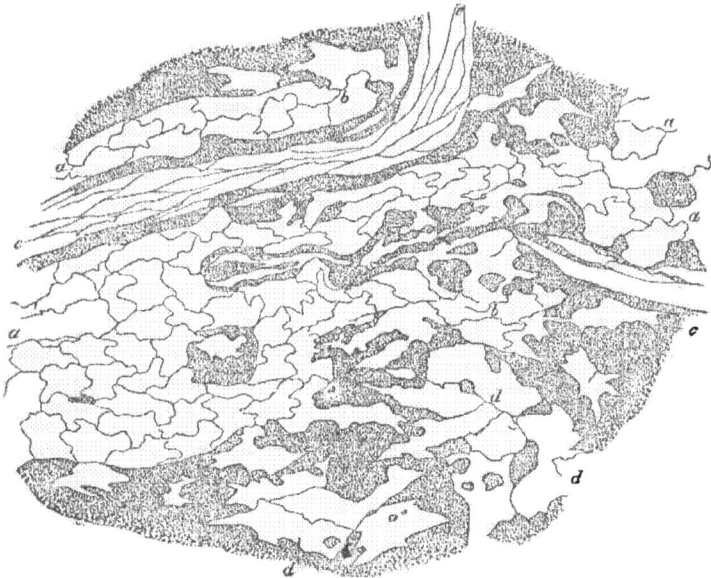

FIG. 78.—Central tendon of the rabbit, treated with solution of nitrate of silver, the most superficial serous layer immediately adjoining the pericardium being shown : *a*, lymphatic capillaries ; *b*, their origin ; *c*, serous canals with communications ; *d*, serous canals equal in width to the origin of the lymphatic vessels ; *e*, blood-vessel with epithelial cells. Magnified 300 diameters. Recklinghausen.

sels with independent walls ; they finally resemble the veins in the largest trunks, except that they possess more muscular tissue than the latter.

The diameter of the lymphatic capillaries is very variable ; they are generally larger than the blood-capillaries, ranging from 0.013—0.045 mm. (Frey). Branches of 0.2256—.2609 mm. may possess three layers (Kölliker). The vessels are richly supplied with valves, which are formed from the intima.

Variations in shape.—Here let us consider an important characteristic of the lymphatic system, viz., its irregularity.

In this respect it contrasts very decidedly with the blood-vascular system. In the calibre of its vessels in different regions, in different parts of the same organ, and even in different parts of the same vessel, it is extremely irregular. A vessel of small calibre may suddenly expand into a saccular shape, which may have its diverticula or branches, or may form a chain of lacunæ. It is true that these dilatations are formed just in front and behind the valves quite regularly, but they are also found everywhere, being, in fact, a characteristic of these vessels.

Topographical peculiarities.—Nor is a uniform direction to be observed in the distribution of these vessels, for while they usually accompany arteries, lying outside the accompanying veins, they frequently take strange courses. A lymphatic may suddenly leave its companions to strike across a comparatively non-vascular field of tissue to share its fortunes with another set of blood-vessels. Respecting the capillary lymphatics, their place seems to be the middle ground between the blood-capillaries, just where we would expect to find this drainage system.[1] They lie deeper in the skin and mucous membrane than the blood-vessels (Recklinghausen). The dispute concerning the question as to whether the smaller lymphatics have a distinct wall or are simple spaces, probably has been largely due to the variation in the structure of the lymphatics in the same tissue or organ in different animals, or in the same animal at different ages.

The *thoracic duct*, which represents the other extreme in the structure of lymphatic passages, has an endothelial layer supported by a reticulum of elastic fibres, which mingles with the next layer, consisting of smooth muscular elements running in every direction, the transverse elements predominating. The adventitia of connective-tissue fasciculi and elastic fibres completes its coats. The muscular layer in man is highly developed compared with quadrupeds (Ranvier).

---

[1] On the external ear of a rat whose blood-vessels are injected with colored gelatine, and whose lymphatic vessels are rendered visible by silver, the larger centrifugal lymph-vessels are seen, even with low powers, to be surrounded by a network of blood-capillaries. The same has been demonstrated in the mesentery, the diaphragm, and the posterior extremities.—Ueber ein die Lymphgefasse um-spinnendes Netz von Blutcapillaren, von Alex. Dogiel. Arch. f. mikroskop.- Anat. Bd. 17 3. Heft, S. 335-340.

The subarachnoid and subdural lymph-spaces and their prolongations.—Axel Key and Retzius have shown that besides the great subarachnoid and subdural lymph-spaces of the brain and spinal cord, connecting with them are spaces enclosing the nerve-fibres of the cord, and, what is still more remarkable, extending outward on the peripheral nerves. The nerves of special sense, the olfactory, the optic, and the auditory, form no exception to this rule. Even the ganglia of the sympathetic system and their fibres have similar spaces, which are in connection with the cord. Nor is this the end of the intricate labyrinth. Each nerve-fibre has a space immediately outside of the sheath of Schwann, between the latter and the so-called fibrillary sheath, through which it communicates with the perineural sheath-space, and through the latter with the lymph-spaces of the central nervous system. That they are true lymphatic spaces is shown by the fact that they are lined by a layer of endothelial cells. Obersteiner demonstrated by injections that the nerve-cells also possess pericellular spaces connected with those of the corresponding fibres, a fact which I can corroborate. Key and Retzius say that this whole lymphatic system is nowhere in direct communication with the ordinary lymphatic system, and that they have never seen the latter injected through the former, except when extravasation occurred. Bogras was the first (1825) to inject the nerves. He used quicksilver, and succeeded in injecting the peripheral nerves up to the ganglia, and made injections from the dura down to the ganglia. He failed with the olfactory, optic, and acoustic. Cruveilhier, and later, Robin, confirmed the fact that such injections are possible. Robin, in 1858, and afterward, His, in 1863, demonstrated the perivascular lymph-spaces of the central nervous system.

Lymphatics of tendons.—Axel Key and Retzius, and also Hertzog, have shown that the tendons possess spaces which may be injected. From the spaces formed by the endotenium and the peritenium, which communicate, connections exist with the deep and superficial lymphatics of the tendon.

The development of the lymphatics is by a process of budding and vacuolation similar to that which takes place in the blood-vessels.

Lymphatic glands.—We now pass to the consideration of the lymphatic bodies called *glands*, *ganglia*, or *nodes*. Their distribution does not concern us here ; it is sufficient to say that they are very variable in size and number in different regions, being supplied to nearly all the lymphatic trunks, with which they are connected by the so-called *afferent* and *efferent branches*. The former usually consist of several small branches ; the latter generally enter as single large trunks.

The shape of the lymph-nodes may be spherical, oval, oblong, or reniform. In the latter, which is by far the most frequent form, the afferent vessels penetrate the capsule on the convex surface, while the efferent branch escapes at the hilus. In the other forms it is difficult to determine which are the afferent and which the efferent vessels. A lymph-node consists essentially of spheroidal and cylindrical masses of reticular tissue, containing lymphoid corpuscles, richly supplied by a blood-capillary system, and sustained in place by a framework of connective tissue, with elastic and sometimes muscular elements, forming a network around the masses for the circulation of lymph, and expanding externally to form a capsule. The gland is usually divided by histologists into a cortical and a medullary portion, the former being simply that part in which the lymphoid masses assume a spheroidal form (the *follicles*), this being the more peripheral portion of the node, or the part farthest from the hilus, when that exists. The *medullary subdivision* represents the remaining portion, and its lymphoid material is in the form of cylindrical or cord-like prolongations from the follicles. The capsule is composed of connective tissue, the fibres of which run in different directions in its external layers, possessing elastic fibres, flat cells, and a slight amount of fat-tissue. The lymphatics of the capsule are found mostly in its outer layers. The inner layers present a more stratified appearance on account of the regularity of their bundles and the interposed connective-tissue cells. An elastic network and smooth muscular elements are found here, and also in the septa, and are developed in some animals to a high degree. It is from the inner layers of the capsule that the septa are given off to form the framework of the node. These consist primarily of trabeculæ, which, passing between the follicles, converge toward the medullary portion, where they interlace with the lymphoid cords of the latter, and may again unite at the hilus (*stroma* of His). They have a structure similar to that found in the portion of the capsule from which they have

their origin. These septa are not complete partitions, but constitute an open framework, which, in consequence of its radiating
arrangement, produces wider spaces in the cortical than in the
medullary portion. To this the follicles correspond by being
broadest at their peripheral portions. It must not be understood that the lymphoid masses, either follicular or cylindrical, are closely embraced by the septa ; they are separated from
the latter, and from the sheath as well, by spaces, the "*investing spaces of the follicular portion*" (Frey), or *sinuses of the*

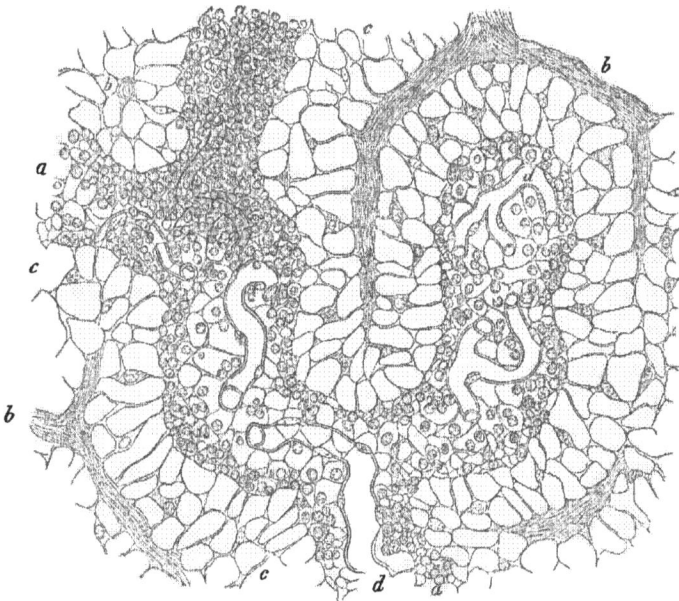

FIG. 79.—Section of the medullary substance of a lymphatic gland from the ox: *a*, follicular cord ; *b*,
trabeculæ ; *c*, path pursued by the lymph ; *d*, blood-vessels. Magnified 300 diameters. Recklinghausen.

cortical substance (Ranvier), and the lymph-passages (Frey)
or *cavernous plexus* (Ranvier) of the medullary portion. These
spaces are maintained by a network of fine fibres (*tenter-fibres*
of Frey) derived from the septa, being given off at nearly right
angles to the latter. The bundles of fibres composing them
divide and reunite, forming meshes, and extend to the follicles
and cords. In reality, they do not end here, but are continued
to form the reticular tissue of these bodies by dividing into a
still finer network, which differs in the different portions only

by slight variations in the size of the meshes and the fineness of
the fibres, the meshes being longer and narrower in the peripheral portions of the follicles and in the cords than in the
central part of the former. This sort of tissue has received
different names : *cytogenous tissue* (Kölliker), *adenoid tissue*
(His), *reticular tissue* (Frey, Ranvier). It is, as the latter name
implies, a network, the fibres of which run in every direction,
being applied to one another in the same manner as the fibres
of the omentum already described. The nuclei, which are
more oval and larger than the lymphoid corpuscles, appear at
the junction of fibres, simply rest upon them, and can be removed by brushing. They are endothelial cells, and in silver-
stained preparations an endothelial layer can be seen to cover
the septa, the reticulum of the lymph-passages, and the follicles in the same manner that the fine bundles of the omentum
are covered ; that is, the spaces between the bundles are nowhere covered, but each bundle is wrapped by these cells.
This can only be seen after the lymphoid corpuscles that occupy
the meshes have been removed by brushing. The endothelial
layer is continuous with that of the afferent and efferent lymphatic vessels, which communicate with the lymph-spaces of
the node, as shown by injections.

    According to Klein, the clinical nature of reticular tissue
does not correspond to connective tissue proper or to elastic
tissue. Filling the meshes of the follicular and cylindrical
portions of the lymphoid masses are the *lymphoid corpuscles*,
two or more in each mesh. Lymphoid corpuscles are also
found in the investing or lymph-spaces, but they are easily
brushed out, while a much longer brushing is required to detach them from the other portions. The corpuscles are somewhat larger than the colorless blood-corpuscles, though variable in size. They possess a single prominent nucleus, which
is readily stained by most coloring matters. The amount of
protoplasm they possess is small. When examined in a moist
chamber at a temperature of 36° to 37° C., some of them exhibit amœboid movements, the small ones having the least
protoplasm around their nuclei being most active (Ranvier).
Klein states that corpuscles are to be found which are larger
than the others, having more protoplasm, and often two nuclei.
He considers them in a more advanced stage of development
than the others.

The *arteries* and *veins* of the lymphatic nodes have their chief entrance at the hilus, with the efferent lymphatic vessels. The main trunks divide to pass into the septa. Still finer divisions pass into the reticular tissue, forming a rich capillary network in the follicles and cylinders, most marked at the surface of these bodies. In the cylinders a single axial arterial branch, surrounded by a peripheral capillary system, may furnish the supply. Another source of blood-supply may be from the capsule ; small branches, both arterial and venous, which ramify in its layers, send finer branches inward, encircling the follicles and traversing the septa and reticulum of the lymph-spaces. The capillaries possess, besides their proper wall, a sheath derived from the reticulum.

Nerves of the lymphatic nodes.—Little is known on this point. Nerve-fibres enter with the blood-vessels in some of the larger glands of man (Kölliker), and non-medullated nerve-fibres have been seen in the lymphatic nodes of the ox. Concerning the lymphatics, they exist, as we have seen, in the outer layers of the capsule, and do not differ from those in other regions, forming a network in the capsule. They are continuous externally with the afferent lymphatics, and internally with the lymph-spaces already described.

The numerous lymphoid organs are all constructed upon a plan similar to that of the nodes, in that they all represent modifications in the arrangement of reticular tissue and its vascular supply.

Injection of a lymphatic gland.—We may obtain an injection of the lymph-passages in the node by puncturing the capsule with an ordinary hypodermic syringe (a method for which we are indebted to Hyrtl), and injecting a mixture of Prussian blue and gelatine (soluble blue, 25, solid gelatine, 1). It is best to inject one of a series of connected nodes, in place, exposing them by dissection in a freshly killed animal. One gland is then injected from the other through the afferent and efferent vessels (Ranvier). They are excised and hardened in Müller's fluid or alcohol ; sections are then made with a microtome, after which they may be washed in water, stained for a few minutes in picro-carminate of ammonia (1 per cent.), again washed, and then mounted in glycerine or Canada balsam.

Method of studying the gland substance.—For the purpose of demonstrating the reticulum of the lymph-spaces and the lymphoid masses, the node must be hardened in alcohol, bichromate of potassa, or (Ranvier's method) placed for twenty-four hours in a concentrated solution of picric acid ; sections are then to be made, after which they are gently brushed and agitated in water with a camel's-hair brush to disengage the lymphoid corpuscles (we are indebted to His for the method of brushing). After staining, preferably with hematoxylin, which exhibits, in a beautiful manner, the lymphoid corpuscles and the darker nuclei of the endothelial layer, they may be mounted in the usual manner.

Ranvier's plan.—The plan particularly recommended by Ranvier is as follows : the node remains for twenty-four hours in a mixture of alcohol (36° Cartier), one part, water, two parts ; then for twenty-four hours in a syrupy solution of gum-arabic, and is afterward hardened in alcohol sufficiently for section cutting in a microtome. Floating them in a shallow, flat dish, in water two or three centimetres deep, the gum is dissolved, and the brush used in a very delicate manner ; the sections may then be stained and mounted, as described above. The degree of hardness, and the force and duration of the brushing process, will determine the result, which practice only will make perfect. The lymphoid corpuscles in the lymph-passages, that is to say, in the parts which fill with the blue injection fluid, as previously described, are first removed, and additional brushing, when the proper degree of hardening has been attained, will enable one to remove these bodies from the follicles and cords, and also to remove the endothelial cells which rest upon the fibres of the reticulum and septa.

Other methods of injecting glands.—A node removed immediately after death and injected by puncture with a 1 per cent. solution of hyperosmic acid, then placed in water for one or two hours, and afterward hardened in alcohol, cut in sections, colored by picrocarminate of ammonia, and mounted, gives good results.

The best method for showing the endothelial layer is by interstitial injection (puncture) with a solution of nitrate of silver, 1—300 ; harden afterward by freezing, and make sections.

Before closing this chapter, let us take a retrospective view of our subject. In doing so, it is almost impossible to avoid associating the connective-tissue cell with other forms which seem to be its antecedents, modifications, or derivatives, viz., the extensive system of branched corpuscles in the matrix of the serous membranes, whose growth and proliferation form large tracts when they possess a sufficient blood-supply, and between which the lymph circulates, affording a channel of escape for the discharged bits of protoplasm, their offspring ; the throwing off of similar bits of protoplasm by the surface endothelium of the serous membranes ; the probable transformation of the branched cells into fat-cells, and the conversion of a branched connective-tissue cell into an endothelial cell, when it reaches a free surface. Again, the fact that similar endothelial cells line the blood and lymph channels, and also cover the reticulum of the lymphatic nodes and follicles, and that in the latter forms, when we have also a rich capillary blood-supply— that is, a supply of oxygen—the accumulation and probable elaboration, if not proliferation, of lymphoid corpuscles goes on in a more extensive manner than in the lymphangeal tracts ; taken together, all point to the idea that they are different forms of protoplasm which have been converted, or are convertible, one into the other under proper conditions of temperature, food-supply, and excitability, the definite limitations of which are but imperfectly known.

In the germinating tracts, superficial and deep, of the serous membranes, in the lymphatic nodes and follicles of the alimentary canal, and also in the lymphoid organs (spleen, tonsils, etc.), we have active forms, reproduction by budding, and division. The formation of the lymphoid corpuscles, which may be considered as so many amœbæ sporting in a nutritious fluid, and engorging themselves with that which is brought to them by the agency of the absorbents and lymph-channels, under conditions favorable to great activity, free to penetrate most of the tissues, and, perhaps, become fixed forms. These processes of activity, when confined to the limits of the organs mentioned, are conducive to life and growth, but occurring in the allied forms that have become fixed, as the corneal branched cells, the connective-tissue cells, or the endothelial cells, to any considerable extent, inaugurate the processes of disease and death. Thus these comparatively indefinite and undifferentiated forms of protoplasm may be said to be keys to life and death.

BIBLIOGRAPHY.

Authors referred to in the text:

BICHAT. Anat. gén. Second edition. 1812.
IBID. Traité des membranes. 1816.
REMAK. Müller's Archiv. 1850.
BRÜCKE. Ueber die Chylusgefässe, etc. Sitzb. der Wiener Akad. 1853.
LEYDIG. Lehrbuch d. Histologie, etc. 1857.
VIRCHOW. Cellular Pathology. 1860.
OEDMANNSON. Virchow's Archiv. Bd. 26. 1863.
CHRZONSZCZEWSKY. Virchow's Archiv. Bd. 31. 1864.
HIS. Archiv f. mikrosk. Anat. Bd. I. 1865.
SCHWEIGGER-SEIDEL and DOIGIEL. Arbeit. a. d. phys. Lab. z. Leipzig. 1866.
KÖLLIKER. Handbuch der Gewebelehre. 1867.
CYON. Arbeit. a. d. Phys. Anstalt. in Leipsig. 1868.
ROBIN. Dict. Ency. Sc. Med. 1870.
RECKLINGHAUSEN. The Lymphatic System. Stricker's Histology. 1872.
KLEIN. The Lymphatic System. 1873.
DYBKOWSKY. Arbeit. a. d. Phys. Anstalt. in Leipsig.
ARNOLD, J. Archiv f. path. Anat. Bd. 58, p. 203. 1873.
THIN. Proc. Royal Soc. Vol. 22. 1874.
THOMA. Centralbl. f. d. med. Wiss. 1875. Archiv f. path. Anat. Bd. 64. 1875.
KEY, AXEL, and RETZIUS. Archiv f. mikrosk. Anat. Bd. IX. 1875. (Abstract of large work on the nervous system.)
HERTZOG. Zeitschr. f. Anat. und Entwick. 1875.
RANVIER. Traité technique d'histologie. 1877 et seq.
DELAFIELD. Path. Studies. New York, 1878—80.
FREY. The Microscope, etc. New York, 1880.

Among the more recent authors that have written on this subject are :
HOGGAN. Proc. Royal Soc. 1876—77. (Two articles.)
LEWIS. Proc. Roy. Society. 1877.
ROBIN and CADIAT. Journ. de l'anat. et de la phys. 1876. No. 6.
BUDGE. Arch. f. mikrosk. Anat. Bd. X. 1876.
RIEDEL. Archiv f. mikrosk. Anat. Bd. XI. 1877.
WITTICH. Mittheil. a. d. k. phys. Lab. 1878.
MIERZYEWSKI. Jour. de l'anat. et de la phys. Paris, 1879.
RENAUT. Comptes rendus Acad. des Sci. Paris, 1879.
WEBER-LIEL. Arch. f. path. Anat. Bd. LXXVII. 1879.
FISCHER. Arch. f. mikr. Anat. XVII. 1879-80.
SITNA. Wien. med. Presse. XXI. 1879.

CHAPTER XIII.

THE LIVER AND BILIARY APPARATUS.

By DR. ABRAHAM MAYER,

Late Curator of the Manhattan Eye and Ear Hospital, New York City, etc.

THE liver is enclosed in a connective-tissue capsule, the peritoneum, which also gives off secondary folds, or duplicatures, called ligaments, by which the organ is held in proper connection with the adjacent parts. The thickness of the capsule is about 0.03 mm., and its free surface is covered with the flattened corpuscles that belong to serous membranes generally. This connective-tissue covering is furthermore composed of thin laminæ, which contain a large number of elastic fibres. At the transverse fissure, where it is continued into the interior of the organ, the same character is maintained. Here it encircles vessels, ducts, and nerves, forming the so-called Glisson's capsule, which, indeed, with its minute ramifications, traverses the whole interior of the gland. The liver contains, in addition to the glandular substance, blood-vessels, lymphatics, nerves, and gland-ducts, the whole held together by the framework of connective tissue just mentioned, which in the human species is but imperfectly developed.

The hepatic lobules.—The glandular parenchyma consists of the so-called hepatic lobules, which in the human liver are not completely separated from one another, for the reason just named. In some of the lower animals, however, this separation is more perfect. In the hog's liver, for example, the septa are so well developed that the lobules are plainly recognizable by the naked eye.

To isolate the human lobules is a matter of some difficulty ; but it can be accomplished by macerating the organ in water from twelve to twenty-four hours.

These lobules are also known as the *hepatic acini*, or *in-*

sulæ of the liver. Their form is irregularly polyhedral, and they usually measure about 4×1 mm. At their bases they are attached to short twigs of the hepatic vein, which have a thickness of from 0.03—0.06 mm., and traverse the lobules in the axes of their long diameters. As the hepatic vein ascends through the lobule, it gives off innumerable capillary branches, almost at right angles to its course. The latter pursue their way to the periphery of the lobule, and hence have a radial direction. These capillaries further subdivide within the lobules, and are united to each other by transverse branches, forming a network with small meshes. At the periphery the capillaries join the ramifications of the portal vein. The latter divides within the liver into numerous branches, which again subdivide at the surfaces of the lobules. Their ultimate ramifications form the boundary lines between adjoining hepatic lobules, and it is for this reason that they have been called *interlobular veins.*[1] For a similar reason the branches of the hepatic vein, which traverse the centres of the lobules, have been called *intralobular*[1] or *central veins*[2] (Fig. 80).

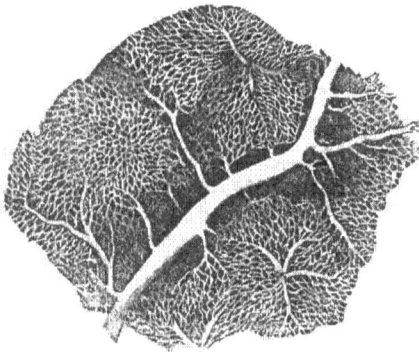

FIG. 80.—Injected liver of rabbit, showing branches to portal vein, capillaries, and the hepatic veins in the centres of two lobules. Frey.

The interlobular veins are contained within *interlobular* or *intermediate* (Hering) *canals ;* these are easily demonstrable in the hog's liver. In this animal the adjoining edges of three or four hepatic lobules combine to form a canal which contains the interlobular vessels. The latter are surrounded by connective tissue, which is continuous with that of the septa between the lobules. In the human liver there is a similar arrangement, but in it the septa of connective tissue do not completely separate the lobules, and, excepting at the inter-

[1] Kiernan : Philosoph. Trans., 1833.
[2] Venæ Centrales, Krugenberg, Müller's Archiv, 1843.

lobular canals, the parenchyma of contiguous lobules appears to coalesce.

Nevertheless, the substance of the human liver can be divíded into distinct lobules, and the terminal branches of the portal veins may be regarded as their natural boundaries (Figs. 80 and 87). Starting with the portal veins, therefore, the course of the blood is as follows : portal veins, interlobular veins, capillaries, intralobular veins, hepatic veins, and inferior vena cava.

Sublobular veins, according to Kiernan, are such branches of the hepatic vein as are placed under the bases of several lobules, and collect the blood from their central veins.

The liver may be injected either through the portal or hepatic veins, or through both. Good specimens may be obtained by injecting the fresh liver of a dog or rabbit with carmine - gelatine through the portal vein, then injecting fluid Berlin blue into the hepatic vein, and afterward hardening the organ in alcohol. The central vein and adjacent capillaries will thus be filled with a blue mass, while the interlobular and portal veins, with the peripheral capillaries, will contain the transparent red mass.

The color of the cut surface of the liver in its natural condition is of a uniform reddish brown tint, and its lobular structure is not readily made out. Usually, however, we find two shades or gradations in color ; one, corresponding to the central veins of the lobules, is of a dark red ; the other, corresponding to the periphery of the lobules, is a lighter and yellowish red.

Occasionally these conditions are found to be reversed, and the difference of color is due to the fact that after death the central and other hepatic veins are filled with blood, while the portal and its branches are empty ; and also because

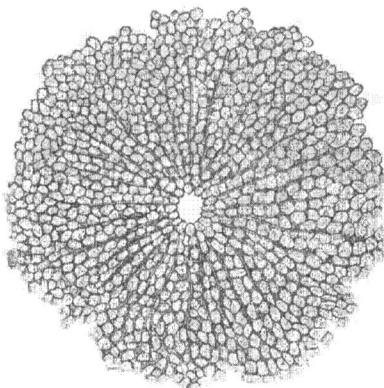

FIG. 81.—Transverse section of a human lobule, showing opening for central vein. Ecker.

the deposit of bile-pigment takes place at the centres of the lobules about the intralobular veins ; whereas a fatty infiltration, such as may occur in normal livers, takes place at the periphery. Not uncommonly the yellowish red color at the boundary of the lobules exists under the form of delicate markings, which are nothing more than the empty interlobular branches of the portal vein.

Kiernan occasionally observed in young subjects that the portal vein was distended with blood, while the hepatic vein was empty. In such cases the periphery of the lobules was of a darker color than their centres.

The blood-vessels of the liver.—These have been partly described above. The hepatic artery, and duct, and portal vein enter the liver at the transverse fissure, enclosed within Glisson's capsule, and continuously subdivide as they push their way through the parenchyma. The subdivisions of the portal vein never anastomose, but are distributed around the surfaces of the lobules, forming their boundaries. At the periphery they break up into capillaries which enter the lobules. These are about 0.02 mm. in diameter, and form a network, the meshes of which are scarcely wider than capillaries. Within the lobule the capillaries unite to form the central vein, and these then empty into branches of the hepatic vein. The subdivisions of the hepatic vein are also devoid of anastomoses, but after traversing the posterior portion of the liver in canals (which they embrace closely), unite to form the hepatic vein. A peculiarity of this latter vein is the fact that its larger branches give off successively small lateral twigs, which enter the bases of the neighboring lobules, so that after dividing such a branch lengthwise it would seem to be pierced by small circular openings, which are the orifices of the lateral branches.

Not unfrequently a central (hepatic) vein will divide into two branches within a lobule, in which case the latter seems to possess two apices, which become joined together as we approach its base. The connection between the portal and hepatic veins takes place only through their capillaries.

The *hepatic artery* is comparatively small. It enters the liver together with the duct and portal vein, and at once breaks up into branches, which, anastomosing with each other, form a large-meshed network. The arterial branches are distributed to the vessels mentioned, which they enclose, and also to the connective tissue which surrounds the latter. The hepatic arte-ry also gives off nutrient branches which supply its own walls, and small twigs, which, piercing the substance of the liver between the lobules, supply the branches of the hepatic vein. The ultimate branches of the artery are contained within the interlobular canals, and break up into capillaries at the periphery of the lobules, which they traverse for a short distance to form a distinct network. There is no communication between the intralobular capillaries of the hepatic artery and those of the portal vein. The former seem destined to supply the adjacent vessels, and probably the small amount of intralobular connective tissue to be spoken of hereafter.

It has been thought by some (Chronszewski, Rindfleisch, and others) that the capillaries of the hepatic artery end midway between the interlobular and central veins, within the lobule. Beale and Kiernan have noticed that an arterial branch here and there enters a lobule; while Theile, Davis, and others describe a capillary network about the periphery of the lobules.

Finally, branches of 0.05 to 0.1 mm. in diameter are distributed to the capsule of the liver, where they break up into capillaries, radiating in all directions and anastomosing with each other to form a large-meshed network, which communicates with the capillaries of the phrenic, mammary, and suprarenal arteries. This plexus empties into small twigs, the so-called inner roots of the portal vein.

The capillaries of the liver may be injected either through the hepatic or portal vein, or both, as before stated. For injecting the hepatic artery the author prefers his cold solution of carmine-glycerine.[1] The gland to be injected must be as fresh as possible. If, for example, a dog be selected for this purpose, the abdomen should be opened and the animal allowed to bleed to death by section of the vena cava. Now introduce into the hepatic artery the canula of a syringe filled with the carmine-glycerine, secure it in place and inject. Harden the organ in alcohol, cut sections, and mount in balsam. The liver will not be uniformly injected, and only those portions can be utilized in which the injected mass seems to be widely diffused.

If, in addition to the artery, the hepatic vein be injected with a blue colored mass, beautiful results may be obtained. Sections in which the lobules are cut transversely show the

---

[1] See chapter on the Kidney.

central veins occupying the position of the axes of the lobules and the capillaries, pursuing a radial course and anastomosing with each other by transverse communications.

Since the capillaries successively divide from the centre toward the periphery, it follows that they are much less numerous at the former than at the latter point. A section through the long axis of an acinus will show that the central vein is divided lengthwise, and that the capillaries are given off from it almost at right angles to its course.

Nearer the summit of the lobule, however, the central vein is seen to break up into diverging capillaries. If the section has been made to one side of the central vein, but yet parallel with its axis, many capillaries will be cut across, more or less transversely, and will then appear as small, circular, or oval rings.

The connective tissue of the liver.—Glisson's capsule is formed of longitudinal bundles of connective tissue which are loosely interwoven. It serves to bind together the hepatic artery, portal vein, and hepatic duct, and also fills out the small spaces left between the ramifications of these vessels (Fig. 82). Sections from a liver hardened in chromic acid or alcohol, and immersed in a dilute solution of caustic potassa, or simply pencilled, show the connective tissue well. About the hepatic vein it is thin and dense, and firmly united to the glandular structure, so that when cut transversely these vessels appear to gape. In the camel the connective tissue is greatly developed,[1] even more so than in the hog. The interlobular septa are very dense and fibrillated ; in the interior of the lobule the connective tissue has a lamellar structure.

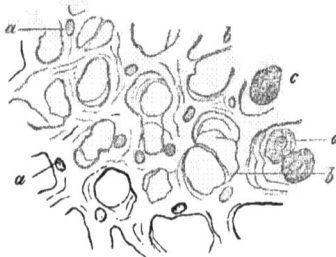

FIG. 82.—Connective tissue of a child's liver, after hardening in alcohol and pencilling : *a, a,* capillary vessels containing a few blood-globules ; *b. b,* connective-tissue fibrils ; *c, c,* liver cells not removed by pencilling. Frey.

According to Ewald and Kuehne, minute bundles of fibrous tissue extend beyond this interlobular connective tissue, and piercing the lobules eventually surround the central veins.

[1] Turner, Wm., Journal of Anat. and Phys., Vol. XI., p. 2.

The liver-cells.—The liver-cells are found lying within the meshes of the capillary network of the lobules. If we bear in mind the shape of the intralobular capillary reticulum, the arrangement of the hepatic cells will be readily understood. The meshes of the capillary network have about the same diameter as the capillaries themselves. Hence it follows that the cells which occupy these meshes must also have the appearance of a reticulum. But inasmuch as the vascular meshes contain two or three liver-cells, it is evident that two neighboring capillaries must be separated from each other by at least one liver-cell. Hence, in sections where the capillaries are cut transversely, their circular openings will be surrounded by a ring of liver-cells, or a circle of capillaries will enclose a mass of glandular substance. In sections which cut the central vein transversely the radiating capillaries will enclose radiating rows of liver-cells. (See Fig. 81.) These are either joined to one another by the intervention of other liver-cells, or they are separated from one another by transverse capillary branches.

On the other hand, in sections where the central vein is cut lengthwise, the (nearly) parallel intralobular capillaries will appear separated from one another by corresponding rows of liver-cells. The glandular substance of the liver would then be composed of small, solid columns or rows of cells united to each other by other cells, thus forming one connected mass, and containing within its meshes the capillary network. In the fresh state the liver-cells appear as spherical or egg-shaped bodies, usually presenting facets. They are somewhat flattened by being pressed against one another (Fig. 83). Corpuscles possessing processes are sometimes found.

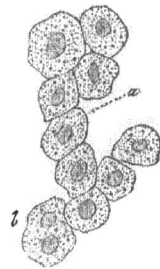

FIG. 83. — Human liver-cells: *a*, with single nucleus; *b*, with double nucleus. Frey.

The hepatic cells are about 0.013—0.02 mm. in diameter, and possess one or two nuclei,[1] which are generally spherical, although they occasionally appear to be flattened; the diameter is 0.006—0.007 mm. The liver-cells do not possess any membrana propria, but a hardened boundary layer seems to exist in its place. It is probable also that the

---

[1] Occasionally three or five nuclei, especially in young subjects (Beale).

cells are bound together by a colloid substance, although this is a point which has not yet been definitely settled.

Sections of a dog's liver, immersed for a short time in dilute osmic acid, will occasionally exhibit a brown or black tracing between adjoining cells. Pressure on the cover glass will part them and leave the darkened material free in the field of vision. I have satisfied myself that this tracing is not of a nerve, biliary duct, or connective-tissue fibril; it is either a portion of the boundary layer of a liver-cell, or, as I suppose, a colloid substance between two cells. This appearance, however, is not constant.

The protoplasm is of a dark brownish or greenish color. It is viscid, and contains numerous granules of small size, in addition to smaller or larger fat-droplets.[1] In livers hardened by chromic acid or alcohol, the shrinkage of the cells causes them to appear polyhedral, and they also seem much darker than in the fresh state. If the portal or hepatic vein has been injected, the cells will show distinct indentations produced by the distended capillaries.

When liver-cells are treated with diluted acetic acid, their protoplasm becomes pale, while their nuclei are rendered more conspicuous. In a dilute solution of caustic potassa the cells swell up, become rounded, and are finally dissolved. With water they also swell up, become paler and more rounded, and at length disintegrate. In the fresh state, by the addition of an indifferent fluid ($\frac{1}{2}$ per cent. solution of chloride of sodium, or iodized serum), the liver-cells are said to show protoplasmic movements. The granular substance of the liver-cells has been shown (by Schiff, in frogs, and by Nasse, in certain mammalia) to consist of an animal *amylum*, which is converted into sugar through the agency of a peculiar ferment.

The fat-droplets may be either small in number and size or quite numerous and large. Not infrequently they coalesce to form larger fat-globules. In the so-called fatty infiltration they are very large, and compose the greater part of the cells. The nuclei are granular, and where two or more of them occupy the same cell, they may apparently be united to each other.

---

[1] According to Kupffer and Klein the substance of the cells is composed of a honeycombed network, *i.e.*, an intracellular reticulum. Klein says the nucleus is limited by a thin membrane, and includes an intranuclear network, containing occasionally one or two nucleoli. The intranuclear network is in continuity with the intracellular one, and the network of contiguous cells are in connection with one another (Klein and Smith : Atlas of Histology).

Division of a nucleus, as described by Kölliker, I have never been able to confirm. When two nuclei are placed in contact, there may be an appearance of division, but the actual process is not easy to see.

Thin liver sections may be stained either in carmine fluid or hæmatoxylon, and preserved in glycerine or balsam.

The larger bile-ducts.—If, for the sake of convenience, we imagine that the hepatic duct enters the liver to be distributed to its substance, we may describe it as giving off two primary branches at the transverse fissure, one passing to the right lobe, the other to the left. As these branches continue their course, following the subdivisions of the hepatic artery and portal vein, they also undergo successive divisions, and at length enter the interlobular canals. In this position their diameter varies between 0.02 and 0.03 mm.

The primary branches do not, however, pass unchanged into the liver tissue. They ramify even before entering the gland, but such vessels are distributed only to the under surface (Henle). Other biliary ducts, given off in the transverse fissure, form a network on the upper surface, as may be demonstrated by injecting the hepatic duct with carmine-glycerine. The branches of these networks then enter the liver-tissue and ramify throughout it, following the subdivisions of the hepatic artery and portal.vein.

As the divisions of the hepatic duct diminish in size, the thickness of their walls undergoes proportionate diminution. The trunk of the hepatic duct comprises an internal layer measuring 0.15 mm. in thickness, and an external layer of 0.2 —0.3 mm. Both of these coats are composed, according to Henle, of interlacing connective-tissue bundles, in which elastic fibres are freely intermixed. These ducts have an internal lining of cylindrical epithelium, which is 0.05 mm. in height. Even where the branches measure only 0.2 mm. in diameter they have cylindrical epithelium surrounded by a single layer of connective tissue longitudinally disposed, in which there are also muscle-corpuscles, distinguished by their long, rod-shaped nuclei (Heidenhain). The most minute biliary passages consist of a structureless membrana propria, which is lined with flattened cylindrical epithelia.

Glands of the ducts.—In the trunk of the hepatic duct and its subdivisions, down to those branches of which the diameter is not less than 0.5 mm., the mucous membrane is provided with numerous irregular excavations, measuring 0.15—0.3 mm. in their long diameter. In this trunk there occur also a great number of pores or orifices, which, on examination, prove to be the mouths of the passages leading from simple and compound gland-like bodies, the so-called glands of the bile-ducts. The *simple glands* consist merely of single vesicles, or alveoli, with afferent passages, all of which are imbedded in the mucous membrane; or of two or more vesicles with a single passage. The compound glands are formed by the union of two or more simple ones, which have a common passage. They are quite large, and their expanded portions lie on the outer surface of the hepatic duct. When filled by injection with gelatine they are visible to the naked eye. The passages pierce the walls of the duct at an acute angle, pursuing a course within its walls, nearly parallel to the duct itself; the opening into the mucous membrane is therefore quite a distance from the gland-vesicles. According to Henle, these compound glands are not found in the larger branches of the hepatic duct, but they occur frequently in the network of bile-ducts situated in the transverse fissure. Allusion has already been made to them. The vesicles measure 0.04 mm. in diameter, and, like the excavations in the larger branches of the duct, are lined with a cylindrical epithelium, in no way differing from that of the duct itself; the afferent passages also possess the same kind of epithelium.

Structures allied to these excavations and glands occur in small number in the bile-ducts[1] which are found in the ligamentum triangulare. and on the diaphragm, where they appear as villous prominences on the duct-walls.

According to Theile, Weber, and others, these bile-ducts represent the last vestiges of an atrophied liver substance, the existence of which dates back to infancy, or perhaps to fœtal life.

The excavations in the larger branches are either simple diverticula of the internal walls, or the openings of lateral bile-ducts; the punctate pores are the orifices of the outlet passages of duct-glands.

Capillary bile-ducts.—When the larger bile-ducts, by con-

---

[1] Vasa aberrantia of E. H. Weber.

tinnous subdivision, have at length reached the interlobular canals, in conjunction with the branches of the portal vein and hepatic artery, they send capillary branches within the substance of the lobule, and thus form an intralobular network. These capillary ducts are of extreme delicacy, measuring only from 0.001 to 0.0012 mm.

In order to demonstrate them fully they should be filled by natural injection. The substance to be employed for this purpose is a solution of pure indigo-carmine. The animal serving for injection (rabbit or dog) should be secured in the manner described in the chapter on the Kidney, where all the necessary manipulations are fully detailed. The best results are obtained by injecting a cold, saturated solution of indigo-carmine into the external jugular vein, directing the stream toward the periphery (brain) ; 5 or 10 ctgms. are to be injected at intervals of thirty to forty minutes, and the injection continued until from 25 to 50 ctgms. have been used, the amount varying according to the size of the animal. It takes a longer time for the elimination of indigo-carmine through the capillary bile-ducts than for the same process by way of the renal tubules, and a larger amount of solution will therefore have to be employed. As soon as large quantities of the indigo solution have been injected into the jugular vein, the animal becomes unconscious and there is a decrease of temperature ; hence, it should be covered over with layers of cotton-batting. After a variable time (three to twelve hours) the animal is killed in the following manner : The abdomen is opened and the cannula of a large syringe filled with absolute alcohol secured in the lumen of the portal vein; the inferior vena cava is then cut across above the entrance of the hepatic vein, and the piston of the syringe pushed home. The liver, which before was of a uniform blue color, now presents a marbled appearance, not unlike that of malachite.

Or, the portal vein may be injected with the writer's carmine-glycerine, the vena cava having been divided as above. In either case the liver is to be removed at once and placed in a vessel containing absolute alcohol, and while immersed in that fluid cut into small fragments. Sections may then be made in a few hours.

The arrangement of the bile-capillaries differs in different animals. In the rabbit, for instance, they lie between the adjoining surfaces of two contiguous cells, and rarely in the canals formed by the edges of three or more cells (Hering [1]). So that while the blood-capillaries occupy the canals previously described, the bile-capillaries form an independent network between the boundary surfaces of the liver-cells (Figs. 84 and 85). In cross sections they may be seen, appearing as small, circular

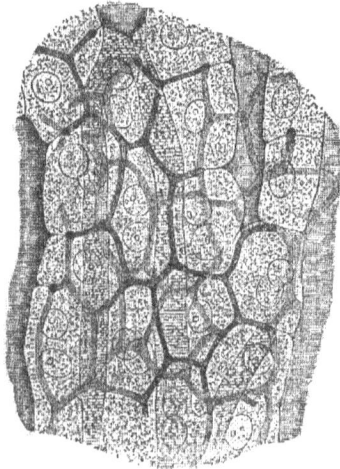 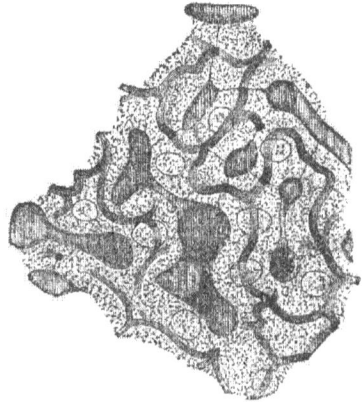

Fig 84.   Fig. 85.

FIGS. 84 and 85.—Injected liver of rabbit. The narrow, reticulated bile-capillaries are shaded with longitudinal, the broader blood-capillaries with transverse lines. Within the boundary line or septum of two contiguous cells the cross-section of a bile-capillary is seen as a dark spot or point. The liver cells contain one or two nuclei. In Fig. 84, the bile-capillaries are slightly distended by the artificial injection ; in Fig. 85, markedly so. Hering.

openings between the cells, while in longitudinal sections they present a linear arrangement (Figs. 85 and 86). In the dog this arrangement is the same, only here the bile-capillaries occur more frequently in the canals formed by the edges of the liver cells.

According to Hering, both in rabbits' and dogs' livers the blood-capillaries are separated from the bile-capillaries by the intervention of at least one liver-cell. Livers in which the bile-capillaries have been injected by the natural method with indigo-carmine do not always demonstrate this. And here it may be remarked, that in artificial or forced injections of the bile-capillaries they are always distended beyond their natural diameters.[2]

---

[1] Hering : Ueber den Bau der Wirbelthierleber, and article on Liver in Stricker's Manual.

[2] Compare Figs. 84 and 85, after Hering. Even in Fig. 84 the bile-capillaries are larger than they ought to be. In an article on the liver by Dr. W. G Davis, in the Amer. Jour. Med. Sci., Vol. LXXVIII., the distention of the capillaries is excessive.

By conjoined natural injection of the bile-capillaries and artificial injection of the portal system with carmine-glycerine by the methods above detailed, very gratifying results are obtained. Care must be taken, however, not to use too much force during the process of injection, and only such portions of the liver should be chosen for sections as show, by their red color, a perfect filling of the portal branches. While the elimination of the indigo-carmine is taking place within the liver of the living animal, the bile-capillaries probably contain the salt in a soluble form. The addition of absolute alcohol at once precipitates this coloring reagent in the form of exceedingly fine stellate crystals, or as finely granular matter, which may in some measure account for the angular character of the biliary capillaries, as seen in such specimens.

FIG. 86.—Liver of a three-months' child, hardened in chromic acid. The capillaries are filled with red blood-corpuscles (indicated by colorless rings) and a few leucocytes. The cross section of a bile-capillary is shown within the boundary line of any two contiguous cells. A similar cross section is shown in the canal formed by three adjoining liver-cells. Hering.

Gentle curves, such as are represented in Fig. 85, never appear. The constringing action of the alcohol on the liver-cells has unquestionably some effect, and therefore modifies the normal appearance.

Natural injections further show the great preponderance of the biliary- over the blood-capillaries. In the liver of a dog, for instance, each liver-cell seems suspended within two or three (rarely four) bile-capillaries, and where the latter are

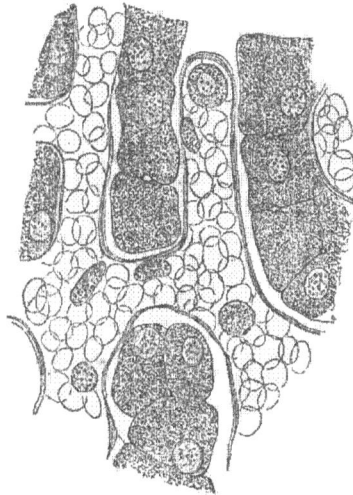

One need only compare Fig. 3 in Davis's article with Fig. 84 of Hering's, which, by the way, is a good illustration.

The first to describe the intralobular network of bile-capillaries were Andrejevic (Ueber der feineren Bau der Leber. Wiener Sitzungsbericht, 1861) and MacGillavry (Zur Anat. d. Leber. Wiener Sitzungsbericht, 1864). Chronszewski was the first to inject the bile-capillaries by natural injection (Virchow's Archiv, Bd. 35). MacGillavry Chronszewski, Budge, and others, described the bile-capillaries as possessing true walls.

joined together the calibre of the capillary is markedly increased. Sections made parallel to the external surface of the liver, immediately under the capsule, generally cut the central vein transversely, and such sections show that the bile-capillaries possess a somewhat radial course (Fig. 87). Human livers can rarely be obtained in a fresh state, and examinations of their bile-capillaries are therefore attended with difficulty.

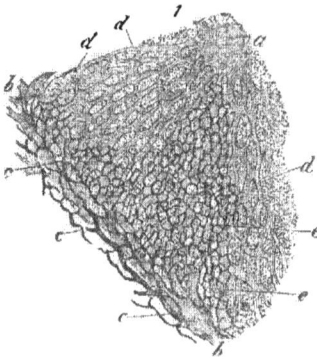

FIG. 87.—Capillary bile-ducts of a rabbit, distended by artificial injection : 1. a portion of a lobule ; *a*, central vein ; *b, b*, interlobular veins ; *c, c*, bile-ducts ; *d, d*, blood-capillaries ; *e, e*, bile-capillaries.

Do the bile-capillaries possess walls of their own ?—This question must be answered in the affirmative. In specimens where the bile-capillaries have been injected by the natural method, cross sections of such capillaries will demonstrate, with high powers, that there is a dot of blue indigo-carmine surrounded by a distinct circle which is perfectly transparent and in marked contrast to the somewhat yellowish color of the adjoining liver-cells. (See Fig. 88.) It is more difficult to see this in sections which cut the capillaries in their longitudinal diameters, but where two or more capillaries unite this halo is again seen. That this appearance is due to the presence of a true wall seems clear, but all doubts will be dispelled by watching the diffusion which takes place in such a section on the addition of a few drops of water under the cover glass. The indigo-carmine becomes dissolved in the water, forming a deep blue liquid which stains the surrounding cells and vessels of a uniform color. While watching a bile-capillary during the progress of this action it appears to

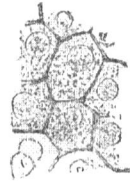

FIG. 88.—Liver of the dog. Natural injection of bile-capillaries, showing double contour of the capillaries, which are only partly filled with injection. Cross sections of the capillaries show a dot of indigo-carmine surrounded by a distinct halo. The woodcut does not show this satisfactorily. In the specimen the lines corresponding to the walls of the capillaries are of the utmost delicacy. Magnified 450 diam.

stand out more prominently than before, and its walls become more distinct. In a few moments the cells will have become swollen by the imbibition of water, and the picture gradually fades, until at length it would be difficult to even locate the original seat of the capillary. I have verified this over and over again. The capillary walls seem to be structureless; at least with a power of 1,400 diameters I have been unable to detect any structure. The membrana propria of the interlobular bile-ducts is continued on to the capillaries within the lobule.

Hering, Henle, and others do not believe that the bile-capillaries possess walls of their own, but suppose them to be contained within the boundary surface of the liver-cells, the latter taking the place of the epithelium of the interlobular bile-ducts. Henle further quotes Schweigger-Seidel (in the *Archiv für path. Anat. und Phys.*, XXVII., 505, 1863), who injected the bile-capillaries with faintly colored gelatine, and showed that by warming the slide the gelatine dissolved without leaving any residue whatever. From what has been said of artificial injections, and recognizing the extreme delicacy of the bile-capillaries, it is not surprising that this result was obtained after injecting a warm solution of gelatine into the capillaries. The walls of these capillaries are homogeneous and exceedingly delicate, so that they are destroyed by a moderate degree of heat. Very soon after death they undergo a sort of liquefaction, and what was before a vessel with true walls is now an open channel, through which an artificial fluid can be made to force its way.

At first the elimination of the indigo-carmine takes place in the bile-capillaries on the external border of the lobule, and somewhat later the capillaries about the central vein become filled. Neither the protoplasm of the liver-cells nor their nuclei ever become stained with the blue solution during the process of elimination; such coloring would be the result of post-mortem diffusion. But the cylindrical epithelium of the glands is colored blue, and indubitably these glands excrete the indigo-carmine, as do the cells of the convoluted tubules of the kidney. Whether they secrete any substance during life, or what that substance may be, has not yet been determined.

Theile, Kölliker, and Kiernan suppose that these glands secrete a mucous substance which becomes mixed with the bile. Henle regards these glands and excavations as reservoirs which are occasionally filled with bile. From what has been said above it would appear that the cylindrical epithelium of the glands eliminates the indigo-carmine, and hence we may suppose that they secrete some fluid or substance during life.

The gall-bladder.—The walls of the gall-bladder are about

2 mm. thick, and are composed of three coats: [1] an internal, *mucous* and *muscular ;* a middle, of *connective tissue ;* and an external, the *serous.* The internal coat, 0.4 to 0.5 mm. thick, is composed of alternating layers of connective tissue and smooth muscle fibres, the most internal being a layer of connective tissue which contains a fine meshed capillary network. The connective tissue is dense and the muscle fibres are arranged in the form of interlacing bands. The internal surface is lined by a layer of cylindrical cells bearing a thickened, striated edge, and the surface is traversed by a network of small intersecting ridges, forming, as it were, a sort of latticework. The middle coat, 0.5 to 1 mm. thick, is formed of connective tissue, the meshes of which are wider on the internal than at the external surface. This coat contains the larger vessels and nerves. The external, or serous coat is thin, and consists of a layer of dense connective tissue and peritoneum. A few mucous glands [2] are found scattered here and there in the walls of the gall-bladder. Sections from this organ, hardened in alcohol, may be stained with the carmine or picro-carmine solution and mounted in glycerine or balsam.

The cystic and common ducts resemble in structure the hepatic duct. The inner surface of the former is thrown into crescentic ridges, and in the region of the neck of the gall-bladder the connective tissue of the internal coat shows a circular arrangement. The ducts contain no muscle fibres.

The lymph-vessels.—These may be divided into a series of superficial and deep channels. The former are situated in the capsule of the liver and form a capillary reticulum with small meshes, the larger branches of which accompany the arteries in pairs and communicate with each other by transverse anastomoses. They are found in Glisson's capsule, and they also form a network somewhat larger meshed than the preceding. They accompany the hepatic artery and portal vein and their branches into the interior of the liver, and form anastomoses with the superficial lymph-vessels. The lymph-canals may easily be injected with colored material (carmine-glycerine) by filling a large hypodermic syringe with the liquid and injecting one of the larger lymph-vessels in the hilus of

---

[1] Henle : Eingeweidelehre.
[2] Luschka : Virchow's Archiv, 1857, and Zeitschr. f. rat. Med., 1858.

the liver. The syringe may be refilled three or four times without removing the canula, and the injection must be made in the direction of the normal lymph-current. In this way the colored liquid will flow backward into the smaller vessels. During the injection of the larger branches their proximal ends should be secured by clamps or ligatures.

The nerves of the liver enter the organ at the hilus and follow the course of the vessels. They are composed mostly of non-medullated elements, a few medullated fibres being found in the larger branches. They cannot be traced into the lobules.

BIBLIOGRAPHY.

KIERNAN. Anat. and Phys. of the Liver. Philos. Trans. 1833.

LAMBRON. Archiv. gén. 1841.

KRUKENBERG. Müller's Archiv. 1843.

WEBER, E. H. Müller's Archiv. 1843. Program. col. fasc., II. Lips., 1851.

THEILE. Wagner's Handwörterb. Bd. II. 1844.

RETZIUS. Müller's Archiv. 1849.

WEDL. Sitzungsber. d. Wiener Akad. 1850.

RAINEY. Quart. Jour. Microsc. Sc. Vol. I. 1853.

GERLACH. Gewebelehre. 1854.

BEALE. Philos. Trans. 1855. Anat. of the Liver. 1856. Archives of Med. Vols. I. and II.

VIRCHOW. Virchow's Archiv. Bd. XI. 1857.

LUSCHKA. Henle u. Pfeuffer's Zeitsch. Bd. IV. 1858.

BUDGE. Reichert u. Du Bois-Reymond's Archiv. 1859.

HIS. Zeitschft. f. wiss. Zoologie. Bd. X. 1860.

WAGNER, E. Archiv d. Heilkunde. 1860. Oester. Zeitschrft. f. prak. Heilkunde, 1861.

EBERTH. Zeitschrft. f. wiss. Zoologie. 1860. Med. Centralbl. 1866. Virchow's Archiv. 1867. Schultze's Archiv f. mik. Anat. Bd. III.

ANDREJEVIC. Sitzungsber. d. Wiener Akad. 1861.

RIESS. Reichert u. Du Bois-Reymond's Archiv. 1863.

SCHWEIGGER-SEIDEL. Reichert u. Du Bois-Reymond's Archiv. 1863.

MACGILLAVRY. Sitzungsber. der Wiener Akad. 1864.

IRMINGER. Zeitschft. f. wiss. Zoologie. Bd. XVI. 1866.

CHRONSZEWSKI. Virchow's Archiv. Bd. XXXV. 1866.

HERING. Sitzungsber. d. Wiener Akad. 1866. Stricker's Handbuch. Bd. I. 1871.

KÖLLIKER. Handbuch d. Gewebelehre. 1867.

VON BIESIADECKI. Sitzungsber. d. Wiener Akad. 1867.

HEIDENHAIN. Studien aus d. phys. Instituts z. Breslau. Heft IV. 1868.

KISSELEW. Med. Centralbl. 1869.

PFLÜGER. Pflüger's Archiv. Bd. II. 1869. u. IV. 1871.
HENLE. Eingeweidelehre. 1873.
LEGROS. Jour. de l'anat. et de la phys. 1874.
COHNHEIM u. LITTEN. Virchow's Archiv. Bd. LXVI. 1876.
EWALD u. KUEHNE. Verhand. Naturhist. med. Vereins zu Heidelberg. 1 Bd. 5
    Hft. 1876.
KOLATSCHEWSKY. Schultze's Archiv. Bd. XIII. 1876.
TURNER. Journ. of Anat. and Phys. Vol. XI. 1877.
WENDT. Med. Centralblatt. No. 15. 1878.
DAVIS. Amer. Jour. Med. Sc. Vol. LXXVIII. 1879.
FRITSCH. Archiv. fur Anat. und Phys. Phys. Abtheil. 1879.
KLEIN and SMITH. Atlas of Histology. Part X. 1879—1881.

CHAPTER XIV.

THE KIDNEY.

By ABRAHAM MAYER, M.D.,

Late Curator of the Manhattan Eye and Ear Hospital, New York City.

General plan of structure.—The glandular substance of the kidney is divided into two parts, an external or convex portion, called the *cortical substance*, or *cortex*, and an internal or concave portion, the *medullary substance*, or *medulla*. This division can be readily seen by cutting a kidney into two equal parts in the line of its long diameter. An intermediate zone, which separates the cortical from the medullary substance, is called the *boundary layer* of the kidney. The whole organ is enveloped in a fibrous membrane, the *capsule*.

The medullary substance contains the pyramids of the kidney, and is therefore also called the *pyramidal portion*. The apex of each pyramid, the papilla, projects into a special arm of the renal pelvis, viz., a calyx; the base or expanded portion is directed toward the cortical substance, and sends prolongations into the latter.

An examination of the *cortical substance* shows it to be composed of two distinct varieties of tissue, running parallel to one another toward the free surface. One has a fibrous appearance, and is composed of cylindrical cords. It is a continuation of the pyramids. These *pyramidal prolongations*[1] (Henle) are also called *medullary* rays (Fig. 89). The other portion, situated between the prolongations, is a granular-looking material, called the *cortical substance proper*, or *labyrinth of Ludwig*.[2] The latter contains numerous small bodies, which are of a distinctly red color when there is a large

---

[1] Ludwig und Zawarykin : Zeitschrft. für rat. Med., 1863. They are also called the prolongations of Ferrein.

[2] Ludwig Stricker's Manual, p. 461.

amount of blood in the kidney ; they are the *Malpighian bodies,* or *glomeruli* (Fig. 89, E).

The boundary layer[1] is characterized by numerous blood-vessels, some of which unite to form an arcade (Fig. 89, C), which is parallel to the convex surface of the kidney, and from which branches are given off to the cortical substance proper.

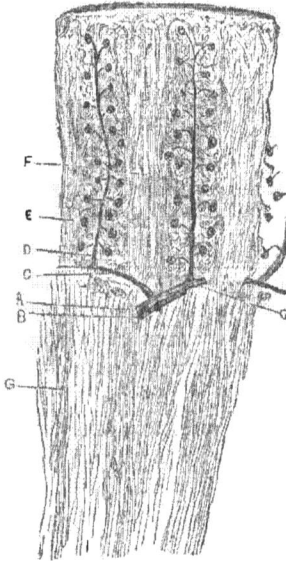

The renal artery, before it enters the hilum of the kidney, divides into branches, which pierce the medulla between the pyramids and ascend toward the cortical substance until they reach the boundary layer. Here they divide obliquely or at right angles to give off smaller branches, which have the direction and arched ppearance above referred to (Fig. 89, C). These arched vessels then send off the branches already mentioned, which traversing the centres of the cortical substance proper, at right angles to the parent stem (Fig. 89, D), extend almost to the capsule of the kidney. On their way they in turn give off smaller twigs, each of which bears a glomerulus upon its extremity (Fig. 89, E). In this way there is an alternate arrangement of pyramidal prolongation and cortical substance proper (Fig. 90). Though the pyramidal prolongations almost reach the capsule of the kidney, they never quite touch it, being separated by the interposition of some cortical substance proper (Fig. 89).

FIG. 89. — Human kidney. Vertical section through cortical and medullary substances: A, branch of renal artery; B, vein, immediately beneath former, but hardly visible in the figure; C, arched arterial branches in the boundary layer; D, artery of the cortical substance proper; E, Malpighian bodies or glomeruli; F, medullary rays or pyramidal prolongations; G, vessels of the medulla, the vasa recta. × 10.

Specimens for study should be made from a fresh kidney, in which the renal artery has been injected with carmine-gelatine, the whole organ having been subsequently immersed in alcohol of 50 per cent. strength. When in that fluid it is to be divided into four or more parts, allowed to remain therein for

---

[1] Henle: Grenzschicht, Eingeweidelehre.

twenty-four hours, afterward transferred to stronger alcohol, then to absolute alcohol, and finally mounted in dammar or balsam. Vertical sections show the arrangement represented in Figs. 89 and 90; transverse sections, the appearance of Fig. 92.

The substance of the kidney is composed of secreting and collecting tubules, vessels, and a stroma, which fills the inter-

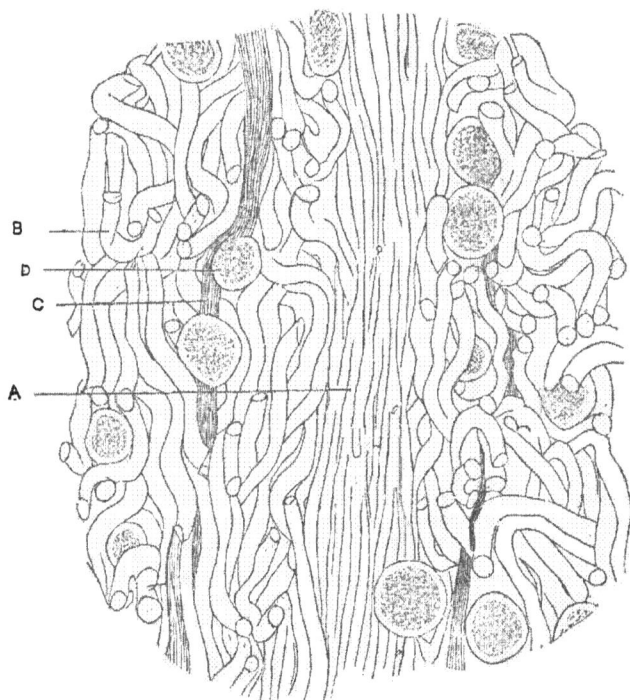

FIG. 90.—Human kidney. Vertical section through cortical portion: A, pyramidal prolongation; B, cortical substance proper; C, artery; D, glomerulus. ×64.

spaces between the tubules, and is more abundant in the medullary than in the cortical substance. In human adults this connective material is found in small quantity and is a sort of colloid substance. In the lower animals it is more abundant, and assumes the character of real connective tissue. In young infants there is said to be a greater proportionate amount of this tissue than in subsequent life.

The renal tubules.—The tubules are found both in the corti-

cal and medullary substances ; they are of different diameters
and pursue either a straight or tortuous course. Some have a
basement membrane (*membrana* or *tunica propria*), on which
the epithelium rests; others appear to have none. The tubules are clothed with epithelium of different varieties. Specimens should be made from a kidney that has lain for twenty-
four hours in a 5 per cent. solution of chromic acid. A small

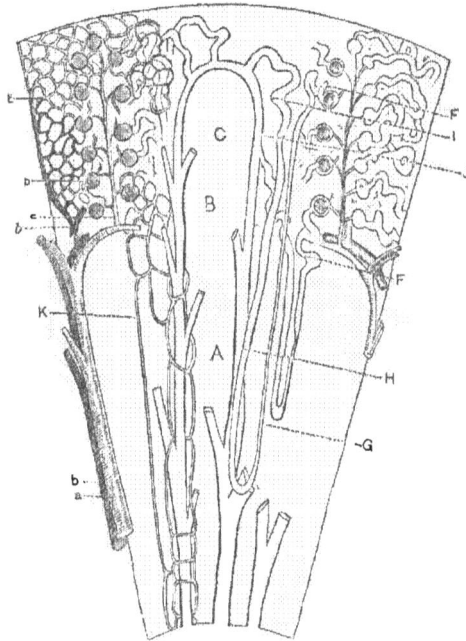

Fig. 91.—Schematic representation of the kidney: A, medulla; B, boundary layer ; C, cortical portion; a, renal artery ; b, renal vein; c, artery penetrating cortex; D, capsule enclosing glomerulus ; E,
capillaries; F, convoluted tubules of first order ; G, looped tubule, descending branch ; H, looped tubule,
ascending branch ; I, convoluted tubule of second order ; J, collecting tubule ; K, vasa recta.

piece of the gland is to be placed on a slide, and a drop of glycerine added ; the tubules may be isolated by teasing with needles.

In Fig. 91 there is a schematic representation of the vascular
distribution and course of the tubules in one of the pyramids.
Each tubule takes its origin in an expansion that surrounds
the glomerulus, and is called *Bowman's* or *Müller's capsule.*[1]

---

[1] Müller, in 1830, described the capsules. but regarded them as vesicles which had
no connection whatever with the uriniferous tubules. Bowman, in Philosoph. Transact., 1842.

It is round or elliptical in shape, and has a diameter of about 0.2 mm. Where the capsule empties its contents into the tubule, there is a slight constriction known as the neck; it is very distinct in some of the lower animals. The canal then enlarges and begins to pursue a tortuous course in the cortical substance; it is now called a *convoluted tube* [1] (Fig. 91, F). It next undergoes sudden diminution in size and passes straight through the medulla until, at a variable point, it bends upon itself, forming a loop; then, ascending, it increases in calibre, and in the cortical substance becomes convoluted for the second time. Those canals that are nearest the glomeruli are called *convoluted tubules of the first order*, the others *convoluted tubules of the second order*. Between these two are the *looped tubules of Henle*, just described, each being divided into a descending and ascending branch (Fig. 91, G and H). The convoluted tubules of the second order terminate by emptying into tubules of greater diameter, called *collecting tubules*, [2] which descend through the cortical and medullary substances, and, receiving other collecting tubules on the way, finally empty into the pelvis of the kidney (Fig. 91, J).

At the base of each pyramid there are a vast number of collecting tubules, but as they successively empty into larger collecting tubes, the area they occupy is thereby diminished; at the apex of the papillæ, where they ultimately discharge the urine into the pelvis of the kidneys, there are only about twenty in number. This gradual coalescence of the tubes gives to the pyramids a conical shape, but the breadth of the base is also partly due to the presence of the looped tubules which pass down into the pyramids for a varying depth.

The larger collecting tubules may be readily injected with Beale's blue fluid [3] or carmine-gelatine, either directly or from the ureters; it will be found, however, that the injection will seldom extend beyond the looped tubules, owing to the small diameter of the descending branches.

---

[1] *Tubulus contortus.* [2] Straight tubules of Bellini.

[3] Glycerine, pure, 2 oz.; tr. perchloride iron, 10 drops; ferrocyan. potassium, 3 grains; strong hydrochl. acid, 3 drops; water, 1 oz. Mix the tincture of iron with one ounce of the glycerine; and the ferrocyanide of potassium, first dissolved in a little water, with the other ounce; mix gradually, and shake during admixture; add the iron to the ferrocyanide; lastly, add the water and hydrochloric acid. Beale: Microscope, p. 87.

Bowman's capsule is composed of a structureless basement-membrane surrounding each glomerulus. Upon the inner surface of these capsules is a continuous layer of flat, epithelioid cells,[1] which are continued over the glomerulus itself.[2] Occasionally an epithelioid cell may be seen between the vessels of the coil composing the glomerulus.

Each capsule is pierced by two vessels, called, respectively, *afferent* and *efferent*. The former enters the capsule and forms

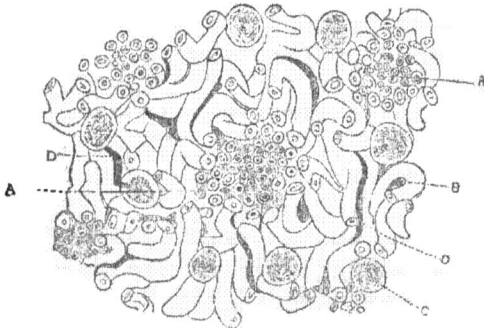

FIG. 93.—Human kidney. Transverse section of cortical portion, showing the alternating arrangement of pyramidal ray and cortical substance proper: A, A, pyramidal rays; B, convoluted tubule; C, glomerulus; D, D, arterial vessels. × 55.

the glomerulus, while the latter makes its exit close to the entrance of the former. The layer of epithelium above described passes over from the inner surface of the capsule on to the glomerulus about the points of entrance and exit just mentioned. On the opposite side, the capsule becomes continuous with a convoluted tubule. To obtain specimens, the renal artery of a fresh kidney should be injected with blue gelatine and then placed in alcohol. Vertical and transverse sections of the cortical substance may then be made. They should be stained in carmine and examined in glycerine, or the artery may be injected with absolute alcohol and the sections stained as above.

The epithelium of the tubules.—The basement-membranes of the convoluted tubules of the first order are in direct continuation with the basement-membranes of the capsules. Their diameter averages 0.04 mm. The epithelium of these canals is

---

[1] Schweigger-Seidel: Die Nieren. Halle, 1865. Henle: Eingeweidelehre, p. 329. Heidenhain: Zur anat. d. Nieren, in Schultze's Archiv, Bd. X., Hft. I. Mayer: Histology of the Kidney. Dis. Inaug., 1876. Also Bowman, Johnson, Frerichs, etc.

[2] Gerlach, Heidenhain.

peculiar, and was first correctly described by Heidenhain. According to this writer, the greater part of the cell-protoplasm assumes the form of small, cylindrical bodies, the so-called *rods of Heidenhain*, giving the epithelium a striated appearance (Fig. 93).

To exhibit these appearances, the cortical substance of a dog's or rabbit's kidney should be cut into small pieces and immersed for twenty-four hours or more in a 5 per cent. solution of the neutral chromate of ammonia. After this time has elapsed, a small piece of the gland is to be placed on a slide and a drop of glycerine added; the specimen may then be teased and examined. Portions of the convoluted tubules will be found floating about in the glycerine, and should be closely scrutinized. By this mode of preparation, individual epithelioid corpuscles cannot be recognized; on the contrary, they seem to merge with one another. The tubule may be regarded as made up of rods transversely disposed, with nuclei embedded in a pulpy mass that appears to fill its lumen, the whole enveloped by the membrana propria. The rods surround the nuclei, and are not all of the same length. They appear to be hollow, as shown by their sometimes containing fatty granules. Here and there in the specimen a separate corpuscle will present itself to the eye; in such instances the rods can readily be made out (Fig. 94, A). In the kidney of the rat these bodies may be isolated with little difficulty (Fig. 94, B). At one end the rods rest against the membrana propria, to which they are attached by a colloid material; their other extremity is lost in the protoplasm of the capsule, which latter lies internal to them and appears to have the character of a pulpy mass containing nuclei. In the dog, the nucleus of each cell is about midway between the lumen and the membrana propria. It is surrounded by rods (Fig. 94, A). In the rat this is not the case (Fig. 94, B). Assuming that the rods begin at the membrana propria, they are directed

FIG. 93.—Convoluted tubule from the kidney of a dog. Neutral chromate of ammonia preparation. The tubule normally appears darker than is represented in the figure. × 450.

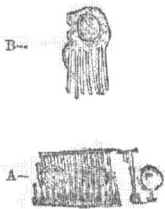

FIG. 94.—Isolated cells from the convoluted tubules exhibiting rod-like epithelium; A, kidney of dog; B, kidney of rat. × 450.

toward the centre of the lumen of the tubule, and the distance between any two adjoining rods at the periphery is necessarily greater than at the centre. For the same reason, also, the rods are more distinctly defined in the former situation ; the micrometer screw will have to be used in tracing them inward.

Transverse sections of the cortical substance may be made by freezing small pieces which have been immersed in a solution of the neutral chromate of ammonia. Such sections should be examined in glycerine, or, better, in a saturated solution of the chloride of potassium in glycerine.[1] The radial direction of the rods is beautifully seen in such specimens (Fig. 95, C),

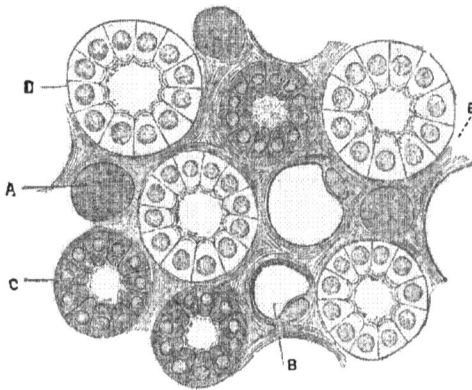

FIG. 95.—Kidney of dog. Transverse section through the medullary portion, about midway between the apex and boundary layer. Neutral chromate of ammonia preparation: A, blood-vessel; B, looped tubule, descending portion; C, looped tubule, ascending portion; D, collecting tubule; E, connective tissue. × 300.

and the individual cells are more clearly defined. Another method of exhibiting these rod epithelia is to inject the artery or vein of a fresh, bloodless kidney with a cold saturated solution of the chloride of potassium, then, after placing the whole organ in alcohol, divide it in small pieces under that fluid. After a day or two sections may be made ; they then should be immersed for a short time in absolute alcohol and clarified by oil of turpentine. Such specimens show the epithelium to perfection and may be preserved for a considerable time. Permanent specimens can be made by substituting resinous turpen-

---

[1] The glycerine should be heated in a porcelain evaporating-dish, the chloride of potassium added, and the whole mixture stirred for several minutes with a glass rod. The glycerine is ready for use after cooling.

tine[1] for the common oil. The renal artery or vein may also be injected with absolute alcohol, and sections prepared as above. But the epithelium suffers in this way, for the alcohol causes the rods to shrink, and the colloid substance between the rods coagulates. Still, the striated appearance is seen near the membrana propria. Another fact which seems to have escaped Heidenhain is that alcohol so injected causes the nuclei of the cells to recede toward the membrana propria by its action on the rods.

• The action of water on the rods is peculiar. A fresh kidney must be used and a portion of the cortical substance placed on a slide, together with a drop of water; it is then to be teased with needles and immediately examined. At first the rods are not distinctly brought into view, but they soon appear with their contours sharply delineated. This appearance, however, does not last very long, for the epithelium soon imbibes water, swells, and then forms an indistinct mass.

In the neck of the convoluted tubules of the frog, coluber, etc., the epithelium is ciliated. In the frog the cilia have great length, but the convoluted tubules do not have the rod epithelium. In the dog, cat, rabbit, etc., the rod epithelium begins at the neck of the tubule and is continued as far as the loops.

The convoluted tubules of the first order, after ramifying in the cortical substance, become continuous with the looped tubules of Henle, as already described.[2] The change takes place in the vicinity of the boundary layer.

The looped tubules.—The looped tubules traverse the medulla for a greater or lesser distance. A few almost reach the apices of the pyramids; others extend but a short distance below the boundary layer, while a third class occupies an intermediate position. Good specimens are obtained by macerating vertical sections of the medulla in a solution of caustic potassa ($\frac{1}{2}$ to 1 per cent.). The potassa destroys the epithelium, the stroma, and the blood-corpuscles, but leaves the basement-

---

[1] Resinous turpentine is prepared as follows: some common oil of turpentine is poured upon a deep plate, so as to form a thin layer, and a piece of fine muslin is snugly fastened over it to keep out the dust. The liquid is now exposed to the action of the air. In a few days, if the weather be warm, or a week or more, if the weather be cold, the turpentine will have become thick, yellow, and resinous, and is now no longer transparent. Resinous turpentine, prepared in this way, forms one of the best preserving agents. Its use will be spoken of further on.

[2] Henle: Eingeweidel., 2te Aufl., p. 316.

membrane perfectly intact. A fresh kidney is necessary, and one ·slightly infiltrated with fat makes the best specimens. Another method is to embed the kidney of a dog or rabbit in powdered chlorate of potassa, adding enough dilute nitric or hydrochloric acid to cover the crystals. After some hours the connective tissue in the gland will have been destroyed. Portions of the medulla should then be placed upon a slide with a drop of glycerine and teased slightly. A great many of the loops are broken in this way, to be sure, but still some will be seen. By this method the epithelium of the narrow branch is not destroyed.

The epithelium of the looped tubules.—The descending branch of the loop is small in diameter (0.02 mm.) and possesses a peculiar distinctive epithelium. The corpuscles are flat, have prominent nuclei, and rest against the membrana propria. The disproportionate size of the nuclei causes the corpuscle to project into the lumen. But these prominences

Fig. 96.—Kidney of dog. Descending portion of Henle's looped tubule.

do not obstruct the passage, for each one corresponds to the space between two on the opposite side of the tubule, so that there is no bar to the urine, but the passage is made more or less spiral (Fig. 96). The corpuscles are of a light color. Specimens should be made from a gland that has been macerated in a 5 per cent. solution of the neutral chromate of ammonia; they should be examined in glycerine. The length of the narrow portion of the loop is variable in man, the pig, and horse.

The second portion of the looped tubule is wider and its epithelium peculiar. In man both the loop and ascending branch are wide, usually ; especially is this the case with loops high up in the medulla ; in the rabbit it is the ascending branch only that has this property. Generally speaking, the length of the broader branch of the loop exceeds that of the narrow portion. The diameter of the broad portion averages 0.04 mm. The epithelium has the same character as that in the convoluted tubules ; it is striated and possesses rods.[1] It is not precisely similar, however. The width of the individual cells is not so great as in the former, and hence the lumen in

---

[1] Heidenhain : loc. cit.   Henle : loc. cit., p. 317.

this portion of the loop is greater than in the convoluted tubules. Specimens prepared with the neutral chromate of ammonia, as before detailed, give good results. Vertical sections may be made from a kidney macerated in the ammonia solution and afterward treated with alcohol ; or, better, from frozen specimens.

The broader extremity of the looped tubule ascends through the medulla into the cortical substance and becomes continuous with a convoluted tubule of the second order (Fig. 91, *i*). These tubules, the *intercalated portions*,[1] greatly resemble convoluted tubules of the first order, as already mentioned. Specimens should be prepared in the same way as those of the latter. The convoluted tubules of the second order, after ramifying in the cortical substance, terminate by emptying into the collecting tubules (Fig. 91, J).

The collecting tubules and their epithelium.—The collecting tubules[2] possess cylindrical epithelia, the bases of which are irregular and present point-like prolongations[3] (Fig. 97), which interdigitate with one another. The nuclei in the smaller collecting tubules are large and very prominent, but the protoplasm which surrounds them is not very abundant. The basement membrane is comparatively thick and exhibits a double contour. The smaller collecting tubules are situated in the cortical substance, a little distance below the capsule. Their diameter ranges between 0.04 and 0.06 mm. The small tubules unite to form larger ones, and these again to form tubules of still larger diameter. The irregular appearance at the bases of the epithelia is the same in the

FIG. 97.—Kidney of dog. Isolated cells of two collecting tubules, showing irregular base and point-like prolongations : *a*, from smallest collecting tubule ; *b*, from one near boundary layer. × 450.

larger trunks as in the smaller branches ; in the former, however, the cells are larger, and the protoplasm more voluminous than in the latter. The nuclei have about the same size in each (Fig. 98). The basement-membrane diminishes in importance in an inverse ratio with the size of the collecting tubules. In the smaller ones it is prominent and possesses a double con-

[1] Schweigger-Seidel : Schaltstücke ; Roth : Verbindungscanäle (connecting tubules).
[2] Open tubules of Henle. Zur Anat. der Niere. Göttingen, 1862.
[3] Heidenhain : loc. cit.

tour; in those of intermediate size it is thin, and has but a single contour; the largest tubes possess no basement-membrane whatever. In the latter the great cylindrical cells are held together by the prolongations above mentioned and a colloid substance. The diameter of the largest tubules at the apices of the pyramids is 0.2 to 0.3 mm., after the first division 0.1 to 0.2 mm., the smallest being about 0.06 mm. The height of the epithelium in the largest tubules is between 0.02 and 0.04 mm. ; in those at the boundary layer about 0.015 mm. Good specimens are obtained by immersing a fresh gland in dilute muriatic or nitric acid for a variable period (six to twenty-four hours), and examining in dilute glycerine. The collecting tubules' should be injected from the ureter with blue or red gelatine, and the whole organ immersed in alcohol, until ready for cutting. Sections made parallel to the collecting tubules produce splendid specimens. The connection between the collecting and convoluted tubules of the human kidney cannot be shown by injection, for the colored fluid thrown in from the ureter rarely reaches the convoluted tubules of the first order. In the lower animals—fishes, frogs, etc.—however, if the ureter be injected under constant pressure the entire length of the uriniferous tubules may be filled with the carmine, or, better, Berlin blue² fluid.

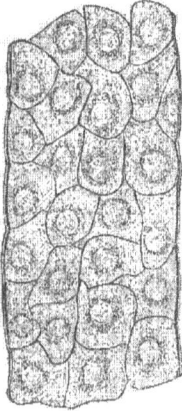

FIG. 98.—Kidney of dog. Small collecting tubule above the boundary layer. × 450.

---

¹ In the pig Henle finds that two large collecting tubules begin at the apex of each pyramid, then run along the outer borders of the cortical substance proper, high up into the cortex, and there unite by forming a loop. Henle states that the convoluted tubules empty into these, or their divisions by intercalated portions, which he calls *communicating tubules* (*Verbindungscanälchen*). Eingeweidel., p. 324.

² This has been done by Frey with fishes and amphibia; by Hüfner with birds, fishes, etc. ; by Gross with fishes and tritons, and by Hyrtl with some sorts of fishes. According to Seraphina Schachowa (Unters. ueber die Niere. Diss. Bern, 1876) the convoluted tubule of the first order is connected to Henle's loop by a spiral tubule, while the ascending portion of the loop exhibits an expanded part immediately above the loop, and a spiral part, which latter becomes continuous with the ascending limb of the loop. Between the ascending part of the loop and the intercalated portion Schachowa describes a new tubule, which she calls the "irregular tubule."

The spiral tubule is lined with an epithelium which has a striated appearance in

The blood-vessels of the kidney.—The renal artery and vein, before entering the hilum, divide and subdivide within the sinus of the kidney. Small branches, which are given off at the hilum, also supply the fibrous capsule of the gland. Veins accompany the arteries as far as the arches already referred to. But here a difference is to be noted. The arteries never anastomose, but form the straight vessels of the cortical substance proper, which again send off twigs to form the glomeruli.

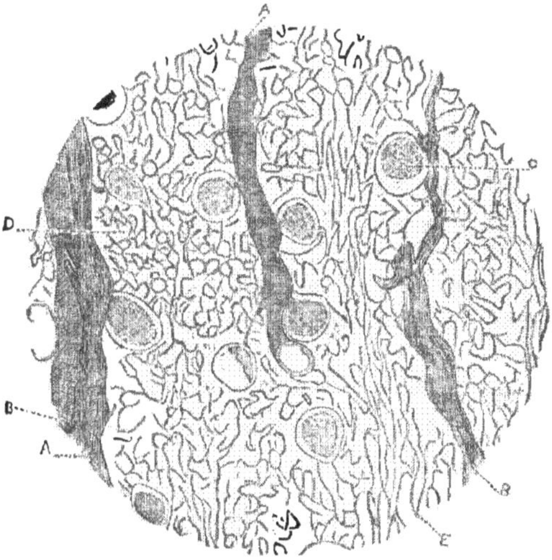

FIG. 99.—Kidney of pig. Injection of artery and vein. Vertical section at boundary layer: A, artery; B, vein: C, glomerulus; D, capillaries of the cortical portion; E, vasa recta formed from capullaries D. × 96.

At the arches, however, the veins anastomose, and a branch accompanies the straight artery of the cortical substance proper (Fig. 99, B). The glomerulus is formed from the arterial twig above referred to (Fig. 89, D). This enters the capsule directly opposite to the point where the latter becomes continuous with a convoluted tubule, and divides into two or more

its first portion. The expanded part of the ascending loop is lined with cells having very thick prominent rods, and whose lumen is exceedingly small.

The *irregular tubule* has an angular, irregular outline, is of very varying diameter, in some portions two, three, or four times as broad as in other portions, a condition due to its peculiar lining epithelia, which are angular and present numerous processes ; the rods are exceedingly thick and prominent.

As yet I have been unable to confirm Schachowa's researches.

branches which subdivide again and again (Fig. 100) to form loops or coils ; these latter unite again and form a vessel equal in size to the one which entered the capsule. The first is called, as already described, the affer- ent ; the second, the efferent vessel, and the glomerulus is formed by the division and reunion of the branches of these two vessels ; the whole form- ing a rounded tuft within the capsule. The vessels of which a glomerulus is composed have the same diameter as small capillaries ; their coats are struc- tureless and provided with elliptical

FIG. 100.—Glomerulus from kidney of pig. Ludwig.

nuclei. The efferent vessels are not veins ; on leaving the cap- sules they break up into capillaries, which anastomose freely with each other and surround the tubules of the cortex, form- ing, in this way, a network with circular meshes (Fig. 99, D).

At the boundary layer the capillaries unite to form vessels which are two to three times larger than the original capillaries. These vessels take a straight course through the medulla to- ward the apices forming the so-called *vasa recta* [1] (Figs. 99, E, and 89, G). The vessels immediately below the boundary layer are arranged in bundles at the side of the pyramidal prolonga- tions, and run parallel with them in that part of the medulla (Fig. 89). They give off branches in the medulla, and near the apices of the pyramids again form a capillary network which surrounds the collecting tubules. The returning vessels (veins) have about the same course, anastomose freely with each other, and empty into the venous arches at the boundary layer. Other veins are formed by the union of capillaries immediately underneath the capsule ; these have a stellate form,[2] the centre of each star indicating the commencement of a vein. Such veins, passing downward through the cortex and receiving branches on the way, empty finally into the venous arches above referred to. The venous arches also give rise to vessels of larger calibre, which run parallel to and accompany the ar- teries of the medulla, and at last unite to form the renal vein.

Injections of the kidney.—The kidney may be injected with gelatine either through the artery or vein. It is best accom-

---

[1] Donders : Physiol., I.   [2] *Venæ Stellatæ*, Verheyen.

plished by the artery, under constant pressure (mercury). Beale's blue injecting fluid [1] answers very well ; the writer's carmine-glycerine fluid [2] also acts exceedingly well, but it is very difficult to obtain a good double injection of artery and vein. I have found the most successful method to be the following : Take a fresh bloodless kidney (dog, pig) and inject the vein under constant pressure with the blue gelatine mass. [3] Next place the kidney in iced water for a few minutes to harden the gelatine, and then attach to the artery a very small constant-pressure injecting apparatus, the receptacle for the injecting fluid containing the writer's carmine fluid. After regulating the amount of pressure, the whole apparatus, with the kidney, is placed within the receiver of an air-pump and the air slowly exhausted. In this way the arteries become filled with fluid. Allow the gland to harden in alcohol and mount the sections in balsam or dammar. Kidneys in which the vein and artery have been injected may have the collecting tubules filled from the ureter with yellow injecting fluid, thus making a triple injection. Sections of kidney hardened in alcohol may be stained with borax-carmine, and afterward bleached in a dilute hydrochloric acid (1 to 10) solution, or a concentrated one of oxalic acid. When the vessels of a kidney have been injected with blue gelatine, staining with carmine gives good results.

Thiersch's yellow injecting fluid is made as follows : Prepare a solution of bichromate of potassa, one part of the salt to eleven parts of water, and a solution of nitrate of lead of the same strength. One part of the potassa solution is placed in a small basin and mixed with four parts of a concentrated solution of gelatine. Two parts of the lead solution are placed in another basin and mixed with four parts of jelly. These are to be slowly and thoroughly mixed together at a temperature of 75° to 90°, and then heated in a water-bath at a temperature of 212° for half an hour or more. Filter carefully through flannel (Beale : Microscope, p. 90).

The kidney stroma.—In the cortical substance the stroma is reduced to a colloid material which binds the tubules together. In the lower part of the medulla, in the fresh state,

[1] See page 205.
[2] Carmine, 5 grammes ; glycerine (anhydrous), 50 grammes ; add caustic potassa until the carmine is dissolved, and neutralize with pure, concentrated muriatic acid.
[3] Gelatine should be first immersed in water until it becomes softened and then gently heated until dissolved. Add soluble Berlin blue, or Beale's blue fluid, until a good color is obtained. Inject while hot.

the stroma is a colorless, transparent substance, which, after immersion for a variable time in a solution of chromate of potassa or ammonia, resolves itself into a thin fibrous reticulum, containing at regular intervals round or elliptical nuclei; [1] these, according to Schweigger-Seidel, belong to stellate or spindle-shaped corpuscles, which may be isolated by maceration in hydrochloric acid. The nuclei are only seen in the lower portion of the medulla ; the fibrous appearance of the stroma is retained some distance beyond this point.

The *nerves* follow the course of the arteries of the kidney and seem to supply only those vessels.

The *lymphatics* at the hilum are derived from the interior of the organ, and from a network of small lymph-branches situated between the bundles of fibres of the capsule. The latter communicate with lymph-canals in the interior of the organ.[2]

The *capsule* of the kidney is a fibrous tissue, containing some few elastic filaments. It is divisible into two layers, an outer and an inner one. The former, about 0.1 to 0.2 mm. in thickness is continuous with the connective tissue which surrounds the blood-vessels at the hilum ; the latter, about 0.025 mm. in thickness, terminates at the points where the papillæ enter the calices. Immediately underneath the inner layer, is a large meshed reticulum of smooth muscle-fibres,[3] some of which traverse the substance of the gland for a short distance.

The *calyx*, at its junction with the papilla, is covered with epithelium, which is continued on to the apex of the papilla ; it contains, in addition, muscle-fibres disposed at right angles to one another, and connective tissue.

Natural injection of the tubules of the kidney by the sulphindigate of soda.[4]—The first to inject the kidney in this way was Chronsczewski ;[5] but his experiments were not very successful, at least so far as the kidney was concerned. Those of Heidenhain[6] which have been confirmed by the writer,[7] give

---

[1] Henle : loc. cit.   [2] Ludwig, in Stricker's Manual.

[3] Eberth : Med. Centralbl., No. 15, 1872.

[4] Commonly known in the laboratory and in commerce as indigo-carmine.

[5] Chronsczewski, in Virchow's Archiv, Bd. XXXI., p. 187; also Bd. XXXV., p. 158.

[6] Max Schultze's Archiv, Bd. X., p. 1, and Pflüger's Archiv, Bd. IX., p. 1.

[7] Mayer : Histol. of Kidney. Prize dissert., 1876.

the most satisfactory results. To insure this desirable end, it is necessary that the sulphindigate of soda be pure.

O. Maschke, of Breslau, the apothecary who manufactures the pure sulphindigate of soda for Prof. Heidenhain, writes to that author as follows: "The indigo-sulphate of soda was prepared from the phœnicin-sulphate of soda. If the latter compound be heated for half to one hour, at a temperature of 60° to 70° C., with five or six times its volume of sulphuric acid of a specific gravity of 1,840, it resolves itself completely into indigo-disulphate of soda and indigo-monosulphate of soda (indigunterschwefelsaures Natron). I have chosen this mode of preparing the salt because the indigo-gelatine and indigo-brown can easily be separated from the phœnicin-sulphate of soda, without marked loss, and in this way I obtain a sufficiently pure substance for future use. An easier method of preparing the salt is the formula given by Crum and Berzelius. One part of best indigo in powder is gradually added to seven or eight parts of pure sulphuric acid, specific gravity 1,840, in a large vessel, and the two thoroughly mixed. After the liquid has ceased to froth, the vessel is covered with an animal membrane and put aside for three days, during which interval it is to be frequently shaken. To this solution thirty to forty volumes of water are added, and the whole carefully filtered. To the resulting clear solution as many parts by weight of crystallized carbonate of soda as there were of sulphuric acid, are added. Owing to the effervescence which now takes place, the vessel in which the mixture is prepared must be of large size. For this reason it is better to substitute the acetate of soda, or chloride of sodium, or simply sulphate of soda, for the formation and precipitation of the indigo-disulphate of soda takes place with any soda salt which does not decompose the indigo-disulphuric acid. The mixture is now filtered, and the precipitate dried over a water-bath. It is then pulverized and treated repeatedly with absolute alcohol, which dissolves any indigo-monosulphate of soda, acetate of soda, or indigo-red, which may have remained." In this way the indigo-carmine is obtained in a pure state. The crystals are copper-colored, but the salt is blue in the pulverized state. The indigo-carmine of commerce is an impure article and cannot be used for natural injection.

For injection, a cold saturated solution of the sulphindigate of soda is used ; the salt may be dissolved in boiling distilled water, and the solution allowed to cool. A dog or rabbit answers for the purpose of injecting. The animal is properly fastened to a board, and the external or internal jugular vein dissected up and exposed. In either of these vessels a canula with stop-cock, previously filled with the indigo-carmine solution, is inserted. The injection into the jugular may be made downward or upward—the latter is preferable. A syringe, graduated in cubic centimetres and containing the solution of indigo-carmine, is now attached to the canula, the stop-cock opened and a small quantity of the solution injected into the vein. Not more than 5 c.c. should be injected at one time. If the animal be a white rabbit, the result of the first injection shows itself in a few seconds, for the animal soon becomes quite blue. After five or ten minutes another 5 c.c. 'of the solution may be injected, and so on until 20 to 50 c.c. of indigo-carmine solution have been employed, the amount varying according to the size of the animal.

The excretion of blue urine takes place soon after the first injection of indigo-carmine. As soon as a sufficient quantity has been excreted the animal is killed in the following manner : The abdomen is opened and the descending aorta looked for ; when found, the canula of a syringe, filled with absolute alcohol, is attached. The jugular vein is now cut across, and while the animal bleeds to death absolute alcohol is injected up the aorta or into the renal arteries. A safer and better way is to inject the renal artery at once with absolute alcohol ; in either case the renal veins should be cut across. The kidney is at once removed, placed in absolute alcohol, and then divided into several pieces, to insure a rapid action of the spirit. While the indigo-carmine is being injected into the jugular vein, the animal should be wrapped up in flannel or cotton-batting so as to be kept warm. No air should be allowed to enter the vein, or the animal may die before the experiment is concluded. Injection of absolute alcohol through the renal artery should be accomplished before the animal has bled to death, or, at least, immediately afterward. When the kidney has been thoroughly hardened, vertical and transverse sections are to be made through the cortical and medullary substances, and examined in glycerine saturated in chloride of potassium ; or, better still, in resinous turpentine.

If the injection of absolute alcohol be delayed, either through lack of skill in the experimenter, or any mishap, the indigo salt within the kidney becomes diffused over the entire organ by absorption of water from the contained vessels, and the whole kidney becomes of a uniform blue color. Such glands must be laid aside, for sections made therefrom, even after immersion in absolute alcohol, are worthless, and will only confuse the microscopist. The absolute alcohol of the shops is not always absolute, as is well known. It has a great affinity for water, and, in handling, rapidly absorbs moisture from the air. To make it absolute, I heat sulphate of copper (pure) at a low red-heat. This drives out the water of crystallization, and changes the color from blue to white. Of this I mix a large spoonful or more, while still hot, with a pint of the so-called absolute alcohol, and tightly cork the vessel, which is then to be shaken occasionally, but not used for a week or more. The affinity that water has for anhydrous sulphate of copper is greater than that of the alcohol, and the latter readily gives it up. As soon as the anhydrous sulphate regains its water of crystallization it assumes a blue color again.

Everywhere in the sections it will be seen that the glomeruli or their capsules are entirely free from color, while all the tubules possessing the rod-epithelium have a more or less blue color, according to the quantity of indigo-carmine excreted. The lumina of the convoluted and other tubules are generally filled with the crystallized indigo-salt. In examining sections, it soon becomes evident that the convoluted tubules and that part of Henle's loop which possesses the rod-epithelium, alone excrete the indigo-salt, while the other tubules merely contain it in their lumen, the salt having been washed down, as it were, from above by the water filtered through the capillaries of the glomeruli.

Instead of using the sulphindigate of soda, Heidenhain, in his second series of experiments, substituted a solution of uric acid in caustic soda. The renal artery was injected with alcohol containing acetic acid. The result showed that urate of soda, like the indigo-salt, was excreted only by the tubules possessing the rod-epithelium. The capsules were entirely free. The addition of acetic acid to the alcohol caused the uric acid to be precipitated in the shape of rhomboid crystals within the tubules. In this condition Heidenhain found them. The hypothesis set down by Bowman, years ago, that the tubules of the kidney excrete the solid constituents of the urine merely, while the glomeruli serve as a filter for the fluid portion, is therefore correct.

If the quantity of indigo solution injected into the jugular be small, and the animal killed soon after, the kidney being treated as above detailed, the microscopic sections exhibit the following appearance: glomerulus and capsule are not acted upon; the narrower branch of the loop and the collecting tubules are free from any crystallized salt, and their epithelium clear. In the convoluted tubules and the broad part of the loop, the following phenomena may also be observed: their lumina are entirely free from any deposit of indigo-carmine, though here and there the rod-epithelium is not stained. In the greater number it is colored of a light blue color. In some the rods and nuclei are uniformly stained; in others the rods alone show the blue color, while the nuclei are not stained. This constitutes the first stage of the excretion of indigo-car-

mine through the kidneys.   If a larger quantity of indigo
solution be injected, and the animal dealt with as above, the
second stage of the excretion is seen.   Here, again, the glomeruli, the capsules, and the collecting-tubules are free from
color, the rod-epithelium stained blue, and their nuclei dark
blue (Fig. 101, F).   In a few of the convoluted tubules and the
ascending broad branches of the loop, crystals of indigo-salt

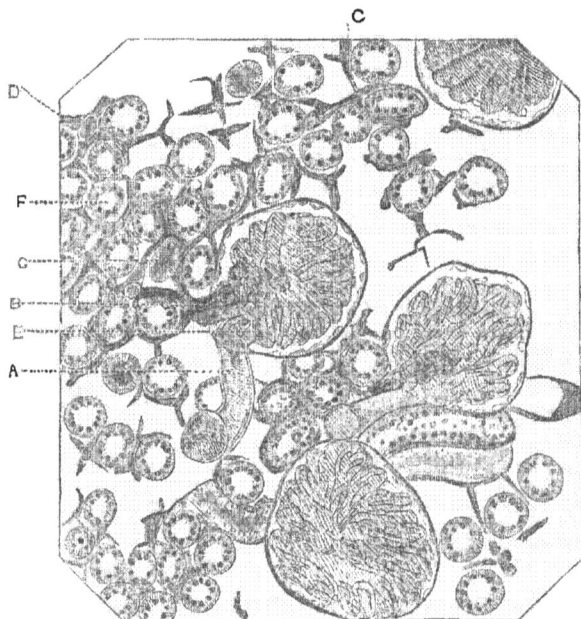

FIG. 101.—Kidney of dog.   Natural injection of secreting portion, artificial injection of artery, vein,
and capillaries.   Transverse section through cortical substance : A, afferent vessel, filled with injected
material ; B, efferent vessel, also filled with injection ; E, glomerulus, injected and lying within its capsule : epithelium of latter distinctly seen : D, capillaries surrounding the convoluted tubules, and distended with the injection ; at this point four capillaries are seen to unite and form a vein ; C, convoluted tubule, filled with crystals of indigo-carmine ; F, convoluted tubule, in which the nuclei have a
dark color.   The striations of Heidenhain are beautifully shown in the convoluted tubules.   × 200.

fill the lumina.   So, also, in some of the descending narrow
branches of the loop.   In the third stage the rods are colorless, while their nuclei are still blue.   Masses of the indigo-
salt fill the lumina of the convoluted, looped, and collecting
tubules ; the glomeruli and their capsules are colorless.   In
the last stage, the salt is contained in the lumina of the collecting tubules only, all the rest of the gland being free from
it, and consequently colorless.   From the above it will be

seen that the rod-epithelium alone excretes the indigo-salt, and it may be presumed, therefore, that the function of the glomeruli is to act as a filter for the fluid portion of the urine. Thus the salt is washed from the convoluted into the collecting tubules, and thence into the pelvis of the kidney. The action of absolute alcohol on a solution of sulphindigate of soda is to precipitate that salt. It is this action within the kidney which fixes the dye, as above set forth.

Beautiful specimens may also be obtained by various modifications of the above process.

The following formulæ and results are given by Heidenhain :

1. Rabbit or dog; section of spinal cord, injection of only 5 c.c. of the indigo solution, the animal being killed after ten minutes. Result : pyramidal portion and boundary layer free from indigo-blue. In the cortical substance, some of the convoluted tubules are filled with the crystalline salt; in the greater number the epithelium is colored of a uniform blue, the nuclei possessing the same tint ; the lumen is usually free.

2. Same conditions as above, excepting that 20 or 25 c.c. of the solution is injected. Medulla free from indigo blue. In the cortex a great many of the tubules are filled with the pigment, while the epithelium is stained blue, the nuclei of a deep blue color.

3. Same conditions as in 2, excepting that the animal is killed one hour after injection. Nuclei of the rod-epithelium stained deep blue, rods clear ; convoluted and collecting tubules filled with crystals of pigment.

Instead of using absolute alcohol for injecting the renal artery, the writer's carmine-glycerine fluid may be employed. After having injected the artery in this way, the kidney is placed in a vessel of absolute alcohol, and divided into small pieces while immersed in that fluid. The glycerine being anhydrous, prevents the diffusion of the indigo-salt within the kidney, while the alcohol fixes the pigment. Sections should be made from the cortex and medulla, and mounted permanently in resinous turpentine. If the glycerine injection has been successful, all the glomeruli and capillaries will be filled with a transparent red mass (Fig. 101). If the indigo excretion has reached the third stage, the collecting tubules in the medulla will be filled with blue crystals of indigo-carmine, and the vasa recta with a red mass, the two arranged in alternate rows. Such specimens leave nothing to be desired in the way of demonstrating the structural relations just described.

BIBLIOGRAPHY.

FERREIN. Mém. de l'acad., p. 502. Paris, 1753.

MÜLLER. De glandularum, etc. Leipz., 1830. And Unters. üb. d. Eingew. d. Fische. Berlin, 1845.

HUSCHKE. Lehre d. Eingeweide. Leipz., 1844.

GERLACH. Müller's Archiv, p. 378, 1845, and p. 102, 1848.

VIRCHOW. Virchow's Archiv. Bd. XII., p. 310. 1857.

BEER. Die Bindesubstanz d. Niere, etc. Berlin, 1859.

LUDWIG. Handb. d. Phys. Bd. II., p. 628. And Wiener med. Wochen. 1804.

ROTH. Diss. Bern, 1804.

CHRONSCZEWSKI. Virchow's Archiv. Bd. XXXI., p. 153. 1864.

SCHWEIGGER-SEIDEL. Die Niere, etc. Halle, 1865.

STILLING. Ein Beitrag, etc., Diss. Marburg, 1865.

HÜFNER. Vergl. Anat. u. Phys. d. Harn. Leipz., 1866.

LINDGREN. Z. f. rat. Med. 1868.

GROSS. Essai sur la structure microscopique des reins. Strassbourg, 1868.

ISAACS. Jour. de la phys. Tome. I., p. 577. 1858.

LUDWIG. Stricker's Manual. 1871.

EBERTH. Centralb. f. d. med. Wiss., p. 227. 1872.

HENLE. Eingeweidel., 2 Aufl. 1874.

FREY. Mikroskop. 6 Aufl. 1877. And Handb. 4 Aufl. 1874.

HEIDENHAIN. Schultze's Archiv. Bd. X. 1874. And Pflüger's Arch. Bd. IX. 1874.

SCHACHOWA. Unters. üb. d. Niere. Diss. Bern, 1876.

NUSSBAUM. Beitr. z. Anat. und Phys. d. Niere Sitzungsber. d. Niederrh. u. Sw. Bonn, 1877.

RUNEBERG. Nord. Med. Ark. XI., 2. No. 13. 1879.

HENSCHEN. Akad. Afhandling in Upsula. Stockholm, 1879.

KLEIN and SMITH. Atlas of Histology. Part XI. 1880.

CHAPTER XV.

THE MALE EXTERNAL AND INTERNAL ORGANS OF GENERATION, WITH THEIR GLANDULAR APPENDAGES.

By Dr. J. HENRY C. SIMES,

Lecturer on Histology, University of Pennsylvania.

Penis.—The copulative organ of the male consists of erectile tissue, and is made up of three bodies, each enclosed in a fibrous membrane, the *tunica albuginea.* Two of these bodies are termed *corpora cavernosa;* the third *corpus spongiosum;* through the latter the urethra passes.

The *tunica albuginea* consists of connective tissue and elastic fibres, with some smooth muscular elements. From the internal surface of this membrane arise numerous trabeculæ, or bands, composed of the same tissue as the membrane; they divide and subdivide, forming a very intricate reticulum. The cavities thus formed freely communicate one with the other, and are lined with a single layer of flattened endothelial plates. This system of intercommunicating lacunæ is in reality nothing but a true venous network. It is in direct communication with the veins of the organ. By the overfilling of these cavities with blood the erectile state is produced.

Externally, the tunica albuginea is surrounded by loose subcutaneous tissue, in which numerous elastic fibres are present. Longitudinal bundles and a few oblique fibres of involuntary muscle are also found in this areolar tissue. The skin covering the penis is thin, and possesses numerous fine hairs, which have an increased length as the root of the organ is approached; they are connected with ordinary sebaceous glands which open into their follicles. Sudorific glands are also present in the skin of this organ. The internal leaf of the prepuce resembles closely a mucous membrane; papillæ are numerous, but there is an absence of hairs, and the sebaceous follicles (Tyson's glands) are sometimes difficult to find in the adult. In new-born children, however, these glands are abundant and well developed. The convoluted glands are here absent.

The extremity of the penis terminates in a cone-shaped body, the *glans penis*, which has a cavernous structure very similar to that in the body of the organ, and differing only in the size of the meshes and the trabeculæ, the former being smaller and the latter more delicate. The external or mucous surface of the glans is covered with a laminated pavement epithelium, the cells of the upper layer being quite flat, those of the middle layer ribbed, while in the lowest layer they are columnar. There are numerous elastic fibres in the mucous membrane of the glans, and many single or branched papillæ are seen, some containing club-shaped nerve-terminations.

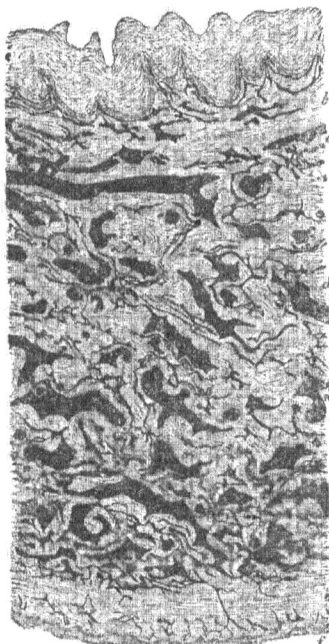

FIG. 102.—Transverse section through the injected glans: *a*, epithelium of the urethra; *b*, tunica mucosa; *c*, corpus cavernosum urethræ; *d*, corpus cavernosum glandis; *e*, mucous membrane of the glans; *f*, epithelium of the glans. Klein.

The system of *blood-vessels* in connection with the penis consists of arteries, veins, capillaries, and cavernous spaces. The modes of communication between these several vascular structures are three : a direct passing of the blood from the larger arterial to the larger venous branches; a somewhat coarse venous reticulum communicating with a system of arterioles; and, finally, a direct capillary anastomosis.

The *lymphatic system* of the penis is represented by lymph-spaces, capillaries, and large trunks. The former, the spaces, are oblong in shape, and occur in the loose subcutaneous tissue surrounding the tunica albuginea ; they communicate with a capillary system, which is disposed in longitudinal meshes. The large lymph-trunks formed from these smaller vessels are situated along the dorsum of the organ, and communicate with the lymph-glands in the pelvis and those of the groin.

The *nerves* and their *terminations* in the penis are derived from the cerebro-spinal and sympathetic systems. In the loose tissue external to the tunica albuginea large medullated fibres are observed; these give off smaller branches which enter the cavernous structure, and may be followed for some distance as medullated or non-medullated fibres. In this same tissue are found, at the root, shaft, and vicinity of the corona glandis, Pacinian corpuscles. They are oval in shape, and have their long diameter parallel to the long axis of the penis. These bodies have also been met with in the cavernous structure. The glans is especially rich in nervous elements, and here are found bodies known as the "*genital nerve-corpuscles*," situated in the tissue of the mucous membrane at the base of the papillæ. These bodies are round in shape, vary in size from 0.1439 to 0.2001 mm. in diameter, and have characteristic constrictions upon their surface, giving them a mulberry-like appearance. The ordinary terminal bulbs of Krause are also met with in this location.

The *urethra* of the male serves as the excretory canal for the urine and seminal fluid. An anatomical division is made into the prostatic, membranous, and spongy parts. The canal is lined with a mucous membrane, external to which there is a fibrous layer rich in elastic fibres, having a cavernous structure; external again to this is the muscular coat, composed of involuntary muscular fibres arranged in two layers, an internal, or longitudinal, and an external, or circular. There are also numerous fasciculi of oblique fibres, which serve to connect the two layers.

The histological structure and arrangement of the three parts of the urethra are unlike, and must be separately studied. (*a*) In the prostatic portion the mucous membrane lies in longitudinal folds. A laminated epithelium covers the inferior wall, while the sides and superior wall are lined with a transitional variety. The prominence of this portion of the urethra, the *colliculus seminalis*, is composed of elastic tissue and smooth muscular cells, which form a cavernous structure. Throughout this spongy tissue, near the surface, are seen glands similar to those found in the prostate. Racemose glands (Littre's glands), imperfectly developed, lined with cylindrical

15

epithelial cells in their acini, and at their orifices with laminated epithelium, are also present. The muscular tissue in
this part of the urethra is intimately connected with that of
the prostate ; its fasciculi have generally a longitudinal direction, and send off oblique bundles into the mucous membrane. (*b*) The membranous por-
tion of the urethra has its mucous
membrane covered by an epithelium similar to that met with in
the prostatic portion. The glands
of Littre are absent. Beneath the
mucous membrane a long-meshed
erectile tissue of a cavernous nature is found. Here the organic
muscular layer is poorly developed, and it is covered by transverse bundles of striped muscular
fibres, the *musculus urethralis.* (*c*)
Passing to the spongy portion, the
mucous membrane is found thrown
into longitudinal folds, which are
in places connected by transverse
ones, forming depressions, known
as the *lacunæ Morgagnii.* These
are not glandular in their nature.
The epithelium covering the mucous membrane in this portion is
mostly cylindrical, but as it approaches the *meatus urinarius*
gradually assumes a pavement

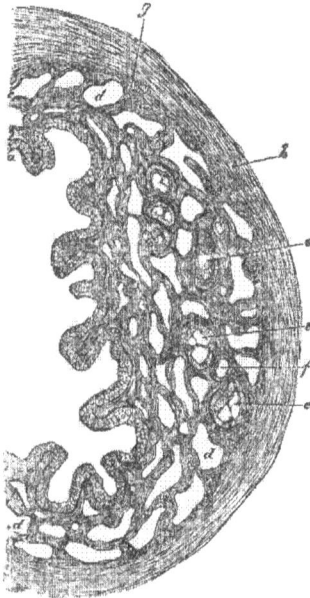

Fig. 103.—Transverse section through
the spongy portion of the urethra (corpus
cavernosum urethræ): *b*, tunica mucosa ; *c*,
muscular cords; *d*, vascular spaces of the
corp. cavern. ; *e*, glands ; *f*, excretory duct
of gland ; *g*, longitudinal muscles ; *h*, tunica
albuginea. Klein.

character. Glands of Littre are found throughout this part.
The muscular elements are even less prominent here than in
the membranous portion.

Well-developed and numerous papillæ are seen projecting
from the mucous membrane of the urethra into the epithelium.
They possess a single capillary loop, or several loops are observed, especially in the fossa navicularis. These papillæ are
absent or imperfectly developed at the points where a transitional
epithelium is met with. Here the capillaries are arranged to constitute a reticulum beneath and parallel to the epithelial covering.

The nerves of the urethra are found forming a network

around the muscular coat, similarly as elsewhere, in connection with smooth muscular fibres. Small nerve-fibres have been traced into the epithelial lining. Collections of ganglionic nerve-cells are found on the posterior surface of the membranous portion; in the dense connective tissue at the posterior portion of the bulb; and lastly, in the network of nerve-fibres around the vessels at the side of the bulb.

The lymphatic system of the urethra is found in the mucous membrane, near the epithelium. It consists of a network of vessels with longitudinally arranged meshes; they are connected with the lymphatic vessels of the bladder, and also open into the lymphatic canals of the glans penis.

Cowper's glands.—These organs, two in number, are situated in the striated muscular tissue which surrounds the membranous portion of the urethra. They are lobulated, oval, and belong to the racemose group of glands. They are composed of acini and excretory ducts which unite to form a single duct for each gland, and discharge into the bulbous portion of the urethra. The acini constituting the several lobules are separated by connective tissue intermixed with smooth muscular fibres; they possess a structureless membrana propria, and are lined with columnar cells, which are imbricated upon their outer thin portions. The ducts are lined with flattened columnar cells, and a layer of smooth muscular fibres is seen running along them. A capillary network surrounds the glandular structure.

The *prostate* may be described as a glandular organ, peculiar in having its stroma composed of involuntary muscular elements. Externally it possesses a connective-tissue envelope which is united to bands of smooth muscular fibres that run in every direction, and constitute the cortical substance of the organ. From this cortex numerous bands or trabeculæ of a similar muscular nature proceed, forming an intricate network, and making up the greater part of the gland; in the meshes of this reticulum is placed the glandular structure. The thickness of the cortex, or the amount of glandular substance, varies according to the position, whether behind or in front of the urethra, and it is found that the glandular structure is comparatively more developed behind and in the lower portions than in front of the urethra.

The arrangement of the glandular elements is similar to
that in the racemose glands, and consists of excretory ducts terminating in glandular vesicles or acini. The ducts which have
their orifices in the urethra at its prostatic portion, and upon
its inferior wall, are here lined with a transitional, or, when
large, with a pavement epithelium, which gradually changes

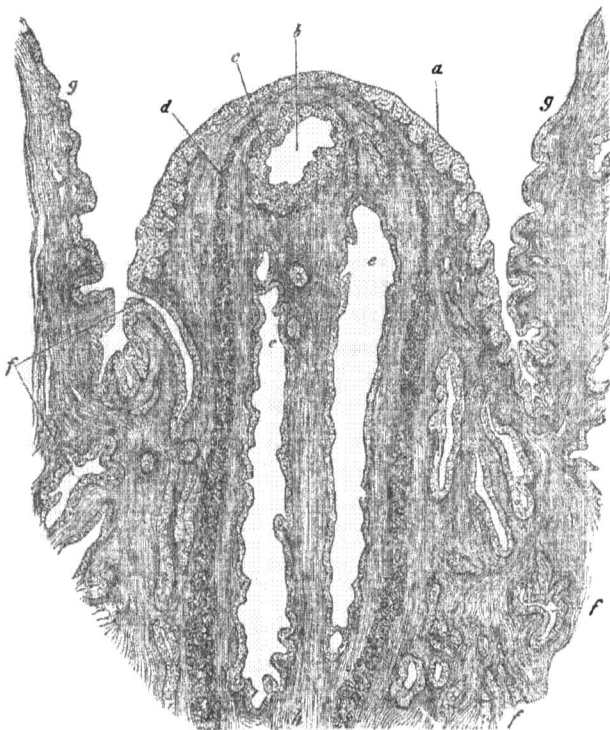

Fig. 104.—Transverse section through the caput gallinaginis: *a*, epithelium of surface; *b*, vesicula
prostatica; *c*, epithelium of the vesicula; *d*, muscles; *e*, ejaculatory duct: *f*, excretory duct of the prostatic glands; *g*, upper wall of the urethra; muscles running vertically. From a child. Klein.

into a columnar variety as the ducts penetrate the organ. The
basement-membrane is structureless, and is invested by a muscular layer. The acini are also lined by a columnar epithelium
and possess a structureless membrana propria; their shape is
usually pyriform, and they have a diameter varying between
0.1254 and 0.23 mm. The epithelial cells of the acini frequently
contain granules of brownish pigment.

Transversely striated muscular fibres are also met with in the prostate, both anterior and posterior to the urethra, extending into the cortical substance, and between the glandular structure in the interior of the gland.

The blood-vessels of the organ come from the large trunks surrounding it; they pass into its structure and form a reticulated capillary system around the glandular substance.

Medullated nerve-fibres are found surrounding the cortex in connection with groups of oval ganglionic centres. Pacinian bodies are also observed in the cortex of the prostate, and in its interior are small medullated nerve-fibres which form a reticulum.

A peculiar structure is found in the upper and posterior part of the prostate. It has the appearance of a duct, with walls resembling an artery, in so far as it consists of an internal longitudinal, a middle circular, and an external longitudinal coat.

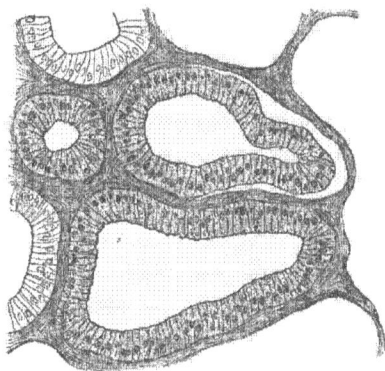

Fig. 105.—Transverse section through the central glandular substance of the prostate. From an adult. Klein.

The middle coat is composed mostly of smooth muscular elements, while the external and internal coats are only partly made up of them. The interior of this structure is filled with a rich vascular network, pigment particles, and smooth muscular fibres.

The *vesicula prostatica*, which forms a cul-de-sac in the middle of the prostate, beneath the middle lobe, opening by a duct at the summit of the *colliculus seminalis*, possesses a fibrous wall in which there are smooth muscular cells and is surrounded by a thin layer of cavernous tissue; it is lined by a laminated epithelium, into which small conical papillæ project; small branched and tortuous glands are also found opening into its cavity.

The *testicles* are glandular organs which secrete the spermatic fluid, and are in the male organism the sexual representatives of the ovaries in the female.

The glandular structure, together with the epididymis of the testicles, is enveloped by a dense fibrous membrane, the *tunica albuginea*. This is surrounded by a serous sac, the *tunica vaginalis propria*. Finally the testicle and spermatic cord are invested by the *tunica vaginalis communis* and the whole is contained in the scrotum.

The tunica albuginea upon its external surface, or that covered by the tunica vaginalis propria, is smooth and shining ; it consists of dense connective tissue with some elastic fibres ; upon the posterior border of the testicle it increases in thickness, and is here termed the *corpus Highmori*, or *mediastinum testis*, which passes into the gland. It also sends off from its whole internal surface numerous bands or trabeculæ, the *septula testis*, which run toward the mediastinum, and divide the interior of the testicle into conical lobules, having their apices directed toward the corpus Highmori. These trabeculæ contain smooth muscular fibres and blood-vessels. It is in these lobules or spaces that the secreting elements of the gland are situated.

The serous sac, or tunica vaginalis, has its visceral layer, the *tunica adnata,* intimately united to the tunica albuginea over the testicle, but it is loosely attached to that over the epididymis. This membrane consists of connective tissue traversed by delicate elastic fibres, and lined on its surface with a layer of polyhedral cells, varying in size and containing oval nuclei with one or two nucleoli. Upon the upper portion of the testicle and sharp edge of the epididymis, the tunica adnata is frequently found to possess tufted excrescences ; these processes are covered by several layers of flattened epithelial cells, or a single layer of round or cylindrical-bodies. A capillary loop is seen extending into the tufts.

The parietal layer of the tunica vaginalis propria consists of connective tissue, elastic fibres, and epithelium, as in the visceral layer.

The *tunica vaginalis communis*, which covers the tunica vaginalis propria, is composed above of a loose, laminated connective tissue, but it becomes more dense below. Between this tunica and the tunica propria unstriped muscular fibres are found, while upon its external surface there are the striped fibres of the cremaster muscle. Small non-vascular pedunculated excrescences are also found upon this surface. The membrane is connected externally by connective tissue with the muscular layer of the scrotum, the *dartos*.

The muscle of the scrotum, the dartos, consists of numerous smooth muscular fibres, arranged singly or forming a more or less continuous layer.

The skin of the scrotum is peculiar in containing considerable pigment, while there is an absence of fat in the subcutaneous tissue. Hairs, large sebaceous follicles, and sweat-glands are also present in the skin of the scrotum.

The *hydatid* of *Morgagni* is a structure found upon the anterior surface of the head of the epididymis, and is thought to be the remains of Müller's duct. It is met with in two forms, either as a vesicle containing a clear fluid (with cells, and nuclei—ciliated epithelial cells are also at times present), and connected to the epididymis by a solid fibrous peduncle, or as a flattened structure possessing scarcely any stalk, which is simple or divided into lobules; the latter form is most frequently seen. At times it is found to communicate with the canal of the epididymis.

Between the head of the epididymis and the vas deferens, situated upon the posterior edge of the testicle, a small organ is seen, consisting of several whitish nodules. Each nodule is composed of a tube forming a number of convolutions and terminating in a club-shaped extremity. The tubes contain a clear fluid and are lined by a cylindrical epithelium, the cells of which are undergoing degeneration. Until ten years of age this organ is fully developed; after this period it experiences degeneration. This structure is known as the *organ of Giraldès*, and represents the remains of the Wolffian bodies.

The glandular or parenchymatous structure of the testicle consists of canals or seminiferous tubules about 0.1128 to 0.1421 mm. in diameter; they are folded on themselves several times so as to constitute lobules, and are situated in the spaces formed by the trabeculæ of the tunica albuginea. The tubules not only are folded but divide and subdivide, anastomose, and terminate by loops. Toward the apices of the lobules the tubules gradually become more straight, fewer in number, and pass into the corpus Highmori, forming the *rete testis*. From the upper part of the rete emerge twelve to seventeen larger tubules which pass through the tunica albuginea, after which they again become convoluted and form a number of conical lobules, named the *coni vasculosi*, which form the head of the epididymis. These tubules gradually unite to form a single canal, which is much convoluted, and develops an elongated body, the body and tail of the epididymis. The convolutions becoming less and less marked, the tube, increased in calibre, then leaves the testicle and ascends, at first somewhat spirally, but soon after in a perfectly straight course, constituting the *vas deferens*. Before this duct is formed, a short cæcal branch, named the *vas aberrans*, is attached to the tube.

The seminiferous tubules either take their origin from blind extremities or anastomoses, the former being more frequently met with in children. Surrounding the tubules there is seen a framework of connective tissue, which proceeds from the septa. This intertubular connective tissue is distinctly laminated, and each lamella is formed of a fenestrated endothelial membrane, and a fenestrated connective-tissue membrane, which thus constitute numerous communicating spaces, that are the rootlets of the lymphatic system of the testis. The number of lamellæ between the seminal tubes varies, and their relation to the tubes is very intimate, but depends upon the amount of fluid present in the interlamellar lymph-spaces. Groups of peculiar cells are found between the lamellæ of the intertubular connective tissue. These cells have been observed by histologists, and by most are thought to be connective-tissue corpuscles. Klein, however, says they are epithelial in nature, and derived from the epithelial columns of the Wolffian body.

In the meshes formed by this reticulated fibrous tissue are located the seminiferous tubules, the membrana propria of which is thought, on the one hand, to be structureless, or, on the other, to be composed of oval, flattened corpuscles, placed at regular intervals, which form an endothelial membrane. The tubules are found filled with corpuscles. Those at the periphery covering the membrana propria are round or polygonal in form, upon transverse section. In children, the cells of the tubules contain a finely granular and pale substance, but in adults they are filled with yellow pigment. Two typical forms of corpuscle are observed, one with dark granular nuclei, the other with bright ones that have or have not nucleoli. The number of nuclei varies; usually there are one or two; but they may reach thirty or more. Many variously formed cells are seen, which fact is held to indicate active proliferation. These bodies are termed seminal cells, and in the embryo are said to possess contractility and amœboid movement.

The seminiferous tubules upon entering the corpus Highmori lose their special external coat, which blends with the connective tissue of this region. Their epithelial lining consists of cylindrical cells with short cilia. After leaving the corpus Highmori and increasing in size, they have an additional coat of smooth muscular fibres, which, further down in the body of the epididymis, consists of two layers, an internal and an external or longitudinal coat. The epithelium lining the canal of the epididymis is composed of cells with long, oval nuclei, and provided with long tufts of cilia. Indeed, the largest cilia found in the human body are upon the large cylindrical cells, which cover the upper part of the canal of the epididymis. Beneath this layer of ciliated bodies is a second of small, polyhedral ones with round nuclei.

The *vas deferens*, which may be considered as analogous in many respects to the excretory duct of a glandular organ, is made up of an external or fibrous coat, a middle or muscular, and a mucous membrane, which is located most internally. Covering this membrane are epithelial elements which differ in the various parts of the duct. At the beginning there is a single layer of cylindrical cells, between which, sometimes, there are spindle-shaped bodies ; the former possess delicate cilia. At about four centimetres from the epididymis the cilia are lost, but the character of the cells remains the same, except that a striated border can be seen in many. In children, a difference exists between the extra- and intra-abdominal portions of the duct. The former, or extra, is lined by a laminated epithelium, composed of a superficial layer of short cylindrical cells, beneath which are one or two layers of round or polyhedral cells. All these corpuscles have a relatively large nucleus. The intra-abdominal portion of the duct has a lining similar to that observed in the adult.

The mucous coat is made up of connective tissue and elastic fibres, the former consisting of intersecting fasciculi, the latter of a close network. The membrane is thrown into two or three longitudinal folds or rugæ. Near the lower end of the vas deferens, in the *ampulla*, the longitudinal folds are connected by transverse ones, and thus depressions are formed.

The *muscular* coat consists of smooth muscular fibres arranged in three layers : an inner, or longitudinal, which is feebly developed ; a middle, or circular, which is substantial in character, and an external or longitudinal. This coat is less developed in young children than in adults.

In the external fibrous coat, or tunica adventitia of the vas deferens, are found bundles of smooth muscular fibres running longitudinally. They are derived from the cremaster internus, which muscle is well developed at the origin of the vas deferens, but gradually diminishes in size as it enters the abdominal cavity.

The vas deferens possesses a dense plexus of medullated nerve-fibres, the spermatic plexus, situated in the tunica adventitia. From this plexus several smaller trunks proceed which penetrate into the muscular and mucous coats. Scattered along these nerve-trunks are seen small ganglion-cells, which are round or oval.

The *blood-vessels* of the testicle come from the internal spermatic artery and enter the gland partly at the corpus Highmori and partly upon its surface. They surround the seminiferous tubules as a capillary plexus of large meshes. The *epididymis* receives its blood from the deferential artery, and also to some extent from the vessels of the testicle. The *vas deferens* possesses a rich capillary network in its muscular coat and also in its mucous membrane beneath the epithelium.

The *nerves* of the testicle come from the internal spermatic plexus ; their mode of termination has not as yet been satisfactorily explained. Letzerich, however, describes fine nerve-fibres in the testicles of mammals ; they penetrate the connective tissue and membrana propria, terminating between this layer and the first row of cells in dark granular masses.

The *lymphatic system* of the testicle consists of a series of lacunæ, lined with endothelial cells, which surround the seminiferous tubules ; in the interstitial connective-tissue, these communicate with canals from which others are given off to the connective-tissue septa of the lobules. Beneath the tunica albuginea another network of lymphatic canals is also found, which penetrate the tunic, especially upon the dorsum of the organ, and finally, uniting with the lymphatics of the epididymis and tunica vaginalis, form several large trunks, which follow the spermatic cord. Distinct networks of lymphatic vessels are found in the vascular and nervous layers of the spermatic cord, and some are seen close to the muscular coat of the vas deferens.

The *seminal vesicles*, designed as receptacles for the fluid secreted by the testicles, are, with some slight modifications, similar in structure to the vas deferens. They are composed of a mucous, muscular, and fibrous coat. The mucous membrane is covered with a superficial layer of cylindrical and a deep layer of polyhedral-epithelial cells, and is thrown into folds, longitudinal and transverse, forming depressions. The muscular coat consists of three layers, an internal or longitudinal, a middle or circular, and an external or longitudinal. The fibrous coat is abundantly supplied with networks of vessels and nerves. Here the ganglionic collections are highly developed, each corpuscle being quite large and containing a single nucleus, or even at times two.

The *ejaculatory ducts* are, histologically, similar to the last described organs. As they approach the prostate their cylindrical epithelium gradually changes into the transitional variety, and subsequently into the laminated pavement, as they approach their point of outlet in the urethra. Their mucous membrane is uneven from the longitudinal and transverse folds. After entering the prostate the muscular substance of the ducts undergoes cavernous transformation.

When the testicle attains its full physiological development, which occurs in man at puberty, there is secreted by the organ a peculiar fluid, the *semen* or *sperma*. This fluid is whitish, slimy, and colorless, and has an alkaline or neutral reaction. Semen examined as discharged from the orifice of the urethra, *in coitu*, appears as a very different fluid, having received the secretions from the various accessory glands of the generative system. It is now more fluid, opaque, strongly alkaline in reaction, and has acquired a peculiar odor. Placed under the microscope there is seen suspended in a hyaline fluid an infinite number of moving thread-like bodies called *seminal filaments, spermatozoa, spermatozoids, seminal elements*, etc. They are divided into a head, body or middle portion, and tail.

The shape of the head is pyriform, the broad part being connected with the body ; each has an average length of 0.0045 mm., and its breadth is about half as much. The middle portion or body is about 0.0061 mm. long, while the tail measures

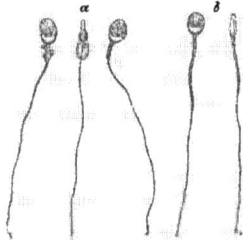

FIG. 106.—Seminal elements of man: a, undeveloped ; b, mature. St. George.

about 0.0406 mm. Both the body and head of the seminal elements seem to be rigid, the terminal thread or tail having an active motion. From this description it will be seen that a comparison of its structure with that of a ciliated epithelial cell is admissible, and indeed quite reasonable.

The way in which spermatozoa are formed is still imperfectly known, and two different views claim our attention. They are as follows : a. The nucleus of the seminal cells moves to the periphery, then at the opposite side the protoplasm of the cell is elongated into a caudal appendage ; the nucleus continuing to advance causes the protoplasm to become more and more elongated, and it is ultimately lengthened into a thread-like tail, while the nucleus, with its thin layer of protoplasm, constitutes the head. b. In this view the columnar or prismatic-shaped cells, the most external layer of cells filling the seminal tubules. are thought to be the spermatozoa-producing elements. The inner remaining cells of the tubules experience no further development. During the active stage of the gland the spermatic cells become elongated, and extend into the centre of the tubule ; their free extremities become enlarged, and have a number of buds or club-like projections, eight to twelve, developed upon them. In each bud is formed a nucleus ; these nuclei eventually become the heads of spermatozoa, and the protoplasm is further developed into the body and tail. The cells from which the spermatozoa have their origin are named *spermatoblasts*.

Klein, in his recent "Atlas of Histology," gives a very extended description of the development of spermatozoa. According to this writer there are several layers of epithelial cells lining the inside of the membrana propria of the seminal tubules. These layers he divides into an outer and inner. The outer, situated next to the membrana propria, embraces the *germ-cells* of Sertoli. The inner layer, those nearer the lumen of the tubule, are the *seminal cells* of Sertoli. These latter are usually arranged in two or more layers, polyhedral in shape when placed closely together, but more spherical when next to the lumen of the tubule; they are uniform in size and contain a single nucleus. The nucleus is spherical, possesses no limiting membrane, and contains a convolution of thick fibrils, or rods, in a transparent matrix. A more minute examination of the nucleus shows that the fibrils are arranged in certain definite forms, which indicate changes preparatory to division, as has been pointed out by Strassburger, Hertwig, Flemming, and others. The various forms, taken by the nucleus before dividing, correspond to what is termed the "convolution," the "basket," the "wreath," the "monaster," or the "dyaster." The entire process of the indirect division of the nucleus is termed by Flemming *karyokinesis*.

Toward the lumen of the tube the above-described cells are seen with their nucleus either dividing or divided into two *daughter-nuclei*. From these daughter-nuclei are developed the daughter-cells, or spermatoblasts, and by an interesting series of changes the spermatozoa are formed.

"The nucleus of the spermatoblasts at first retains its spherical shape, but is invested in a distinct membrane, the convolution of fibrils changes into a honey-combed reticulum, sometimes with one or two nucleoli, and the nucleus is not placed in the centre but in the periphery of the cell."

"Next the nucleus becomes uniform in its substance and transparent, all traces of a reticulum have disappeared. The cell-substance has collected at one end of the nucleus as an elliptical granular mass, and appears separated from it by a transparent, clear bag."

"In the next stage the nucleus becomes flattened and discoid, so that when viewed from the surface it is broad and circular, but appears narrow and staff-shaped when seen in profile. The cell-substance at this time is drawn out into a cylindrical or club-shaped *granular body*, separated from the nucleus by a shorter or longer *clear tube*, the former clear bag. At the front part of the nucleus is seen a short and tapering curved projection, and at its hind end—viz., that directed toward the clear tube and cell-substance—there is also to be found a short-pointed process extending into the clear tube just named."

"In the next stage the nucleus becomes more flattened and

oblong. In the last stage the granular body has become changed into a long, thin, and homogeneous filament."

"In what relation do, then, these different parts of the fully formed spermatozoön stand to the parts of the developing element—that is, the spermatoblast? A comparison shows at once that the head of the ripe spermatozoön is the changed nucleus of the spermatoblast; that the filament, or tail, is derived from what has been mentioned above as the granular body of the original cell. The middle piece of Schweigger-Seidel is an outgrowth of the nucleus of the spermatoblast, that is, of the head, the spermatozoön, and the *clear tube* of the developing spermatozoön, described above as embracing the hind part of the nucleus and separating the latter from the granular body, is the sheath which, in some instances (triton and salamander), is observable on the middle piece of the fully formed spermatozoön."

In short, the head of the spermatozoön is derived from the nucleus, while the tail has its origin from the body of the spermatoblast.

BIBLIOGRAPHY.

COOPER, A. Obs. on the Struct. and Dis. of the Testis. London, 1830.

WAGNER. Müller's Archiv. 1836.

PANIZZA, B. Osservazioni anthropo-zoot.-fisiol. Pavia, 1836.

VALENTIN. Ueb. d. Verl. d. Blutgef. im Penis d. Menschen. Müller's Arch. 1838.

KOBELT. Die männl. u. weibl. Wollustorgane. Freiburg, 1844.

KÖLLIKER. Gewebelehre und Verhandl. d. Würzb. med.-phys. Ges. 1851.

KOHLRAUSCH. Zur Anat. u. Phys. d. Beckenorgane. Leipzig, 1854.

SAPPEY. L'urèthre de l'homme. 1854.

LEYDIG, F. Zur Anat. d. männl. Geschlechtsorg. in Zeitschr. f. wiss. Zool. Vol. II. And Histologie. 1857.

JARJAVAY. Rech. anat. sur l'urèthre de l'homme. Paris, 1857.

MERKEL. Göttinger Nachrichten. No. 1, p. 7. 1863. And Arch. f. mikr. Anat. Vol. I., p. 309. 1865.

ST. GEORGE, v. LA VALETTE in Arch. f. mikr. Anat. Vol. I., p. 403. 1865. And Stricker's Manual.

PETTIGREW, in Proc. Roy. Soc. Vol. XV., p. 244. 1866.

SCHWEIGGER-SEIDEL, in Virch. Arch. Vol. XXXVII., p. 225. 1866.

BALBIANA. Journal de l'anat. et de la phys., p. 218. 1868.

LETZERICH, in Virch. Arch. Vol. XLII., p. 570. 1868.

STIEDA. Ueber den Bau des Menschen-Hoden, Arch. f. mikros. Anat. Vol XIV., p. 17. 1877.

SERTOLI. Sulla struttura di canalicoli seminif. dei testicoli. Arch. p. le scien. med. Vol. II., p. 107. 1877.

MENZEL. Ueber Spermatozoen. Arch. f. klin. Chir. Vol. XXI., p. 518. 1877.

VALENTIN, in Zeitschr. f. rat. Med. Vol. XVIII., p. 21. Vol. XXI., p. 89. 1879.

LANGER, in Wien. Sitz. Vol. XLVI., p. 120. 1879.

ROUGET. Compt. rend. Vol. IV., p. 902. 1879.

FREY, HEINRICH. Histology and Histochemistry of Man. 1880.

KLEIN, E., and SMITH, E. NOBLE. Atlas of Histology. 1880.

CHAPTER XVI.

THE FEMALE EXTERNAL AND INTERNAL ORGANS OF GENERA TION, WITH THEIR GLANDULAR APPENDAGES—PLACENTA.

By Dr. J. HENRY C. SIMES,

Lecturer on Histology, University of Pennsylvania.

THE external female genitals are the labia majora, labia minora, and clitoris.

The *labia majora* are folds of skin, the subcutaneous tissue of which contains a large amount of adipose tissue. Their internal surface has the nature of a mucous membrane, while externally it is similar to the common integument. Here hairs, sebaceous glands, remarkable for their large size, and sweat-glands, are found. The papillæ, vessels, nerves, and Pacinian corpuscles do not differ from those found elsewhere in the skin.

The *labia minora* may be considered as folds of mucous membrane. They are covered by a laminated pavement-epithelium and the deepest layer contains pigment granules. Conical vascular papillæ are seen beneath the epithelium. In the connective-tissue framework of the mucous membrane smooth muscular elements are found. Capillary networks are seen on the surface beneath the epithelium, and in the substance of the membrane, from which arise small veins, constituting a plexus, and giving this structure the character of an erectile tissue. Upon the external surface of the folds are found sebaceous glands without hairs. These glands are absent at birth. There is no adipose tissue in the labia minora.

The *clitoris* is covered by a mucous membrane which is a continuation of that of the labia minora, and to which it is similar in structure, in so far as epithelium, mucous tissue, and papillæ are concerned. The mucous membrane covering the glans of the organ is found to have those peculiar nerve-terminations in its structure, the *genital nerve-corpuscles*, which have been described as existing in the mucous membrane of the glans penis.

Beneath the mucous membrane of the clitoris are found the *corpora cavernosa* and *glans;* the latter is in connection with both *bulbi vestibuli*, which correspond to the corpus spongiosum urethræ of the male. These structures consist of erectile or cavernous tissue, which, like that in the penis, is made up of a vascular network, mostly venous in character, and erectile in nature ; they are also surrounded by a fibrous tunic analogous to the tunica albuginea of the penis.

The *vestibule* has its mucous membrane, which is a continuation of the mucous membrane of the clitoris, thrown into a number of folds. Opening upon its surface are numerous orifices of racemose mucous glands. These glands are collected into groups around the orifice of the urethra and vagina. They consist of branched ducts, which at their deeper parts are developed into a number of acini ; they are lined with a simple epithelium ; at their orifices they have the laminated pavement-epithelium of the mucous surface. These glands vary in diameter between 0.5 mm. to 2.5 mm. The vessels of the vestibule form a network near the mucous surface, and are connected to the capillary loops in the papillæ.

Opening upon each side of the vaginal entrance is the orifice of the duct belonging to the *gland of Bartholine.* These organs, two in number, are analogous to Cowper's glands in the male. They belong to the racemose group, and are composed of ducts and acini, which have an epithelium lining of cylindrical cells.

The *hymen* consists of a duplicature of the mucous membrane of the vagina. Its laminated epithelium is similar to that of the vestibule. The papillæ are numerous, long, simple or multiple, and project from 0.2 to 0.3 mm. into the epithelial covering. The vascular and nervous supply is very abundant.

The *vagina* consists of an external coat of connective tissue, a middle coat of muscular tissue, and an internal mucous coat. The mucous membrane is uneven, thrown into ridges and papillary elevations, which are especially well-marked in the neighborhood of the vaginal entrance. The epithelium lining the canal is a laminated pavement-epithelium, into which the vas-

16

cular papillæ of the mucous membrane extend. In the latter coating are found numerous elastic fibres in the fasciculi of connective tissue; bundles of smooth muscular cells are also present. Tubular glands, lined with ciliated columnar epithelium at their fundus, have been described as existing in the mucous membrane of the vagina by Preuschen. Hennig also speaks of similar glands being present in this membrane. The submucous tissue is very vascular and loose in texture. The muscular coat consists of an internal longitudinal and an external circular layer of smooth muscular fibres, between which are many oblique connecting fasciculi. The external fibrous tissue is loose in texture, and has embedded in it the external venous plexus.

The *vascular system* of the vagina is composed of arteries, veins, a venous plexus, and capillaries. The plexus is met with in the folds of the vagina. It is a cavernous structure possessing smooth muscular fibres, and has an arrangement of trabeculæ similar to that found in other erectile organs.

The lymphatics and nerves of the mucous membrane of the vagina are abundant. The latter form networks in which there are found ganglion-cells, in groups or single; as in the male genitals, these cells are of two sizes. The ultimate terminations of the nerve-fibres are as yet undetermined. The fluid secreted by this membrane has an acid reaction.

The *urethra* possesses a mucous membrane covered by a transitional epithelium at its upper portion, the superficial layer of cells being short cylinders, which gradually become shorter, until the deepest layer is seen made up of rounded cells. The lower portion of the canal has a lining of laminated pavement-epithelium similar to that of the vestibule. The mucous membrane has numerous papillæ extending into the epithelium. In this layer are seen at places many lymph-corpuscles, sometimes amounting to an infiltration, when it may be considered as adenoid in nature. The submucous · tissue is mostly composed of venous networks; it is in fact a cavernous tissue. As in the male, there are present in the mucous membrane the glands of Littre, seen especially abundant near the *meatus urinarius*. The muscular coat of the urethra consists of an internal longitudinal and an external circular layer of smooth muscular fibres; in the external layer are also the transversely striated muscular fibres of the urethral muscles. The external fibrous coat of the urethra consists of wavy connective-tissue fasciculi, which have a longitudinal and circular course.

The *uterus* possesses an external covering of serous membrane, the peritoneum ; anteriorly it is more intimately connected with the organ than posteriorly, while at the sides the layers are separated, in order to permit the passage of blood-vessels, lymphatics, and nerves into the uterine substance. The tissue composing the greater part of the uterus is formed of smooth muscular fibres, the arrangement of which is very irregular, but three more or less distinct layers have been described. The external one, which is relatively thin, consists mostly of fibres running longitudinally, although many circular fasciculi are seen. The middle layer exceeds the others in thickness, its fibres take a longitudinal, transverse, or oblique direction, while the internal layer is essentially circular, and forms the sphincters of the uterus. The contractile elements of these muscular layers are intimately united together by a cementing substance, forming fasciculi or bundles, which are again held together by connective tissue in which elastic fibres are found. The shape of the cells in the normal uterus is fusiform, frequently very long, and in transverse section round or oval, with several angles. The nucleus is always single, rod-like or oblong in shape.

The *mucous membrane* lining the uterus is closely connected to the muscular tissue. It has no connective-tissue framework of fibres, but its structure resembles the stroma of lymphoid organs, in which the framework is made up of spindle and fusiform cells. The surface of this membrane varies in different parts ; at the fundus and body it is smooth, except at the orifices of the Fallopian tubes, where there is a slight folding ; in the canal of the neck it is thrown into numerous branching folds, the *plicæ palmatæ*. At the upper end of the isthmus of the cervix a distinct border indicates the termination of the mucous membrane of the body. The epithelium covering this portion of the membrane is columnar in shape, and provided with short cilia. There are found in the mucous membrane of the fundus and body numerous tubular glands, which are either simple tubes or they divide about their middle, and terminate in blind ends; frequently they have a spiral course, corkscrew-like; but generally their direction is vertical to the plane of the membrane; they open into the cavity of the uterus. The existence of a membrana propria in these *glandulæ utriculares* is denied by some, or if present it is only toward the orifice of the gland. In the pregnant organ, however, an extremely delicate, structureless membrane, in which oval nuclei are found, is thought to represent such a structure. The cells lining these glands are prismatic in shape, their broad ends directed outward; the slender extremities projecting into the lumen of the gland are provided with cilia.

The mucous membrane lining the canal of the cervix is denser and thicker than that of the body. It possesses a connective-tissue investment which lies between it and the muscular layer, and it also differs from the lining of the body in the presence of folds, which constitute the plicæ palmatæ. The epithelium covering this portion of the uterus is made up of cylindrical ciliated cells, in the upper two-thirds of the canal, but as the external *os uteri* is approached it gradually assumes the laminated pavement variety. Minute papillæ, provided with a capillary loop, are found in the lower half of the canal. The folds of membrane consist of a firm fibrous tissue, a few smooth muscular elements, and a scanty amount of elastic fibres. Here are also located the mucous follicles of the cervix, or, as some histologists consider them, depressions only of the mucous membrane; they are lined with a cubical epithelium, and possess a structureless membrana propria, which is intimately connected to the connective tissue. From an occlusion of the orifices of these follicles there are developed small retention cysts containing mucoid fluid, usually round or oval, and measuring 0.3 to 0.5 mm. in length; they are known as the *ovula Nabothi*. The fluid secreted by the mucous membrane of the uterus differs from that of the vaginal mucous membrane in having an alkaline reaction.

The mucous membrane covering the intra-vaginal portion of the uterus is a continuation of the vaginal mucous membrane, consisting of a similar structure, and composed of a connective-tissue framework with papillæ projecting into its covering of laminated pavement-epithelium. At times this portion is found to contain the ovula Nabothi.

The uterus is a very vascular organ; a capillary network is

found in the muscular coat and mucous membrane. In the latter such reticula are seen to surround the glands. The veins are very large, possess delicate walls, and are valveless. In the cervical portion, a more regular distribution of vessels is met with, and their walls are unusually thick.

Numerous lymphatic vessels are found beneath the peritoneal covering of the uterus, and arched passages are seen ending in loops or blind extremities under the mucous membrane of the cervix. Lymph clefts and vessels are also met with in the intermuscular connective-tissue.

The nerves of the uterus are derived from the genital spermatic ganglia. On the posterior wall of the neck a large ganglionic mass is met with, from which most of the nerves have their origin. Nervous filaments may be followed as far as the mucous membrane, and a few histologists have traced them into the papillæ of the cervix, while in the muscular coat they are said to terminate in the nuclei of the muscular elements.

During the physiological function of menstruation and gestation the uterus experiences certain modifications. In the former there is an increase in the size of the organ, owing mostly to the great increase of blood in the vessels ; the glands of the mucous membrane are also increased in size. The discharge of blood during this period is due either to a rupture of the distended capillaries, or a diapedesis, in which the walls remain uninjured. On microscopical examination of the menstrual fluid it is found to contain, besides the blood-elements, numerous uterine epithelial cells.

The modifications of the uterus during gestation occur especially in the muscular elements, which are greatly hypertrophied, and there is also a new formation of them. The blood-vessels, lymphatics, and nerves also experience an increase in size, the latter by a thickening of their perineurium. The mucous membrane of the body of the uterus during gestation is separated from the uterus, previously becoming thicker, softer, and more vascular, and constitutes the *decidua*. The cervical portion of the mucous membrane does not participate in this metamorphosis ; it retains its epithelium, and secretes a mucous plug, which fills the canal of the cervix during pregnancy. Subsequent to delivery a new mucous membrane and glands are developed on the cavity of the uterus, and the hypertrophied and newly formed muscular elements undergo retrograde development and fatty metamorphosis.

The *Fallopian tubes*, or temporary ducts of the ovary, consist of an external covering furnished by the peritoneum, rich in connective tissue and blood-vessels ; a muscular coat made up of an outside layer of longitudinal, and an inside layer of circular involuntary muscular elements ; and, finally, an internal mucous membrane. A division of the tube is made into two parts: that toward the uterus, into which it opens, the much narrower portion, is the *isthmus*, while the free half is the *ampulla*, which terminates in the *fimbriæ*. The mucous membrane, upon transverse section of the tube, in the narrow portion, is seen thrown into simple longitudinal folds, while in the ampulla the folds are much more complicated, and in a transverse section have a dendritic appearance. The epithelium covering the mucous membrane consists of ciliated columnar epithelial cells. The movements of the cilia occasion a current in the direction of the uterine opening. There is an absence of glands in the mucous membrane of the Fallopian tubes. The same histological elements are present in the fimbriæ as in other portions of the tube, of which they are a direct continuation.

The *ovary* for histological study may be divided into two parts, the cortex and medullary substance ; covering the cortex is a layer of columnar epithelial cells, named the ovarian or germ epithelium (Fig. 107). In a perpendicular section, the germ-epithelium is here and there seen to extend down into the substance of the organ and form tubes—the *ovarial tubes*. The cortical substance or parenchymal zone consists of several layers of dense connective tissue, in which are found ovarial tubes and *ovarian follicles*. The most external follicles are imperfectly developed, while those lying deeper are more highly developed and contain the ovum. Internal to the cortex is the medullary substance or vascular zone, in which are numerous blood-vessels, giving it the nature of a cavernous tissue.

The stroma of the ovary consists of fibrillar connective tissue. In the vascular zone it is somewhat loose in texture, and contains a network of elastic tissue. There are also found in this zone fasciculi of smooth muscular fibres, which follow the large and medium sized arteries, at times constituting a sheath for the vessels. In the stroma of the parenchymal zone the connective-tissue forms an outer layer of short, dense fibres

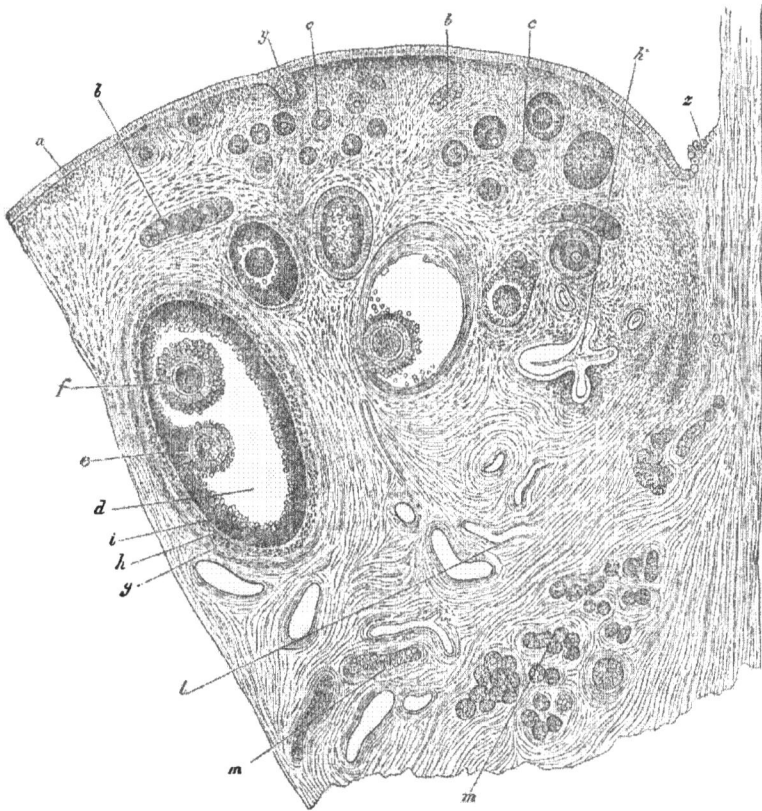

FIG. 107.—From the ovarium of a rather old bitch; portion of a sagittal section. *a*, germ-epithelium; *b, b*, ovarial tubes; *c, c*, younger follicles; *d*, older follicle; *e*, discus proligerus, with egg; *f*, epithelium of a second egg in the same follicle; *g*, tunica fibrosa folliculi; *h*, tunica propria folliculi; *i*, follicular epithelium (membrana granulosa); *k*, collapsed degenerated follicle; *l*, vessels; *m, m*, cell-tubes of the parovarium, both longitudinal and transverse sections; *y*, tubular sinking in of the germ-epithelium into the substance of the ovary; *z*, commencement of the germ-epithelium close to the lower border of the ovary. Waldeyer.

which run in every direction, and an inner one abounding in cells, in which the follicles are seen.

The blood-vessels enter the ovary at the hilum. The arteries have a spiral, corkscrew-like course through the organ. At the hilum the veins form a convoluted mass, the bulb of the ovary. A capillary reticulum surrounds the follicles, and is situated in their internal membrane.

The stroma of the hilum contains numerous lymphatics, which have an arrangement similar to that of the veins. Surrounding the follicles in their external lamina is found a dense network of lymphatics.

The nerves enter the ovary at the hilum with the arteries, and they have been followed into the stroma between the large follicles, but their ultimate terminations have not as yet been ascertained.

The follicles of the ovary, or *Graafian follicles*, consist of a connective-tissue wall separable into two layers: an internal, which contains the small capillaries, and an external, containing the large blood-vessels and lymphatics. The outer layer is made up of the same connective tissue as the stroma of the ovary, in which are numerous spindle-shaped cells. The internal layer consists of connective tissue, in which are numerous and variously shaped cells, fusiform, stellate, and small round bodies, the latter possessing amœboid movement; there are also seen larger round or polygonal-shaped cells. This layer of corpuscles is the *membrana granulosa*. Within the follicle, and distending it, is an albuminous fluid holding a few bodies in suspension. Situated in the follicle, usually at that part most distant from the surface of the ovary—although this is not a rule without exception, since it is also found immediately below the most superficial part of the follicle—the ovum is found surrounded by a collection of cells of the granular membrane, known as the *discus proligerus*. Two kinds of cells form the discus proligerus, the follicular and egg epithelium; the latter lie in immediate contact with the vitelline membrane, and are closely adherent to it.

An examination of the mature ovum demonstrates it to measure 0.28 to 0.1379 mm. in diameter; it is spherical in shape, and is a typical cell, consisting of an investing membrane, the vitelline membrane, or zona pellucida, which is a dense, transparent, homogeneous substance, apparently pierced by numerous minute pores. This membrane is probably developed from the cells of the discus proligerus, and from the layer described as the egg epithelium. The cell-contents, protoplasm, or vitellus is a granular mass composed of albuminous and fatty particles, and a more or less distinct reticulum of fine fibrils. Within the vitellus is seen the nucleus or germinal vesicle (also presenting a delicate reticulum of fibrils), situated eccentrically, spherical in shape, measures 0.037 to 0.451 mm. in diameter, shining, transparent, and contains the nucleolus or germinal spot, which is a highly refractile body, finely granular, supposed to be non-vesicular, and measures 0.0046 to 0.0068 mm. in diameter.

The mature Graafian follicle, which is seen on the surface

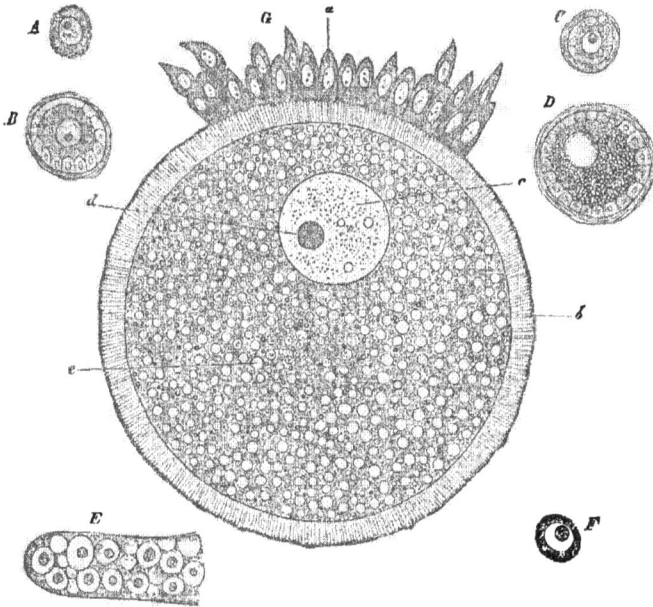

FIG. 108.—*A*, primordial egg of the human being: 8 months' fœtus. *B*, primordial follicle of the rabbit. *C*, primordial follicle of a dove. *D*, a somewhat older follicle of the same animal; commencement of the formation of the subordinate yolk. *E*, blind end of the ovary of an ascaris nigrovenosa; germinal vesicles (some of which possess a germinal spot and Schrön's "granule") in a diffuse mass of protoplasm. *F*, egg of the ascaris nigrovenosa from about the middle of the ovary; Schrön's granule; commencement of the deposition of yolk-matter. *G*, egg from a follicle (3 mm. in diam.) of the rabbit: *a*, egg epithelium; *b*, striated zone with radiating striæ; *c*, germinal vesicle *d*, germinal spot; *e*, yolk. Waldeyer.

of the ovary, giving rise to a prominence, ruptures during the menstrual period and empties its contents, viz. : the ovum, fluid contents, and discus proligerus into the Fallopian tube. The cause of the rupture is an increase in the contents of the follicle, and a fatty metamorphosis of the cells of the wall of the follicle. As a result of this rupture of the Graafian vesicle, there is formed a yellow body, the *corpus luteum*, which

reaches its full development in a few weeks after the ruptur-
ing of the follicle, or when impregnation has occurred after the
lapse of two or three months. It consists of a central portion,
at first red, becoming gray, and a peripheral portion, yellow in
color, thrown into folds. These folds are made up of the internal membrane and cells. The central portion in a fresh
corpus luteum consists of a very vascular tissue, in which are
seen numerous large cells, containing a red coloring substance
and hæmatoidin crystals. A retrograde metamorphosis occurs
in the yellow body, supposed to be due to a want of nutrition
caused by a wasting of the 'arteries, and there only remains a
white cicatrix, the *corpus albicans*. The time required for
the disappearance of a corpus luteum when impregnation has
taken place—a true corpus luteum—is several months, lasting
to the end of gestation ; but for the disappearance of a false
corpus luteum, or when impregnation has not occurred, it only
requires a few weeks. It is, however, to be remembered, that
every Graafian follicle with its contents does not reach full development ; most of them experience fatty or colloid metamorphosis.

The ovaries have their origin from the Wolffian bodies. A
thickening of the epithelial covering is early observed upon
the side of these bodies ; at the same time and place a cellular
projection growing from the connective tissue of the organ is
noticed. From this increase of epithelium the Graafian follicles and ova are developed, later the ovarial epithelium ; from
the connective tissue is built up the vascular system of the ovary.

The Graafian follicles are developed from collections of cells,
irregular in shape, or, as they are named, *ova chains*, consisting
of small-sized peripheral cells, which later form the membrana
granulosa, and the primordial ova ; these last are recognized
by their large size, granular or reticulated protoplasm and
central position. The ova chains are sometimes enclosed in a
homogeneous membrana propria, forming a tubular structure,
as in the cat ; this membrane, however, is not found in all animals. These chains are developed by an ingrowth of the epithelial cells covering the surface of the ovary.

The *parovarium*, or remains of the Wolffian body, situated
in the broad ligament, is made up of twelve to fifteen tubules,
which possess a membrana propria, lined by a single layer of
ciliated epithelium, and contain a transparent substance.

The *placenta* is divided into a uterine and fœtal portion. The former consists of cells irregular in shape, containing one or several nuclei, and at times one or more nucleoli. These cells are separated by an intercellular substance, either hyaline, granular, or fibrous in nature. Fusiform cells, in which a rod-shaped nucleus is seen, are also found, and are thought to indicate the presence of smooth muscular elements. The tufts upon the surface of the uterine placenta, which divide and sub-divide, pass quite deeply into the fœtal placenta, yet no direct transformation of them into the fœtal tissue can be demonstrated ; they appear to terminate in fibrillated tissue, which contains none of the cellular elements of the uterine placenta.

The blood-vessels of the uterine placenta are arteries and veins, with no intermediary capillary system ; they communicate by means of sinuous spaces, limited by placental tissue only. These spaces are said to possess a delicate limiting wall ; this statement, however, has not been confirmed.

The fœtal placenta is developed from the chorion, the villi or tufts of which growing into the uterine follicles are covered by a columnar epithelium. The blood-vessels in the villi do not lie directly in contact with the wall of the villus, but are separated from it by a perivascular space. Besides a direct communication of the arteries and veins, there is also a capillary system present in the villi. Connective tissue accompanies the vessels into the villi from the chorion. The variety of connective tissue here met with is the mucoid, consisting of round, spindle, and stellate-shaped cells, with a structureless intercellular substance. There is a direct transformation of this mucoid connective tissue into the connective tissue of the chorion.

BIBLIOGRAPHY.

BISCHOFF. Beitr. zur Lehre v. d. menschl. Eihüllen. 1834.
VALENTIN, in Müller's Arch., p. 526. 1838.
GOODSIR. Anat. and Path. Researches. Edinburgh, 1845.
KOBELT. Der Nebeneierstock des Weibes. Heidelberg, 1847.
STEINLIN. Ueber d. Entw. d. Graaf. Foll. u. Eier d. Säugeth., Mittheil. d. Zü-
    richer naturf. Gesellsch. 1847.
ROBIN. Arch. génér. de méd. Vol. XVII., p. 258 and 405. 1848. And Vol.
    XVIII., p. 257. Also Gaz. méd. No. 50. 1855.
RAINEY, in Phil. Trans., II. 1850.

252 MANUAL OF HISTOLOGY.

SCHRÖDER VAN DER KOLK. Waarnemingen oves het Maaksel van de menschl. Placenta, etc. Amsterdam, 1851.

SMITH, TYLER-. Med. Chir. Trans. Vol. XXXV., 378. 1852.

REMAK. Unters. ueb. d. Entwick. d. Wirbelthiere. Berlin, 1855. Med. Centr. Zeit. No. 42. 1861. No. 3. 1862.

KLEBS, in Virch. Arch. Vol. XXVIII. 1863.

PFLÜGER, E. Ueb. d. Eierstöcke d. Säugeth. u. d. Menschen. Leipzig, 1863.

SPIEGELBERG. Virch. Arch. Vol. XXX., p. 466. 1864.

KAMENEW. Unters. d. Blutgef. d. Mutterth. d. Placenta, Medicinsky Westnik. No. 13. 1864.

CORNIL, in Jour. de l'anat., p. 386. 1864. Unters. aus d. phys. Labor. zu Bonn, p. 173. Berlin, 1865.

POLLE. Die Nervenverbr. in d. weibl. Genital. Göttingen, 1865.

HIS, in Arch. f. mikr. Anat. Vol. I., p. 151. 1865.

ST. GEORGE, V. LA VALETTE, in Arch. f. mikr. Anat. Vol. II., p. 56. 1866.

PÉRIER. Anat. et phys. de l'ovaire. Paris, 1866.

STRICKER. Wien. Sitz. June, 1866.

LANGHANS, in Virch. Arch. Vol. XXXVIII., p. 543. 1867.

FRANKENHÄUSER. Die Nerven. d. Gebärmutter. Jena, 1867.

JASSINSKI. Zur Lehre ueb. d. Struct. d. Placenta. Virch. Arch. 1867.

VIRCHOW. Bildg. d. Placenta, in Gesamm. Abhandlungen. 1853.

BIDDER. Ueb. Hist. d. Nachgeb., in Holst's Beitr. z. Gynäcol. II. 1867.

ERCOLANI. Giamb. delle gland. otricolare, etc. Bologna, 1868.

PLIKOL, in Arch. f. mikr. Anat. Vol. V., p. 445. 1869.

FRIEDLÄNDER. Unters. ueb. d. Uterus. 1870.

HENNIG. Der Catarrh d. inn. weibl. Geschlechtsorg. 1870.

WALDEYER. Eierstock. u. Ei. Leipzig. 1870.

LOTT and A. ROLLET. Untersuchungen. II. Leipzig, 1871.

LANGHANS. Unters. ueber d. menschl. Placenta. Arch. f. Anat. u. Phys. 1877.

LEOPOLD. Stud. ueb. d. Uterus-schleimhaut. Arch. f. Gyn. Vol. XI., p. 110 and 443. 1877. Also Vol. XII., p. 169. 1877.

HENNIG. Ueber Drüsen der Vagina. Arch. f. Gyn. Vol. XII., p. 488. 1877.

FOULIS. The Development of the Ova, and the Structure of the Ovary, etc. Jour. of Anat. and Phys. Vol XIII., p. 353. 1878–79.

FREY, HEINRICH. Histology and Histochemistry of Man. 1880.

KLEIN, E., and E. NOBLE SMITH. Atlas of Histology. 1880.

CHAPTER XVII.

THE RESPIRATORY TRACT.

By BENJAMIN F. WESTBROOK, M.D.,

Lecturer on Anatomy and Physician to Department for Diseases of Chest, Long Island College Hospital.

THE respiratory tract includes the nares and, perhaps, the pharynx, but as the latter is more commonly associated with the function of deglutition, and the former contain in their upper portions the organs of one of the special senses, they have been assigned to other portions of this work. This chapter is devoted exclusively to the consideration of those parts which are concerned in the respiratory process. As the pleura forms a part of the lung, and facilitates the movements of breathing, its structure may properly be described under this section.

The air-tubes are in general made up of three layers: an outer of connective tissue and elastic fibres; a middle, muscular and cartilaginous; and an inner of mucous membrane. Their structure is more complex in the upper, and simpler in the lower portions of the respiratory passages.

The larynx.—The *muscles* of the larynx are of the striped or voluntary variety.

The *ligaments* and *membranes* are composed of yellow elastic fibres with some white fibrous tissue. Their structure can be easily demonstrated by the process of teasing or by employing the reagents ordinarily used for this class of tissues. The lateral thyro-hyoid and the inferior thyro-arytenoid ligaments have the following peculiarities of structure: the lateral thyrohyoid ligament usually encloses a small piece of hyaline cartilage about the size and shape of a large grain of wheat. It is known as the *cartilago triticea*. In adult males it is usually calcified. It may be incorporated either with the cornu of the hyoid bone or with the superior cornu of the thyroid cartilage.

The inferior thyro-arytenoid ligaments, or *true vocal cords*, are made up almost entirely of yellow elastic fibres stretched across from the thyroid cartilage in front, to the vocal processes and adjacent anterior borders of the arytenoids behind. The elastic bundles originate, anteriorly, in a mass of connective tissue which occupies the angle of the thyroid. Posteriorly, many of the fibres are prolonged into the arytenoid cartilage, converting that part of it into reticular tissue. These ligaments are continuous below with the lateral crico-thyroid membranes, and are described by some anatomists[1] as their superior borders.

The innermost fibres of the internal thyro-arytenoid muscle mingle with the outer fibres of this ligament, some ending in or taking their origin from them. The intimate relation between the muscle and the ligament can be seen in a vertical section through the larynx.

Of the laryngeal cartilages, the three larger are of the hyaline variety. Horizontal sections show a broad central area with two zones between it and either the outer or inner surface. The appearance of the zones or bands is thus described by Rheiner:[2] "1. A thin peripheral portion, appearing to the naked eye as a narrow, bluish, opalescent band, which consists of a transparent and longitudinally striated matrix with elongated cartilage-cells arranged parallel to the surface. 2. The intermediate layer, a narrow, whitish, opaque band, consisting of a dull yellowish ground-substance with numerous large mother-cells containing fatty daughter-cells. 3. The broad central layer, with a perfectly transparent homogeneous matrix and few cells. The intercellular substance increases, relatively to the contained cells, from without inward, and, in the interior, presents numerous large spaces in which no cells are found. In the thyroid and cricoid cartilages the outer peripheral zone is thicker and more easily distinguished than the inner."

The following peculiarities are to be noted : the central portion of the thyroid, viz., that part which forms the anterior projection or angle, is distinguished by the great number and small size of its cells. It is penetrated by numerous fibres[1]

---

[1] Quain's Anatomy, eighth edition, Vol. II., p. 284.

[2] Quoted by Merkel in Anatomie u. Phys. des mensch. Stimm- u. Sprach-Organs. Leipzig, 1863, S. 166.

from that mass of connective tissue from which the vocal cords take their origin. After prolonged maceration in some alkaline solution, this cartilage can be separated into three parts— two lateral and an anterior or median.

The arytenoids are not composed exclusively of hyaline cartilage. The vocal process, as already mentioned, presents a yellow reticulated structure, the fibres of which are continuous with those of the true vocal cords. The apex has also a reticular structure when there is no joint between it and the cartilage of Santorini. The elastic tissue is then continuous with that which connects it with the *corniculum.* A horizontal section through the arytenoid at the level of the vocal process shows the reticular structure of the process, the hyaline character of the body of the cartilage, and the gradual transition from one to the other.

The three cartilages already described are subject to calcification and partial ossification. This occurs more frequently and at an earlier age in the male than in the female. It also begins at a later date in those who have been castrated. It makes its first appearance at the points of muscular attachment. As the cartilages undergo calcification they increase in size, so that the calcified larynx of old age is larger than that of the young adult. The matrix also splits up into a fibrous texture, not affected by acetic acid.

The *cornicula laryngis* or cartilages of Santorini and the cuneiform cartilages of Wrisberg, as well as the sesamoid cartilages (when they exist) are of the reticulated variety. The cartilago triticea is hyaline and prone to calcification.

The *epiglottis* consists of reticular cartilage. On transverse section, however, the intercellular substance is seen to be a spongy elastic substance, granular on section ; at the periphery yellow fibres are present. The elastic cartilage should be examined with a high power.

The *mucous membrane* of the larynx varies in its structure in different situations. On the laryngeal surface of the epiglottis it is thin.

The epithelium in the upper half is in several layers. The deepest cells are somewhat columnar or pyramidal in form, while the superficial ones are flat. The lower half is covered by a stratified, columnar, ciliated epithelium. The epithelium rests upon a thin, apparently structureless basement-membrane.

The mucosa is made up of delicate connective-tissue fibres, enclosing in their meshes a series of lymph-spaces. Connective-tissue cells are also found here, and some elastic fibres. There are a few small papillæ in the upper portion. The submucous layer is thin, contains many elastic fibres, and is continuous with the perichondrium. It contains the racemose mucous glands, whose ducts open upon the surface. Some of the larger glands are lodged in the depressions of the cartilage, and some are even situated on its anterior aspects, their ducts passing through to the posterior side.

In the submucous tissue there are lymphatic follicles, some of which are arranged about the mucous glands and their ducts.

The membrane covering the false vocal cords, arytenoid cartilages, and ary-epiglottic folds, as well as that lining the ventricles and inferior compartment of the larynx is thicker and more loosely attached to the subjacent parts. It is covered by stratified columnar, ciliated epithelium, except upon the edge of the false vocal cords and over the inner surfaces of the arytenoids, where it is of the pavement variety. The mucosa contains a large amount of lymphoid tissue, which holds in its meshes lymphoid cells. Closed lymph-follicles are also found in the submucous tissue of the false vocal cords and on the floor of the ventricle.[1] That portion of the mucous membrane which covers the true vocal cords is thin, more closely attached, and has no mucous glands. In its anterior half it has numerous small papillæ (0.07 to 0.08 mm. in height, Coÿne) projecting at the edge and on the superior and inferior surfaces of the cord. They are composed of connective tissue, with many elastic fibres. Their vascular supply is slight. The membrane in this situation is covered by stratified pavement-epithelium, continuous posteriorly with that which covers the inner surfaces of the arytenoids. Numerous racemose glands send their ducts obliquely upward and inward to discharge their secretion upon the upper and under surfaces of the vocal cords.

In front of the corniculum laryngis, on either side, is a collection of racemose glands surrounding the cartilage of Wrisberg. Another collection is found between the arytenoids.

The epithelium can be examined, either by scraping it from the surface, or in sections. The mucous glands are best seen

---

[1] Coÿne : Archiv. d. Physiologie, p. 92, 1874.

in sections of the hardened larynx. They are lined by cubical glandular epithelium. The capillary blood-vessels of the laryngeal mucous membrane are small with wide meshes, giving the membrane a paler appearance than that of the pharynx.

The lymphatics are numerous in the mucous and submucous layers. They may be injected with Berlin blue, by puncturing the submucous tissue.

In the nervous filaments are ganglion cells. The mode of termination is not definitely known. But in the mucous membrane of the epiglottis end bulbs have been found. The methods of examination will be found elsewhere.

The trachea and primary bronchi.—The rings of the trachea and bronchi are composed of hyaline cartilage. Longitudinal sections of these rings show that the cells lying near the periphery, underneath the perichondrium, are flattened, and arranged with their long axes parallel to the surface. Internally they are oblong and perpendicular to the former.

The ends of the incomplete rings are connected, posteriorly, by a layer of smooth muscular fibres, which are attached to the fibrous tissue of the perichondrium. The attachment is to the inner aspect of the ends of the cartilages, so as to·throw the muscular layer forward of the most posterior projection of the rings.

These muscular fibres also exist in the spaces between the rings, where they are attached, on either side, to the fibrous tissue of the tube. Outside of the transverse fibres are a few filaments which have a longitudinal direction. They are attached to the fibrous membrane.

The fibrous membrane which encloses the cartilages and completes the framework of the tube is composed of connective tissue containing a considerable portion of elastic tissue, particularly in its external portion. The outer layer of the fibrous membrane encloses both the cartilages and the muscle fibres. The inner layer is·thin and lies between the rings and the glandular layer.

The mucous membrane is covered by several layers of epithelial cells, the deeper being more or less spherical or ovoid, whilst the superficial ones are columnar and ciliated. The columnar cells, losing their cilia, are continued into the ducts of the mucous glands. These glands are very numerous, and often of considerable size. They are racemose, the acini being

lined with cubical epithelium. Owing to the distention of some
of the gland-cells by mucus or by the action of reagents, they
assume a rounded form, and the nuclei are pressed against the
attached ends of the cells. Such corpuscles are known as
"goblet" cells. Some of the larger glands project posteriorly
outside of the fibrous membrane, but the great majority of them
are situated internally to that structure, and then form a distinct layer, the "glandular layer." They are most abundant
in the spaces between the cartilages. Their ducts pierce the

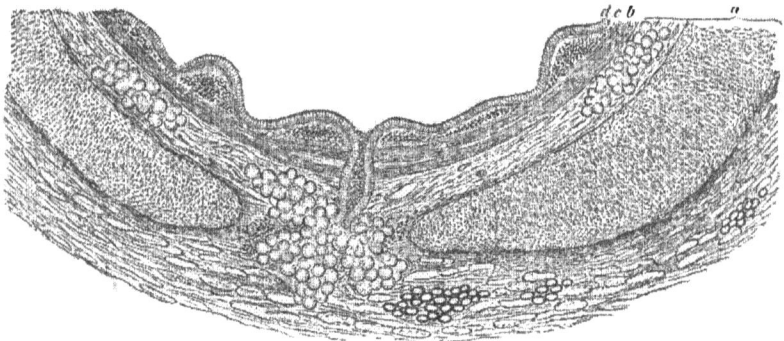

Fig. 109.—Transverse section of bronchial twig, 6 mm. in diameter: *a*, outer fibrous layer; *b*, muscular layer; *c*, inner fibrous layer (mucosa); *d*, epithelium. Magnified 30 diameters. F. E. Schulze.

mucous membrane obliquely, so that the entire length of a
duct is not usually found in a section of the tracheal wall.
At short intervals, between the columnar cells of the surface,
other cells are found, of a spindle shape, or somewhat stellate.
These cells send processes upward to the surface and downward into the basilar membrane, where they become continuous with other branched cells. The prolongation which passes
upward to the surface is usually single, though it may occasionally send off a delicate filamentary branch, which is lost in
the cement substance between adjacent cells.

The process, sometimes double, which passes downward
connects with a tissue in the mucosa which resembles the
lymph canalicular system of other parts. It is made up of
a network of branched cells, or connective-tissue corpuscles,
which line a series of spaces, that in turn communicate with
the lymphatic capillaries of the mucous membrane. Sikorsky
injected a watery solution of carminate of ammonia into the

bronchial tubes of cats and dogs while the animals were living, and found, *post-mortem*, that the carmine had penetrated through the interepithelial cells above described into the lymphatic vessels below.

The interepithelial cells have a small nucleus which stains more deeply with hæmatoxylon than do the nuclei of the ordinary epithelial cells. In vertical section they are more opaque than the epithelia, and, when seen on the surface of the membrane, appear as dark spots among the ciliated cells.

The lymphatic capillaries join to form larger trunks which run along the sides of the bronchi communicating freely with each other and with those of the neighboring blood-vessels. They are called by Klein the *peribronchial lymphatics*.

Beneath the mucosa, and between it and the mucous glands, are numerous bundles of yellow elastic tissue having a longitudinal direction. Some of the bands are quite thick, particularly in the posterior wall, and raise the mucous membrane in longitudinal folds.

The mucous membrane of the trachea and bronchi has a rich network of capillaries. The racemose glands are also supplied with a vascular network which ramifies in the fibrous tissue by which they are surrounded. The natural injection of these vessels, which occurs in cases of bronchitis in the human subject, is often sufficient for their examination.

The mode of termination of the nerves has not been ascertained.

The trachea should be hardened in chromic acid or Müller's fluid, followed by alcohol. The sections may be stained in hæmatoxylon. In order to preserve the ciliated epithelium, it is well, as Professor Rutherford suggests, to cut the sections with the freezing microtome. The lymphatics can be injected by puncture.

The smaller bronchi and lungs.—Beyond the primary bronchi (or first division of the trachea) the muscular fibres encircle the tubes inside of the cartilaginous and fibrous layer ; indeed, the primary divisions show the first sign of this new arrangement. The cartilages change from incomplete rings to irregularly shaped plates, which are found on all sides of the tubes, but their microscopic structure remains unaltered. The longitudinal elastic fibres are contained between the muscular and mucous coats. The tubes divide and subdivide generally in a dichotomous manner, diminishing gradually in calibre, the combined area of the branches, however, always exceeding that of the trunk from which they spring. No change occurs in their structure, except a gradual thinning of their walls, until they reach a diameter of about 1 mm., when the cartilages disappear and the attenuation is more marked. The circular muscular fibres continue to exist, as also the longitudinal elastic fibres, but the mucous glands disappear. After a still further division the tubes are diminished to a diameter of .20 to .30 mm., the muscular fibres become more sparse, and the epithelium is reduced to a single layer of low, somewhat cubical cells, which are still ciliated. These are the lobular bronchi, each one going to a single pulmonary lobule. The lobular bronchi each give off ten to fifteen smaller tubes, known as the *terminal bronchi* or *bronchioles*. They are straight and cylindrical, their walls are very thin and delicate, and their epithelial cells gradually lose their cilia and become flattened plates. Each bronchiole leads to a smaller division of the lobule, called an *acinus* or *lobulette*.[1] The bronchioles divide into short canals, the *alveolar passages*, usually three for each acinus. Their walls are thin and bulge outward on all sides, forming, externally, little projections or

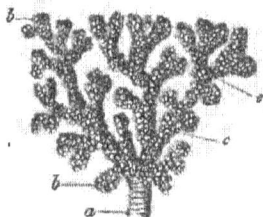

FIG. 110.—A system of alveolar passages with infundibuli from an ape's lung: *a*, terminal bronchial twig ; *b*, *b*, infundibula ; *c*, *c*, alveolar passages. Magnified 10 times. F. E. Schulze.

elevations ; internally, shallow depressions or cavities which open into the calibre of the tube. They also give off secondary branches, called *infundibula*, which have groups of such little cavities attached to, and opening into them. The little cavities are the *alveoli* or air-cells of the lung. From this description it will be seen that each lobule has ten to fifteen acini or lobulettes, and that the lobulette is made up of alveoli or air-cells, which open into common spaces or infundibula, which in turn communicate with the alveolar passages. The alveoli, which are connected with the infundibula, are called *terminal alveoli ;* those which open on the sides of the alveolar passage are called the *parietal alveoli.* The latter are called, by Dr. Waters, the *bronchial alveoli.* The alveolar passages, infundibula,

---

[1] Dr. Waters : The Anatomy of the Human Lung, London, 1860.

and alveoli have a flat pavement epithelium resting on an apparently structureless basement-membrane. Outside of this are numerous elastic and muscular fibres, curving around the cavities, and holding in their meshes the capillary blood-vessels. The muscular fibres are very numerous in the walls of the alveolar passages and infundibula. The alveoli have a diameter of .1 to .4 mm., but their size varies greatly according to the degree of inflation of the lungs.

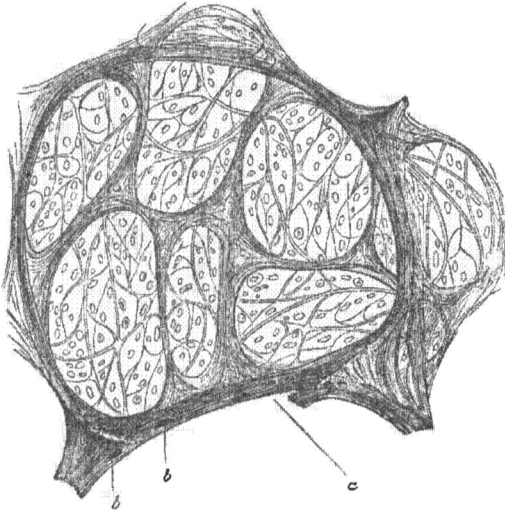

Fig. 111.—Section through an infundibulum : a, entrance from the alveolar passage into the infundibulum; b, nuclei of smooth muscular cells. Magnified 30 diameters. F. E. Schulze.

The epithelium in the alveoli of the fetal lung is columnar in shape, so that a section of such a lung resembles a section of a glandular organ. But when the alveoli are distended at birth, the cells change their form. In transverse sections, either real or optical, of the alveolar walls, the epithelial plates project more or less into the cavity, according to the degree of distention of the lung. This change of shape undoubtedly occurs during life with the alternating expansion and contraction of the thorax, and should be taken into account in considering the pathological changes of inflammation, collapse, etc. By injection of a weak solution of silver nitrate ($\frac{1}{4}$ per cent.) into the bronchi of a fresh lung, and its subsequent immersion in alcohol, the lines between the epithelial plates can be demonstrated. The nuclei can be stained with carmine.

Some of the cells are converted into hyaline plates. The alveolar epithelium of the human lung is not so readily demonstrated as that of animals, principally because too long a time usually elapses between death and the post-mortem dissection. In some traumatic cases an autopsy can be made early, and as

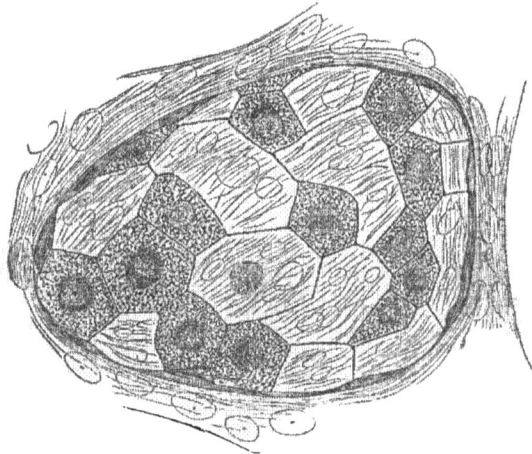

Fig. 112.—Interior of an alveolus. Lung injected with a solution of nitrate of silver to show the lines between the alveolar epithelial cells. F. E. Schulze.

favorable opportunity had of examining these structures. They can be shown very well in fresh sections cut with Valentin's knife.

The spaces between the alveoli and acini contain the elastic fibres mentioned above, together with a few oval connective-tissue nuclei and muscular elements. The lobules are held together by thin septa of connective tissue. The connective tissue is also found in the angles of division of the lobular bronchi and bronchioles.

The muscle-cells may be identified by their elongated, fusiform nuclei. A further proof of their existence is found in certain cases of cirrhosis of the lung, in which many distinct muscular fibres are found in the new connective tissue.[1]

The branches of the pulmonary artery follow the course

---

[1] Buhl: Lungenentz. Tuberculosis, u. Schwindsucht, München. 1873, S. 358.

of the bronchi as far as the lobules. The lobular branches are *terminal arteries*—*i.e.*, they do not anastomose with each other. They break up into very small branches, which encircle the alveoli and supply the capillary plexuses of their walls. These capillaries are very small, and the network so fine that, when injected, the open spaces are not as wide as the vessels themselves. This, however, will vary with the degree of distention of the lung. Between two adjacent alveoli only one

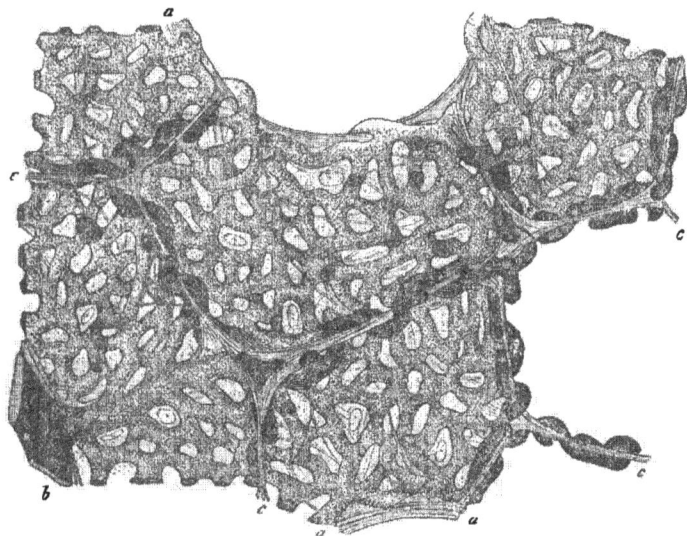

FIG. 113.—Section of human lung injected through the pulmonary artery : *a, a,* free alveolar margins ; *b,* small arterial branch ; *c, c,* alveolar walls seen in transverse section. F. E. Schulze.

capillary plexus is found, the branches of which are seen to pursue an undulating course, projecting, first, into the cavity on one side, then into that on the other. These unite again into veins which run irregularly through the lobules to unite upon the bronchi and follow their course to the root of the lung. The peculiarities of the pulmonary veins are, 1st, that their united calibre does not exceed (if it equals) that of the arteries ; 2d, that they have no valves. The bronchial vessels supply the coats of the bronchial tubes and the surrounding connective tissue and the pulmonary pleura.

But the line of demarcation between the bronchial and pulmonary circulations is indistinct on the venous side, as injections thrown into the bronchial arteries fill the pulmonary veins and capillary plexuses and overflow into the pulmonary arteries.[1]

It appears from this that part of the blood from the bronchial arteries does, or may, return through the pulmonary veins. In their course through the lung, the pulmonary arteries lie upon the upper and anterior aspect of the bronchial tubes, while the veins are found on their inferior surface. The bronchial arteries follow the tubes and divide with them.

The lymphatics of the alveolar septa are a series of lacunar spaces lined by branched connective-tissue corpuscles, whose nuclei have already been described as being visible in ordinary sections of the lung.

In sections of a lung treated with silver nitrate the forms of the cells are distinguishable. According to Klein the processes of these cells pass upward between the epithelial plates of the alveoli so as to bring the cells into direct communication with the cavity, just as we have seen the interepithelial cells of the bronchial mucous membrane send certain processes upward between the columnar epithelia and others downward to the cells of the lymph lacunæ. On examining the epithelium of an alveolus, small, round, dark spaces are seen between the cells ; these are said by Klein to be the projecting processes of the branched cells of the lymph lacunar system. The ends of these processes, both here and on the bronchial mucous membrane, are called *pseudostomata*, in contradistinction to the true stomata of the serous membranes.

The small spaces, or lacunæ, open into lymphatic radicles, which have a regular endothelial lining. These pass inward toward the root of the lung, upon the bronchi and the walls of the vessels. On the vascular walls they communicate freely with each other, and at times completely invest the vessel with a lymphatic sheath like that of the cerebral vessels. In this situation they are called *perivascular* lymphatics. The perivascular and peribronchial lymphatics communicate freely. At the surface of the lung there is a plexus immediately beneath the pleura (*subpleural* lymphatics) from which trunks of some size run to the root of the lung. They communicate with the perivascular system and with the pleural cavity. The final termination of all these channels is in the bronchial glands.

---

[1] Dr. Waters.

The nerves of the lungs are derived from the sympathetic and pneumogastric. Their mode of termination is not known. For the examination of the general structure of the lung it may be inflated and dried pretty rapidly in the sun or by a fire. For more careful examination it should be hardened in chromic acid, Müller's fluid, or alcohol. The hardening fluid should be injected into the air-passages.

In order to distend the vesicles it is well, before placing the lung in the hardening fluid, to inject the bronchi with simple gelatine. The vessels may also be injected with a colored mass. The lungs of the lower animals are used for these demonstrations, owing to the difficulty of obtaining normal human lungs in a perfectly fresh condition. The investigation of the lymphatics is attended with great difficulty. They may be demonstrated by the puncture method. Klein found that on injecting the blood-vessels, under high pressure, with Berlin blue or silver nitrate, some of the capillaries ruptured, and the fluid passed into the perivascular lymphatics.

The pleura.—The pleura, like the other serous membranes, consists of a connective-tissue ground-substance covered by a single layer of polygonal endothelial cells. In the costal pleura the subserous connective tissue is more abundant, and its attachment to the thoracic wall is not so firm as is that of the pulmonary pleura to the lung. The structure of the pleura is most conveniently studied in the smaller mammals. It can also be demonstrated in young children.

To demonstrate the endothelium of the surface, the thorax of a recently killed animal should be opened, care being taken not to rub or otherwise injure the pleura. The surfaces are to be washed by pouring distilled water over them, in order to remove the serum, and then a weak solution of silver nitrate ($\frac{1}{4}$—$\frac{1}{2}$ per cent.) allowed to flow over them. After a few moments the surfaces are bathed with pure water. The diaphragmatic or mediastinal portion is then excised with scissors, immersed in distilled water or glycerine, and exposed to the daylight until it takes a light reddish-brown color. It may now be floated on to a slide, carefully smoothed by traction at the edges, and mounted in glycerine. The portion excised should be large, so that it can be manipulated without touching the part which is to be examined. For this reason it is well to take with it some of the surrounding structures, *e.g.*, the

entire diaphragm, with the mediastinal portion, together with
the heart and pericardium.

It will be seen that the endothelium is composed of a great
number of polygonal plates whose edges are glued together by
a substance which has been stained brown or black by the silver. Nuclei are seen in many of them, or they can be shown
by staining with carmine or hæmatoxylon. Small openings
are to be seen in certain localities surrounded by cells of a
more cubical form, with large, distinct nuclei. In other places
small dark spots are seen between the cells. The openings are
known as *stomata*, and communicate with lymphatic vessels
running beneath the endothelium. The dark spots are *pseudo-
stomata*, and are similar in their nature to the pseudo-stomata
of the alveoli and bronchial mucous membrane ; *i.e.*, they are
the ends of processes of the branched cells of the ground-substance reaching up between the endothelial plates. In order
to demonstrate the *ground-substance* or connective-tissue layer
of the pleura, the fresh surface is carefully pencilled with a
soft brush dipped in the fluid of the abdominal cavity, or in
artificial serum. After washing with distilled water, the solution of silver nitrate is poured over it, and it is treated as before. On examination, the branched connective-tissue cells
are seen communicating with each other by their processes.

Blood-vessels and lymphatics are also seen, and in a favorable place the endothelium of the latter is seen to be continuous
with the branched cells. These cells line the cavities of the
connective tissue, and belong to the lymph lacunar system.

The lymphatic vessels accompany the blood-vessels, sometimes ensheathing them. They are identified by the shape of
their endothelial cells, which are wider and more polygonal in
form than those of the veins. It will be seen from this description that the serous membrane is a lymphatic structure. Its
cavity communicates by means of the stomata with the lymphatic vessels below, while, by means of the pseudo-stomata,
it communicates with the lacunar spaces which are lined by
the branched cells. To demonstrate the pulmonary pleura,
the lungs should be excised, moderately distended with air
(which is retained in them by ligature of the trachea), treated
with silver nitrate, as already described, and then immersed in
alcohol. After a few days sections are made parallel to the
surface.

If the lung be pencilled before it is treated with the silver solution the deeper structures can be examined. The sections should be mounted in glycerine with the external surface upward. The appearances here are similar to those already described. The capillary lymphatic-vessels communicate with the superficial pulmonary branches forming the *subpleural lymphatics*.

The endothelial cells of the pulmonary pleura vary in shape according to the degree of distention of the lung. In the lung which has been inflated before hardening, the cells appear as flat plates, but in the atelectatic lung of a fœtus, or the collapsed lung of an animal that has breathed, they are cubical or even columnar in shape. This difference is most marked in the guinea-pig, owing to the presence of a layer of muscular-fibres beneath the pleura of that animal. The tops of the cells which have this pyramidal shape are not flat as in true columnar epithelium, but rounded. This change of shape simply indicates that the cells accommodate themselves to changes of space. These changes, in a lesser degree, must be occurring constantly during life, with the movements of respiration. On the costal pleura, the stomata are only found in the intercostal spaces.

Attached to the lower border of the lung are minute appendages, the "*pleural appendages*," forming a sort of fringe connected with the pleura. Some are visible to the naked eye, some microscopic. The larger are made up of connective tissue and blood-vessels, and, exceptionally, nervous fibres in the larger ones. They are covered by round cells, sometimes resembling epithelium. The smallest ones are structureless, and in general have no epithelial covering.[1]

BIBLIOGRAPHY.

COŸNE, P. Recherches sur l'anatomie normale de la muqueuse du Larynx. Archives de Physiologie, p. 92. Paris, 1874.

STIRLING. Nervous Apparatus of the Lung. Brit. Med. Journal. Vol. II., p. 401. 1876.

CADIAT. Des rapports entre le dévelop. du poumon et la structure. Jour. de l'anat. et de la Phys., No. 6, p. 591. 1877. And, Structure et dével. du poumon. Gaz. Méd. de Paris, No. 17, p. 214. 1877.

---

[1] Luschka : Anatomie des Menschen, Bd. I., S. 298.

GRANCHER. Note sur les lymphat. du poumon. Gaz. Méd. de Paris, No. 9, p. 103. 1877.

AEBY. Die Gestalt d. Bronchialbaumes u. die Homol. d. Lungenlappen beim Menschen. Med. Centralbl., No. 16, p. 290. 1878.

SEILER, C. Researches on the Anatomy of the Vocal Cords. St. Louis Med. and Surg. Journal, p. 333. April 5, 1880. And, Minute Anatomy of the Larynx, Normal and Pathological. Archives of Laryngology. Vol. I., Nos. 1 and 2, and to be continued. 1880.

KÖLLIKER, A. Bau der Lunge des Menschen. Verh. der phys.-med. Gesellschaft in Würzburg. N. F. XVI. 1-24. 1881.

PANSCH, A. Unteren u. oberen Pleuragrenzen. Arch. f. Anat. 111-121. 1881.

CHAPTER XVIII.

THE SKIN.

BY A. R. ROBINSON, M.D.,

Lecturer on Normal Histology in the Bellevue Hospital Medical College, New York.

General plan of arrangement.—The *integumentum commune*, or skin, forms the external covering of the body, which it mechanically protects, and at the same time is endowed with certain physiological functions. The surface of the skin in some parts of the body is smooth and soft ; in others it is more or less uneven and rough. This latter condition depends upon the presence of pores, hairs, furrows, and ridges. The pores correspond to the surface openings of the hair-follicles, sebaceous and sweat-glands. The hairs vary in amount of development according to their situation. In the so-called hairy regions they are largest ; other parts are provided only with a soft down (lanugo hairs). There are no hairs on the palms of the hands and soles of the feet, the dorsal surfaces of the terminal phalanges of the fingers and toes, the glans penis, and inner surface of the prepuce. The furrows are either long and deep, or short and superficial. The former are chiefly found in the flexures of the joints, and correspond to the folds in the derma produced by movements of the joint. The latter run between the papillary elevations, and, by crossing each other, divide the surface into a number of polygonal or lozenge-shaped fields. This division is well-marked on the backs of the hands. These superficial furrows are more developed on the extensor than on the flexor surfaces of the extremities, and in the lumbar region more than on the anterior surface of the abdomen. Their direction is dependent on the degree of the tension of the skin. The ridges correspond to the papillæ, and are most developed on the palmar surfaces of the last digital phalanges. The color of the skin varies in

individuals according to race, and in the same individual according to the part of the body. The dark skin of some races
depends upon the presence of pigment in the cells of the rete
Malpighii. In the white race, dark pigment is usually present in greatest quantity in the areolæ of the nipples and in
the scrotum and labiæ.

General structure.—The skin is composed of the following parts: epidermis, corium, subcutaneous connective tissue,

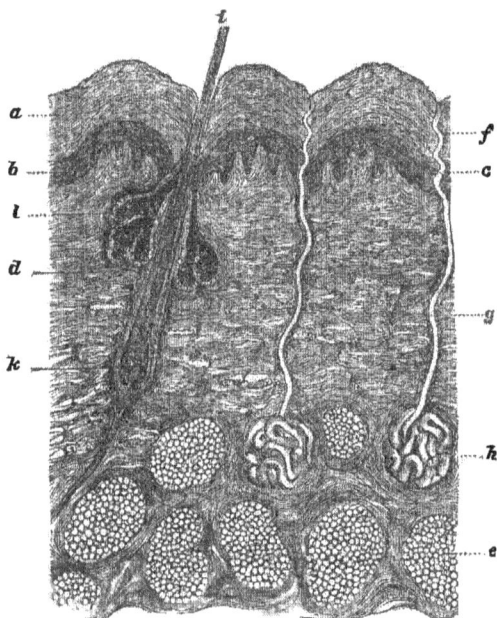

FIG. 114.—Diagrammatic perpendicular section through the normal skin: *a*, epidermis; *b*, rete Malpighii; *c*, papillary layer; *d*, corium; *e*, panniculus adiposus; *f*, spirally bent end of excretory sweat-
duct: *g*, straight portion of excretory duct of sweat-gland; *h*, coil of sweat-duct; *i*, hair-shaft; *k*, root
of hair; *l*, sebaceous gland. After Neumann.

blood-vessels, nerves, lymphatics, sweat and sebaceous glands,
hairs, and nails.

A perpendicular section through the skin shows (Fig. 114)
three well-marked layers; the most superficial is called the
epidermis proper, *a*, *b ;* the middle layer is the corium or cutis,
d ; and the deepest layer the subcutaneous connective tissue, *e.*
The limit of the epidermis at its place of union with the corium
is sharply defined, but the corium and subcutaneous connec-

tive tissue gradually merge into each other, the boundary between them being only an artificial one.

Commencing with the epidermis, we will describe in detail the minute structure of the different tissues and organs of the skin, omitting only the lymphatics.

Description of the different layers.—The *epidermis* is generally subdivided into several layers, with specially distinctive names for each layer; but though such a division has some practical value, histologically it is incorrect, as the cells of the lowest layer are transformed, at some period of their existence, in their movement toward the free surface, into the cells of the other layers. Examination with high powers also shows that the changes in the molecular constitution or chemical condition of the cells of the epidermis — changes which produce differences in their appearance — are

FIG. 115.—*a*, rete cells; *b*, granular layer; *c*, stratum lucidum; *d*, corneous layer; *e*, inter-papillary rete Malpighii; *f*, cutis papilla.

quite gradual. Consequently, sharply defined layers are not found. For practical reasons, however, it is well to adopt the usual classification. In Fig. 115 these layers are shown.

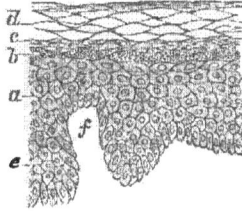

Another division is into Malpighian and corneous layers only, the former comprising the rete and the granular layer, and the latter the stratum lucidum and corneous layer. The Malpighian layer, as compared with the corneous layer, presents a more or less dark, granular appearance, while the latter is homogeneous, and its cells have a lamellar arrangement.

The *rete Malpighii* consists of nucleated corpuscles, rich in protoplasm, granular in appearance, and disposed more or less in parallel strata, the elements of the different layers differing somewhat from each other as regards their size and shape. The lowest layer consists of columnar-shaped cells arranged palisade-like, with their long axes more or less perpendicular to the surface of the corium. Where the papillæ are well developed, this perpendicular arrangement is not so marked. The base of some of these bodies terminates in a pointed extremity, which passes a short distance into the underlying corium. Each of them has an oval nucleus. The cell-body consists of a small quantity of slightly granular, shining protoplasm. The corpuscles of this layer are not united to each other by bands, as in the other layers. The next two or three strata consist of more or less polygonal-shaped bodies, each with a spherical nucleus. The cells of these layers are large, their contours sharply defined, and they contain more or less pigment. It is this substance deposited in the corpuscles that gives the characteristic color to the different races of mankind. Their cell-bodies are larger in proportion to the nucleus than in the first layer. In the succeeding layers the cells increase in size and are more granular in appearance, the cells and nuclei become flatter as they approach the granular layer, and, finally, lie with their long axes parallel to the surface. The granular structure which in the lowest layer is most marked around the nucleus, gradually extends toward the margin of the cells, as the surface is approached, so that finally a clear area is seen around the nucleus, whilst the remainder of the cell-body is markedly granular. At the same time the cell-body becomes firmer and the nucleus smaller.

All the cells of the rete Malpighii, except those of the first row, are united to each other by filaments (Martin, Bizzozero,

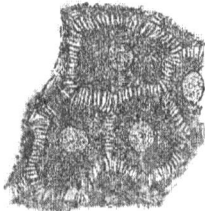

Fig. 116.—"Prickle" cells of the rete.   × 1600.

Heitzmann), the so-called *prickles* of Max Schultze (Fig. 116). These uniting filaments or bands vary much as regards their size and length in different parts of the body. They are most distinct wherever the Malpighian layer is well developed, but are thicker and longer in the lower rows of cells than in the upper. At the stratum lucidum they cease to exist. Between neighboring corpuscles the length of these bands is in direct proportion to the distance between the borders of the cell-bodies. Hence, where three or four cells meet at one place, as in the centre of Fig. 116, the minute filaments are much longer than those uniting the bodies of closely adjoining cells. Examining these prickle-cells with the microscope, alternate dark and light bands are seen between the cell-borders. With a low power, these light bands appear to consist of spaces between the connecting filaments, the dark lines being the connecting filaments, but with a high power the latter can be recognized as spaces between the former. The light bands can be traced from the surface of one cell to the surface of another, whilst the dark lines are the spaces between these

bands. These connecting cords sometimes divide and anastomose with each other, forming a sort of network between the
cells. In this case, the dark spaces do not always extend
from one cell-body to another, since they may correspond to
the space between anastomosing filaments. These bands are
therefore not the prickles of adjoining cells, which interlock
with each other, but are true connecting filaments between
cells of a common origin, and which have not yet become separated from each other. The connecting bands or fibres gradually diminish in length and thickness from below upward, and
finally cease to exist when the granular layer is reached.

The spaces between the bands are filled with an intercellular albuminous substance, and they may be regarded as
minute channels for the conveyance of nutriment to the cells
of the epidermis. The above view of the "prickles" corresponds very closely with that held by Dr. Martin, and differs
from that of later observers, who maintain that the dark lines
are connecting bands, and the light lines the spaces between
them.

Owing to the close union of the Malpighian elements it is
very difficult to isolate them. Perhaps the best way to accomplish this result is by long immersion in iodized serum. Fig.
117 represents a cell isolated in this manner. Here
the bands have been torn apart and the cell-surface is
studded with thorn-like projections. Hardening in
chronic acid, with subsequent boiling in a moderately

Fig. 117.—Iso-
lated "prickle"
cell.

strong solution of potash, causes a separation of the
mucous layer from the corium and a falling apart of the rete
cells (Biesiadecki). The structure of the corpuscles, however,
can be best studied when their normal relations with each
other are preserved. Variations in the number of cellular layers are of normal occurrence in the rete, although this portion
of the skin shows the least variation as regards its thickness.
The arrangement of the elements in these different strata is the
same in all parts of the body, and appears to be independent
of the thickness of this layer.

As regards the direction of the long axes of the cells there
is a gradual passing from the perpendicularly seated cells of
the first layer to the horizontally lying cells of the uppermost
row. The lower surface of the rete adapts itself to the upper
surface of the corium, and between the papillæ projects down-

ward and forms the interpapillary rete Malpighii. Wandering
lymphoid cells are frequently present in the rete. They are
especially numerous in some pathological conditions. They
(Fig. 118) are elongated spindle-shaped bodies lying between
the rete cells, and sending out minute processes. They color
deeply in carmine, have a
small nucleus, and are most
numerous in the lower part
of the rete mucosum.

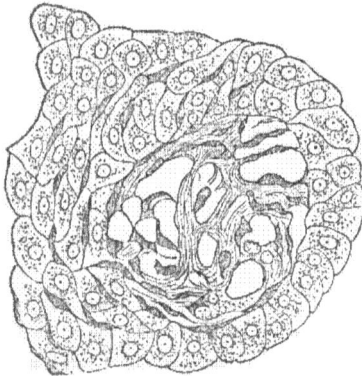

The *granular layer* (Fig.
115, *b*) consists of one or two
strata of flattened, granular-
looking bodies, which, in
perpendicular section appear
spindle - shaped, with their
long diameter parallel to the
free surface of the epidermis.
In this stratum the cells are
no longer connected with each
other by bands, as in the preceding layer. The nuclei of

FIG. 118.—Horizontal section of skin through a
papilla. The migrating cells are observed as dark
bands between the epithelial cells and amongst the
connective tissue of the papilla. Pagenstecher.

these corpuscles are very distinct, and flattened in the same
direction as the cell-body. The latter has a very coarsely granular appearance, which is most marked near the nucleus, and
gradually diminishes in degree as the periphery of the cell is
approached. The structure of these bodies is best shown with
hæmatoxylon.

The *stratum lucidum*, also called the *stratum of Oehl*, is
composed of at least three layers (Fig. 115, *c*). It presents a
clear, homogeneous, or striated appearance. Within the flattened cells composing it, a staff-shaped nucleus is found. The
cells of this layer are formed from those of the granular stratum. In their movement to the free surface the latter become
less granular and the inter-granular substance grows more transparent and shining (Unna). This change from a granular to a
homogeneous translucent appearance commences around the
nucleus, whence it gradually extends to the periphery of the
cell. The nucleus, also, usually becomes invisible.

In vertical section the *corneous layer* appears (Fig. 115, *d*)
to be composed of wavy fibres and horny, transparent cells
of various sizes and shapes. This variation in bulk and form

depends in great measure upon the thickness of the layer.
The nearer we approach to the stratum lucidum, the more distinct are the cells. If the layer is very thin the cells appear
as elongated, flat, or curved bodies, giving to this part of the
epidermis a fibrous appearance. When the corneous stratum
is thick these cells present various forms and sizes. The corpuscles of the lower layers color slightly in carmine, are polygonal or spindle-shaped, and frequently contain a shrivelled
nucleus. As the surface is approached they grow flatter and
drier, are more bent upon themselves, and color less and less in
carmine. The nucleus also becomes invisible. The most superficial layers are composed of elongated, flat, dried-up cells,
the so-called *epidermic scales.* These bodies are best studied
after they have been subjected to the action of liquor potassæ,
which causes them to swell up.

The corpuscles of the stratum corneum are arranged in layers as in the other parts of the epidermis, but the elements
forming a layer are more closely united with each other than
with those of the adjoining layers. Hence this stratum can be
separated into lamellæ, as occurs in some pathological states
of the skin. It accompanies, for example, the formation of
some vesicles, where the exuded liquid, prevented from passing toward the surface, accumulates between the layers, and
thus separates them from each other.

The corneous layer participates in the elevations and depressions of the underlying layers. This causes the undulating or wavy appearance of the lamellæ, as observed in sections
where the papillæ are well developed. It varies greatly in
thickness in different parts of the body, and reaches its greatest development on the palms of the hands and soles of the feet.
Its thickness does not depend upon the rete Malpighii, as it
sometimes forms a thin layer where the rete is thick, and vice
versa.

The *subcutaneous connective-tissue layer* of the skin consists principally of connective-tissue bundles, which, coming
from the underlying fasciæ of the muscles or from the periosteum, pass in an oblique direction to the corium. These
fasciculi are generally cylindrical in form, and variable in size;
by their anastomoses or divisions they form larger or smaller
networks, with correspondingly large or small interfascicular
spaces. Generally large bundles anastomose with each other

in this layer, and hence a loose connective tissue is formed. Within this layer adipose tissue is found in greater or less quantity. The *fat-cells* are collected into masses or lobules, the number of cells which form a lobule varying greatly in number. Each of these latter may be regarded as a fat-gland, as it is provided with an afferent artery, a capillary plexus between the corpuscles, and one or more efferent veins. Several lobules are sometimes united together in the form of an acinous-like gland, and are likewise seen to be surrounded by a general sheath of connective tissue. The individual fat-cells are round, flattened, polyhedral, or oval-shaped, the form depending upon the degree and direction of the pressure exerted upon them. Owing to the amount of fat-tissue so often found in this layer, it has been called the *panniculus adiposus.* Such fat-lobules are absent in the penis, scrotum, labiæ minoræ, eyelids, and pinna. The corresponding spaces in these regions are traversed by fine connective-tissue bands or single fibrils. From this adipose tissue fat-columns pass upward in a somewhat oblique direction to the bases of the hair-follicles, especially to those of the fine hairs. Their long axes form a slight angle with the axes of the follicles, and they are nearly parallel to the erector pili muscles (Warren). In cases of starvation, in the so-called wasting diseases, and in all acute diseases attended with excessive loss of tissue, the fat-cells disappear to a greater or less extent. The skin, in such instances, becomes correspondingly flaccid and wrinkled. Adipose tissue gives to the skin its tension and fulness, and to the body its appearance of roundness or plumpness. Obesity consists in an excessive production of fat-cells.

The interfascicular spaces differ in size in proportion to the amount of lymph present, and to the closeness of the anastomoses between the bundles. In œdema the lymph-spaces are increased in size proportionately to the increased amount of liquid present. The interfascicular spaces all communicate with each other, as is shown by the rapidity with which a hypodermically injected liquid can be dispersed by manipulation.

The *connective-tissue cells* of this layer and of the corium consist of branched cells (Ravogli) which surround the white fibrous bundles and send in processes between the fibres. According to some observers, these cells are epithelioid in character. The *elastic-tissue fibres* are developed from the processes of the branched cells.

Besides connective-tissue fibres and cells, *lymphoid corpuscles* are present in this layer. They exist in greatest number near the blood-vessels and glands. In this situation they are of a roundish form, but in the parts distant from the blood-vessels they are more or less spindle-shaped, and are to be regarded as wandering cells.

The convoluted part of the sweat-glands and the lower part of the hair-follicles of deep-seated hairs lie in this layer.

Blood-vessels, lymphatics, and nerves are present. The *blood-vessels* are large, and after giving off small branches to the hair-follicles, sweat-glands, and fat-lobules, pass upward to the corium.

Pacinian corpuscles are found in connection with some of the nerves. For a description of these bodies the reader is referred to the article on the nerves.

The principal part of the *corium* consists of white fibrous and elastic tissue, the latter increasing in amount with advancing age. Here the white fibrous tissue forms a much denser, firmer structure than in the previous layer. It consists of deep oblique, and superficial horizontal bundles. The latter comprise fine bundles of connective tissue which run parallel with the surface of the skin, and by their division and anastomoses form a very fine network with small interfascicular spaces. From this layer bundles pass upward into the papillæ, and these form a second denser network. The deeper layer is formed by a continuation upward of the subcutaneous connective-tissue bundles. These pass upward in an oblique direction, and as they reach the corium divide into fasciculi. Here they continue to divide and anastomose with each other and with fibres from the horizontally running bundles. The anastomoses are very close ; hence, the corium is formed of a dense network of connective tissue, except in those parts which are traversed by blood-vessels, lymphatic vessels, nerves, hair-follicles, and sebaceous and sweat glands. Immediately around the hair-follicles, sweat-ducts, and sebaceous glands the connective tissue is dense, and the fibres run parallel with the direction of the organs. Owing to the greater size of the connective-tissue bundles in the lower part of the corium, and the consequent looseness of the network formed by their anastomoses, this part of the corium has been called the *pars reticularis corii*, in contradistinction from the finer network formed in the upper part, to which the name *pars papillaris* has been applied. But neither between these two parts nor between the subcutaneous layer and the corium is there any sharp dividing line, the transition being a gradual one.

As already mentioned, the size of the interfascicular spaces depends upon the closeness of the anastomosis between the bundles and fibres. The direction of the bundles corresponds with that taken by the blood-vessels.

The connective-tissue corpuscles of the corium resemble those found in the subcutaneous layer, and also bear the same relation to its connective-tissue bundles. From the upper portion of the corium fibres pass upward to make the papillæ. The form of the papillæ is very variable in different parts of the body. Where they are most developed, as on the inner surface of the terminal phalanges of the fingers and toes, they are conical in shape. In some other regions they form only slight elevations on the corium, giving a wave-like appearance to its upper surface. They consist of a close network of white, fibrous connective tissue combined, especially in the central part of the papilla, with a large number of elastic fibres. Those papillæ which contain tactile corpuscles are called nerve-papillæ.

The corium is separated from the stratum mucosum by a thin, transparent basement-membrane, containing oval nuclei. Its under surface is not sharply defined, and from it prolongations pass upward between the cylindrical cells of the rete, giving this surface a notched appearance similar to that observed on the inner margin of the internal sheath of the hair-follicle.

Elastic fibres are present in large numbers in the corium, especially in its upper part, where they form a network around and between the white fibrous tissue-bundles. In the lower part of the corium they form a large network, which becomes finer as the surface is approached. The number of elastic fibres increases with advancing years. With this increase of elastic fibres there is a corresponding decrease of the white fibrous connective-tissue cells (Ravogli). Numerous wandering cells are met with in the corium, especially in the vicinity of the blood-vessels and glands. Hair-follicles, sebaceous glands, sweat-ducts, nerves, lymphatic vessels, and non-striated muscles are also present in this layer. For a fuller description of the intimate structure of the connective-tissue bundles and cells, see the subject of connective tissues.

Blood-vessels.—Only the corium and subcutaneous tissue are provided with blood-vessels. The *arterial blood-vessels* supplying the skin form two parallel horizontal layers, a superficial and a deep one. The deep layer lies in the subcutaneous tissue, and consists of large vessels running parallel to the general surface. From this horizontally lying deep layer, branches are distributed to the sweat-glands and fat-follicles of this region. The principal branches, however, pass perpendicularly or obliquely upward through the corium to its upper part, and form immediately beneath the papillæ (after free branching and anastomosis) a superficial horizontal layer, the *stratum subpapillare.* From the vessels ascending through the corium branches are given off to the hair-follicles, sebaceous glands, and general tissue of the corium. From the stratum subpapillare small branches pass upward into the papillæ, where they become capillary vessels, which proceed to the summit of the papilla. (See Fig. 119.) Before reaching this point, however, they frequently divide into two or more branches. Frequently, those papillæ in which tactile corpuscles are seated have no blood-vessels.

Fig. 119.— Blood-vessels of the papillæ: *a,* stratum subpapillare; *b,* papilla.

The *veins* are arranged on the same plan as the arteries : they form a superficial and a deep layer, and have their origin in the papillæ. From the superficial layer larger vessels pass downward, receiving blood from the veins of the hair-follicles, sebaceous glands, and the general tissue of the corium, thus forming a deep subcutaneous layer or venous network.

Nerves.—Medullated and non-medullated nerve-fibres are present in the skin. They are found in combination in the nerve-trunks of the subcutaneous tissue, the medullated fibres being most numerous in those regions of the skin where the Pacinian and tactile corpuscles are most abundant. In the subcutaneous connective-tissue region, and in the lower part of the corium, some nerve-fibres leave the nerve-trunks and pass to the glands, blood-vessels, and Pacinian corpuscles found in this region. In the corium some of the fibres lose their medullary

sheath, and afterward continue their course as non-medullated
fibres. The nerve-bundles pass upward in a more or less oblique
direction from the subcutaneous connective tissue through the
corium to the subpapillary network of blood-vessels, around
which they form a plexus. From this subpapillary plexus
medullated fibres run upward and pass into the tactile corpuscles.

The non-medullated nerve-fibres form a reticulum around
the blood-vessels of the pars reticularis corii and the capillaries of the papillæ. They consist of thick or fine, smooth,
varicose fibres with numerous nuclei. These fibres proceed
from the network around the subpapillary blood-vessels upward toward the rete Malpighii, and either pass directly into
the rete or run for a short distance parallel to its under surface, and then finally enter that layer. Within the epidermis the fibres run between the cells and terminate in a manner
not yet definitely known. Their mode of division and termination within the epidermis is probably similar to that occurring
in the cornea. Within the papillæ the nerve-fibres frequently
divide before entering the rete.

The manner of distribution and termination of the non-
medullated nerve-fibres can only be studied successfully in tissue stained with gold chloride. The tissue must be fresh, and
a weak solution of the gold chloride used. When sufficiently
stained the tissue is placed in distilled water slightly acidulated with acetic acid and exposed to the light.

The Pacinian corpuscles are found in greatest abundance in
the skin of the fingers, toes, palm of the hand, sole of the foot,
but also occasionally in other regions of the skin. Their structure is described in the article on the nervous system.

Tactile corpuscles.—As already mentioned, some of the
medullated nerve-fibres forming the plexus surrounding the
subpapillary blood-vessels, pass upward and enter the so-called
tactile corpuscles. These corpuscles are generally seated in the
papillæ, but occasionally they are found in the subpapillary
region, *i.e.*, the upper part of the corium. The majority of
the papillæ containing such corpuscles have no blood-vessels.
They are more or less oval in form, and can be easily recognized under the microscope by their dark contours and by the
oblique lines produced by the transversely running connective-
tissue fibres of the outer surface of the corpuscle. There may

be two or more corpuscles within a single papilla (Thin), but each corpuscle invariably has a special nerve passing into it. Frequently, however, an appearance as if two corpuscles were present is produced by a single corpuscle having the shape of a figure 8. The medullated nerve-fibre, in passing to the corpuscle, pursues a more or less curved course, and usually enters it at or near its lower extremity. It may, however, enter at any part of the corpuscle, and sometimes winds around it for a considerable distance before entering. After entering the corpuscle the medullary sheath is lost, and its course now becomes difficult to pursue, except in the case of very small or young corpuscles. The intimate structure of these bodies and the arrangement of their formative elements are still matters of discussion and uncertainty. The external portion of a corpuscle appears to be composed, in great part, of larger or smaller bundles of white, fibrous connective tissue anastomosing with each other and running transversely, or in a spiral direction, to the long diameter of the corpuscle. This part of the corpuscle differs, as regards irregularity of surface, with the size and the manner in which the fibrous fascicles divide and anastomose. The coarser the bundles and the anastomoses the more irregular will be its surface. Between the fibres are found oval or round bodies which color deeply in gold, and have been regarded as elastic elements (Thin). Other observers consider them as connective tissue, or nerve-fibres. Some of these bodies undoubtedly represent the nerve-fibre in transverse or oblique section ; for the nerve pursues a more

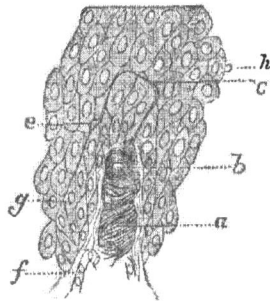

FIG. 120.—Tactile corpuscle, showing termination of nerve : a, corpuscle; b, nerve, cut obliquely; c, apparent division of nerve-fibre; e, similar appearance as at c; f, blood-vessel; g, rete cells; h, nerve-fibre cut transversely.

or less zigzag course within the corpuscle, and, consequently, a section of the body will probably show the nerve cut across in one or more places (Fig. 120, b). The arrangement of the elements forming the central part of the corpuscle is not yet thoroughly understood. These bodies have hitherto been usually regarded as end-organs—that is, it has been believed that the medullated nerve-fibre terminates within the corpuscle, hence the name, tactile corpuscle. Observers, however, have

not agreed as to the mode of termination of the nerve, and
some have maintained that it has not been clearly proven that
they really do terminate in the corpuscle. From specimens
which I have recently obtained I am led to believe that the
nerve does not terminate within the corpuscle, but passes on
into the rete Malpighii.

The best corpuscles for studying this point are small ones,
as in these a section is more likely to include the entire upper
extremity of the corpuscle at the same time that it is not too
thick for examination with the microscope. Even in a small
corpuscle, however, unless the nerve passes onward in a direct
level with the corpuscle after leaving it, the nerve, in a vertical
section, will be cut across, and it will, therefore, be impossible
to follow it from the corpuscle into the rete. I believe the
nerve frequently, perhaps generally, changes the direction of
its course after leaving the corpuscle, and hence we often see
a transverse section of the nerve at the upper extremity of the
corpuscle. In Fig. 120 is seen the location of the termination
of the nerve-fibre as observed in one of my specimens. In
one place its course between the rete cells was very indistinct,
though recognizable. The nerve passed obliquely upward between the cells of the rete to the space between the second
and third rows of cells, where it assumed a longitudinal direction. At the commencement of the curve the nerve appeared to have undergone division (c). After passing a short
distance horizontally it ran almost perpendicularly downward,
and near g was lost to view. At e it appeared to have again
undergone division. According to the appearances here figured the corpuscles are not the structures in which the nerve
terminates, the latter passing from the corpuscle (as a non-
medullated fibre) into the epidermis, where it divides and
probably terminates in the same manner as the other nerves.
This mode of termination cannot be regarded as strange, as we
have already seen that some medullated nerve-fibres lose their
medulla deeper in the corium, and afterward continue their
course as non-medullated fibres.

The tactile corpuscles are found in greatest number in
the ends of the fingers. They are also present on other parts
of the hand and on the foot, and sometimes in the lips and
nipple.

The sweat-glands.—The sweat-glands—*glandulæ sudorif-*

erœ—are found in the skin of all parts of the body except that of the glans penis and margin of the lips. They are most numerous in the palms of the hands and the soles of the feet, where they number, according to Krause, 2,685 to 2,736 to the square inch.

A sweat-gland is composed of two parts, viz.: the gland proper, or secreting part, and an excretory duct. The gland proper lies in the subcutaneous tissue, and consists of the lower part of the sweat-gland rolled and coiled upon itself into a more or less globular form, the tube terminating in a cul-de-sac, the blind extremity generally lying in the centre of the coil. The diameter of the secreting tube is greater than that of the excretory duct. The former is composed of secreting cells, unstriped muscular fibres, and a basement-membrane. The cells (glandular or secreting epithelial cells) are polygonal in shape and form only a single layer. They are strongly granular in appearance and have a very distinct nucleus. Their basal end is sometimes notched where they are inserted into the basement-membrane. In normal conditions these bodies are never found in the sweat-fluid, but in inflammation of the surrounding connective tissue they frequently become separated from the basement-membrane. Oil-globules are frequently seen in the cell-body, and are to be regarded as a normal constituent of the corpuscles.

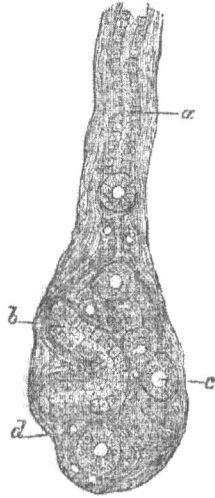

FIG. 121.—Lower part of a sweat-gland: *a*, excretory duct; *b*, coil of secreting-tube; *c*, secreting-tube cut transversely; *d*, blood-vessels cut across.

The basement-membrane is a thin, transparent structure, lying beneath the epithelial cells and composed of flat endothelial elements, as shown by the action of silver nitrate on the fresh tissue.

In certain glands, especially those of the axilla, a layer of unstriped muscular fibres is found external to the basement-membrane. These fibres are present in only a small number of sweat-glands; by their contraction they assist in the expulsion of the secreted sweat. They are the smallest unstriped muscular fibres met with in the human body.

The sweat-glands are surrounded by a somewhat loose fibrous connective tissue, from which fibres pass inward and form a closer network between the coils of the gland. Some of the fibres run parallel, and others transversely or obliquely, to the long diameter of the convoluted tube. A large number of lymphoid cells are always present in this interglandular connective tissue. The sweat-glands are richly supplied with blood-vessels.

The excretory duct passes upward from the gland proper in a more or less vertical direction through the different layers of the skin to its free surface, where it opens with a funnel-shaped orifice. In passing through the corium it pursues a straight or slightly wavy course, and enters the lowest part of the inter-papillary rete. The structure of this part of the excretory duct differs from that of the gland proper, in the shape of the cells, the absence of muscle-fibres, and the presence of a cuticula. This cuticula lines the inner surface of the epithelial coating and limits the lumen of the duct. As the rete Malpighii is entered there are generally two or more layers of cells lining the duct, the number increasing as the rete is approached. The transition from secreting cells to lining cells is gradual, so that the presence of a cuticula decides the nature of the tube. The basement-membrane corresponds in structure with that of the gland proper. The fibres of surrounding connective tissue run parallel with the duct.

As the duct approaches the rete Malpighii its epithelial cells increase in number and form two or more layers, which are really only a continuation downward of the cells of the rete. When the duct enters the rete it loses its basement-membrane and is formed only of the cells of the mucous layer, which have become more or less flattened and spindle-shaped. The direction of the duct through the rete is sometimes straight and sometimes spiral.

In passing through the stratum corneum the duct pursues a spiral direction on account of the horizontally flattened cells of this layer (see Fig. 114, f), and the number of spirals present depends upon its thickness. The largest number is found in the palms of the hands and soles of the feet, where it may amount to twenty or more, whilst on some parts of the body there is not even a single complete spiral. The wall of the duct is formed of the cells of the corneous layer, and the duct opens on the free surface at the summit of the ridges.

The formation of the sweat-glands commences in the fifth month of fœtal life by the pushing of epithelial cells from the rete mucosum into the cutis. In the seventh month the epithelial cells form a canal, and the lower end of the tube becomes dilated and somewhat twisted. In the ninth month the tube is coiled upon itself to form the gland proper. According to Ranvier, who believes that the muscular fibres lie between the epithelial cells and the basement-membrane, the muscle-cells arise from the external cells of the gland proper by a process of simple differentiation. The lumen of the tube is formed not by a softening down of the central cells, but by the formation of the cuticula, which occurs first at the lowest part of the excretory duct (Ranvier).

The sebaceous glands.—The sebaceous glands are seated in the corium and are in close connection with the hair-follicles. When the hairs are large the sebaceous glands appear as appendages to the hair-follicles into which their ducts enter, and by which their contents are carried to the free surface. As regards the small downy, or lanugo hairs, they may be said to open into the ducts of the sebaceous glands, the ducts of the latter having in this case a much greater diameter than in the previous instance. They also open directly on the free surface.

The sebaceous glands are almost without exception acinous glands, the number of lobules forming a single gland, ranging from two to twenty, or more. The largest glands are seated in the nose, cheeks, scrotum, about the anus, and in the labia. Occasionally the secreting portion of a sebaceous gland consists of a single tubule, or sac, whose duct opens into a hair-follicle.

Every sebaceous gland is composed of two parts, viz.: the secreting portion, or gland proper, and the duct. The gland proper is formed of a basement-membrane, or sac, externally, and secreting cells, or their products, internally. The basement-membrane is continuous with the transparent membrane described as lying directly beneath the rete Malpighii and above the corium, and has a similar structure. This basement-membrane passes from the sebaceous gland to the hair-follicle, where it forms the inner layer of the hair-sac. The membrane of the sebaceous gland is surrounded externally by bands of dense connective tissue containing blood-vessels, nerves, and lymphatics.

The secreting part of the gland (Fig. 122, *f*) is composed of layers of cells very similar to the cells present in the epidermis, those of the outer part corresponding to the cells of the rete Malpighii. The first layer of cells, viz., those seated upon the basement-membrane, is composed of cylindrical, or cubical, cells, like those of the rete. They have a very distinct nucleus. Further inward the cells become larger, more or less polyhedral in form, and contain fat, which obscures or conceals the nucleus. If the fat is extracted the nucleus can be seen lying in the centre of the space previously occupied by the fat. The nearer the centre of the gland the greater the quantity of fat in the cells. The most external layer of cells contains but a small quantity. In the centre of the gland, free fat, fat-crystals, and remnants of epithelial cells are found.

The duct of the sebaceous gland is similar in structure to that of the gland proper. Externally is the basement-membrane, lined inside by epidermis-like cells, containing more or less fat, and enclosing a central cavity through which the sebaceous matter passes to reach the hair-follicle or the free surface. The contents of this canal are fat, fat-crystals, and remnants of epithelial cells. Internal to the polyhedral cells of the duct are the cells of the corneous layer of the epidermis, which diminish in number in proportion to the distance from the free surface.

In large hairs the duct of the sebaceous gland opens at an acute angle into the hair-follicle near its upper third, and the gland proper lies about on a level with the middle third of the hair-follicle.

At the place of union of the hair-follicle with the sebaceous gland the cells of the latter become continuous with the cells of the external root-sheath of the hair. This latter root-sheath becomes continuous above with the cells of the rete Malpighii.

The development of the sebaceous glands commences at the third month of fœtal life, as a projection downward and outward of a part of the external root-sheath of the hair, at the place where the future opening of the duct will be situated.[1] It consists, at first, entirely of epithelial cells, which by subsequent multiplication and further projection downward, form the sebaceous gland.

Muscles.—Striated and non-striated muscles are present in the skin. The former are found both in the smooth and in the bearded parts of the face, and also in the nose. They arise from the deeply seated muscles, and passing vertically, or more or less obliquely, upward between the hair-follicles and the glands of the skin, terminate in the corium.

The non-striated muscles are very numerous, and run either in a parallel or in an oblique direction to the general surface of the skin. Those lying parallel with the general surface run either in a straight or circular direction. When they run in a straight direction and anastomose with each other they form a network, as in the scrotum, prepuce, and perinæum. The straight running muscles are found, especially in the scalp and in the axilla, both above and below the sweat-glands. Where the muscles have a circular course, as in the areola of the nipple, a continuous ring muscle is formed.

The majority of the muscles running in an oblique direction have a special relation to the hair-follicles. The muscle arises from the internal sheath of the hair-follicle and passing obliquely upward, skirting the lower surface of the sebaceous gland, terminates in the upper part of the corium (Fig. 122, *n*). Occasionally two muscles, situated on opposite sides, arise from a single hair-follicle sheath. A muscle in its course upward frequently divides into two or more bundles, these secondary bundles afterward pursuing different directions from each other, and sometimes uniting with fibres from other muscles, form a network in the corium. Sometimes an entire muscle, or a secondary bundle, passes upward into a papilla of the cutis and is inserted into the dense fibrous connective tissue directly beneath the rete Malpighii. Occasionally several secondary bundles run nearly parallel with each other and terminate either separately in the corium, or conjointly, after uniting.

The skin is provided with other muscles which have no special relation to the hair-follicles, but pass more or less vertically upward from the subcutaneous tissue to be inserted in the corium.

The number of muscles present in the skin varies in different regions of the body. They are most numerous in the scrotum. The order of frequency in the different parts of the body is as follows: Scrotum, penis, anterior part of perinæum, scalp,

forearm, thigh, arm, shoulder, forehead, abdominal wall, axilla, fore-leg, face, volar and dorsal surfaces of the hands and
feet (Neumann). They are less
developed on the flexor than on
the extensor surfaces.

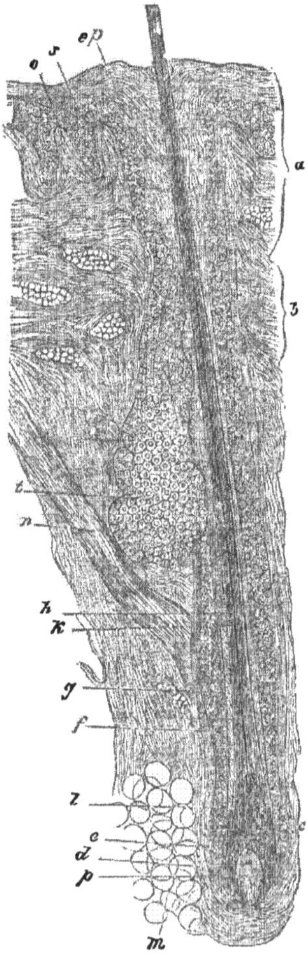

The size of the individual muscles varies according to the person
and the region of the body. It is
impossible, therefore, to recognize
with certainty a slight hypertro-
phy or atrophy of these structures.

For information as to their
blood, lymph, and nerve supply
see the article on unstriped muscle.

The hair.—The parts to be
studied in connection with the hair
proper are the *hair-follicle* and
the *hair-papilla.* The hair proper
is a cylindrical structure seated
within the hair-follicle and upon
the hair-papilla. Its base lies
embedded either in the subcutaneous connective tissue or in the
corium. The portion of the hair
proper within the follicle is called
the *root* of the hair, and the remainder the *shaft* of the hair.
The true hair-follicle includes all
that part of the hair-sac below
the place where the sebaceous
duct enters the hair-follicle. It
is of very variable size and consists of a blind extremity and a
funnel - shaped orifice (*a*). The
follicle is narrowed just below
this funnel - shaped orifice and
forms the so-called neck of the
hair-follicle (*b*). This is the nar-
rowest part of the follicle, and

Fig. 122.—Hair from beard: *a*, canal of exit; *b*, neck of hair-follicle; *c*, lower part of hair-follicle; *d*, external sheath of hair-folli-cle; *e*, internal sheath of hair-follicle: *f*, ox-ternal root-sheath of hair; *g*, internal root-sheath of hair; *h*, cortical substance; *k*, me-dulla of hair; *l*, root of hair: *m*, fat-cells; *n*, arrector pili; *o*, papillæ of skin; *p*, papilla of hair; *s*, rete mucosum; *t*, sebaceous gland; *ep*, stratum corneum, which is continued into the follicle. Biesiadecki.

is the place where the duct of the sebaceous gland enters.
From the neck downward the hair-follicle increases in size, be-

ing largest at its lower end, where it rests upon the papilla. Below the neck we have the follicle and the root of the hair.

The follicle consists, anatomically, of three layers: the external, middle, and internal hair-follicle sheaths.

The *external sheath* of the follicle (*d*) consists of connective-tissue fibres, which extend from the upper corium and running parallel to the long axis of the hair-follicle surround the base of the latter and send some fibres into the papilla. The fibres forming the inner portion of this sheath are arranged much more closely than the fibres forming the external part. In this latter situation there is no sharp dividing line between the sheath and the surrounding loose connective tissue, the one merging gradually into the other. Within this sheath run the special blood-vessels and nerves of the hair-follicle.

The *middle sheath* of the follicle consists of a few transversely running connective-tissue fibres, between which lie oval nuclei imbedded in a granular substance. These latter, probably, represent organic muscle-cells. This sheath begins at the neck of the follicle and, surrounding its lower part, passes also within the papilla. In this tissue is a close network of blood-capillaries. Nerves have not as yet been observed, though they probably exist.

The *internal sheath* of the follicle is composed of a transparent, homogeneous-looking structure—the basement-membrane, which is not altered by the action of acids or alkalies. It is merely a continuation of the transparent membrane found between the rete mucosum and the corium, which it resembles in its structure. It contains neither blood-vessels nor nerves. The external surface is smooth, but the internal surface has a notched appearance, caused by prolongations inward between the cells of the external root-sheath of the hair.

The *hair-papilla* is formed from the stroma of the hair-follicle sheaths, especially from that of the middle sheath. It consists of connective-tissue fibres, between which are found numerous round cells. The internal follicle sheath separates it from the root of the hair. Within the papilla are found one or more arteries and veins besides non-medullated nerve-fibres. The papilla has a narrow neck, a thicker body, and a conical apex. It is, on an average, twice as long as it is broad. The breadth is in direct proportion to the length of the hair.

The hair-follicles and hairs stand obliquely to the surface of the skin. Their direction varies in different regions of the body, and depends upon the structure of the connective tissue of the corium and the degree of its tension. The contents of the hair-follicles are the external and internal root-sheaths and the hair proper.

The *external root-sheath* (*f*) adjoins the inner follicle sheath and consists of rete cells continued into the hair-follicle from the general rete mucosum layer of the skin. This sheath does not extend as far as the lowest part of the follicle, generally ending about on a level with the apex of the hair-papilla, though it is sometimes continued as far as the base of the latter. All the different kinds of cells present in the epidermis are also found in this sheath as far down as the neck of the follicle. Beyond this point the cells of the rete Malpighii only enter into its formation. The number of rows of cells forming it is subject to great variation. It diminishes as the base of the follicle is approached, so that finally the sheath is formed of a single row of cells. At the neck of the follicle the sheath is usually narrower than directly above or below this point, owing to the pressure to which the cells are here subjected. Their form is very similar to that of the corresponding cells of the rete mucosum. Those of the deepest row are cylindrical, and those of the second row polyhedral. In the other rows the cells are flatter, with the exception of the most internal row, where all these bodies are large and round. This last row is not subject to the same changes as the others, and has been considered to be a distinct, independent row of cells (Unna). The nuclei of all the cells color strongly in carmine, hæmatoxylon, etc. Nerve-fibres have been described as running between the cells of this sheath (Langerhans).

The *internal root-sheath* (*g*) lies in direct contact with the external root-sheath. It is usually described as consisting of two layers, an external one, also called the *sheath of Henle*, and an internal one, or *sheath of Huxley*. Strictly speaking, this division into two sheaths is incorrect, as it has been shown (Unna) that the two sheaths supposed to be distinct. have a common origin from the cylindrical epithelial cells surrounding the neck of the hair-papilla at its lowest part. These cells color very deeply in carmine. They surround the root of

the hair like a sheath. In the thick hairs of the beard the
sheath consists of three rows of cells—the external row, afterward forming Henle's sheath, and the two inner rows of cells,
the sheath of Huxley. In finer hairs there are only two layers of
such cells. These corpuscles are originally similar in structure,
having a very granular appearance and an indistinct nucleus.
The sheath is thinnest where the hair-papilla is broadest.
The cells of the external layer (Henle's) become paler and lose
their nuclei earlier than those of the inner layer, so that on a
level with the upper part of the papilla there is a marked difference in the appearance of the two layers of cells. Formerly
it was supposed (Biesiadecki) that Henle's sheath commenced
at this point and was a product of the external root-sheath,
corresponding in this respect with the corneous layer of the
epidermis. The cells of Huxley's layer afterward become
transparent also and lose their nuclei, and can then no longer
be distinguished from the cells of Henle's layer. The internal
root-sheath is now formed of transparent, non-nucleated, spindle-shaped, or flattened bodies which surround the hair-cuticula as far as the neck of the hair-follicle.

Within the internal root-sheath lies the *hair proper*, which
consists of a knobbed extremity, the root of the hair, and a
cylindrical portion, the shaft. Between the hair proper and
Huxley's layer lies the hair-cuticula. This latter consists of
two rows of cells—an external one, closely united with Huxley's layer, and an internal one, united to the hair-shaft. They
both arise from the cylindrical cells seated directly upon the
upper part of the neck of the papilla to the inside of the cells
producing the internal root-sheath. The cells of the inner
cuticula (the hair-cuticula) are at first round, then cuboid in
form, and finally, long and prismatic. Above the papilla they
are more elongated, and commence to overlap the cells above
them. With the flattening out of the cells they assume the
form of rhomboid or ovoid plates, so that above the free surface of the skin one cell partly covers the bodies of four or five
others. At first they lie perpendicularly to the long axis of the
hair, but afterward they are parallel with it. Above the papilla
they form spiral rows around the hair shaft, so that in any section of this part the cells appear of a long cylindrical or spin-
dle-shape. The external or root-sheath cuticula consists at
first of round cells which afterward flatten and lie in the same

direction as the flat cells of the previous cuticula. Before the
internal root-sheath is pierced by the growing hair both cuti-
culæ are composed of similar cells.

The *root of the hair* consists of cells closely resembling
those of the rete mucosum. The corpuscles seated directly
upon the basement-membrane of the papilla are cylindrical in
form, and the more superficial ones polyhedral. Near the hair-
shaft they are spindle-shaped and firmer. The lower cells of
the central part of the root of the hair are round, have a large
nucleus, and a small amount of cell-body. Afterward the cell-
body increases in size. They bear a close resemblance to embryonic corpuscles and color deeply in carmine. In the upper
part of the root of the hair the cells of the external part of the
bulb become oblong, spindle-formed, and, finally, are lengthened
out like fibres, in which condition they
form the fibrous part of the hair-shaft.
The pigment in the root of the hair is
sharply limited externally by the cells
of the hair-cuticula.

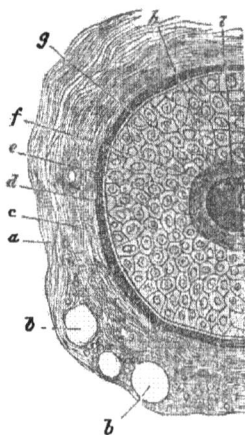

FIG. 123.—Transverse section of
the hair beneath the neck of the hair-
follicle : *a*, external sheath of the hair-
follicle ; *b*, transversely cut blood-vessels ; *c*, inner sheath of hair-follicle ;
d, basement-membrane of hair-follicle;
e, external root-sheath ; *f*, cells of Henle's layer ; *g*, cells of Huxley's layer ;
h, cuticula ; *i*, hair-shaft. Biesiadecki.

The *shaft of the hair* consists of a
central part or medulla, and a fibrous
portion covered by the hair-cuticula.
The medulla consists of polyhedral
cells containing fat and pigment granules. Toward the free end of the hair
it becomes smaller, and finally ends
near the point. The fibrous portion
forms the principal part of the hair-
shaft, and consists of flattened, fusiform cells, containing numerous spindle-shaped granules.

From the foregoing description of
the hair and its follicle it is clear that
in transverse sections it will present
different appearances, according to the
situation in which the section is made. A description of transverse sections in different regions of the hair is here unnecessary. We reproduce, however, above, a figure from Biesiadecki,
which will sufficiently explain this matter (Fig. 123).

A hair increases in length by the formation of new elements
in its root, and they, by their subsequent elongation and move-

ment upward, push the shaft of the hair and its cuticula before them. The structure of an adult hair can be best studied in the stiff, gray hairs of the beard. For the study of the origin of the root-sheaths young hairs should be chosen. There are still many points in regard to the structure of the skin and its appendages which appear to be rather doubtful, owing to our insufficient knowledge. The first development of the hair-follicle takes place at the end of the third or beginning of the fourth month, and it originates as a projection downward of the cells of the rete mucosum. It is seen as a finger-shaped collection of rete cells surrounded by the connective tissue of the corium. The papilla is formed later. By the numerical increase of round cells the follicle is enlarged, and the external cells are pushed sideward, thus forming the external root-sheath. The origin of the other parts of the hair has been already described. The first hairs are always of the lanugo kind—that is, they are fine hairs, with a very short hair-follicle. In certain regions the hairs always remain fine; in other parts they give place to thicker ones. In the latter case a prolongation downward of the external root-sheath takes place. This forms the hair-papilla. The papilla of the first hair atrophies, the hair falls out, and its place is occupied by a thick hair. The permanent hair grows to a certain length, which varies in different persons and in different parts of the body. If a hair has reached its proper term of existence it falls out and is replaced by a new hair, which grows from the old papilla. A hair ceases to be produced when no new cells are formed in the hair-root. The last-formed cells become converted into the hair proper, and form a conical or knobbed extremity to the lower end of the hair-shaft.

The nails.—The nail is merely a modification of the epidermis, and differs from the stratum corneum only in being harder and firmer. It is a longish, four-sided, hard, elastic, transparent, dense, flat body, situated in a fold of the skin on the dorsal surface of the terminal phalanges of the fingers and toes. It is slightly curved in its long diameter, the convex surface being above and the concave below. Its posterior and two lateral sides are connected with the other structures of the skin; the anterior side is free. The fold of skin in which the posterior and two lateral surfaces are imbedded increases in depth from before backward, and at the posterior margin is continued forward for a short distance on the surface of the nail. This fold of skin is called the *nail fold*, and the tissue upon which the nail is seated is termed the *bed of the nail*. That part of the nail imbedded in the flesh posteriorly is the *root* of the nail, and the remainder its *body*. The flesh underlying the root— the corium—is called the *matrix*, and that underlying the body of the nail the bed of the nail proper. The matrix and bed of the nail proper are separated by a more or less convex line, generally easily seen through the nail and known as the *lunula*. The bed of the nail is composed of corium and rete Malpighii tissue. There is no fat in its subcutaneous tissue. The rete here dips down between the papillæ of the corium as in other parts of the skin. The papillæ in the matrix project forward, and are shorter and closer together than in the bed of the nail

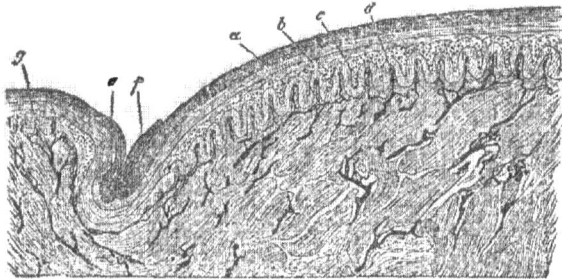

FIG. 124.—Transverse section of the nail through the bed of the nail proper: *a*, nail; *b*, loose corneous layer beneath it : *c*, mucous layer; *d*, transversely divided nail ridges; *e*, nail-fold without papillæ; *f*, the horny layer of the nail-fold which has pushed forward on the nail; *g*, papillæ of the skin of the finger. Biesiadecki.

proper. In this latter structure the papillæ also project forward (Fig. 124, *d*) and increase in length as the free margin of the nail is approached. The rete Malpighii covers the papillæ of the nail, forming cones, which fill the space between the papillæ. In the bed of the nail proper the transition from rete cells to horny cells is very rapid, whilst in the matrix it is gradual. Consequently, this portion of the nail is softer than the other. It is from the matrix that the nail is formed, and from the corneous cells of the body of the nail that the nail is made thicker. The soft cells are directed forward and become more horny as they advance. The under surface of the nail-fold covering the posterior part of the nail is provided with epidermis, which is continued forward a short distance on the upper surface of the nail.

The tissue of the nail is nourished by blood from the bed of the nail and from the nail-fold. Nails grow more rapidly in children than in adults, and more rapidly in summer than in winter. The rapidity of growth varies according to the person and the particular nail. The rate of growth in individual nails can be learned by observing the rate of progress toward the free margin of the white spots seen on nails.

The nail begins to form in the third month of intra-uterine life as a fold covered with a layer of embryonic epidermic cells. In the fourth month a layer of new cells, which afterward become the horny cells of the nail, appear between the rete Malpighii and the embryonic epidermic corpuscles. At the fifth month the epidermic covering disappears and the nail lies exposed. Between the sixth and eighth months the nails are somewhat firm, but do not quite extend to the ends of the fingers. At the eighth month the nails are well developed and extend to the extremities of the fingers.

For the microscopical study of the horny part of the nail, sulphuric acid, or caustic soda, or potash must be employed to soften the corpuscles. For the other structures of the nail no special procedure is necessary.

BIBLIOGRAPHY

WAGNER. Müller's Archiv. 1852.

MEISSNER. Beiträge z. Anat. u. Phys. d. Haut. Leipzig, 1853.

OEHL, E. Annali univ. di med. 1857.

KRAUSE. Die term. Körp. d. einf. Sens. Nerven. Hannover, 1860.

SCHROEN. Contrib. alla anat. fisiolog. e patholog. della cute umana. Torino, 1865.

AUFFHAMER. Wurzburger Verhandlungen. Band I. 1869.

THOMSA. Arch. f. Dermat. 1873.

LOTT. Ueber den feineren bau u. die phys. Regeneration des Epithels. Leipzig, 1874.

THIN. Journal of Anat. and Phys. Vol. VIII. 1874.

HEYNOLD. Ueber die Knäueldrüsen des Menschen. Virchow's Archiv. Bd. LXI. 1874.

UNNA, P. Archiv f. mikrosk. Anat. XII. 1876.

FISCHER, E. Ibid.

RAVOGLI. Med. Jahr. Wien. H. I. 1879.

RANVIER. La France médicale. January, 1880.

CHAPTER XIX.

THE CENTRAL NERVOUS SYSTEM.

By R. W. AMIDON, M.D., New York City.

THE *spinal dura mater* is a serous membrane. Its structure from without inward is: first, loose connective tissue; then dense fibrous tissue; lastly, a layer of lymph-vessels and endothelium. If one tears, with forceps, a shred from the outer surface of the dura mater, fresh or hardened, stains with hæmatoxylon, teases, and examines in glycerine, there is seen a loose network of connective-tissue bundles containing free and fixed connective-tissue cells, blood-vessels, minute nerves, and some fat-cells. This layer is continuous with the loose adipose tissue which normally surrounds the dura mater. The denser tissue next in order may be treated in the same way, and perhaps a few spindle-shaped connective-tissue cells and elastic fibres may be isolated.

On transverse section, however (a very difficult thing to make, by the way), the bulk of the membrane is seen to be a dense mass, 0.5—1.0 mm. thick, composed of longitudinal and horizontal connective-tissue bundles, interspersed here and there with elastic fibres. In this layer blood-vessels and nerves are very scanty and small.

Next, immerse a piece of dura mater, as fresh as possible, in a one per cent. solution of nitrate of silver. Leave it for several hours, and then expose it for a few minutes to the sunlight. When a brown tint is developed on the inner surface, remove it, wash it in distilled water, and strip off the internal surface with forceps.

The shreds of tissue thus obtained show beautifully the structure common to all serous membranes: first, a delicate endothelial layer (see Fig. 125), consisting of flat, unequal, irregularly shaped cells, most of which are furnished with large, round nuclei ; here and there are seen stomata marked by an aggregation of nuclei, which are all located at the edge of the cells surrounding a stoma ; secondly, irregularly disposed lymph-spaces and vessels. The lymph-spaces appear as irregular, transparent patches lying just under the endothelium, and the lymph-vessels are seen as varicose channels, which begin by a blind extremity, anastomose freely, receive tributaries, and, finally, empty by a constricted orifice called a stoma. Their walls are in places thin, but more often thick and irregular from the aggregation of masses of protoplasm along the sides. The capillary lymphatic radicles are lined by a very delicate endothelial layer, which can only be demonstrated in completely successful silver preparations. Some are seen to contain lymph-corpuscles, others are found empty.

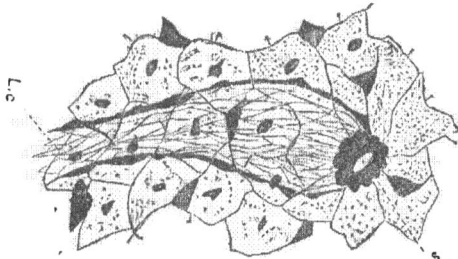

FIG. 125.—Diagram representing the internal surface of the dura mater treated with nitrate of silver. Shows endothelium with nuclei and intercellular masses of protoplasm and a lymph-channel, L.c., lined by delicate endothelial cells, which terminates at S, an opening called a stoma about which is an aggregation of nuclei. × 300.

The *spinal arachnoid* is also a serous membrane, much more delicate, however, than the dura mater. Its extreme thinness allows it to be examined in the fresh state or stained by carmine or hæmatoxylon. It is seen to be essentially a large-meshed connective-tissue network, containing many elastic fibres. Good silver preparations demonstrate an endothelial coat and a lymph system similar to, but more delicate than that of the dura mater. It is doubtful whether blood-vessels exist in the arachnoid in its normal state.

The spinal *pia mater* consists of a small amount of connective tissue, holding together a vascular plexus. It is firmly adherent to the cord, dips into all its fissures, and is intimately connected and continuous with the connective-tissue framework of the cord. The pia mater is best studied by means of fresh specimens stained in hæmatoxylon, as this demonstrates beautifully the different coats of the small vessels.

The spinal fluid should be clear, and contain only a few lymph-corpuscles ; but it usually, when examined post-mortem, contains some blood-corpuscles and swollen epithelial cells.

General histology of the spinal cord.—The spinal cord is composed of connective tissue, blood-vessels, nerve-structures, and epithelium.

The connective-tissue framework or *neuroglia* of the cord is constructed as follows : At tolerably regular intervals the pia mater at the periphery of the cord sends off prolongations which form septa, dividing the white substance into a large number of prisms (base outward). From each of these septa smaller branches spring, forming a delicate network, or stroma, which encloses the nerve-fibres. Generally one, but sometimes two or more fibres are contained in the same mesh.

At the points of junction of these ultimate fibres are seen, here and there, small branching cells, the so-called *spider-* or *neuroglia-cells*. This fibrous structure reaches to the central gray matter and penetrates it by very delicate processes, which chiefly accompany the nerve-fibres.

Three large prolongations of pia mater are of constant occurrence, viz., the *posterior median septum* and a less complete septum on either side, dividing the posterior column into two ; the larger, anterior, or *column of Burdach ;* and the smaller, posterior, or *column of Goll.* The connective-tissue elements are best brought out by hæmatoxylon.

The blood-vessels of the cord are derived from its pia mater, follow its prolongations, and are most numerous in the gray matter, especially that of the anterior horns. In transverse sections there will be seen a clear space about all the blood-vessels. This is the perivascular space or lymph-channel, in which all the blood-vessels are contained. During life these sheaths probably serve a double purpose : an auxiliary nutrient function by lymph-circulation ; and a means of accommodating the ever-varying degrees of vascular distention. In some diseases they become enormously dilated. They are all connected with the space between the pia mater and the cord, and an injection forced into this space will follow the blood-vessels for long distances. These perivascular spaces are also said to be lined with endothelium.

The vessels of the cord present no other peculiarities. Their structure is best brought out by the use of a dilute hæmatoxylon solution, or by the slow carmine staining. The perivascular canals may be more clearly demonstrated by forcing a colored gelatine injection at any point under the spinal pia mater—care being taken, if the cord is cut, to secure the ends of the sections by ligatures.

Nerve-elements of the cord.—The consideration of the nervous elements of the cord will now be taken up in a general way, and the peculiarities of different regions explained later.

The *white substance* of the cord contains, besides the blood-vessels and neuroglia already mentioned, myelinic nerve-fibres of different sizes. These fibres pursue a vertical course, with the exception of those forming the *root-radicles* and commissures.

On examination with a low power, the white substance, in a transverse section stained with carmine, seems to be a collection of minute rings, each with a red dot in the centre. More highly magnified, the transverse section of a nerve-fibre appears as a delicate, rather irregular circle, on the circumference of which, in some cases, are seen nuclei resembling those of the sheath of Schwann, but which are really nuclei of the neuroglia. Next comes a broad ring of colorless, transparent material, the medullary or myelinic-sheath, which very often exhibits concentric lamination. Lastly, usually in the centre, is seen the solid axis-cylinder.

When these fibres pursue a more or less horizontal direction they give the appearance of broad, clear bands traversed by longitudinal red fibres (axis-cylinders). The myelinic fibres average about 5 μ[1] in diameter. Fibres, when isolated by teasing, present the varicose aspect of myelinic nerve-fibres, which lack the sheath of Schwann. To demonstrate this they are best treated when in the fresh state by osmic acid (see p. 114), the result being a black myelinic sheath and brownish axis-cylinder.

The *gray matter* is composed of nerve-cells, medullated and non-medullated nerve-fibres, and an amorphous matrix. The most striking elements are the cells of the anterior horns. These, whether teased from specimens fresh or hardened in chromic acid, or whether examined in sections, always present the same general appearance. They are large, multipolar cells, having a slightly granular, protoplasmic body, a large, oval

---

[1] μ = micromillimetre = $\frac{1}{1000}$ millimetre.

nucleus, and a round nucleolus. These cells are polyhedral in form, as is shown by the fact that sections made in all directions give them the same pyramidal or polygonal outline. In nearly all the large cells there is in some part of the body an aggregation of granules, which are often distinctly pigmented, giving the appearance of a heap.

Striations of the body have been frequently described and depicted (Schultze, Schmidt, etc.), and this appearance has been attributed by some to plications of a very delicate investing membrane, by others to expansions of the ultimate nervous fibrillæ, of which the axis-cylinder was thought to be composed. The motor cells average about 40 μ. in diameter. The cell-processes vary in number. Most of them are bifurcating. One, however, connected with nearly every cell, can be followed for a long distance without dividing, and when the cell is situated near the anterior rootlets this process joins them and acquires a myelinic sheath. This is called the *axis-cylinder process*. The branching processes are called the protoplasmic processes, and are supposed by some to freely anastomose with those of other cells. This anastomosis, if it exist at all, is very delicate, and difficult of demonstration.

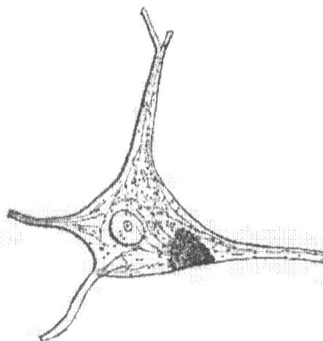

FIG. 126.—Diagram of a motor-cell from the anterior horn of a human cord in the cervical enlargement. × 500.

A certain number of the cells of the anterior horns, especially those located in the lateral region of the cornua, present an elongated, fusiform aspect, and appear to have but two processes. The nerve-cells in the posterior horns are of an elongated oval or fusiform shape, their long diameter corresponding in direction with that of the posterior horn. They are very much smaller than the anterior cells, and less numerous. Their average diameter is about 15 μ. They are seldom seen to have processes.

The *myelinic nerve-fibres* of the gray matter are seen principally in the anterior horns, and converging from the cell-groups to form the anterior root-radicles. Here and there fibres appear in transverse section, which, singly or in bundles, pursue a longitudinal direction.

Amyelinic fibres are found everywhere in the gray matter pursuing various courses. The *gray commissure* is composed almost completely of amyelinic fibres connecting the lateral gray masses.

Besides the above-described elements the gray substance seems to have a structureless or slightly granular matrix, in which the other elements are embedded. In the study of the spinal gray matter osmic acid and carmine preparations are by far the most useful, although much is to be learned by the examination of fresh specimens teased in serum. To study the cells, cut out a piece from the anterior horn of a fresh cord and tease in serum. A preliminary treatment with osmic acid or ammoniacal carmine is sometimes advantageous.

The *epithelium of the spinal cord* lines the central canal. The most internal layer is of the cylindrical, ciliated variety. On account of the difficulty in obtaining fresh specimens the cilia are never seen in the human cord, though they undoubtedly exist. The epithelial cells, as they do exist in the human cord, have a square base, taper to a slender thread toward the apex, which penetrates the layer of young, round epithelial cells, and is lost in the granular central gray matter. The cells of the second layer are round, granular, and thickly crowded.

The *subepithelial tissue*, for some distance around the central canal, consists of embryonal cells in a granular matrix.

The *central canal*[1] has no constant shape, varies greatly in size, and is often choked with desquamated epithelium. Its position, as its name indicates, is in the middle of the gray commissure, on a line passing between the anterior fissure and posterior septum. The general features of the spinal cord having been pointed out, the peculiarities of different regions will now be shown.

Special study of the different portions of the cord.—The cord will be studied from below upward. The mode of study will mainly be by sections made after Clarke's method. The cord, after slitting the dura mater with the scissors up the front and back, is cut in segments 3 ctm. long, which adhere

---

[1] Sometimes double. See Seguin: Am. Jour. Med. Sci., p. 427. 1872.

to the undivided dura mater. Thus prepared it is suspended in Müller's fluid (see p. 15), or dilute chromic acid (see p. 14), until hardened. The segments are then embedded in a microtome (see p. 16), and horizontal, transverse sections made. These are washed in distilled water and stained with carmine or hæmatoxylon (see p. 23). A few minutes' immersion in alcohol previous to this manipulation makes the tissues take the coloring more quickly. After staining and washing, dehydrate the sections with alcohol and absolute alcohol, make transparent with oil of cloves, and mount in Canada balsam or dammar varnish (see p. 23).

Hidden in the cauda equina is found the *filum terminale*, which is the end of the cord. Sections near its end exhibit little of the structure of the cord. At a point where it is 1.5 mm. in diameter it presents the appearance of a peripheral nerve, except that it has an opening—the central canal—in its centre. Its transverse section shows a collection of large and small myelinic nerve-fibres pursuing a vertical direction.

A little higher up, where the filum measures 2 mm. in diameter, there is little difference, except that the central canal is nearer the surface (anterior) and surrounded by a small amount of gray matter. Now and then there are seen small, oval nerve-cells in the region posterior and external to the central canal. A little higher still, where the filum is 3 mm. in transverse and 2 mm. in antero-posterior diameter, back of the central canal on each side, where the future posterior horn is to be, there is a small collection of spindle-shaped cells.

Sections from a region a little above this present an entirely different picture. The gray substance is here much more developed and occupies the larger part of the section. It is divided into a club-shaped anterior horn, containing a few large polyhedral cells, and a posterior horn which is rounded and formed of peripherally directed nerve-fibres and oblong nerve-cells. From this point up sections gradually become more circular and develop more and more a resemblance to the structure of the cord, until, at a point where the sections are about 3.5 mm. in diameter, the anterior fissure and posterior septum become well marked. The anterior horns contain few cells, and the fibres emanating from them pursue a very oblique course downward through the anterior columns.

From the lateral gray matter arise bundles of nerve-fibres

which curve around the posterior horn, and, meeting similar fibres from the posterior columns, together form the posterior nerve-root. These two bundles form an arciform structure surrounding the round extremity of the posterior horn. (See Fig. 127.) The gray commissure occupies one-third the diameter of the cord. The central canal is large, slit-like, and antero-posterior in direction. To summarize then, there seems to be in the filum terminale, especially its lower portion, a preponderance of the posterior or sensory part of the cord.

About two centimetres from the end of the cord nearly the same picture is presented. The transverse section is circular and about 6 mm. in diameter. Many large nerve-cells appear at the outer side of the anterior cornua, mostly at their junction with the posterior horns. Fibres from

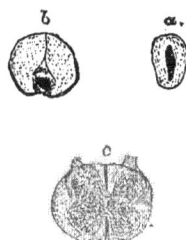

Fig. 127.—Three sections of the filum terminale: *a*, its transformation into the coccygeal nerve; *b*, section higher up before the giving off of the last sacral filaments; *c*, its commencement.

this cell-group, instead of running a direct course, curve backward and inward (see Fig. 127), then run forward and emerge from the anterior horns. Many oval cells appear in the posterior horns, which now reach the surface of the section, and the posterior roots begin to show their origin from the posterior columns and horns.

In the *lumbar enlargement* transverse sections have a circular shape. (See Fig. 128.) The white substance here predominates, and has but one peculiarity, which will be noticed in greater or less prominence throughout the remainder of the cord. At the bottom of the anterior fissure is a broad band of white substance called *the white commissure*. This is formed of myelinic nerve-fibres, which pursue a course from the base of the anterior horn of one side, forward, across the median line and downward to join the anterior column of the opposite side at a lower level. (See Fig. 129.) The anterior horns in the lumbar region are large and square, as are also the cells contained in it. *The gray*

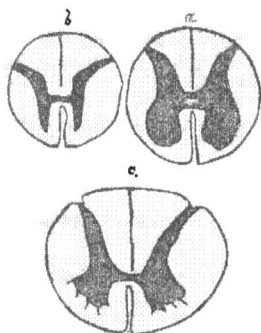

Fig. 128.—Three diagrams showing the relations of gray and white matter in different regions of the cord: *a*, lumbar enlargement; *b*, mid-dorsal region; *c*, cervical enlargement.

commissure is narrow, and the central canal has its long diameter placed transversely to the cord.

Transverse sections in the *dorsal region* are circular and 8 mm. in diameter. The white commissure is thin, otherwise the same structure as in the lumbar region is observed. The anterior horns are narrow and sparsely filled with rather small multipolar cells. No continuous tracts of nerve-fibres can be traced through the anterior columns, as their course is so oblique (downward) as to give almost a transverse section of the bundles. The posterior horns, just behind the gray commissure, are swollen out, and contain a number of large nerve-cells—some multipolar, some oval. They approach the type of the cells in the posterior horns. This collection of cells is called the *column of Clarke.*

Transverse sections in the *cervical enlargement* measure about 14 mm. The antero-posterior diameter is about 11 mm. The white commissure in this region presents about the same characteristics as in the lumbar region. The anterior horns are fan-shaped; the anterior roots curve forward, outward, and downward. The central canal is triangular. The posterior horns are slender, and contain a few small nerve-cells. The posterior roots are also more intimately connected with the posterior horns than lower down.

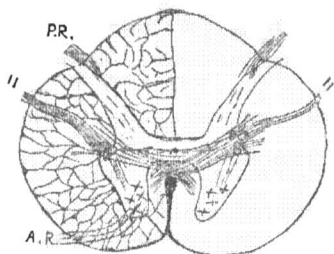

Fig. 129.—Diagram of transverse section of the cord in the upper cervical region, showing coarse connective-tissue reticulum in left half of diagram, commencing decussation of the lateral columns across the base of the anterior horn into the opposite anterior column, taking the place of the anterior commissure lower down, and the root of the spinal accessory, 11: A.R. = anterior root; P.R. = posterior root. In this figure and in others small crosses must be understood as nerve-cells.

In *the upper cervical region* the gray matter assumes more the shape of the dorsal gray matter. In the lateral region, at the junction of the anterior and posterior horns, longitudinal bundles of myelinic nerve-fibres begin to appear. These bundles curve over (see Fig. 129), and pass rather obliquely upward and outward through the lateral columns, emerging nearer the posterior than the anterior horns. They are joined by fibres curving back from the cells of the anterior horns, and also emanating from the central gray matter. In this structure is seen the first appearance of the spinal portion of the spinal accessory root-fibres. The longitudinal bundles mentioned evidently come from cells of the anterior horns lower down. Some of the fibres, passing back from the anterior horns to join the root, are seen to arise directly from the motor cells.

In taking leave of the cord, the introduction of a diagram[1] showing its regional anatomy, looked at from a physiological standpoint, is deemed advantageous. It will enable the microscopist to properly record localized lesions.

In studying the spinal cord by means of horizontal transverse sections, it is of the utmost importance, particularly in pathological cases, to know which is the right or left side, and whether one is looking at the upper or under surface of a section. Of so much importance is this knowledge, that some means must be employed to acquire it.

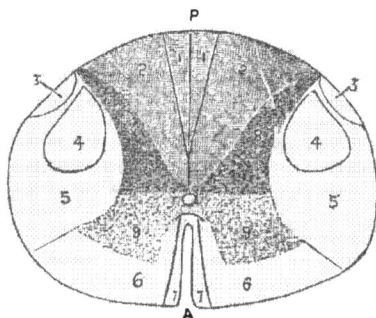

FIG. 130.—Diagram of transverse section of the spinal cord; A, anterior median fissure; P, posterior median septum; 1, columns of Goll; 2, columns of Burdach; 3, direct cerebellar column; 4, crossed pyramidal column; 5, lateral column; 6, anterior fundamental column; 7, direct pyramidal column; 8, posterior gray horns; 9, anterior gray horns; stippled part, gray matter: shaded part, æsthesodic system; unshaded part, kinesodic system.

One of the best means is a method devised by Dr. E. C. Seguin, and published in the translator's note appended to Schultze's article on the spinal cord, in the American translation of Stricker's "Histology," p. 647. He there recommends, before placing the segment of the cord in the microtome, that a slight longitudinal incision be made in the right lateral column. By this means all the sections have a nick in the right lateral column, and can easily be placed. This method, however, has many drawbacks. One is that it is a process easily forgotten during the manipulations. Another more serious drawback is the fact that, make the incision slight as you can, the resulting nick often causes extensive fissures and crumbling of the lateral column or whole section, especially in pathological or over-hardened specimens.

The requirements by the new method are two: 1st, the sections must be nearly horizontal; and 2d, they must be suf-

---

[1] Dr. E. C. Seguin: Lectures on Localization, in N. Y. Medical Record, April 27, 1878, p. 323.
    20

ficiently well stained and transparent to demonstrate the constituent parts of myelinic nerve-fibres. The mode of determination depends entirely on the fact that the anterior roots
pursue an obliquely descending course through the anterior
columns, and for this reason horizontal sections cut the anterior rootlets obliquely. (See Fig. 131.)

What is the natural inference to draw from this fact? It is
this: let the reader look at the *upper* surface of a transverse
section of the spinal cord and bring the anterior roots into the
field ; that is, let him look *down* the anterior column. He
readily perceives that the central ends of the anterior root-
fibres are nearer his eye than the peripheral ends. He sees
that while the central ends are *at* the focus, the peripheral
ends are *beyond* the focus, and he needs to bring the eye nearer
to define them. This nearing the focus also gives the fibre-
bundle an apparent peripheral motion, while increasing the
focal distance causes an apparent central motion.

The application of this method to a chance section is easy.
Suppose we examine the anterior
columns of a section and find by
focussing that the central ends of
the anterior root-fibres are farther
from the eye than the peripheral
ends. We will immediately know
we are looking *up* the cord or at
the *under* surface of the section.
Now, all it is necessary to do is
to turn over the section, either in
your mind or on the slide, and put
the anterior horns forward. The
section is then in position.

In sections of the cord where
the anterior roots do not show, the
posterior roots may be used in a similar way, as they, too, pursue a slightly descending course. Their use is not so easy, as
the fibres are short and pursue a slightly wavy course. In
sections or fragments of sections, where neither of these structures avail, a study of the course of the fibres in the anterior
white commissure will lead to detection. These fibres pursue
a course downward and across the median line, from the base of
one anterior horn into the anterior column of the opposite side.

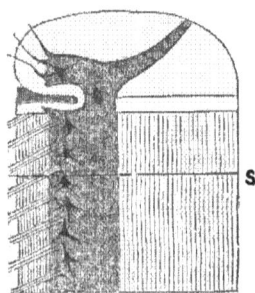

Fig. 131.—Diagram of vertical section of human cord through the anterior and posterior columns and the anterior horns. It is intended to demonstrate how a transverse, horizontal section. S, cuts the anterior nerve-roots obliquely. (From *Archives of Medicine*, August 1, 1879, p. 70.)

In sections of the upper cervical region the spinal accessory roots may be made use of, remembering, however, that they pursue a course obliquely upward through the lateral columns.

The application of these rules to the medulla will be pointed out later on.

NOTE.—To demonstrate the obliquity of the anterior rootlets, find, by a transverse section, the exact direction of the anterior rootlets, and then make longitudinal sections through the anterior column and horn on this line.

THE MEDULLA OBLONGATA.

In the upper part of the cervical region changes take place in the arrangement of the elements of the cord transforming it into the medulla oblongata. The changes are as follows: before the external signs of decussation appear, it is seen that the fibres of the lateral columns change their vertical course and bend forward and inward. This fact is demonstrated by the oblique sections of bundles and fibres. A little higher these bundles and fibres can be traced across the gray matter behind the anterior horn

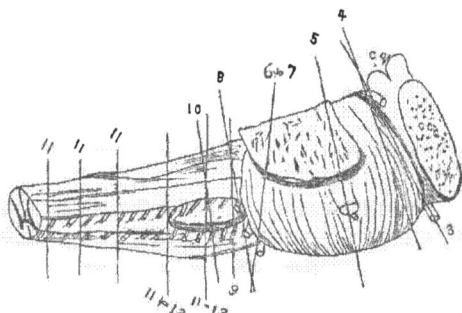

FIG. 132.—Diagram of the medulla, pons, etc., natural size, to show the direction of sections for displaying the different nuclei and roots: 11′, line of section to show the early decussation of the lateral columns and spinal accessory tract; 11, line of section to show the spinal accessory tract and decussation of the pyramids; 11 & 12. region of the spinal accessory and hypoglossal; 10, pneumogastric; 9, glosso-pharyngeal; 8, acoustic; 6 & 7, abducens and facial; 5, trigeminus; 4, patheticus; 3, motor oculi; c, q., corpora quadrigemina; c. c., crus cerebri.

into the opposite anterior column, which is to become by this addition the anterior pyramid. The *decussating fibres* take the place of the anterior commissure lower down, and the fibres pass upward and forward across the median line. The fibres of the anterior columns do not decussate at all, but give way to and mingle with the fibres from the lateral columns.

The shape and structure of the anterior horns are about the same as lower down. The posterior horn expands suddenly at its peripheral extremity into a bulbous termination (see Fig. 133), from which the posterior root emerges. *The central gray matter* between the two horns is traversed and intersected by the decussating fibres from the lateral columns. Numerous prolongations from this gray matter spread out into the lateral columns, presenting a coarse reticulum, called the *formatio*

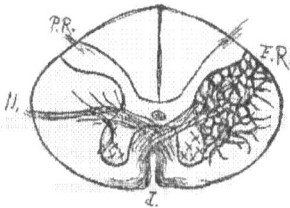

Fig. 133.—Diagram of transverse section of human medulla below external decussation of pyramids, showing bulbous posterior horns: *P R*, formatio reticularis; 11, spinal accessory root and decussation of the lateral columns.

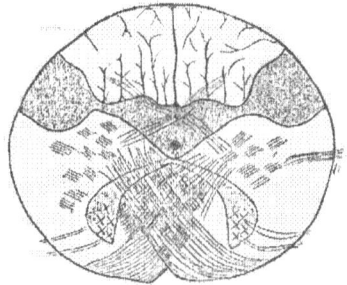

Fig. 134.—Diagram. Decussation of the pyramids, shows decussation of the lateral columns, the swelling of the posterior horns, the shrinkage of the anterior horns, the spinal accessory root 11, and a partial decussation of the posterior columns behind the central canal.

reticularis. The gray commissure is very broad, the central canal having its long diameter directed antero-posteriorly.

In sections at the decussation of the pyramids proper, *i.e.*, where they are seen to decussate externally, a slightly different picture is presented. The lateral columns have nearly disappeared, having now almost all entered into the decussation, which is here very broad (see Fig. 134), and presents a peculiar zigzag appearance from the interweaving of bundles of fibres from the opposite lateral columns. These fibres, after curving around the anterior columns for a short distance, seem to disappear by assuming a vertical direction. The club-shaped extremities of the posterior horns remain, while the rest is pushed back into the posterior columns, and contains many large cells.

The anterior horns are also displaced backward, pushed back by the anterior columns increased in size by the addition of the lateral columns. Hence, the anterior roots have a longer path through the anterior columns and approach the type of the hypoglossal nerve-roots seen a little higher up. (See Fig. 135.) The spinal accessory nerve curves out and back from the lateral gray matter where a group of cells is situated.

Let us next take up a section involving the lower end of the olivary body. We have the following view presented. The section is slightly cordiform. (See Fig. 135.) The decussating fibres at the base of what remains of the anterior fissure, which has all along become shallower, now forms the commencement of the *raphe*, a structure which extends all through the rest of the medulla and pons, separating the two motor tracts. The union of the lateral and anterior columns now nearly complete, forms the anterior pyramids. The fibres here have a general vertical direction, except that a broad band which emerges from the decussation at the bottom of the anterior fissure, curves around the margin of the anterior pyramid, and then, sometimes in the substance, sometimes at the surface of the medulla, almost completely surrounds it, the bundle becoming longitudinal on the posterior surface. These bear the name of *the arciform fibres*. The rest of the white matter is so cut up as to render it hardly divisible into regions. The central canal, which is very long antero-posteriorly, has almost coalesced with the gradually deepening posterior furrow soon to become the fourth ventricle.

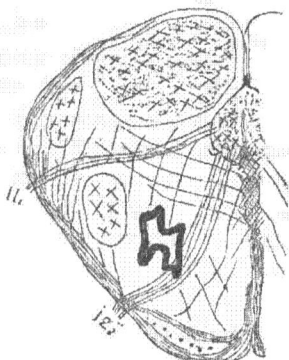

Fig. 135.—One half of section at lower end of the olives: 11, upper spinal accessory root; 12, lower hypoglossal roots.

The gray matter originally in the cord is now collected about the central canal. Anterior and external to the central canal there is a small group of multipolar cells. This is the remnant of the anterior horns, which have been continually crowded back by the accumulation of fibres in the anterior pyramids. These cells in every respect are similar to those in the anterior horns. Their processes give origin to fibres which course forward in two or three bundles through the white matter of the anterior pyramids, and emerge at about the junction of the anterior pyramids and the lateral white mass.

A little farther back in the gray matter, behind the central canal, is a small group of nerve-cells the remains of the spinal accessory nucleus, from which a few fibres run in a straight course outward and slightly backward, through the lateral white matter. Additional collections of gray matter now begin to appear. In the posterior region is a large tract (see Fig. 135) containing scattered groups of many small cells evidently connected with the arciform fibres. This is probably a part of the lower origin of the pneumogastric. A little in front and external to this is a small group of larger nerve-cells which help to form the lower sensory origin of the fifth nerve. Still farther forward in the lateral region is a large collection of multipolar nerve-cells. Although this group is traversed in many directions by fibres, single and in bundles, still it seems to give rise to fibres which run back and upward, evidently to curve upon themselves and join the peripheral fibres of the spinal accessory root. (See Figs. 135 and 137.)

Farther forward still there is a collection of small cells arranged in a wavy line (see Fig. 135), the commencement of the olivary nucleus. Through this the roots of the hypoglossus all pass. Some seem to be lost in it, others appear to arise from it, but this is probably due to the arrangement of roots often seen to curve into the nucleus and then out again. As this is the first appearance of the olivary body, it will be well here to describe it.

THE OLIVARY BODY.

The olivary nuclei are situated in the medulla, under the oval projections on its anterior surface called the olivary bodies. The nucleus consists of a strip of gray matter arranged in general like a piece of fluting folded on itself, so as to form almost an ellipse. From the concavities of the fold on either side proceed bundles of fibres, the external ones joining the formatio reticularis, the internal ones passing into the raphe. Their connection with the hypoglossal roots is probably not important. The intimate structure of the olivary fold is that of a dense gray matrix holding numerous small polyhedral cells having delicate protoplasmic processes.

Let us now go a trifle higher (see Fig. 137), and observe that in sections the central canal, which has all along been elongating and receding backward, now opens into the apex of the fourth ventricle. There is now, therefore, quite a deep notch in the posterior part of the section, covered with the same cylindrical epithelium which lined the central canal. On each side, and in front of the bottom of the fourth ventricle, lies a large group of multipolar cells, the *hypoglossal nucleus*, from which bundles of fibres course forward through the olivary body, which is here much enlarged and more complex than in the last section. On the inner side of the hypoglossal roots in the olivary region is an elongated mass of gray matter containing small cells, called the *parolivary nucleus*. There is an oval group of fusiform cells at, behind, and external to the hypoglossal nucleus, from which indistinct and broken bands of fibres pass outward to emerge from the lateral region of the medulla. This constitutes the *upper spinal accessory nucleus* and root. Behind this nucleus, forming the

FIG. 136.—Diagram showing structure of one fold of the olivary nucleus; C, centripetal fibres; P, peripheral fibres. × 64.

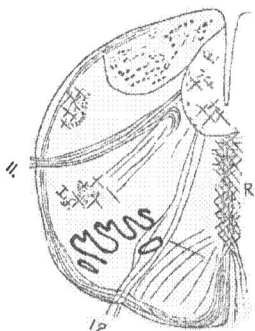

FIG. 137.—One-half transverse section of the human medulla at the point of fusion of the central canal and the posterior fissure to form the fourth ventricle; 11, spinal accessory root; 12, hypoglossal root; R, raphe.

eminence on each side of the fourth ventricle, is a large mass of gray matter containing a great number of small nerve-cells, which also seems to be, rather indistinctly connected with the spinal accessory root. External to this nucleus is a continuation of the collection of large cells seen in the section lower down, the lower sensory nucleus of the fifth. In front of the spinal accessory root is seen a group of multipolar cells not so large as in preceding sections. The peripheral circular fibres in this region are confined to the anterior and external aspect of the medulla, and are still seen to be in connection with the raphe by the arcuate fibres which traverse obliquely the intervening nervous tissue.

From this point to the middle of the olives, sections differ little, except that in this space the root-fibres of the spinal accessory seldom appear, although figured by most writers. The region formerly occupied by the spinal accessory nucleus contains a group of small cells which form part of the pneu-

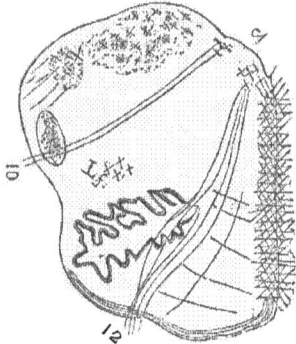

mogastric nucleus. The fibres between this nucleus and the point of exit of the pneumogastric root run so obliquely upward, that no direct connection between them can be traced.

It is in sections at the middle of the olives that the pneumogastric begins to appear distinctly. Most of its fibres seem to be connected with a small group of cells situated in the gray matter, at the junction of the funiculi graciles and the restiform body. The gray mat-

FIG. 138.—One-half transverse section of the human medulla through the middle of the olives; 4, fourth ventricle; 10, pneumogastric root; 12, hypoglossal root.

ter of the restiform bodies is filled with small cells and contains many fibres having a peripheral direction posterior to the pneumogastric root—the beginning of the auditory nucleus and root. The olivary body here reaches its highest development and greatest dimensions.

Behind the olivary body is a small group of cells, from which scattered fibres pass backward and inward toward the pneumogastric nucleus. But most of them are lost by assuming a longitudinal direction. This is probably the lower facial nucleus, to be described farther on. The arciform fibres are chiefly confined to the surface of the anterior pyramids and the olivary bodies. The fibres of the raphe pursue, in great part, an antero-posterior direction.

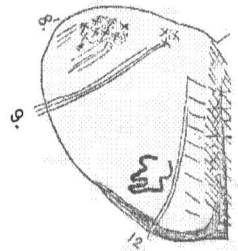

FIG. 139.—One-half transverse section of the human medulla through the upper part of the olives bringing the glosso-pharyngeal tract (9.) and the lower part of the acoustic nucleus (8/) into view

Sections through the medulla at the upper part of the olivary bodies differ little from the former sections. But a small segment of the olivary bodies is present, and only a few of the hypoglossal roots remain. (See Fig. 139.) External to the remains of the hypoglossal nucleus is a nucleus of small cells giving origin to a bundle of fibres, which pass out laterally just as does the pneumogastric lower down. This is the *glosso-pharyngeal nerve and root*. Farther still from the median line, in the floor of the fourth ventricle, is seen a group of small cells, the commencement of the acoustic nucleus. Scattered nerve-cells arising here pursue an obliquely forward and outward direction, making the lower margin of the auditory root.

Transverse sections of the medulla just at the edge of the pons bring the acoustic region into view; the upper olivary body is here visible. Behind this are scattered a few large cells, from which fibres pass backward to form higher the *facial root*.

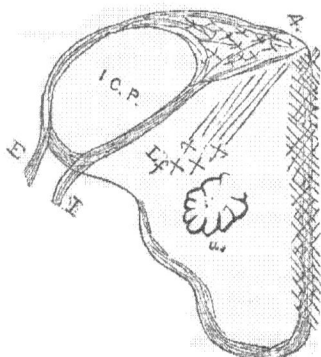

FIG. 140.—One-half transverse section of the human medulla just below the edge of the pons, showing acoustic nucleus and roots which enclose the inferior cerebellar peduncle I. C. P.: I, internal root; E, external root; *v*, upper olivary nucleus; Lf, lower facial nucleus, *s diams.*

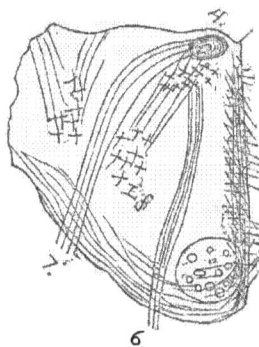

FIG. 141.—Diagram of a transverse section just above the edge of the pons, having the obliquity given it in Fig. 132, 6 & 7: 6, abducens root; 7, facial root. For other explanations, see text.

Occupying the floor of the fourth ventricle is a large mass of gray matter, from which the acoustic arises. This gray matter contains many small round and some multipolar cells. The nerve has two roots, one internal, the other external. (See Fig. 140.) The former arises from fibres emerging from the raphe near the fourth ventricle and from the gray matter just external to it, and pursues a course downward and forward through the lateral white matter. This root, at its point of emergence, is joined by fibres from the posterior root curving around the surface of the medulla, like, if not identical with, the arciform fibres. The external root has also one origin from the gray matter near the median line, and curving outward on the floor of the fourth ventricle (forming the *lineæ transversæ*) it receives additions from the lateral gray mass, and emerges from the medulla a little behind the internal root, which, however, it soon joins.

It is seen that the two roots embrace a column of white matter, which is the *inferior peduncle of the cerebellum.* (See Fig. 140.) In sections just above the edge of the pons, having the oblique direction given in Fig. 132, the region of the sixth and seventh nerves comes into view. The view presented here is different from that in the medulla below. In place of the narrow band of arciform fibres which covered the anterior region of the medulla, nearly the anterior half of this section is composed of transverse, arciform fibres. Imbedded in this structure is a longitudinal bundle of white matter, the continuation of the anterior pyramid. The posterior half of the section contains the structures under consideration.

From a group of multipolar cells at the floor of the fourth ventricle, some distance from the median line, several bands of fibres pass forward and slightly outward, in a somewhat similar way to the hypoglossal roots lower down. This is the *nucleus and root of the abducens nerve.*

Internal to and behind the abducens nucleus, in almost all sections, is seen an oval bundle of what at first sight appears to be longitudinal nerve-fibres. Closer examination, however, shows the fibres to be not straight but looped, and in successful sections the following appearances are presented. Behind the anterior pyramids and outside of the abducens root is seen a group of multipolar cells occupying the same location as the group called the lower facial nucleus, lower down. Arising from

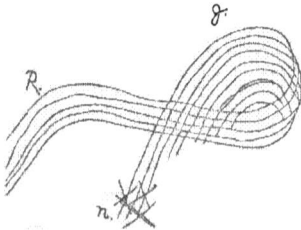

Fig. 142.—Diagram of course of fibres in the "genu" of the root of the facial nerve; *n,* fibres coming from the nucleus; *g,* the "genu," or coil where the fibres change their direction R, the root proper of the facial nerve.

this, and pursuing a course backward and inward, are numerous fibres ; these reach the oval bundle before mentioned, enter it, curl upon themselves (see Fig. 142), and emerge at about their point of entrance. The fibres mentioned as appearing longitudinal undoubtedly come from the lower facial nucleus, and curl upon themselves like the rest.

Some fibres (commissural) join the root from the raphe, and others seem to arise from the abducens nucleus, though this is denied by many authors. The fibres which seem to arise from the abducens nucleus are probably fibres from the anterior nucleus of the facial, which do not traverse the coil ("genu," as it is called), but enter the root directly.

The facial root thus formed goes directly outward at first toward the external angle of the fourth ventricle, then turns sharply forward to emerge at the junction of the pons and medulla external to the sixth root. Many authors, first of whom was Clarke, describe an inferior nucleus of the facial nerve, supposing it to innervate the lips and mouth, basing their assertions as much on the seat of lesion in labio-glosso-pharyngeal paralysis as on anatomical evidence. There can be but little doubt as to its existence, and probably it corresponds to the group of cells seen in Figs. 137 and 138.

Sections of the pons above this point soon begin to show traces of the fifth nerve. (See Fig. 143.) The picture we get in transverse sections at the emergence of the fifth root is, in front, two large bundles of longitudinal nerve-fibres surrounded by the arciform fibres and separated by the raphe; behind, the gray matter of the fourth ventricle, which here is pentagonal in shape and is covered in by the base of the cerebellum, the inferior vermiform process.

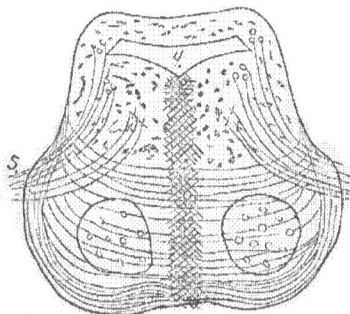

Fig. 143.—Diagram showing origin and course of the trigeminus nerve.

Emerging from the gray matter in front of the external corner of the ventricle, and also joined by fibres from above and below, is a large bundle of fibres which pursue a diagonal course outward and forward, to emerge from the side of the pons. This is the *sensory root of the fifth nerve.* Internal to this root, just after its formation, is seen in successful sections a large group of multipolar cells sending off fibres, *the motor root*, which join the sensory root and emerge with it. A collection of large, oval, pigmented cells here underlie the exterior part of the fourth ventricle and form *the locus cæruleus.* It seems to have an indistinct connection with the trigeminal sensory root, and Meynert makes it one of its points of origin.

The sensory root is reinforced by fibres from a group of large oval cells external to the fourth ventricle and by the so-called descending branch (Meynert), which is seen in transverse section in the same location coming from regions still higher up. Some fibres also come from the raphe and arcuate fibres, and others from the lower sensory origin of the fifth, which occupies a lateral position in all the sections up from the spinal accessory region of the medulla.

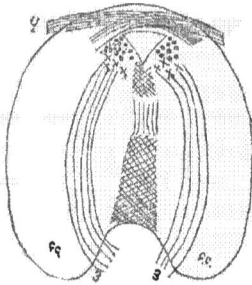

FIG. 144.—Diagram showing origin of the third and fourth nerves from the gray matter about the aqueduct of Sylvius; c. c., crus cerebri; 3, third nerve; 4, fourth nerve.

Higher in the pons, where the anterior motor tracts or pyramids, before mentioned, begin to separate into the crura cerebri, the fourth nerves are seen. They are supposed to arise from a nucleus at the floor of the fourth ventricle lower down, curve around the outer wall of the ventricle, decussate in the median line in the valve of Vieussens, and pass from the pons behind the tubercula quadrigemina. From this point they curve forward around the crura, on the outer side of which they appear at the base of the brain.

At about this point and a little higher are seen bundles of fibres emerging from the gray matter containing small cells, in front of the fourth ventricle, diverging and pursuing an arcuate course through the crura, to converge again and emerge from the inner side of each crus. (See Fig. 144.) This constitutes the nucleus of origin, the course and point of emergence of the third nerve—a view hard to get unless just the right obliquity is given to the section.

Imbedded in the crus, in the region through which the third nerve passes, is a collection of pigmented cells forming *the locus niger*. Higher the crura separate and enter their respective hemispheres. Their further course is better shown by a transverse vertical section of the hemispheres at the large part of the thalamus opticus. (See Fig. 145.)

Here we see a great part of the substance of the crus flattened in form passing upward, between the optic thalamus and a gray mass called the *nucleus lenticularis*, forming what is denominated *the internal capsule.* The posterior third of the internal capsule is distributed to the posterior part of the hemisphere, and when destroyed produces loss of sensibility on the opposite side of the body. The anterior two-thirds of the internal capsule is distributed to the middle or motor region of the hemisphere, and its destruction causes a paralysis

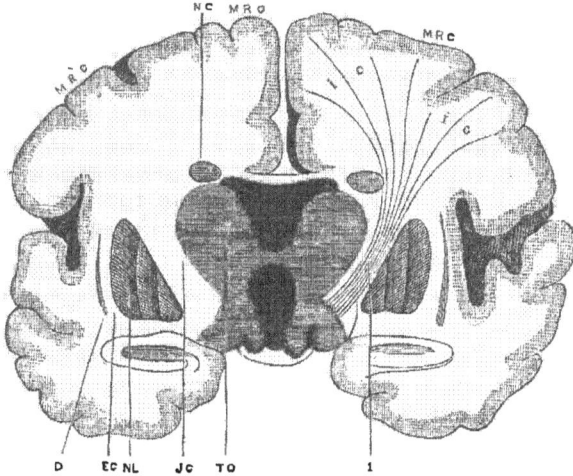

FIG. 145.—Modified from Charcot's diagram to show position, relation, and distribution of the internal capsule as seen in a vertical transverse section of the brain on a level with the greatest development of TO, thalamus opticus; IC, location of the internal capsule: NL, nucleus lenticularis; EC, external capsule; D, claustrum; NC; nucleus caudatus; MRC, motor regions of cortex cerebri; 1, fibres representing the radiation of the internal capsule vertically to the motor region of the cortex.—From "Lectures on Localization," by Dr. E. C. Seguin: New York *Medical Record*, p. 142, August 24, 1878.

of the opposite side of the body. The fibres expanding from the internal capsule, joined by those emanating from the ganglia at the base and the corpus callosum, form a fan-shaped expansion of white fibres called *the corona radiata.*

THE CEREBELLUM.

The white centre of the cerebellum, formed from the expansion of the peduncular tracts, incloses a collection of gray substance, the *corpus dentatum.* This body, visible in all sections, bears some resemblance to the olivary body in the medulla, on account of its irregular, dentated outline. Its greater consistence causes it to stand out in a section from the surrounding tissue. In intimate structure this body consists

of a collection of small fusiform and polyhedral cells with
minute processes, imbedded in a basis-substance much more
dense than the surrounding white matter. The body is made
to appear striated in a peripheral direction by bundles of
fibres and blood-vessels pursuing a parallel course.

The surface of the cerebellum, deeply gashed by sulci and
their subdivisions, presents, on section, its well-known compound, arborescent appearance. This arrangement of the gray
matter causes the greatest possible surface to come in contact with the blood-current furnished by the pia mater, and
hence secures the greatest nutrition of the elements of the
cortex. The gray matter of the cortex is easily divisible into
an external or granular layer, a middle or cellular layer, and
an internal or nuclear layer. The latter consists of a vast
number of small granular cells about the size of white blood-
corpuscles, which take staining fluids with great avidity. The
middle stratum is a clear space in which there is a single layer
of large corpuscles, called the *cells of Purkinje*, 10 to 40 μ. in
diameter. They
are scattered at
some distance
from each other,
and present pe-
culiarities pos-
sessed by no other
cells in the body.
The cells are of
large size, vary-
ing in form from
fusiform to flask-

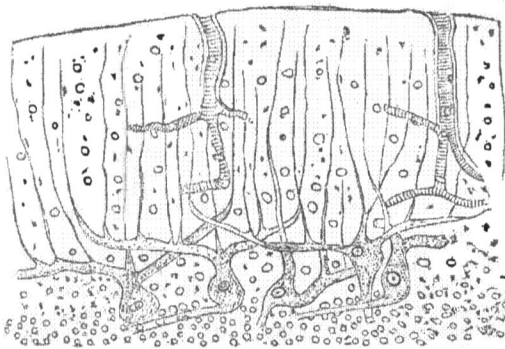

FIG. 146.—Diagram of the cerebellar cortex, showing the large cells of
Purkinje.

shaped, accord-
ing to the plane of
the section. Their central side is round, and in most cases has
no processes. Often the usual rounded contour of the cell-
body is broken by an angle, seemingly the remains of a broken
process. Here and there a large non-branching axis-cylinder
process is seen emerging from the base of a cell and pursuing
a course parallel to the cortex. That these basal processes
exist in all cases, and ultimately acquire a myelinic sheath,
there is no doubt. (See Fig. 146.)

From the peripheral side large arborescent processes spring, which pursue quite a direct course through the external or granular layer and disappear when near the periphery. The primary processes, one or two in number, have a tendency to spring from the cell-body at an obtuse angle, and give off at almost right angles to themselves the straight peripheral pro-cesses already mentioned. The nuclei of these cells are oval and coarsely granular; the nucleolus is round and small.

The cortex proper consists of a granular matrix vertically striated by the cell-processes and parallel blood-vessels. There is also a moderate sprinkling of small round cells and nuclei similar to those in the third layer. The cortex is very vascular.

THE CEREBRAL GANGLIA.

As examples of these structures the optic thalami and corpora striata may be taken. They are collections of gray matter through which part of the fibres, emanating from the crura to help form the corona radiata, pass.

In the *corpus striatum* these fibres pass through in bundles visible to the naked eye, which gives to this body its striated appearance. These bundles radiate toward the periphery of the body, thus leaving ever increasing spaces between them. These spaces at the base of the body, at the point of entrance of the bundles from the crura, are narrow, filled with nerve-fibres running in horizontal, vertical, and diagonal directions, seemingly commissural in nature, and multipolar cells few in number, large, and resembling somewhat cells of the anterior horns of the spinal cord, whose processes mingle with the fibres mentioned. Nearer the periphery of the organ, where the bundles of fibres are more widely separated, the intervening mass of fibres and cells abruptly changes to a finely granular gray matrix, holding in its substance numerous small blood-vessels and small nerve-cells, mostly round—some, however, triangular in shape, similar to those of the second layer of the cerebral cortex. They have large nuclei and many delicate processes.

The *optic thalami* consist of a mixture of gray matter and fibres, not, however, so regularly arranged as in the corpus striatum. The gray matter contains a few oval cells having many delicate processes.

The cerebral ventricles.—Continuous with the central canal

of the cord, and doubtless like it in function, the cerebral ventricles resemble it in their structure. They are lined throughout with a structure called the *ependyma*. This consists first
of a finely granular layer covering all the nervous matter
bounding the ventricles. Besides the minute granules, this
layer contains a few small nuclei here
and there, but no fibres. On its free
surface rests a single layer of cylindrical epithelium. The cells of this
layer have square free ends, while
they are anchored by one or more
delicate processes which emerge from
the attached end and pierce the subjacent granular-matrix. These epi-
thelia in the fresh state undoubtedly have cilia. This layer
of epithelium is apt to be arranged in folds, giving a section
of the ependyma a wavy appearance.

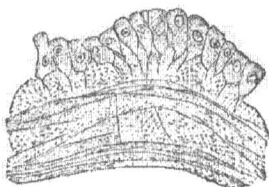

FIG. 147.—Diagram illustrating the
structure of the ependyma of the cerebral ventricles.

The *choroid plexus* of the lateral ventricles has for its basis
an artery which enters the descending horn of the lateral ventricle from the base of the brain. This artery gives off along
its course short arterial trunks which repeatedly subdivide, and
each ultimate arteriole terminates in a convoluted capillary
loop, resembling the Malpighian tuft of the kidney. Some
of the twigs seem to end in a cæ-
cal extremity; but it is doubtful
whether they do, the preparations
giving this appearance being probably artificial. The peculiarity of
the choroid plexus is that all the
vessels composing it, large and
small, are covered by a layer of
polyhedral epithelial cells, each
having one, sometimes two large
nuclei. This presents a beautiful
example of the so-called tesselated
epithelium, each cell being sepa-

FIG. 148.—Diagram showing structure
of the choroid plexus of the lateral ventricles.

rated from its neighbor by a transparent intercellular substance. This epithelial covering causes the tufts of the choroid
plexus to resemble, in a degree, the villi of the chorion. The
best plan in studying the choroid plexus is to use hæmatoxylon, or alcoholic specimens slightly teased.

The cerebral dura mater differs from the spinal in the fact that, its outer surface serving as periosteum, it lacks the layer of loose connective tissue present in the spinal dura mater. Its bulk consists of two layers of dense fibrous tissue running in opposite directions. The inner serous surface is coated with endothelium and lymphatics. The outer or periosteal surface is the most vascular. The cerebral differs from the spinal arachnoid only in being perhaps a little more closely attached to the pia mater. The pia mater of the brain is extremely vascular, and shows more beautifully than the spinal membrane the system of perivascular spaces.

The cerebral cortex.—The cerebral cortex is a thin sheet of gray matter spread on the outer surface of the hemispheres. The outer surface of the hemispheres is grooved by furrows (sulci) less deep in proportion to their size, and less regular than those of the cerebellum. The convolutions produced by these sulci, although seemingly very irregular, still have a certain symmetry in different brains by which they can be classified and named. A definite knowledge of these facts is necessary for an understanding of the current literature on the subject and of properly recording cases.

The fetal hemisphere at an early date is smooth. Furrows soon begin to appear, the first and most important of which is the *fissure of Sylvius*, extending upward and backward, from about the anterior third of the base of the brain, and the *fissure of Rolando*, running from near the posterior extremity of the fissure of Sylvius upward to the superior longitudinal fissure. One after another the other fissures appear, till in the adult brain they seem innumerable. Even here, however, there is a certain constant arrangement of fissures and convolutions on which a nomenclature may be based.

The original fissures of Sylvius and Rolando remain. From the anterior inferior part of the frontal lobe three furrows run obliquely upward and backward toward the two fissures just named, dividing the frontal region into the three frontal convolutions, while a convolution in front of the fissure of Rolando receives the name of the *ascending frontal* or *anterior central convolution*. A similar convolution behind the fissure is called the *ascending parietal or posterior central convolution*. The parietal region is irregularly divided from above downward, as is also the temporo-sphenoidal and occipital region. The base of the brain is also divided into a series of basal frontal, temporal and occipital convolutions. By far the most important region of the cortex, according to our present knowledge, is that along the fissures of Sylvius and Rolando, the so-called *motor tract of the hemispheres.* The exact physiological functions of the anterior frontal, the occipital, temporal, and basal

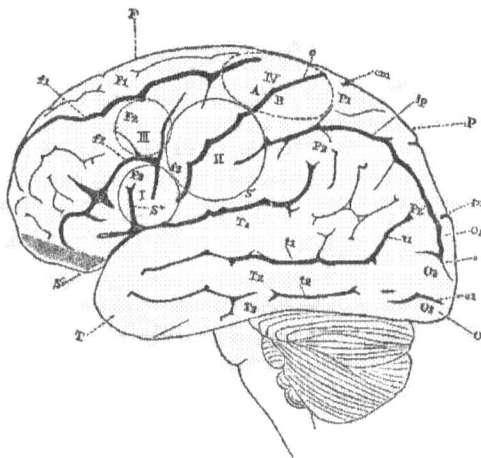

FIG. 149.—Modified from Ferrier; letters and figures the same: S, fissure of Sylvius; c, fissure of Ronaldo; po, parieto-occipital fissure; A, ascending frontal gyrus; B, ascending parietal gyrus; F₂, third frontal gyrus; P₂′, gyrus angularis; circle I., seat of lesions which (on the left) cause aphasia; circle II., seat of lesions which convulse or paralyze the upper extremity of the opposite side; dotted circle III., seat of lesions which probably convulse or paralyze the face on the opposite side; dotted oval IV., seat of lesions which probably convulse or paralyze the lower extremity of the opposite side. These districts receive their blood-supply chiefly from the middle cerebral artery.—From Lectures on Localization by Dr. E. C. Seguin: N. Y. *Medical Record,* October 19, 1878, p. 301.

regions of the hemispheres, is not known, inference, however, making them the seat of general and special sense, vaso-motor, psychic centres, etc., etc.

The middle or fronto-parietal region, however, is the proven seat of motor centres for the face, limbs, and body, and the faculty of articulate language. The centre for speech occupies the region at the base of the third frontal convolution and the *island of Reil* on the left side, a similar location on the right side being occupied by a centre for articulatory movements. A little higher on the ascending frontal and parietal convolutions is an area having control over the movements of the tongue and face. Still higher is found a larger space, the centre for the arm of the opposite side. A larger space at the junction of the fissure of Rolando and the superior longitudinal fissure, including a tract on the inner aspect of the hemisphere, called the *paracentral lobule*, is the centre for movements of both extremities, especially the lower. On account of the anatomical variability of the convolutions in different brains, these centres must be allowed some latitude, and should not be made so small and exactly located as they are by some authors. Their location has been pretty definitely determined, however, by experimentation on animals, and lesions in man, such as traumatisms, neoplasms, abscesses, hemorrhages, atrophy following amputations, retarded development, etc.

Possessing such important properties we should naturally expect the cerebral cortex to be a very complex structure, and so it is.

Minute structure of the cortex.— In order to get a satisfactory view of the elements of the cortex, great care has to be exercised in making sections. It is not enough to make a section exactly perpendicular to the cortex. The plane of the section must exactly coincide with the direction of the fibres of the corona radiata as they enter the convolution. This can be rather easily accomplished by paying close attention to the arrangement of the white

Fig. 150.—Diagram showing the elements and relation of parts in the cerebral cortex. (See text.)

and gray matter in the piece from which the sections are to be made. Cuts with any obliquity will give erroneous impressions as to the exact shape and structure, especially of the cellular elements of the cortex. The cortex cerebri is generally divided into five layers, but it is easily divisible into three only.

The *outer layer*, lying immediately under the pia mater, is more transparent than the rest, and is composed of a fine network of neuroglia containing many quite large openings, giving it a spongy appearance. It also contains a few large, round nuclei, and a small number of triangular nerve-cells.

The *second layer*, thicker than the first, consists of a gray basis-substance, dense and granular, holding an immense number of small, triangular and conical cells, their apex being di-

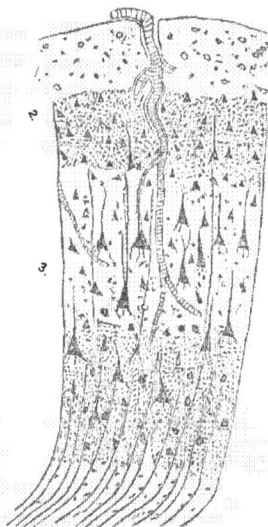

rected toward the periphery and often drawn out into a slender axis-cylinder process, while from their base several delicate processes are given off. These cells all have large nuclei and nucleoli. Here and there are seen larger conical cells, which will be described with the next layer. The characteristic feature of the second layer, however, is the presence of a great number of small, round cells and free nuclei similar to those in the third layer of the cerebellar cortex.

In the *third layer* the matrix is still more dense, and contains, besides a few small triangular cells, round cells, and free nuclei, a large number of large conical corpuscles, the so-called "giant cells" of the cortex, the distinguishing feature of this layer. When isolated from their surroundings these cells appear like cones which taper gradually from a broad base to a very slender apex, which, when it attains the size of an axis-cylinder, can be traced for a long distance without showing a division. This undoubtedly terminates in a myelinic nerve-fibre. The base of the cell is not square, but crenated and notched by the giving off of numerous delicate basal processes which are lost in the granular matrix.

The cells all have nuclei and nucleoli, most of which are round, but some of which seem also to have a triangular shape corresponding to the cell-body. The cells average 25 μ. in diameter. A great difference is made in the apparent shape of the cell by obliquity of the section. If the line of section is moderately oblique, it shortens the cells; if still more oblique, it makes them very short and blunt; while if the section is at right angles to their axis, all the cells appear round and of various sizes. In the deepest parts of this layer the giant-cells gradually disappear, and the gray matter of the cortex merges into the white matter. In the two inner layers of the cortex there are seen many fibres and bundles of fibres having a vertical direction, which, with the blood-vessels (the largest of which being perpendicular to the surface), give the cortex a somewhat striated appearance.

We see, then, that the only difference between the second and third layers of the cortex is the greater number of small cells in the second and the greater number of large cells in the third, while the division of the third layer into three, as is accepted by most authors, seems purely arbitrary, there being a gradual gradation into the white substance.

Some writers[1] lay much stress on the difference of structure of the cortex in different regions of the hemisphere. It is true that, in the non-excitable or sensory regions, the cortex is thinner and perhaps less highly organized; but here are met the same elements as form the cortex in the motor region (centre, for the arm, for instance). (See Fig. 150.) Even the giant-cells are found less numerously than in the motor regions. Another fact demands attention, that is, that the structure of the cortex is the same at the bottom of a fissure as on the surface of a convolution, and for this reason lesions of the sides and bottom of fissures should receive as much attention as those of the surface of the convolutions, implicating, as they do, equally important structures.

BIBLIOGRAPHY.

SPINAL CORD.

CLARKE, J. L. Researches into the Structure of the Spinal Cord. Philosoph. Transactions. 1850.

DONDERS, F. C. Dissertatio anatomica inauguralis de cerebri et medullæ spinalis systemata vasorum capillari in statu sano et morboso. 1853.

JACUBOWITSCH, N. Mittheilungen über die feinere Structur des Gehirns und Rücken-marks. Breslau, 1857.

JACUBOWITSCH, N. Further Researches Into, etc. Breslau, 1858.

BIDDER, F., und KUPFFER, C. Untersuchungen über die Textur des Rückenmarks, etc. Leipzig, 1859.

VAN DER KOLK, SCHROEDER. Minute Structure and Functions of the Spinal Cord and Medulla Oblongata, and on the Proximate Cause and Rational Treatment of Epilepsy. New Sydenham Society. London, 1859.

STILLING, B. Neue Untersuchungen üeber den Bau des Rückenmarks. Cassel, 1859.

LUYS, J. Recherches sur le système nerveux cérébro-spinal; sa structure, ses fonctions et ses maladies. Paris, 1865.

HIS, W. Zum Lymphsystem. Leipzig, 1865.

HIRSCHFELD, LUDOVIC. Traité et iconographie du système nerveux et des organes des sens de l'homme. Paris, 1866.

JOLLY, F. Ueber die Ganglienzellen des Rückenmarks. München, 1866

KÖLLIKER, A. Éléments d'histologie humaine. Traduit par Marc Sée. Paris, 1868.

---

[1] See Betz: Anatomischer Nachweis zweier Gehirncentra. Centralblatt für die Medicinischen Wissenschaften, August 1 and 8, 1874, pp. 578 and 595. He finds " nests " of enormous cells in the motor area, especially of the paracentral lobule.

HENLE, J. Handbuch der Nervenlehre des menschen. Braunschweig, 1871.

GERLACH, J. The Spinal Cord. Translated by Dr. E. C. Seguin, in Stricker's Histology. 1872.

SCHULTZE, MAX. The General Character of the Structures Composing the Nervous Substance. Translated by Henry Power. Stricker's Histology. 1872.

RETZIUS, GUST. och KEY, AXEL. Studier i nervsystemets anatomi. Stockholm, 1872.

ERB, W. H. Diseases of the Spinal Cord and Medulla Oblongata (Anatomical Introduction). Ziemssen's Cyclopædia of Medicine. Vol. XIII. American Edition. 1878.

SEGUIN, E. C. Lectures on the Localization of Spinal and Cerebral Diseases. N. Y. Medical Record. 1878.

FORT, J. A. Leçons sur les centres nerveux. Paris, 1878.

HUGUENIN, G. Anatomie des centres nerveux. Traduit par Dr. Th. Keller. Paris, 1879.

BRAIN.

BERLIN, RUDOLF. Beitrag zur Structurlehre des Grosshirnwindungen. Erlangen, 1858.

KUPFFER, GUST. De cornus ammonis textura. Dorpat, 1859.

CLARKE, J. L. Researches on the Intimate Structure of the Brain, Human and Comparative. 1857 and 1867.

ARNDT, RUDOLF. Studien über die Architektonik der Grosshirnrinde des Menschen. Bonn, 1867-68.

JENSEN, JULIUS. Die Furchen und Windungen der menschlichen Grosshirn Hemisphären. Berlin, 1870.

MEYNERT, T. The Brain of Mammals. Stricker's Histology. Am. edition. New York, 1872.

HITZIG, EDWARD. Untersuchungen über das Gehirn. Berlin, 1874.

CHARCOT, J. M. Leçons sur les localisations dans les maladies du cerveau. Paris, 1876.

BENEDIKT, MORIZ. Anatomische Studien an Verbrecher-Gehirnen. Wien, 1879.

BOYER, H. DE. Etudes topographiques sur les lésions corticales des hémisphères cérébraux. Paris, 1879.

FERRIER, DAVID. The Localization of Cerebral Disease. New York, 1879.

STRICKER und UNGER. Untersuchungen über den Bau der Grosshirnrinde. Wiener Anzeiger, 1879.

BEVAN LEWIS and CLARKE, H. The Cortical Lamination of the Motor Area of the Brain. Proceedings of the Royal Society, Vol. XXVII. 1879.

CEREBELLUM.

HESS, N. De cerebelli glorum textura. Dorpat, 1858.

SCHULTZE, F. E. Ueber den feineren Bau der Rinde des kleinen Gehirnes. Rostock, 1863.

CENTRAL NERVOUS SYSTEM.

DEITERS, OTTO. Untersuchungen über Gehirn und Rückenmark des Menschen und der Säugethiere. Braunschweig, 1865.

DEECKE, THEODORE.   Perivascular Spaces in the Nervous System.   American Journal of Insanity.   January, 1874.

WALDEYER.   Beiträge zur Kenntniss der Lymphbahnen des Centralnervensyst. Arch. f. mikr. Anat.   1879.

KESTEVEN, W. H.   The Structure and Functions of the Olivary Bodies.   St. Bartholomew's Hospital Reports.   1879.

SÉE, MARC.   Sur la communication des cavités ventriculaires de l'encéphale avec les espaces sous-arachnoïdiens.   Revue mensuelle.   1879.

BROCA, P.   Localisations cérébrales.   Revue d'anthropol.   1879.

BETZ.   Structure de l'écorce cérébrale.   Rev d'anthrop.   2. S.   IV. 426–438.   Paris, 1881.

LAEHR.   Pacchionischen Granulationen.   Allg. Ztg. f. Psychiat.   XXXVIII. 101–105.   1881.

SPITZKA, E. C.   Notes on the Architecture of the Oblongata.   New York Med. Journ.   XXXIV. 233–240.   1881.

CHAPTER XX.

THE EYE.

By C. H. WILLIAMS, M.D., Boston, Mass.

THE *eyelids* are very complicated structures. Their external coating is formed of skin, which is modified for the special
purpose it has to serve in this situation. Beneath the skin is a
loose sheet of connective tissue ; still more internally is the little *orbicularis palpebrarum* muscle ; behind this again is loose
connective tissue, which shades off gradually into the *tarsus*.
This latter is not formed of cartilage, as was formerly supposed, but of dense fibrous tissue. The *conjunctiva tarsi*
lines the inner surface of the tarsus. The skin of the lids
exhibits the usual layers of horny, serrated, and cylindrical
epithelium. At the upper portions the papillæ are sparsely
developed and short, but they gradually increase in size and
number as they approach the free edges. A peculiarity of this
skin are the pigment-cells, which are scattered throughout the
cutis. They are more abundant in brunettes than in blondes.

At the confronting margins of the lids are found the *cilia*
or *eyelashes*, which resemble the ordinary larger hairs in their
formation and mode of growth ; they are placed in two or
three rows, are well supplied with pigment, and have a definite
direction given to them by the deep follicles from which they
grow.

Ordinary sweat-glands are quite numerous, especially in the
upper portions of the lid ; at the lower border we occasionally
find them in a modified form, opening into sebaceous follicles
near or just behind the cilia ; they have a long and wide orifice, and the tubules are filled with fine granular matter, containing occasional roundish masses resembling particles of
albumen.

Beneath the cutis is a loose connective-tissue layer through which numerous blood-vessels and nerves pass; behind this, and covering the whole extent of the lid, are bundles of the orbicularis palpebrarum; some small fasciculi of this muscle are also found at the lower and inner angle of the lid, enclosing the openings of the Meibomian glands. These bundles, known as the *musculus ciliaris Riolani*, have fibres which are among the smallest of the striped variety of muscular tissue.

Behind this layer is a thin sheet of loose connective tissue, which merges without any sharp boundary line into the *tarsus;* this latter body forms a leaf-shaped plate about twenty millimetres in length by one millimetre in thickness, and is composed of very dense connective-tissue fibres separated only by minute lymph-spaces; it has few blood-vessels or nerves, and serves to give the requisite stiffness to the looser tissues of the lid.

The *Meibomian glands* are imbedded in the tarsus. Their excretory ducts, which are directed at right angles to the palpebral margin, have their openings on the surface of the lid near its posterior angle. They are lined with epithelium, which at the external orifice is similar to that in the superficial parts of the skin; more internally it is serrated, while in the acini of the gland it has a cuboidal shape. These glands have a straight central tube, around which the acini are clustered, and into which they discharge the sebum, a material composed of epithelial cells that have undergone fatty degeneration. This oleaginous substance serves to moisten the edges of the lid and to prevent the overflow of tears.

Above the Meibomian glands, and in part imbedded in the tarsus, are the acinous glands, which have their openings on the surface of the *conjunctiva fornicis*. Above these glands the smooth muscular fibres of the little *palpebralis muscle of Müller* are inserted, through a tendon, into the upper part of the tarsus; the fibres of this muscle are quite large and have peculiar irregular cells with pigmented nuclei scattered throughout them.

To prepare sections from the lids they should be pinned flat on a piece of cork and then immersed in Müller's fluid [1] for eight days. After being washed in water they are placed in absolute alcohol until sufficiently hard; or they may be hard-

---

[1] See chapter on General Methods.

ened by placing in the ordinary ½ per cent. solution of chloride
of gold. This last method shows very clearly the nerves of
the lid and conjunctiva, which take a deep violet or mauve
color. For rapid work the lids may be hardened in a saturated
solution of picric acid. They may then be stained with picro-
carmine or hæmatoxylon, and mounted in glycerine or balsam.
(See chapter on General Methods.)

The *caruncula lachrymalis* is a small, rounded mass of
skin; it is placed between the lids at their inner angle, and
contains hairs, vessels, and glands, such as are found elsewhere in the cutis. Its office is to prevent the overflow of tears.

The conjunctiva.—Just behind the tarsus, and separated
from it by a thin layer of fibrillated connective tissue, is the
conjunctiva, which, after lining the inner surface of the lid,
passes backward as a loose connecting fold (*fornix*) to the
sclera, over which it is reflected forward as far as the margin
of the cornea. The conjunctiva consists of an external or
epithelial layer and a tunica propria or proper investing membrane. There is also a subconjunctival layer.

The lower portion of the conjunctiva, where it takes its
origin from the margin of the lid, is quite smooth; but near
the upper edge of the tarsus it becomes more or less infiltrated
with lymph-cells, and is thrown into numerous folds, which
have sometimes been mistaken for glands. The epithelial elements of this part vary much in shape; in general there are
two layers: a superficial one, composed of cylindrical bodies
which are a continuation of the superficial strata of the skin,
and a deeper one of small, round cells, representing the changed
cylindrical elements of the Malpighian layer or rete mucosum.

The tunica propria consists of fine connective-tissue fibres,
in which a few elastic fibrillæ are interspersed. The subconjunctival layer resting immediately upon the tarsus is very
thin. That part of the conjunctiva forming the fornix has an
abundant subconjunctival tissue, which is composed of loose
elastic fibres and vessels; the epithelial layers are also thicker
here, and small racemose glands, supposed to secrete mucus,
are also found there.

On the conjunctiva covering the bulb the epithelium contains here and there the large mucus-cells corresponding to
the goblet-cells of the intestines. It gradually begins to change
its character and passes over into the variety which is seen in

the cornea, and, in fact, is continuous with it. The tunica propria has an abundant supply of blood-vessels, and is loosely connected with the sclera by fibres, which become more numerous and firm in the vicinity of the corneal margin.

The nerves of the conjunctiva may be seen by cutting small pieces of fresh conjunctiva from a pig or calf and examining them in aqueous humor, or in a 1 per cent. aqueous solution of common salt—care being taken to support the cover-glass at the sides, in order to avoid pressure. The nerve-fibres can then be seen passing under the epithelium ; they can be distinguished with certainty by their annular constrictions (*anneaux constricteurs*) ; after penetrating a short distance, however, they lose their medullary sheath and form open networks under the epithelium ; a few fibres find their way toward the surface between the epithelial cells.

The gold method is of special use in exposing the finer nerve-branches. The question of the manner in which the nerves ultimately end is still a point in dispute.

The *lymph-spaces of the conjunctiva* are quite numerous, especially near the corneal border ; here they are narrow, and finally pass forward to unite with the lymph-spaces of the cornea, from which they can be injected by means of a solution of alkanet-root in turpentine.[1]

The normal conjunctiva does not have any true papillæ, but on the tarsal portion the surface often has small papilliform projections covered with epithelium.

The cornea.—This tunic is covered with stratified epithelium (*a*), comprising layers of flat, serrated, and cylindrical cells. Directly beneath these is the anterior limiting or *Bowman's membrane* (*b*) ; this is a clear, homogeneous stratum, which differs from the substantia propria of the cornea only in containing no lymph-spaces or cells. It can be divided up into the same fine fibres as the cornea itself, and its inner border has no distinct limit, the fibres passing directly into the corneal tissue ; when this layer has been destroyed, as by a perforating ulcer or wound, it is not regenerated.

The substantia propria of the cornea (*b*, *c*) is made up of lamellæ, like the leaves of a book ; these lamellæ, which at first appear homogeneous, can be separated into fine fibres, just

---

[1] See chapter on General Methods.

like other connective-tissue membranes, by dissolving out the cementing substance in a 10 per cent. solution of common salt.

With the exception of the *fibræ arcuatæ*, which curve forward through several strata in the anterior portions of the cornea, the fibres pursue the same direction as the layers ; but, although most of the fibres run parallel to the surface of the cornea, yet they may have a different direction in each layer,

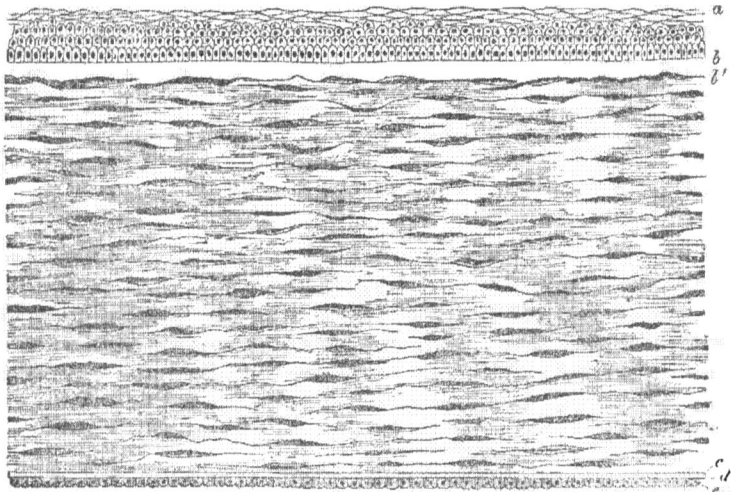

FIG. 151.—Meridional section through the cornea of the human adult, from an eye hardened in Müller's fluid. The section was colored with carmine, and made transparent by the oil of cloves. Rollett.

so that when viewed from above the fibres will appear to cross one another. This explains the formation of the stellate figures which are sometimes observed after the injection of fatty substances into the cornea, or by the infiltration of bacteria between the fibrils.

In the interfibrillar material are found the lymph-canals and spaces, which contain the *fixed corneal corpuscles* (Fig. 152). These spaces are stellate and broad when seen from above, but thin and spindle-shaped on side view ; they have numerous branches and branchlets given off from them at right angles (lymphatic channels) (Fig. 152, A). The spaces and branches usually lie in the plane of the lamellæ, anastomose freely with one another, and are filled with the corneal corpuscles and lymph (Fig. 152, B).

In life these fixed bodies nearly fill the lymph-spaces and conform to their size and shape ; they are flat corpuscles, usually nucleated, and have short, sharp-pointed processes, which pass out into the minute lymph-canals. In the lymph-spaces of the cornea are also found, even in normal conditions, a few migratory cells, resembling white blood-corpuscles ; they are very numerous when the cornea has been irritated, and can be seen in a frog's cornea, which has been kept five to fifteen minutes in serum or aqueous humor in a moist chamber, and examined without pressure on a warm slide.

Beneath the substantia propria of the cornea we find the *posterior limiting layer*, or *Descemet's membrane* (*d*) (Fig. 151). This is transparent, apparently homogeneous, rolls up when cut, is intimately connected with the posterior fibres of the cornea proper, and is lined on its inner surface with endothelium (*e*). It contains no cellular bodies, but, like the anterior limiting layer, can be separated into fibrillæ, and appears to represent a concentration of the corneal fibres rather than a separate structure.

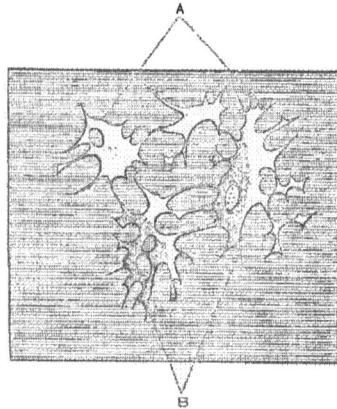

Fig. 152.—Lymph spaces and canals, A ; fixed corneal cell, partly filling these spaces, B. After Waldeyer.

The endothelium is a single layer of flat cells lining the anterior chamber. Blood-vessels are found only in the normal cornea at the periphery, where they form a fine network connecting with the conjunctival and scleral vessels.

The nerves enter the cornea at the posterior part of the periphery ; they soon lose their neurilemma and medullary sheath, and pass forward obliquely, as small axis-cylinders, toward the epithelial layer ; here they divide up into branchlets, often having a ganglionic enlargement at the point of division. Under the epithelium these delicate fibres form a network which sends some very minute filaments upward between the epithelial cells. Their further course is unknown.

To separate the cornea into its constituent fibres, small pieces should be soaked for twenty-four hours in a concentrated pi-

eric acid solution; they can then be washed in water and easily
picked to pieces. In order to see the arrangement of the fibrillæ
in the different layers, the cornea of a rabbit should be pricked
with a needle in several places; then some highly infectious
fluid, as the exudation in puerperal peritonitis, is to be brushed
over the surface, and in a few days an infiltration will have
taken place throughout the interfibrillar substance. We shall
then see the lines of pus-cells crossing one another in different
directions, and sometimes collections of micrococci forming
stellate figures.

A very delicate preparation of the fixed corneal cells may
be made by removing a fresh cornea, and then immersing it
from three to six hours in aqueous humor, in a moist chamber.
In examining it take care, as before mentioned, to avoid any
pressure upon the cover-glass.

It is easier, however, to demonstrate the cells and lymph-
spaces by staining with silver or gold. To do this the nictitating membrane of a live frog should be cut off or held to one
side by an elevator; the exposed cornea is then placed near the
mouth of a test-tube, in which some water has been raised
to the boiling point; when the epithelium begins to appear
opaque it should be carefully wiped off with a fine cloth; a
⅓ per cent. aqueous solution of nitrate of silver is then applied;
when the cornea has become thoroughly white by this method,
it is to be removed, washed in a weak solution of common salt,
placed in distilled water, and exposed to the light until it becomes brown. It should then be cut at the edges and mounted
in glycerine. In ten or fifteen minutes it will be transparent
and ready for examination. Instead of removing the epithelium by steam, a solution of silver nitrate (⅓ per cent.) may be
used, the lids being held out of the way until the epithelium
appears whitish; this outer layer is then removed, and the
same process repeated as before. The substantia propria assumes a brown color, and the corpuscles appear as lighter spaces
in it. The nuclei may be exposed by hæmatoxylon.

The best preparations, both for the lymph-spaces and the
nerves, are made with chloride of gold. A fresh cornea, preferably one from a live pigeon, is removed immediately after
decapitation and immersed for five minutes in lemon-juice,
then washed in distilled water, placed for fifteen minutes in a
1 per cent. solution of chloride of gold, again washed, and this

time soaked for twenty-four hours (well protected from the light) in a 2 per cent. solution of formic acid. After another washing in distilled water the cornea should be cut in two and placed in glycerine; one portion can then be separated into thin layers, by tearing with fine forceps or needles.

Examine in glycerine for the corneal corpuscles, nerves, and lymph-spaces, which latter appear dark on a light blue or red background; or the piece may be imbedded in wax or some such material, and sections made parallel to the surface of the cornea. The remaining half of the specimen is to be imbedded or held in liver or pith. Transverse sections may then be made. These will exhibit on lucky sections the fine plexuses of nerve-filaments under the epithelium, with occasional fibres passing up between the individual corpuscles. The different layers of the cornea will be well shown, also the narrow corneal cells (as seen on side view), together with the remains of the endothelial layer on the inner surface.

The peripheral portions of the cornea are particularly interesting. We have here the transitions from cornea to conjunctiva and sclera, the origin of the ciliary muscle, the ligament of the iris, and the numerous vessels of the part.

The epithelium of the cornea (a) forms a gradual transition into the epithelium of the conjunctiva, but the anterior limiting membrane (Bowman's) becomes thinner as it approaches the edge of the cornea, until finally it merges with the fibres of the anterior corneal layers into the tunica propria of the conjunctiva.

No sharp boundary line has been demonstrated between the cornea and the sclera. Under the microscope the fibres appear to have no distinct limit; the lymph-spaces also of the cornea are continued directly into the sclera, and the scleral and corneal fixed corpuscles are much the same.

The *posterior limiting membrane* (*Descemet's*) (c), like the anterior, becomes gradually thinner and loses itself in a small bundle of scleral fibres which surround the edge of the membrane and form the anterior support to the *ligamentum pectinatum iridis*.

The endothelium (Fig. 153 e,) passes uninterruptedly over this ligament (e') and is reflected forward over the anterior surface of the iris (e'') to the edge of the pupil.

In the angle between the iris and cornea, forming buttresses, as it were, to hold the iris in position, is the *ligament of the iris* (*d*), composed of loose connective tissue with an abundant open meshwork, enclosing spaces (*Fontana's spaces*), (*f*), which, on the one hand, connect with the anterior chamber by small openings lined with endothelium, and on the other with the lymph-spaces of the cornea and sclera, as may be shown by injecting a solution of aniline blue into the anterior chamber.

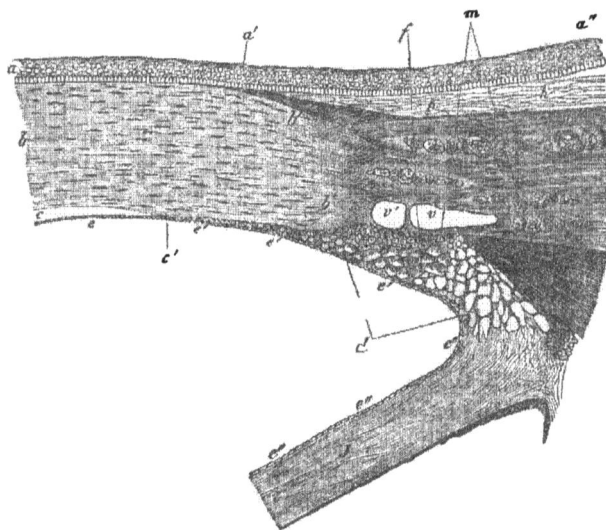

FIG. 153.—Corneal margin from a meridional section of the human eye: *a, a'*, external epithelium of the cornea ; *a', a''*, epithelium of the conjunctiva bulbi ; *b, b', b'*, corneal tissue ; *b', b', b'', b''*, sclerotica ; *k, k*,conjunctiva ; *v, v'*, canal of Schlemm ; *c, c'*, membrane of Descemet ; *d*, process of the iris ; *J*, iris ; *e*, endothelium of the membrane of Descemet ; *e'. e', e'*, of the ligamentum pectinatum iridis ; *e'', e'', e''*, of the iris ; *f*, meshwork of the space of Fontana ; *m*, musculus ciliaris. Rollett.

At the inner part of the sclera, close to its junction with the cornea and the ligament, is the *canal of Schlemm* (*v, v'*), a ring-shaped passage, oval on section. It is lined with a single layer of endothelium, varies in size in different specimens, often appearing as if divided into two parts, and, according to Waldeyer, probably connects with the anterior chamber and also with the scleral veins.

Through this passage and *Fontana's spaces* the fluid of the anterior chamber is supposed to escape from the globe, and it is worthy of note that in glaucoma, with increased intra-ocular tension, we find the iris attached to the periphery of the cornea over a circular space which would entirely cover these probable channels of exit.

Preparations of these parts can be made from eyes which have been placed in Müller's fluid while quite fresh and allowed to remain in it three to four weeks, the fluid being renewed from time to time. Hæmatoxylon is well adapted for coloring them, and they may be preserved in glycerine.

The sclera.—In the sclera we find the same minute structures as in the cornea, *i.e.*, bundles of fibres, cementing substance, lymph-spaces, and fixed corpuscles. The fibres, however, are not laminated, as in the cornea, but run in various directions, weaving a very dense tissue, so that the lymph-canals have a correspondingly tortuous course.

Chemically there is a difference between the two, as the sclera is found to yield on boiling a true connective-tissue gelatine; the cornea, on the other hand, a substance resembling chondrine. We find also in the sclera, near the foramen for the optic nerve, a few pigment-cells.

The sclera is covered by the conjunctiva from the corneal border to the insertion of the recti muscles, and the fibres of the subconjunctival tissue pass directly into it. From the entrance of the optic nerve to these muscular insertions, and even passing up between them, the scleral portions of *Tenon's capsule* form the covering, which consists of delicate filaments of connective tissue passing directly into the sclera itself. On the inner surface the sclera is covered with a large-celled endothelium lining the *perichoroidal space*. At the round opening for the entrance of the optic nerve, the outer fibres of the optic nerve sheath pass directly into the outer scleral layers; the inner portions of the sheath partly mingle with the inner layers of the sclera, and partly, after the addition of some true scleral fibres, form the *lamina cribrosa*, a fine, sieve-like network of fibrous tissue, which stretches across the opening in the sclera on a level with its inner surface. This lamina can be easily shown in specimens where the delicate nerve-fibres which pass through its openings have been macerated out.

The sclera is perforated in the equatorial region by the trunks of the *venæ vorticosæ;* they are accompanied by the lymph-vessels which form the connection between the perichoroidal and Tenon's lymph-spaces. The direction of the canal through which they pass is so oblique that it is supposed to be

22

easily contracted in diameter by any increase in intra-ocular pressure.

The arteries of the sclera, with their thick adventitial coats, the peculiar sheaths of the veins and capillaries, as also the nerves, are best studied in hematoxylon preparations. A solution of silver nitrate (a quarter to one per cent.) will expose the endothelial cells, while sections of the tissue may be made from specimens preserved in alcohol or Müller's fluid.

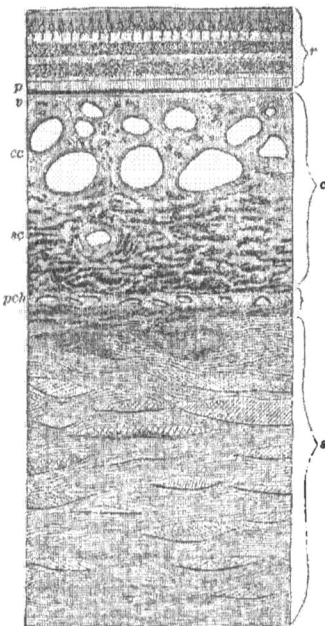

The *tunica vasculosa*, consisting of the choroid, ciliary body, and iris, forms one continuous membrane through which the principal blood-supply of the eye is carried.

The choroid.—This tunic lines the sclera from the entrance of the optic nerve to the junction of sclera and cornea, and is united to it at those points ; over the remaining portion there is a loose connection formed by scattered fibres and the numerous vessels and nerves which pass through the sclera to the choroid. The meshes of the open network between the layers of the choroid and the sclera form lymph-sacs — the perichoroidal spaces—which connect with the sac enclosed in Tenon's capsule, and this in turn unites with the supra-vaginal space surrounding the sheath of the optic nerve. The choroid consists of several layers, with limits not distinctly marked.

FIG. 154.— Sclera, *s*; choroid, *ch*; retina, *r*; perichoroidal space, *pch*; lamina suprachoroidea, *sc*; lamina chorio-capillaris, *cc*; lamina vitrea, *v*; layer of pigment-cells between choroid and retina, *p*. After Merkel.

The *lamina suprachoroidea* (Fig. 154, *sc*) lies next the sclera, and consists of fine elastic and connective-tissue fibres, holding in their meshes pigmented and transparent cells: the first are stellate, often with projecting arms by which several are joined together ; the latter resemble lymph-corpuscles.

The layer of large vessels is traversed by branching arteries and veins ; between them are numerous pigmented corpuscles, while the whole is held together by the firm connective-tissue network which extends throughout the entire choroid.

The *lamina chorio-capillaris* (*cc*) consists of a network of fine vessels.interspersed with pigment, and extends over the whole inner portion of the choroid.

The *vitreous* layer (*v*) is very closely connected with the lamina chorio-capillaris; though it appears homogeneous, fibres may be detected in it after long maceration in a ten per cent. solution of common salt. Where this layer covers the ciliary processes the surface is no longer smooth, but has fine, elevated ridges upon it; here the membrane also is thicker, and is more easily affected by reagents.

The dense lamina of hexagonal pigment-cells between the choroid and retina has sometimes been classed with the former, although it belongs more properly to the retina.

The *long* and *short posterior*, and the *anterior ciliary arteries*, furnish the numerous blood-vessels which constitute the great mass of the choroid.

The short posterior ciliary arteries, four to six in number, give off some twenty branches which penetrate the sclera, pursuing a straight course near where the optic nerve enters; then, continuing their course in a tortuous manner, they divide into fine networks which supply the greater part of the lamina chorio-capillaris. About the entrance of the optic nerve they also form a network of fine vessels, and even send occasional branches to anastomose with vessels from the sheath and centre of the optic nerve.

The two *long ciliary arteries* penetrate the sclera in a very oblique course, a little anteriorly to those last mentioned, and in the horizontal meridian; they pass forward in the outer lamina of the choroid without branching until they reach the ciliary muscle; here they divide, and penetrating the muscle, form near the periphery of the iris a circle (*circulus arteriosus iridis major*) by uniting with the artery of the opposite side.

The *anterior ciliary arteries*, eight to ten in number, arising from muscular branches of the ophthalmic artery, penetrate the sclera near the insertion of the recti tendons; they also unite with the circle just described, which forms the principal ' distributing point for the vessels of the iris and ciliary body. From this circle also are sent back a few small branches to unite with the choroidal capillaries, and there is formed the sole connection between the short posterior or choroidal arteries proper and those which supply the circulus arteriosus. A small amount of the blood which returns from the capillaries of the choroid, ciliary body and iris finds its exit from the eyeball through the veins accompanying the anterior and posterior ciliary arteries, but by far the larger part is collected by the large veins in the outer layers of the choroid (venæ vorticosæ), converging so as to form four or six great trunks, which perforate the sclera obliquely in the equatorial region, and empty into the ophthalmic vein.

The long and short ciliary nerves supply the tunica vasculosa with fibres from the third and fifth pair and the sympathetic. The long nerves, two or three in number, are branches of the nasal division of the ophthalmic nerve ; the short, ten to fifteen in number, arise from the ciliary ganglion. These nerves penetrate the sclera near the optic nerve, and then, passing forward on the outer portion of the choroid, form, in the ciliary muscle, a fine plexus with ganglionic corpuscles at the nodal points of the meshes ; from this plexus fibres are distributed to the cornea and iris.

At the junction of the anterior and middle thirds of the eyeball the choroid undergoes a change, the membrane becomes thinner, the capillaries turn back toward the veins, only a few vessels continuing forward in a straight course.

In this region the retina also undergoes a change and loses all its nervous elements, the connective tissue supporting fibres alone being continued forward under the name of the *pars ciliaris retinæ*. The very narrow zone between the points where these changes occur and the irregular line formed by the beginning of the ciliary processes is called the *orbiculus ciliaris*, and the line of origin of these processes the *ora serrata*.

The ciliary body.—Crossing the orbiculus, the choroid is seen raised in radial folds, some seventy in number, which increase in size until they reach the thickness of a millimetre. This increase is caused by the development of smooth muscular fibres in addition to the usual constituents of the choroid.

These fibres arise just behind the canal of Schlemm, from the sclera and cornea ; passing backward, they together form a ring, which on section appears as a right-angled triangle, with the base turned toward the anterior chamber, and the hypothenuse toward the vitreous (Fig. 155).

This triangle consists largely of the fibres of the ciliary muscle, which are divided into meridional fibres, or those which occupy the side next the sclera, and radial fibres, which pass

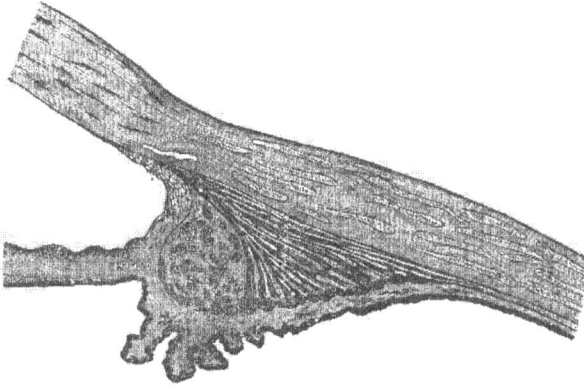

Fig. 155.—Section through the ciliary region of a hypermetropic eye.   Ivanof.

from the point of origin to the hypothenuse ; the circular fibres of Müller's muscle lie next to the base of the triangle, and are concentrically arranged.

In highly myopic eyes the meridional and radial fibres

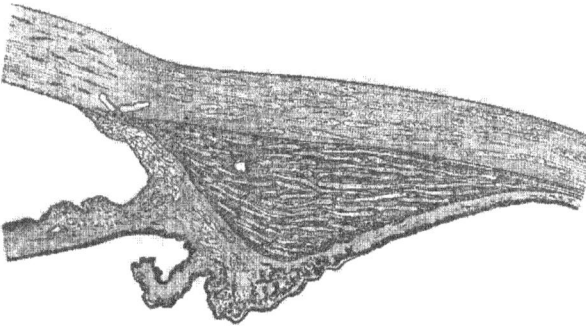

Fig. 156.—Section through the ciliary region of a myopic eye.   Ivanof.

are strongly developed (Fig. 156), while the circular fibres are scarcely seen, and the angle of the ciliary body at the point of origin is changed from a right to an acute angle.

In very hypermetropic eyes, on the contrary, the circular fibres are abundantly developed (Fig. 155), the meridional fibres are shorter, while the angle at the point of origin of the muscle becomes somewhat obtuse, so that by these changes one can determine, even in a microscopic section, what considerable refractive error the eyes have had.

The meridional fibres are either prolonged some distance into the stroma of the choroid and end in a delicate fringe, or they terminate at the anterior and outer layers of this membrane in stellate knots with fine anastomosing branches.

The radial fibres form a looser network than the last, but also have the same terminal interlacement of their fibres ; the circular fibres form fewer anastomoses, and only those bundles which lie next to the radial fibres are extensively connected with them.

The nerves of the ciliary body are derived from the plexus formed in its stroma by the ciliary nerves ; the vessels are largely supplied from the circulus iridis major, lying in the anterior part of the body.

The *iris* arises from the anterior side of the ciliary body, and from the connective tissue surrounding the fibres of the ciliary muscle ; it is also attached to the cornea and sclera by the ligamentum pectinatum. (See Fig. 153).

It consists of a loose connective-tissue stroma, which supports a rich vascular network, a complete muscular structure. and the nerves. It is covered anteriorly by a continuation of the endothelium of the cornea, and posteriorly by a thick layer of pigment-cells continuous with those which line the ciliary body. The vessels arise from the circulus, have adventitial coats which are thick in proportion to their calibre, and pass radially to the margin of the pupil, where they form a network of fine capillaries, the *circulus arteriosus iridis minor*, ending finally in veins which return in the same general direction as the arteries, but lie beneath them, emptying finally into the venæ vorticosæ.

Near the margin of the pupil, and forming a ring about it 1 mm. in breadth by $\frac{1}{16}$ mm. in thickness, is the *sphincter muscle of the iris*. It is composed of unstriped muscular tissue, and is situated in the posterior portion of the iris.

The *dilator muscle*, at its inner border, is in close connection with the sphincter, and its fibres run radially to the periphery of the iris, where they are woven into a thick anastomosing circle.

The nerves of the iris are derived from the ciliary plexus; at the periphery they divide and scatter in various directions: the pale fibres to the posterior layers, forming a fine network about the dilator muscle; the fibres with a medullary sheath to the anterior portion; another set supplies the sphincter muscle—these being, in the order of description, the branches possibly of the sympathetic, sensory, and of the third pair.

The posterior surface of the iris, which, near the pupil, rests upon the anterior capsule of the lens, is covered with a thick layer of densely pigmented cells, the *uvea*, which can rarely be so separated as to determine their shape, and which appear to have no distinct limiting membrane behind them.

This layer extends from the pupil, where it meets the endothelium of the anterior surface, back to the pigment of the ciliary body, with which it is continuous and from which it can be distinguished by having no connective tissue covering it. The pigmented cells, which are more or less thickly scattered through the stroma of the iris, determine the color of the anterior surface.

Transverse sections through the sclera and choroid are best made from eyes hardened in Müller's fluid. An eye which has been injected with colored gelatine, introduced through the aorta after that vessel has been tied beyond the carotids, will show the fine meshes of the chorio-capillaris, when the pigment-layer covering the choroid has been brushed away under glycerine. Such injections are best made on albinotic rabbits.

Good sections of the ciliary body can be made from eyes hardened in alcohol or Müller's fluid, and the blood-vessels can be easily seen in injected specimens. The muscular tissue of this body and the iris may be examined in specimens treated with a 30 to 40 per cent. solution of potash. Carmine may then be used to color. The vessels of the iris are best seen in the eyes of a young albino rabbit, injected with colored glycerine or Berlin blue.

The *retina* lines the whole inner surface of the choroid as far as the ora serrata; it is composed of nervous elements, connective tissue, and blood-vessels.

The following division into well-marked layers from within outward has been generally adopted. (See Fig. 157).

a, membrana limitans interna.
b, optic nerve fibre-layer.
c, ganglion-cell layer.
d, inner granular layer.
e, inner nuclear layer.
f, outer granular layer.
g, outer nuclear layer.
h, membrana limitans externa.
i, layer of rods and cones.
Pigment layer.

The fibres of the optic nerve generally lose their medullary sheath at the lamina cribrosa, and proceed thence as naked axis-cylinders through the opening in the choroid to the level of the retina, where they spread over its entire inner surface to form the nerve-fibre layer, which is thick in the vicinity of the nerve, but gradually decreases as it approaches the ora serrata, where it ends.

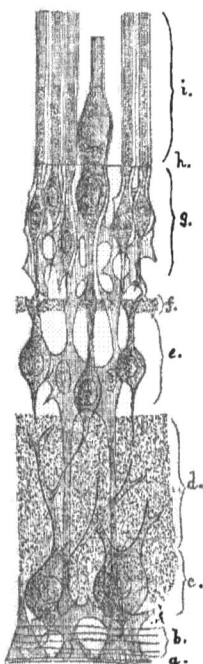

At the *macula lutea* the fibres do not form a distinct layer, but, curving toward this spot from above and below, are lost in the layer of ganglion-cells, either entering them or passing on to the inner granular layer.

The *ganglion-cell layer* consists of large branching cells in most places but one row deep, though near the macula there may be two or more layers. They are very transparent, have no visible cell-wall, and are provided with a varying number of projecting arms; when fresh they contain fine granular matter with a clear, large nuclei and nucleoli, and appear finely fibrillated.

Fig. 157.—Transverse section of the retina. After Zehender.

They receive an axis-cylinder on their inner side, and on the outer send out branches which ultimately divide into fine fibrillæ, and are lost at the inner granular layer in a tangled network. It is probable, however, that some of these fibres are connected with the cells of the inner nuclear layer.

The *inner granular layer* partly surrounds the ganglion-cells and forms a sort of spongy network between these and the inner nuclear layer; its composition is still a matter of doubt, but it appears to be made up of a more or less homogeneous substance, in which are numerous fine openings filled with some material of a peculiar refractive power. It does not belong to the nervous substance of the retina, and when placed in a 10 per cent. solution of common salt, dissolves, leaving the supporting connective-tissue fibres unaffected.

The *inner nuclear layer* is made up of numerous oval cells with large nuclei; they belong mostly to the nervous tissue, but scattered among them are also cells of the supporting connective-tissue framework.

The nerve-cells resemble small bipolar ganglion-cells, having two fine processes, the inner of which probably connects with the ganglion-cell layer, or directly with the optic nerve fibres. Near the macula these cells are more numerous; toward the ora serrata they gradually decrease in number.

Next comes the *outer granular layer*, a thin stratum resembling the inner in appearance and composition; here the fine fibres from the outer and inner nuclear layers become lost in a tangled mass.

Between this layer and the *membrana limitans externa* is the *outer layer of nuclei*, made up of a number of oval cells, connected more or less closely with the inner ends of the rods and cones.

The larger nerve-fibres, which pass through the outer granular layer, are joined to the nuclei of the cones, which lie directly within the membrana limitans and are connected to a prolongation of the base of the cones themselves. The smaller fibres pass to the nuclei of the rods, which form an irregular layer at varying distances from the limiting membrane, and from which fine tangled fibres pass to the base of the rods. These nuclei resemble those of the inner layer; they contain a small amount of granular matter with a nucleus and nucleolus, and sometimes exhibit, as the result of post-mortem changes, peculiar transverse stripes.

Directly beyond the membrana limitans externa, and resting upon it, are *the rods and cones*, each composed of an outer and inner member.

The rods are small, cylindrical bodies of high refractive power; when fresh they appear homogeneous, but with the

beginning of decomposition, which occurs very quickly, the
inner half appears as if filled with a finely granular substance,
while the outer exhibits transverse striations, and finally
breaks up into small disks, which can only be distinguished
from those of the outer segment of the cones by their red color
(visual purple of Kühne), which soon fades on exposure to
light.

The inner segment of the cones is larger than that of the
rods ; it tapers rapidly toward the outer part, where it is filled
with a peculiar oval-shaped body ; the outer segment does not
equal that of the rods in height, but divides into similar disks.

The *pigment-layer*, in which the ends of the rods and cones
are imbedded, consists of a single layer of hexagonal cells,
more densely pigmented in the part next the retina, and by
some observers said to be provided with fine processes, which
are lodged between the rods and cones. This pigment is more
dense at the macula and varies with the color of the person,
being most abundant in negroes, whereas it is absent in albi-
nos ; from this layer, according to Kühne, the visual purple
of the rods is reproduced.

At the *macula lutea*, which is situated a little to the outer
side of the entrance of the optic nerve, the ganglion-cell and
inner nuclear layers have their greatest thickness. The fibres
which pass from the outer granular to the outer nuclear layer
are lengthened and run in a more horizontal direction toward
the *fovea*, which forms a slight depression in the centre of the
macula.

Over this fovea the layers of nerve-fibres and ganglion-cells
are absent, and the other laminæ become so much thinned
that the membrana limitans interna approaches nearly to the
nuclear layer ; the rods are also absent, and the cones become lengthened and slightly convergent.

The *membrana limitans interna* lies between the retina and
vitreous body ; it is a transparent homogeneous structure, and
from its outer surface spring the connective-tissue fibres which
form the supporting framework for the nervous part of the
retina.

These fibres arise in the form of thin fenestrated plates,
connected together by numerous arms ; they soon contract,
however, to smaller radiating bands, which surround the ganglion-cells and pass on to the inner nuclear layer, where they

contain occasional nuclei. From this point they again expand into broader sheets, which, after surrounding the outer nuclei, are united to form the membrana limitans externa. This membrane lies just at the base of the rods and cones, and it is provided with numerous holes, through which those structures pass ; from its outer surface fibres extend up between the rods and cones to form supporting sheaths.

The blood-vessels of the retina come from the *arteria centralis retinæ*, which usually divides into two or more branches at the entrance of the optic nerve ; these vessels lie in the layer of nerve-fibres, and, arching above and below the macula, give off numerous fine branches, from which capillaries penetrate as far as the inner nuclear layer. The larger retinal vessels are surrounded by lymph-spaces, which probably unite with those of the optic nerve.

At the periphery the retina becomes much thinned, and at the ora serrata the nervous elements are discontinued, the connective tissue alone being prolonged over the ciliary body to its anterior angle, thus forming the *pars ciliaris retinæ.*

This membrane consists of long cylindrical cells of varying shapes ; they rest on the pigment and are covered by a thin stratum, which sends processes between them and seems to be a prolongation of the membrana limitans interna of the retina.

It is very difficult to prepare good sections of the retina, but the following plan is recommended : enucleate with care the eye of a frog or some small animal, and immediately suspend it in a well-stoppered bottle containing a small bit of solid osmic acid ; when sufficiently hard the posterior portion of the eye can be cut in pieces and sections made by imbedding or holding between pieces of liver.

Another method is to place the eye unopened in Müller's fluid for some two weeks, frequently changing the fluid ; afterward harden in alcohol. Sections may then be made in the same manner as before.

To obtain the separate constituents, place a fresh retina in a $\frac{1}{10}$ per cent. aqueous solution of osmic acid for fourteen days, then in glycerine for seventeen days ; after this, place a small piece on a slide in glycerine, with the cover-glass so arranged that no pressure is made upon the specimen ; now tap gently on the centre of the glass until the motion of the fluid causes the retina to fall apart.

The *optic nerve*, after leaving the optic canal, passes through the orbit surrounded by three coverings, continuations of the cerebral membranes.

The *dural coat*, composed of dense connective tissue with a few elastic fibres, forms the outer covering ; the fibres are attached to the periosteum, where the nerve leaves the bony canal, and where it enters the eyeball they are continued directly into the outer layers of the sclera.

Within this covering, and separated from it by a very narrow space, are the delicate fibres of the arachnoidal coat, and the lymph-space between the two is called the *subdural space*.

Within the arachnoidal coat, and separated from it by a wide lymph-space, is the *pial coat* closely surrounding the nerve-fibres, and sending processes of connective-tissue between their bundles. This membrane passes into the inner layers of the sclera, and also sends numerous fibres to the lamina cribrosa. Its outer surface is covered with endothelium, and between it and the *arachnoid coat* is the *subarachnoid space*, which reaches to the inner layers of the sclera, and is continuous with the same space in the brain.

The optic nerve itself, closely surrounded by its *vagina fibrosa*, passes forward through the orbit, receiving the central artery and vein at about 15 to 20 mm. from the sclera. These vessels pass to the centre of the nerve and lie in a connective-tissue sheath until they emerge on the inner surface of the eyeball to branch over the retina.

On cross-sections of the nerve, bundles of connective tissue are seen to pass inward from the pial sheath and form a cross-network, through the openings of which the nerve-fibres pass. On longitudinal sections the connective tissue appears in irregular fenestrated sheaths ; this tissue can also be demonstrated by macerating thick sections in a ½ per cent. solution of chromic acid and then brushing out the nerve-elements.

These nerve-filaments themselves are extremely small, but vary somewhat in size. They consist of an axis-cylinder surrounded by its medullary sheath; they are grouped in large bundles which pass through the meshes of the connective tissue. The fibres appear to be held together by a kind of homogeneous albuminous substance—*neuroglia*, and have on their surface occasional nucleated corpuscles, distinguished from those of the connective tissue by being larger and more irregular in shape.

Blood-vessels are found not only in the centre of the nerve, but also scattered through various parts of the connective tissues.

At the lamina cribrosa there is an anastomosis with the vessels of the *circle of Haller*, which, coming from the short posterior ciliary arteries, forms a vascular circle in the sclera, about the entrance of the optic nerve.

Where the nerve-fibres pass through the sieve-like openings of the lamina cribrosa they lose their medullary sheath, and from that point pass on to the nerve-fibre layer of the retina as transparent axis-cylinders; but in rare cases the sheaths are continued from the optic disk some little distance over the retina, and are seen with the ophthalmoscope as very white patches radiating out from the disk, or following the vessels and gradually fading into the general color of the fundus by a fine, fringe-like border.

The *vitreous body* is a transparent, jelly-like mass, of spherical shape, with a depression at the anterior part, in which the lens rests. It is bounded behind and on the side by the retina, in front by the lens with its attachments, and appears to have no true hyaloid limiting-membrane of its own. It is very difficult to demonstrate any definite structure in this substance; toward the periphery it appears to be arranged somewhat in concentric layers, but in the centre is more homogeneous.

From the optic disk to the lens there is a small canal about 1 mm. wide in front and spreading out behind; it is lined with very transparent cells, and filled with a substance more fluid than the rest of the vitreous; it marks the position of the *arteria hyaloidea*, which is usually obliterated at about the seventh foetal month.

The vitreous body also contains numerous corpuscles, especially near the periphery; these consist of round lymph-cells, stellate cells, with one or more nuclei, and irregular arms, and of branching cells which seem to have a transparent vesicle filling up a part of their interior. The vitreous contains no nerves, and after birth no blood-vessels; it may be examined fresh or hardened in a ½ per cent. solution of chromic acid. Sections may be colored blue with aniline, and preserved in glycerine.

The *lens* (Fig. 158) is a transparent, biconvex body, sur-rounded by a structureless, elastic capsule, which is thicker in front where it touches the iris, and thinner behind where it rests in the *fossa patellaris* of the vitreous.

The inner surface of the anterior capsule is covered with a single layer of hexagonal epithelial cells, which become longer near the equator of the lens, and gradually pass over into the lens-fibre.

After birth these fibres consist of long, transparent tubes, on section resembling flattened hexagons closely joined together by their serrated edges; they are arranged in concentric meridional layers with their broad side out-ward. They do not pass around the entire circumference of the lens, but arise on the anterior surface from three lines, which, uniting at the axis, make a figure like an in-verted Y, with the arms set at an angle of about 20° to each other; on the posterior surface this star is reversed, the Y standing upright. In adult life the rays are more numerous, and the fluid contents of the tubes become more solid and of greater refractive power, espe-cially toward the centre of the lens.

FIG. 158. — Meridional section through axis of the human lens. Babuchin.

On a meridional section of the lens one sees the concentric ar-rangement of the lens-fibres, and near the equator a collection of nuclei (*the nuclear zone*). These nuclei belong to the lens-fibres, each one of which originally had one, although in adult life they are found more abundantly in the peripheral region.

The fibres of the supporting ligament of the lens (*the zonula ciliaris*) are attached to the anterior and posterior capsule near the equator; from here they converge to the apex of the ciliary body, to which they are fastened.

The fibres form for the most part an anterior and posterior layer, and have occasional nuclei, especially toward the ora serrata; between these layers is the *canal of Petit*, the result of post-mortem changes, which quickly destroy the delicate fibres that ordinarily fill this space.

Specimens for study may be made in the following way : harden an eye for fourteen days in Müller's fluid ; then open, remove the lens, and preserve in alcohol. Sections may be made in any direction ; they should be colored with hematoxylon and mounted in glycerine.

To examine the epithelium under the anterior capsule, a piece of capsule should be peeled off from a fresh lens and examined with or without previous staining. Single lens-fibres or groups of fibres may be obtained by macerating a portion of lens in dilute sulphuric acid ($\frac{1}{4}$ per cent.), or in a $\frac{1}{4}$ per cent. solution of chromic acid, after which it can be easily separated into its elementary parts.

The *lachrymal gland* is situated under the upper and outer edge of the orbital wall, resting partly in a shallow fossa of the frontal bone, to which it is attached by firm bands of connective tissue.

It is an acinous gland, divided into a larger upper portion (*glandula Galeni*), some 20 mm. long, 10 wide, and 5 thick, and a lower part of about half the size (*glandula Monroi*) ; they are supplied with blood by a branch of the ophthalmic artery, and with nerves from the fifth pair.

The connective tissue which envelops the gland also ramifies through its substance, dividing it into numerous small alveoli, in which are the true secreting cells of the gland, and from which fine ducts pass out to coalesce, and finally discharge on the free surface of the conjunctiva fornicis at its upper and outer part.

The upper part of the gland is quite dense, but in the lower portion the alveoli are less closely packed, and often nearly surrounded by the orbital fat. The alveoli are covered by a fine membrane composed of flat cells with numerous branches or processes, which spread in various directions and serve to unite the cells of the investing membrane, and also the different alveoli ; they form a shell which is surrounded on its outer side by a distinct lymph-space, and on its inner surface is lined by the secreting cells of the gland.

If these lymph-spaces have been injected with Berlin blue, and especially if the blood-vessels are injected with some other color, the arrangement of the lymph-spaces can be very well

seen.   The openings from the alveoli are at first lined with
fine, flat cells ; then, as the tube grows larger, they assume the
character of cylindrical epithelium.

BIBLIOGRAPHY.

GRAEFE U. SAEMISCH.   Handbuch der gesammten Augenheilkunde.   Vol. I.
     Leipzig, 1874.
J. ORTH.   Cursus der normalen Histologie.   Berlin, 1878.
A. ALT.   Lectures on the Human Eye.   New York, 1880.

CHAPTER XXI.

THE EAR.

By DRS. WILLIAM F. WHITNEY and CLARENCE J. BLAKE, of Boston.

FOLLOWING the natural order are to be considered, first, the external ear with the meatus externus ; secondly, the middle ear with the Eustachian tube; and thirdly, the internal ear (membranous labyrinth and cochlea).

External ear.—This includes the auricle, the meatus externus, and the membrana tympani.

The *auricle* is formed by a cartilaginous plate, 1–2 mm. in thickness. The fine elastic fibres of this plate, which is of the reticular variety of cartilage, can be traced into the perichondrium, and even into the subcutaneous tissue. Both perichondrium and subcutaneous tissue are rich in elastic fibres, the latter varying greatly in amount in different parts of the ear, being very sparingly developed on the concave surfaces, where the skin is closely adherent to the perichondrium, and immovable in consequence, but more abundant on the convex surfaces, where the skin is movable ; it forms, together with the fat enclosed in its meshes, the bulk of the lobule.

The cutis covering the auricle is a direct continuation of that covering the face, and is well provided with downy hairs and sebaceous glands. These latter reach their greatest development in the depressions of the auricle, especially the concha.

The *external meatus* consists of a cartilaginous and an osseous portion. The former only differs in structure from the auricle into which it passes, in the presence of the ceruminous glands. These are tubular glands, having a coil at the bottom. They consist of a membrana propria, on which is a layer of cubical epithelium, and are the analogues of the sweat-glands. In the osseous portion of the meatus the glands are sparingly found, and the hairs are fewer and finer. Otherwise there is

23

no difference between the two portions, except that the cartilage is replaced by bone.

The ear of a new-born child can be easily removed with the cartilaginous part of the meatus, and when hardened in Müller's fluid and afterward in alcohol, and imbedded in paraffine or hardened liver, furnishes sections which, when colored with hæmatoxylon, show the different relations very clearly. The osseous portion must first be decalcified by allowing the bone to hang freely in a weak ($\frac{1}{2}$ per cent.) solution of chromic acid, often renewed, during several months. The specimens are then to be well washed, hardened in alcohol, and prepared as above.

At the inner end of the external meatus, and separating it from the middle ear, is stretched the membrana tympani. The tympanic ring, with the membrane attached to it, is to be carefully separated from the surrounding parts by means of bone-scissors, and placed for five to fifteen minutes in a weak solution (two to five per cent.) of formic or acetic acid. It should then be well washed in distilled water, and the external layer of epithelium removed by a camel's-hair brush, and finally stained with hæmotoxylon and mounted in glycerine. In specimens thus prepared there are to be distinguished three layers, viz.: an external or cuticular layer, a middle or fibrous layer (membrana propria), and an internal or mucous layer.

The cuticular layer is composed of simple pavement-epithelium, without glands or hairs. It is thickest at the periphery, and over the handle of the hammer, and along its edge.

The fibrous layer (membrana propria) consists of two sets of flattened, spindle-shaped fibres, with long, thin connective-tissue corpuscles imbedded in them, and which have a close analogy with the fibres of tendons. The outer series, lying directly beneath the cutis, radiates from the handle of the hammer toward the periphery, while the inner series circles about the handle. At the periphery the two series interlace with each other and with a few fibres coming from the cuticular and mucous layers to form the so-called tendinous ring, in which are also to be found a few scattered cartilage-cells. This ring is joined to the annulus tympanicus by a thin periosteum. (The handle of the hammer is joined to the membrana tympani by a cartilaginous formation which stands in close relation to the membrana propria. This is a shallow groove of hyaline

cartilage, in which the handle of the hammer lies, kept in place
by the mucous layer which passes over and is firmly adherent
to it ; the upper part of this furrow ends in a sort of cartilaginous cap, into which the processus brevis fits.) Transverse
sections made after hardening the membrane in Müller's fluid
and alcohol, and then imbedding, give the best idea of these
relations.

The inner or mucous layer is formed of flat epithelium, supported on a reticulated layer of connective tissue, and directly
continuous with the epithelial lining of the middle ear. The
arterial supply is furnished by a small arteriole, which follows
the handle of the malleolus, and gives off lateral capillaries
anastomosing with others coming from small branches which
enter at the periphery. The blood is collected into venous
trunks which pass out in a similar manner. Fine nerves are
said to be found in close connection with the vessels. They
apparently come from the sympathetic system.

The middle ear.—In order to obtain a clear idea of the relations and structure of the middle ear a fresh temporal bone,
with the soft parts still adherent, must be decalcified by soaking for a long time in a ¼ per cent. solution of chromic acid,
which should be frequently changed ; it is then to be washed
in distilled water for twenty-four hours, and hardened in alcohol, when it will be ready for cutting.

A section from a specimen thus prepared shows that the
whole middle ear is lined by a layer of pavement-epithelium,
supported upon two layers of connective tissue, one serving as
a submucous layer and the other as a periosteum. This tissue is thrown into ridges corresponding to the bony prominences, in the hollows of which the vessels and nerves lie. According to Kessel the submucous layer is provided with oval
expansions, recalling the Pacinian bodies found in the mesentery of the cat. The existence of muciparous glands in the
human tympanum has yet to be confirmed. A plexus of nerves
is described as distributed in the subepithelial tissue, in the
nodal points of which are found scattered ganglion-cells. The
lining of the tympanum passes directly into that of the mastoid
cells, and has there the same general arrangement.

The Eustachian tube.—In direct communication with the
tympanum stands the Eustachian tube, composed like the external ear of a cartilaginous and an osseous portion. The car-

tilage, which gives the name to the anterior part of the tube that stands in connection with the pharynx, is in the form of a hook (Fig. 159, 2), with its short end directed downward and inward. At the bend of the hook the opposing surfaces of cartilage cannot quite apply themselves to each other, and there is thus left a little air-space between them, which Ruedinger has termed the safety-tube (Fig. 159, 9). The cartilage is of the hyaline variety, with small cells, which are much smaller and more numerous at the periphery, thus forming a sort of peri-

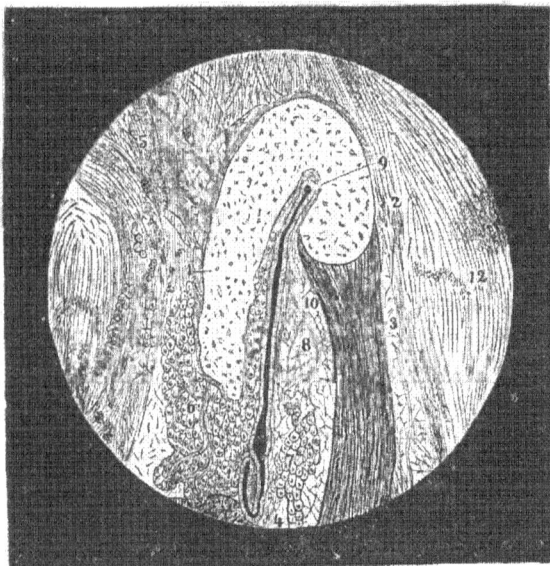

FIG. 159.—Transverse section of Eustachian tube and surrounding parts: 1, median cartilaginous plate; 2, lateral cartilaginous hook; 3, musculus dilator tubæ; 4, musculus levator veli palatini; 5, fibro-cartilago basilaris; 6 and 7, acinous glands; 8, deposit of fat in the lateral wall; 9, safety-tube; 10, accessory fissure; 11, fold of the mucous membrane; 12, adjacent tissues. Ruedinger.

chondrium. The cartilage is joined to the osseous portion by a narrow band of fibro-cartilage.

The musculus dilator tubæ (Fig. 159, 3), which goes to form the membranous (muscular) portion of the tube, is joined to the short end of the hook along the whole length of the cartilaginous portion. The muscle is of the striped variety, and is inserted into the perichondrium by means of a very short, flat tendon.

The entire tube is lined with a mucous membrane (Fig. 159, 11), continuous at one end with that of the pharynx, and at the other with that of the tympanum. This membrane consists of several layers of cylindrical epithelial cells, the upper or inner of which have their broad surfaces directed inward and carry cilia. In the other layers the epithelia are wedge-shaped. The epithelium rests upon a basement-membrane, beneath which is a layer of connective tissue (Fig. 159, 5), in which lie the muci-parous glands (Fig. 159, 6, 7), which are similar to those of the pharynx and œsophagus, and lined with wedge-shaped epithelium. These glands are absent in the safety-tube. A plexus of nerves arising from the pharyngeal and tympanic plexuses has been demonstrated, the final distribution of which to the glands is probable.

Before leaving the middle ear a short mention of the os-sicula and their mode of articulation is in place. The bones are composed of an internal spongy and an external compact portion. The former is very rich in blood-vessels. These bones are covered in early life by the mucous membrane only, but in later life there is also a thin periosteum to be seen. Their articulation with each other is constructed similarly to that of the larger joints; *i.e.*, their articular ends are sur-rounded by a capsule in which is a synovial fluid. The method of union of the foot-plate of the stapes with the fenestra ovale is a little more complicated. The bottom and edges of the plate are covered with a thin film of hyaline cartilage. The edges of the window are also covered with cartilage, which is united to that of the plate by means of a fine network of elastic tissue. The base of the plate rests upon a firm connective-tissue layer, a continuation of the periosteum lining the inside of the scala tympani, and called the ligamentum baseos-stapedis.

The muscles connected with the ossicula belong to the striped variety, and are connected to the bones by tendons, which are covered by the mucous membrane wherever they pass through the tympanum.

The internal ear.—The internal ear consists of two portions, to which the auditory nerve is finally distributed, and which are the essential parts concerned in the perception of sound. These are the membranous labyrinth and the cochlea.

In man and the higher vertebrates both of these parts are enclosed within bony walls, a circumstance which makes their histological study a matter of considerable difficulty. In fishes, however, although the cochlea is represented merely by a small

diverticulum (the lagena), the membranous labyrinth is fully
developed, and, as it is large and easy of access, has always
been a favorite object for demonstration.   Its method of preparation will be given here, while that for the cochlea will be
described farther on.

The membranous labyrinth.—Our knowledge of this part
has been chiefly derived from studies upon the pike (esox lucius), perch (perca fluviatilis), or cod (gadus morrhua).   The
head is divided longitudinally in the median line, and the brain
carefully removed by means of the handle of a scalpel, when
there is seen directly behind the eye a second cavity filled with
a grayish translucent mass, composed principally of fat and a
sort of mucous tissue.   This can be removed with the aid of
fine forceps, and there is usually drawn out at the same time
more or less of the semicircular canals with their ampullæ and
the remains of the utricle and saccule.   With a little practice,
and by carefully freeing the canals from the short, bony channels by which they are held in place, the membranous labyrinth, with a portion of the acoustic nerve, can be removed
entire.

Within the utricle and saccule are found the otoliths, con-
cretions of lime.   After the lime has been removed by means
of a weak acid, they show a coarse, fibrillated structure on
section.   These serve as a ready means of distinguishing between the saccule and utricle, as the largest otolith (called
sagitta) and the smallest (asterix) occupy the saccule, the
former lying on the expansion of the acoustic nerve in the saccule proper, while the latter lies on the expansion of the nerve
in that part of the saccule called the lagena, and which corresponds to the cochlea of the higher animals.   The medium-sized
stone (lapillus) lies upon the expansion of the nerve in the utricle.   The otoliths are embedded in a mucilaginous mass lying
directly upon the termination of the nerve.   In the higher animals they are represented by cretaceous particles in the macula
acustica.

The labyrinth thus removed is to be placed, during twenty-
four hours, in a 1 per cent. solution of osmic acid, and then
carefully washed in distilled water.   In order to obtain the .
separate cells, the point where the nerve enters (known by its
darker color) is to be carefully teased with fine needles and
examined in glycerine.   To obtain good sections, the por-

tions of the canal where the nerve terminates, and the similar portion of the saccule and utricle, are to be placed for twenty-four hours in a saturated solution of gum arabic in water, and then directly into strong alcohol for twenty-four hours longer, when they will be ready for embedding. The sections, made with a sharp razor, kept well wet with alcohol, are to be deprived of their gum by passing a stream of distilled water beneath the cover-glass, the water being replaced by a solution composed of one part of a saturated solution of acetate of potash and four parts each of glycerine and water.

The structure and arrangement of the semicircular canals, except at the points of expansion of the nerve, is as follows: In the osseous fishes the canals lie embedded in a mass of adipose tissue, and are held in place by very short bony tubes; in the cartilaginous fishes (shark, skate) they lie in canals hollowed out in the cartilage, while in man and the higher vertebrates they are surrounded by bony walls.

In man the membranous part does not entirely fill up the bony canals, but is adherent to the lining periosteum at one point, and to the rest of the wall by bands of connective tissue (called *ligamentum labyrinthi canaliculorum et sacculorum*), in the interstices of which the perilymph circulates. In the fishes the walls of the tubes and ampullæ, as well as of the utricle and saccule, are composed of what has been termed spindle-cartilage. This consists of a homogeneous ground-substance, like that of ordinary cartilage, in which lie embedded long, spindle-shaped connective-tissue corpuscles, anastomosing with each other in all directions, like the corpuscles of the cornea. The whole is lined with a pavement-epithelium. In man the structure is different. Here there are to be distinguished three layers, viz., externally, a layer of connective tissue, composed of fibrous tissue with numerous nuclei. This is connected at one point with the periosteum, and passes into the ligamenta labyrinthi canaliculorum at the other points of the circumference; secondly, of a hyaline layer, the tunica propria; this is raised into papilliform projections in certain parts of the tube. The internal layer is composed of simple pavement-epithelium.

The distribution and termination of the nerve is as follows in the fishes: The acoustic nerve divides into two branches, the cochlear and vestibular, each of which gives off three filaments. Those from the cochlear portion supply the saccule, lagena, and ampulla frontalis; those from the vestibular branch go to the utricle and the ampullæ of the horizontal and sagittal semicircular canals. The termination of the nerves in the saccule and utricle is called *macula acustica*, and in the ampullæ, *crista acustica*.

The macula is a small, roundish spot, slightly projecting above the surface. Thin sections through it show the presence of three layers of cells. Directly upon the wall proper of the canal lies a single row of small, round epithelial cells with large nucleoli (Fig. 160, 1). Next come several rows of cells hav-

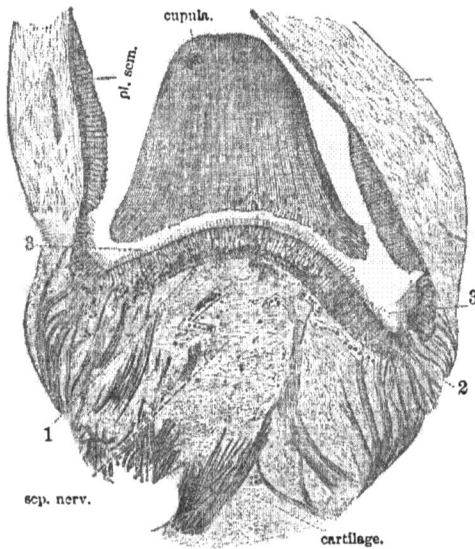

FIG. 160.—Section through the ampulla frontalis of esox lucius: 1, basal cells; 2, cells with thread-like prolongations: 3, cylindrical cells, with cilia. After Kuhn.

ing a round or oblong (spindle-shaped) central portion, from which are given off two filiform prolongations, the one passing inward and standing in close connection with a fine plexus of nerves lying in the layer of round cells mentioned above; the other also passing inward, but ending either as a free cilium between the layer of cells next to be described, or being joined to their inner extremity (Fig. 160, 2, and Fig. 161).

The inner layer consists of several rows of cylindrical epithelial cells, having the end, which is directed inward, tapering into a fine filament connected with those of the middle layer, as already described. The free surface of these cells is provided with numerous hairs (Fig. 160, 3).

The arrangement of the cells in the crista acustica is essentially the same as that of the macula, with the exception that the crista rests upon an infolding of the wall called the septum nerveum (Fig. 160, sep. nerv.), and has on each side two half - moon - shaped prominences of cylindrical epithelium called the plana semilunata (Fig. 160, pl. sem.), into which no nerves have been traced. At the point where the macula and plana semilunata pass into the epithelium lining the rest of the canal, there is found an intermediate form of cell, larger than the ordinary epithelium, and separated one from another by a fine web of connective tissue. These have received the name of protoplasmic cells, but as yet their function has not been discovered.

Covering the crista in the place of an otolith is a gelatinous mass in the form of a cup, having a striated appearance, and into which the fine hairs of the internal surface project. This is considered as a cuticular formation, and is supposed to act as a damper (Fig. 160, cupula).

The nerve, after passing through the wall at the point opposite the crista or macula, loses all its sheaths, and forms a fine plexus in the outermost layer of cells, and

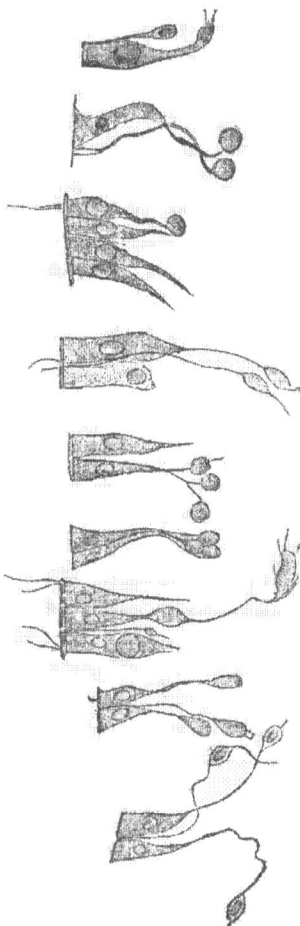

Fig. 161.—Separate cells from the macula, showing the connection of the cylindrical cells with the cells having thread-like processes, and also the passage of these processes to the surface between the cells. Kuhn.

this plexus has been found to communicate with the inner filaments of the middle layer of cells, the internal filaments of which ended as free cilia or were joined to cells of the inner layer which were provided with cilia upon their free surface. This can be best understood by a study of Figs. 160 and 161. In man the arrangement, as well as can be followed, is almost identical with that of fishes.

The cochlea.—There is no easy method of obtaining good preparations of the cochlea, but that by which the best results have been obtained is as follows : The portion of the temporal bone containing the internal ear from a recently killed animal (young cat, dog, or bat) is hardened for twenty-four hours in ½ to 1 per cent. solution of osmic acid in distilled water, then placed in Muller's fluid for a week, and decalcified by a 0.01 per cent. solution of chloride of palladium. After decalcification it is to be washed in distilled water for a few minutes, then soaked for twenty-four hours in a concentrated aqueous solution of pure gum arabic, and finally placed directly in strong alcohol for twenty-four hours. After this hardening the preparations are ready to be embedded in soap or hardened liver, and cut. The razor is to be kept well wet with alcohol while cutting. The sections are to be placed directly upon a slide, and the gum removed by passing a stream of distilled water under the covering-glass.

Small portions of the lamina spiralis can also be taken from the fresh cochlea, after opening it carefully with the bone-forceps, and placed in the vapor of osmic acid or in a ½ to 1 per cent. solution of the same for a few (twelve to twenty-four) hours. The preparations thus treated may be teased in glycerine, and the separate cells obtained.

The sections are to be made in a direction parallel with the long axis of the cochlea, and if the central shaft (modiolus) is cut through, the following picture will be presented : On each side of the modiolus are seen sections of the canal of the cochlea, divided by a thin partition (the lamina spiralis, Fig. 162, *L sp*) into an upper portion (the scala vestibuli, Fig. 162, *SV*) and a lower (the scala tympani, Fig. 162, *ST*). The scala vestibuli is further subdivided by means of a delicate membrane, named after its discoverer the membrane of Reissner (Fig. 162, *f*, *f₁*), which passes off at an angle from the middle of the lamina spiralis and is inserted into the wall of the cochlea.[1] The portion of the canal thus cut off forms the ductus cochlearis (Fig. 162, *e*, *e₁*), and in it lies the peculiar body in which the nerve terminates, and which is called the organ of Corti.

The scala tympani is a blind canal, having at one extremity the membrane which covers the fenestra rotunda, and at the upper part terminating in the cupula of the cochlea, where it

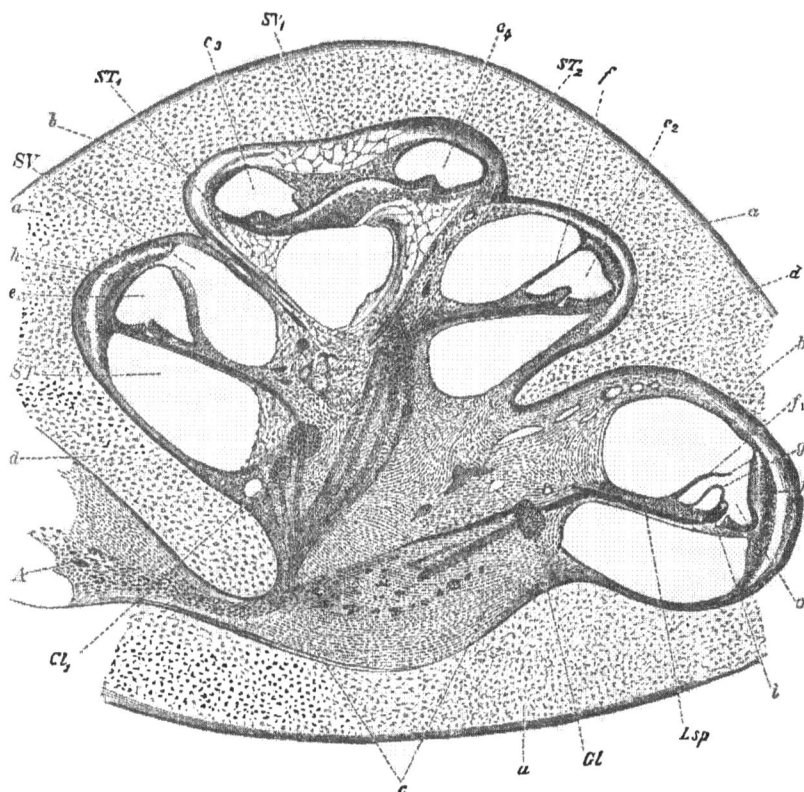

FIG. 162.—Section of the cochlea of a human embryo at the fourth month. *a. a, a,* cartilaginous incasement of the cochlea; *b. b,* perichondrium; *c,* mucoid tissue matrix of the modiolus; *d, d,* cartilaginous septa of the individual turns of the cochlea; *e—e₄,* sections of the ductus cochlearis; *f, f₁,* Reissner's membrane; *g,* membrana tectoria, somewhat lifted up from the subjacent parts; *h,* rudiment of the stria vascularis; *i,* rudiment of the subsequent organ of Corti; *L sp,* lamina spiralis; *Gl, Gl₁,* ganglion spirale with various efferent and afferent bundles of nerves; *ST,* scala tympani; *SV,* scala vestibuli; *ST₁, SV₁, ST₂,* mucoid tissue where later the scalæ of the last cochleal turn will be. ³⁄₁. Waldeyer.

is said to enter into communication with the scala vestibuli by a minute opening, the helicotrema.

The scala vestibuli stands in direct communication with the perilymphatic space of the vestibular sacs, while the ductus cochlearis is in communication with the saccule by means of a slender canal (the canalis reuniens). The walls of the two scalæ are formed of a thin periosteum, on the surface of which there can be shown, by means of the silver method, a layer of endothelium. This proves that the canals are of the nature of serous cavities.

The lamina spiralis is composed of an osseous and a membranous portion. The osseous portion reaches about one-half the distance from the modiolus to the opposite wall, and on its outer and vestibular portion is a mass of connective tissue called crista spiralis (Fig. 163, *Cr.*), the upper lip of which is called labium vestibulare (Fig. 163, *Lv.*), while the lower lip is called labium tympanicum (Fig. 163, *Lt.*); the space between the two lips has received the name of recessus internus. The crista spiralis is divided by a number of parallel furrows, which gives the surface a regular toothed appearance when seen from the vestibular surface. Hence, the portions between the furrows are called "auditory teeth."

The under (vestibular) of the two lips is connected with the membrana basilaris (Fig. 163, *Hn*, *Zp'*), which is composed of two layers of finely fibrillated connective tissue, and is covered on its tympanic surface by a layer of endothelium, and on the surface turned toward the ductus cochlearis by the organ of Corti and its supporting cells. The inner layer of this fine connective tissue is directly continued into the bases of the pillars of the organ of Corti next to be described.

The organ of Corti, so named from its discoverer, is a complicated arrangement of cells in which the nerve terminates, and of other cells and their modifications, which apparently act as supports to these and as modifiers of the sound. The cells proper, in which the nerve terminates, have received the name of hair-cells, from the ciliated appendages which they carry (Fig. 163, *a*, *a''*, *a''*, *a''*), while the peculiar modified cells which are their chief support are called the pillars.

The pillars (Fig. 163, *fi*, *fa*) are two slender, slightly shaped bodies, of a finely fibrillated structure, showing, however, in their early stages, the presence of nuclei. They stand upon the membrana basilaris, and are apparently to be directly followed into the fine layer of connective tissue beneath them. They are arranged in two rows, named inner and outer, according to their situation as regards the modiolus. The pillars are inclined toward each other, and the space between them is named the tunnel. The head of the outer is a little enlarged and rounded, lying in a shallow depression in the head of the inner pillar, thus resembling a ball and socket-joint (Fig. 163, gia). The heads of the pillars, when seen from the surface, have

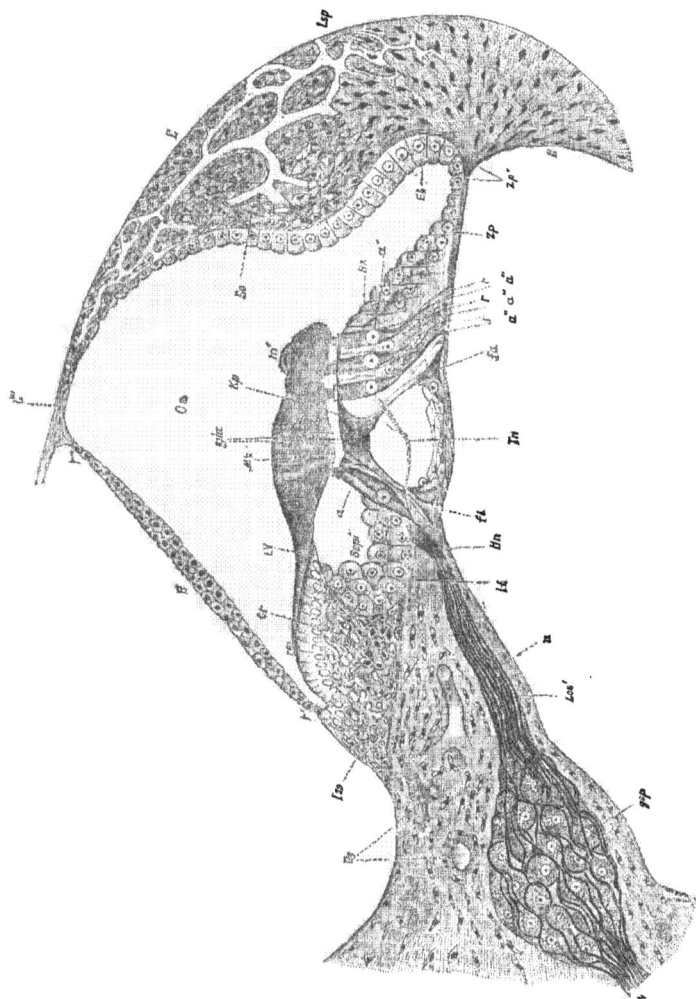

FIG. 163.—Section through the ductus cochlearis of a young dog: R-r', Reissner's membrane; Los and Los', vestibular and tympanic plates of the osseous lamina; gsp, ganglion spirale; n, fine nerves passing through the habenula perforata at Hn; Cr, crista spiralis; Lv, its vestibula or upper lip; rm, Mt, m', the membrana tectoria (Corti's membrane); $Sept$, recessus internus clothed with epithelium; fi and fa, inner and outer pillars of Corti, a and a'', a'', a'', inner and outer hair-cells, between the latter are seen the flask-shaped cells, r, r, r; Tu, nerve passing through the tunnel to reach one of the outer hair-cells; Hz, Henson's prop-cells; Sp, Zp' zona pectinata; gia, inner and outer heads of the pillars of Corti; Kp, plate called phalynx, which, when joined with its neighbors, forms the lamina reticularis, in which the ends of the hair-cells are supported; Lsp, ligamentum spirale; Sv, stria vascularis. After Lavdowsky.

prolongations shaped a little like the bones of the fingers, and hence called phalanges (Fig. 163, *Kp*). These enclose spaces between them, through which the ends of the hair-cells project. The network thus formed is called the lamina reticularis, and gives a very peculiar appearance when this portion of the organ is viewed from above.

Corresponding to the pillars are rows of hair-cells termed inner and outer—a single row of the former (Fig. 163, *a*) and four rows of the latter (Fig. 163, *a''*, *a''*, *a''*). The shape of the cells of the inner row is cylindrical, having their base prolonged into a fine thread expanding into a foot-stalk, which passes into the membrana basilaris. The top of the cell which passes through the opening in the lamina reticularis is provided with fine cilia. The four rows of cells in connection with the outer pillar are of the same shape as those of the inner row, but, in addition, are joined at their lower part to peculiar cells shaped like a flask, large and rounded at the bottom, and tapering to a long and narrow neck. The tops of these cells reach to the lamina reticularis, but do not pass through it (Fig. 163, *r*, *r*, *r*, and *b*). Immediately adjoining the outer rows of hair-cells are several rows of cylindrical epithelial cells (Henson's prop-cells) (Fig. 163, *Hz*), which pass gradually into the short cubical epithelium forming the zona pectinata (Fig. 163, *Zp* to *Zp'*) adjoining the epithelial lining of the ductus cochlearis.

The course of the nerve has already been followed to the ganglion spirale. From this point a number of fine trunks pass through a canal in the osseous portion of the lamina spiralis to the lower lip of the crista, which they leave as naked axis-cylinders by a number of small holes, called the habenula perforata (Fig. 163, *Hn*). After entering the ductus cochlearis they divide into two chief bundles, one distributed to the inner hair-cells, and the other, passing between the bases of the inner pillars, crosses the tunnel and then again passes between the outer pillars, and terminates finally in the outer hair-cells. Beyond the fact that they apply themselves directly to the surface of the hair-cells, their mode of ultimate ending is not known.

From the upper edge of the crista spiralis, lying directly upon it and covering the whole of the organ of Corti, is the membrana tectoria (Corti's membrane) (Fig. 163, *Mt*), a homogeneous mass in which indistinct striations are to be seen. This is of the nature of a cuticular formation, and probably acts as a damper, preventing excessive vibrations of the organ of Corti.

BIBLIOGRAPHY.

RUEDINGER. The Eustachian Tube, etc. Stricker's Histology, New York. 1872.

TRAUTMANN. Der gelbe Fleck am Ende des Hammergriffes. Arch. f. Ohrenheilk., Vol. XI., p. 99. 1876.

URBANTSCHITSCH. Zur Anat. d. Gehörknöchelchen des Menchen. Arch. f. Ohrenheilk., Vol. XI., p. 1. 1876.

POLITZER. Ueber Anastomosen d. Gefässbezirk d. Mittelohres u. d. Labyrinths. Arch. f. Ohrenh., Vol. XI., p. 237, 1877, and Wien. med. Woch., No. 30. 1876.

WEBER-LIEL. Die Membrana tympani secundaria. Monatsschr. f. Ohrenheilkunde, No. 4. 1876.

LAVDOWSKY. Ueber d. akust. Endapparat d. Säugethiere. Arch. f. mikros. Anat., Vol. XIII., p. 417. 1877.

KUHN. Untersuch. über den häutigen Labyrinth der Knochenfische. Arch. f. mikr. Anat., Vol. XIV., p. 264. 1877.

MOLDENHAUER. Beitr. zur. Anat. u. Entwickel. d. Menschl. Gehörorganes. Arch. f. Ohrenheilkunde, Vol. XI., p. 225. 1877.

DORAN. Morphology of the Mammalian Ossicula Auditus. Trans. Linn. Soc., London, Second series, Vol. I. 1877.

UEBER-LIEL. Der Aqueductus cochleæ beim Menschen. Monatsschr. f. Ohrenheilk., Vol. XIII., No. 3, p. 33, 1878-79, and Virch. Arch., Vol. LXXVII., p. 207, 1879; also Arch. f. Anat. u. Phys., Phys. Abtheilung, p. 188. 1878.

CISOFF. Ueber d. Gehörlabyrinth d. Knorpelfische. Sitz. d. Naturf. Gesellsch. an d. K. Universit. zu Kasan. May, 1879. (Russian.)

PRITCHARD. The Organ of Corti in Mammals. The Lancet, 1876, p. 552, and Proc. Roy. Soc., Vol. XXIV., No. 168, p. 346, 1878; also The Termination of the Nerves in the Vestibule and Semicircular Canals of Mammals. Quart. Journ. Micros. Sc., New Series, No. 64, Vol. XXI., p. 398. 1879.

MINOT, C. S. Recent Investigations of the Histology of the Scala Media Cochleæ. American Journal of Otology. April, 1881.

PART III.

CHAPTER XXII.

THE NASAL FOSSÆ, PHARYNX, AND TONSILS.

By D. BRYSON DELAVAN, M.D.,

Member of the American Laryngological Association.

The vestibulum nasi is that part of the nasal canal which
is surrounded by the anterior cartilages of the nose. It is covered by a continuation of the exterior skin, which gradually
assumes the characteristics of a mucous membrane and possesses several layers of pavement-epithelium, the uppermost
of which is composed of horny cells. This epithelium extends
backward to the anterior margin of the inferior turbinated
bone and the commencement of the inferior nasal duct, where
it becomes ciliated. The integument has also vascular papillæ,
with both simple and compound loops, and in the lower part
of the nose long, stiff hairs (vibrissæ), as well as large sebaceous
follicles. It is sparingly supplied with blood-vessels. The
nerves are derived from the trigeminus, and consist of filaments, which probably end in terminal bulbs.

The respiratory region.—The nasal fossæ proper, with the
exception of a limited part known as the olfactory region, may
be regarded as a continuation of the respiratory tract. Each
fossa communicates with four sinuses: the frontal, the sphenoidal, the maxillary or antrum Highmorianum, and the posterior ethmoidal. The mucous membrane covering the respiratory region and its accessory sinuses is called the Schneiderian
or pituitary membrane. It is devoid of papillæ, and is covered
with a cylindrical ciliated epithelium, like that of the trachea,

the ciliary current being invariably toward the choanæ (posterior nares). It contains, also, goblet-cells. Under the epithelium is a true membrana mucosa, which forms at the same time a periosteum for the bones, and is composed almost entirely of connective tissue, scantily permeated, if at all, with elastic tissue-elements. The mucous membrane may be divided into two varieties : a thinner membrane, covering the internal surface of the turbinated bones and the accessory sinuses, and the thicker membrane of the nasal fossæ proper.

The thinner membrane contains many acinous glands. In the adjacent cavities they are less abundant, excepting upon the internal wall of the maxillary sinus. Here, and in the sphenoidal sinus, the glands consist of several cylindrical tubes with connecting single oblong acini. The epithelium of the latter is pyriform, while in the tubes it is cylindrical. The mucous membrane itself is pale in color, and scantily supplied with blood-vessels. Special nerve-terminations have been described in these sinuses. These are probably nothing more than terminations of fibres from the great sympathetic, having at their extremities ganglionic cellules.

The thicker membrane covers the lower part of the nasal septum and the inferior and middle turbinated bones. It is lined with the same ciliated epithelium, and in the anterior two-thirds of the turbinated bones forms only a delicate, slightly corrugated covering for the subjacent parts. Posteriorly, however, its surface is thrown into numerous thick folds, evidently designed to increase the extent of surface of the mucous membrane.

The membrana mucosa forms a fibrous network, which passes between the glands and vessels and connects the mucous membrane with the periosteum. Its characteristics resemble more nearly those of periosteum, so that it may properly be classed as a part of the latter. The glands of this region vary somewhat from the acinous type, and are composed of tortuous tubules, having many sinuses and oblong offshoots. They are lined on their inner surface with low cylindrical epithelium, and sometimes assume a circular, sometimes an oval or tubular shape in the microscopic section. The thickness of the pituitary mucous membrane is due not only to its mucous glands, but more particularly to the existence in it of true erectile tissue, as well as venous plexuses. (See p. 160). These are

24

most abundant at the posterior extremity of the inferior turbinated bones. Some of these vessels are prolonged throughout
the continuity of the bone on the lateral as well as the median
side, to appear with greater frequency at the anterior extremity, without, however, regaining the number or size which they
possessed at their origin. Where they are less numerous the
remaining space is almost entirely occupied by large mucous
glands.

In the bony framework of the inferior turbinated bone, large,
bright interspaces are seen in the fine trabecular substance,
which are filled with fibrous tissue containing pale lymphoid
cells. In this fibrous tissue are usually found transverse sections of delicate vessels, the walls of which are apparently
composed of fibrous tissue. In order to reach the outer surface these vessels either perforate the bone or lie in recesses
separated from the soft parts only by the periosteum. In the
middle three-fifths of the bone, where the osseous structure
contains the largest cavities, we find in the vicinity of the vessels large, round, and polygonal, glistening cells, analogous to
marrow-cells. A recent author believes most of the above-
mentioned vessels to be lymphatics. The arteries of the inferior turbinated bone do not number more than three or four,
and are derived from the posterior nasal artery.

The olfactory region is situated in the uppermost portion
of the nasal cavity. Its inferior limit in man has not yet been
accurately determined. According to the generally received
views of Schultze and Ecker, it is probably limited to the roof
of the nasal fossæ, the superior turbinated bone, and the corresponding part of the septum. The mucous membrane of this
region is of a dull, yellowish brown color, and is perceptibly
thicker and softer than that of the respiratory region. This
color proceeds from fine pigment-molecules, which are embedded partly in the bodies of the cylindrical epithelial cells,
and partly in the cells of an especial gland-formation found
here. Soon after death, however, it becomes unrecognizable.
Under the microscope the olfactory region is seen to be bounded by a tolerably well-defined, serrated border, although isl-
ands of ciliated epithelium, such as is found in the respira- •
tory region, are frequently found scattered about in different
parts of it. The differences of structure in the olfactory mucous membrane depend upon the character of the epithelium,

the occurrence of peculiarly constructed glands—Bowman's glands—and upon the relations of the nerves.

The fundamental layer of the mucous membrane is composed of a finely fibrillated connective tissue, rich in cells, the arrangement of which is determined by the numerously distributed glands, nerves, and vessels which it contains. As in the other regions of the nasal cavity, the mucosa seems to pass, without a well-defined limit, into the periosteum. In many places aggregations of small pigmented nuclei are found, some in the shape of long strips lying near the nerve-branches, some in other situations, in rounded or irregular groups.

The olfactory epithelium attains a considerable thickness. It consists of a single layer of very elongated cells, which Schultze has proved to be of two kinds, epithelial cells and olfactory cells.

The *olfactory cells* are slender, delicate structures, in which may be distinguished a cell-body and two prolongations going in opposite directions—the one to the periphery, the other centrally. The bodies of the olfactory cells are not all located in the same plane of the epithelial stratum. The majority, however, occupy its deeper portions. The cell-body appears spindle-shaped or pyriform. It is finely granulated, and has in its central and widest portion a spherical, light-colored, ill-defined nucleus. The peripheral prolongation is generally rod-shaped, but now and then presents slight sinuosities. It is sharply outlined and homogeneous, and its free extremity, in some animals (amphibia and birds), has a tuft of the most delicate hairs, which project above the surface of the epithelium. In man this is not the case. The opposite prolongation is extremely delicate and perishable, and, by some methods of preparation, resembles the finest nerve-fibrils, sometimes covered with varicosities, at others entirely smooth. It runs continuously and undivided as far as the base of the epithelial stratum, where it appears to meet the final radiations of the olfactory nerve, partly intertwines with these radiations, and then escapes further investigation.

The *indifferent epithelial cells* appear in the form of an elongated cylinder with a very fine, granulated cell-body and an ellipsoid nucleus. Near the latter the cell suddenly contracts into a slender, very pale, centrally directed prolongation, the inferior end of which becomes somewhat wider, and branches into a number of delicate filaments, by means of which the cell is attached to the fundamental layer of connective tissue. These widened extremities of the cells often contain a brownish, partly nuclear, partly diffused pigment. Viewed upon the plane surface, the number of olfactory cells is apparently larger than that of the cylindrical cells. Each one of the latter, however, is generally surrounded by six of the olfactory cells, which completely fill the intermediary spaces between the cylindrical bodies. Both varieties of cells are so accurately adjusted to each other that, especially in the wider portion of the epithelial cells, fine longitudinal furrows may be seen, into which the peripheral continuations of the olfactory cells have been received.

The surface of the epithelium is covered by a delicate membrane, discovered by Von Brunn, and called by him the membrana limitans olfactoria. He has compared it to the membrana limitans externa of the retina, and describes its free surface as being plane and even, while its lower surface covers completely the rounded terminations of the epithelial cells. The peripheral prolongations of the olfactory cells pass through this membrane, and terminate with bare extremities at the level of its free plane.

The olfactory nerves.—The branches from the olfactory ganglia which emerge through the apertures of the lamina cribrosa are composed entirely of non-medullated filaments, which resemble embryonic nerve-fibres. They next anastomose in the deeper layers of the mucous membrane, and form a dense plexiform meshwork, which sends fine branches toward the surface. In these branches the axis-cylinders are broken up into numerous, very fine, varicose fibrils, which ascend to the limit of the epithelial layer, where they are lost. Most authors agree with Schultze that there is a distinct connection between the nerve-fibrils and the olfactory cells. Exner believes that the nerve-fibrils connect with the epithelial cells also. He argues, moreover, that intermediary forms, between the two varieties of epithelium, are found, which would prove that they are not different structures, but one and the same. Neither of these views has yet been established.

Bowman's glands, peculiar to the olfactory mucous membrane, are found in it in large numbers. They occupy almost the whole thickness of the mucous membrane, their bodies being located in the deeper layers of the connective tissue. In man their shape varies somewhat from that of simple tubules, as several glandular tubes ordinarily unite in a common excretory duct, so that, in some cases, the gland almost appears racemose. The glandular cells are partly round, partly irregular in shape, and have many pale nuclei, together with a brownish-colored pigment.

THE PHARYNX.

The mucous membrane of the pharynx is, in general, similar to that of the mouth. It consists essentially of a stratified pavement-epithelium, a rather loosely woven submucosa, which contains aggregations of mucous glandules, and a tunica propria composed of fibrillary connective tissue and furnished with papillæ. The papillæ are smaller than those found lower down in the œsophagus. The mucous glandules are most abundant in the superior part of the pharynx. The mucous membrane of the vault of the pharynx, and in the vicinity of the isthmus of the fauces, where it becomes continuous with the mucous membrane of the nasal cavity, to some extent assumes the characteristics of the latter. In this region the connective tissue is more or less thickly interspersed with lymphoid cells. It is provided, moreover, with ciliated cylindrical epithelium. In adults this epithelium extends some distance backward until it passes into the stratified pavement variety. In children, however, ciliated epithelium lines the whole naso-pharynx. In the upper and lateral parts of the pharynx are found certain aggregations of adenoid tissue, most abundantly in the vault of the pharynx, extending from one Eustachian tube to the other. This tissue is generally quite diffuse, but is identical in its structure with the lingual follicular glands and with the tonsils, and from this resemblance it has derived the name "pharyngeal tonsil."

THE TONSILS.

The tonsil consists essentially of a reduplication, more or less extensive, of the oral mucous membrane, containing in its folds an abundance of the so-called adenoid tissue.

Its *gross structure* varies in different animals. In some the organ is entirely absent. Its simplest form is found in the rabbit, where it resembles a large lingual follicular gland. In man its usual shape is ovoid. Its average vertical diameter is 20 mm., and its transverse diameter 13 mm. Its surface is perforated by a varying number of slit-like and circular depressions, the common orifices of the system of cavities which it contains. If the tonsil of the rabbit be considered a single follicular gland, we have in man a multiplication of this to the number of from eight to eighteen, the interval between each gland forming a "lacuna tonsillaris," crypt, or one of the system of cavities mentioned above. There are also in the interior of the tonsil single larger cavities, each of which includes several follicular folds and procures their common discharge at the periphery. The crypts generally are filled, more or less, with a yellowish substance composed of fat-molecules, detached pavement-epithelium, lymph-corpuscles, small molecular granules, and cholesterin-crystals, which probably proceed from retained and decomposed epithelial matter, and perhaps now and then from the bursting of follicles whose cells have increased by proliferation and have undergone retrograde metamorphosis and fatty degeneration. In its minute anatomy the tonsil is for the most part like other so-called adenoid glands. In common with the rest of the oral cavity, it is invested with a thick covering of pavement-epithelium, which rests upon a delicate endothelioid basement-membrane. Following this is a tolerably compact mucosa, formed of interlacing bands of fibrous connective tissue and containing many connective-tissue corpuscles. In the normal adult tonsil this structure is so delicate that sometimes it is hardly recognizable. From it bands of connective tissue extend centrally into the larger tonsillary folds, and the whole forms essentially both an enclosure and a framework for the adenoid tissue or proper substance of the gland, as well as a nidus for its vessels. The minute structure of the adenoid tissue of the tonsil does not differ from that of other follicular glands (those of the intestine, etc.), described elsewhere. Occasionally in the tonsil the adenoid tissue extends so near the periphery as to penetrate the mucosa and encroach upon the epithelial layers. This is especially the case in the walls of the crypts, where the epithelium commonly exists in a modified form, or is altogether wanting. The tonsil is supplied abundantly with racemose mucous glands, which are most numerous in the neighborhood of the hilus. Here, also, may be found small bundles of muscular fibres apparently independent.

BIBLIOGRAPHY.

KÖLLIKER. Ueber das Geruchsorgan von Amphioxus. Müller's Archiv für Anat. und Physiol. 1843.

KOHLRAUSCH. J. Müller's Archiv, pp. 8, 140. 1853.

ECKER. In Berichte über die Verhandlungen zur Beförderung der Naturwiss. No. 12. Fribourg, 1855.

SCHULZE, MAX. Ueber die Endigungsweise der Geruchsnerven und die Epithelial-gebilde der Nasenschleimhaut. Monatsberichte der königl. Acad. der Wissensch. Berlin, 1856.

ECKER. Ueber die Geruchsschleimhaut des Menschen. Zeitschrift f. wiss. Zoologie. VIII., p. 305. 1856.

ECKER, A. Bericht über die Fortschritte, Anatomie und Physiologie f. d. Jahr 1856, p. 117. Von Henle und Meissner.

TODD and BOWMAN. The Physiological Anatomy of Man. II. London, 1856.

SEEBERG. Disquisitiones Microscopicæ de textura membranæ pituitariæ nasi. Diss. Inaug. Dorpati, 1856.

KÖLLIKER. Ausbreitung der Nerven in der Geruchsschleimhaut von Plagiostomen. Sitzber. der physik.-med. Gesellschaft, T. VIII., pp. 81. Würtzburg, 1857.

ERICHSEN. De textura nervi olfactorii ejusque ramorum. Th. inaug. Dorpat, 1857.

HOYER. De tunicæ mucosæ narium structura. Berolini, 1857.

ECKHARDT. Ueber Endigungsweise der Geruchsnerven. Beitrag zur Anatomie und Physiologie. 4. Abhand., p. 97. 1858.

GASTALDI. Nuovi Ricerche sopra la terminazione del nervo olfactorio, in memorie de l'Acad. reale della Scienza de Torino. XVII., p. 372. 1858.

FUNKE, O. Lehrbuch der Physiologie. 2. Auflage. 1858.

KÖLLIKER. Handbuch der Gewebelehre. 3. Auflage, p. 680. 1859.

HOYER. Ueber die mikroskopischen Verhältnisse der Nasenschleimhaut. In Müller's Archiv f. Anat. und Physiolog., 1861, p. 287; 1860, p. 6.

CLARKE, LOCKHART. Ueber den Bau des Bulbus olfactorius und der Geruchs-schleimhaut. Zeitsch. f. wissens. Zoologie. XI. 1862.

WALTER, G. Ueber den feineren Bau des Bulbus olfactorius. Virchow's Arch., T. XXII., p. 261. 1862.

HENLE. Handbuch der systematischen Anatomie des Menschen. Bd. II. Braunschweig, 1866.

ZERNOFF. Ueber das Geruchsorgan der Cephalopoden. Bull. de la Soc. imp. des sc. nat. de Moscow. 2e série. XLII. 1869.

EXNER. Weitere Studien über die Structur der Riechschleimhaut bei Wirbelthieren. Sitzungsberichte der k. Akad. der Wissenschaften. Wien. Band LXV, 3. Abth. 1872. Et Bd. LIII. 1867–1869.

376 MANUAL OF HISTOLOGY.

HEIDENHAIN, A. Ueber die acinösen Drüsen der Schleimhäute, ins besondere der Nasenschleimhaut. Diss. Inaug. Breslau, 1870.

SCHULZE, MAX. Untersuchungen über den Bau der Nasenschleimhaut. In Abhandlung. d. naturforsch. Gesellschaft. VII. Halle, 1872.

BABUCHIN. Das Geruchsorgan. In Stricker's Handbuch. 1872.

MARTIN. Studies from the Physiol. Lab. in the University of Cambridge. I. 1873.

CISOFF. Zur Kenntniss der Regio Olfactoria. Centralblatt. 1874.

BIGELOW, H. J. On the Anat. of the Turbinated Corpora Cavernosa. Boston, Med. and Surg. Journal. April, 25, 1875.

SHOFIELD, R. N. A. Taste-Goblets in the Epiglottis of the Dog and Cat. Journal of Anat. and Physiol. X., p. 475. 1876.

HÖNIGSCHMIED. Ztschr. f. wiss. Zool. XXIX., S. 255. 1877.

DAVIS, C. Die becherförmigen Organe des Kehlkopfes. Arch. f. mikroskop. Anat., XIV., S. 158. 1877.

PODWISOTZKY. Anatomische Untersuchungen über die Zungendrüsen des Menschen und der Säugethiere. Inaugural Dissertation. Dorpat, 1878.

LÖWE. Beiträge zur Anatomie der Nase und Mundhöhle. S. 20. Berlin, 1878.

ZUCKERKANDL. Ueber die norm. med.-path. Anat. der Nasen- und angrenzenden Höhlen. All. Wien. med. Ztg., No. 51. 1879.

STEINBRÜGGE, H. The Histology of the Inferior Turbinated Bones and of the Tele-angiectatic Fibromata Arising from These. Archives of Otology, New York, Oct., 1879.

CHAPTER XXIII.

THE MOUTH AND TONGUE.

By D. BRYSON DELAVAN, M.D.,

Member of the American Laryngological Association.

WITH the exception of a few remarkable modifications, the structure of the mucous membrane of the buccal cavity is the same throughout.

The *tunica propria* consists of fibrillated connective tissue, made up of tolerably minute bundles of intertwining filaments. Between these appear many delicate, elastic fibres. Toward the epithelium this structure becomes less distinct, and an exceedingly delicate, filamentous network is developed. The connective-tissue cells with their nuclei, on the other hand, become more marked. The surface of the tunica propria contains many slender papillæ, which penetrate more or less deeply into the epithelial covering. They have, also, the above-mentioned filamentous structure, but contain few cellular elements.

The transition of the tunica propria into *submucous connective tissue* is, in general, hardly perceptible. The latter, however, contains fewer elastic filaments and broader bundles of connective tissue. The *epithelium* lining the buccal cavity is, throughout, stratified pavement. The mucous membrane of the mouth varies in different regions as to the thickness of its different strata, the height of its papillæ, and the condition of the submucous tissue. It is thickest and firmest in the gums and near the palate—particularly in the posterior section of the hard palate—and thinnest in its reduplications, *e.g.*, the frœnum linguæ, glosso-epiglottic fold, and the pillars of the fauces. Its firmness in the above places is due to the density of the submucosa, which forms, with the underlying periosteum, one compact mass of connective tissue.

Elsewhere the mucosa is looser, so that the mucous membrane is readily thrown into folds. It is thickest wherever it has intervening layers of glands. In some places, especially in the lips and soft palate, the submucosa is crossed by bundles of striped muscular fibres, which are connected partly with the submucosa, and partly with the tunica propria. The *papillæ* of the mucous membrane are most developed at the margin of the lip and its immediate vicinity, as well as on the gums, attaining here a height of 0.5 mm., and often terminating in a double point. In the reduplications of the mucous membrane (the frænum linguæ, etc.), and partly in the region of the hard palate, the papillæ are very small, sometimes rudimentary. The thickness of the epithelial layer is proportionate to the height of the papillæ. Beginning at the vermilion border of the lips, and going backward, the epithelial covering becomes progressively thicker, and is thickest at the posterior margin of the lip, decreasing rapidly on the posterior surface. Upon the cheeks and on the anterior surface of the hard palate the epithelium is of medium thickness; it is thinnest on the floor of the mouth and on the above-mentioned reduplications. There are, however, deviations in these proportions, especially in the hard palate, where the papillæ are in some cases absent. Moreover, the tunica propria sometimes assumes an almost tendinous character. Certain important aggregations of glands, the so-called *mucous glandules,* are found lodged in the submucous connective tissue of the mouth. These are the labial, buccal, palatal, and molar glandules. They are found as white, sharply defined knobs, visible to the naked eye upon the posterior surface of the lips, as well as upon the cheeks, palate, and bottom of the buccal cavity. In some cases they are aggregated into a few large clusters, while in others they are more scattered and smaller. The orifices of their ducts are best seen in the lining membrane by everting the lips or cheek. They belong to the acinous type, and have a short duct, generally somewhat curved, relatively wide, but somewhat contracted at the orifice. The greatest width of the tubes is at their place of segmentation. On the branches themselves are smaller ramifications, which either terminate directly with globular or ellipsoid alveoli, or previously divide into one or more twigs. It often happens that a small group of acini, with a narrow common duct, situated near a larger duct, discharge into the latter near the surface of the mucous membrane, appearing like a small accessory glandule. The walls of the glandules consist of a structureless basement-membrane, upon the interior surface of which are superimposed cylindrical, clear, almost homogeneous-looking cells, with oblong nuclei.

As for the connection of the buccal mucous membrane with the underlying structures, different conditions obtain in different regions. Its connection with the hard palate and gums has been described above. Where it is superimposed upon a sharply defined muscle, e.g., over the floor of the mouth, and over the sublingual gland, it passes into the connective-tissue sheath of the part.

The *blood-vessels* of the mucous membrane are arranged in two systems of superficially extended networks. The deeper one, located in the submucosa, is composed of the mutually anastomosing branches of the afferent and efferent vessels. From this network many smaller vessels penetrate into the tunica propria, which, by division into still smaller branches, and by frequent anastomoses with one another, form the more superficial and finer-meshed vascular net. In both nets the venous and arterial branches run tolerably parallel. From the superficial network very fine branches enter the papillæ, where, according to their size, they form either capillary nets or simple loops.

The *lymphatics* form wide networks in the submucosa, and narrow nets in the tunica propria. Single small vessels cross those of the vascular nets. That lymphatics penetrate the papillæ is doubtful. The *nerves* of the buccal mucous membrane form in the submucosa more or less dense plexuses, in which many separations of the single nerve-fibrils may be noticed. Thence numerous filaments, partly isolated, partly arranged in small bundles, and always medullated, ramify, and radiate in wider ramifications toward the superficial layers of the mucous membrane. A certain number of *nerve-fibrils* approach the papillæ, to implant themselves either at their bases or at the centre of their apices, sometimes even at their extremities, in the terminal bulbs of Krause. Such fibrils are most abundant in the lips and in the anterior surface of the velum palati, and in smaller quantity in the cheek and bottom of the mouth. Nerve-fibrils may sometimes be seen also with double contours, which wind, during their course, into a coil in the superficial layers of the mucous membrane.

THE TONGUE.

Although the mucous membrane of the tongue is, in the general details of its construction, similar to that of the rest of the buccal cavity, it nevertheless presents some striking peculiarities, mainly due to the configuration of its upper surface. This is covered by many closely aggregated prominences of the mucous membrane—the *lingual papillæ*—which give it a roughened, fungoid appearance. Upon the under surface of the tongue the papillæ are absent, but the mucous membrane here contains a large number of follicular glands. The lateral edges of the tongue are here and there covered with lingual papillæ, which are often arranged in rows, and toward the base of the tongue are replaced by the so-called *fimbriæ linguæ*. Besides simple papillæ, analogous to those of the skin, the lingual mucosa is studded with three distinct varieties of compound papillæ—the filiform, the fungiform, and the circumvallate. These are distinguished from the ordinary papillæ of the mucous membrane, not only by their large size and their peculiar shapes, but also by their complicated structure, by the arrangement of their secondary papillæ, and the conditions of their epithelial coverings. Between these three forms are several intermediary ones. The *filiform papillæ* are found all over the dorsum of the tongue, anterior to the line of the circumvallate papillæ. Not only in different individuals, but also in the same tongue, there are marked variations in their form. At the tip and lateral edges of the tongue they are always smaller, and their filaments are wanting or merely rudimentary. Toward the centre of the tongue they gradually become larger and more abundant, and attain their highest development in the angle made by the circumvallate papillæ.

Their shape is that of a truncated cone, which has at its free extremity a central hollow or depression, around which is arranged, in a circular manner, a collection of thread-like projections, or secondary papillæ. Like the rest of the mucous membrane of the tongue, they are covered with stratified pavement-epithelium. In the secondary papillæ of the larger filiform papillæ the epithelium is of the horny variety, and its arrangement is imbricated, the lower margin of each scale overlapping the upper border of the scale next below it. In the axes of the filiform papillæ large-sized arterial and venous capillaries extend. Each secondary papilla contains a vascular loop. The papillæ of smallest size contain a fine network of vessels, and in the posterior part of the tongue simple capillary loops. Neither the filiform papillæ nor their secondary papillæ contain nerve-fibrils. The latter are found, however, at the base of the papillæ, where they end in rounded terminal bulbs.

The *fungiform papillæ* are larger than the filiform, and their epithelial covering is much thinner. They appear as rounded prominences, somewhat constricted at the base, and covered upon the sides and top with many cone-shaped secondary papillæ. The free surface of some fungiform papillæ is smooth, the secondary papillæ being farther apart. These are found most commonly at the lateral edges of the tongue, and are the so-called lenticular papillæ. The distribution of the fungiform papillæ is rather irregular, and it varies in different individuals. At the base of the tongue, and generally at its lateral portions, between the filiform papillæ, they are sometimes scarce and sometimes quite abundant. Toward the tip of the tongue they are smaller, while they are larger in the region of the circumvallate papillæ. They are covered with several layers of pavement-epithelium, the deeper strata of which are formed by smaller polygonal prickle-cells. In this epithelial covering, upon the surface of the fungiform papillæ, are constantly found peculiar bodies, called the "taste-goblets."

The *taste-goblets* vary in size and shape in different animals, and also in the same animal, according to the locality in which they are found. They usually resemble a short-necked flask, their longest diameter being the longitudinal. The lower part of the taste-goblet rests upon the submucosa ; the body, and more especially the part which corresponds to the neck of the flask, is surrounded by epithelial cells. Every taste-goblet has at the surface of the epithelium an opening called a *porus*, which word is frequently used not only to designate the exterior opening, but also for the entire short canal in the epithelial layer. The diameter of the porus is from .0064 to .0198 mm. It is surrounded by two and sometimes by

three similarly formed cells. Sometimes the porus is formed
by a single perforated cell. The short canal in the epithelial
cells is surrounded in like manner. In each taste-goblet two
varieties of cells may be distinguished—the exterior or superficial cells, called roof- or supporting-cells, and the interior, or
central cells, called taste- or rod-cells. The roof-cells, which
may be considered as modified epithelial cells, surround the
taste-goblets as petals envelop a bud. Their arrangement with
relation to one another is imbricated. The cells themselves
are long, narrow, spindle-shaped, and curved, and each one
has a well-marked nucleus. The peripheral end of the cell is
pointed, while the central extremity is sometimes ramified.
The taste- or rod-cells are long, slender, and highly refractive.
A nucleus of unusual size almost entirely fills their bodies, while
their extremities pass into two distinct prolongations—the peripheral or superior, and the central or inferior. The peripheral
prolongation is moderately broad, and has a short, delicate
extremity, which resembles a small rod or hair. Hence the
name rod-cell. These rods are located inside the short canal,
and rarely project above the porus. The inferior prolongation
is divided into several rootlets. The connection of nerve-filaments with the taste-goblets has never yet been conclusively
demonstrated, although all authorities agree as to the probability of such connection. Many aggregations of ganglionic
cells, of greater or less size, are found in the course of the
nerve-bundles, near the circumvallate as well as near the filiform papillæ. In the fungiform papillæ the nerves enter the
axis of the papillæ as small trunks, composed of fibres with
double contours. These divide into single nerve-filaments,
some of which terminate in bulbs, which are located in the lateral surfaces of the fungiform papillæ, under the secondary
papillæ. The fibrils which run into the axis pass into pale terminal filaments, and disappear in a brush-like extremity in a
granular mass composed of neurilemma—its nuclei, and numerous circular granules—the gustatory granules. These last
consist of a globular nucleus, surrounded by a very small
amount of cell-protoplasm. The resemblance of the above to
the interior roof-cells of the acoustic terminal apparatus, and
to the rods and cones of the retina, is striking.

The conical or secondary papillæ are of the same general
construction as the fungiform throughout; but they present

the following differences of appearance : their epithelial covering is thicker, and stratified somewhat after the manner of the filiform papillæ, the taste-goblets are absent upon their surface, and the nerve-fibres, so far as they can be traced, terminate in bulbs.

The *circumvallate papillæ*, about nine in number, are situated at the back part of the tongue. They form an irregular row on each side and incline slightly from before backward toward the median line. At their point of junction is the *foramen cæcum* of Morgagni. Each circumvallate papilla consists of a broad, flat elevation of the mucous membrane, which is surrounded with a fossa. Its surface is covered with small secondary papillæ, and the epithelium is like that of the fungiform papillæ. Taste-goblets are found abundantly upon the lateral edges and toward the centre of the papillæ. The blood-vessels are arranged as in the fungiform papillæ, and each secondary papilla contains a vascular loop. The nerves are derived from the glosso-pharyngeal. They consist of single pale nerve-fibres, which form a network in the centre of the papillæ and ascend toward its peripheral surface.

The *papillæ foliatæ*, or fimbriæ linguæ, consist of several folds of the mucous membrane at the lateral edges of the tongue. Between them are scattered a few fungiform papillæ, and they contain a considerable number of taste-goblets. Many excretory ducts of acinous glands empty at the bases of these folds.

The sublingual mucous membrane includes that of the floor of the mouth. Both are of the same structure, and pass into each other by means of a reduplication, the frænum linguæ.

The secreting glands of the root of the tongue are of two varieties—serous and mucous. The mucous glands are like those elswhere in the buccal cavity. Their ducts are sometimes lined with ciliated epithelium. The glands themselves are not found in the neighborhood of the taste-goblets. The serous glands, on the other hand, are found most abundantly in those parts of the tongue which are most richly supplied with taste-goblets. Their ducts open into the grooves which are lined by the taste-goblets.

The follicular glands, which form the collections of adenoid tissue found at the base and at the sides of the tongue, are not true glands, but rather elevations of the mucous membrane caused by circumscribed collections of adenoid tissue found in the tunica propria. They resemble glands, in that they generally possess a cavity of variable size which terminates at the surface of the follicle. The mass of adenoid tissue which composes the follicle is surrounded by fibres of connective tissue, which are sometimes so compactly woven as to form almost a capsule around it. Sometimes this capsule is wanting, but a gradual transition of the two neighboring forms of tissue is never seen. Above, the adenoid tissue extends as far as the epithelium, so that the papillæ of the mucous membrane either disappear altogether or are only to be found occasionally, and then of small size. This adenoid tissue is in all its essentials similar to that found in the tonsils, the vault of the pharynx, and at scattered points in the adjacent tissues.

The so-called mucous corpuscles of the saliva are probably lymph corpuscles which have escaped from the adenoid tissue just mentioned.

BIBLIOGRAPHY.

ALBINUS. Academicarum Annotationum. Lib. I. S. 58. (Quoted by J. Hönig-schmied.) Leidæ, 1754.

BOPP. Die Verrichtungen des fünften Nervenpaares. Leipsig, 1832.

ELSÄSSER, in F. Majendie Lehrbuch der Physiologie, aus dem Französischen über-setzt mit Anmerkungen und Zusätzen von D. C. L. Elsässer. 3 Aufl. I. Tü-bingen, 1834.

MAYER, J. F. C. Neue Untersuchungen aus dem Gebiete der Anatomie und Phy-siologie. S. 25 und 26. Bonn, 1842.

BRÜHL. Ueber das Mayer'sche Organ an der Zunge der Haus-Säugethiere oder die seitliche Zungenrücken-Drüse derselben. Vierteljahrschrift für wiss. Veter-inärkunde. I. S. 165. Wien, 1851. Kleine Beiträge zur Anatomie der Haus-Säugethiere. Wien, 1850.

KÖLLIKER, A. Microscopische Anatomie. II. Specielle Gewebelehre. 2. Hälfte. 1. Abth. Leipzig, 1852.

SCHWALBE. Das Epithel der Papillæ vallatæ. Vorläufige Mittheilung. Arch. f. microscop. Anat. III. S. 504. 1867. Derselbe Ueber die Geschmacks-organe d. Säugethiere und des Menschen. Arch. f. microscop. Anat. IV. S. 154. 1867. Und M. Schultze, Erklärung der Entdeckung der Schmeck-becher von G. Schwalbe betreffend. Arch. f. mikroskop. Anat. VIII. S. 600. 1872.

LOVEN. Beiträge zur Kentniss vom Bau der Geschmackswärzchen der Zunge. Arch. f. mikroskop. Anat. IV. S. 96. 1867.

SCHWALBE. Zur Kentniss der Papillæ fungiformes d. Säugethiere. Centralblatt f. d. med. Wiss. Nr. 28. S. 433. 1868.

VON WYSS. Ueber ein neues Geschmacksorgan auf der Zunge des Kaninchens. Centralblatt f. d. med. Wiss. Nr. 35. S. 548. 1869. Derselbe, Die becherförmigen Organe der Zunge. M. Schultze. Arch. für mikroskop. Anat. VI. S. 238.

KRAUSE. Die Nervenendigung in der Zunge des Menschen. Göttinger Nachrichten. S. 423. 1870.

VERSON. Beiträge zur Kentniss des Kehlkopfes und der Trachea. Sitzgsbr. der wiener Acad. 1 Abth. LVII. S. 1093. 1868. Derselbe, Kehlkopf und Trachea in Strickers Handbuch der Lehre von den Geweben. I. S. 456. Leipzig, 1871.

HÖNIGSCHMIED, J. Beiträge zur mikroskop. Anatomie der Geschmacksorgane. Ztschr. f. wissensch. Zool. XXIII. S. 414.

EXNER. Med. chirurg. Rundschau. Juni Heft. S. 400. Wien, 1872.

DITLEVSEN. Undersøgelse over Smaglögene paatungun hos patte dyrene og mennesket. Kopenhagen, 1872. Referat in Hoffmann und Schwalbe Jahresb. I. Lib. S. 211. 1872.

HÖNIGSCHMIED. Ein Beitrag üb. die Verbreitung der becherförmigen Organe auf der Zunge der Säugethiere. Centralbl. f. d. med. Wiss. No. 26. S. 401. 1872.

HENLE. Handbuch der system. Anatomie des Menschen. II. 2. Aufl. S. 873. 1873.

VON EBNER, RITTER. Die acinösen Drüsen der Zunge und ihre Beziehungen zu den Geschmacksorganen. Gratz, 1873.

SERTOLI, E. Osservazioni sulle terminazioni dei nervi del gusto. Gazetta Medico-Veterinaria. IV. 2. Separatabdruck. Deutsch in Molesch. Unters. XI. 4. Heft. S. 403. 1874.

HOFFMANN, A. Ueber die Verbreitung der Geschmacksorgane beim Menschen. Arch. f. pathol. Anat. LXII. S. 516. 1875.

WATSON, W. SPENCER. Diseases of the Nose and its Accessory Cavities. London, 1875.

VON BRUNN. Untersuchungen über das Riechepithelium. Arch. f. mik. Anat. No. 11. 1875.

KRAUSE, W. Allgemeine und mikroskop. Anat. Hannover, 1876.

VOLTOLINI. Address delivered December 15, 1876, before the Silesian Association for National Culture.

KRAUSE. Lehrbuch. Hannover, 1876.

KÖLLIKER. Ueber die Jacobson'schen Organe des Menschen. Festschrift zu Rineckers Jubiläum. Leipzig, 1877.

PONCHET et TOURNEUX. Précis d'histologie humaine. 1878.

LUSCHKA. Das Epithelium der Riechschleimhaut des Menschen. Centralbl. f. die med Wissenschaft. Nr. 22. 1877.

WUNDT. Lehrbuch der Physiologie des Menschen. Stuttgart, 1878.

25

CHAPTER XXIV.

THE ALIMENTARY CANAL.

By EDMUND C. WENDT, M.D.,

Curator of the St. Luke's and St. Francis' Hospitals, etc., New York City.

THE human alimentary canal is a tube of great length, extending from the mouth to the anus. There are considerable variations of its calibre in the different regions of the body through which it passes. The two external openings of the digestive tract are continuous with the cutaneous surface of the body. Throughout its entire extent we find several superimposed layers or membranes, which are from within outward: 1, a mucous membrane with its submucosa; 2, the muscular coat; and 3, a fibrous layer. In addition to these fundamental strata, we encounter certain special structures, which characterize the various parts of the canal. The buccal cavity and pharynx are elsewhere described; we begin, therefore, with a consideration of

THE ŒSOPHAGUS.

The walls of this section of the tract are directly continuous with those of the pharynx, and have an average thickness of from three to four millimetres. In the œsophagus, in addition to the four pharyngeal coats, a new layer appears between the epithelial stratum and the submucous tissue. This new structure has received the name of muscularis mucosæ. Hence, the different layers of the œsophagus are from within outward:

1. The mucous membrane.
2. The muscularis mucosæ
3. A submucous layer.
4. The muscular coat.
5. A fibrous envelope.

The *mucous membrane* presents comparatively long, conical papillæ of more or less dense connective tissue, containing looped blood-vessels, and lined throughout by stratified pavement-epithelium. These papillæ attain a marked degree of development in the adult only. In infancy their future presence is indicated by a wavy outline at the internal attached border of the epithelial stratum. This latter portion of the mucous membrane contributes 0.22 —0.26 mm. toward the entire œsophageal thickness of about 4.0 millimetres.

The *muscularis mucosæ* consists chiefly of longitudinal, unstriped muscle-cells. They are disposed in bundles of different sizes, separated by varying amounts of connective tissue. Toward the inferior portion of the œsophagus these bundles approach each other, displacing the interposed tissue, and forming finally one continuous muscular layer. The thickness of this layer varies between 0.2 and 0.3 mm.

FIG. 164.—Transverse section through the lower part of the œsophagus of the newly-born child: *a, a,* epithelium ; *b,* mucosa ; *c,* muscularis mucosæ ; *d,* submucous tissue ; *e,* layer of circular muscular fibres : *f,* longitudinal muscular layer ; *g,* external fibrous layer ; *h, h,* two of the ganglia of Auerbach, Klein.

The *submucous layer* is made up of fasciculated connective tissue and elastic fibres. It contains groups of fat-cells, and lodges the mucous glands. The latter closely resemble the glands found in the mouth. They consist of pyramidal or polygonal secreting-cells with conspicuous rounded nuclei, and ducts lined by cylindrical epithelia. The lower portion of the œsophagus contains smaller and more superficial acinous glands. In this region they are also found in greater abundance, and around the cardiac orifice they form almost a complete ring.

The *muscular coat* has an inner circular and an outer longitudinal layer. In man it is formed of both varieties of muscle-cells, the striped and unstriped. The upper portion is composed of striped muscle only, whereas the lower half consists exclusively of the unstriped variety. Below the upper one-eighth of the œsophagus smooth muscle-cells first begin to be blended with the other variety ; they rapidly increase as we proceed

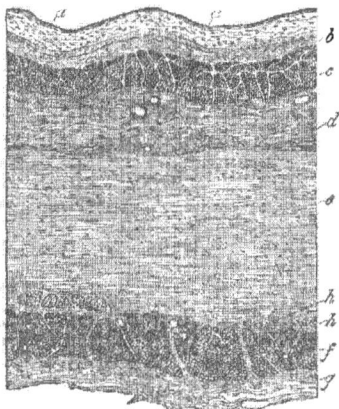

downward, until at about the middle of its course the striped fibres entirely disappear, being replaced by continuous layers of unstriped muscle-cells.

The *fibrous envelope* consists of connective tissue and elastic fibres, arranged so as to form a thin, peripheral, sheath-like membrane.

Blood-vessels and *lymphatics* are found in less abundance in the œsophagus than in the mouth and pharynx. The former are arranged in the shape of capillary networks in the mucosa. The papillary loops, already mentioned, take their origin from these reticula. The larger branches are found in the submucosa. The lymphatics occur as plexuses; one is situated superficially in the mucous membrane, and communicates by capillary vessels, with a second larger one, placed in the submucosa. The glands are said to have special lymphatics.

Nerves.—An elaborate account of the mode of distribution of nerves in the œsophagus is given in Ranvier's "Leçons d'anatomie générale," 1880, p. 366 et seq. The following brief summary gives the main points : Nervous filaments proceeding from the pneumogastrics find their way to the striped muscles, where they terminate in the well-known eminences ordinarily found in that tissue. These terminal bodies are seen to be very numerous, a fact which corresponds to the importance and complexity of nervous action concerned in the process of deglutition. The terminal distribution in the unstriped muscle presents no striking peculiarity. Between the two layers of the muscle-coat we find an arrangement analogous to Auerbach's ganglionic plexus, but the ganglia and their nerve-cells are larger and appear to be more numerous than in the intestine. The nerve-fibres proceeding from the vagus are medullated ; those from the ganglionic plexus belong of course to the non-medullated variety.

THE STOMACH.

The *serous covering* of this organ has the same general structure as all visceral peritoneum, being composed of a connective-tissue membrane lined by flat endothelial cells.

The *muscular coat* of the stomach is divisible into three layers, composed of, 1, external longitudinal fibres ; 2, middle circular ; and 3, internal oblique fibres. All of these belong exclusively to the unstriped variety of muscle-cells. A thickening of the inner circular layer constitutes the pyloric sphincter.

The *submucous layer* is composed of loose connective tissue, and it is for this reason that the mucous membrane is so freely movable over the muscular coat. It is, moreover, owing to this peculiarity that, whenever and wherever muscular contraction takes place, the mucous membrane presents numerous folds, ridges, and elevations. Thus, we may find in a perfectly healthy stomach appearances quite analogous to those described by pathologists as the so-called *état mamelonné* of gastritis.

The *muscularis mucosæ* frequently presents two layers of unstriped muscle-cells—an outer longitudinal and an inner circular one. In some regions we observe only one layer of longitudinal muscle-cells.

The *gastric mucous membrane* is covered by a single layer of columnar epithelium, containing goblet-cells in greater or less abundance. These goblet-cells

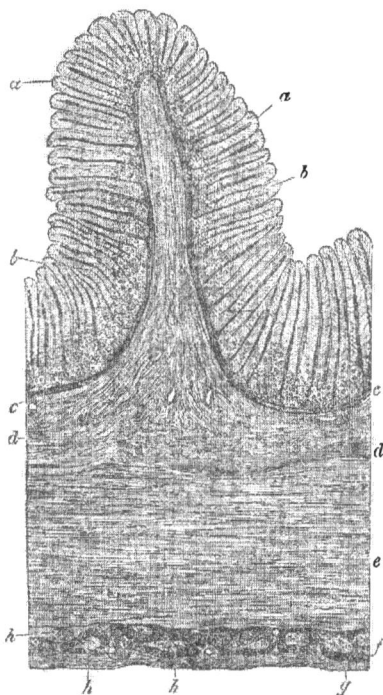

Fig. 165.—Transverse section through the fundus of the stomach in a child: *a, a,* cylindrical epithelium; *b, b,* peptic tubes; *c, c,* muscularis mucosæ; *d, d,* submucous tissue; *e,* circular muscular layer; *f,* longitudinal muscular layer; *g,* peritoneum; *h, h,* ganglion of Auerbach. Klein.

represent ordinary epithelia, which appear to be bulged out by mucoid contents. At the cardiac extremity of the stomach there is a sharp, serrated line of demarcation between the œsophageal and gastric epithelial lining. The surface-epithelium forms one continuous stratum, and is continued down into the ducts of the gastric glands. The latter occur in two distinct varieties, viz., peptic glands and pyloric glands.

The *peptic glands*, also called gastric glands, are cylindrical tubules, nearly straight or slightly tortuous, with often a single rounded cæcal extremity. However, the latter is sometimes double by dichotomous division, or we find many such blind terminal branches. Hence, we may speak of *simple* peptic glands and *compound* peptic glands. They are all placed vertically to the surface, and consist of a homogeneous basement-membrane with a lining of secreting epithelia. (Fig. 166.) The basement-membrane contains flattened nuclei, and at its inner aspect it is furnished with flat, branching adventitial cells. Each gland is divisible into a duct and gland proper. The latter, again, consists of a neck, body, and fundus.

Usually, two, three, or even more of these glands, have a common duct. The length of the entire structure varies in the different gastric regions from 0.4—2.0 mm., in accordance with the thickness of the entire mucous membrane in the respective parts. The duct, amounting to about one-fourth of the whole length of the tube, is lined with one continuous layer of columnar epithelial cells, similar to the surface epithelium of the rest of the stomach. The neck, the thinnest portion of the minute tube, has similar cells; but they appear shorter, darker, and have a smaller ovoid nucleus. As regards its breadth, the body stands about midway between

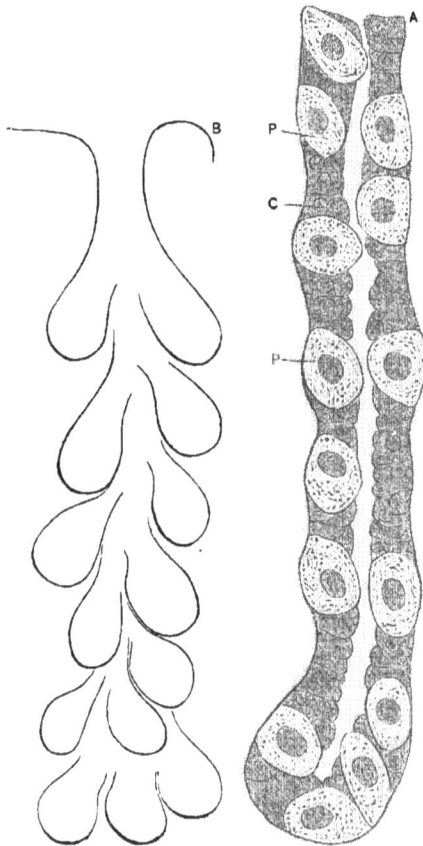

FIG. 166.—A, simple gastric gland: P, parietal; and C, chief cells B, compound gastric gland. Only the outline, denoting the membrana propria, is drawn.

the neck and the fundus, which latter is the thickest portion of the entire gland. In the neck we also find, in addition to the cells already described, other corpuscles placed externally to the former. They are the parietal cells (Heidenhain), or delomorphous cells (Rollett), the former variety being termed chief cells (Heidenhain), or adelomorphous cells (Rollett), or simply peptic cells. The parietal cells occur as spheroidal, oval, or polygonal, rather opaque, sometimes very granular bodies, which lie beneath the basement-membrane, but commonly outside the layer of ordinary chief cells. In the body of the gland-tube we again meet with these two forms of lining-corpuscles. Here, however, the columnar or chief cells are longer than in the neck, and their bodies generally appear more transparent, while the nuclei, again spheroidal, are situated nearer the external than the internal border. Klein describes the substance of these cells as consisting of a delicate reticulum, with a small amount of a hyaline interstitial substance in its meshes. The same author, also, invariably finds an intra-nuclear network. Others have been less fortunate in finding such appearances. The parietal cells of the body in all respects resemble those of the neck. As the fundus is approached their number grows comparatively less.

The *pyloric glands*, which some histologists insist on calling mucous glands, are lined throughout by a single layer of epithelium. This is composed of the ordinary columnar cells of the gastric surface. But the corpuscles here appear to be somewhat compressed, so that they seem less transparent than elsewhere. They are known to undergo certain changes during their passage from activity to rest. Examined in the latter condition, we find them more granular, and apparently smaller or shorter, than during and immediately after secretion. These glands have long ducts, each one serving for several secreting tubules. Their bodies are branched, and usually appear somewhat tortuous. When such glandules become somewhat more complex and grow larger (a change which normally takes place in the duodenum), they are called Brunner's glands.

Dr. Edinger has recently (*Archiv f. mikr. Anat.*, Vol. XVII., p. 193) asserted that the gastric glands contain in reality only one kind of cellular element. He based his opinion on results obtained by treating the almost living mucous membrane with osmic acid, after Nussbaum's method. By him the chief cells are said to develop into parietal cells, through an increase of their volume and a filling up with the gastric ferment. The considerations which led him to form this opinion are as follows : 1, the occurrence of bodies which represent transition-forms between chief cells and parietal cells ; 2, the analogy of this assumed metamorphosis of gastric corpuscles (*i.e.*, the conversion of chief cells into parietal cells), with similar changes, known to occur in other glands during active secretion ; 3, the fact that many animals which secrete pepsin have only the parietal cells ; 4, the results of an examination of the mucous membrane of starving animals, which revealed only the chief-cell form of gastric corpuscles ; and 5, the apparent discrepancy in the descriptions of these bodies by competent histologists—some observers regarding the chief cells, others the parietal cells, as exclusively pepsinogenous.

Still more recently, Stöhr has (*Verhandl. d. phys.-med. Gesel. in Würzburg*, 1881, p. 101) studied the histology of the gastric epithelium. His specimens were derived from the fresh stomach of a criminal immediately after execution of the latter. The man had taken no nourishment for some hours before his death. The principal conclusions of Stöhr are : 1, the epithelia of the mucous glandules are not destroyed during the process of secretion, but, like those of the true gastric glands, continue their existence ; 2, the parietal groups of cells represent those portions of the mucous corpuscles which have not undergone mucoid metamorphosis, being made up of unaltered protoplasm.

From the above contradictory statements it appears that even to-day our intimate knowledge of the gastric mucous membrane, and especially its epithelia, is far from being in a satisfactory condition. It will have to be reserved for future investigations to dispel the uncertainty still existing with regard to some of the most interesting details of the physiologico-histological characteristics of the inner coat of the stomach.

The *blood-vessels* of the stomach have an arrangement similar to that of the œsophagus. In the mucous membrane, however, we find abundant plexuses of capillary vessels surrounding the gastric glands. These networks intercommunicate, and just beneath the surface-epithelium they become especially

close. From this point the veins take their origin. The venous rootlets unite in a stellate manner to form larger branches,
which descend almost vertically and empty into a venous reticulum situated between the glandular layer and the muscularis
mucosæ, and just above a similar arterial network.

Lymphatics abound in the stomach. They appear to
arise from superficial loops, which, anastomosing between the

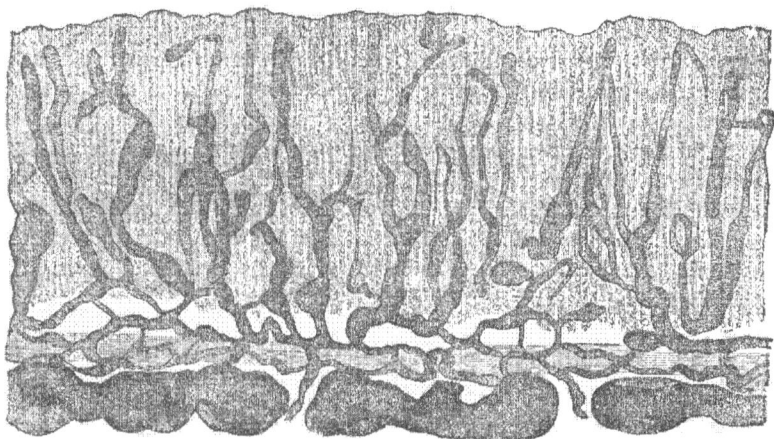

Fig. 167.—Lymphatics of the gastric mucous membrane of the human adult. Frey.

glandular tubules, reach the fundal zone of these structures.
There they form a network, and this is in communication
with a plexus of larger vessels, situated in the submucous
tissue.

The distribution of the *gastric nerves* does not differ materially from that of the small intestine, in the description of
which this matter will receive more particular attention. Ganglion-cells are frequently found both in the muscular layer
and the submucosa; in the latter we have a tolerably distinct
plexus of nerve-filaments and ganglion-cells.

Of the normal occurrence in the walls of the stomach, of
true lymphoid follicles, the author has been unable to find
convincing evidence. Nevertheless some writers assert that
they are always to be found there.

THE SMALL INTESTINE.

The *serous coat* presents no structural characteristics peculiar to itself, closely resembling the gastric peritoneum. It encloses a muscular coat and the mucous membrane, which are held together by connective tissue. The average thickness of these layers does not, in man, exceed 1.0 mm., of which three-fourths belong to the muscular, and one-fourth to the

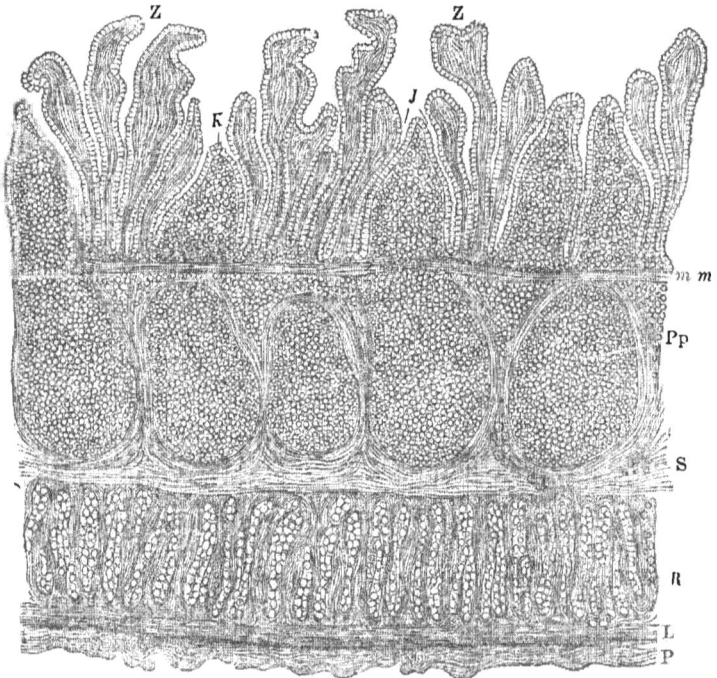

FIG. 168.—Longitudinal section of the small intestine of a rabbit: Z, Z, villi; J, crypts; Pp, a Peyer's patch; K, cap of a follicle; S, submucosa; *m, m*, muscularis mucosæ; R, circular muscular layer; L, longitudinal muscular layer; P, peritoneum. Verson.

mucous coat. Of course, the contracted or relaxed condition of the intestinal tube at the time of measurement will appreciably influence these figures. But they represent the general ordinary average.

The *muscular coat* has an external longitudinal and an internal circular layer. Between the two we find Auerbach's plexus myentericus of flat nerve-fibres, which will be described farther on. The muscle-coat becomes gradually thinner as we pass from the duodenum to the ileo-cæcal valve. In the formation of this thickened fold the longitudinal layer does not participate.

The unstriped muscle-cells have an average length of 0.255 mm., and are about 0.005 mm. broad. They are arranged in bundles, surrounded by connective-tissue bands, with which elastic elements are abundantly interwoven.

The *mucous membrane* is thrown into folds, and is studded with closely placed projections, called villi. The general direction of these folds, the *valvulæ conniventes Kerkringii*, is parallel to the transverse course of the circular muscle-layer. They run parallel to one another, or join at acute angles.

The *villi* jut out into the lumen of the intestinal canal, as variously shaped projections, of an average length of 0.04—0.6 mm., and an average breadth of 0.06—0.12 mm. In general their form may be said to be conical or cylindrical; but we always encounter a great variety of shapes, in accordance with the varying states of contraction in the muscularis mucosæ. Each villus consists of a large-meshed reticulum of connective tissue, infiltrated, as it were, with leucocytes, and containing flattened corpuscles, which resemble endothelial cells. One or several spaces, situated in the centre of every villus, constitute the origin of the lacteal tubes. According to Brücke, these chyle-vessels are covered by thin, but

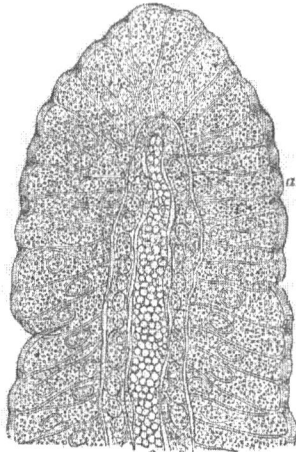

FIG. 169.—Section of a villus from the intestine of a rabbit: *a*, epithelium; *b*, stroma; *c*, central cavity. Verson.

not continuous bundles of smooth muscle-fibres. Their walls show only a single layer of ordinary endothelial cells, with clear oval nuclei. The free surface of the villi, like that of the stomach, is covered by a single layer of columnar epithelium. Each cell presents, in the recent state, a finely striated hyaline band at its unattached border. This structure has, at different times, received various interpretations, and even now opinions are much divided as to its true significance. Some histologists regard the striæ as indicating so many minute pores for purposes of absorptive transmission; others believe that the juxtaposition of numerous delicate rods explains the peculiar appearance; and Klein has lately asserted them to be merely prolongations of the fibrils of the cell-substance composing the epithelia. These striæ are always seen to run parallel to the long axis of the cells.

Krause also described as of normal occurrence, a basal process extending at an obtuse angle from the attached surface of these bodies, and inserted into the delicately serrated border of the villi. Near its attached border each epithelium presents a bright ovoid nucleus, with one or more distinct nucleoli. Besides the ordinary corpuscles, we find interposed between them the so-called goblet-cells. These are derived from the former by mucoid infiltration of the cell-body, which is therefore conspicuously bulged out. Lymph-corpuscles also occur between the epithelia.

Immediately beneath this layer we find a delicate, homogeneous *basement-membrane*, composed of flattened cells, resembling endothelia.

The *muscularis mucosæ*, or muscle of Brücke, is made up of a single or double layer of smooth muscle-cells. When double, an inner circular may be distinguished from an external longitudinal coat, both being always very attenuated.

The *submucous layer* is formed of connective tissue, the supporting framework of which contains lymphatics, blood-vessels, nerves, and often groups of fat-cells.

The *glands of the small intestine* are those of Brunner and the crypts of Lieberkühn. In addition to these, however, there occur numerous lymphoid follicles, which, when found singly, are known as the *solitary follicles*, and, when grouped together, as agminated glands, or *Peyer's patches*. The solitary or closed follicles are real lymphoid glands, and, like these, consist of reticulated connective tissue, the meshes of which are replete with lymph-corpuscles. The jejunum, ileum, and colon all contain such follicles, but the agminated glands occur in the ileum, abounding especially at its lower part. Around each follicle we find a ring of villi and glands, which arrangement goes by the name of *corona tubulorum* (Müller). The follicles receive an enveloping layer of fibro-connective tissue.

Brunner's glands lie in the submucosa, where they form closely crowded tubules, separated by a small amount of connective tissue. Smooth muscle-cells, starting from the muscularis mucosæ, are often seen to pass between them. These convoluted tubules resemble and correspond to the gastric glands, but have here attained a much greater degree of development.

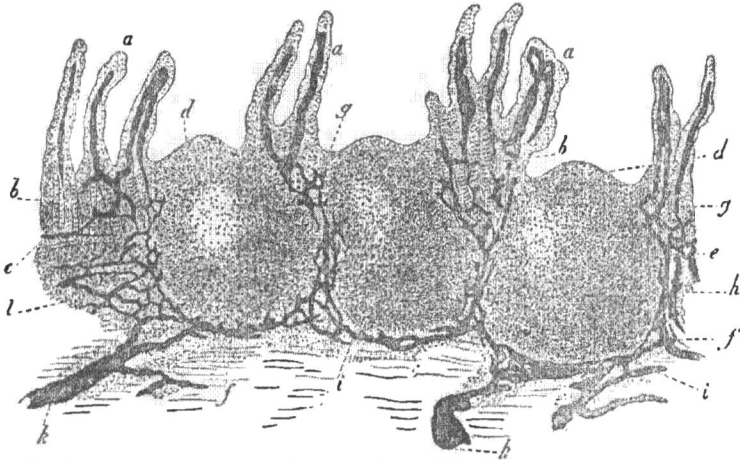

FIG. 170.—Vertical section through a human Peyer's patch, with its lymphatics injected: *a*, intestinal villi with their lacteals; *b*, Lieberkühnian glands; *c*, muscular layer of the mucous membrane; *d*, apex of the follicle; *e*, middle zone of the follicle; *f*, basis portion of the follicle; *g*, continuation of the lacteals of the intestinal villi into the mucous membrane proper; *h*, reticular expansion of the lymphatics in the middle zone; *i*, their course at the base of the follicle; *k*, continuation into the lymphatics of the submucous tissue; *l*, follicular tissue in the latter. Frey.

They also appear to have been pushed down, as it were, from the mucous into the submucous layer.

An individual gland consists of its long duct lined by columnar epithelium, and the branched tubules, which frequently have terminal clusters, resembling true acini. They are, however, only secondary or tertiary diverticula, so that Brunner's glands really conform to the compound tubular type of secreting structures (Renaut). Each ultimate diverticulum has an external membrana propria composed of flattened endothelial cells, and a lining of cylindrical, columnar, or prismatic secreting epithelia, containing oval nuclei.

Histologists have described minute capillary channels proceeding from the central lumen of the gland, between the secreting-cells, ending just underneath the membrana propria. The author believes these intercellular channels, as they have

been called, to be the artificially altered cement-substance always present between such adjacent cells. Brunner's glands
abound only in the duodenum, but a few may occasionally be
seen lower down the intestine. Their ducts, after traversing
the muscularis mucosæ, ascend almost vertically between the
crypts, opening on the free surface of the mucous membrane. -

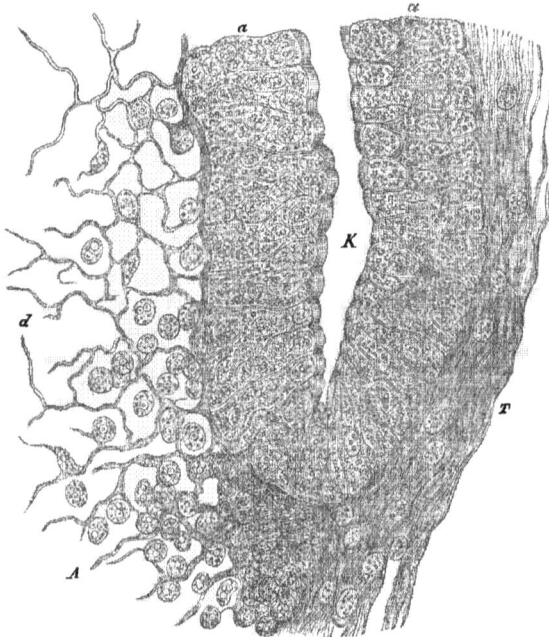

Fig. 171.—Crypts and interfollicular connective tissue, from the intestine of the rabbit: K, crypt:
a, a, epithelium; d, adenoid tissue, from which the cells have been removed by pencilling; T, fibrous
tissue on the opposite side. Verson.

These crypts represent open spaces within the so-called
follicles of Lieberkühn, which are tubular glands placed vertically in the intestinal mucous membrane, existing throughout
its entire extent.

They form a continuous layer, except where the upward
projection of a lymph-follicle creates an interruption. These
glands open at the base of the villi, the epithelial covering of
the latter being continued down into the tubular depressions
which they constitute in the mucous membrane. The cells of
this stratum naturally appear broader at their attached than at

their free extremities. A continuation of the villous basement-membrane forms the membrana propria of the crypts of Lieberkühn. External to this we find the surrounding connective tissue, which is disposed in reticula, containing many leucocytes in its meshes. Hence it is also known as adenoid tissue.

The *blood-vessels* enter and leave the intestine at the mesenteric margin. The arteries, generally accompanied by one or two veins, pierce the muscle-coat, giving off branches which form networks in those layers, then enter the submucosa, where they run parallel to the surface of the mucous membrane, and finally send off vertical arterioles at the base of the villi. The latter ascend on one side of the villus, and then suddenly divide into a dense capillary network. This division takes place near the middle, the capillaries then spreading out to the apex and periphery. Here they become quite superficial, being covered by the epithelial lining only. The venous rootlets of the villus are generally two, or even three in number. About the glands and follicles we encounter special networks with variously shaped meshes.

Lymphatics are found in all the layers of the intestinal canal. Those of the serous coat empty into the large mesenteric trunks. In an inward direction we also find a network of lymph-capillaries between the two layers of the muscle-coat. The submucous layer contains the perifollicular lymph-sinuses situated at the base of these bodies, and a reticulum of larger channels, many of which are found provided with valves. The lymphatics of the mucous membrane are present in the shape of capillary networks surrounding the intestinal glands.

In the villi we note, as already stated, one or more central lacteals, communicating at the base of these structures with the lymph-vascular networks situated around and between the glands.

The *nerves* of the intestine are known as the *plexus of Auerbach*, and of *Meissner*. The former, situated between the circular and longitudinal fibres of the musculosa, is composed of flattened nerve-branches, made up of numerous ultimate fibrils. Small nodules, containing characteristic ganglion-cells, are also found, while little twigs are given off from the plexus myentericus, to be distributed to the layers of the musculosa.

The *plexus of Meissner* is situated in the submucous tissue. Its component nerves are less flattened, but are likewise provided with ganglia containing variously shaped ganglion-cells. This plexus also gives origin to the secondary networks of the muscularis mucosæ, and is besides connected by certain branches with Auerbach's plexus.

The histological structure of the colon, broadly speaking, very nearly resembles that of the preceding section of the alimentary canal. The lining epithelium of the mucous membrane presents the same characteristic appearances as in the

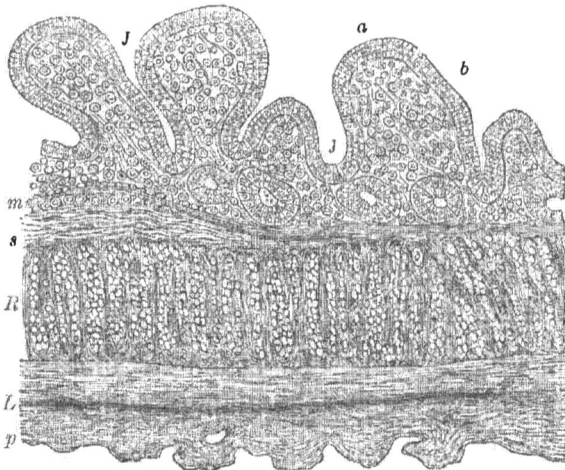

FIG. 172.—Section of the large intestine of a rabbit: *J*, crypts of Lieberkühn ; *a*, epithelium ; *b*, mucosa ; *m*, muscularis mucosæ ; *s*, submucosa : *R*, circular muscular layer ; *L*, longitudinal muscular layer ; *p*, peritoneum. Verson.

small intestine. The mucosa of the colon is, however, devoid of villi ; but it shows numerous crescentic folds. The muscularis mucosæ will be found to answer to the description already given of that layer in the small intestine.

The submucosa also shows the same morphological composition, but appears to be much richer in deposits of fat-cells. Aggregations of lymph-follicles are not generally found, but large, conspicuous solitary glands abound throughout.

The crypts of Lieberkühn are identical with the glands of

the same name found in the small intestine. As we approach the rectum an increase in their length becomes apparent.

In the *vermiform appendix* we find the collection of solitary lymph-follicles so closely placed that the space left between adjoining glands does not equal in diameter that of these structures themselves.

The longitudinal layer of the muscle-coat is quite thin between the tæniæ coli, or flat longitudinal bands of the large intestine. These bands themselves represent thickened layers of the musculosa. It appears that the circular fibres are especially developed in the portions between the sacculi of the cæcum and colon.

The *blood-vessels* are arranged after the same plan as in the small intestine. In the submucosa are contained large trunks, running parallel to the surface. Capillaries arise from these, and ascend almost vertically between the crypts of Lieberkühn, the capillary network surrounding those structures being only moderately developed.

As regards the *lymphatics*, they have a distribution similar in all essential respects to that found in the small intestine.

The *nerves* likewise imitate in their structure and arrangement those encountered in the small intestine. Meissner's plexus appears to be provided with comparatively large ganglia and relatively small component cells. The plexus of Auerbach also attains conspicuous development in the large intestine.

THE RECTUM.

The internal sphincter ani represents a thickening of the circular layer of the muscle-coat. In its upper portion the rectal mucous membrane is like the same structure of the large intestine. Lower down we find the columnar epithelium gradually replaced by stratified pavement-epithelium.

The follicles of Lieberkühn are large and long. Finally, the mucous membrane gradually passes into the ordinary integument surrounding the anal orifice.

The blood-vessels, lymphatics, and nerves resemble in their distribution those of the colon, and are devoid of characteristic peculiarities.

26

BIBLIOGRAPHY.

BŒHM.   De glandularum intest. struct. penit.   Berol., 1835.

HENLE.   Symbol. ad anat. vill. intest.   Berol., 1837.

BISCHOFF.   In Müller's Archiv, p. 503, 1838.

WASMANN.   De digestione nonnulla.   Berol., 1839.

MIDDELDORPF.   De glandulis Brunnianis.   Vratisl., 1846.

BRETTAUER and STEINACH.   Unt. über d. Cylinderepithel.   Vienna, 1857.

LEYDIG.   Histologie.   1857.

AUERBACH.   Ueber einen Plexus myentericus.   Breslau, 1862.

AUERBACH.   Virch. Arch., Vol. XXXIII., p. 340. 1865.

LETZERICH.   In Virchow's Archiv, Vol. XXXVII., p. 232.   1866.

EIMER.   Zur Geschichte der Becherzellen.   Berlin, 1868.

SCHWALBE.   Arch. f. mikros. Anat., Vol. VIII., p. 92.   1872.

HEIDENHAIN.   Arch. f. mikros. Anat., Vol. VIII., p. 279.   1872.

GERLACH.   Ber. d. sächs. Ges. der Wiss.   Leipzig, February, 1873.

KRAUSE.   Handb. d. menschl. Anat., Band I.   1876.

F. HOFFMANN.   Die Follikel des Dünndarms beim Menschen.   Munich, 1878.

SERTOLI.   Contribuzioni all' anatomia della mucosa gastrica.   Arch. di med. veter. Fasc. 3, p. 15. 1878.

RÜDINGER.   Beitr. z. Morphol. d. Gaumenseg. u. des Verdauungsapp.   Stuttgart, 1879.

H. SEWALL.   Devel. and Regen. of the Gastric Gland, Epithel., etc.   Journal of Phys., Vol. I., p. 321.   1879.

EDINGER.   Zur Kenntniss d. Drüsenzellen d. Magens.   Arch. f. mikros. Anat., Vol. XVII., p. 193.   1879.

RANVIER.   Les muscles de l'œsophage.   Journ. de micrographie, III., p. 9.   1879.

RENAUT, G.   Note sur la structure des glandes à mucus du duodenum.   Gaz. méd. de Paris, No. 41, 1879, and Progrès méd., No. 23, p. 439.   1879.

RANVIER.   Leçons d'anat. générale.   Paris, 1880.

P. STÖHR.   Ueber das Epithel. des menschl. Magens.   Verhandl. der phys.-med. Gesellschaft in Würzburg, p. 101.   1881.

CHAPTER XXV.

THE SPLEEN, PANCREAS, THYMUS, THYROID AND PINEAL GLANDS, AND PITUITARY BODY.

By C. L. DANA, A.M., M.D.,

Professor of Physiology in the Woman's Medical College, New York City.

THE SPLEEN.

General structure.—This organ is composed of connective tissue and muscular fibres, containing Malpighian corpuscles, pulp-substance, blood-vessels, lymphatics, and nerves. An outline of the general arrangement of these several elements will make subsequent details clearer.

Within its peritoneal investment the spleen has, in the first place, an elastic fibrous capsule; this envelops the organ and passes into its interior at the hilum. From the internal surface of the capsule are given off fibrous bands and processes—the trabeculæ, which interlace and form a fine network. In the meshes of this network is a soft, reddish substance—the *splenic pulp*. The arteries, entering at the hilum, run along the trabeculæ and end in capillaries, which gradually break up in the parenchyma. Attached to the walls of the arterioles and bathed in the spleen-pulp are little bodies, called the *Malpighian corpuscles*. The veins begin in the pulp, and, gradually enlarging, pass out alongside the arteries. The blood thus passes out of the capillaries into the spleen-pulp, and from thence is collected by the veins. It passes through the blood-paths in the pulp much as the lymph passes through lymph-paths in the lymphatic glands.

This unique structure is now to be considered in detail.

The *peritoneal* or *serous coat* of the spleen resembles the peritoneum elsewhere. It is, in man especially, very firmly adherent to the fibrous coat beneath it, and closely invests the organ. It is reflected off at the hilum to form the gastro-splenic omentum, and also at the upper border, where it invests the suspensory ligament.

The *fibrous coat*, or capsule of the spleen, is white in color, and thicker than the serous coat. It is composed of fibrous tissue, which is permeated very extensively by elastic fibres. Mingled with them are a few smooth, muscular elements. At the hilum this fibro-muscular coat surrounds the vessels and nerves and passes into the substance of the spleen with them, forming what is called the "capsule of Malpighi." It invests the arteries and veins as far as their finer branches, and gives off fibrous processes, which have a diameter of $\frac{1}{10}$ mm. to 2 mm., and which help to make up the trabecular framework of the spleen. This framework is formed by processes sent off from the internal surface of the spleen's fibrous coat, which join with the processes sent off from the capsule of Malpighi, and interlace until a firm network is made. In this structure lie embedded the spleen-pulp and the Malpighian corpuscles. The fibrous sheath of the veins has a somewhat peculiar arrangement. It becomes at once intimately adherent to the venous walls, uniting them closely with the surrounding parenchyma. As the veins grow smaller this fibrous coat splits into bands containing muscle-cells, which lie longitudinally along the vessel-wall. These bands do not entirely surround the vessel, however, but allow the thin endothelium and intima to be seen between them. They finally leave the veins to join the trabecular framework. The tissue composing this framework is made up, like the capsule, of elastic and other fibres, with a good many smooth muscle-fibres arranged longitudinally along their course.

Malpighian corpuscles.—The Malpighian or spleen corpuscles are so intimately connected with the arteries that it will be necessary first to trace in part the course of the latter. The arteries of the spleen enter at the hilum, enclosed in a common sheath with the veins and accompanied by the lymphatics. They divide and subdivide very rapidly. When they have reached a diameter of about two-tenths of a millimetre, the veins leave them and take an independent course. At this point of separation, or even sooner, the outer connective-tissue coat of the artery begins to be transformed into the ordinary adenoid tissue; the fibrillæ become more delicate and interlace in a coarser meshwork; in the interstices are lymph-cells and at the nodal points are small nuclei. Klein describes large, flattened endothelioid cells, "endothelioid plates," fixed upon the reticulum. This lymphoid tissue surrounds the artery in a loose coat of variable thickness. At certain points there is a local hyperplasia of it; it becomes massed into little ovoid or spherical bodies, which are called Malpighian corpuscles. These have a diameter of $\frac{2}{10}$ to $\frac{1}{10}$ mm. They are attached like buds to the artery, or, not rarely, the artery pierces them centrally or eccentrically. When thus pierced the lymphoid change in the arterial coats extends much deeper. The corpuscles resemble very closely the follicles in the solitary glands of the intestine, as well as those of the lymphatic glands (Fig. 173). They are composed of the same retiform connective tissue, in the meshes of which are lymphoid cells, with occasionally yellow or brown pigment. This retiform tissue becomes denser near the external part of the corpuscle, but no distinct enveloping membrane exists. Indeed, the external surface is generally connected by fibrillæ with the

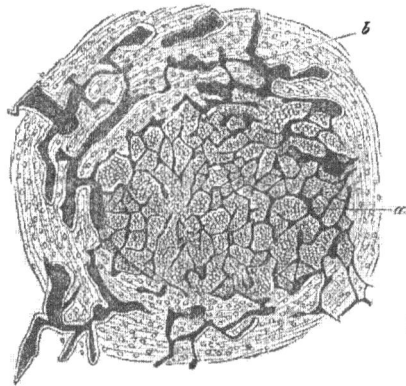

FIG. 173.—From the spleen of the Tropidonotus natrix: *a*, follicle, with its capillary plexus; *b*, septum, with venous plexus. Müller.

branching cells of the spleen-pulp surrounding it. Toward the centre the retiform tissue is more open. The cells within the meshes are lymph-cells of various sizes. They have an average diameter of $\frac{1}{100}$ mm. The smaller ones have a single nucleus, the larger may have several. An arterial twig enters the corpuscle either from the attached artery or from the outside. It divides at once into capillaries, which, as a rule, have no regular arrangement. They receive an adventitia of lymphoid tissue. Most of them soon lose this adventitia, their walls become rich in nuclei, branching processes are given off, and the structural character of the vessel is lost. They finally break up entirely, and their contents pass out at the periphery of the corpuscles into the meshes of the pulp. It is to be noted that the Malpighian corpuscles are the only parts of the spleen where capillaries exist to any extent. The arteries going to the pulp for the most part break up at once.

The spleen-corpuscles differ from the lymph-follicles, particularly, in having fewer capillaries, no lymph-paths, and in containing pigment in their meshes. The number of Malpighian corpuscles in a spleen of ordinary size, as estimated by Sappey, is about ten thousand ; but this applies to lower animals. In man they are smaller and less numerous. Protracted disease is thought to diminish the number.

The spleen-pulp.—This is a soft, reddish brown substance, looking, when squeezed out, like grumous blood. On exposure to the air it acquires a redder hue. Under the microscope it is found to present a honeycombed appearance, in the meshes of which are numerous lymph-corpuscles, fragments of red blood-corpuscles, so-called nuclei, and pigment-granules. Thus, we have really only a modified form of adenoid tissue. Klein considers that the network is made up of the large, flat endothelioid cells above referred to. Processes branching from these and uniting with each other form the meshes. I have been unable to make out the structure as Klein describes it, and his own observations and plates do not demonstrate it satisfactorily. The branching endothelioid cells are connected with the breaking-up and the beginning of the blood-vessels, but do not form the whole pulp reticulum.

The fibrillæ of this retiform tissue are connected with the external surface of the Malpighian corpuscles, with the lymphoid tissue that ensheaths the small arteries, with the fibrous trabeculæ of the spleen itself, and with the cell-nuclei of the walls of the arterioles, capillaries, and venous radicles. From these points they branch and interlace, enclosing the cellular and other elements in their meshes. These branching fibrillæ are, as in other lymphoid tissue, of a pale, granular appearance. The cells enclosed in the meshes are not crowded so closely together as are those in the Malpighian corpuscles (Fig. 174). They are of different sizes ; the small ones are sometimes described as free nuclei. The larger ones have one, two, or more nuclei within them. These larger cells often contain red blood-globules in various degrees of disintegration, a fact which gives rise to the opinion that one of the functions of the spleen is to destroy them. The pigment-granules are found both without and within the cells, and occasionally even stain the nodal nuclei of the sustentacular tissue. The pigment is yellowish, brown, or black, and there is enough of it to give a characteristic dark color to the gross appearance of the spleen. In addition to the pulp-elements mentioned, there are, according to Fremke and Kölliker, small, yellowish nucleated cells, which are possibly young red bloodglobules.

The pulp-substance thus described has arterioles and capillaries ending and veins beginning in it. The blood flows from the former, through the spaces between the cells, into the latter. Here is every opportunity, therefore, for the blood to recruit itself with new white corpuscles, and to enrich itself with albuminous and pigmentary matter from disintegrated red globules. The analyses of the blood in the splenic vein seem to show that it does do this.

FIG. 174.—From the sheep's spleen (double injection): *a*, reticular framework of the pulp; *b*, intermediate pulpcurrent: *c*, its continuation into the venous roots with incomplete walls; *d*, venous branch. *Frey*.

Blood-vessels.—We have already described, to a certain extent, the general arrangement of the blood-vessels, but some further particulars remain to be noticed.

The splenic artery, the largest branch of the cœliac axis, passes to the spleen in a course so tortuous as to shorten its length in a straight line by one-third. It enters the gastrosplenic omentum, divides generally into six branches, and passes into the spleen at the hilum, where, in common with the vein, it becomes surrounded by the capsule of Malpighii. The branches then rapidly subdivide and decrease in size, but without anastomosing. When about two-tenths of a millimetre in diameter they leave the veins and receive their sheaths of lymphoid tissue and Malpighian bodies, as has been described. They then end for the most part in capillaries, which pass to the Malpighian bodies and there break up in the way above described. But there are other capillaries which pass into the pulp-substance, where their walls gradually melt away, so to speak, into the retiform tissue that surrounds them. If one follows this change with a microscope, he will see the capil-

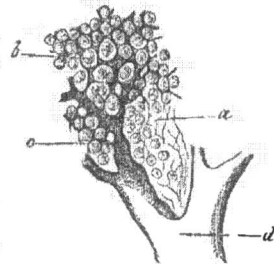

lary tube becoming thinner and more freely studded with nuclei ; from some of these nuclei processes are sent out which connect with the fibrillæ of the pulp. At this stage injections into the capillaries pass freely out into the surrounding tissue. The exact point where the capillary wall merges into the sustentacular tissue can hardly be determined.

The venous radicles begin in a somewhat similar way to that in which the capillaries end (Fig. 174). The sustentacular fibrillæ (endothelioid plates ?) appear to arrange themselves, first of all, in a circular manner, occasionally interlacing at right angles (Fig. 175). Lying within and upon the fibrillæ thus arranged are oval cells with prominent nuclei. These nuclei are often connected with the sustentacular fibrillæ outside. These cells are not adherent to each other at first, but, as the radicle becomes more perfect, they unite to form a complete wall ; the external layer of circular fibrillæ then becomes metamorphosed into a tunica intima ; finally, the thick oval cells are replaced by flat endothelial cells, and the complete venule is formed.

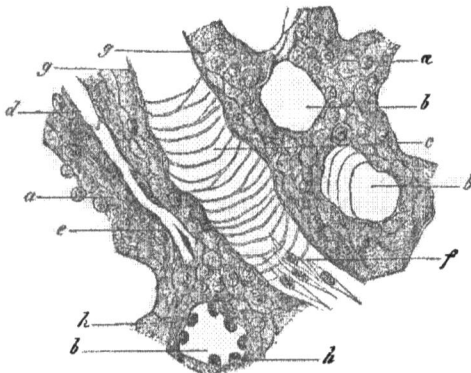

FIG. 175.—From the pulp of the human spleen, brushed preparation (combination): *a*, pulp strand with the delicate reticular framework : transverse section of the cavernous venous canal ; *c*, longitudinal section of such an one ; *d*, capillary vessel in a pulp tube, dividing up at *e* ; *f*, epithelium of the venous canal ; *g*, side view of the same ; *h*, its transverse section. Frey.

Having shown how this vascular channel begins, we turn, for convenience of description, to its other end. The splenic vein enters the hilum, just as the artery does. As it subdivides, however, it loses both tunica adventitia and tunica media. The internal tunic remains and becomes firmly united with the fibrous trabeculæ of the spleen, so that, on section, the venous wall does not collapse, but appears like a part of the parenchyma. After several subdivisions the veins begin to anastomose, and they finally form a closely reticulated arrangement of like-sized vessels having an average diameter of $\frac{1}{100}$ to $\frac{2}{100}$ mm. These are called the cavernous veins. The branches from them subdivide, pass into the pulp, and end in the venous radicles we have described.

It is proper to state that some authors (Gray, Billroth, Kölliker) believe that the capillaries connect directly with these cavernous veins, pouring the blood into the lacunæ which they form. Others (Key, Stieda) believe that the sustenacular tissue of the pulp is not composed of branching fibrillæ, but of collapsed capillaries, which connect the arteries with the venous radicles. Such views cannot now be sustained.

The lymphatics of the spleen occur in two sets : one, the trabecular, forms a close plexus in the external capsule and sends deep branches along the trabeculæ, to communicate with the deep or perivascular set. This perivascular set arises from the lymphoid sheaths of the arteries, and at first has no distinct channels. True lymphatics are soon formed, however, which run along the arteries, generally one on each side. At the hilum they unite with the trabecular set, and, passing along the gastro-splenic omentum, enter the neighboring lymphatic glands.

The nerves are derived from the solar plexus (right and left semilunar ganglia and right pneumogastric). They enter the hilum and follow the course of the arteries ; along their terminal ramifications, according to Müller, are oval ganglia, through which a single fine capillary runs. On section of the nerves of the spleen the organ dilates, and on electrical stimulation it contracts.

Development.—The spleen is present in all vertebrates except the *septocardia* and *myxenoids* (Müller).

The organ is developed entirely from the mesoblast, and, according to Peremeschko, is intimately related in its origin with the pancreas, from which it is an offshoot. Its shape can be recognized in the twelfth week. The capsule, trabeculæ, and retiform connective tissue, are first formed ; then the cells and Malpighian bodies appear, the latter at about the middle of intra-uterine life.

Preparation of spleen for microscopical examination.— The methods of preparing the spleen for examination are in general like those for preparing lymphoid tissue anywhere. The organ is very soft, and the object to be aimed at is to harden it without interfering too much with its intimate structure. A good method is that of Klein. The spleen should be

first washed out with ½ per cent. solution of common salt until
the fluid from the vein is clear. Then inject $\frac{1}{10}$ per cent. solution of osmic acid or Müller's fluid for twenty minutes. Then
place the spleen in Müller's fluid for ten days, at the end of
this time small bits should be cut off and hardened in alcohol,
when it may be stained and mounted in the ordinary way.
The spleen of man is best prepared (E. Klein) by placing small
bits in a large excess of ⅓ per cent. chromic acid for a week.
Then change it to a ¼ per cent. solution, and in three days from
this to a ½ per cent. solution. Finally, bits are to be placed in
alcohol and hardened in the usual way.

I have obtained excellent sections, however, which answered
very well for demonstrations, by freezing the spleen of the
living cat with the ether-spray, making sections at once, and
staining them with Bismarck brown. In this way the retiform
tissue even may be seen.

THE PANCREAS.

The pancreas is a compound racemose gland. It is composed of a central duct, which sends off branches that divide
and subdivide until they end after the usual manner of racemose glands, by opening into collections of little vesicles or
acini. This mode of structure divides the gland into small
lobules, between which runs areolar connective tissue. The
same tissue envelops the whole organ.

In each of the lobules will be found a number of acini
grouped around the terminal extremity of a duct. These
acini consist of a basement-membrane; lining this and almost
filling the acinus are cubical epithelial cells. The basement-
membrane is composed of flat, stellate cells. Owing to their
branching, they do not form a completely homogeneous membrane. The epithelial cells lining the acini are nucleated and
compressed closely together. Their internal portion, next the
lumen, is granular; the external part is clear. This granular
part represents (Heidenhain) the mother-ferment, zymogen,
which is transformed subsequently into trypsin. It varies in
extent with the activity of the gland. During such activity
the cell is smaller and the granular part less. Between the
cells (Langerhaus, Saviotti) fine intercellular passages similar

to those in the liver-lobules have been described (Fig. 176). These intercellular passages are claimed by some, however, to be branching processes from the cells of the basement-membrane. Others regard them as albuminous cement substances, holding the secreting corpuscles together.

Langerhaus describes branching centro-acinal cells connected on either side with similar inter-epithelial cells. (See Pituitary Body.)

The excretory duct of the pancreas is composed of a basement-membrane lined with cells; at the lower portion small mucous glands open into it. The basement-membrane is thickened with fibrous tissue at first; but, as the duct divides up into smaller branches, this disappears. The lining cells are columnar in shape near the mouth of the duct; passing back, however, they grow shorter and more flat. Finally, on reaching the acini, they resemble endothelial cells, and, as such, line the axial cavity of the acinus. Here they form the centro-acinal cells referred to above.

FIG. 176.—Glandular canals of the rabbit's pancreas, after Saviotti: *a*, Larger excretory duct; *b*, that of an acinus; *c*, finest capillary ducts. Frey.

The blood-vessels of the pancreas are numerous, and form a close capillary plexus around the basement-membrane of the acini.

The lymphatics probably arise from between the acini. They pass out with the blood-vessels.

The nerves are supplied from the solar plexus; through this fibres come from the vagus. They end, according to Pflüger, in a manner similar to that of the salivary glands; fine terminal filaments pass through the basement-membrane into the lining cells of the acini. Section of the vagus stops the

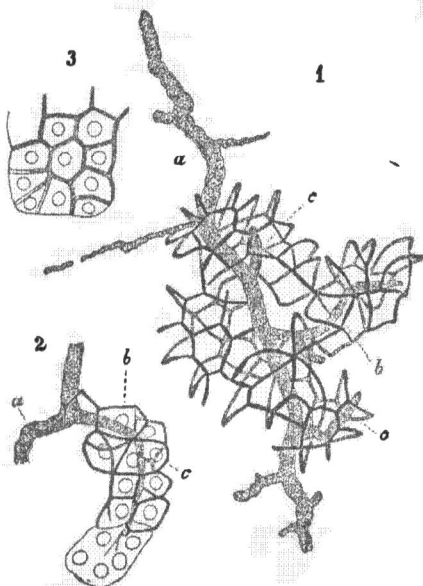

secretion of the pancreas for a short time ; stimulation of its central end does the same. On section of all the nerves going to the gland, there is a paralytic flow of the pancreatic juice.

Development.—The pancreas appears very early in fœtal life, developing from a mass of mesoblastic tissue in the duodenal wall. It is probable that hypoblastic tissue from the same region passes into it from the ducts.

THE THYMUS GLAND.

The thymus gland is an organ whose function is unknown ; it may be classed, however, on account of its structure, with the lymph-glands, its tissue being of the adenoid type. It is loosely enclosed in a vascular connective-tissue capsule, which sends septa and processes into the interior of the organ. These divide it up into small lobules of the size of a pin's-head to that of a pea. Within the lobules are the characteristic elements of the gland—the follicles—which are also known as the acini, alveoli, or granules. Running spirally through each of the two long lobes is a central band or canal, and, upon unravelling the gland, the various lobules are seen to be arranged about this.

· *The fibrous capsule* is made up chiefly of white connective tissue, mingled with which there are fine elastic fibres and stellate connective-tissue cells. At a few of the nodal points of the larger reticulating fibres are found peculiar cavities, lined with fusiform cells and containing a few lymph-corpuscles. They are probably connected with the lymphatics, and the fibrous capsule seems, as a whole, to be slightly touched with a lymphoid metamorphosis. The external surface of the capsule is covered with a single layer of flat epithelial cells. Deep in the capsule is a rich plexus of vessels, and scattered sparingly through it are medullated nerve-fibres.

The follicles.—Enclosed in each of the lobules, and making up its substance, are from ten to fifteen, or even fifty (Frey), small, spherical or polyhedral bodies. These are the follicles of the gland. They are from $\frac{1}{10}$ to $\frac{5}{10}$ mm. in diameter, and resemble very much the follicles in the lymphatic glands and Peyer's patches, but present a more embryonal aspect. They are held closely together by the surrounding tissue, which sends septa down between them for a short distance (Fig. 177). On section each follicle is found to be composed of a cortical and medullary portion. The medullary portion is often only a cavity, and, as a rule, is found to connect, by a passage through the cortex, with a general cavity in the centre of the lobule. This latter cavity again connects with the spiral central canal. The follicle is composed of reticular connective tissue, in whose meshes are cells and the thymic juice. The reticulum forms an adventitia for the blood-vessels. In the cortical portion this reticular tissue is made up of small, nucleated cells, with long, fine, branching processes. In the medullary portion, when present, the reticular cells have large nuclei, and their processes are coarse and short. Within the meshes of the structure thus described are cells, fat-globules, capillaries, and a peculiar, transparent, acid, viscid, albuminous fluid — the thymic juice. The cells are: 1, lymph-corpuscles, which exist in the greatest abundance; 2, large, granular, nucleated cells of various sizes—many of these have long processes, and they help to form, partly by a

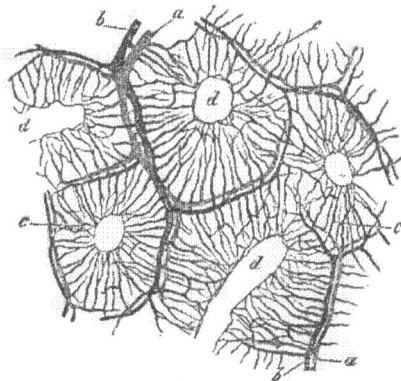

Fig. 177.—Portion of the calf's thymus, after His: The rings of the arterial branches (a) and venous branches (b) with the capillary net-work (c) and the cavities of the acini (d). Frey.

process of vacuolation (Watney), the concentric corpuscles; 3, giant cells; 4, the concentric corpuscles of Hassall. These last consist of one or more cells, around which are arranged concentric layers of flat, epithelioid cells. This concentric envelope suggests the epithelial cylinders seen in carcinomatous growths. One or two of these corpuscles may be enclosed in another common envelope, thus forming a compound concentric corpuscle. These corpuscles are strongly refractive, and are readily stained with carmine. They lie near the arteries, and have an intimate relation with them. According to Afanassien, indeed, they are developed from the endothelium of the arterial wall. There is a vascular plexus about the follicles, from which capillaries pass into the interior, forming a fine network. They generally pass in as far as the medullary portion or central cavity, and form a ring about this.

The central canal, or band of the thymus, is lined with a vascular membrane, and communicates with the central cavities of the lobules and follicles. Along its interior the bulgings of attached vesicles, or groups of the same, may be seen.

Many authorities consider that the central cavities in the follicles and lobules are produced artificially by the breaking down of the very delicate tissue. There is much probability that this is the case. More investigation, however, is needed, and meanwhile the cavities and canals are described as above, since it is extremely rare to find a human thymus in which they do not appear to exist, no matter how careful the preparation.

The blood-vessels.—The thymus is not a very vascular gland. Its arteries are distributed in the capsule and along the central band. From these parts they pass unaccompanied, as a rule, by the veins, to the interlobular tissue, and are distributed to the follicles, as has been described.

The lymphatics accompany the blood-vessels along the central band. From there it is stated (His) that they pass to the interlobular tissue and are distributed around the follicles, communicating by minute channels with the centre of the follicle. This latter point, however, lacks confirmation.

Development.—The thymus gland is found in all vertebrates except *amphioxus* (Huxley). It is developed, like the lymphatic glands, from the mesoblastic layer, and can be seen early in fœtal life. It appears first as a closed tube, which is probably (Quain) a mass of embryonic cells enclosed in a membranous capsule. Along this projections bud out which are gradually transformed into lobules. By the twelfth week it has become well developed.

The thymus is an organ of fœtal and infant life only. It grows rapidly until the second year, when it begins to undergo a fatty degeneration and atrophy. By the seventh or eighth year it is a small, fatty mass. This degeneration of the thymus takes place in all the animals which have the gland.

THE THYROID BODY.

The thyroid body is a dark red, vascular organ, composed of two lobes. It seems very possible that we may now legiti-mately call it a secreting gland, whose product acts upon the red blood-cells, and is carried away by the lymphatics.

The entire organ is enclosed in a thin, but firm, fibrous capsule. This sends off processes to the interior, which interlace, forming a sponge-like network. This network is thin, however, and does not make up much of the substance of the gland. A few elastic fibres run in it. Enclosed in the meshes of the framework thus formed are the vesicles of the gland. These are very numerous and make up the bulk of the organ. They are minute, spherical, ovoid, or flattened bodies, whose diameter is from $\frac{2}{100}$ mm. in the embryo to 2 mm. in the adult, and are grouped into small lobules of various sizes. They consist of a homogeneous connective-tissue basement-membrane, lining which is a single layer of epithelial cells, the whole enclosing a yellowish, transparent, viscid fluid. The lining-cells, in adults, measure about $\frac{2}{100}$ mm. in height and $\frac{1}{100}$ mm. in width. They contain nuclei, and sometimes nucleoli. They are loosely connected to the basement-membrane, and, with extra-uterine life, begin to break away into the interior of the vesicle. Baber describes fine, longitudinal striæ passing from the base toward the apex of the cell. These cells have a tendency to undergo colloid degeneration. The cell-body swells up, and bursting, the contents spread out in the vesicle-cavity, there to undergo or complete the metamorphosis (Fig. 178) mentioned. According

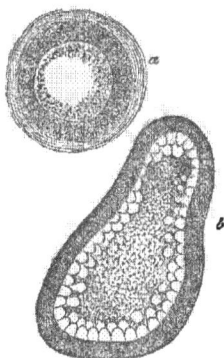

FIG. 178.—Colloid metamorphosis: *a*, Gland vesicle of the rabbit; *b*, commencing colloid metamorphosis of the calf. Frey.

to Baber, however, the cells which undergo this degeneration come from the connective tissue surrounding the vesicles. They pass through the vesicle-wall into its cavity, and there gradually break up. This change goes on at the expense of the vesicle-wall and the intervesicular tissue, so that in time the gland, without being much enlarged, may appear, on section, almost like a single colloid mass.

The normal fluid contents of the vesicle coagulates with heat and alcohol, without losing its transparency. Floating in it are granules, cells, and occasional translucent, curiously shaped bodies called sympexions (Robin). The cells come from the vesicle-wall and the intervesicular tissue. Many of them have lost their nuclei. The "sympexions," if they uniformly occur, have not been shown to have any significance.

Baber has recently announced the very interesting fact that large numbers of colored and colorless blood-corpuscles are to be found in the vesicle-cavities of the thyroid of man and lower vertebrates. The colored cells, which largely preponderate, are in a state of partial disintegration. This explains the yellowish color of the vesicle-contents, and the inference is drawn that the thyroid has the function of destroying red blood-corpuscles.

The blood-vessels of the thyroid are quite numerous. They ramify in the capsule along the trabeculæ, and finally form a rich plexus about the vesicles, but do not penetrate the interior. The walls of the veins are united firmly to the fibrous reticulum of the gland, so that when a section of them is made they do not collapse.

The lymphatics form large and numerous trunks, both on the surface and in the interior of the organ. They originate by cœcal extremities lying in the tissue between the vesicles. These unite to form trunks which surround the lobules, and give off branches that pass to the capsule. There a thick, peripheral network is formed, from which lymph-trunks pass to the thoracic and right lymphatic ducts. They contain a viscid substance like that in the vesicles themselves, and it seems probable that they have something to do with carrying off this fluid.

The nerves are from the middle and inferior cervical ganglia, but not (Frey) from the pneumogastric. They enter the gland along the trabeculæ and pass between the vesicles. Ganglion-cells, either single or in groups, are met with in their course. The mode of termination is not known, more than that they seem to dwindle away into fine, terminal fibres, that are lost in the connective tissue.

THE PINEAL GLAND.

The pineal gland, or *conarium*, is a small body, about the size of a pea, resting upon the nates and covered by the back part of the corpus callosum. It consists of a fibrous capsule and framework, lying in which are vesicles, cells, blood-vessels, and sabulous matter. There is generally a cavity near the base of the gland.

The interior of the structure is divided into a cortical and medullary portion. The former is composed of little vesicles, resembling those of the pituitary body. The central portion is filled with nerve-cells and sabulous matter, the latter lying in the cavity at the base. The nerve-cells are of two kinds: one, large, $\frac{1}{15}$ mm. in diameter, and giving off long processes; the other, very small, $\frac{1}{150}$ mm. in diameter, and giving off processes, in the adult. Nerve-fibres run among these cells, and connect them to the medullary substance of the cerebral lobes and to the crura cerebri. They are considered, by Meynert, to be ganglion-cells giving origin to fibres in the crura cerebri.

The sabulous matter is composed of corpora amylacea and of earthy salts combined with animal matter. The earthy salts are: phosphate and carbonate of lime, phosphate of ammonia, and magnesia (Stromeyer).

There is no doubt that the pineal gland contains considerable nervous tissue. It is not yet determined, however, whether it should be considered a ganglionic centre or a structure of similar character to the suprarenal capsules.

THE PITUITARY BODY.

The pituitary body (*hypophysis cerebri*) is notable for the peculiarity of its development and its uniform presence in all vertebrates. It is a small, reddish gray, vascular mass, ovoid in shape, and situated in the sella turcica. It is composed of two lobes, anterior and posterior, the former being the larger. In structure, the body, in its anterior lobe, has some resemblance to the suprarenal capsules, being composed of a connective-tissue framework, in which lie blood-vessels and closed vesicles. These latter consist of a homogeneous membrane enclosing nucleated and nucleolated cells, mostly epithelial in character. These cells generally line the interior of the vesicle and nearly fill its cavity, so that on section the vesicle looks somewhat like an acinus of the pancreas. In the centre there is often a branched nucleated corpuscle connected with a similar cell on one or the other side (Klein). The cells vary much in size. In the connective tissue around the vesicles are lymphatic spaces and blood-vessels.

The posterior lobe is smaller, darker, and more vascular than the anterior. During fœtal, and perhaps infant life, it has a cavity in its interior lined with ciliated epithelium and connected by the infundibulum with the third ventricle.

Development.—The pituitary body is formed by a diverticulum from the future mouth (buccal epiblast), which projects up to be transformed eventually into the anterior lobe ; and another diverticulum from the wall of the vesicle of the third ventricle, which projects down to form the posterior lobe (Quain). Epiblastic and mesoblastic tissue are thus united in the organ. The posterior lobe retains its nervous elements in the lower animals, but in man contains little besides connective tissue and blood-vessels.

BIBLIOGRAPHY.

THE SPLEEN.

MÜLLER, WM.   Ueber den feineren Bau der Milz   Leipzig und Heidelberg, 1865.

PEREMESCHKO.   Beiträge zur Anatomie der Milz, und Ueber die Entwicklung der Milz.   Sitzungsberichte der k. k. Akademie.   Zu Wien, 1867.

STRICKER, S.   Manual of Histology.   1872.

QUAIN.   Elements of Anatomy.   New York, 1877.

BACELLI.   Venous Circulation of the Spleen.   Med. Times and Gaz., Vol. I., p. 562.   1878.

SAPPEY.   Traité d'anatomie descriptive.   3me éd. rev. et amél.   1879.

RANVIER, L.   Traité technique d'histologie.   1879 et seq.

KLEIN, E.   Quarterly Jour. Mic. Science.   No. LX., p. 363.   1875.   Also, Atlas of Histology.   Par. XIII.   1880.

FREY.   Histology.   1880.

THE PANCREAS.

PFLÜGER, E. F. W.   Stricker's Manual of Histology.   1872.

RENAUT, J.   Sur les organes lympho-glandulaires et le pancréas des vertèbres.   Compt. rend. Acad. des Sciences.   Vol. LXXXIX., p. 247.   Paris, 1879.

FOSTER, M.   Physiology.   1880.

THE THYMUS GLAND.

WATNEY, H. Note on the Minute Anatomy of the Thymus. Proc. Roy. Soc., Vol. XXVII., p. 369. London, 1878.

AFANASSIEN. Structure of Thymus. Archiv für mikroskopische Anatomie, Band XIV., Heft 134.

THE THYROID BODY.

BOECHAT, P. A. Thesis on the Structure of the Thyroid Gland. 1873.

BABER, E. CRESWELL. Researches on the Minute Structure of the Thyroid Gland. Philosophical Transactions Lond. Roy Soc., Vol. CLXVI., Pt. 2, p. 557. 1876. Proc. Royal Soc., Vol. XXVII., p. 56. London, 1878.

ZEISS, OTTO. Mikroskopische Untersuchungen über den Bau der Schilddrüse. Strassburg, 1877.

POINCARÉ, M. Contribution à l'histoire du corps thyroïde. Jour. de l'anatomie, p. 122. 1877.

KLEIN, E. Atlas of Histology. Par. XIII. 1880.

THE PITUITARY BODY.

Journal de médecine, de chirurgie et de pharmacologie de Bruxelles, Vol. LXIX., p. 305. 1880.

KLEIN, E. Atlas of Histology. Par. XIII. 1880.

CHAPTER XXVI.

THE THICK CUTIS VERA.

By J. COLLINS WARREN, M.D.

THE portions of the skin usually selected for histological purposes are those in which the papillæ or hairs are best shown. The glands are also carefully described ; but little attention, however, has been given to the anatomy of the cutis vera as an organ by itself, consequently those parts have not been examined where it is found in its most highly developed form.

The skin varies greatly in thickness ; on the inside of the arms and thighs, and on the anterior aspect of the body generally, it is much thinner than behind. In the former case, particularly in delicate women, it is exceedingly soft and pliable, a thin fold being easily raised and rolled between the thumb and finger. In the latter it is exceedingly thick in the back and shoulders of hardy adults, appearing as a veritable hide, being much thicker than the skin of many pachydermatous animals. Here it measures 5.5 mm. and even more in thickness ; when tanned it resembles sole leather. This structure is composed of bundles of fibres interwoven in various directions. On the surface of these bundles lie the flat connective-tissue cells, disposed in rows and occupying the intervals, the tissue being somewhat analagous to tendon. The cutis is, in fact, a sort of tendon or aponeurosis ; from its under surface it sends out fibrous prolongations of considerable size, and in some animals these are actually attached to muscles.[1] In man we find them dipping down into the subcutaneous fat, in the back forming a very dense and firm mesh-work. Fatty tumors

---

[1] M. Renaut : Anatomie générale de la peau ; Annales de Dermatologie et de Syphilographie ; Tome neuvième, No. 5 ; Satterthwaite : New York Medical Journa], July, 1875.

growing in this part of the panniculus adiposus are, for this reason, extremely difficult to enucleate.

The papillæ are but imperfectly formed, and are represented by an undulating line. At short intervals are the follicles of the lanugo hairs, which penetrate only the superficial layers of the cutis, the sweep of whose fibres would be otherwise unbroken were it not for the existence of a structure, hitherto undescribed,[1] which connects the bases of the hair-follicle with those parts in which we find the root of the longer hairs imbedded —the panniculus adiposus. This consists of a nearly vertical cleft, or slender columnar-shaped space, extending from the last-named structure in a somewhat oblique direction through the deeper and middle layers of the cutis, and terminating at the base of the follicle which rests upon it. This space is occupied by adipose

Fig. 179.—Section of skin from back of an adult, showing columnar adiposa and lanugo hair. Magnified about eight diameters: a, epidermis; b, erector pili muscle; d, fat-column; e, sudoriparous gland; f, cutis vera; g, adipose tissue; h, hair; k, cone fibrous; p, lateral cleft.

tissue in its entire length; hence, the term "fat-columns," or "fat-canals,"[2] would seem to be an appropriate name.

The length of this space (in very lean individuals the fat is absent, and we then see a delicate mesh-work of connective tissue, and the trunk of a blood-vessel) is about 4 mm.; its width rather exceeds that of the hair-follicle above. Its long axis is placed at a slight angle to that of the follicle, which in most cases is nearly perpendicular to the surface, and is nearly parallel to that of the erector pili muscle (b). At about the middle of this axis are given off two horizontal prolongations, usually partially filled with fat-tissue, appearing like a pair of

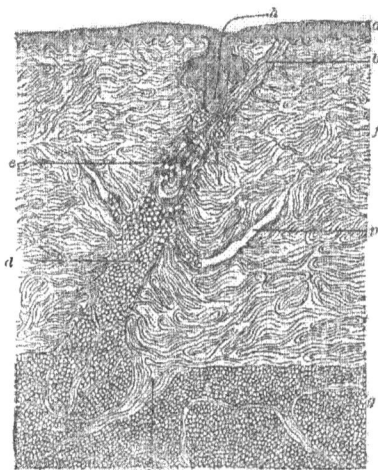

---

[1] In the latest treatises of the skin, no such structure is described. See Die Hautkrankheiten für Aerzte und Studirende von Dr. Gustav Behrend. Berlin, 1879; Pathologie und Therapie der Hautkrankheiten von Dr. Moriz Kaposi. Wien, 1879.

[2] Note on the Anatomy and Pathology of the Skin, by J. C. Warren. Boston Medical and Surgical Journal, April 19, 1877.

extended arms, or the remaining branches of a leafless trunk (p). Near this point is suspended the coil of a sweat-gland (e), held in place by a few delicate fibres which find their insertion at the top of the canal or cleft. The duct of the gland runs to the top of this space, whence it may be traced to the side of the hair-follicle, whence it finds its way to the surface. (In dogs the sweat-duct opens directly into the follicle, a short distance from its mouth.) The fibres of the cutis appear, in vertical sections, to terminate abruptly at its edges. There does not appear to be any structure resembling a "limiting membrane." At its base there is sometimes a slight widening of the cleft, and on the side toward which its axis leans, the fibres of the cutis collect to form a bundle which penetrates the subcutaneous fat (*Cône fibreux de la peau*—k, Fig. 179). The upper extremity is rounded off in somewhat dome-shape.

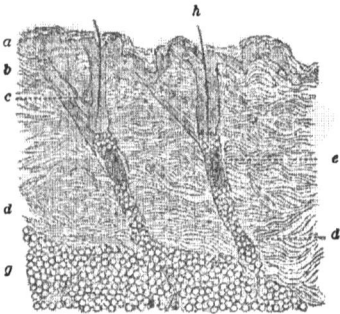

Fig. 180.—Section of skin from the shoulder of an infant, magnified seventeen diameters: *a*, epidermis; *b*, erector pili muscle; *c*, sebaceous gland; *d*, fat-column; *e*, sudoriparous gland; *g*, adipose tissue; *h*, hair.

The erector pili muscle, taking its origin from the papillary layer of the cutis, is inserted partly into the base of the follicle, which its fibres embrace, and partly into the apex of the fat-canal; in some sections the fibres seem to penetrate this space, but probably surround it, although some of them may be attached to those delicate bands of fibrous tissue which traverse the column of fat-cells. The muscle lies on the side corresponding with the inclination of the hair externally, and appears almost continuous in its direction with the fat-column beneath it.

The sebaceous gland lies between the muscle and the follicle at the apex of the angle made by them ; a lobe is found also on the opposite side.

The number of these columns corresponds to the number of hairs, as they are not found elsewhere. In some sections of skin, half an inch in length, as many as five may be counted ; they are seen to best advantage in the thickest portions of the skin, but may be found on the shoulders and arms, breast, abdomen, and lower extremities. At some points they appear as slight indentations in the section ; at others as long canals. They are well shown in the skin of an infant (Figure 180), and in a fœtus of nine months. In the pig, the lower border of the cutis appears to the naked eye, when seen in section, like the teeth of a saw. Under the microscope, the apex of each indentation contains the bulb of a hair. In thick hides these indentations become clefts or canals, and we find frequently a sweat-gland situated at about the middle of each. The canals are oblique, as are also the hair-follicles, and the axes of the two are more nearly parallel than those in the human subject.

In thin skins the canals are either so short as hardly to pass for such, or, if the hair is not of sufficient length to extend to the bottom of the cutis, absent. A thick skin and the existence of downy hairs are, then, the conditions necessary for the presence of this structure in its most marked forms. I have not found them in the face, although in some individuals they probably exist there, nor in the thinner skin already alluded to. In the lip of the rat the long hairs are imbedded in a transparent, mucous-like connective tissue, and their roots are surrounded by numerous bands of muscle. It is interesting to note the fact, that under each root are to be found vertical rows of fat-cells, arranged end on end like the beads of a rosary, but there appears to be no cleft in the surrounding tissue to enclose them. In order to obtain a preparation of skin which shows these structures in their entire length, the section must be made vertical to the surface, and in a direction which corresponds with the inclination of the cleft of the hair above the surface. This coincides with the fine folds or "grain" of the skin. Sections made in any other direction give but a fragment of the canal, which appears then nearly as an isolated lobule of adipose tissue. Even with these precautions it is difficult to obtain a good specimen, unless the razor is guided by the eye and, as in embryonic skin, the canals are not large enough to be seen, it is greatly a question of luck whether a good section can be obtained.

The blood-vessels are well shown by an injection of Berlin blue in the fœtus near full term. In each canal, as well as in the intervals between them, the arterioles which nourish the cutis ascend from the subcutaneous system of vessels, which forms a fine net-work in the panniculus adiposus. Those in the canals, on reaching the lateral clefts, bifurcate, giving a

branch on either side, which anastomoses sparingly through
subdivisions with the adjacent arterioles in the middle layer of
the cutis, and give origin to the papillary and sub-papillary
network of capillaries, which here can be considered as one
and the same. At the point of bifurcation of the main vessel,
branches are given off which ascend farther in the canal and
form a delicate net-work surrounding the sudoriparous gland
("Wundernetz"). The anastomosis of the vessel about the
hair-follicle is particularly rich and fine, and unites intimately
with the superficial layer of capillaries. The hair-follicle, with
its subjacent fat-column, thus forms the centre of a rich system
of arterioles and capillaries, which extend from the panniculus
adiposus to the papillæ.

The lymphatics.—The following experiments were made to
determine the question of the presence of lymphatics in these
canals, and also to observe to what extent fluids and particles,
pressed up from below, could be forced to the surface.

Skin was taken from the body of a lean adult, twenty-four hours after death.
A small amount of the loose areolar tissue was left adherent to its lower surface. The skin being prepared by warming for a few minutes in water of
about 90° F., Berlin blue was injected, by means of a subcutaneous syringe,
into the loose areolar tissue, which was rapidly distended by the fluid. The
specimen was then thrown into strong alcohol. A similar fragment of skin
was stretched like a drum, over the end of a brass cylinder, to which it was
firmly attached by an open brass cap and screws. The cylinder being held
vertically, Berlin blue was poured upon the skin, the upper surface of which
looked downward. A rubber cork, perforated by a glass tube, was securely
fastened to the top of the cylinder, and the tube was connected with an apparatus designed to exert any atmospheric pressure required. Pressure sufficient
to raise a column of mercury twenty-eight millimetres was continued for an
hour and a half, the skin being pressed out with great force in dome-shape
at the bottom of the cylinder, which was kept during this time in blood-warm
water. The specimen was then placed in alcohol. It was observed that the
injection mass had gone, at one or two points, to the surface, and on making
vertical sections of the skin the next day, the cutis was found to be penetrated
by the mass in vertical blue lines, which united at various intervals by horizontal branches, occasionally so numerous as to present an almost continuous
blue surface. The subcutaneous areolar tissue was almost uniformly colored
blue.

Opinions on the character and distribution of the lymphatics of the skin seem to differ. For instance, Neumann describes them as vessels distributed through the skin in two

horizontal layers—a superficial and a deep one—the vertical connection between the two being found only at comparatively rare intervals.[1] Renaut regards the skin as a lymphatic sponge, the minutest ramification being but the space between the bundles of fibres ; the coarser differing from these in having an endothelial lining (connective-tissue cells ?), there being in neither case a true wall, which is found only in the lymphatic vessels of the subcutaneous tissue.[2] Vertical sections taken from the specimens of skin injected by puncture, showed a similar, but not so complete an injection, as was effected by

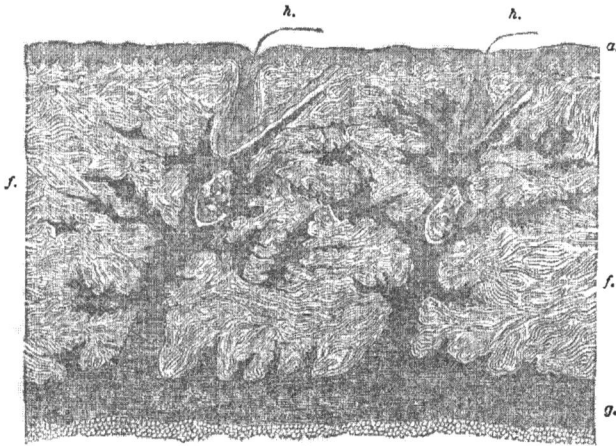

FIG. 181.—Injected lymph-system magnified about eight diameters : *a*, epidermis; *f*, cutis vera ; *g*, adipose tissue ; *h*, hair.

the present method. The latter seems to possess special advantage, as a larger lymph surface is exposed at one time.

Fig. 181 shows the route taken by the Berlin blue, which, as will be seen, ascends in nearly vertical columns through the fat-canals to the base of the hair-follicles, going round the sides of the sweat-gland. When a slight amount only had passed into the canal, a medium power of the microscope showed the blue lying in and staining the tissue accompanying the ascending blood-vessel in the so-called "perivascular space." The lateral clefts were filled with the mass,

[1] Zur Kenntniss der Lymphgefässe der Haut, von Isidor Neumann.
[2] Renaut. Op. cit.

which extended far enough to communicate with that coming from an adjacent column. From this point there is a delicate and freely anastomosing network, marking out the spaces between the bundles of fibres of the cutis. The lateral anastomosis, lower down, is not so free, and in the uppermost layers, owing probably to the compression of the bundles of fibres, there is little blue to be seen. From the top of the canal the injection surrounds the base of the hair-follicle, on one side ascending vertically and giving off horizontal branches, and on the other following the interval between the lower border of the erector pili muscles and the fibres of the cutis. The main route is through the canals, there being no penetration from below elsewhere. A similar method of injection of these spaces is seen in certain forms of disease. A subcutaneous, round-celled sarcoma infiltrating the skin, gave a similar configuration. Also that form of congenital nævus which develops in the panniculus adiposus, and in a few days after birth begins to appear on the surface. Another instance is that variety of purulent infiltration of the subcutaneous tissue, which is most frequently seen under thick skin and known as carbuncle. The wandering cells find their way to the surface through these canals, and thus give the characteristic, punched-out appearance to the skin.

It is evident from these examples that a free communication exists between the interspaces of the fibrous bundles of the cutis, and the subcutaneous tissue, and that this is effected by no closed system of vessels.

The special function of these canals is not so evident. In addition to furnishing a route for the blood-vessels and lymphatics, there would seem to be some connection with the hair and its apparatus. The constant relation which they bear to this structure, and the erector pili muscle, would suggest an arrangement designed to facilitate the action of the muscle, according to Biesiadecki.[1] This muscle, by its contraction, raises the hair from the position which it occupies, nearly horizontal to the surface, to a vertical one. Any movement of the root of a lanugo hair would be well nigh impossible, imbedded in the dense tissue of the cutis, were it not for a yielding structure like that of the columns, an elongation of which

---

[1] Stricker's Handbuch der Lehre von den Geweben des Menschen und der Thiere.

would aid the contraction of the muscle. In specimens where the muscle is found in a state of contraction, the hair-follicle is bent like a bow, the root being drawn through the arc of a circle. The presence of fat near the hair-bulb is made possible by this structure, a condition which is constant with all hairs. That the fat is not an incidental feature of their structure, which might be considered merely a cleft for the transmission of vessels, is rendered probable by the observation of rows of fat-cells beneath each hair in the lip of the rat, where no special channels exist, and, also, by the fact that such columns of fat do not accompany the nutrient vessels of the skin, in those parts where the hairs are not found. It seems, therefore, probable, that this structure has some bearing upon the nutrition of the hair.

Sweat-glands are found not only in these canals, but elsewhere in the thick cutis ; the coil of the gland is then usually situated at a level a little below the middle of the cutis vera, and not in the subcutaneous adipose tissue, as in thin skin.

CHAPTER XXVII.

URINARY EXCRETORY PASSAGES; SUPRARENAL CAPSULES.

By EDMUND C. WENDT, M.D.,

Curator of the St. Luke's and St. Francis' Hospitals, etc., New York City.

THE renal pelvis, the calices, ureters, and bladder, all consist essentially of three layers, which are an inner mucous membrane, a middle muscular coat, and an external fibrous layer. In the

RENAL PELVIS

we find the *mucous membrane* lined with stratified epithelium, the cells of which are large and variously shaped. Three different forms are readily distinguished. The most superficial layer consists of flat or polyhedral cells of various sizes, each one containing a round or oval nucleus, or, as frequently happens, two nuclei. Peculiar dark granules, often of large size, surround the nucleus, and are quite distinct from the finely granular protoplasm of these cells. Then comes a layer of conical or club-shaped bodies, each one again furnished with a round or oval nucleus. Every cell also possesses a long basal process, which appears to attach it to the subjacent tissue. The bulbous portion of these corpuscles is turned outward in the direction of the surface. Wedged in between the processes just mentioned we find the third variety of cellular elements. These are oval or rounded bodies containing ellipsoid nuclei. At the renal calices we find a sharp line of demarcation between the cylindrical columnar epithelium of the papillary ducts and the stratified pavement epithelium of the pelvis. The epithelial layer has a thickness here of 0.045–0.09 mm.

The connective-tissue portion of the mucous membrane is devoid of papillæ, contains sparse elastic fibres, and is rich in fixed corpuscles, the inoblasts of Krause. There is no true basement-membrane. Below this stratum we find a submucous layer, which is abundantly furnished with elastic tissue, and contains a few simple acinous glands with ducts having a lining of cylindrical epithelium.

The *muscular coat* is composed of bundles of smooth muscle-cells forming an inner layer, with a peripheral direction of its constituent anatomical elements, and an outer layer concentrically arranged. The "papillary sphincter" is but a thickening of this latter layer.

The *external fibrous layer* forms a thin connective-tissue membrane, not always clearly marked here, whereas in the ureters and bladder it is found to be well developed.

The *blood-vessels* of the pelvis are derived from the renal artery and vein, and form capillary networks characterized by polygonal meshes. The lymphatics and nerves are found to have the same distribution as in the ureters.

THE URETERS

have a structure which closely resembles that of the renal pelvis. The *mucous membrane* shows the same varieties of epithelium; its connective-tissue components are similarly arranged; and the external investing membrane is composed of the same kind of tissue already described. But in addition to the two *muscular layers*, which here attain a greater development, we find a third muscle coat, so that we can now distinguish an internal and external longitudinal from a middle circular layer of muscular elements.

Engelmann has described a close reticulum of blood capillaries lying immediately under the epithelial stratum, but its existence is made doubtful by the negative statements of other authors.

Glandular bodies are not found in the ureters. The peripheral layer of fibrous connective-tissue possesses conspicuous elastic bundles in the lower portion of the ureters.

The distribution of the *blood-vessels* is like that of the pelvis already described. The *lymphatics* are well developed here, forming several networks in the different layers of the ducts. *Nerves* are likewise readily distinguished, some of the nerve-fibres being also furnished with ganglion cells. Their mode of termination in the muscular layer is not definitely known, but may be assumed to resemble that of ordinary smooth muscular-tissue.

THE BLADDER

has the same type of structure as the ureters, but contains, in addition, a serous covering in its upper portion. The different coats of the bladder are, however, much thicker than the corresponding layers in the other urinary excretory passages.

The *epithelial* lining of the mucous membrane shows the three varieties of its cellular elements in a clearly defined manner.

The *connective-tissue* stratum presents no noteworthy peculiarities, if we except the comparative abundance of simple acinous glands.

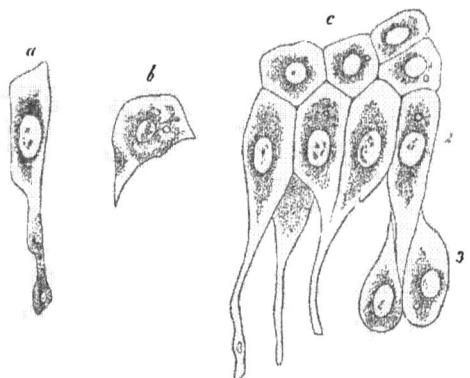

The bundles of muscle-cells in the *muscular-coat* interlace, forming irregular, long-stretched meshes. This irregular arrangement prevents the distinct recognition of successive layers, each with a largely prevailing direction. Nevertheless,

FIG. 182.—Epithelium of the urinary bladder. *a*, a cell of the second layer; *b*, a cell of the first layer; *c*, shows the first, second, and third layers of the epithelium in connection. Obersteiner.

we find in the external portion of the muscle-coat some predominance of longitudinal bundles, together with an abundant supply of elastic fibres. The anterior wall and vertex of the bladder show this arrangement very conspicuously, in fact the muscle-fibres have here received a separate name, that of *detrusor urinæ*. The vesical neck shows a tolerably distinct thickening of its circular muscle-fibres, which is known as the *sphincter vesicæ*. It should always be borne in mind that the arrangement of the muscular coat is apt to vary in different individuals, the description here given will, however, be found to apply to the majority of cases.

The *blood-vessels* form a capillary network in the mucous membrane, which is situated about midway between the epithelial stratum and the muscular coat. In other respects they present no peculiarity worthy of note.

The *lymphatics* are less abundant in the bladder than in the ureters. They, also, lack noteworthy peculiarities or special features of interest.

Plexuses of *nerve-fibres* are found in the subserous connective-tissue, and also in the muscular coat. Microscopic ganglia and groups of ganglion cells are also met with.

SUPRARENAL CAPSULES.

The suprarenal capsules (*glandulæ suprarenales*) are small flattened bodies, two in number, situated somewhat above and

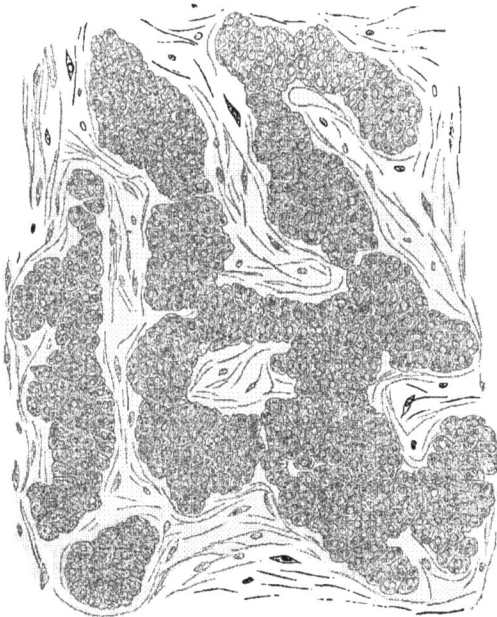

Fig. 183.—Cellular groups and trabeculæ of the cortical substance, from the suprarenal capsule of the Frog. Eberth.

in front of the upper end of either kidney. They are usually triangular or semilunar in shape, although round and oval forms are also met with. In structure they resemble the so-called blood-vascular glands, but their function is not known. They belong to the ductless variety of glands.

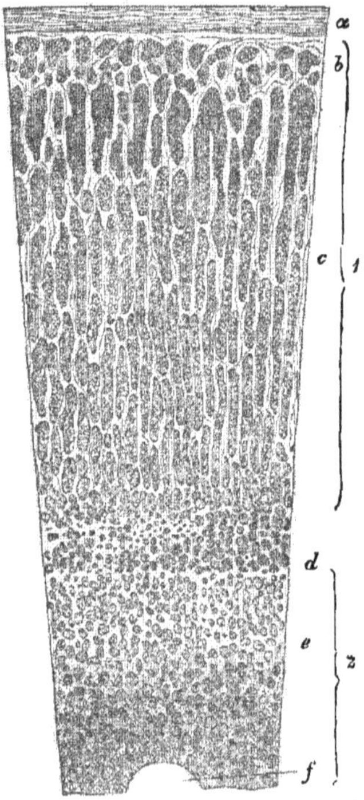

Fig. 184.—Perpendicular section through the suprarenal capsule of man : 1, cortex; 2, medulla; *a*, capsule; *b*, layer of outer cell-groups; *c*, layer of cell-trabeculæ (zona fasciculata); *d*, layer of inner cell-groups; *e*, medullary substance; *f*, transverse section of a vein. Eberth.

Each suprarenal body consists of a capsule inclosing the parenchyma, which shows a cortical and medullary substance. The *capsule* is formed of ordinary connective tissue containing many delicate elastic fibrils. Externally it is surrounded by loose connective tissue, containing a greater or less proportion of adipose tissue, and internally it sends out trabeculæ, which traverse the entire organ, thus constituting and completing its frame-work.

The *cortical substance*, as its name implies, occupies the external portion of the suprarenal body. It has an average thickness in man of 0.28 to 1.12 mm., is of a yellowish color, and may be divided into three layers or zones. The limits of demarcation between these layers are much less marked, however, than the corresponding boundary line between the cortical and medullary portions. In the human being the external layer of the cortex is distinctly separate from the middle one, but the latter shows no such sharp limit against the innermost layer. The cortex is a friable substance, and its broken surface presents a striated appearance. Owing to rapid post-mortem changes, the cortex in man is usually found to be separated from the medullary portion by a dirty brownish substance, containing modified blood and cortical corpuscles.

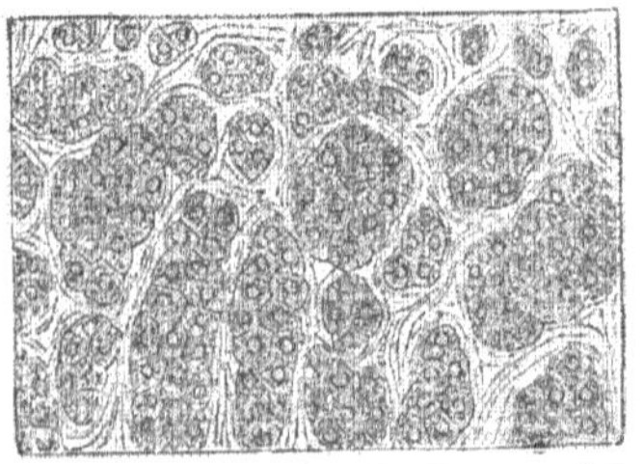

Fig. 185.—Single cells and cell-groups of the outermost cortical layer. Human suprarenal capsule. Eberth.

The three layers of the cortex are an external one, or *zona glomerulosa ;* a middle one, or *zona fasciculata ;* and an internal one, or *zona reticularis.*

The *external layer* consists of rounded or oval groups of cells, separated by delicate connective-tissue trabeculæ, which spring from the capsule. Similar cells are found throughout the entire cortex. They have been called the parenchymatous bodies or cells, although a better name is cortex corpuscles. In structure they resemble ordinary cells, consisting of poly-

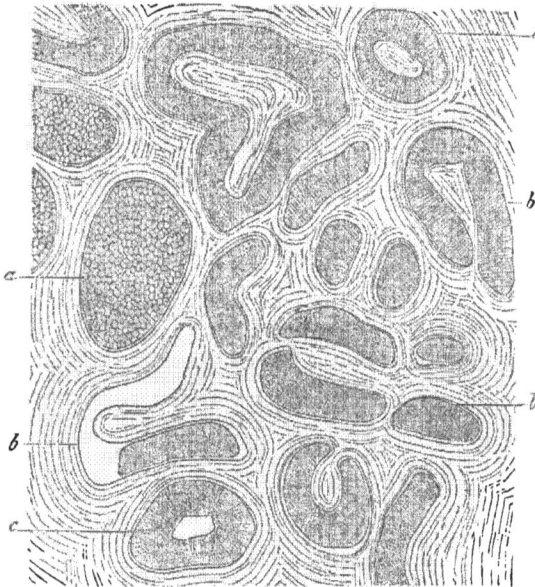

FIG. 186.—Horizontal section through the outermost cortical portions of the suprarenal capsule of the Horse. *a,* blind termination of a cylinder ; *b,* groove-shaped and cylindrical cortical trabeculæ ; *c,* stroma. Eberth.

hedral masses of protoplasm furnished with spherical nuclei and conspicuous nucleoli. Their protoplasm has a coarsely granular character, and, as a rule, contains more or less fat in greater or smaller droplets.

The *middle layer* contains cortical corpuscles which are arranged in almost parallel rows, and are so closely packed that this portion acquires a distinctly striated appearance. These cellular columns have received various names. By Ecker they were called gland tubules, Kölliker termed them cortical cylin-

28

ders, Eberth described them as cylindrical cell-trabeculæ, or cortical trabeculæ, and Krause named them cellular pillars. These cellular rows, columns, or streaks, are by no means always cylindrical, for on cross-section they frequently present a semilunar, oval, or bean-shaped appearance. Their inner and outer terminations have a rounded shape, and near the former place they seem to anastomose with one another. At

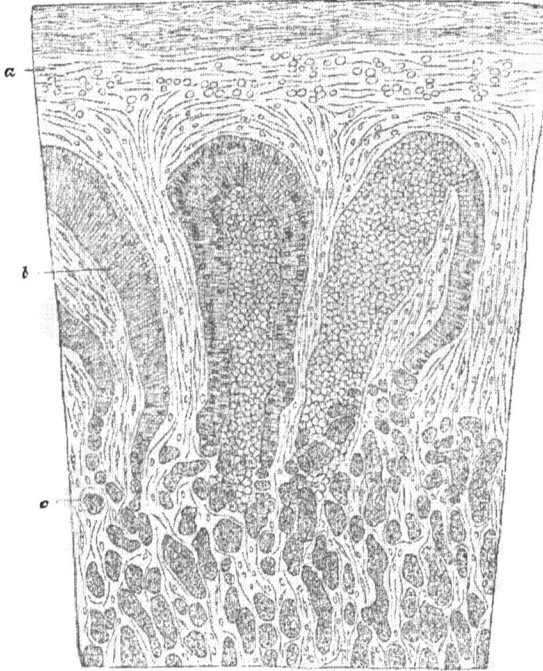

FIG. 187.—Vertical section through the the cortical portion of the suprarenal capsule of the Horse. *a*, capsule; *b*, cell-trabeculæ; *c*, cell-groups. Eberth.

the peripheral end they sometimes appear groove-shaped, or in horse-shoe form.

Connective-tissue processes communicating with the capsule are found between the cell columns, but the latter are not completely isolated by them. These connective-tissue streaks also send off transverse or oblique fibres, so that occasionally the cells of the middle layer seem to be inclosed in basket-like meshes. In addition to fat-droplets, granules of pigment are found in the cells of the innermost portion of the middle layer.

The *internal layer* is made up of irregularly arranged cortical corpuscles. Nearly all the cells of this layer contain pigment granules. The connective-tissue here forms a reticulum, with variously shaped meshes, which contain greater or smaller heaps of cells.

The *medullary substance* has a whitish-gray appearance, and is of a more delicate consistency than the cortex. It consists

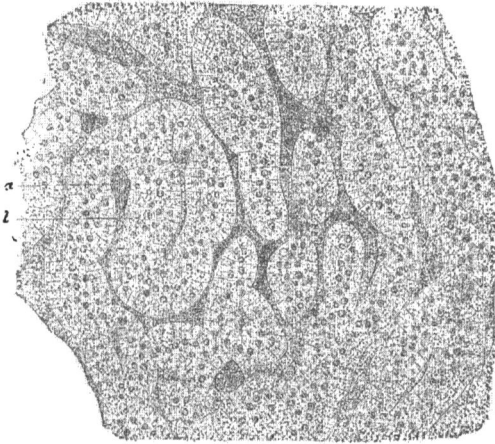

FIG. 185.—Vertical section through the medullary substance of the suprarenal capsule of the Cow. a, blood-vessels ; b, trabeculæ of medullary cells. Eberth.

of a network of connective tissue, which contains in its meshes the medullary corpuscles. These are pale cells with spherical nuclei and large nucleoli. They may assume various shapes. In man they are generally of an irregularly stellate or polygonal form. Their protoplasm is finely granular, and they contain, as a rule, much less fat and pigment than the cortical corpuscles. Kölliker finds that they resemble the nerve-cells of the central nervous system, but he adds that they cannot be regarded as such nerve-elements. The medullary cells assume a yellow or brownish color when treated with chromate of potash or chromic acid. Since the cortex corpuscles are not thus colored, this peculiarity may serve to distinguish one cellular variety from the other.

The connective-tissue framework of the medulla is called its stroma, and its meshes in man have an oval or rounded form, so that, as a rule, the cell-groups have a similar shape. On the whole, we find a smaller proportion of connective tissue in the medulla than in the cortex.

The *blood-vessels* of the suprarenal capsules occupy the stroma, and are found in great abundance. The arterial vessels arise from the aorta, the phrenic and renal arteries, and the cœliac axis. About twenty small branches pierce the capsule, and are distributed mainly to the cortex. The medullary substance is very rich in venous plexuses. Capillary networks are found in both cortical and medullary portions. The veins uniting form one principal branch, which passes out at the hilus of the organ. The right suprarenal vein empties its blood into the vena cava inferior, the left one into the vena renalis sinistra.

Lymphatics were seen by most observers only at the surface of the suprarenal capsules. Klein, however, has recently asserted that there exists between the cells "an anastomosing system of narrower and broader clefts, channels, and lacunæ, which belong to the lymphatic system." This applies to the zona fasciculata. In the other portions of the organ the same writer also finds lymph-spaces, and lymph-sinuses, occupying the regions "between the septa and trabeculæ of the framework on the one hand, and the cell-groups on the other."

The *nerves* occur in comparatively greater abundance in these organs than in any other glandular structures of the human body. Kölliker was able to count thirty-three branches in a single suprarenal capsule of a man. They are derived from the renal plexus, the pneumogastric and phrenic nerves, and semilunar ganglion. Very fine or medium-sized, dark-bordered fibres are commonly encountered, and they abound especially in the medulla. Ganglion-cells are also frequently seen, and Virchow has traced them into the interior of the organ. In the cortical substances they are of rare occurrence. The terminal distribution of the nerves has not been hitherto ascertained, and it appears to be still a matter of doubt whether they terminate in the suprarenal body at all.

Development.—In mammals the suprarenal capsule has an independent origin in a collection of tissue between the Wolffian bodies behind the mesentery and in front of the abdominal aorta. (Kölliker.) The mesoderma at this point assumes a special structure. Certain of its cells form more or less cylindrical masses with a reticulated appearance. Between these cellular groups a network of blood-vessels is soon found, so that the whole structure is now not unlike embryonal hepatic tissue. In rabbits, Kölliker saw the first traces of these bodies about the twelfth or thirteenth day. On the sixteenth day they had already attained a length of 1.56 mm., and occupied a position along the vertebral column from the first to the fourth and part of the fifth lumbar vertebra. On cross sections of embryos sixteen days old, Kölliker found that the suprarenal capsules were distinctly separate at their upper borders, whereas their lower ends were joined together to form a single organ. The same writer also found a nervous ganglion at the coalesced central portions of somewhat older embryos.

Behind the suprarenal capsules a second sympathetic ganglion was discovered. Remak and v. Brunn do not in all respects corroborate the statements of Kölliker. The latter was unable to ascertain any existing relationship between the nervous system and the suprarenal capsules.

BIBLIOGRAPHY.

BERGMANN. De glandulis suprarenalibus. Diss. inaug. Göttingen, 1839.

ECKER. Der feinere Bau der Nebennieren beim Menschen und den vier Wirbelthierklassen, 1846. Article "Blutgefässdrüsen" in Wagner's Handwörterbuch der Physiologie, Bd. IV. 1849.

H. FREY. Art. "Suprarenal Capsules" in Todd's Cyclopædia of Anat. 1849.

REMAK. Untersuchungen ueber der Entwickelung d. Wirbelthiere. Berlin, 1853-1855.

VIRCHOW. Zur Chemie der Nebennieren. Virchow's Archiv, 1857.

LEYDIG. Lehrbuch der Histologie, 1857.

B. WERNER. De capsulis supraren. Dorpat Dissertatio. 1857.

VULPIAN. Gaz. méd., p. 659. 1856; p. 84, 1857. Gaz. hebd., p. 665, 1857.

G. HARLEY. The Histology of the Suprarenal Capsules. Lancet, June 5th and 12th, 1858.

BARKOW. Anat. Unters. ueber die Harnblase. 1858.

PALLADINO. Estratto del bulletino dell' ass d. natur e med. Anno I., No. 5. Napoli.

BURCKHARDT. Virchow's Arch., Vol. XVII., p. 94. 1859.

G. JOESTEN. Archiv für phys. Heilkunde, S. 97. 1864.

A. MOERS. Virchow's Archiv, Bd. XXIX., S. 336.

HENLE. Anatomie des Menschen. Bd. 2. 1866.

ARNOLD, JUL. Ein Beitrag zu der feineren Structur und dem Chemismus der Nebennieren. Virchow's Archiv, Bd. 35, S. 64. 1866.

HOLM. Ueber die nervösen Elemente in den Nebennieren. Sitzungsberichte der Wiener Akademie. Ed. 53, 1. Abtheilung. 1866.

GRANDRY. Structure de la capsule surrénale. Journal de l'anatomie et de la physiologie. 1867.

KÖLLIKER. Handbuch der Gewebelehre. 5. Aufl. 1867.

EBERTH. Stricker's Archiv.

KISSELEFF. Centralblatt. No. 22. 1868.

BOUVIN. Over der bouw en de beweging der Ureteres. Utrecht, 1869.

ENGELMANN. Zur Phys. d. Ureters. Pflüger's Arch., Vol. II., p. 243. 1869.

OBERSTEINER, in Stricker's Manual.

UNRUH. Archiv f. Heilkunde, p. 289. 1872.

v. BRUNN. Archiv f. mikr. Anat., Vol. VIII., p. 618. 1872.

EGLI. Arch. f. mikros. Anat., Vol. IX., p. 653. 1873.

HAMBURGER. Zur Histol. d. Nierenb. u. d. Harnleiter. Arch. f. mikr. Anat., Vol. XVII., p. 14. 1879.

See also the text-books of Frey, Krause, Kölliker, and Henle.

BRAUN. Ueber Bau u. Entw. der Nebennieren bei Reptilien. Zool. Anzeiger, Vol. II., No. 27, p. 238. 1879; und Arbeiten aus d. zool.-zootom. Institut in Würzburg, Vol. V., p. 1. 1879.

KÖLLIKER. Entwickelungsgeschichte des Menschen. Leipzig, 1879.

KLEIN, and S. NOBLE SMITH. Atlas of Histology. 1880.

CHAPTER XXVIII.

THE MAMMARY GLAND.

By W. H. PORTER, M.D., and EDMUND C. WENDT, M.D., of New York City.

General considerations.—By virtue of its intimate association with the function of reproduction, this organ occupies a
distinctly peculiar position among the glands of the body. In
the male it persists through life in the same rudimentary form
which characterizes the mamma of both sexes at birth. Only
in the female, and in her only at certain times, does this organ
attain its complete histological maturity. It may be borne in
mind, however, that in a few anomalous cases, male beings supplied with fully developed mammary glands have been observed.

After conception, and as pregnancy advances, progressive
evolution takes place within the mamma. This unfolding
process at length culminates in exaggerated tissue-metamor-
phosis, which in other organs we should scarcely hesitate to
call pathological. In fact, Virchow and his followers all maintain that the secretion of milk is the direct result of a fatty
degeneration of mammary epithelium, and similar in all essential
respects to the processes involved in the elaboration of the sebaceous material from the cutaneous glands of that name. Billroth, indeed, calls the mammæ cutaneous fat-glands (*Hautfett-
drüsen*), and he does this in consideration of the mode of their
development, and because they are placed immediately beneath the integument. In spite of these statements, however,
we must maintain that the mammæ are radically different from
ordinary sebaceous glands, and that the processes of secretion
in the two sets of glands are quite distinct. The grounds on
which we base this opinion will be amplified farther on. The
secretory activity of the gland, consisting in the elaboration
of milk, is, as a rule, called into play only during the period

of rapid growth and development already alluded to. In exceptional instances, however, lacteal fluid may be secreted during the extra-puerperal period.

The mammæ belong to the class of compound acinous or racemose glands, and, like the other organs of this group, consist of a framework or stroma, and a proper secreting structure or parenchyma. As they appear to the naked eye, the bulk of the breasts is not their secreting parenchyma, but ordinary adipose tissue. This fills out the intervals between the lobes and lobules, and gives to the entire organ its smooth, round form. The different lobes have separate secretory ducts, which open upon the nipple. These ducts ramify throughout the substance of the gland tissue, and ultimately carry upon their terminal branches the clusters of secreting vesicles, called acini or alveoli. According to Zocher and Hennig, the true glandular substance has not a rounded shape, but shows a grouping into three principal divisions, one of which extends far up in the direction of the axilla. It is separated from the axillary lymphatic glands only by a small amount of adipose tissue. This would explain the ease, readiness, and frequency with which these glands become implicated in malignant disease of the mamma.

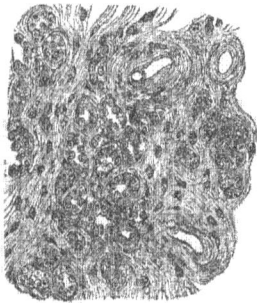

FIG. 189.—Terminal vesicles and stroma from the gland of a nursing woman. Langer.

Since the glands at birth differ very widely from the mammæ of adult women, and still more widely from those of pregnancy, it will be convenient to consider the histology of the organ under different aspects. This will be necessary, however, only with regard to the acini and the epithelia therein implanted, as these alone show such wide morphological divergencies in the different phases of existence.

The *nipple* (teat, *mamilla*, *papilla mammæ*) is the one structure belonging to the mamma which is least liable to modifications of tissue due to age and sex. It generally assumes the shape of a pigmented conical or cylindrical projection, at the apex of which the galactophorous ducts have their terminal openings. It is composed principally of a rather loosely woven connective tissue, containing abundant corpuscles, and provided with elastic fibrils. This conjunctive tissue forms a supporting framework for the milk-ducts traversing the nipple. The latter show walls of rather dense fibrous tissue, with a large proportion of elastic elements, and are provided with a lining of one row of short cylindrical cells. As the external orifice is approached, these cells begin to take on the character of the ordinary epidermic corpuscles of the integument. Partsch has found in many animals that the secreting parenchyma accompanied these ducts almost to their mamillary orifices.

The occurrence of unstriped muscle in the nipple, accords with the fact of its erectile properties. But the exact mode of distribution of these elements is still a matter of controversy among histologists. From the researches of Winkler and Kolessnikow, recently confirmed by Partsch, it would appear that they occur not in the ducts themselves, but form an incomplete ring around and external to the same. In or around the smaller galactophorous ducts, muscle-cells cannot be unmistakably recognized, though some authors have described their occurrence there.

As regards the structure of these smaller *galactophorous ducts (ductus lactiferi*, milk-ducts) it is quite simple. Their membranous walls consist of a delicate and closely woven reticulum of connective tissue, with a large admixture of fine elastic fibres. Henle, Meckel, and Kolessnikow have described smooth muscle-cells in these canals, but, as already stated, Partsch and others have denied their existence. At any rate, on cross-sections the contracted condition of some of the larger ducts results in a stellate appearance of their lumina, whereas the smaller ducts always appear round or oval.

The larger ducts traced into the gland tissue are found to be provided with saccular dilatations immediately beneath the nipple. These *milk-reservoirs (sinus ductuum lactiferorum, sacculi lactiferi*, or *ampullæ*) may be 5 to 8 mm. broad, and thus become distinctly perceptible to the naked eye. Below these dilatations the ducts again grow narrower, and by numerous divisions and subdivisions form a system of ramifying tubes, which terminate in the secreting alveoli. The structure of the larger ducts does not materially differ from that of the smaller ones. Their walls are, of course, considerably thicker, and there is found in addition a greater proportion of elastic tis-

sue. All the different kinds of ducts show a lining composed
of a single layer of short cylindrical cells, containing ellipsoid
nuclei. The character of the lining cells is, however, gradually
changed as the acini are approached, near which it merges into
the alveolar epithelium by insensible gradations.

Surrounding the nipple is a variously pigmented ring, called
the *areola mammæ*. Its surface is slightly corrugated, and
this circumstance, taken in connection with its pigmentation,
results in the production of the marked contrast it presents to
the very white and soft integument covering the other portions
of the female mamma. The areola is also provided with abundant unstriped muscle-fibres. Some of the latter surround the
nipple in concentric rings, others pursue a radial course. The
sudoriferous and sebaceous glands of the areola are conspicuously developed, and lanugo hairs are also found. The familiar changes which go on in the areola simultaneously with
the development of pregnancy, are mainly due to increased
blood-supply and additional pigmentation. The areola is also
provided with small granules of secreting parenchyma. Some
of these grains empty the products of their secretory activity
by special recurrent ducts into the main excretory canals. But
there are others which have special openings upon the free surface of the areola. Usually, little papillary eminences mark
the presence of such orifices. These scattered bits of mammary parenchyma are known as the *glandulæ aberrantes* of
Montgomery. Kölliker and others regard them as largely
developed sebaceous glands.

The *arteries* of the mamma are chiefly derived from the
internal mammary artery and the long thoracic. The veins
empty into the thoracic branches and cephalic vein. Both
arterial and venous vessels proceed subcutaneously from the
periphery to the nipple, whence branches are given off in a
posterior direction. They are not guided in their course by
the distribution of the milk-ducts, but are distributed to the
glandular parenchyma in such a way that each lobule has its
own separate supply. Finally, under the areola the veins of
the nipple form a circular anastomosing chain, known as the
circulus venosus of Haller. Capillary vessels surround the
acini, forming networks with rather close meshes. Of course,
the varying states of expansion and contraction in the ultimate
alveoli, which conditions correspond to phases of activity and

rest, will materially affect the size and shape of the capillary networks. They are, however, much less distinct and conspicuous during the period of lactation than in the quiescent state of the gland. Rauber found in the glands of pregnant animals that the blood-vessels were not in immediate contact with the walls of the secreting vesicles, being separated from them by interposed lymph-channels. Coyne, Langhans, and Kolessnikow have also described these perialveolar lymph-spaces. Their presence is, indeed, readily demonstrated by injections with nitrate of silver solutions. In actively secreting glands these channels are sometimes packed with leucocytes, which also infiltrate the stroma of the organ.

Lymphatics are plentiful in the mammary gland. We find them subcutaneously, as well as deep in the interior of the organ. Coyne, in 1874, described the perialveolar lymph-spaces, already mentioned, for the human mamma, and Kolessnikow, in 1870, perialveolar lymph-spaces for the mammary gland of the cow. Langhans succeeded in injecting a rich network of periacinal lymph-vessels, likewise lymph-channels around the excretory ducts and the lacteal sinuses. The largest lymph-vessels are retro-glandular. They are without valves. The lymph-vessels of the nipple resemble those of the skin. There seems to be no free communication between the lacunal and interstitial spaces of connective tissue of the glands, and the proper lymph-channels.

The principal lymph-vessels of the mamma, both deep and superficial branches, proceed to the glands of the axilla. But some of the mammary lymphatics also communicate, through intercostal branches, with the thoracic lymphatic glands. These are points worthy of remembrance in studying the mode of dissemination in mammary tumors.

Nerves abound less in the secreting structure of the mamma than in its integumentary apparatus. The majority are of spinal origin, although the sympathetic system is by no means excluded from representation. Branches from the fourth, fifth, and sixth intercostal nerves—the so-called *rami glandulares*—accompany the milk-ducts, and ramify within the organ. Satisfactory evidence concerning the manner of their ultimate termination has, however, not been hitherto obtained. Most of the nerves in the interior of the organ belong to the vascular or vaso-motor variety, and many are seen to accompany the blood-vessels. Eckhard has given the most elaborate description of the nerve-supply of the human mamma.

Structure of fully expanded gland.—Immediately before, during, and after lactation, the mamma appears as a distinctly lobulated organ, having a pinkish or yellowish hue, and resembling in consistence the human pancreas or salivary gland.

The different lobuli are made up of numerous ultimate acini, having, as a rule, a rounded, pyriform, or slightly polyhedral shape. They are of nearly uniform size, and are closely placed, being separated from one another by only sparing amounts of connective tissue, and the capillary vascular channels therein contained. Elastic fibres and smooth muscle-cells also occur, though not constantly, between the alveoli of the lobules. Lymphoid elements, as well as branched connective-tissue corpuscles, are always encountered there in greater or less abundance. In addition to these elements, large granular corpuscles containing nuclei are found. They are most numerous along the course of the blood-vessels, and appear to be identical with the so-called plasma cells of Waldeyer. Creighton, however, also describes similar cells in the interior of the alveoli, and believes that both are identical, maintaining that they are derived from the acinous epithelium.

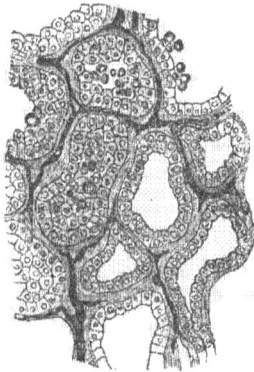

FIG. 190.—Transverse section through the terminal vesicles of the gland in a nursing woman, showing interalveolar capillaries. Langer.

According to this author's description, such cells are " not infrequently seen in the tissue outside a lobule in rows three or four deep ; again, they are found in the interfascicular spaces among the lymphoid-cells," that have been already mentioned. These large, granular, and nucleated corpuscles are said to be filled with a bright yellow or golden pigment. Now, Creighton has pointed out that the periodical subsidence of the mammary function is accompanied by the formation of much corpuscular waste material. And the production of these remarkable yellow cells, which finally leave the gland by way of the lymph-vessels, is, according to him, but a final phase of this process.

The mammary epithelium which paves the acini has been variously described as consisting of flat polyhedral (Reinhard);

cubical, cylindrical (Kolessnikow); small polyhedral (Langer); and prismatic (Kehrer) cells. This discrepancy of opinion receives its explanation from the fact that the epithelial cells

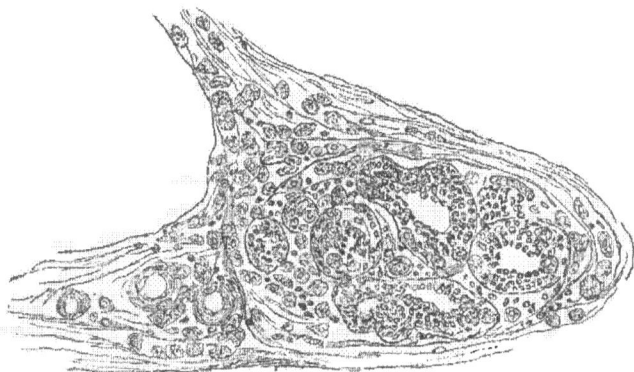

FIG. 191.—Lobule of a mamma near the resting state. Numerous large pigmented cells within the acini and in the interlobular fibrillar tissue. Creighton.

have a different appearance in the various conditions intervening between full activity and complete rest of the gland.

Creighton has given a very satisfactory description of mammary epithelium. He states that in the fully expanded gland "the floor of an acinus in section is covered by a mosaic of polyhedric epithelial cells, usually to the number of fifteen or twenty, while in the larger elongated acini as many as thirty may be counted. The cells are usually pentagonal or hexagonal, and the corners are sometimes rounded. In each cell there is a central round nucleus, which colors brightly with the staining fluid, and a broad fringe of protoplasm, which stains less deeply." The nucleus varies in its relative size, generally having a diameter equal to about one-third that of the entire cell.

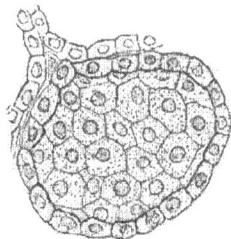

FIG. 192.—Fully expanded acinus, showing mosaic of polyhedral cells. Creighton.

"In a profile view of an acinus, the epithelium appears as a circlet of oblong cells, in which the nucleus at the centre occupies almost the entire thickness of the cell. The mammary epithelial cell may therefore be described as a flattened polyhedric body, with a thickness about one-half of its breadth. The substance of the nucleus is apparently homogeneous, with a deeper line of staining round the margin ; a nucleolus is not always prominently seen.''

Structure of involuted mamma.—Having thus briefly indicated the main histological features of a fully evolved gland, we are now prepared to examine the mamma in a condition of advanced involution. By involution, in this sense, is meant the periodical return to inactivity, and not to final retrograde metamorphosis, which culminates in complete senile atrophy. The glandular lobules, then, in the involuted organ are again found to be composed of closely crowded alveoli. But all the lobules appear to have become smaller, and their acinous components are likewise shrunken. The basement-membrane of the latter does not appear to be materially altered, but its cellular contents are considerably changed. In place of the beautiful mosaic characteristic of the active gland, there now appears only an aggregation of nucleated corpuscles to the number of five or ten. Creighton describes them as "nothing else than a somewhat irregular heap of naked nuclei, with no fringe of protoplasm round them, and in size little, if at all, larger than the nucleus alone of the perfect epithelium." This description, however, applies only to hardened specimens, for in fresh preparations the nuclei, as a rule, show a broader or narrower surrounding zone of protoplasm. As regards the diameter of the involuted acini, it is about one-fourth that of the actively secreting alveoli.

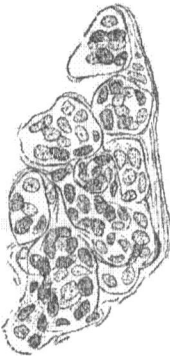

FIG. 193. — Involuted mammary lobule, showing the nuclear contents of the alveoli. Creighton.

Owing to the shrinkage in the glandular parenchyma, the blood-vessels and excretory ducts, as already stated, are more prominent in an involuted than in an active gland.

It is not our purpose here to trace, step by step, the various processes by which a gland passes from the resting state to that condition of complete evolution which is alone compatible with active secretion. For the details of this interesting subject, the reader is referred to the work of Creighton. We may, however, very briefly summarize this author's account of the trans-formations in question. The one essential circumstance characterizing the whole change is a process of vacuolation, which Creighton assumes to take place in the secreting cells. "The

most definite and unmistakable form of vacuolation is the sig-
net-ring type." This process is, according to him, a true one
of endogenous cell formation, resulting in this instance in the
formation of milk. Moreover, large, granular, nucleated cells,
filled with a bright yellow or golden pigment, "found both
within the alveoli and in the interfibrillar spaces without them",

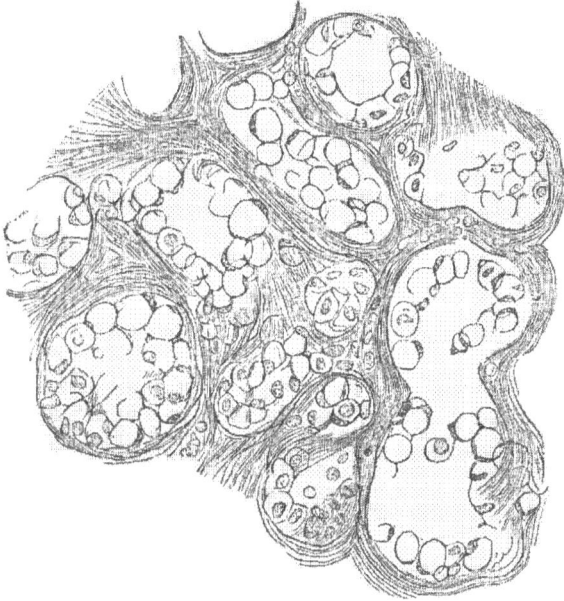

FIG. 194.—Vacuolation of alveolar epithelium. From the udder of a ewe shortly after the end of lactation. The cells *in situ* are vacuolated cells, with the usual thin and, for the most part, uncolored hoop
or ring of the vacuole, and the deeply stained peripheral mass. Creighton.

characterize the last stage of involution, "and the pigment
that belongs to them is to be .found strewn over the lobules
that have reached the resting state." Finally, Creighton asserts that "the various forms of cells that characterize the
various stages of involution must have resulted from a transformation *de novo* of the renewed epithelium, and not from
successive changes upon the same cell." Each epithelial cell,
therefore, that is used up in the formation of milk, has been at
one time a perfect polyhedral corpuscle or fully equipped cell,
and "has rapidly undergone the cycle of changes whereby
its whole substance has been converted into milk."
A distinguishing feature of one stage of evolution which

deserves to be mentioned, is "the presence in the cavities of
the acini of a peculiar granular material, the coagulated condition of a fluid." Partsch has also described the occurrence
of this granular mass within the alveoli, and he states that the
secreting epithelia, though of normal size, were furnished with
shrunken nuclei, and showed numerous light spots, as if the
cells were perforated and sieve-like. It
would appear that this writer has observed the stage of vacuolation without, however, interpreting the same in
Creighton's sense.

Creighton also describes in certain
glands the connective-tissue stroma as
crowded with cellular elements, which
he considers equally with the pigmented
corpuscles as waste-cells of the secretion. Others (Winkler, Brunn, and particularly Rauber) have assigned a far
different significance to these bodies, as
will appear farther on. Finally, Creighton explains that the secretion of the
mammary gland "may be said to be produced by a transformation of the substance of successive generations of
epithelial cells, and in the state of full activity that transformation of the substance is so complete, that it may be called a
deliquescence."

FIG. 195.—Acini from a partly
expanded gland, some of them
filled with a granular material.
From the mamma of a pregnant
cat. Creighton.

Although Creighton's investigations did not extend to the
human mammary gland, there is ample ground for the belief
that changes of evolution and involution similar to those which
he has described in animals, constantly take place in the human female as well. And even if we accept only some of his
views on the inter-relations of physiological action and histological appearance, the discrepancy still existing in the descriptions given by different authors will receive a more rational
explanation than has hitherto been offered by writers on this
subject. Certainly some of his assertions appear rather fanci-
ful in their far-reaching novelty, nevertheless they deserve the
attentive consideration which we have, at least, in part bestowed
on them.

From the results of our own examinations, we are unable

to concede in all respects the correctness of Creighton's inter-pretations. The evidences of epithelial destruction for purposes of milk secretion, are not positive and convincing. In the Harderian gland, as well as in the mamma, we have observed the extrusion of fat-droplets from cells replete with them without destruction of the cell itself. Partsch agrees with us in assuming that the cells may burst or otherwise discharge their contents, and yet retain enough protoplasm to maintain their vitality ; and also that the vital contractions of the protoplasm may force out the oil-globules without destruction of the epithelium. What Creighton has called vacuolation does not mean death to the cells concerned in this action, for they retain their nuclei and sufficient protoplasm to become re-established as perfect epithelia. That this reformation of old epithelium takes place, is proven by the fact that a new formation by proliferation has never been observed, and by the additional circumstance that the mammary acini never show more than a single layer of lining-corpuscles, and, moreover, always show this layer complete.

In this, as in many other respects, the mamma closely resembles the Harderian gland, more particularly of the rodentia, as described by one of the writers in a monograph. The basement-membrane of the acini in every particular also corresponds in the two kinds of glands, being in both a homogeneous, apparently structureless membrane, with superimposed branched adventitial cells, the so-called *Stützzellen* of German writers. A basket-shaped reticulum, such as has been described by Boll, Langer, Kolessnikow, Moullin, and others, is never found to constitute this *membrana propria*, although artificially, appearances simulating a structure of this kind are readily obtained, and have been interpreted by several histologists as natural occurrences.

In the cutaneous sebaceous glands the secreting vesicles are filled with several superimposed layers of epithelia, and it is this circumstance which leads to an entirely different mode of secretion. For there it would indeed appear that the cells undergoing fatty degeneration become detached from their bases and find their way into the narrow lumen of the acinus. The older or inner generation of cells thus vanishing is replaced by new corpuscles formed by gradual proliferation from the peripheral zone.

29

Rauber's views on the mamma and the lacteal secretion are
somewhat startling, but must occupy our attention here. From
a series of very carefully conducted examinations, principally
on the glands of guinea-pigs during and after pregnancy, he
feels justified in concluding that milk owes its orgin to the
entrance of countless leucocytes into the lumen of the gland-
vesicles. The emigrated lymphoid elements, he believes, penetrate the alveolar walls, passing through the single layer of
epithelial cells which line them. Arrived in the interior of an
ultimate acinus, the leucocytes undergo fatty metamorphosis,
and thus at length furnish the most essential and characteristic
ingredient of milk, viz., the milk-globules. Rauber, therefore,
discards the notion that the formed particles of the lacteal
secretion originate in the glandular epithelium, and represent
the elaborated products of its functional activity. He also
denies that previously formed milk globules, or colostrum corpuscles, ever pass through the alveolar walls. Thus the primitive opinion advanced by Empedocles, describing milk as white
pus, is in a measure revived, and milk is held to be directly
derived from the white corpuscles of the blood.

Preparations of mammary glands taken from animals still
suckling their young, according to him, invariably show the
intraglandular lymph-vessels replete with leucocytes, the stroma similarly infiltrated, identical corpuscles in greater or less
abundance within the vesicles, and transitional forms between
lymphoid-corpuscles and milk-globules. These claims, granted
to be facts, and considered in conjunction with the circumstance that epithelial proliferation is not seen, would certainly
go far to make Rauber's theory seem a somewhat plausible
one. Nevertheless, we require corroborative evidence from
others, before his views can be accepted as anything more than
an ingenious hypothesis.

Rauber has also described the occurrence of a delicate striation within the epithelial cells of the alveoli. These striæ are
said to be in all respects similar to those found in the secreting
elements of certain portions of the salivary glands and the
tubules of the kidneys.

As regards the *corpuscles of Donné*, or *colostrum bodies*,
most authors regard them as the products of desquamation of
the alveolar epithelium, the latter being in a condition of fatty
degeneration (Winkler, De Sinéty, Buchholtz, and others).

Some histologists, like Stricker, hold that oil-globules may be expelled from the interior of fat-filled cells without disintegration of their protoplasmic bodies. It is an undoubtable fact that colostrum corpuscles, when managed with proper precautions, may be seen to yield droplets of fat under the microscope, just as amœbæ reject similar contained particles. Rauber, however, maintains that these bodies represent leucocytes in various stages of fatty metamorphosis, and he calls such corpuscles, when found in the gland vesicles, *galactoblasts*.

In the gland of Harder, one of the writers has found the spacious gland vesicles lined with very large epithelia; and these cells were in many animals entirely fat-filled. They secreted a greasy substance not unlike thick milk. Yet destruction of the cell-body did not occur, at least evidences of such a process could not be obtained. Partsch has therefore anticipated the authors in their conclusion that the secretion of milk is accomplished in much the same way in which the creamy products of the Harderian gland are formed, *i.e.*, without total destruction of epithelial cells. According to our view, then, and it nearly coincides with the opinion of Stricker, Winkler, and especially Partsch, the cells containing the fat-globules may, indeed, burst and discharge their contents, but the nucleus and sufficient protoplasm are retained to enable the epithelium to recuperate, and in the course of time again and again discharge its contents. Along with this mode of milk secretion, a second process occurs. This consists of the gradual extrusion of oil-droplets, the cell body remaining entirely intact, since the mere vital contractions of the protoplasm suffice to drive out one milk-globule after another.

When the activity of the gland is suddenly heightened in the period immediately before childbirth, some few epithelial cells are desquamated. These, appearing in the milk of most women, are identical with the bodies known and described as colostrum corpuscles.

Of other anatomical constituents of normal milk, we only find the *milk-* or *oil-globules*. They are suspended in the fluid emulsion which milk truly represents, in countless numbers. They vary in size from 0.002 to 0.009 mm. A very delicate fringe of protoplasm adheres to their periphery, and it is for this reason that they may appear to become stained when submitted to the action of proper dyes.

DEVELOPMENT OF THE GLAND.

Like the other cutaneous glands of the body, the mamma
is first formed by a proliferation inward of certain epidermal
cells.   In other words, the breast results from a downward
extension of epiblastic corpuscles. The first unmistakable indication of the future gland is seen about the third or fourth month
of pregnancy. At that time it consists of a solid plug, or pro-

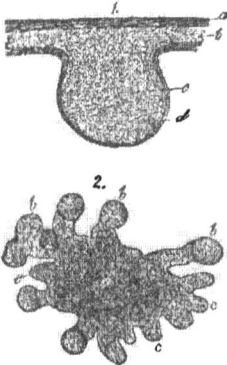

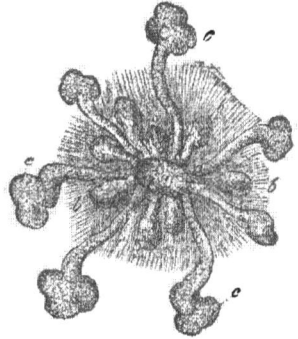

FIG. 196.—1. Rudimentary form of gland
in human fœtus: a, b, epidermis; c, aggregation of cells; d, connective tissue layer. 2. From
a seven-months' fœtus: a, central substance;
b, larger, and c, smaller outgrowths. Frey.

FIG. 197.—Embryonal mamma: a, central mass, with b. and c, variously shaped
outgrowths. Frey.

cess, extending downward from the rete-mucosum of the skin.
This has been called *Drüsenfeld*, by Huss. From the internal
end of this solid process, sprouts, or offshoots, are developed,
and they represent the future separate glands constituting the
mature organ. These buds have a pyriform, or club-like shape,
and are surrounded by ordinary embryonal connective tissue.
The further growth of the gland takes place by a process of
continuous extension and subdivision, but indications of the
latter are not always found at birth. Ducts are already visible
in the new-born infant, but the aggregations of cells representing the future acini, remain without lumina for a much longer
period.

Th. Kölliker describes as a constant occurrence, especially
marked in the breasts of female infants, the dilatation of a
greater or smaller number of milk-ducts. Such ectatic-canals

have their lumina filled with desquamated epithelial cells, and a whitish, granular material. Formerly, these occurrences were considered to be exceptional, and were regarded as having a pathological significance. During the first year of extra-uterine life, this characteristic process of progressive dilatation may assume such large dimensions, that the mamma may come to resemble cavernous tissue, the ectatic spaces of which are paved with flattened epithelium. Within certain limits, Kölliker regards this as a perfectly normal physiological event. But he adds that an exaggerated process of this kind may result in early mastitis. Such an occurrence, he thinks, may explain the rudimentary development of the breasts observed in some women of otherwise normal growth.

The post-embryonal growth of the mamma has been carefully studied by Langer, and his results and conclusions having been confirmed by the investigations of Kölliker, Huss, and others, must still be received as representing the true condition of things, in spite of the novel and heterodox views advanced by Creighton.

Up to the time of puberty, the growth of the breast is very gradual and quite insignificant, even in females. Then, however, the ducts begin to rapidly ramify in all directions, and, by offshoots from various points, true acini are at length developed. But they remain of small size until the stimulus of

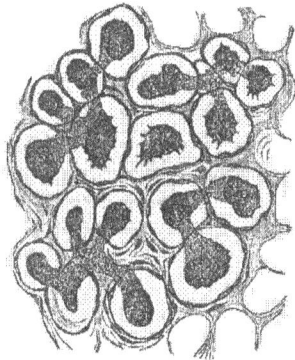

FIG. 198.—Transverse section of glandular vesicles in a virgin. Langer.

pregnancy causes a further evolution. In the male, the existing ducts, as a rule, atrophy with advancing age. The evolution changes which the mamma undergoes during pregnancy, have already been set forth, and there remain to be considered only those final phases of metamorphosis which take place in the climacteric period of life.

These are readily understood, consisting essentially of a complete atrophy of all the secreting acini. Simultaneously with these atrophic changes the epithelia of the galactophorous ducts become flattened, and finally shrink, so as to form only squamous plates, which line the ramifying processes of connective tissue representing the former lactiferous canals. The terminal portions of these larger duct-remnants are sometimes connected with minute channels, the latter being the remnants of collapsed smaller ducts. In some measure we find a compensatory production of fat, which partly replaces the faded acini. The breasts of old women, therefore, consist of fibrous tissue, with a large proportion of elastic elements, fat-cells, and the remnants of the ducts. It may be remarked that the latter frequently show cystic dilatations, the cavities being filled with a dirty, slimy fluid. The blood and lymph-vessels, but especially the latter, participate in the general atrophy of the tissues.

This succinct account concerning the histogenesis of the mammary gland, does not, as already intimated, represent the unchallenged opinion on its first development. For Creighton, in the remarkable work already cited, radically opposes the view that the mamma takes its origin from the epiblast. He believes, on the contrary, that it starts from the mesoblast, or connective-tissue layer of the embryo, and not the upper epithelial layer or epiblast. According to him, moreover, and his conclusions are based on developmental studies, chiefly of the guinea-pig's gland, the process may be justly described as a centripetal one, whereas the current view represents this gland-develpoment as essentially centrifugal. We have already expressed our adherence to the current view, attributing this growth to extension from a central point. Nevertheless, it seems proper to briefly give the conclusions of Creighton, especially since they appear to be singularly corroborative of the account given by Goodsir of this process, as early as 1842, an account which has apparently remained almost unnoticed by workers in this branch of scientific medicine.

Creighton then concludes his inquiry as follows :

" 1. The mammary acini of the guinea-pig develop at many separate points in a matrix-tissue. The embryo cells from which they develop are of the same kind that give origin to the surrounding fat-tissue. The process of development of the mammary acini is, step-for-step, the same as that of the fat-lobules."

" 2. The ducts of the mamma develop from the same matrix-tissue, by direct aggregation of the embryonic-cells, along predetermined lines. The ducts develop, in the individual guinea-pig, before the acini, whereas, in the phylogenetic suc-

cession, the ducts are a later acquisition. This reversal of the
order of acquisition of parts is in accordance with the principle stated by Herbert Spencer, that 'under certain circumstances the direct mode of development tends to be substituted
for the indirect.' "

Hints regarding the histological study of the mamma.—
The evolution of the mammary structure progresses *pari passu*
with the development of its functional activity. It is the stimulus of pregnancy which determines both. Nevertheless,
even during the period of its fullest physiological bloom, *i.e.*,
during lactation, variations in the degree of functional activity
normally take place. Moreover, the same gland may contain
lobules which are comparatively at rest, and others which are
at the full height of activity. This should always be borne in
mind in interpreting the results of histological inspection of
this organ, lest erroneous impressions be conveyed.

The alveolar epithelial cells will, therefore, not be found
alike in the different acini, nor yet even in the same vesicle.
We may find cuboidal cells, and cylindrical ones, and flattened
corpuscles, and in addition, various transitional forms between
these types.

The nucleus will appear round, or oval, and about 6–7 μ in
diameter. Sometimes two nuclei may be found in one cell.
The radiating striation observed by Rauber in many cells, has
already received mention. It is a noteworthy fact that the
cells themselves contain only a very small proportion of fatty
granules, whereas the intra-alveolar lumen is often replete
with the same.

In order, then, to study the histology of the gland at the
high-water-mark of its functional activity, animals should be
chosen which have either just given birth to their young,
or are about to do so. For the normal conditions of the
human mamma are rapidly transformed by post-mortem change,
if not previously altered in consequence of the disease which
caused the death of the individual. The organ may be examined fresh, or else hardened and then cut in sections to be
stained and mounted in the ordinary manner.

BIBLIOGRAPHY.

RUDOLFI. Bemerkungen ueber den Bau der Brüste. Abhandl. der Berliner Akad. 1831.

DONNÉ, AL. Du lait, etc., en particulier de celui des nourrices. Paris, 1837.

COOPER. Anatomy of the Breast. 1839.

GÜTERBOCK. Ueber die Donneschen Corps granuleux. Müller's Archiv. 1839.

HENLE. Ueber die mikroskop. Bestandth. d. Milch. Froriep's Notizen. 1839.

FETZER. Ueber die weiblichen Brüste. Würzburg, 1840.

NASSE. Ueber die mikroskopischen Bestandtheile der Milch. Müller's Archiv. 1840.

GOODSIR. Anatom. and Pathol. Observations. 1845.

REINHARDT. Ueber die Entstehung der Körnchenzellen. Virchow's Archiv. Vol. I. 1847.

WILL. Ueber die Milchabsonderung. Erlangen, 1850.

LANGER. Ueber den Bau und die Entwickelung der Milchdrüse. Denkschr. d. Wien. Akad. 1851. Also article on the Mammary Gland, in Stricker's Histology.

LUSCHKA. Zur Anatomie der Männl. Brustdrüsen. Müller's Archiv. 1852.

ECKHARD. Beitr. zur Anat. u. Phys. 1. Band. 1. Heft. Giessen, 1855.

VIRCHOW. Die Cellularpathologie, p. 305. 1859.

DUVAL. Du mamelon et de son auréole. Paris, 1861.

GRUBER. Ueber die Männliche Brustdrüse. Memoiren d. Petersburger Akad. 1866.

STRICKER. Ueber contractile Körper, etc. Sitzber. d. Akad. Wien. Vol. LIII. 1866.

ZOCHER. Beitr. zur Anat. u. Phys. d. weibl. Brust. Leipzig, 1869.

HENNIG. Beitrag. zur Morphologie der weibl. Milchdrüse. Arch. f. Gynäkol. Vol. II., p. 331. 1871.

HUSS. Beiträge zur Entwickelung der Milchdrüse beim Menschen, etc. Jenaische Zeitschrift, Vol. VII., 2. 1873.

LANGHANS. Die Lymphgefässe der Brustdrüsen in ihren Beziehungen zum Krebse. Arch. für Gynäkologie, Bd. VIII., S. 181. 1875. Also, Zur pathologischen Histologie der weiblichen Brustdrüse. Virchow's Archiv, p. 132. Bd. 58. 1873.

COYNE. Sur les lacunes lymphatiques de la glande mammaire. Soc. de Biologic. 21. Nov., 1874. Also, Sur les lacunes lymphatiques de la glande mammaire. Gazette Hebdom., p. 775. 1874.

DE SINÉTY. Recherches sur les globules du lait. Arch. de Phys. 1874.

VON BRUNN. Göttinger Nachrichten, No. 19. 1874.

LABBÉ and COYNE. Traité des tumeurs bénignes du sein. 1876.

BUCHHOLTZ. Das Verhalten der Colostrumkörper, etc. Göttingen, 1877.

DE SINÉTY. Sur le dévelop. et l'histol. comp. de la mamelle. Gaz. méd. de Paris, No. 6, p. 68. 1877.

KOLESSNIKOW. Die Histologie der Milchdrüse der Kuh. Virchow's Archiv. Bd. 70, p. 531. 1877.

SCHMID, H. Zur Lehre von der Milchsecretion. Würzburg, 1877.

WENDT. Ueber die Hardersche Drüse der Säugethiere. Strassburg, 1877.

WINKLER. Bau der Milchdrüse. Jahresber. d. Ges. f. Natur. u. Heilkunde. Dres-

den, 1874. Beitr. zur Histol u. Nervenverth. in d. Mamma. Archiv f. Gynäkol. Vol. XI. 1877.

KÖLLIKER, TH. Beiträge zur Kenntniss der Brustdrüse. Verh. d. phys.-med. Ges.
zu Würzburg. 1879.

RAUBER. Ueber die Absonderung der Milch. Sitzber. d. naturf. Gesel. zu Leipzig, pp. 30–34. 1879. Also, Bemerkungen ueber den feineren Bau der Milchdrüse. Schmidt's Jahrb. 1879.

RAUBER. Ueber den Ursprung der Milch. Leipzig, 1879.

BILLROTH. Die Krankheiten der Brustdrüsen. Deutsche Chirurgie. Lieferung
41. 1880.

PARTSCH. Ueber den feineren Bau der Milchdrüse. Breslau, 1880.

MOULLIN. The Membrana Propria of the Mammary Gland. Journ. of Anat. and
Phys. April, 1881.

SAEFFTIGEN, A. Zur fein. Anat. d. Milchdrüse während der Lactationsperiode.
Méd. biol. acad. imp. d. sc. de St. Petersb. XI. 13–40. 1881.

TALMA, S. Beitrag z. Histogenesis d. weibl. Brustdrüse. Arch. f. mikr. Anat.
XX. 145–159. 1881–82.

REIN, G. Untersuch. u. d. embryonale Entwicklungsgeschichte der Milchdrüse.
Ibid. XX. 431–501. 1881–82.

APPENDIX A.

THE LYMPHATIC SYSTEM.

By W. R. BIRDSALL, M.D.

THE principal contributions which have been made to this subject, since the chapter on the lymphatic system was written, are by Drs. George and F. E. Hoggan, in several articles cited below, including observations on the lymphatics of the pancreas, the bladder, and of cartilage, besides the article previously referred to on the lymphatics of muscular tissue and the skin. The views of these authors are decidedly at variance with those of many observers. They hold that the injection methods are not suited to demonstrate the course of the lymphatics, as the injection fluid follows channels in the connective tissue which are not true lymphatics. By an ingenious method of warming mounted specimens, from which the water had not been entirely removed by alcohol, they were able to trace the flow of the vapor thus formed along the interstices of the connective tissue external to the lymphatics, which, in their opinion, represent what others have described as lymphatics or "plasma channels." They regard silver staining as the only reliable method, for it alone reveals the crenated outline of the endothelial cell, which they consider the necessary element in the constitution of lymphatics. Gold and hæmatoxylon solutions are used as accessories in double staining. The details of these methods are too extended to be recited here, but should be read in the original by the student. They devise what they term "histological rings," consisting of an outer ring, which crowds over an inner one, upon which the membrane or tissue has been spread, in the same manner that the parchment head of a tamborine or drum is stretched. All reagents are applied to

the specimen while so fastened, even to the abstraction of
water by alcohol, and rendering transparent by oil of cloves.
When possible, the tissue is not detached from the body of the
animal until the specimen is finished.   Very small and lean
animals are used, as rats and mice.

They have "failed to find evidence of the existence of such
structures as 'stomata,'" and believe that the peri-vascular
and peri-neural sheaths "have no existence in fact," while
they consider erroneous the view that the "branched cells stand
in formal connection with lymph-channels ; or that the cells or
cavities in which they lie are lymphatic radicles."

Klein has contributed an article on the lymphatics of the
skin, in which he reiterates his former assertions, and combats
the opposing views just referred to.

BIBLIOGRAPHY.

Hoggan, G. and F. E. On the Lymphatics of Cartilage and of the Perichondrium.
   Jour. Anat. and Phys., XV., 121–136.   London, 1880–81.
Ibid. On the Comparative Anatomy of the Lymphatics of the Mammalian Urinary
   Bladder. Ibid., XV., 355–377.
Ibid. On the Lymphatics of the Pancreas. Ibid., XV., 475–495. 1881.
Klein. On the Lymphatics of the Skin. Quart. Jour. Mic. Sci. 1881.
Jourdain. Sur les sacs-sous-cutanées et les sinus lymphatiques de la regione cepha-
   lique dans la rana temporaria. Compt. Rend., Acad. d. Sc. XCIII., 597–
   600. Paris, 1881.

APPENDIX B.

THE SALIVARY GLANDS.

By EDMUND C. WENDT, M.D.,

Curator of the St. Luke's and St. Francis' Hospitals, etc., New York City.

General remarks.—Modern physiological research has imparted a new stimulus to histological investigations. For the fact is now well established that, in many tissues and organs, functional activity, alternating with rest, represent phases of life, each accompanied by distinctly recognizable morphological changes. No organs or class of organs have been more carefully, industriously, and, withal, ingeniously studied, in this direction, than the salivary glands. But although abundant new evidence has thus been accumulated, it cannot be said that the testimony of different authors has so far succeeded in harmonizing conflicting views and contending theories. It will be the aim of the writer to avoid, as much as possible, theoretical and controversial reasonings, and present the subject in its present aspect of real knowledge.

All the glands constituting this group belong to the compound acinous type. Here, at the very outset, we are confronted by the assertions of Grot and Klein, who positively declare that the salivary glands are exclusively made up of convoluted tubules. From the repeated examination of numerous specimens of different glands, the writer is satisfied that the acinous preponderates very decidedly over the tubular form, and hence it is more correct to give them the former name.

It may also be mentioned, in this connection, that Bermann has described the normal occurrence of a compound tubular mucous gland found in intimate relationship with the submaxillary of man and several animals. Heidenhain, however, demonstrated that the organ described by Bermann really corresponds to the sublingual gland.

The salivary glands lie enclosed in a connective-tissue *capsule* of varying thickness. From this envelope trabecles are given off, and, traversing the organ in all directions, divide it into secondary lobes and lobules. In this supporting frame-work leucocytes are found in greater or less abundance, surrounding the inter-lobular ducts and vessels. In addition, large plasma cells (Waldeyer), or Ehrlich's corpuscles (*Mastzellen*), are commonly encountered. The excretory ducts form a system of ramifying tubes, terminating in the secreting acini or vesicles.

THE ACINI (*Alveoli, Ultimate Secreting Vesicles*).

Each acinus consists of a membrana propria (basement membrane) lined by a varying number of secreting cells.

In fresh specimens, derived from recently killed animals, the *membrana propria* invariably appears as a very delicate, translucent, and apparently structureless membrane. In sections of hardened glands, flattened, oval nuclei are found studding this membrane.

Boll, Heidenhain, Lavdovsky, and, in fact, most recent authors, assert that the membrana propria is composed of flat, branching cells, which form a basket-like reticulum, containing the secreting corpuscles. The writer cannot agree to this view. Branching, nucleated bodies of the kind described by these authors are, indeed, readily visible after suitable modes of preparation. But they usually lie outside of the membrana propria, being superimposed to afford the necessary additional strength to this extremely delicate membrane. Pflüger described them as multipolar ganglion cells. But his views are clearly erroneous, having been refuted by all later investigators, with but few exceptions. One of these, Kupffer, claims to have succeeded in demonstrating the direct entrance of nerve-fibrils into the glandular acini in the cockroach (*blatta orientalis*). But even this author failed to corroborate the assertions of Pflüger with regard to man and the higher animals.

According to the observations of the author the membrana propria is a nucleated connective-tissue membrane. In the fœtus it is first formed in the following way : Solid proliferating plugs of epithelia, representing the future parenchyma, grow into the surrounding embryonic tissue. The layer of connective-tissue cells immediately adjoining the epithelia gradually assumes a flattened shape. At length these corpuscles coalesce and form a richly nucleated membrane. In later life some of the nuclei atrophy and disappear, but a certain number usually persist. For this reason the membrana propria in adult glands appears as a homogeneous membrane, containing a varying number of nuclei. The branched cells are superimposed, or lie beneath it; but while they are found to adhere to it, they, nevertheless, do not form true constituent elements of the membrane in question.

THE SECRETING CELLS.

The epithelia of the proper gland substance, usually line the basement membrane, in a single layer of nucleated, pyramidal, cuboidal, or polyhedral cells. In structure they differ rather widely in the various glands belonging to this group. It will be well, therefore, to consider, separately, first the cells of the albuminous glands, and then those of the mucous type.

1. *Albuminous glands.*—Formerly these were known as "serous" glands, since the product of their secretion was apparently a serous fluid. Recently, however, Heidenhain has demonstrated the abundant presence of albuminoid matter therein. Glands of this type are, therefore, more properly called albuminous. The parotid gland of man and mammals generally, the lachrymal glands, the submaxillary glands of certain animals, and the larger portion of the human submaxillary gland, are included in this category.

In fresh specimens the cells of their alveoli appear to be so completely filled up with darkly granular matter that their boundaries are either invisible or quite obscure. Sections of hardened glands, however, show the intercellular boundary lines clearly marked. The form of these corpuscles is now seen to be either somewhat rounded or polygonal. Each one is, as a rule, provided with a pale, spherical nucleus, occupying a peripheral position, *i.e.*, approaching the membrana propria. In hardened specimens of resting glands, the nuclei commonly assume a stellate or angular form, the result of shrinkage. As regards the size of the salivary epithelia, their average diameter is 0.015 mm., the nuclei measuring 0.006 mm. It should be borne in mind, however, that many cells fall considerably below this average, whereas others measurably exceed it.

2. *The mucous glands.*—In the simplest glands of this type, the alveoli contain a single layer of large, clear, transparent, columnar cells, almost identical in appearance with the so-called goblet cells of the alimentary canal. In recent specimens the nucleus is found round or oval, but in hardened glands it appears quite flat. In all cases it almost lies in contact with the membrana propria.

But the glands of this variety contain, in addition to the simple mucous cells just described, smaller and

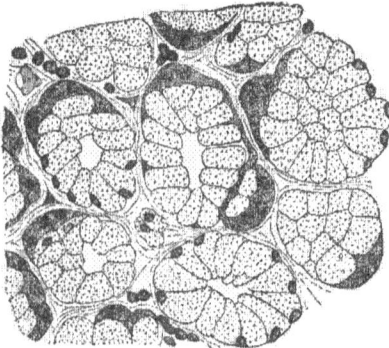

Fig. 199.—Section of mucous gland at rest, showing crescents of Giannuzzi. Lavdovsky.

very granular bodies, which are known as the *crescents* or *lunulæ* of Giannuzzi. They usually occur in semilunar groups, and are found external to the mucous cells, and just beneath the basement membrane. The individual cells of such groups are not always provided with a nucleus. In some, however, two nuclei appear.

Isolated mucous cells (maceration of fresh gland in iodized serum or chromate of ammonia), appear to be furnished with a distinct cell-membrane.

A protoplasmic process also juts out from the vicinity of the nucleus. While *in situ* these processes are placed in apposition to the membrana propria. They become deeply tinged in stained specimens. The contents of these mucous cells is a clear substance, containing a few granules, and giving the characteristic micro-chemical reactions of mucin.

As regards the granular crescents, their behavior under the application of different chemical reagents leaves no doubt as to the albuminoid nature of their cell-substance. There is an infinite variety in the proportion of albuminous cells to crescents. For we find in some glands a very marked preponderance of one variety of corpuscular elements over another, whereas in others they are about equally distributed.

Having thus briefly indicated the characteristic appearances of the cellular constituents of the alveoli, as found in glands which had been at rest before being examined, we are now prepared to appreciate the *morphological changes occurring in the active organs.*

In the quiescent state of the gland, then, the protoplasm of its alveolar cells is gradually converted into a material resembling the ultimate product of secretion. It is but natural, therefore, to find in gland cells, which have enjoyed prolonged rest, a small proportion of protoplasm. In fact, as has been already stated, the quiescent gland is marked by the coarsely granular appearance of the secreting corpuscles, and by a

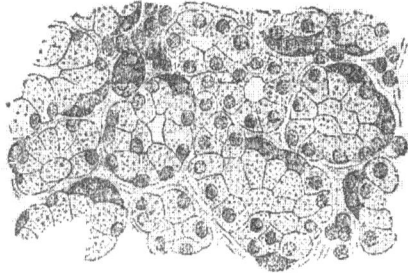

FIG. 200.—Mucous gland with changes due to incipient secretion. Lavdovsky.

more or less complete obscurity both of cell-boundaries and nuclei. In the mucous glands this is due to the abundant presence of mucigenous material, destined later to become converted into mucin.

But let a proper stimulus now waken the dormant activity of the gland, and interesting changes are at once inaugurated. The cells gradually lose their granular aspect, distinct boundary lines become visible, and the nucleus appears. In glands exhausted by protracted secretion or excessive stimulation, we accordingly find conspicuous nuclei, shrunken alveolar corpuscles, and small granular cells closely resembling the crescents of Giannuzzi. The entire alveolus appears reduced in size. At length, in typical mucous glands, the large, clear, mucous cells are found to have entirely disappeared. Heidenhain and his followers have concluded, from these easily

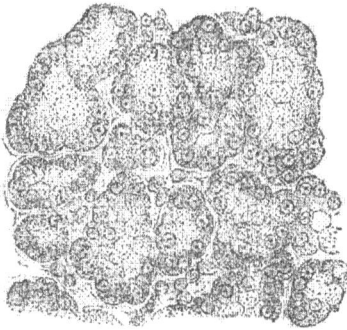

FIG. 201.—Mucous gland with structural alteration of advanced secretion. Lavdovsky.

demonstrable and constantly recurring phenomena, that the
mucous cells suffer actual destruction, and that restitution of
the alveolar epithelium occurs in consequence of proliferation
of the parietal cells.

The writer cannot accept this interpretation. His own observations point to the probability that actual disintegration of the
secreting cells occurs only under pathological conditions. The
mucous cells disgorge the mucin which has been formed within
them by protoplasmic metamorphosis, they alter their appearance considerably, but nevertheless they continue to exist. It
is by a constant renewal of their protoplasm that they are thus
able to secrete for a period of indefinite length. Destruction
and recuperation, growth and decay, are thus constantly taking place at the same time and in the same cell.

EXCRETORY DUCTS.

The lobar, and larger interlobular ducts have essentially
the same structure. That is, we find a basement membrane
lined with a double layer of large columnar cells, and surrounded by a varying amount of connective tissue. The
nucleus is oval and sharply defined, and it is generally found
in the middle of the cell. A longitudinal striation is often
distinctly seen in these epithelia, giving them the appearance
of being traversed by minute rodlets. Lateral anastomoses
have been described between these rodlets by Klein. In
fact, this author finds networks of various kinds in all the
cellular constituents of glands, and even in most nuclei. But
his assertions in this respect are not confirmed by most recent
authors, and certainly in fresh specimens, such reticula are
conspicuously absent. When they do occur it seems that they
are but the anatomical expression of protoplasmic coagulation.

The interlobular ducts or salivary tubes (*Speichel-Röhren*) of
Pflüger have only a single layer of columnar epithelia, the external portion of which (that nearest the basement membrane)
is characterized by longitudinal fibrillæ, or rods. At about
the middle of each cell, there is a large, round or oval nucleus.

Between the intralobular ducts of larger calibre and the alveoli, there is found still another variety of excretory channels.
These are the intermediate or intercalated ducts. They are

lined with relatively long, spindle-shaped corpuscles (parotid gland), or small, cuboidal cells (submaxillary of different animals).

Quite recently Klein has also described "a distinct, narrow, short bit," found intermediate between the salivary tubes and the intercalated part. This he calls the neck, and points out the similarity of such an arrangement with the transition of the duct into the alveolus of the pyloric glands.

A structure of this kind is indeed often seen, but it is also frequently

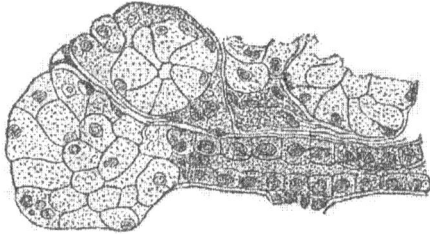

FIG. 202.—Glandular acini with intercalated portion of duct. Ebner.

absent, so that we are not justified in regarding it as a constant anatomical feature. Finally, the presence of smooth, muscle fibres in the main ducts is a fact which deserves to be mentioned.

Blood-vessels and lymphatics.—A beautiful and dense capillary plexus surrounds the acini of the salivary glands. But the vascular walls are not in immediate contact with the membrana propria, being separated therefrom by lymph-spaces. When the latter contain much fluid, the distance between capillary wall and basement membrane will thus be materially greater than when only a small amount of liquid is present in these lymph-channels. The arteries and veins are devoid of peculiarities deserving of special mention.

In addition to the perivascular lymphatics, just mentioned, there are found channels around the ducts and acini. Both sets of vessels are connected, however, by abundant anastomoses. Valves are present in these lymph-vessels, and lateral pouches corresponding to them. This gives rise to a sacculated appearance, which is so characteristic of their course.

Nerves.—Medullated fibres are readily seen to enter the salivary glands at the hilus. They follow the course of the main duct, forming a plexus around its larger ramifications. From this reticulum, which is provided with collections of ganglia of varying dimensions, secondary medullated fibrils arise, and are distributed between the smaller lobules. Ganglion cells, but of smaller size, are still found here. Non-medullated fibres are at length given off from the other nerves, and may be traced to the acini. But concerning their terminal distribution, we have as yet no definite knowledge, only a number of more or less acceptable statements and theories.

Most conspicuous among these is Pflüger's, because couched in words of most positive assurance. Briefly stated, this author regards the secreting cells as the real nerve terminations. And he bases this conviction on what he claims to have actually seen, viz., the direct entrance of axis cylinders into the glandular epithelia.

But, with a few exceptions, presently to be mentioned, all recent observers have failed to corroborate Pflüger's assertions.

These exceptions are Patenko, who claims to have seen nerve-endings in the uterine glands; Kupffer, who, as already stated, saw similar terminations in the so-called salivary bodies of the cockroach (*blatta orientalis*), and Openchowski. The latter asserts that, in the glands of the nictitating lid of frogs, he has discovered unmistakable evidence of the direct entrance of nerve-fibrils into secreting epithelia. Such fibres, he says, are continuous, with an intracellular reticulum. Finally Palladino, ten years ago, described somewhat similar appearances.

It does not seem desirable to enter more fully into the various details of pending controversies concerning the termination of nerves in different glands. What has been briefly described, is what we actually see, and not the imaginary pictures drawn by enthusiastic observers.

Intra-alveolar networks and capillary secreting ducts have been very minutely described by different authors. As regards the latter there can be no doubt that an albuminoid intercellular cement-substance, which may be displaced by any fluid injected with sufficient force into the main duct, has given rise to appearances simulating the existence of minute channels between the secreting cells. In the light of our present knowledge it may be definitely asserted that capillary excretory ducts, possessed of walls of their own, do not constitute real structural features of the salivary glands.

The same also applies to the reticulum which many have claimed to exist within the acini of all these glands. Protoplasmic coagulation, resulting from the different hardening processes and methods of preparation, must be held accountable for the net-like appearance referred to. In the living gland such a reticulum is not found.

BIBLIOGRAPHY.

GIANNUZZI. Bericht d. Sächs. Gesel. d. Wiss. 1867.

KÖLLIKER. Gewebelehre. 1867.

PFLÜGER. Die Endigung d. Absonderungsnerven in den Speicheldrüsen. Bonn, 1869. Also, Stricker's Manual.

BOLL. Beitr. z. mikrosk. Anat. d. Drüsen. Berlin, 1869.

KRAUSE. Arch. f. Anat. u. Physiol., p. 9. 1870.

EWALD. Beitr. z. Histol., etc., d. Speicheldrüse, etc. Berlin, 1870.

EBNER. Ueber die Anfänge d. Speichelgänge. Arch. f. mikros. Anat. Vol. VIII. 1872.

EBNER. Die Acinösen Drüsen. d. Zunge. Graz, 1873.

KUPFFER. Arch. f. mikros. Anat. Vol. IX. 1873. Also, Beitr. z. Anat. u. Phys. Leipzig, 1875.

NUSSBAUM. Die Fermentbildung in d. Drüsen. Bonn, 1876. Also, Ueber den Bau u. die Thätigkeit d. Drüsen. Arch. f. mikros. Anat. Vol. XIII. 1877.

LAVDOVSKY. Zur fein. Anat. d. Speicheldrüsen. Arch. f. mikros. Anat. Vol. XIII. 1877.

LANGLEY. Untersuch. aus d. phys. Inst. zu Heidelberg. Vol. I. 1878.

BERMANN. Ueber d. Zusammensetzung d. gland. Submax. Würzburg, 1878.

HEBOLD. Beitr. zur Secret. u. Regeneration d. Schleimzellen. Bonn, 1879.

BEYER, G. Die Glandula sublingualis, etc. Diss. Breslau, 1879.

LANGLEY, J. N. On the Changes in Serous Glands during Secretion. Jour. Phys., Vol. II., p. 261. 1879. Also, On the Structure of Serous Glands in Rest and Activity. Proc. Roy. Soc., p. 377. 1879.

HEIDENHAIN. Studien d. phys. Inst. zu Breslau. IV. 1868. Also, Vol. V. of Hermann's Handbuch d. Physiologie. 1880.

NITOT, E. Recherches anat. sur la glande Sous-max., etc. Arch. de Phys. Vol. VII., p. 374. 1880.

OPENCHOWSKI. Histologisches zur Innervation der Drüsen. Arch. Physiol. Vol. XXVII., p. 223. 1882.

KLEIN. On the Lymphatic System and Minute Structure of the Salivary Glands and Pancreas. Quart. Jour. Micros. Soc. April, 1882.

INDEX.

484

INDEX.

www.ingramcontent.com/pod-product-compliance
Lightning Source LLC
Chambersburg PA
CBHW020448270326
41926CB00008B/528